Corporate Social Responsibility

As a relatively young subject, corporate social responsibility has unsurprisingly developed and evolved in numerous ways since the first edition of this textbook was published. Retaining the features that made the first edition a top selling text in the field, the new edition will continue to be the only textbook available which provides a ready-made, enhanced course pack for CSR classes.

Authoritative editor introductions provide accessible entry points to the subjects covered – an approach that is particularly suited to advanced undergraduate and postgraduate teaching that emphasizes a research-led approach. New case studies are integrated throughout the text to enable students to think and analyze the subject from every angle. The entire textbook reflects the global nature of CSR as a discipline and further pedagogical features include chapter learning outcomes; study questions; 'challenges for practice' boxes and additional 'further reading' features at the end of each chapter.

This highly rated textbook also now benefits from a regularly updated companion website that will feature a brand new 'CSR Case Club' presenting students and lecturers with further case suggestions with which to enhance learning; lecture slides; updates from the popular Crane and Matten blog; links to further reading and career sites, YouTube clips and suggested answers to study questions.

Andrew Crane is the George R. Gardiner Professor of Business Ethics at the Schulich School of Business at York University, Canada.

Dirk Matten is Professor of Strategy and holds the Hewlett-Packard Chair in Corporate Social Responsibility at the Schulich School of Business at York University, Canada.

Laura J. Spence is Professor of Business Ethics and Director of the Centre for Research into Sustainability at Royal Holloway, University of London, UK.

Corporate Social Responsibility

Readings and cases in a global context

Second edition

Edited by

**Andrew Crane, Dirk Matten and
Laura J. Spence**

Routledge
Taylor & Francis Group

LONDON AND NEW YORK

First edition published 2008
Second edition published 2014
by Routledge
2 Park Square, Milton Park, Abingdon, Oxon OX14 4RN

Simultaneously published in the USA and Canada
by Routledge
711 Third Avenue, New York, NY 10017

Routledge is an imprint of the Taylor & Francis Group, an informa business

British Library Cataloguing in Publication Data
A catalogue record for this book is available from the British Library

Library of Congress Cataloging in Publication Data
Corporate social responsibility : readings and cases in a global context / edited by
Andrew Crane, Dirk Matten and Laura Spence. — 2nd.
     p. cm.
   Includes bibliographical references and index.
  1. Social responsibility of business. 2. Business ethics. I. Crane, Andrew, 1968–
  II. Matten, Dirk. III. Spence, Laura J., 1968–
  HD60.C6915 2013
  658.4′08—dc23   2012040250

ISBN: 978–0–415–68324–1(hbk)
ISBN: 978–0–415–68325–8(pbk)

Typeset in Perpetua and Bell Gothic
by Keystroke, Station Road, Codsall, Wolverhampton

Printed and bound by CPI Group (UK) Ltd, Croydon, CR0 4YY

Contents

List of illustrations   ix
Acknowledgements   xiii

**SECTION A   UNDERSTANDING CORPORATE SOCIAL
RESPONSIBILITY** 은 개념   1

1   Corporate social responsibility: in a global context   3
    Crane, Matten and Spence

2   The case for and against CSR   27
    Crane, Matten and Spence

    Reading 1: Smith, N. C. (2003) 'Corporate social responsibility: whether
    or how?' *California Management Review*, 45(4): 52–76.   35

    Reading 2: Karnani, A. (2010) 'The case against corporate social
    responsibility', *Wall Street Journal*, Aug 23: 1–5.   61

3   What is CSR? Concepts and theories   66
    Crane, Matten and Spence

    Reading 1: Garriga, E. & Melé, D. (2004) 'Corporate social responsibility
    theories: mapping the territory', *Journal of Business Ethics*, 53(1-2): 51–71.   74

    Reading 2: Schwartz, M. S. & Carroll, A. B. (2008) 'Corporate social
    responsibility: a three-domain approach', *Business Ethics Quarterly*, 13(4):
    503–530.   104

4   Responsibilities to stakeholders   133
    Crane, Matten and Spence

    Reading 1: Freeman, R. E. (1984) 'Stakeholder management: framework
    and philosophy', Chapter 3, *Strategic management. A stakeholder approach*,
    Boston: Pitman.   140

    Reading 2: Mitchell, R. K., Agle, B. R., & Wood, D. J. (1997) 'Toward a
    theory of stakeholder identification and salience: defining the principle of who
    and what really counts', *Academy of Management Review*, 22(4): 853–886.   168

    Integrative case 1: Vodafone: Africa calling   **203**
    Crane, Matten and Spence

SECTION B   APPLYING CSR ⌐ᵢ᷄⌐₇   **211**

5   CSR in the marketplace   213
    Crane, Matten and Spence

    Reading 1: Prahalad, C. K. & Hammond, A. (2002) 'Serving the world's
    poor, *profitably*', *Harvard Business Review*, 80(9): 48–57.   221

    Reading 2: Crane, A. (2012) Ethical consumers and the CSR Marketplace
    Revised and updated from Crane, A. (2005) 'Meeting the ethical gaze:
    issues and challenges in orientating towards the ethical market', in
    Harrison, R., Newholm, T., & Shaw, D. (eds) *The ethical consumer*,
    London: Sage.   235

6   CSR in the workplace   253
    Crane, Matten and Spence

    Reading 1: Utting, P. (2007) 'CSR and equality', *Third World Quarterly*,
    28(4): 697–712.   260

    Reading 2: Bhattacharya, C. B., Sen, S., & Korschun, D. (2008) 'Using
    corporate social responsibility to win the war for talent', *MIT Sloan
    Management Review*, 49(2): 37–44.   277

7   CSR in the community   291
    Crane, Matten and Spence

    Reading 1: Valente, M. & Crane, A. (2010) 'Public responsibility and
    private enter prise in developing countries', *California Management
    Review*, 52(3): 52–78.   299

    Reading 2: Porter, M. E. & Kramer, M. R. (2002) 'The competitive advantage
    of corporate philanthropy', *Harvard Business Review*, 80(12): 56–69. 328

8   CSR in the ecological environment   349
    Crane, Matten and Spence

    Reading 1: Hart, S. L. (1997) 'Beyond greening: strategies for a sustainable
    world', *Harvard Business Review*, January–February: 67–76.   358

Reading 2: Pinkse, J. & Kolk, A. (2009) 'Business strategies for climate change', Chapter 5 in *International Business and Global Climate Change*, London: Routledge.   371

Integrative case 2: HSBC: banking on CSR?   **391**
Crane, Matten and Spence

SECTION C   MANAGING CSR 借理   **399**

 9   CSR reporting and auditing   401
     Crane, Matten and Spence

     Reading 1: Zadek, S., Pruzan, P. & Evans, R. (eds) (2003) 'How to do it', Chapter 3 in *Building corporate accountability: emerging practices in social and ethical accounting, auditing and reporting*. London: Earthscan.   409

     Reading 2: Unerman, J. (2007) 'Stakeholder engagement and dialogue', in J. Unerman, J. Bebbington, & B. O'Dwyer (eds), *Sustainability accounting and accountability*: London: Routledge, 86–103.   424

10   Developing CSR strategy   443
     Crane, Matten and Spence

     Reading 1: Husted, B. W. & Allen, D. B. (2011) 'How do we build corporate social strategy?', Chapter 4 in *Corporate social strategy: stakeholder engagement and competitive advantage*, Cambridge: Cambridge University Press, 64–85.   451

     Reading 2: Galbreath, J. (2006) 'Corporate social responsibility strategy: strategic options, global considerations', *Corporate Governance*, 6: 175–187.   472

11   CSR, partnerships, and self-regulation   488
     Crane, Matten and Spence

     Reading 1: Peloza, J. & Falkenberg, L. (2009) 'The role of collaboration in achieving corporate social responsibility objectives', *California Management Review*, 51(3): 95–113.   495

     Reading 2: Gond, J.- P., Kang, N., & Moon, J. (2011) 'The government of self-regulation: on the comparative dynamics of corporate social responsibility', *Economy and Society*, 40(4): 640–671.   516

     Integrative case 3: CSR masala at the Tata Group   **545**
     Crane, Matten and Spence

12   The future of CSR in a global context   553
     Crane, Matten and Spence

     Index   573

List of tables and figures

Chapter 1

Table 1.1:   CSR definitions   6
Figure 1.1: Core characteristics of CSR   9
Table 1.2:   Differences in CSR among large and small firms   12

Chapter 3

Table 3.1:   Basic types of CSR   67
Table 3.2:   Corporate social responsibilities theories and related
             approaches (Reading 1)   94
Figure 3.1: Carroll's (1991) Pyramid of Corporate Social Responsibility
             (Reading 2)   105
Figure 3.2: The Three-Domain Model of Corporate Social Responsibility
             (Reading 2)   110
Table 3.3:   Examples of legal motives and possible responses (Reading 2) 113
Figure 3.3: The Three-Domain Model of Corporate Social Responsibility:
             Corporate Examples (Reading 2)   121
Figure 3.4: Corporate Social Responsibility "Portraits" (Reading 2)   126

Chapter 4

Table 4.1:   Managerial model versus stakeholder model of the firm   135
Exhibit 1:   Stakeholder map of a very large organization (Reading 1)   143

Exhibit 2:   Specific stakeholders in a very large organization
              (Reading 1)   144
Exhibit 3:   'Stakes' of selected stakeholders in XYZ company
              (Reading 1)   144
Exhibit 4:   Possible stakeholder role set of employees and government
              officials (Reading 1)   145
Exhibit 5:   Typical indirect or coalition strategies (Reading 1)   146
Exhibit 6:   Classical stakeholder grid (Reading 1)   148
Exhibit 7:   'Real world' stakeholder grid (Reading 1)   149
Exhibit 8:   Typical strategic planning process schematic (Reading 1) 154
Exhibit 9:   Stakeholder management capability = f (Stakeholder map,
              organizational process, stakeholder transactions) (Reading 1) 158
Exhibit 10:   The 'stakeholder dilemma' game (Reading 1)   162
Table 4.2:   Who is a stakeholder? A chronology (Reading 2)   172
Table 4.3:   Sorting of rationales for stakeholder identification (Reading 2) 176
Table 4.4:   Key constructs in the theory of stakeholder identification and
              salience (Reading 2)   184
Figure 4.1:   Qualitative classes of stakeholders (Reading 2)   187
Figure 4.2:   Stakeholder typology: One, two, or three attributes present
              (Reading 2)   189

Chapter 5

Figure 5.1:   The world pyramid (Reading 1)   226
Table 5.1:   The high-cost economy of the poor (Reading 1)   228
Figure 5.2:   Orientations to the CSR Marketplace (Reading 2)   239

Chapter 6

Figure 6.1:   Recommended shifts in CSR management approach
              (Reading 2)   283
Figure 6.2:   Employee reactions to CSR (Reading 2)   287

Chapter 7

Table 7.1:   Case sampling (Reading 1)   303
Exhibit 1:   Public responsibility strategies (Reading 1)   308
Appendix A: Case Illustrations (Reading 1)   323
Appendix B: Methodology (Reading 1)   324
Exhibit 2:   A convergence of interests (Reading 2)   332
Exhibit 3:   The four elements of competitive context (Reading 2)   333
Exhibit 4:   Maximizing philanthropy's value (Reading 2)   337

Chapter 8

Exhibit 1:   Ecological footprints (Reading 1)   360
Exhibit 2:   Major challenges to sustainability (Reading 1)   362
Exhibit 3:   The sustainability portfolio (Reading 1)   369
Exhibit 4:   Building sustainable business strategies (Reading 1)   370
Table 8.1:   Factors that influence corporate positions on climate
              change (Reading 2)   374
Figure 8.1:   Strategic options for climate change (Reading 2)   381

Chapter 9

Table 9.1:   Typology (Reading 1)   416
Box 9.1:   The eight principles of quality (Reading 1)   416
Figure 9.1:   Social and ethical disclosure: Assessing progress
              (Reading 1)   420
Table 9.2:   Quality rating against basic principles and elements
              (Reading 1)   421
Figure 9.2:   A staged hierarchical model of the Social and
              Environmental Reporting (SER) process (Reading 2)   428

Chapter 10

Figure 10.1: Husted and Allen's seven-step model of CSR Strategy
              Development   448
Figure 10.2: CSR strategic options (Reading 2)   478
Figure 10.3: Considerations for CSR strategy in a global context
              (Reading 2)   484

Chapter 11

Figure 11.1: Strategic factors for CSR collaboration strategies
              (Reading 1)   500
Table 11.1:   Five CSR-government configurations (Reading 2)   523
Table 11.2:   The changing social responsibility doctrine in Western
              Europe (Reading 2)   529
Figure 1:   CSR management at the Tata Group   547

Chapter 12

Figure 12.1: Future developments in CSR   555
Figure 12.2: Basic dimensions of CSR related regulation   561
Table 12.1:   Top five activities of CSR professionals in the UK   565

Acknowledgements

Writing and researching in the field of CSR inevitably brings you into contact with a lot of intelligent and creative people who inspire you to develop your ideas in interesting and unexpected ways (you also get to meet a good few weirdoes, but that's another story). We have been extremely lucky to have worked with and learnt from some of the best CSR thinkers around, and so would like to take this opportunity to thank all the faculty, students, and practitioners who have contributed to our understanding of this fascinating and sometimes exasperating subject. This goes in particular to everyone at the Centre of Excellence in Responsible Business at the Schulich School of Business, the Centre for Research into Sustainability at Royal Holloway, University of London, and also to our former colleagues and students at Brunel University and in the International Centre for Corporate Social Responsibility at the University of Nottingham.

The genesis of this book can be traced to a cocktail bar in Honolulu, where our initial editor for the first edition, Jacqueline Curthoys alerted us, during the course of a few Mai Tais to the urgent need for a CSR textbook that didn't treat its readers like they were stupid, but also didn't try and confuse them with too many long words. Now in its second edition, the course of the book has been a little bumpy, as we've been through five editors, four babies, one career change, and two transatlantic relocations. Sometimes, things just don't go the way you plan! But it is with great pleasure that the second edition of the book now hits the shelves. In helping us get there, we'd particularly like to offer our thanks to: Shanthini Jayakumar and Mary Rizzo at York University for their tremendous administrative support; Sarah Glozer for her first class work on the companion website materials; Satyameet Ahuja for his excellent research for the case studies; and Chijioke Uba for preparing the index. The editorial team at Routledge has also been unstinting in their support for the project, so thanks to Terry Clague, David Varley and Rosie Baron for your patience and encouragement, and to Emma Hart for guiding us through the production process.

The editors and publishers wish to thank and acknowledge the following authors, journals and publishers that have assisted us in allowing materials to be cited and shared in the readings:

1   Reprinted from *California Management Review*, 45(4), 'Corporate social responsibility: Whether or how?' by Smith, N. C., pp. 52–76, ©2003, by the Regents of the University of California. By permission of The Regents.

2   Reprinted from *Wall Street Journal*, 'The case against corporate social responsibility' by Karnani, A., pp. 1–5, Aug 23, 2010, with permission from Dow Jones and Company, Inc.

3   Reprinted from *Journal of Business Ethics*, 53(1–2), 'Corporate social responsibility theories: mapping the territory' by Garriga, E. & Melé, D., pp. 51–71, ©2004, with permission from Springer Science and Business Media.

4   Reprinted from *Business Ethics Quarterly*, 13(4), 'Corporate social responsibility: a three-domain approach' by Schwartz, M. S. & Carroll, A. B., pp. 503–530, ©2008 with permission from Philosophy Documentation Center.

5   Reprinted from *Stakeholder management: framework and philosophy* by Freeman, R.E., 'Strategic Management. A stakeholder approach', Chapter 3, ©1984, with permission from the author. Reproduced by permission of Cambridge University Press.

6   Reprinted from *Academy of Management Review*, 22(4), 'Toward a theory of stakeholder identification and salience: defining the principle of who and what really counts' by Mitchell, R. K., Agle, B. R., & Wood, D. J., pp. 853–886, ©1997 with permission from the Academy of Management.

7   Reprinted from *Harvard Business Review*, 80(9), 'Serving the world's poor, profitably' by Prahalad, C. K. & Hammond, A., pp. 48–57, ©2002, with permission from Harvard Business School Publishing.

8   Reprinted from *MIT Sloan Management Review*, 49(2), 'Using corporate social responsibility to win the war for talent' by Bhattacharya, C. B., Sen, S., & Korschun, D., pp. 37–44, ©2008, with permission from Tribune Media Services International.

9   Reprinted from *Third World Quarterly*, 28(4), 'CSR and equality' by Utting, P., pp. 697–712, ©2007, with permission from Taylor & Francis Books.

10   Reprinted from *Harvard Business Review*, 80(12) 'The competitive advantage of corporate philanthropy' by Porter, M.E. & Kramer, M.R., pp. 56–59, ©2002, with permission from Harvard Business School Publishing.

11   Reprinted from *California Management Review*, 52(3), 'Public responsibility and private enterprise in developing countries' by Valente, M. & Crane, A., pp. 52–78, ©2010, by the Regents of the University of California. By permission of The Regents.

12   Reprinted from *Harvard Business Review*, 75(1) 'Beyond greening: strategies for a sustainable world' by Hart, S. L., pp. 67–76, ©1997, with permission from Harvard Business School Publishing.

13   Reprinted from *International Business and Global Climate Change* by Pinkse,
      J. & Kolk, A., 'Business strategies for climate change', Chapter 5, ©2009,
      Routledge. Reproduced by permission of Taylor & Francis Books.

14   Reprinted from *Building corporate accountability: emerging practices in social
      and ethical accounting, auditing and reporting* by Zadek, S., Pruzan, P., &
      Evans, R. (eds), 'How to do it' by Zadek, S., Pruzan, P., & Evans, R., Chapter
      3, ©2003, with permission from Earthscan.

15   Reprinted from *Sustainability accounting and accountability* by J. Unerman,
      J. Bebbington, & B. O'Dwyer (eds), 'Stakeholder engagement and dialogue'
      by Unerman, J., pp. 86–103, ©2007, Routledge. Reproduced by permission
      of Taylor & Francis Books.

16   Reprinted from *Corporate Social Strategy: Stakeholder Engagement and
      Competitive Advantage* by Husted, B. W. & Allen, D. B., 'How do we build
      corporate social strategy?' by Husted, B. W. & Allen, D. B., Chapter 4, pp.
      64–85, ©2011, with permission from authors. Reproduced by permission of
      Cambridge University Press.

17   Reprinted from *Corporate Governance*, 6, 'Corporate social responsibility
      strategy: strategic options, global gonsiderations', by Galbreath J., pp.
      175–187, ©2006. Reproduced by permission of Emerald Group Publishing
      Limited.

18   Reprinted from *California Management Review*, 51(3), 'The role of collab-
      oration in achieving corporate social responsibility objectives' by Peloza, J. &
      Falkenberg, L., pp. 95–113, ©2009, by the Regents of the University of
      California. By permission of The Regents.

19   Reprinted from *Economy and Society*, 40(4), 'The government of self-
      regulation: on the comparative dynamics of corporate social responsibility'
      by Gond, J. P., Kang, N., & Moon, J., pp. 640–671, ©2011. Reproduced by
      permission of Taylor & Francis Books UK.

The publishers have made every effort to contact authors/copyright holders of works
reprinted in *Corporate Social Responsibility: Readings and cases in a global context*.
This has not been possible in every case, however, and we would welcome correspondence from those individuals/companies whom we have been unable to trace.

SECTION A

Understanding corporate social responsibility

Corporate social responsibility, or CSR for short, is a much discussed and debated subject in contemporary business. It is also frequently found in the discourse of governments, public sector organizations, non-government organizations (NGOs), and even intergovernmental organizations such as the UN, the World Bank, or the International Labour Organization. CSR, it seems, is pretty much everywhere.

This means that, apart from anything else, there is much to gain from an academic study of CSR. After all, the different people and organizations that deploy the language or tools of CSR may well want, or even mean, different things when they get involved with CSR. For some, it represents a misguided attempt to divert money that should rightly go to shareholders; for others, it is little more than a smokescreen behind which large multinationals can maintain a discredited, unsustainable business model while appearing to be responsible to the outside world; for still others, it represents a genuine opportunity to help leverage millions out of poverty in the world's poorest countries. Ultimately, corporations may do good, or harm, or perhaps even very little, when they practise CSR.

The academic study of CSR therefore seeks to get behind the spin of CSR and explore some of these different perspectives with real substance. In this first part of the book, we will start this process by developing a robust understanding of CSR – i.e. what it means, what it looks like in different national and organizational contexts, what some of its basic underlying principles are, what kind of ways we can theorize about it, and so on. We will also begin to explore some of the very different opinions on CSR that people have, and perhaps more importantly, what lies behind these different perspectives. To integrate and apply some of this knowledge, we provide an in depth case study on Vodafone, the mobile telecommunications company, and its experiences in Africa.

In this section, then, we will develop an understanding of CSR in five main stages:

- Introducing CSR
- The case for and against CSR
- CSR concepts and theories
- Responsibilities to stakeholders
- *Vodafone: Africa Calling* case study

It is important to recognize that in building an understanding of CSR, our aim is not to convince anyone that CSR is necessarily right or wrong, or even that some approaches to CSR are better than others. Our aim is to explore different facets of the subject, and different perspectives, in an objective way that enables anyone interested in CSR to get a clearer picture of the area and make their own mind up as to what is good or bad about a particular approach. CSR is a complex, and ultimately *contested* concept that is hard to pin down – but at the same time, one that rewards greater investigation. Therefore, once we have built this foundation of understanding of CSR in Section A, we will turn in Section B to how CSR is applied in different arenas of the business – the workplace, the marketplace, the community, and the ecological environment – before exploring CSR management in Section C. This first section is crucial though: without an adequate understanding of CSR and its many guises, it is very difficult to evaluate specific responsibilities or management practices.

Chapter 1

Corporate social responsibility: in a global context

IN THIS CHAPTER WE WILL:

- Examine the rise to prominence of corporate social responsibility
- Analyze different definitions of corporate social responsibility
- Outline six core characteristics of corporate social responsibility
- Explore corporate social responsibility in different organizational contexts
- Explore corporate social responsibility in different national contexts
- Explain the approach to corporate social responsibility adopted in the rest of the book

Introduction: the recent rise of CSR

The role of corporations in society is clearly high on the agenda. Hardly a day goes by without media reports on corporate misbehaviour and scandals or, more positively, on contributions from business to wider society. A quick stroll to the local cinema and films such as *Inside Job*, *Margin Call*, and *Wall Street 2*, reflect a growing interest among the public in the impact of corporations on contemporary life.

Corporations are clearly taking up this challenge. This began with 'the usual suspects' such as companies in the oil, chemical, and tobacco industries. As a result of media pressure, major disasters, and sometimes governmental regulation, these companies realized that propping up oppressive regimes, being implicated in human rights violations, polluting the environment, or misinforming and deliberately harming their customers, just to give a few examples, were practices that had to be reconsidered if they wanted to survive and prosper. Today, however, there is virtually no industry, market, or business type that has not experienced increasing demands to legitimate its practices to society at large. For instance, banking, retailing, tourism, food and beverages, entertainment, and healthcare industries – for long considered to be fairly 'clean' and uncontroversial – now all face increasing expectations that they institute more responsible practices.

In the context of the global economic crisis, which began in 2008 and reverberated for a number of years thereafter, questions regarding the responsibilities of business have moved still further to the fore of the media, political and public interest. The focus here has been on financial institutions primarily, whose imprudent practices are largely held to blame for igniting a wave of economic recession. As governments bailed out failing businesses and popular protests such as 'Occupy Wall Street' spread globally, companies in the financial sector faced a new era of scrutiny of their values, goals, and purpose.

Companies have responded to this agenda by advocating what is now a common term in business: corporate social responsibility. More often known simply as CSR, the concept of corporate social responsibility is a management idea that has risen to unprecedented popularity throughout the global business community during the last decades. Most large companies, and even some smaller ones, now feature CSR reports, managers, departments, or at least CSR projects, and the subject is increasingly promoted as a core area of management, next to marketing, accounting, or finance.

If we take a closer look at the recent rise of CSR, some might well argue that this 'new' management idea is little more than a recycled fashion, or as the old saying goes, 'old wine in new bottles'. And, in fact, one could certainly suggest that some of the practices that fall under the label of CSR have indeed been relevant business issues at least since the Industrial Revolution. Ensuring humane working conditions, providing decent housing or healthcare, and donating to charity are activities that many of the early industrialists in Europe and the US were involved in – without necessarily shouting out about them in annual reports, let alone calling them CSR. The involvement of business in social issues is not the prerogative of the West. In India, for example, companies such as Tata can pride themselves on more than 100 years of responsible business practices, including far-reaching philanthropic activities and community involvement (Elankumaran et al, 2005). What we discover then in the area of CSR is that while many of the individual policies, practices, and programmes are not new as such, corporations today are addressing their role in society far more coherently, comprehensively, and professionally – an approach that is contemporarily summarized by CSR.

As well as the rise to prominence of CSR in particular companies, we have also witnessed the emergence of something like a CSR 'movement'. There has been a mushrooming of dedicated CSR consultancies, all of which see a business opportunity in the growing popularity of the concept. At the same time, we are witnessing a burgeoning number of CSR standards, watchdogs, auditors, and certifiers aiming at institutionalizing and harmonizing CSR practices globally. More and more industry associations and interest groups have been set up in order to coordinate and create synergies among individual business approaches to CSR. Meanwhile, a growing number of dedicated magazines, newsletters, social media and websites not only contribute to providing an identity to CSR as a management concept, but also help to build a worldwide network of CSR practitioners, academics, and activists.

Defining CSR: navigating through the jungle of definitions

In the context of such an inexorable rise to prominence of CSR, the literature on the subject, both academic and practitioner, is understandably large and expanding. There are now thousands of articles and reports on CSR from academics, corporations, consultancies, the media, NGOs, and government departments; there are innumerable conferences, books, journals, and magazines on the subject; and last, but not least, there are literally millions of web-based formal and social media contributions dealing with the topic from every conceivable interest group with a stake in the debate.

How then to best make sense of this vast literature so as to construct a coherent account of what CSR actually is? After all, few subjects in management arouse as much controversy and contestation as CSR. For this reason, definitions of CSR abound, and there are as many definitions of CSR as there are disagreements over the appropriate role of the corporation in society. Hence there remains a lack of consensus on a definition for CSR (Lindgreen & Swaen, 2010). The CSR page on Wikipedia, the online encyclopaedia, has been in more or less permanent dispute since 2007 (Ethical Performance, 2007) and continues to be challenged for its neutrality.

Table 1.1 provides just a few examples of the many different ways that CSR is described and defined by different organizations across the globe. As this clearly shows, there are some similarities in the way that different actors understand CSR, as well as considerable differences. Moreover, although we often look to academic research to provide clarity among so much ambiguity, this diversity is also reflected in scholarly definitions of CSR. For example, one early writer on CSR, Keith Davis described CSR as 'the firm's consideration of, and response to, issues beyond the narrow economic, technical, and legal requirements of the firm' (Davis, 1973), while a few years later Archie Carroll (1979) defined it much more broadly to include exactly those elements that Davis excluded: 'the social responsibility of business encompasses the economic, legal, ethical, and discretionary expectations that society has of organizations at a given point in time.'

This heterogeneity in CSR definitions has continued unabated. While the Carroll definition given above is arguably the most commonly cited one, it remains contested, as we will see later in Chapter 3. Therefore, others have taken a different route and rather than specify particular responsibilities, have offered more general definitions that seek to include the different opinions on CSR that are evident across the literature, and across practice. For instance, Brown and Dacin (1997) define CSR as a company's 'status and activities with respect to its perceived societal or, at least, stakeholder obligations', while Matten and Moon (2008) suggest that CSR 'empirically consists of clearly articulated and communicated policies and practices of corporations that reflect business responsibility for some of the wider societal

CWS 1.1

Visit the companion website for links to CSR organizations, interest groups and web forums

Table 1.1: CSR definitions

Name of the organization	Type of organization	Definition	Source
International Labour Organization	Non-governmental organization (international)	CSR as a way in which enterprises give consideration to the impact of their operations on society and affirm their principles and values both in their own internal methods and processes and in their interaction with other actors.	www.ilo.org/ wcmsp5/groups/ public/---ed_ emp/---emp_ ent/---multi/ documents/ publication/wcms _116336.pdf
Corporate Responsibility Coalition (CORE)	NGO coalition (UK)	Corporate Social Responsibility (CSR) has been promoted by business as a way of realising its 'social responsibilities' beyond making a profit for its shareholders. In contrast to this view, NGOs and trade unions tend to dismiss CSR as a public relations tool at best, and at worst a means for corporations to avoid the creation of regulatory and legal mechanisms as a means of ensuring that they adhere to acceptable standards of conduct.	CORE (2011)
Grameen Bank	Social enterprise (Bangladesh)	Businesses are identifying themselves with the movement for Corporate Social Responsibility (CSR), and are trying to do good to the people while conducting their business. But profit-making still remains their main goal, by definition. Though they like to talk about triple bottom lines of financial, social, and environmental benefits, ultimately only one bottom line calls the shot: financial profit.	Yunus & Weber (2009)
General Electric	Business organization (US)	GE businesses depend on the infrastructure, skills and institutions of stable, prosperous societies and healthy environments. To succeed as a global business, we need to be a part of building these societies where we operate. We do this through the products and services we create, the way we work with employees, customers, suppliers and investors, the public policies we advocate and the philanthropic partnerships we support.	www.ge citizenship.com/ about-citizenship/

Table 1.1: Continued

Name of the organization	Type of organization	Definition	Source
Tata	Business organization (India)	Jamsetji Tata and those who followed in his immediate wake set the CSR mandate for Tata companies: to look beyond the generation of products and profits to serving the communities in which they functioned.	www.tata.com/ pdf/COH_2009/ coh_foreword.pdf
Foreign Affairs and International Trade	Governmental organization (Canada)	Corporate Social Responsibility (CSR) is defined as the way companies integrate social, environmental, and economic concerns into their values and operations in a transparent and accountable manner. It is integral to long-term business growth and success, and it also plays an important role in promoting Canadian values internationally and contributing to the sustainable development of communities	www. international.gc. ca/trade- agreements- accords- commerciaux/ds/ csr.aspx?view=d
Chinese Ministry of Commerce	Governmental organization (China)	A concrete action taken by Chinese companies to implement the political aspiration of the new Communist Party collective leadership – putting people first to create a harmonious society	www.ethicalcorp. com
Department for Business, Innovation and Skills	Governmental organization (UK)	The voluntary actions that business can take, over and above compliance with minimum legal requirements, to address both its own competitive interests and the interests of wider society.	BERR (2009)
MVO Nederland (CSR Netherlands)	NGO (Netherlands)	The Corporate Social Responsibility approach means that the company takes responsibility for the effects of the business' activities on people and the environment. The company makes conscious choices in order to find a balance between People, Planet and Profit. Businesses can even go a step further and focus on new market opportunities, growth and innovation with a view to profiting people, society and the environment. Voluntary commitment to society.	www. mvonederland.nl/ content/pagina/ wat-mvo

Table 1.1: Continued

Name of the organization	Type of organization	Definition	Source
Nike	Business organization (US)	It's not just about getting better at what we do – addressing impacts throughout our supply chain – it's about striving for the best, creating value for the business and innovating for a better world.	http://nikeinc.com/pages/responsibility
World Economic Forum	Business association (International)	We believe that corporate global citizenship is fundamentally in the enlightened self-interest of global corporations since their growth, prosperity and sustainability is dependent on the state of the global political, economic, environmental and social landscape.	www.weforum.org/issues/corporate-global-citizenship
European Commission	Governmental organization (EU)	The responsibility of enterprises for their impacts on society. Corporate social responsibility concerns actions by companies over and above their legal obligations towards society and the environment. Certain regulatory measures create an environment more conducive to enterprises voluntarily meeting their social responsibilities.	Commission of the European Communities (2011)
World Bank	International organization (international)	Corporate Social Responsibility (CSR) is the commitment of business to contribute to sustainable economic development, working with employees, their families, the local community and society at large to improve quality of life, in ways that are both good for business and good for development	http://info.worldbank.org/etools/docs/library/57434/public policy_econference.pdf
Business for Social Responsibility	Not-for-profit business association (US)	Business decision making linked to ethical values, compliance with legal requirements, and respect for people, communities, and the environment around the world.	www.forensicsolutions.info/page20.html
CSR Asia	Social enterprise (Asia)	We believe CSR is a company's commitment to operating in an economically, socially and environmentally sustainable manner whilst balancing the interests of diverse stakeholders.	www.csr-asia.com

good. Yet the precise manifestation and direction of the responsibility lie at the discretion of the corporation.'

In this book, we will not seek to simply follow one of these definitions, nor will we provide a new improved one that will simply add to the complex jungle of CSR definitions. In the contested world of CSR, it is virtually impossible to provide a definitive answer to the question of what CSR 'really' is. Therefore, our intention is to identify some core characteristics of the CSR concept, which we hope will help to delineate its essential qualities, and will provide a focus for the definitional debates that continue to surround the subject.

Core characteristics of CSR

The core characteristics of CSR are the essential features of the concept that tend to get reproduced in some way in academic or practitioner definitions of CSR. Few, if any, existing descriptions will include all of them, but these are the main aspects around which the definitional debates tend to centre. Six core characteristics are evident (see Figure 1.1):

Figure 1.1: Core characteristics of CSR

Voluntary

Many characterizations of CSR typically see it as being about voluntary activities that go beyond those prescribed by the law. The Dutch group MVO Nederland (CSR Netherlands) and the UK government follow this line. Although the Business for Social Responsibility definition emphasizes CSR as legal compliance, many companies are by now well-used to considering responsibilities beyond the legal minimum, and in fact the development of self-regulatory CSR initiatives from industry is often seen as a way of forestalling additional regulation as the NGO coalition CORE argues. The case of companies such as McDonald's, KFC, Pret A Manger, and Pizza Hut agreeing in 2011 to introduce calorie labelling in the UK on out-of-home food and beverage items (as part of a Department of Health voluntary programme) is a good example of such a CSR initiative that has arguably been introduced to head off potential regulatory action – such as New York's mandatory calorie labelling on menus introduced in 2008 (Triggle, 2011).

Critics of CSR, therefore, tend to see the element of voluntarism as CSR's major flaw, arguing that legally mandated accountability is where attention should really be focused, as the CORE definition demonstrates.[1] There are some indications, however, of a shifting tide in this respect. The EU, for example, has revised its definition of CSR from 'a concept whereby companies integrate social and environmental concerns in their business operations and in their interaction with their stakeholders on a voluntary basis' (Commission of the European Communities, 2002) to acknowledging the role that the legislative environment can make in enabling CSR (Commission of the European Communities, 2011).

Internalizing or managing externalities

Externalities are the positive and negative side-effects of economic behaviour that are borne by others, but are not taken into account in a firm's decision-making process, and are not included in the market price for goods and services. Pollution is typically regarded as a classic example of an externality since local communities bear the costs of manufacturers' actions. Regulation can force firms to internalize the cost of the externalities, such as pollution fines, but CSR would represent a more voluntary approach to managing externalities, for example by a firm investing in clean technologies that prevent pollution in the first place. Much CSR activity deals with such externalities (Husted & Allen, 2006), including the management of human rights violations in the workforce, minimizing carbon emissions, calculating the social and economic impacts of downsizing, or reducing the health impacts of 'toxic' or otherwise dangerous products, etc. For example, a study commissioned by the Egg Corporation of Australia in 2011 maps out the carbon footprint of cage eggs compared with free-range eggs, and other protein sources such as pork and beef.[2]

Multiple stakeholder orientation

CSR involves considering a range of interests and impacts among a variety of different stakeholders other than just shareholders. The assumption that firms have responsibilities to shareholders is usually not contested, but the point is that because corporations rely on various other constituencies such as consumers, employees, suppliers, and local communities in order to survive and prosper, they do not *only* have responsibilities to shareholders. While many disagree on how much emphasis should be given to shareholders in the CSR debate, and on the extent to which other stakeholders should be taken into account, it is the expanding of corporate responsibility to these other groups that characterizes much of the essential nature of CSR, as illustrated by the CSR Asia definition in Table 1.1. We will discuss stakeholder management in much more depth in Chapter 4

Alignment of social and economic responsibilities

This balancing of different stakeholder interests leads to a fourth facet. While CSR may be about going beyond a narrow focus on shareholders and profitability, many also believe that it should not, however, *conflict* with profitability. Although this is much debated, many definitions of CSR from business and government stress that it is about enlightened self-interest where social and economic responsibilities are aligned. See, for example, the definitions of the Canadian Foreign Affairs and International Trade, and General Electric. This feature has prompted much attention to the business case for CSR – namely, how firms can benefit economically from being socially responsible.

Practices and values

CSR is clearly about a particular set of business practices and strategies that deal with social issues, but for many people it is also about something more than that – namely a philosophy or set of values that underpins these practices. This perspective is evident in both the BSR and Chinese Government definitions of CSR given in Table 1.1. The values dimension of CSR is part of the reason why the subject raises so much disagreement – if it were just about what companies *did* in the social arena, it would not cause so much controversy as the debate about *why* they do it.

Beyond philanthropy

In some regions of the world, CSR is mainly about philanthropy – i.e. corporate largesse towards the less fortunate. But the current debate on CSR has tended to emphatically claim that 'real' CSR is about more than just philanthropy and community giving, but about how the entire operations of the firm – i.e. its core business functions – impact upon society. Core business functions include production, marketing, procurement, human resource management, logistics, finance, etc. This debate rests on the assumption that CSR needs to be integrated into normal business practice rather than being left simply to discretionary activity. The attempt to consider how CSR might be 'built in' to the core business of firms as opposed to 'bolted on' as an added extra has become a major theme in the CSR practitioner world (Grayson & Hodges, 2004). According to Wayne Visser (2010), for example, CSR needs to become the 'new DNA' of business.

These six core characteristics, we would suggest, capture the main thrust of CSR. However, as we will now discuss, the meaning and relevance of CSR will vary according to organizational and national context.

CSR in different organizational contexts

The variety of definitions and perspectives on CSR discussed in the previous section is partly credited to the fact that CSR is practised in a broad range of different organizational contexts. In the following we will explore these contexts by analysing the role and relevance of CSR in all three main sectors of modern economies, i.e. the private sector, the public sector, and the civil society or third sector (including non-governmental organizations, social enterprises, charities). It should be noted that there is an issue of terminology here, since the 'corporate' aspect of CSR does not in a literal sense apply to small businesses, public sector organizations, NGOs and the like, but the acronym is nevertheless commonly used in a generic sense and we continue to do so here.[3]

CSR and the private sector

The main arena of CSR, as indicated by the 'corporate' in CSR, is the business world. Within that arena, however, we have a plethora of different types, industries and organizational forms. In the following section, we will have a look at one of the main distinctions, namely between large corporations and small- and medium-sized enterprises (SMEs) – see Table 1.2.

Table 1.2: Differences in CSR among large and small firms

	Large firms	Small firms
Formalization of CSR	Formal, bureaucratized	Informal
Main actors in CSR	Shareholders, external stakeholders	Owner-manager, employees
Aims of CSR	Build corporate brand and manage public legitimacy	Build trust, networks and personal relations

Arguably, the language of *corporate* social responsibility indicates that CSR is predominantly a concept that applies to large corporations, typically owned by shareholders and run by employed managers. Certainly the seminal contributions on CSR, as discussed in Chapters 2 and 3 of this book, conceive CSR against the backdrop of these large corporations. Therefore, as entities in which ownership and control are separated (Berle & Means, 1932), one of the prominent issues for thinking about CSR in the context of large corporations is the question of whose interest the company should be run on behalf of by managers: just the interests of the owners or also the interests of society at large, represented by different groups such as customers, employees or local communities?

One could also argue that large corporations are far more visible and thus far more vulnerable to criticism from the public than smaller firms (Spence, 2007). A large company that wants to behave socially responsibly therefore may well have formal policies on its responsibilities and how these are managed. On the whole, then, CSR in large corporations typically results in a fairly structured and formalized approach. CSR policies will be translated into codes of conduct for employees or suppliers; there will normally be committees and managers responsible for CSR; and many large companies involved in CSR will document their engagement in a dedicated annual report. In such a report, the corporation discharges accountability for how exactly they have dealt with different interests and expectations of society.

If we turn to SMEs, however, we will find a rather different picture, with evidence suggesting that they tend not to communicate externally about their CSR activities (Nielsen & Thomsen, 2009). There are a number of reasons that account for these differences (see Spence, 1999). First, SMEs are informal in nature, lacking the need for bureaucratic systems and structures due to the advantages of small size and the proximity of business partners and stakeholders. All business systems, including CSR, are rather informal and ad hoc in nature as opposed to the structured, formalized and codified approach of large corporations.

Second, unlike large corporations – who, due to size and branding, are often quite visible and vulnerable to criticism – SMEs are generally rather invisible and fall under the radar of wider society. Their key relationships with society are the personal relations developed between the owner/manager and, for instance, his or her employees, suppliers, customers, or neighbours. These personal relations, however, are of crucial importance to the SME and therefore much of what we could identify as CSR in this context is targeted at building good personal relations, networks, and trust (Spence & Schmidpeter, 2002).

Third, the common owner-managed nature of the small firm means that there is no separation of ownership and control, unlike in publicly traded large firms. Accordingly, managers are not obliged to serve shareholders or seek to maximize their return on investment. Owner-managers typically enjoy the autonomy of running their own firm and are not seeking to maximize profit as their reward (Spence & Rutherfoord, 2001). This frees them to invest time and resources according to their, and importantly their employees' (seen as key stakeholders) interests. As noted above, however, the CSR activities embedded in the firm are not reflected in external reporting. Nielsen & Thomsen (2009) capture this paradox poetically, 'SMEs have no interest in turning their local and authentic practice into a forced marketing and branding exercise.'

Overall, it is probably fair to say that given the importance of SMEs, which in much of the world account for the majority of private sector employment and GDP in their countries, the CSR literature has so far paid disproportionate attention to larger organizations (Morsing & Perrini, 2009). This gap in research is highlighted further where family businesses – also a majority form in the private sector and relevant to both large and small firms – are taken into account. A range of issues related to the mixing of public and private objectives and the influence of succession issues and family legacy have important impacts on CSR which are yet to be fully understood (Mitchell et al, 2011).

CSR and the public sector

At first sight, one would not necessarily expect CSR to be an issue for public sector organizations, such as government ministries, agencies or local administrative bodies. After all, it is 'corporate' social responsibility. However, in most industrialized countries, governments still supply a large amount of all goods and services, somewhere between 40–50 per cent of the GDP in many countries. Consequently, the same demands made upon corporations to conduct their operations in a socially responsible fashion are increasingly applied to public sector organizations as well. For example, public sector organizations face the similar environmental demands, similar claims for equal opportunities for employees, and similar expectations for responsible sourcing as do private companies. Consequently, we increasingly find public sector organizations adopting CSR policies, practices and tools very similar to those found in the private sector.

In some ways, these demands for social responsibility in the public sector could be considered more pronounced due in part to the public service ethos (Van der Wal et al, 2008). Public organizations, such as schools, hospitals, or universities, by definition have social aims and are mostly run on a not-for-profit basis. This establishes the social dimension of their responsibility at the core of their operations. Furthermore, given the size of many public bodies and agencies, as well as their quasi-monopolistic position in many areas of services, they are likely to have an impact on society that is often far beyond the impact of a single large corporation. Consequently, the claim for responsible behaviour on the part of public bodies has grown, as has the demand for greater accountability to society in the public sector. Just as private sector companies are exhorted to become more accountable in their reporting and communication to the public, so we now witness a steady rise in the use of typical CSR instruments, such as social auditing and reporting, by public bodies (Ball, 2004). The United States Postal Service, for example, has been publishing social responsibility and sustainability reports since 2008.[4]

Apart from incorporating CSR into their own operations, many government organizations also take an active role in promoting CSR within their sphere of influence, including going beyond their borders. For example, the Sino-German CSR project is the first bilateral project of its kind to focus exclusively on CSR in China. One of the major objectives of the project is to strengthen key government institutions in their efforts to improve framework conditions for CSR in China.[5]

A similarly pronounced role in promoting CSR has been adopted by the European Union. In a part of the world where CSR is still largely considered a novel, Anglo-Saxon idea, the European Commission has invested considerable effort in defining and promoting CSR in Europe, convening a multi-stakeholder dialogue which resulted in a widely discussed White Paper in 2002 (Commission of the European Communities, 2002) and a new CSR strategy in 2011 (Commission of the European Communities, 2011). We will discuss in more depth the broader role of government in CSR in Chapter 11.

CWS 1.2

Visit the companion website for more examples of CSR initiatives by governments in different countries

CSR and civil society organizations

Intractably linked to the rise of CSR is the role of civil society organizations (CSOs). These non-governmental organizations (NGOs) have primarily social goals and may include social enterprises, charities, and community organizations. The sector is also sometimes called the third sector (alongside the private and the public) or the not-for-profit sector. Many of the initial demands for more responsible business behaviour – such as the protection of the environment, improvements in working conditions in sweatshops in the developing world, or prevention of human rights violations in countries with oppressive regimes – have been brought to the attention of the wider public by CSOs such as Greenpeace, Save the Children, or Amnesty International. Traditionally then, the role of NGOs in the CSR arena has been more that of a police officer or watchdog, a constant critic exposing corporate misbehaviour and mobilizing pressure against allegedly irresponsible practices. This role continues to be an important function of those CSOs whose skills in raising awareness and publicly exposing corporations can be such a major reputational risk for 'responsible' companies.

Increasingly, however, companies have responded to these challenges and have tried to take on board the criticisms of CSOs. In a considerable number of cases, this has resulted in a changing relation between business and CSOs: rather than just being critic and opponent, CSOs have also built partnerships with business in order to contribute to more socially responsible behaviour on the part of corporations. Although such relationships are not without their challenges (Jamali & Keshishian, 2009), within these partnerships, corporations can bring their considerable financial resources to the table while CSOs can offer their expertise and public legitimacy, among other things (Elkington & Fennell, 2000). Moreover, a number of broader industry- or countrywide standards for responsible corporate behaviour have emerged from business-CSO partnerships. A prominent example here is the Marine Stewardship Council,[6] a set of rules and practices for sustainable fisheries, which was initially set up by the NGO Worldwide Fund for Nature (WWF) and the company Unilever (Clay, 2005). Indeed, many of the voluntary approaches to self-regulation seen today come into existence with some degree of NGO involvement (Doh & Teegen, 2003).

Another civil society organizational form which has prospered in recent years is the social enterprise (see Chapter 12 for more details). Social enterprises and social entrepreneurs vary in type and form with as many definitions as CSR, but have a clear primary goal of social or environmental benefit, although they may operate in the private sector (Zahra et al, 2009). One of the most readily recognized social enterprises globally is the Grameen Bank,[7] which is a community development bank and gives very small loans (microcredit) to those at the very bottom of the economic scale – usually women – initially in Bangladesh but now further afield. While not uncontroversial, the work and ideas behind the Grameen Bank (Yunus & Weber 2009) have had such an impact globally that its founder, Mohammad Yunus was awarded the Nobel Peace Prize in 2006. Challenging the developed-developing country divide, Grameen Bank also operates in developed countries with, for example, Grameen Scotland opening in 2012.

With the continued growth of NGOs such as Oxfam, Greenpeace, or Amnesty International – many of which are global organizations with multimillion budgets and thousands of members and employees – CSR has also becomes a topic for these organizations to apply to themselves. Since they claim to campaign 'in the public interest', there is a growing demand to improve their public accountability (Unerman & O'Dwyer, 2006). The relationship of social enterprises to CSR is similarly a complex one, with research still emerging, not least because of the assumption that social enterprises are inherently 'doing good' (Nicholls, 2009). In addition, social enterprises are as varied in size as private sector organizations, with vast multinationals such as Ashoka and Grameen grouped together with many and varied micro community-based organizations.

CSOs as well as corporations need to be transparent about their causes, their funding, and their tactics, and to provide their supporters and the general public with some degree of say in how they represent these causes. This becomes more pronounced as business itself has increasingly moved towards setting up CSOs that represent specific business interests, such as the World Business Council for Sustainable Development (WBCSD), the Global Business Coalition on HIV/AIDS (GBC) or the Global Climate Coalition (GCC). While on the outside, these organizations often look like CSOs, they are in fact far different from normal grassroots CSOs, and have therefore been dubbed by some as 'astroturf NGOs' (Gray et al, 2006). Arguably, the challenge of putting policies and practices in place for enhanced public accountability and transparency – in other words, implementing CSR – is one of the key future tests for CSOs.

CSR in different regions of the globe

The meaning of CSR not only differs from sector to sector (as we have discussed in the previous section), but it also differs quite substantially from country to country (Freeman & Hasnaoui, 2011). To put CSR 'in a global context' (as our subtitle suggests) it is essential to understand the specific regional and national contexts in which companies practise CSR. In the following section, we will therefore discuss some basic characteristics of CSR in different regions of the globe. It should be noted that the categories developed/developing/transitional/emerging – are not definitive. In particular, the rise in economic power of the 'BRIC' economies – Brazil, Russia, India and China – where economic growth is far greater than in the US and Western Europe at the beginning of the 2010s, leaves a global economy in flux and transition.

CWS 1.4

Visit the companion website for more examples of CSR initiatives and approaches in different countries

CSR in developed countries

In its most well-known guise, CSR is essentially an American idea. It was in the US that the language and practice of CSR first emerged. Also, most of the academic literature on the topic, and most of the key ideas discussed in the first section of this book, originate from there, although they have been built on and developed by contributors from around the world. The main reason for this lies in the specific characteristics of the US business system (Matten & Moon, 2008). That is, American society is characterized by fairly unregulated markets for labour and capital, low levels of welfare state provision, and a high appreciation of individual freedom and responsibility. Consequently, many social issues, such as education, healthcare, or community investment have traditionally been at the core of CSR. Philanthropy is high on the agenda with, for instance, corporate community contributions by US companies being about ten times higher than those of their British counterparts (Brammer & Pavelin, 2005).

In other parts of the world, most notably Europe, the Far East, and Australasia, there has always been a stronger tendency to address social issues through governmental policies and collective action. Many issues that US companies would typically boast about as CSR on their websites, such as the provision of healthcare or fighting climate change, have not appeared until recently on the screens of continental European companies. The reason for this is that these issues have traditionally been considered a task for governments. In other words, the corporate responsibility for social issues has been the object of codified and mandatory regulation. CSR for European companies, therefore, has predominantly come on the agenda through their overseas operations (where regulatory frameworks are different from Europe), and it is fair to say that even until the present day, multinational corporations (MNCs) rather than domestic companies can be considered to be the leading actors in European CSR. The US-Europe differences in CSR are likely to persist and the way corporations address CSR issues, such as global warming, the provision of affordable medicine to the developing world, or the use of genetically modified organisms in food production, remains markedly different on both sides of the Atlantic (Doh & Guay, 2006).

Countries such as Japan, and to a lesser degree South Korea and Taiwan, are considered fairly similar to continental Europe in terms of the institutional context for CSR. They are characterized by high bank and public ownership, patriarchal and long-term employment, and coordination and control systems based on long-term relations and partnerships rather than on markets. The Japanese 'Keiretsu', the

Korean 'Chaebol', or the (mostly state-owned) Taiwanese conglomerates have a legacy of CSR similar to European companies – including life-long employment, benefits, social services, and healthcare – not so much as a result of voluntary corporate policies, but more as a response to the regulatory and institutional environment of business.

The reasons for the rise of CSR in Europe and in these developed economies in the Far East in recent years are several. To begin with, MNCs with their home base in such countries are challenged to implement more CSR in their operations located in countries with poor governance and low levels of state provision of public services, human rights protection, or environmental protection. Furthermore, some of these developed economies have undergone substantial overhauls of their welfare systems and regulatory frameworks, resulting in lesser degrees of state attention to social issues and more discretion for private actors. The United Kingdom is probably the best example here, where radical reforms that liberalized labour and capital markets, together with the privatization of public services and publicly owned companies, contributed to a significant surge in CSR (Moon, 2004). Increasingly, corporations in the UK have assumed responsibility for regenerating local communities, addressing unemployment, sponsoring schools and education, as well as improving public transparency and accountability. This shift was formalized in the flagship commitment for the 'Big Society' – i.e. local community empowerment – by Prime Minister David Cameron in the early 2010s.[8]

In addition to these domestic political changes, globalization also represents a powerful booster of CSR. The rise of global investors linking their investment decisions to 'socially responsible investment' criteria, the growth in global NGO activism scrutinizing corporate behaviour, and intensified exposure of business by the media have all boosted growing attention to CSR in Europe and elsewhere (Matten & Moon, 2008). It can also be observed that in most developed countries we have specific domestic CSR issues that shape the debate in the respective context. For instance, many European countries see CSR specifically with regard to the protection of the natural environment, while the CSR debate in the Far East prominently features issues of corporate governance and transparency in large conglomerates (Webb, 2006). Often the CSR debate in a country reflects longstanding and ongoing deliberations in society at large: for instance in Australia and South Africa, considerable expectations have been directed towards companies to address and uphold rights of aboriginal and black people respectively, or to contribute to their economic empowerment more generally.

CSR in developing countries

The activities of Western MNCs in developing countries have also been a major driver behind the recent surge in CSR over the last two decades. Many companies use developing countries as a source of cheap raw materials and, in particular, cheap labour. Against this backdrop, campaigns against Shell's role in Nigeria and Nike's poor labour practices in its Asian supply chains in the 1990s triggered significant changes toward more responsible practices in many MNCs. Problems still persist, however, with Apple facing substantial criticism for the low pay in one of its major suppliers Foxconn in China resulting in a spate of suicides in 2010, and front-page headlines in the *New York Times* in 2012.

Developing countries are broadly characterized by various features that can offer considerable scope for the exercise of CSR. These include low standards for working conditions and environmental protection, high corruption, oppressive regimes with low regard for human rights, poor provision of healthcare and education, as well as low levels of per capita income and foreign direct investment. Although this is not a fair representation of all developing country contexts at all times, the main challenge for MNCs from the developed world when they are faced with such circumstances lies in conducting their business in a way that would be considered socially responsible in their respective home countries

It is important to recognize though that a growing number of *domestic* companies in developing countries have also developed an interest in CSR. The main CSR issues these companies are concerned with include contributions to enhance the infrastructure of health, education, and transport, and to serve as examples of good governance. The development of microfinance has been an important contribution in this respect, encouraging small scale enterprise and the empowerment of marginalized groups. Such initiatives have moved beyond the realm of CSOs and are now engaged with by mainstream commercial banks such as HSBC (see Integrative case 2).

The debate in the Global South has begun to shift from understanding CSR as aid, towards thinking of responsible behaviour more in terms of development. Arguably, one of the main reasons why these countries are poor is the absence of economic activity and growth – and it is here where one of the main responsibilities of business can be seen. Implementing CSR in this sense would therefore require MNCs to conduct business and bring foreign direct investment to developing countries in the first place, and then ensure that the wealth created is locked into development. So, for instance, the World Business Council for Sustainable Development issued an in-depth report on how business supports the implementation of the United Nations' Millennium Development Goals[9] (WBCSD, 2005). Many of the points raised in the report do not refer to business 'sharing' its wealth with these countries but business being present in these countries and contributing to economic growth and prosperity.

This role of MNCs, however, is not uncontested. Many critics argue that profit-maximizing corporations have only very limited interest in these more political goals, and that evidence of MNCs contributing positively in the developing world is at best sketchy (Frynas, 2005). Ultimately, according to the sceptics, responsible corporate behaviour in the developing world is an issue that cannot be left to the voluntary discretion of business people but needs to be addressed by more stringent regulation in their home countries in the global North (Aaronson, 2005).

CSR in emerging/transitional economies

Between those two major categories of developed and developing countries there is a third category that deserves attention from a CSR perspective. Most countries of the former communist bloc have changed from a planned and government run economy to a capitalist market system. While the social responsibility of state-operated business in the former model was far-reaching, including broad provision of education, healthcare, housing and a plethora of other services, the transition to a market economy has seen many of these former conglomerates dismantled and transformed into shareholder-owned companies. While there is a range of different approaches to CSR in these countries, one might argue that in some respects, Russia and China represent the more extreme cases. In the Russian context, the societal acceptance of the market remains an issue with large corporations often tainted by an image of fraud and corruption, and where mutual suspicion between business, the state and the people is rife. Perhaps unsurprisingly in this context, research has found that Russian managers do not see CSR as a relevant topic for business or for other stakeholders. Challenging the Western understanding of CSR, Russian managers are more likely to perceive CSR in terms of responsibilities that are taken for granted elsewhere, such as abiding by the law, paying taxes and providing employment (Kuznetsov et al, 2009).

In China, the CSR movement has emerged since the new millennium, in a context of a legal framework for companies to abide by ethical and socially responsible codes, and the beginning of a wave of CSR reports by State Owned Enterprises starting in 2006 when the Shenzhen Stock Exchange also published its 'Socially Responsible Guidelines for Listed Companies'. Po (2009) attributes all these developments and the rise of CSR to supply chain demands and China's increasingly important role in the world and the desire to match this role with an appropriate national image in terms of social responsibility. There is also the argument that the cultural legacy of Confucianism is in keeping with many elements of CSR. Against this positive backdrop, however, it should not be forgotten that there remain serious and seemingly intractable problems relating especially to the environment, labour and human rights and product safety in China (Po, 2009).

The 'Arab Spring', which started at the end of 2010, saw a wave of protest and a string of dictators overthrown, leading to the emergence of several new governments across North Africa and the Middle East. The economic, business and socio-political outcomes of these transitions have yet to fully take shape, but it is notable that companies, especially technology firms, played a significant role both in supporting and constraining pro-democracy movements at this time. The Egyptian revolution, for example, was lauded as a 'Facebook revolution' and one of its more prominent leaders was a Google executive (Smith, 2012). Internet service providers and mobile phone providers (including Vodafone, see Integrative case 1), however, across the region were at various times forced by the authorities to close down service in order to restrict protestors' ability to organize. Social responsibility (or the lack of it) might therefore go further than just adapting to the existing institutional context, but also include playing a role in the transformation of political systems in transitional economies.

Conclusion

In this chapter we have discussed the development of CSR, and its rise to prominence. We have also examined the maze of definitions that have been used to delineate CSR in order to develop some core characteristics of the concept. Finally, we explored the meaning and relevance of CSR in different national and organizational contexts.

What should certainly be clear by now is that the term 'corporate social responsibility' is very difficult to pin down precisely – it can have many meanings, applications, and implications, and these are rarely agreed upon by those who take an interest in the debate. This may not make our lives any easier when studying CSR, but it certainly makes it more interesting!

In this book, we have adopted a deliberately broad perspective on CSR in order to provide a well-rounded introduction to the subject. Included in the following chapters are those that espouse a view of CSR thoroughly embedded in a pro-corporate 'business case for CSR' as well as those that argue for a more political view of CSR that attends to the need to make corporations more accountable to the societies in which they operate. The point of this text is not so much to suggest that any of these perspectives is necessarily 'better' or more 'correct' than another. Rather it is to provide an insight into the richness and diversity of the CSR literature. Editing a collection of readings on CSR allows us to present some of this heterogeneity whilst simultaneously providing some guidance as to how to 'read' and contextualize the different contributions. After all, it is clear that many of the authors writing about CSR in this book are engaging in a discussion about CSR for different ends, and bring with them very diverse assumptions about the nature and purpose of the corporation. The introductions to the readings will offer some useful insight on these purposes and assumptions, at least as far as we see them.

The book is organized into three sections, dealing with respectively:

- Understanding CSR
- Applying CSR
- Managing CSR

In designing this structure, it is evident that our main focus is around the actual performance of CSR by organizations, although the book also offers considerable theoretical insight on CSR by bringing out key conceptual issues as they pertain to particular CSR practices and principles. The applied approach that we take is also demonstrated by the three integrative case studies that appear at the end of each section. These are intended to bring together some of the main issues that arise in the different chapters in each section, and offer some fascinating insights into the challenges of CSR in a global context.

Ultimately, the theory and practice of CSR as presented in this book represents a work in progress. The subject has risen to prominence only relatively recently, and has been disseminated across the globe with remarkable speed. The way in which CSR is understood, practised, and institutionalized in the global context is ever-changing and open to substantially different interpretations. This book offers a multifaceted, and relatively comprehensive account of CSR as it stands today, but this account is by no means the only or the final one.

Challenges for practice

Take a close look at a company you work for or with which you are familiar.

1. Is CSR part of the stated company mission?
   a) If not, where if anywhere does CSR make an appearance in the business? Does this match your experience?
   b) If CSR is a part of the mission, what relative importance is assigned to it? Does this match your experience?
2. Who is assigned responsibility for CSR and how do you think this affects CSR in practice?
   a) Is the system hierarchical or a more matrix-based approach?
   b) To whom do those responsible for CSR report and at what level are they in the organization?
   c) How much resource is assigned to CSR compared to, say, marketing?
3. Would you say that CSR is integrated into the business?
   a) Do performance appraisal and reward mechanisms include CSR measures?
   b) Are the financial and CSR reports integrated?
   c) Are sanctions applied if codes are not complied with?
   d) Is there regular training and discussion on CSR issues?

Study questions

1. What is CSR and why has it risen to prominence in the past decade?
2. What are the six main characteristics of CSR? How do definitions of CSR vary around the core characteristics?
3. Select four corporations and four NGOs and research their perspectives on CSR on the web. To what extent is there overlap and divergence in their view of CSR? What can account for these similarities or differences?
4. 'CSR is only relevant for large private sector companies.' Critically discuss, providing examples from SMEs, the public and civil sectors.
5. Can or should CSR be transferred to developing and emerging economies? What are the benefits and drawbacks of this for the countries concerned?

Further reading

Carroll, A. B. (1999) 'Corporate social responsibility – evolution of a definitional construct', Business & Society, 38(3): 268–295.
This paper gives a thorough and wide ranging overview of the first 50 years of CSR research.

Porter, M. & Kramer, M. (2011) 'Creating shared value', Harvard Business Review, January–February: 62–77.
This article has gained substantial attention from the business world and is potentially a game-changing contribution to the CSR debate in terms of the language and rhetoric of 'shared value'. As an approach it has its critics, but is certainly an important article in the contemporary CSR field.

Endnotes

1   The Corporate Responsibility (CORE) Coalition is a collection of UK NGOs including WWF (UK), Amnesty International, Action Aid, and Friends of the Earth, that 'work to make changes in UK company law to minimize companies' negative impacts on people and the environment and to maximize companies' contribution to sustainable societies' (www.corporate-responsibility.org).
2   www.abc.net.au/rural/content/2011/s3395026.htm (Accessed 30 August, 2012).
3   This limited applicability of the 'corporate' label might contribute to the preferred use of terminology such as 'sustainability' in many organizations, which has many common features with CSR and is often used interchangeably. For details on the various terms for CSR see Chapter 3.
4   http://about.usps.com/what-we-are-doing/green/report/2010/welcome.htm (Accessed 30 August, 2012).
5   www.chinacsrproject.org/ (Accessed 30 August, 2012).
6   www.msc.org (Accessed 30 August, 2012).
7   www.grameen-info.org (Accessed 30 August, 2012).
8   www.cabinetoffice.gov.uk/big-society (Accessed 30 August, 2012).
9   www.un.org/millenniumgoals (Accessed 30 August, 2012).

References

Aaronson, S. A. (2005) '"Minding our business": what the United States Government has done and can do to ensure that US multinationals act responsibly in foreign markets', Journal of Business Ethics, 59: 175–198.
Ball, A. (2004) 'A sustainability accounting project for the UK local government

sector? Testing the social theory mapping process and locating a frame of reference', *Critical Perspectives on Accounting*, 15(8): 1009–1035.

Berle, A. A. & Means, G. C. (1932) *The modern corporation and private property*, New York: Transaction.

BERR (2009) 'Corporate responsibility report', London: HM Government.

Brammer, S. & Pavelin, S. (2005) 'Corporate community contributions in the United Kingdom and the United States', *Journal of Business Ethics*, 56: 15–26.

Brown, T. J. & Dacin, P. A. (1997) 'The company and the product: corporate associations and consumer product responses', *Journal of Marketing*, 61(1): 68–84.

Carroll, A. B. (1979) 'A three dimensional model of corporate social performance', *Academy of Management Review*, 4: 497–505.

Clay, J. (2005) 'Exploring the links between international business and poverty reduction: a case study of Unilever in Indonesia', Oxford: Oxfam GB, Novib Oxfam Netherlands, and Unilever.

Commission of the European Communities (2002) 'Communication from the Commission concerning corporate social responsibility: a business contribution to sustainable development', Brussels, 02.07.2002 COM(2002) 347 final.

Commission of the European Communities (2011) 'Communication from the Commission to the European Parliament, the Council, the European Economic and Social Committee of the Regions: a renewed EU strategy 2011–14 for Corporate Social Responsibility', Brussels, 25.10.2011 COM(2011) 681 final.

CORE (2011) 'CORE values: why the UK needs a Commission for Business, Human Rights and the Environment', The Corporate Responsibility Coalition. Available from http://corporate-responsibility.org/wp-content/uploads/2011/04/CORE values.pdf (Accessed 30 August, 2012).

Davis, K. (1973) 'The case for and against business assumption of social responsibility', *Academy of Management Journal*, 16: 312–322.

Doh, J. P. & Guay, T. R. (2006) 'Corporate social responsibility, public policy, and NGO activism in Europe and the United States: an institutional-stakeholder perspective', *Journal of Management Studies*, 43(1): 47–73.

Doh, J. P. & Teegen, H. (eds) (2003) *Globalization and NGOs: transforming business, government, and society*, Westport, CT: Praeger Publishers.

Elankumaran, S., Seal, R., & Hashmi, A. (2005) 'Transcending transformation: enlightening endeavours at Tata Steel', *Journal of Business Ethics*, 59(1): 109–119.

Elkington, J. & Fennell, S. (2000) 'Partners for sustainability', in J. Bendell (ed.) *Terms for endearment: business, NGOs and sustainable development*, Sheffield: Greenleaf, 150–162.

Ethical Performance (2007) 'CSR combatants dig in for the battle of Wikipedia', *Ethical Performance*, 8(9): Downloaded from www.ethicalperformance.com/ news/article.php?articleID=4328 (Accessed 30 August, 2012).

Freeman, I. & Hasnaoui, A. (2011) 'The meaning of corporate social responsibility: the vision of four nations', *Journal of Business Ethics*, 100: 419–443.

Frynas, J. G. (2005) 'The false developmental promise of corporate social responsibility: evidence from multinational oil companies', *International Affairs*, 81(3): 581–598.

Gray, R., Bebbington, J., & Collinson, D. (2006) 'NGOs, civil society and accountability: making the people accountable to capital', *Accounting, Auditing & Accountability Journal*, 19(3): 319–348.

Grayson, D. & Hodges, A. (2004) *Corporate social opportunity: seven steps to make corporate social responsibility work for your business*, Sheffield: Greenleaf.

Husted, B. W. & Allen, D. B. (2006) 'Corporate social responsibility in the multinational enterprise: strategic and institutional approaches', *Journal of International Business Studies*, 37(6): 838–849.

Jamali, D. & Keshishian, T. (2009) 'Uneasy alliances: lessons learned from partnerships between businesses and NGOs in the context of CSR', *Journal of Business Ethics*, 84(2): 277–295.

Kuznetsov, A., Kuznetsova, O., & Warren, R., (2009) 'CSR and the legitimacy of business in transition economies: the case of Russia', *Scandinavian Journal of Management*, 25(1): 37–45

Lindgreen, A. & Swaen, V. (2010) 'Corporate social responsibility', *International Journal of Management Reviews*, 12(1): 1–7.

Matten, D. & Moon, J. (2008) '"Implicit" and "Explicit" CSR: a conceptual framework for a comparative understanding of CSR', *Academy of Management Review*, 33(2): 404–424.

Mitchell, R., Agle, B., Chrisman, J., & Spence, L. J. (2011) 'Toward a theory of stakeholder salience in family firms', *Business Ethics Quarterly*, 21(2): 235–255.

Moon, J. (2004) 'CSR in the UK: an explicit model of business-society relations', in A. Habisch, J. Jonker, M. Wegner, & R. Schmidpeter (eds) *CSR across Europe*, Berlin: Springer, 51–65.

Morsing, M. & Perrini, F. (2009) 'CSR in SMEs: do SMEs matter for the CSR agenda?' *Business Ethics: A European Review*, 18(1): 1–6.

Nicholls, A. (2009) '"We do good things, don't we?": "Blended Value Accounting" in social entrepreneurship', *Accounting, Organizations and Society*, 34: 755–769.

Nielsen, A. & Thomsen, C. (2009) 'Investigating CSR communication in SMEs: a case study among Danish middle managers', *Business Ethics: A European Review*, 18: 83–93.

Po, Ip (2009) 'The challenge of developing a business ethics in China', *Journal of Business Ethics*, 88: 211–224.

Smith, C. (2012) 'Egypt's Facebook revolution: Wael Ghonim thanks the social network', *Huffington Post*, 11 February 2012, www.huffingtonpost.com/2011/02/11/egypt-facebook-revolution-wael-ghonim_n_822078.html (Accessed 30 August, 2012).

Spence, L. J. (1999) 'Does size matter? The state of the art in small business ethics', *Business Ethics: A European Review*, 8(3): 163–174.

Spence, L. J. (2007) 'CSR and small business in a European policy context: the five "C"s of CSR and small business research agenda 2007', *Business and Society Review*, 112(4): 533–552.

Spence, L. J. & Rutherfoord, R. (2001) 'Social responsibility, profit maximisation and the small firm owner-manager', *Small Business and Enterprise Development*, 8(2): 126–139.

Spence, L. J. & Schmidpeter, R. (2002) 'SMEs, social capital and the common good', *Journal of Business Ethics*, 45: 93–108.

Triggle, N. (2011) 'Calorie counts on menus "prompt healthy choices"', BBC, 26 July, www.bbc.co.uk/news/health-14295093 (Accessed 30 August, 2012).

Unerman, J. & O'Dwyer, B. (2006) 'On James Bond and the importance of NGO accountability', *Accounting, Auditing & Accountability Journal*, 19(3): 305–318.

Van der Wal, Z., de Graaf, G., & Lasthuizen, K. (2008) 'What's valued most? Similarities and differences between the organizational values of the public and private sector', *Public Administration*, 86: 465–482.

Visser, W. (2010) 'The age of responsibility: CSR 2.0 and the new DNA of business', *Journal of Business Systems, Governance and Ethics*, 5(3): 7–22.

WBCSD (2005) *Business for development: business solutions in support of the Millennium Development Goals*, Geneva: World Business Council for Sustainable Development.

Webb, T. (2006) 'Is Asian corporate governance improving?' *Ethical Corporation*, May: 25–26.

Yunus, M. & Weber, K. (2009) *Creating a world without poverty: social business and the future of capitalism*, New York: Public Affairs.

Zahra, S., Gedajlovic, E., Neubaum, D., & Shulman, J. (2009) 'A typology of social entrepreneurs: motives, search processes and ethical challenges', *Journal of Business Venturing*, 24(5): 519–532.

Chapter 2

The case for and against CSR

IN THIS CHAPTER WE WILL:

- Map out the longstanding debate in favour and critical of CSR
- Highlight the nature of the modern corporation and its impact on CSR
- Evaluate the role of governments with regard to the socially responsible behaviour of corporations
- Understand and evaluate the key arguments against CSR
- Understand the key arguments in favour of CSR

Introduction

CSR is a peculiar beast. Not only is it pretty hard to nail down in terms of a definition – as we have seen in Chapter 1 – but there is also considerable disagreement among academics, managers and politicians as to whether CSR should be considered a legitimate activity of private companies to begin with. As Milton Friedman (1970) famously put it: 'the social responsibility of business is to increase its profits'!

This ambiguity should not come as a surprise since the contested nature of CSR is part and parcel of its very essence. This has little to do with the fact that CSR is still a rather new topic for practice, teaching and research. As we will see in this chapter, the controversies around our topic are rooted in wider controversies about the nature of the 'S' in CSR and how responsibilities between the core actors in a specific society (i.e. nation, local community, industry) should be defined and distributed.

Nothing has brought those controversies more to the fore than the financial crisis of the late 2000s and early 2010s. Since Lehman Brothers went into bankruptcy and the entire banking and financial system in the US and Europe threatened to fall apart in 2008, the debate about the wider societal impacts and responsibilities of private business and its managers has risen up the agenda like never before. Rather than just letting financial institutions reap the consequences of their poor decisions, governments across the world assessed the wider contribution of the sector towards society as too important and their core firms as 'too big to fail' (Sorkin, 2009). The financial crisis then has not just reinvigorated the old debate about the role and importance of business in society, but has also raised concerns about the status of CSR as a business practice. Whether it is Bank of America[1] in the US or the Royal Bank of Scotland[2] in the UK – most of the main firms involved in the crisis and receiving government bailouts had (and still have) extensive CSR programmes. The question many critics therefore asked was how it was possible that such companies could behave so recklessly in the marketplace while still upholding the image of a responsible member of society?

These controversies are further fuelled by two phenomena we briefly mentioned in Chapter 1. First, historically – as the reading by N. Craig Smith (in this chapter) elaborates in more detail – many of the activities labeled 'CSR' today have been practised by companies long before the fairly recent take-up through explicit CSR programmes. When companies such as Cadbury in England or Krupp in Germany provided housing, healthcare or education to their workers and their families or when industrialists such as Carnegie or Duke in the US funded universities in the nineteenth century they were doing pretty similar things to what contemporary firms currently feature as part of their CSR policies. Second, geographically, the notion of what a 'responsible' business looks like differs widely across different regions and countries. Japanese companies provide some fairly lavish benefits for their employees because of longstanding traditions and customary practices – but they hardly refer to this as CSR. German manufacturers have rather extensive environmental policies and practices in place – but they do so because they are an 'implicit' element of their regulatory framework rather than an element of a cunning 'CSR strategy' (Matten & Moon, 2008).

All this makes CSR somewhat elusive in nature, which in turn drives a considerable debate about whether businesses should or indeed can be responsible for their social impacts. This debate has become increasingly complex for two main reasons. First, the nature of the corporation has changed significantly over time and is still rather diverse globally. While the social provisions of nineteenth-century industrialists were mostly paternalistic initiatives of individual business leaders, today's CSR is carried out by huge corporations that are owned by hundreds and thousands of largely anonymous shareholders. Second, many of the early CSR activities by wealthy industrialists ultimately provided a standard for governments to issue legislation that made the provision of, for instance, decent working conditions, fair wages, and access to education a mandatory right for their citizens. These political changes resulted in extensive welfare state provision in most industrialized countries. This resulted in a situation where the care for the public good was mainly a responsibility of the state and if companies were involved then it was chiefly by complying with laws to this effect. The main points of contention between advocates and adversaries of CSR therefore focus on (1) the nature of the modern corporation and (2) the adequate role of the state. We will have a look at both issues in turn.

Understanding the nature of the modern corporation

As we discussed already in Chapter 1, the first major wave of debate on CSR started in the US in the 1950s. By this time, most big corporations were no longer owned by individual business people or their families but by shareholders with shares being traded on capital markets. The key debate in this context is in whose interest the company should be managed: should a corporation just pursue the interests of its owners, i.e. their shareholders, or the interests of wider society as well. It is well worth noting then that the terminology of *corporate* social responsibility reflects this focus on big businesses and while many of the issues discussed in CSR also apply to smaller businesses, the key trigger of the debate was the rise of the modern corporation which became manifest after the Second World War in the US and beyond in most industrialized countries.

Much of the literature on CSR, in particular as discussed in Chapters 3 and 4 in this book, can be seen as making the case for the legitimacy of the interests of societal groups beyond (but including) shareholders. The reading by Smith in this chapter provides an overview over this side of the argument. On the other hand, there has always been the argument that a company should just do what their owners want it to do – and as their chief interest is to maximize the value of the shares and/or the amount of their dividend, the economic goals of a business should be paramount. The article by Aneel Karnani in this chapter can be considered as a recent contribution to this side of the argument.

Interestingly, the resurgence in the debate on CSR at the beginning of this century was triggered mostly by corporate *ir*responsibility towards shareholders in the context of corporate scandals in the US (e.g. Enron, WorldCom) and Europe (e.g. Parmalat, Ahold). While the debate in essence did not surface fundamentally new arguments, it provided some more contextualization of the issues for the twenty-first-century business environment. In particular the compatibility of capitalism with wider societal interests (Child, 2002; Handy, 2002) and the need for change in business research and education (Gioia, 2002; Ghoshal, 2005) were centre-stage of the debate. While these scandals have given considerable mileage to CSR in business practice, many critics eloquently reiterated the necessity of business to focus on its core economic functions of producing goods and services while maximizing the returns for their primary legitimate interest groups, namely shareholders (Henderson, 2001; Sternberg, 2000). The 2008 financial crisis and its aftermath, although initially also mostly infringing shareholders' interests, has led to a much larger, and yet unresolved, debate. The crisis precipitated a global recession that affected numerous other sectors of the economy, for instance the automotive industry in North America and Europe. Furthermore, since many governments have spent considerable funds on 'rescuing' the banking system and other big corporations (e.g. General Motors in the US), the capacity of nation states to steer and

CWS 2.1

Visit the companion website for links to more material on the historical development of CSR

CWS 2.2

Visit the
companion
website for
links to more
on the financial
crisis as well
as to a number
of movies
which have
been made
based on the
events on Wall
Street during
this period

invigorate their local economies has suffered considerably, leading to a global recession of unknown length as of writing.

The role of government

A main concern of CSR critics from the very beginning has been the contention that responsibility for wider societal interest should not be located in the hands of business managers. Perhaps best known is Nobel Laureate Milton Friedman's (1970) trenchant critique of CSR, where he argues that private business should just stick to making profits rather than interfering with the job of governments. This view of government has always been at the heart of those criticisms. As recent as 2005, *The Economist* opened a special section on CSR with the grudging admission that 'CSR has won the battle of ideas' – but not without hastening to add 'That is a pity' (Crook, 2005). The central reason for this assessment was put this way:

> The proper guardians of the public interest are governments, which are accountable to all citizens. It is the job of elected politicians to set goals for regulators, to deal with externalities, to mediate among different interests, to attend to the demands of social justice, to provide the public goods . . . and to organise resources accordingly.
>
> (Crook, 2005: 18)

The gist of this CSR-scepticism then is that the central arbiter of the wider welfare of society is the (democratic) government of a country. The decision on which social causes should be met, what labour standards should be considered adequate, or what education should look like – to name some examples – is ultimately the domain of government. Private actors, most notably corporations, simply do not have the mandate to decide on these issues; rather it should be society as a whole through its democratically elected representatives. In essence then these critics argue that if there is a problem in society which managers could potentially address through CSR, it should not be at the discretion of individual managers, dedicating their shareholders' money to these causes; rather it should be an issue taken up by regulators resulting in changes in the legal framework of the corporation – if that is what society as a whole wants.

This argument is quite powerful. However, it overlooks one of the key reasons which has put CSR on the agenda over the last two decades. As we will discuss in more detail in Chapter 11, globalization and other socio-political factors have fundamentally changed the way in which societies are governed. Many governments are now reluctant to impose extra regulation on business for fear of losing employment and tax income, since companies find it easier to relocate to more 'business friendly' countries – a phenomenon sometimes referred to as the 'race to the bottom' because it can result in a drive to find locations with ever lower social and environmental standards. This is reflected in a statement by US President, Barack Obama in one of his weekly addresses where he specifically urges businesses to take on responsibility for providing growth and employment in the US rather than offshore:

> Businesses have a responsibility, too. If we make America the best place to do business, businesses should make their mark in America. They should set up shop here, and hire our workers, and pay decent wages, and invest in the future of this nation. That's their obligation.
>
> (Yager, 2011)

Furthermore, as we will see in the paper by Valente and Crane in Chapter 7, businesses in developing countries often face governments that are either undemocratic or are otherwise unwilling, or simply unable, to implement existing regulation to look after the public interest. It is no surprise that many companies – as the case studies in this volume illustrate – take up CSR because of their global operations in contexts of poor societal governance on the part of governments.

CWS 2.3

Visit the companion website for links to more material on the 'race to the bottom' by companies looking for lower social and environmental standards

Introducing the readings

The two readings that follow offer a good introduction to both sides of the argument on CSR. As we have discussed above, the two key contested areas have pretty much remained the same over the years and the two papers were accordingly written relatively recently by two distinguished academics. In their own way, they represent simple but quite comprehensive overviews of the respective sides of the debate, and thus present a succinct summary of a controversy which has accompanied the field of CSR for more than four decades.

CSR as an established part of contemporary business practice

INSEAD and former London Business School professor N. Craig Smith's reading signals a sea change in attention to CSR and places it firmly in the business mainstream. Smith takes the reader through some historical overview about CSR and presents the key business arguments in favour of this emerging practice: CSR can reduce costs, enhance revenues, and help mitigate a number of business risks, in particular reputational risk. The article, however, also turns the attention to the normative side of CSR. Using the pharmaceutical company GSK as an example, Smith shows that in some cases CSR might be more a reflection of wider normative expectations of society towards corporations, rather than a result of a clear-cut business case.

The overarching bracket of Smith's argument is linked to the necessity of a company to maintain their social 'licence to operate' as a fundamental condition of all potential business success. The latter point is arguably becoming more widespread in the contemporary business debate on CSR after the financial crisis. As the *Financial Times* observed 'a pre-recession argument for corporate responsibility was that it gave companies a moral "licence to operate". Some skeptics regarded this as a bit of a joke. Few do now' (Skapinker, 2009). Concerns around the licence to operate have boosted CSR in many companies just because the public trust in the private sector has so much declined in the aftermath of the financial crisis.

The case against corporate social responsibility

Aneel Karnani's argument against CSR starts exactly at Smith's core point: if CSR in all its manifestations is simply a fundamental way to protect and enhance the firm's profitability – it is just a good business practice and nothing more. CSR in this sense then is a nice sounding label of business as usual, a handy disguise of clear-cut corporate self-interest behind the cloak of alleged interest in the public good. Karnani's argument is interesting as much of his work has not focused on CSR as such; rather he is probably best known as a vocal critic of the 'bottom of the pyramid' approach (e.g. Karnani, 2007, see the reading by Prahalad and Hammond in Chapter 5). Companies that claim an interest in serving poor consumers by selling them goods at a profit, goes his argument, are not doing this out of altruism but rather plain self-interest. He does not blame business for this, rather Karnani argues that the way publicly owned companies are set up they do not have another option.

Karnani's argument is strongly reminiscent of the argument against CSR posed by Milton Friedman more than 40 years previously. Both primarily attack the professed motivations of companies in practising CSR. Like Friedman, Karnani is deeply sceptical of whether companies can, or even should, be expected to trade profits for the pursuit of the public good. His key solution for companies to behave in socially responsible ways thus comes from outside. Governmental regulation, the coercive power of civil society, and government controlled forms of self-regulation are, in his view, the better avenues to create socially beneficial corporate behaviour.

Challenges for practice

Take a close look at a company you work for or with which you are familiar.

1. Reflect on the role of the government in the home country of the company.
   a) What is the basic provision of public goods, such as education, health-care, safety, infrastructure (roads, public transport, telecommunication) by the government?
   b) What is the legal framework for the company with regard to product safety, employee healthcare and the environment? Is it well enforced?
   c) What are the general public expectations of companies in the country?
2. Looking at the paper by N. Craig Smith, in which areas of CSR is the company active? If it is not, in which areas could it be useful to think about CSR?

   a)   Is there potential for the company to reduce costs through CSR?
   b)   Are there opportunities for new areas of revenue through CSR?
   c)   Are there any risks to the brand or other parts of the business which
        could be managed through more CSR?
3. Reflect on the 'financial crisis' that has been ongoing since 2008. Was
    the company affected or involved in any way? What relation has the crisis
    had to CSR in the company?
4. Next time you get a chance, talk to your colleagues or superiors about
    CSR, try to find out if they are in favour or against it. Analyse their argu-
    ments in the light of the readings in this chapter. How would you categorize
    them and how would you evaluate them?

Study questions

1.   What are the key arguments for and against CSR? Answer the question using
     the arguments brought forward by Aneel Karnani and Craig Smith.
2.   Both Smith and Karnani have different assumptions about:
     a)   The nature of the modern corporation;
     b)   The role and capacity of governments.
     Describe and discuss both aspects in the respective articles. Which approach
     do you think is most realistic for business in the twenty-first century?
3.   Is there a difference between the social responsibility of a small, private-owned
     family business and a large, publically-traded corporation?
4.   The EU Commission has supported CSR in various initiatives over the last
     decade, for example with the European Alliance for CSR.[3] In similar vein, the
     Chinese[4] and Indian[5] governments recently released a number of initiatives to
     further CSR in their countries. Think about reasons why governments could
     be interested in encouraging CSR. What are the benefits and drawbacks of
     such an approach?
5.   The debate for and against CSR is decades old. How do you think the financial
     crisis of 2008 and its aftermath have affected the arguments for and against
     CSR?

Further reading

Friedman, M. (1970) 'The social responsibility of business is to increase its profits', *The New York Times Magazine*, 13 September: 70–71, 122–126.

This short magazine article is a classic in the CSR literature. It is a frequently cited cornerstone of arguments against CSR from a management perspective. It is based on the assumption that private companies have a very specific, economic mandate in society. Beyond this mandate, the impact of business on society should not be at the discretion of unaccountable managers but in the hands of publicly elected and accountable governments.

Banerjee, S. B. (2007) 'Corporate social responsibility: the good, the bad and the ugly', *Critical Sociology*, 34(1): 51–79.

This academic analysis offers a thorough critique of CSR from the school of thought of 'critical management'. As such, Bobby Banerjee comes to conclusions that on the surface are similar to Friedman's above. The foundations of his arguments though are rather different and his critique is more radical: CSR in this paper is not just a misnomer or a misconstrued venture for the public good; rather it is unpacked as the very tool that disguises and enables forms of corporate irresponsibility and exploitation.

Endnotes

1   See, for example, its CSR Report 2010 at www.bankofamerica.com (Accessed 30 August, 2012).
2   See www.rbs.com/sustainability.html (Accessed 30 August, 2012).
3   ec.europa.eu/enterprise/policies/sustainable-business/corporate-social-responsibility/european-alliance/index_en.htm (Accessed 30 August, 2012).
4   www.dlapiper.com/foreign_enterprises_csr_compliance/ (Accessed 30 August, 2012).
5   www.nfcgindia.org/pdf/CSR_Voluntary_Guidelines_2009.pdf (Accessed 30 August, 2012).

References

Child, J. (2002) 'The international crisis of confidence in corporations', *Academy of Management Executive*, 16(3): 145–149.
Crook, C. (2005) 'The good company', *The Economist*, 374 (22 January): 20.
Friedman, M. (1970) 'The social responsibility of business is to increase its profits', *The New York Times Magazine*, 13 September: 70–71, 122–126.

Ghoshal, S. (2005) 'Bad management theories are destroying good management practices', *Academy of Management Learning & Education*, 4(1): 75–91.

Gioia, D. A. (2002) 'Business education's role in the crisis of confidence in corporations', *Academy of Management Executive*, 16(3): 142–144.

Handy, C. (2002) 'What's a business for?' *Harvard Business Review*, 80(12): 49–56.

Henderson, D. (2001) *Misguided virtue: false notions of corporate social responsibility*, London: Institute of Economic Affairs.

Jensen, M. C. (2010) 'Value maximization, stakeholder theory, and the corporate objective function', *Journal of Applied Corporate Finance*, 22(1): 32–42.

Kapstein, E. B. (2001) 'The corporate ethics crusade', *Foreign Affairs*, 80(5): 105–119.

Karnani, A. (2007) 'The misfortune at the bottom of the pyramid', *Greener Management International*, 51: 99–110.

Matten, D. & Moon, J. (2008) '"Implicit" and "explicit" CSR: a conceptual framework for a comparative understanding of corporate social responsibility', *Academy of Management Review*, 33(2): 404–424.

Skapinker, M. (2009) 'Why corporate responsibility is a survivor', *Financial Times*, 20 April.

Sorkin, A. R. (2009) *Too big to fail: the inside story of how Wall Street and Washington fought to save the financial system – and themselves*, New York: Viking.

Spence, L. J. (2007) 'CSR and small business in a European policy context: the five "C"s of CSR and small business research agenda 2007', *Business and Society Review*, 112(4): 533–552.

Sternberg, E. (2000) *Just business: business ethics in action* (2nd edn), Oxford and New York: Oxford University Press.

Yager, J. (2011) 'Obama: businesses have responsibility to help economy grow', *The Hill*, 5 February, thehill.com (Accessed 18 June, 2012).

CORPORATE SOCIAL RESPONSIBILITY: WHETHER OR HOW?

N. Craig Smith

While corporate social responsibility (CSR) was widely discussed in the last forty years of the twentieth century, the idea that business has societal obligations was evident at least as early as the nineteenth century. In Britain, visionary business leaders in the aftermath of the Industrial Revolution built factory towns—such as Bourneville (founded by George Cadbury in 1879) and Port Sunlight (founded by William Lever in 1888 and named after the brand of soap made there)—that were intended to provide workers and their families with housing and other amenities when many parts of the newly industrialized cities were slums. A similar pattern also emerged in the United

States—George Pullman's town built on the outskirts of Chicago was described as "the most perfect city in the world."[1]

Consider Saltaire, founded in 1851 by Sir Titus Salt (1803–1876) just outside Bradford, then the world's wool textile capital. In the mid-nineteenth century, Bradford was also known as the most polluted town in England, with factory chimneys churning out black, sulphurous smoke and factory effluent and sewage being dumped into the local river that also provided the town's drinking water, leading to cholera and typhoid. Average life expectancy in Bradford was only 20 years. Daniel Salt and Sons was one of the most important textile companies in Bradford and the largest employer. In response to conditions in the city and needing a suitable site for a new factory, Titus Salt moved from Bradford and built a new industrial community called Saltaire. By the time of his death in 1876, this included 850 houses for his workers, each served with fresh water from Saltaire's own reservoir, as well as a park, church, school, hospital, and a library.

Unfortunately, Saltaire was the exception rather than the rule and the "dark Satanic mills" described by William Blake (1757–1827) were more the norm. Moreover, this was a form of paternalistic capitalism; like Lever and Cadbury, Salt also wished to promote moral virtue among his workers. As an account of the founding of Saltaire observes, "Bradford was polluted, unhealthy and immoral; at Saltaire the physical, material, and moral improvement of the workers was to be promoted by a good employer."[2] Nonetheless, while Salt would not have been familiar with the term, he clearly supported the fundamental idea embedded in corporate social responsibility, "that business corporations have an obligation to work for social betterment."[3]

Salt and other philanthropic industrialists of the Victorian period were motivated by a desire to do good, but they were also motivated by enlightened self-interest. Salt recognized that his mill workers would be more productive if he offered an improved work environment and better living conditions. He also realized that Saltaire would be less vulnerable to the political unrest and militancy evident at that time among some sections of the population in Bradford, and strikes and other disputes were rare in Saltaire. Indeed, historian Styles asked: "Was Salt's paternalism (consciously or not) ultimately a device for securing a compliant, captive workforce which could be indoctrinated into disciplined behavior that ensured continued profits?"[4] While acknowledging that the realization of Salt's vision secured the continuing profitability of his business, Styles rejects these pejorative interpretations of Salt and Saltaire: "It fulfilled the obligations he believed he owed his workers."[5]

Key Characteristics of CSR

CSR refers to the obligations of the firm to society or, more specifically, the firm's stakeholders—those affected by corporate policies and practices. Saltaire and other early examples of paternalistic capitalism reveal three important characteristics of CSR. First, it is not a new idea, the hype surrounding it today notwithstanding.[6] Second, although there is a clear difference between CSR stemming from a desire to do good (the "normative case") and CSR that reflects an enlightened self-interest (the "business case"), a firm's reasons for engaging in CSR might reflect a mixture of these motivations. Third, while there is substantial agreement that CSR is concerned with the societal obligations of business, there is much less certainty about the nature and scope of these obligations. Salt's ideas for social betterment did not meet with universal approval and he opposed legislation to prohibit child labor. Even corporate champions of CSR today, such as Starbucks meet with criticism from NGOs (non-governmental organizations) and others.[7] As Sethi observed nearly 30 years ago, the operational meaning of CSR is supremely vague.[8]

Prominence of CSR

Historical origins notwithstanding, CSR has never been more prominent on the corporate agenda. It has been one of the leading topics at recent World Economic Forum (WEF) meetings. A report from the WEF observes that the three key pressures of "corporate competitiveness, corporate governance, and corporate citizenship, and the linkages between them, will play a crucial role in shaping the agenda for business leaders in the coming decade."[9] It continues:

> In the face of high levels of insecurity and poverty, the backlash against globalization, and mistrust of big business, there is growing pressure on business leaders and their companies to deliver wider societal value. This calls for effective management of the company's wider impacts on and contributions to society, making appropriate use of stakeholder engagement.[10]

Similarly, the World Business Council for Sustainable Development (WBCSD), a coalition of 120 international companies, refers to the increasing calls for business to assume wider responsibilities in the social arena and claims that CSR "is firmly on the global policy agenda."[11] Among the many other organizations that are advocating greater attention to CSR are the International Business Leaders Forum (IBLF), Business for Social Responsibility (BSR), and Business in the Community (BITC).[12]

Governmental organizations also are involved. In the U.K., the government has appointed a minister for CSR and in its second report on CSR, published in 2002, the Department of Trade and Industry (DTI) states: "The Government has an ambitious vision for corporate social responsibility: to see private, voluntary, and public sector organizations in the U.K. take account of their economic, social, and environmental impacts, and take complementary action to address key challenges based on their core competences—locally, regionally, nationally, and internationally."[13] The European Commission adopted a new strategy on CSR in July 2002. Announcing the policy paper, Anna Diamantopoulou, Commissioner for Employment and Social Affairs commented: "Many businesses have already recognized that CSR can be profitable and CSR schemes have mushroomed. However, the EU can add value in at least two key ways: by helping stakeholders to make CSR more transparent and more credible, and by showing that CSR is not just for multinationals—it can benefit smaller businesses too."[14]

A Shift in the Debate on CSR?

Historically, there have been periods of heightened interest in CSR in the past, such as the late 1960s and early 1970s.[15] At that time, business organizations such as The Conference Board in the U.S. and the Confederation of British Industry in the U.K. issued calls for business to give greater attention to CSR. What is different today is that these calls are more broadly expressed, more specific, and more urgent. The calls are coming from business associations with the express purpose of promoting CSR (e.g., WBCSD, BSR, IBLF) as well as the general business associations and they are also coming from governmental organizations (e.g., U.K.'s DTI). Often, these calls include concrete recommendations for action, such as CSR audits and stakeholder engagement (e.g., WEF, WBCSD).

The urgency stems from a realization that the criticism of business is more far-reaching than ever before. This is in part because, with globalization, business itself is more pervasive and more powerful. The extent of this criticism is evidenced, for example, by protests at global meetings of the World Trade Organization since Seattle in 1999 as well as actions targeting individual firms.[16] Moreover, the demands for greater social responsibility are coming from mainstream quarters of society, as well as protesters at global meetings.[17] In 2002, the accounting and governance scandals associated with Enron, WorldCom, and other major corporations have further damaged the public standing of business.

However, criticism of business is also more far-reaching because more is expected of business today, with the growing recognition of the failure of governments to solve many social problems and, for this and other reasons, the diminished scope of government (at least in the U.S. and Europe). The private sector is increasingly called upon to address social problems and, accordingly, shoulder greater social responsibilities in addition to righting the wrongs for which it is more directly responsible, such as pollution or inadequate product safety.[18]

The terrorist attacks in the U.S. on September 11, 2001 have also added to the urgency of the calls for greater attention to CSR, with businesspeople seemingly now more attuned to global inequities. A survey of 264 *Fortune*

1000 CEOs found that 52% believed that corporations acting responsibly to communities around the world can reduce support for terrorist groups.[19]

The CSR responses of individual firms appear to be more widespread and more substantive than we have seen in the past. Most large corporations now at least espouse a commitment to CSR and in some cases their initiatives appear to go substantially beyond corporate philanthropy and corporate communications that attempt to defend the firm's societal impacts.[20] Certainly, CSR is no longer the preserve of Public Affairs or restricted to smaller firms that champion CSR in line with social enterprise goals, such as the Body Shop or Ben and Jerry's. Even corporate critic Naomi Klein talks of a "massive shift" in a more socially responsible direction by many multinationals, though she views the response as haphazard and inadequate.[21] The impression created overall is that the debate about CSR has shifted: it is no longer about whether to make substantial commitments to CSR, but how?

This article examines the pressures for greater attention to CSR. Should firms be making a substantial commitment to CSR? More specifically, is there a requirement for some firms to make a greater commitment to CSR, but not others? Does an increased requirement for some firms also indicate the form that CSR should take? What other challenges need to be overcome in the development and execution of CSR initiatives? It suggests that is the answer to *whether* to make a substantial commitment to CSR lies the clues as to *how* such a commitment should be made. Of critical consideration is the extent to which arguments in general for greater attention to CSR have specific application to individual firms. CSR strategy for any given firm may be best formulated through an understanding of where these arguments do or do not apply to that organization.

Some firms may find that there is a compelling business case for making a substantial commitment to CSR. For these firms, greater attention to CSR may even be inescapable and the challenge is developing CSR initiatives consistent with a strategic purpose, deciding on their form and scope, and overcoming major potential obstacles to their implementation. For other firms, the business case may be less evident and the case for greater attention to CSR must be made on normative grounds.

Developing Country Access to Essential Medicines

A detailed example drawn from the pharmaceutical industry more clearly differentiates between the normative and the business case for CSR. It also illustrates the extent to which CSR can have profound implications and how, for some multinational corporations, it may even assume a strategic significance. Pharmaceutical companies are well known for their philanthropic activities. These activities extend beyond support for charities and include giving away large quantities of their products. Often cited is the example of Merck's development of a treatment for onchocerciasis ("river blindness"), a tropical disease that afflicts people in some of the world's poorest regions. In 1978, the World Health Organization (WHO) estimated that 340,000 people were blind as a result of the disease, a further one million had some visual impairment, and around 18 million were infected. Merck discovered a treatment and although there was no commercial market for the drug, invested tens of millions of dollars in its development. In 1987, Merck set up the Mectizan Donation Program to organize the free distribution of the drug in collaboration with WHO, the World Bank, and other partners. Around 25 million people a year are treated under the program and avoid the risk of premature blindness.[22] Other pharmaceutical companies have since developed similar initiatives. GlaxoSmithKline (and Merck) donate large quantities of medicines as part of a program in conjunction with WHO to eliminate Lymphatic Filariasis ("elephantiasis"), Novartis donates drugs as part of a program to eliminate leprosy, and Pfizer makes azithromycin available for the treatment of trachoma.[23] Although large numbers of people have been treated under such programs and undoubtedly have an improved quality of life as a result, this did not prevent the industry's vilification over its response to the HIV/AIDS crisis, particularly in the context of South Africa.[24]

More than 4 million people in South Africa are HIV infected. In 1997, the South African government announced plans to permit the distribution of generic versions of patented HIV/AIDS drugs that were estimated to be 1/50th of the cost of the patented versions (that were averaging $12,500 per patient per year). However, this plan was accused of violating the government's obligations under the TRIPS (Trade-Related Aspects of Property Rights) agreement, to which it was a party as a member of the World Trade Organization. The following year, a consortium of drug companies brought suit against the South African government and named individuals as defendants, including Nelson Mandela. Accused of putting profits before people, the industry stated that "the case is nothing to do with blocking access to medicines, or price fixing. It's about patents. Patents do not block medicines. They stimulate research and development."[25] Nonetheless, in a humiliating back down in April 2001, the pharmaceutical companies dropped the case. As the *Boston Globe* commented, "With their boardrooms raided and their executives being hounded in the streets, 39 of the world's largest drug makers caved to public pressure. . . . It was hailed as a stunning triumph for the developing world: A $360 billion industry was brought down by a country that represents just half of one percent of the pharmaceutical market."[26]

GlaxoSmithKline (GSK) was a major target of protesters. It is the second-largest pharmaceutical company with sales of $27.5 billion in financial year 2000 and 108 manufacturing sites in 41 countries. It serves 140 global markets and has an annual R&D budget in excess of $4 billion. It is the market (and R&D) leader in the HIV/AIDS category and the company that (as Burroughs Wellcome) had first introduced drugs for the treatment of HIV/AIDS. According to WHO, AIDS is the second biggest killer of all infectious diseases worldwide and 95% of HIV/AIDS sufferers live in the least developed countries that represent only 10% of the world's population. It was estimated that more than 53 million men, women, and children had been infected worldwide as of 2001 and in that year alone five million people became infected with HIV, three million died of AIDS, and forty million were living with the AIDS virus on a daily basis. Two-thirds of those infected live in Sub-Saharan Africa.

Following the South African court case, GSK and other pharmaceutical companies heavily discounted their HIV/AIDS medicines to developing countries. The industry fear, however, was that this move threatened the central tenets of its business model. Investments in R&D and profits— consistently among the highest of any industry—depended upon the monopolistic pricing of patent-protected drugs. Moreover, discounting in developing country markets raised the possibility of downward pressure on prices in the lucrative developed country markets, particularly as HIV/AIDS was not restricted to developing countries (unlike most tropical diseases) and information on price differentials and drug profit margins would become widespread. There was also the prospect of parallel imports—discounted drugs distributed in developing country markets finding their way back to developed country markets. Some industry leaders spoke of firms focusing their efforts on lifestyle drugs such as Prozac or Viagra rather than killer diseases such as HIV/AIDS and they could see little incentive for continued R&D on tropical diseases.

The South African court case and the access problem reveal an industry in crisis over the scope and meaning of social responsibility. Sophia Tickell, Senior Policy Advisor at the NGO, Oxfam observed that the industry's critics were able to argue convincingly that "a business model is unacceptable if it makes the defense of industrialized country markets a greater priority than the health of poor people in developing countries."[27] The access issue is now a strategic consideration for every major pharmaceutical company. In the last two years, the industry has moved, albeit reluctantly, from having well-regarded programs of philanthropy, such as donating medicines for tropical diseases, to having to rethink its business model to incorporate CSR at the core.

In the specific case of GSK, CEO Jean-Pierre Garnier stated that the protection of intellectual property was not an obstacle to access to drugs. In June 2001, GSK rolled out a detailed access strategy. It made commitments in three areas: to continue investment in R&D on diseases that affect the developing world; to offer sustainable preferential (not-for-profit) pricing arrangements in least developed countries (LDCs) and Sub-Saharan Africa for currently available medicines that are needed most (for HIV/AIDS and other diseases, such as malaria); and, to take a leading role in community activities that promote effective healthcare.[28] Several NGOs welcomed the new policy. Tickell commented: "This is really positive. It is better than all the other initiatives the industry suggested." Nonetheless, others remained concerned and even some investors have questioned whether GSK has done enough.[29]

Pressures for Greater Attention to CSR

Normative or Business Case?

Business leaders can be expected to say that CSR is important, especially in today's social and political climate.[30] Garnier, however, appears to have done much more than this. At GSK's annual meeting in May 2001, campaigners from Oxfam, dressed in lab coats, had called for GSK to do more for LDCs by donating a percentage of drug revenues to a global health fund established by Kofi Annan, the United Nations Secretary General. Garnier's response was unprecedented. He defended GSK's actions on the access issue and then suggested that the company's priority was public health, not simply share-holder value:

> Some months ago, when the newly merged GlaxoSmithKline was formed, I said that I did not want to be head of a company that caters only to the rich. I made access to medicines in poorer countries a priority and I take this opportunity to renew that pledge. We have 110,000 people who go to work every morning because they are pro-public health. We have to make a profit for our shareholders but the primary objective of any policy put forward in the industry is public health.[31]

The quote suggests a normative, moral basis for GSK's response to the access issue. Simply put, "it is the right thing to do." In this respect, it is consistent with the motives earlier attributed to Salt and long-standing ideas about business as a good citizen. More formally, a normative basis for CSR may be found in theories of moral philosophy. Thomas Donaldson, for example, draws on social contract theory. His social contract for business is founded on consent —that corporations exist only through the cooperation and commitment of society. This suggests an implicit agreement between the corporation and society. He asks: "If General Motors holds society responsible for providing the condition of its existence, then for what does society hold General Motors responsible? What are the terms of the social contract?"[32] The simplest form of the contract is to specify what business needs from society and what, in turn, are its obligations to society. This approach can be used to ground the "license to operate" argument that the WEF and others advance in support of CSR.[33] With the access issue, it might be used to develop a normative basis for justifying actions by the pharma-ceutical industry to assist HIV/AIDS victims in LDCs.

However, as with Salt and other examples of paternalistic capitalism, there are quite possibly mixed motives underlying GSK's response to the access issue. Garnier acknowledged a requirement to make a profit for shareholders. Conceivably, this requirement might be met through its actions on access or, perhaps more likely, these actions reduce the risk of eroding shareholder value. Clearly, for example, shareholders' economic interests would be served if GSK's access policy motivates employees and these effects more than outweigh the costs associated with increasing access (including the possibility of reduced profit margins on HIV/AIDS drugs in developed country markets). More important, perhaps, is avoiding the potential scenario where the industry's business model is fundamentally changed and government regulation dictates its every action.

It might be suggested that the pharmaceutical industry example is a special situation. GSK does, after all, produce life-saving products (though firms in other industries are also under pressure to give away their products in LDC markets). Further, HIV/AIDS is a pandemic that, if infection continues on its current trajectory, is projected to affect more than half the world's population. This view bolsters the normative case for action on access, but it also helps explain why external forces such as NGOs have pressured the industry and strengthened the business case as a result.[34] Some might even argue that action on access was unavoidable. However, while this example might be considered extreme in certain respects, it does illustrate the increased pressures for attention to CSR that many firms face today.

Traditional Arguments for CSR

Arguments advanced in support of CSR have long recognized enlightened self-interest as well as beliefs about corporate good citizenship and a beneficial social role of business.[35] CSR can be in the enlightened self-interest of business in many ways (though not necessarily in the same way for any given firm). Paternalistic capitalism benefited from the improved living conditions employees found in its factory towns. The modern corporation has benefited from CSR as a result of avoiding or pre-empting legal or regulatory sanctions, such as DuPont's profitable exploitation of more environmentally friendly chlorofluorocarbon (CFC) alternatives.[36] CSR also has benefited firms through direct or indirect economic efficiencies. For example, Starbucks' employee turnover is said to be less than a third that of the average for the retail food industry. This is attributed to Starbucks' socially responsible practices (including a full benefits package for part-time employees) and provides economic efficiencies due to lower costs of staff recruitment and training.[37]

Added Pressures

Along with heightened societal expectations and demands of business, the globalization of large corporations has led to firms increasingly operating in countries with very different and generally much lower standards of living than found in their domestic base. More extensive media reach coupled with advances in information technology (e.g., NGO use of web sites) has allowed rapid and widespread exposure of alleged corporate abuses in even the most remote corners of the world, as both Shell (oil spills in Nigeria exposed on television documentaries) and Nike (exposure of sweatshop labor conditions in its subcontractor operations in Asian LDCs) have learnt to their cost.

Democracy is now more widespread. In part, and more obviously, this came with the collapse of communism. However, there is also a sense that people now "matter" in places where—to those in power—they didn't matter before. Hitherto, their rights were few, politically and in actuality. While there are still many countries where democracy is largely absent in the formal sense, some elements of democracy are possible when NGO and media attention is given to corporate complicity in human rights abuses. For example, the U.S. firm Unocal has been judged legally liable for the abuse of Myanmar villagers by military security guards when they were forced to build an oil pipeline.[38]

Thus, while the traditional arguments for CSR remain important, there are additional pressures for attention to CSR today. A critical consideration for many firms is reputational risk, heightened by the greater visibility and criticism of corporate practices, particularly by NGOs.[39] As a result, the business case for CSR is much stronger. Consider the approach of Starbucks. While acknowledging a normative case, Starbucks emphasizes a business case for CSR as follows:

> Consumers are demanding more than "'product" from their favorite brands. Employees are choosing to work for companies with strong values. Shareholders are more inclined to invest in businesses with outstanding corporate reputations. Quite simply, being socially responsible is not only the right thing to do; it can distinguish a company from its industry peers.[40]

Safeguarding the corporate reputation and brand image have become ever more important as markets have become more competitive and reputations and image have become more vulnerable. Simply put, firms may be penalized by consumers—and others—for actions that are not considered socially responsible.

Reputational Risk in Consumer Markets

Boycotts are one manifestation of this pressure. In the 1990s, the business press reported both that consumer boycotts work and that they were increasing in number. *The Economist*, for example, observed: "Pressure groups are besieging American companies, politicizing business, and often presenting executives with impossible choices. Consumer boycotts are becoming an epidemic for one simple reason: they work."[41] Research has found that product boycott announcements are associated with significant negative stock market reactions.[42] Stock market reactions reflect investor beliefs about boycotts having an effect on sales, both directly and indirectly, through harm to the firm's and brand's reputation.

Recent prominent consumer boycotts include the European boycott of Royal Dutch/Shell in 1995 over its plan to dump the Brent Spar oil platform at sea. As a result of the boycott, Shell suffered widespread adverse publicity, as well as up to a 50% decline in sales in some markets.[43] It agreed to the demand by Greenpeace that it abandon sea disposal. However, Shell's decision to dismantle the oil platform on land was almost certainly *less* socially responsible than the planned disposal at sea, and Greenpeace later admitted that it had overestimated the pollution risk of the platform.[44] Shell's problems were compounded by public reactions to reports of environmental harm as a result of its operations in Ogoniland, Nigeria, and the company's apparent failure to use its influence to prevent the execution by Nigerian authorities of Ken Saro-Wiwa and eight other Ogonis, who had been protesting Shell's presence in Ogoniland as well as on a broader array of social and political issues. Criticism of Shell by environmentalists and human rights activists and the associated boycotts were said to be key contributors to a fundamental transformation in the company efforts to meet its social and ethical responsibilities.[45]

Another example is the ongoing multi-country boycott of Nike over alleged sweatshop conditions at Asian suppliers. Nike is a market leader in the footwear and apparel industry with sales of $9 billion. Ten years ago, Nike asserted that because it did not own its overseas contractors, workplace standards inside their factories were not its responsibility. However, a campaign by NGOs led to the admission by Phil Knight, Nike's CEO, that "Nike has become synonymous with slave wages, forced overtime, and arbitrary abuse." In 1997, in a remarkable reversal, Knight announced that three Indonesian suppliers were to be terminated over workplace conditions and stated: "Good shoes come from good factories and good factories have good labor relations." Today, while the extent to which Nike sales have suffered is unclear, it continues to fight attacks on its image. It has over 90 people employed in CSR positions and invests heavily in independent third-party audits of its suppliers, the results of which it agrees to publish even though they might be unfavourable.[46]

Boycotts may be only the most manifest example of a broader phenomenon of consumer behavior influenced by perceived CSR lapses.[47] Surveys of consumers report that many claim to be influenced in their purchasing decisions by the CSR reputation of firms. For example, a 1999 survey of 25,000 consumers in 23 countries found that 40% had at least thought about punishing a specific company over the past year they viewed as not behaving responsibly.[48] Academic research by Brown and Dacin found that "negative CSR associations ultimately can have a detrimental effect on overall product evaluations, whereas positive CSR associations can enhance the product evaluations."[49] According to Sen and Bhattacharya, key moderators of consumer responses to CSR are individual consumer-specific factors (such as consumers' personal support for

CSR issues and their general beliefs about CSR) and company-specific factors (such as the CSR issues a company chooses to focus on and the quality of its products).[50] Their findings highlight the likelihood of differences across consumers in their response to CSR and differences in the type of CSR practices that might serve to generate favorable consumer sentiment. This heterogeneity in responses to CSR points to the likelihood that firms differ in their exposure to reputational risk in consumer markets.

Firms may be rewarded by increased patronage if they have a reputation for being socially responsible. No longer is this the preserve of a handful of companies serving a small segment of consumers, such as Ben and Jerry's, Stonyfield Farms, and the Body Shop. There is also evidence to suggest that some consumers will pay a premium for CSR. One of the more noteworthy successes of the ethical shopping movement is the growth in sales of free-range eggs, now accounting for 35% of sales in the U.K. although they are 25% more expensive than eggs laid by battery hens. However, at least some of the preference for free-range eggs is attributed to salmonella fears, with free-range eggs seen as safer. Fair trade coffee is another example, accounting for retail sales of $64 million in the U.S. and Canada in 2002, with imports up 50% over 2001. In the U.K., fair trade coffee is 12% of the roast and ground coffee market. Cafedirect, the leading U.K. supplier, attributes its success to product quality and offering a premium product as well as adherence to fair trade principles.[51]

Overall, however, evidence to suggest that a significant proportion of consumers will pay more for CSR is scant. According to the Co-operative Bank's Ethical Purchasing Index, the combined U.K. market share of "ethical products" (e.g., fair trade products) over seven food and non-food segments is approximately 1.5%, equating to £7 billion in sales in 2001. Research by the Bank suggests that while around 30% of consumers might claim to be ethical consumers, few products that make ethical claims (e.g., to protect the environment or animals) have a market share greater than 3%.[52]

It is possible that the potential for CSR to provide competitive advantage may be more diffuse and more widespread than these figures suggest. CSR might make a big difference at the margin for many firms given the increased competitiveness of consumer markets. Frank Walker of Walker Information has observed: "As more and more organizations meet the quality requirements of the marketplace . . . the consumer will want to know what the company behind the product or service stands for in today's society, and to make certain that they are not contributing to any corporation that is harming society, its resources, or its people."[53] In highly competitive markets, CSR might provide a valuable basis for differentiation. Hence, a broad array of firms now include environmental claims within their advertising (e.g., automobile manufacturers).

Reputational risk would appear to be largely but not solely a concern for consumer goods companies. Many B2B firms face similar pressures indirectly because of the reputational concerns of their customers, be they retailers or further removed from the consumer in the supply chain. Retailers such as Home Depot in the U.S. and B&Q in the U.K. have pressured suppliers on environmental impacts. For example, 22% of B&Q's sales are of timber and timber-related products, over 99% of which are independently certified as coming from well-managed (sustainable) forests.[54] There is also some evidence of social criteria in B2B purchasing independent of supply chain considerations, and public sector procurement is also increasingly subject to social criteria.[55]

Reputational Risk in Labor and Equity Markets

Product markets are not the only source of pressure, employees and investors have concerns about company CSR practices as well as consumers.[56] In the labor market, some employees express a preference for working for more socially responsible companies.[57] It has long been known that tobacco companies have difficulties recruiting the best talent. This effect has become more widespread, particularly in tight labor markets, as potential and current employees consider the corporate social performance of their employer. For example, Edward Jones was the number one company in *Fortune* magazine's 2002 list of best U.S. companies to work for. Its employees praise the company's ethics, with 97% citing its management's honesty. Moreover, employees who are aware of a firm's CSR activities have been found to be more likely to speak highly of it.[58] Belief in the potential value placed by employees on CSR is clearly evident in the GSK example.

Reputation is also important in equity markets. According to the Social Investment Forum, $2.32 trillion or nearly one out of every eight dollars under professional management in the United States was involved in socially responsible investing in 2001.[59] The Dow Jones Sustainability Index (introduced in 1999) and FTSE4Good (2001), list companies that meet socially responsible investing criteria. However, critics have questioned their inclusiveness: 76% of the FTSE 100 stocks qualify for the U.K. FTSE4Good index.[60] Nonetheless, the growth in investing and listing of companies according to social responsibility criteria has led to a substantial increase in social and environmental reporting by firms. Around 80% of FTSE-100 companies now provide information on their social or environmental policies. In France, legislation introduced in 2002 makes such reporting mandatory. Increasingly, companies are setting up elaborate reporting mechanisms to measure their social and environmental performance. Advising business on its ethical and social responsibilities is a multi-million pound business in the U.K. alone, with most of the consulting operations formerly associated with leading accounting practices offering services in the area as well as more specialist consultancies.

Thus, a powerful set of external forces and changes have contributed to the recent rise in prominence of CSR: increased societal expectations of business voiced, in part, by powerful NGOs; a diminution of the power and scope of government; globalization; heightened media reach, assisted by advances in information technology; and the greater spread of democracy. Prior peaks of interest in CSR have generally coincided with economic prosperity and interest has diminished at times of recession.[61] However, the depth of current societal concern about corporate practices seems unprecedented and some important developments, such as globalization, are likely to be long lasting and their influence on CSR sustained. Many companies appear to be doing more in response to the pressures for increased attention to CSR, especially in light of their apparent importance within ever more competitive product, employment, and equity markets and the potential for reputational risk. However, there are those who question greater corporate attention to CSR.

Dangers of Do-Gooding Executives

Consider Garnier's statement of aspirations for GSK: "The pharmaceutical industry today sells 80% of its products to 20% of the world's population. I don't want to be a CEO of a company that caters only to the rich. . . . I want those medicines in the hands of many more people who need them."[62] The forthright expression of such a vision was uncharacteristic for a pharmaceutical industry executive. It is also the sort of statement that deeply troubles CSR critics such as David Henderson and Ethan Kapstein.[63] They suspect that "do-gooding" executives are pursuing personal visions of a better world using shareholders' money and often with insufficient regard for the likely effectiveness or possible ill-consequences of their initiatives. Kapstein acknowledges that it is hard to argue against making drugs available to patients who desperately need them, but is concerned about what this means for the industry: "the possible adverse consequences of this decision need to be considered. If the giveaway means lower profits for manufacturers—and thus less incentive for innovation— this victory will prove a hollow one for future patients with deadly and debilitating diseases."[64]

Forty years ago in *Capitalism and Freedom*, Friedman claimed that "there is one and only one social responsibility of business—to use its resources and engage in activities designed to increase its profits so long as it stays within the rules of the game, which is to say, engages in open and free competition, without deception or fraud."[65] Friedman's famous dictum on corporate social responsibility was part of an attack on much broader conceptions of the social role of business, which Friedman viewed as fundamentally subversive.

There is more to commend Friedman's arguments than his critics generally allow.[66] First, he was not opposed to the idea that firms have societal obligations that must be fulfilled. He was only opposed to activities that went beyond a narrowly defined role for the corporation. In this way, the uncertainty about the societal obligations of the firm, discussed at the outset of this article, is substantially diminished. Friedman believed that business satisfied its social responsibilities through conventional business activities, primarily producing needed goods and services at prices that people could afford. In this respect, his argument can be traced back to Adam Smith, who recognized that in the pursuit of self-interest the businessperson is "led by an invisible hand to promote an end which was no part of his intention."[67]

Second, Friedman reasoned that a more expansive role for the corporation was a worrisome departure from the competitive model of capitalism. More specifically, he argued that CSR amounted to spending someone else's money (notably shareholders' or customers') and muddied decision making by diluting the focus on profit and placing the firm at a competitive disadvantage as a result. He also questioned whether managers were competent to engage in social issues, whether the imposition of their values in the social arena was desirable and whether they were potentially usurping the role of government. However, it is now widely accepted that Friedman's position was founded on an inaccurate economic model and was unrealistic in its attempt to isolate business from society when the two are so interdependent. As Mintzberg wrote: "the strategic decisions of large organizations inevitably involve social as well as economic consequences, inextricably intertwined . . . there is no such thing as a purely economic strategic decision."[68]

Nonetheless, there are grounds for concern about some CSR initiatives. On the one hand, there is so often little real substance to what some firms claim to do.[69] The amount spent touting a firm's CSR achievements is sometimes more than the amount spent on the CSR activity itself.[70] On the other hand, there is the issue of the legitimacy of substantive corporate involvement in social issues—"Do we want corporations playing God?"This is perhaps today the most potentially valid of Friedman's original criticisms of CSR, though it can be argued that corporate power is increasingly held in check by NGOs, whose legitimacy, in turn, relies on public support.

CSR in the Shareholders' Interest

Friedman's most powerful argument against CSR was always that it was not in the shareholders' interest and many managers still find this idea appealing. However, the business case for CSR—if supported—makes this argument largely moot. Roger Martin has observed that firms often engage in CSR "precisely because it enhances shareholder value" and, more specifically, that some CSR activities "create goodwill among consumers in excess of their price tag."[71] Margolis and Walsh found that nearly 100 studies have examined the relationship between corporate social performance (CSP) and corporate financial performance (CFP) over the last 30 years.[72] Most studies point to a positive relationship between CSP and CFP. Of the 80 studies that examined whether CSP predicts CFP, 42 found a positive relationship, 19 found no relationship, 15 studies reported mixed results, and only 4 studies found a negative relationship. Not surprisingly, it is generally inferred that CSR does produce financial dividends for firms, but this conclusion needs to be treated with caution because there are major methodological problems associated with such studies.

Formulating a Response

How any individual firm formulates a CSR strategy should reflect an understanding of whether (and why) greater attention to CSR is warranted by that particular organization. The WBCSD advises that a "one-size-fits-all" approach to CSR strategy (e.g., universal codes) may not provide the right answer.[73] Equally, however, the generally asserted reasons for greater attention to CSR also may not have universal application. Consider the following examples:

- Du Pont's leadership in the development of CFC alternatives might *not* have been enlightened self-interest were it not also the market (and R&D) leader in the category; similarly, GSK's leadership on the access issue might make less (business) sense if it were not also the leading provider of drugs for the treatment of HIV/AIDS, tuberculosis, and malaria (three of the top five killer diseases overall and especially prevalent in LDCs).
- While reputational risk is particularly relevant to global brands in consumer markets, firms with smaller, local brands might be less vulnerable, especially if the corporate name differs from the brand name familiar to consumers; equally, firms in B2B markets far removed from consumers as end users have much less reputational risk, especially if their products are marketed as commodities.
- Employees typically do prefer to work for socially responsible firms, but tobacco companies have been able to attract people by paying more, despite the pariah status of the industry; similarly, many investors stick with tobacco stocks because of their generally high levels of return.
- A mining company has every reason to be concerned about environmental impacts threatening its "license to operate," but this is far less of a concern for a financial services company.

The purpose here is not to identify the many criteria by which we might assess a firm's vulnerability to criticism for CSR failings (there are consultancy organizations dedicated to providing this service). However, if a business case is to be advanced for CSR initiatives, the organizational fit with any given rationale requires close scrutiny. This applies equally to elements of a CSR strategy intended to enhance the firm's reputation and exploit an upside potential of CSR.[74] Consider some of the questions that should be asked by a firm planning to develop a more socially responsible version of an existing product:

- How likely is it that these improvements would be in advance of a regulatory requirement to be instituted in this industry? (There might be advantages from developing and launching the product ahead of a change in regulations.)
- How responsive is the firm's customer base to CSR? Research would be required to ascertain whether a more socially responsible version of an existing product would appeal to the intended market segment— there is likely to be considerable variation in the extent to which a firm's served market responds to various possible CSR initiatives (e.g., not tested on animals, more environmentally benign, manufactured with materials from fair trade sources).
- Would customers be willing to pay more for the new product? (Generally, few consumers will pay a premium for CSR.)
- If the firm's customer base is CSR-responsive, but unwilling to pay more, would the improvement provide a sustainable advantage relative to competitors? Could it be easily copied?

Similar questions would need to be formulated with CSR initiatives intended to satisfy investors, employees, or other stakeholders. The decision on increased attention to CSR is thus likely to be highly idiosyncratic, a function of both the characteristics of the individual firm and its fit with the elements of potential CSR initiatives.

Developing the Right CSR Strategy

Clearly, a firm's social responsibility strategy, if genuinely and carefully conceived, should be unique, despite the sameness of the growing number of corporate reports on CSR.[75] As well as a fit with industry characteristics, it should reflect the individual company's mission and values—what it stands for— and thus be different from the CSR strategy of even its closest competitors.[76] Many company CSR statements do not seem to be reflective of a deep commitment to CSR or, at least, they suffer from a failure to identify the issues that matter most for measurement, management, and reporting.[77] Phil Watts, Group Managing Director of Royal Dutch/Shell Group, has observed that "CSR is not a cosmetic; it must be rooted in our values. It must make a difference to the way we do our business."[78] Shell's CSR report, published annually since 1998, is a good example of a company that provides quantified evidence of its social and environmental performance.[79]

While there is not a generic CSR strategy, there are common elements. There will be substantial overlap among the stakeholders identified by any firm—all will at minimum identify obligations to customers, employees, suppliers, and the community. However, the characteristics of these stakeholders and the form of the obligations of any specific firm to that stakeholder group are likely to vary considerably. For example, at the core of British Telecom's CSR strategy is a belief in a "better world" where everyone has access to the benefits of information and communications technology (ICT), a belief that is said to shape BT's obligations to its stakeholders. This is reflected not only in a commitment to improved levels of customer satisfaction for all its customers, but also to services for elderly, disabled, and low income customers that increase their access to ICT in excess of regulatory requirements.[80] The first CSR report from Westpac, an Australian bank, also identifies obligations to customers but is markedly different.[81] It includes a newly introduced Personal Customer Charter, with commitments to transparency of fees and services and to privacy. It also reports on the bank's performance in areas such as accessibility and availability of banking services (e.g., banking services in rural areas, new ATM technology for vision impaired consumers), complaint resolution rates, and responsible lending (e.g., data on accounts overdue).

Developing the right CSR strategy requires an understanding of what differentiates an organization—its mission, values, and core business activities. At British Telecom, a "hot topic" is the digital divide and CSR initiatives address digital inclusion, with attention to capability (people having the skills to use digital technology) as well as connectivity (physical access).[82] Contribution to the community finds a different guise at Starbucks. All proceeds (and a minimum of $75,000) from the Georgetown Starbucks in Washington, D.C., are donated to The Starbucks Memorial Fund. Established following an armed robbery of the store in 1997 that left three employees dead, the Fund contributes to violence prevention and victim assistance programs in the D.C. area. More recently, attention has been focused on coffee sourcing and particularly the plight of poorer small farmers, who are now being supported through a commitment to buying fair trade coffee (one million pounds in 2002–2003).[83] Not surprisingly, the CSR initiatives of Shell and other firms in resource extraction industries (e.g., BP, Rio Tinto) reflect the profound impact these firms can have upon the natural environment coupled with the human rights issues often directly or indirectly associated with their activities.[84]

Stakeholder Engagement

In figuring out a CSR strategy, stakeholder engagement must be at the core.[85] As noted earlier, there can be considerable uncertainty about a firm's obligations to its stakeholders. However, if CSR is fundamentally about obligations to stakeholders, their engagement is more likely to lead to informed management thinking and decision making. The form this engagement should take can be subject to much debate. Some might view stakeholders as having a substantial input on decision making, while others see stakeholders as more of an information resource, with it being "management's job to manage." Either way, engagement is critical. As WBCSD put it:

> The essence of corporate social responsibility is to recognize the value of external stakeholder dialogue. Because of this, we place stakeholder engagement at the center of CSR activity. CSR means more than promulgating a company's own values and principles. It also depends on understanding the values and principles of those who have a stake in its operations.[86]

However, this assumes a skill set and openness on the part of management that may not exist. The values of NGO members, for example, are often dramatically different from those of corporate executives. Their objectives as well as perspectives on issues are also likely to differ. In many cases, at least with hot issues, management and representatives of stakeholder groups talk past each other. There is also the assumption of a willingness on the part of the stakeholder groups to participate in such a dialogue. It is not unusual for some groups to refuse to engage with management. There is little prospect of many animal rights activists, for example, getting involved with firms they describe as "evil," such as drug testing laboratories.

One response to this problem has been for firms to recruit talent from the non-profit sector, though this is still unlikely to work in the case of extreme issues. Shell provides a good example of a firm promoting openness. Shell explains that it is committed to open and transparent debate with its stakeholders. "Tell Shell" provides a global discussion forum with e-mail postings on topics and issues related to Shell. Postings are both critical and supportive of Shell, with occasional postings by the firm in response or to raise issues.[87]

Given the right people, the firm must still identify which representatives of stakeholder groups it should engage with. Here the problem is, in part, one of the "squeaky wheel gets the grease." WBCSD suggests that firms need to consider the legitimacy, the contribution, and influence of the group and the likely outcome, including whether engagement is likely to result in a productive relationship.[88] Appropriate mechanisms for engagement also need to be determined.

Measurement of Social Performance

Formulating CSR strategy also requires an understanding of the firm's current CSP. This includes developing appropriate metrics for measuring social and environmental performance and goal setting. Shell refers to "key performance indicators" (KPIs), which are "benchmarks used to drive improvements whilst independently measuring progress against clearly defined goals."[89] As well as providing metrics, the use of KPIs gives substance to Shell claims of a commitment to CSR. As these KPIs are often developed in collaboration with stakeholders, such as NGOs, reports of how the firm is delivering on that commitment have credibility. However, there are major challenges to be overcome. Clearly firms can report on readily quantifiable performance measures, such as greenhouse gas emissions or hours worked by employees. It is more difficult to develop KPI's where more qualitative data is all that is available, as, for example, with many aspects of support for human rights or company impacts on other species (e.g., biodiversity, treatment of animals).

Implementation of CSR Programs

Having formulated CSR strategy, CSR programs need to be determined. This is where potentially abstract visions of CSR must become concrete. Many challenges are likely in the execution of those programs. To return to the pharmaceutical industry example, after GSK determined that it would do something about access, management had to develop appropriate programs to make medicines available to those without. Yet even with this decision made, its societal obligations were uncertain. Where to begin? Many tricky decisions must be made, for example, with respect to beneficiaries (assessments of needs, treatment/disease categories), scope of the program (where? what scale?), and form of distribution (which channels? free or at cost?).

GSK has made its drugs more widely available in LDCs. However, in the HIV/AIDS category, take-up is pitifully low: only 30,000 of the estimated 28.5 million people with the disease in sub-Saharan Africa receive the anti-retroviral drugs that have made it treatable in developed countries. It is unlikely that take-up would be much higher if they were given away. A far bigger obstacle to access is the limited healthcare infrastructure in LDCs and, for HIV/AIDS medications, their strict monitoring and compliance regimen.[90] Further, GSK is already facing a problem of parallel imports. Drugs destined for Africa at prices close to marginal cost have been illegally re-exported and resold in the Netherlands and Germany.[91] While there are remedies, such as stricter enforcement of laws on illegal re-importing and dual-branding strategies, this problem represents a substantial challenge to GSK's implementation of a two-tiered pricing structure.

How Much Is Enough?

Consider the example of Nike and its commitment to monitoring workplace conditions of its suppliers. The scale of this monitoring task is huge; Nike has over 800 contract suppliers, employing over 600,000 people in 50 countries. For companies making a substantial commitment to CSR, a key strategic and implementation question is: How much is enough? For Nike, this extends to more specific issues such as: What level of resources should it devote to monitoring? How frequently should sites be audited? How should it respond to the dilemmas that often arise in this context, such as the use of child labor? If children above a set age are to employed by its suppliers, should it provide funding for their schooling?

Similarly, how far should GSK assist in drug distribution and administration, given infrastructure shortcomings in many LDC markets? Should GSK be involved in healthcare problems that are unrelated to drug therapy, such as the availability of clean water? How much should be invested in R&D to develop medicines for tropical diseases, when only losses are foreseeable for these potential products?

No Good Deed Goes Unpunished

Despite careful attention to whether a CSR strategy fits a given organization and situation, it still has the potential to backfire. Sometimes, this can be due to the firm having drawn attention to itself as a result of taking a stand on CSR, such as the recent protests at Starbucks. At other times, it might result from poor implementation. Consider companies that identify an opportunity to contribute to education. On the face of it, this would be a welcome or at least innocuous activity and highly appropriate for some firms in light of their core business activities. Yet CSR initiatives in this area have been viewed as highly controversial. For example, both Coca-Cola and Pepsi bottlers have signed contracts with public school districts in the U.S. that provide millions of dollars of much-needed support for educational purposes in exchange for exclusive distribution rights. Following protests from parents concerned about children's sugar-laden diets and the commercialism of schools, Coca-Cola announced plans to discourage its bottlers from such deals.[92] CSR initiatives can make worthwhile contributions to social problems. However, as this example indicates, and consistent with the concerns expressed by Friedman, the indirect cost of such initiatives may be an imposition of corporate values. Critics of the factory towns of paternalistic capitalism had similar concerns. Failings of the public school system notwithstanding, many might argue that it is the role of government to provide adequate funding for schools and to provide a commercial-free learning environment.

Another example is Microsoft, a company that has various CSR initiatives addressing the "digital divide." It has offered to give away its software to schools in developing countries. In South Africa, for example, the offer to give its software to all 32,000 public schools would entail the loss of most of the $2 million of annual revenues from this sector. However, such programs have been criticized as an attempt to foster and retain captive markets for its products.[93] Microsoft's motives have been impugned; as one critic observed: "Businesses are opportunistic and driven by shareholder interests. . . . There is a fine line between charity and exploitation." If this reaction is typical, then there is a problem for advocates of the business case for CSR. If a business case exists for a CSR initiative, then there is always the prospect of it being attacked as cynically self-serving (and, if there is not a business case, shareholders might question why the firm is engaged in it).

Perhaps, in these cases, there are solutions that would permit corporate involvement in funding public schools and to help bridge the digital divide. Greater social acceptance might be forthcoming through more appropriate implementation. For example, one measure proposed by Coca-Cola was to reduce the amount of advertising on vending machines.

Conclusions

Few firms adopt the normative case for CSR and assert a moral basis for obligations beyond those to stockholders, at least without also claiming a business case (those that do are mostly privately held). It has been claimed by U.K. business leaders, for example, that a company should "balance and trade off the competing claims of customers, suppliers, employees, investors and the communities in which it operates."[94] The implication of this view of the firm balancing stakeholder interests—a fiduciary duty to share-holders notwithstanding—is that the interests of shareholders might in some instances be considered secondary to those of other claimants, not an argument that sits easily with many managers of public corporations. Nonetheless, some managers might well choose to exercise their discretion consistent with beliefs about management action on social issues.[95] Ultimately, if such action is grounded in an accurate assessment of society's best interests, then the normative case may well also be consistent with the long-term interests of the firm, though there is no guarantee of this.

Many firms have found the business case for greater attention to CSR to be compelling, particularly given reputational risk and other pressures of the contemporary business environment. For some corporations (e.g., in the mining and pharmaceutical industries) CSR may be unavoidable and it appears to have assumed strategic significance. However, it is unclear whether this is peculiar to these industries or an early warning of pressures likely to be faced more broadly. This article has argued that the widely touted *general* rationale for making a more substantial commitment to CSR must be assessed relative to the *specific* vulnerabilities and opportunities of a particular organization. This assessment, in turn, should help clarify societal obligations and thereby (if the business case is persuasive) inform the formulation of a CSR strategy and decisions about specific CSR programs. Nonetheless, there remain major challenges in developing and imple-menting CSR strategy, especially the measurement of corporate social performance and engaging with stakeholders. There are also possible questions about the legitimacy of CSR initiatives. Concerns might be voiced about the appropriateness of management action on social issues and there may be a backlash against a well-intentioned CSR initiative; concerns that become all the more important if CSR assumes a more central role in corporate strategy. These challenges might well undercut an otherwise convincing business case.

While a business case might be identified for many CSR initiatives, what of those that do not appear to offer any return to shareholders? Martin has proposed that, absent an economic incentive, collective action is required that would involve other firms as well as governments and NGOs.[96] For GSK and the access issue, this suggests a requirement for involvement of other parties because of the limited economic incentives for action by the pharmaceutical industry alone (the problem also demands the collaboration of multiple participants, such as healthcare organizations and governments, because of the specialized skills or resources they can bring). However, it is unclear as yet whether these other parties will come to the table; the response from governments to requests for contributions to Kofi Annan's global fund is modest, to date.

Notes

Financial assistance provided by London Business School is gratefully acknowledged.

1. Margaret Crawford, *Building the Workingman's Paradise: The Design of American Company Towns* (New York, NY: Verso, 1995); "The Strange Death of Corporationville," *The Economist*, December 23, 1995, p. 73.
2. John Styles, *Titus Salt and Saltaire: Industry and Virtue* (Shipley, England: Salts Estates Ltd., 1994), pp. 12–13.
3. William C. Frederick, "From CSR1 to CSR2: The Maturing of Business-and-Society Thought," *Business and Society*, 33/2 (1994): 151.
4. Styles, op. cit., p. 38. Crawford [op. cit.] suggests that this motivation was evident in the founding of a number of American company towns.
5. Styles, op. cit., p. 39.
6. As Frederick [loc. cit.] writes: "By the mid-1920s, business representatives and executives were beginning to speak of the need for corporate directors to act as trustees for the interests, not just of stockholders, but other social claimants as well . . . Corporate philanthropy, the history of which stretched back into the 19th century, was accompanied by a growing belief that business and society were linked together in organic, if not yet well understood, ways."
7. Since March 2001, thousands of activists are said to have taken part in protests outside Starbucks's cafes in over 300 cities in the U.S., Canada, New Zealand, and England over the poverty of third world coffee farmers and other issues. See, for example, <www.obgo.org/starbucks.htm>.
8. S. Prakash Sethi, "Dimensions of Corporate Social Performance: An Analytical Framework," *California Management Review*, 17/3 (Spring 1975): 58–64. See note 9 on the meaning and terminology of CSR.
9. World Economic Forum's Global Corporate Citizenship Initiative in partnership with The Prince of Wales International Business Leaders Forum (WEF), "Responding to the Challenge: Findings of a CEO Survey on Global Corporate Citizenship," <www.weforum.org/corporatecitizenship>, January 2003, p. 2. Also see "Global Corporate Citizenship: The Leadership Challenge for CEOs and Boards," <www.weforum.org/corporatecitizenship>, January 2002. In the latter document, the WEF acknowledges the use of different terminology for what it refers to as

"corporate citizenship," including "corporate responsibility," "sustainable development," and the "triple-bottom-line." Each can have nuances of meaning (e.g., the term sustainable development often is used to emphasize environmental impacts). In this article, the term corporate social responsibility is used to be consistent with the established academic literature of the field.

10. WEF (2003), op. cit., p. 2.

11. WBCSD, "Corporate Social Responsibility: Meeting Changing Expectations," report from World Business Council for Sustainable Development, March 1999, <www.wbcsd.ch>, p. 2.

12. The sheer volume of publications emanating from organizations advocating CSR in itself speaks to the increased prominence of the topic.

13. UK Government Department of Trade and Industry, "Business and Society: Corporate Social Responsibility Report 2002," <www.dti.gov.uk>, p. 4.

14. Institute for Global Ethics, "Europe Tackles Corporate Social Responsibility," <www.globalethics.org/newsline>, July 30, 2002.

15. See, for example, David Vogel, *Lobbying the Corporation: Citizen Challenges to Business Authority* (New York, NY: Basic Books, 1978); S. Prakash Sethi, *Up Against the Corporate Wall: Modern Corporations and Social Issues of the Seventies* (Englewood Cliffs: Prentice Hall, 1974).

16. Naomi Klein, *No Logo* (London: Flamingo, 2000); Noreena Hertz, *The Silent Takeover* (London: Random House, 2001).

17. Roger L. Martin, "The Virtue Matrix: Calculating the Return on Corporate Responsibility," *Harvard Business Review*, 80/3 (March 2002): 68–75; Steve Hilton and Giles Gibbons, *Good Business* (New York, NY: Texere, 2002).

18. Many U.S. and global firms are responding by devoting significant time and resources in support of community involvement projects. See David Hess, Nikolai Rogovsky, and Thomas W. Dunfee, "The Next Wave of Corporate Community Involvement: Corporate Social Initiatives," *California Management Review*, 44/2 (Winter 2002): 110–125.

19. Survey by Jericho Communications in 2002, <www.jerichopr.com/releases/jericho3>.

20. SustainAbility, *Trust Us: The Global Reporters 2002 Survey of Corporate Sustainability Reporting* (London: SustainAbility and the United Nations Environment Program, 2002); Hess et al., op. cit.

21. Klein, op. cit., p. 434.

22. <www.merck.com/about/philanthropy/9.htm>.

23. Sophia Tickell, "Why Philanthropy Is Not Enough: Lessons from the Pharmaceutical Industry," in Roger Cowe, ed., *No Scruples: Managing to be Responsible in a Turbulent World* (London: Spiro Press, 2002).

24. Much of the following discussion of this example is based on N. Craig Smith and Anne Duncan, "GlaxoSmithKline and Access to Essential Medicines," London Business School case study, January 2003.

25. "Drug Price Wars: Helping the Poor will Help the Industry," *The Guardian*, April 18, 2001.

26. Kurt Shillinger, "AIDS Drug Victory Sours in South Africa: Government Still Refusing to Supply AZT," *Boston Globe*, April 23, 2001, p. A8.

27. Tickell, op. cit., pp. 65–66.

28. "Facing the Challenge: Our Contribution to Improving Healthcare in the Developing World," GlaxoSmithKline, Brentford, United Kingdom, 2001.

29. CalPERS, America's largest pension fund, has asked GSK to evaluate its "humanitarian efforts" and report whether it is offering the "lowest possible prices for its (HIV/AIDS) drugs (in developing countries), including licensing generics, without hurting its long-term business." See Chris Gaither, "Investing With an Agenda: CalPERS Social, Corporate Activism Drawing Attention in Bear Market as Some Fear Its Aggressive Tactics May Cost Governments, Firms Money," *Boston Globe*, April 20, 2003, p. E1.

30. One noteworthy exception is Lee Raymond, CEO of Exxon, who has taken a markedly different and public position on the environmental impacts of the oil industry than Exxon's "greener" competitors, Shell and BP. *The Economist* writes: "Judged by his financial record alone, Mr. Raymond could claim to be the most successful oil boss since Rockefeller of Standard Oil . . . what happens to Mr. Raymond's reputation in the years to come will be a barometer of the relative strengths of red-blooded capitalism and of the kinder, gentler, greener, more socially responsible—and perhaps less profitable—version." See "The Unrepentant Oilman," *The Economist*, March 13, 2003.

31. Smith and Duncan, op. cit.

32. Thomas Donaldson, *Corporations and Morality* (Englewood Cliffs, NJ: Prentice Hall, 1982), p. 42.

33. WEF (2003), op. cit.

34. For an alternative viewpoint, see Ian Maitland, "Priceless Goods: How Should Life-Saving Drugs Be Priced?" *Business Ethics Quarterly*, 12 (October 2002): 451–480. Maitland argues against restraints on drug pricing and profits, suggesting it is precisely because life-saving drugs are priceless that firms should be free to charge market prices for them.

35. See, for example, Robert D. Hay, Edmund R. Gray, and James E. Gates, *Business and Society* (Cincinnati: South-Western Publishing, 1976).

36. Thomas Hoffman, "Say Goodbye to Ozone-Wrecking Chemicals," *Computerworld*, June 5, 1995, p. 105.

37. John Leming, "Workers Benefit from Tight Market; Service Industries Offer Employees Health Cover to Lure Them on Board," *Journal of Commerce*, June 15, 1998, p. 5A; <www.starbucks.com/aboutus/CSR_FY01_AR.pdf>. This is not intended to suggest that caring for employees always pays, there are many examples to the contrary. See Aaron Feuerstein and Malden Mills example in Martin, op. cit.

38. Pui-Wing Tam, "Myanmar Human Rights Suit Is Reinstated," *The Wall Street Journal*, September 19, 2002.

39. John Elkington, *Cannibals with Forks* (Oxford: Capstone Publishing, 1999). Debora L. Spar and Lane T. La Mure, "The Power of Activism: Assessing the Impact of NGOs on Global Business," *California Management Review*, 45/3 (Spring 2003): 78–101.

40. <www.starbucks.com/aboutus/CSR_FY01_AR.pdf>.

41. "Boycotting Corporate America," *The Economist*, May 26, 1990, p. 69.

42. Wallace N. Davidson, III, Abuzar El-Jelly, and Dan L. Worrell, "Influencing Managers to Change Unpopular Corporate Behavior Through Boycotts and Divestitures: A Stock Market Test," *Business and Society*, 34/2 (1995): 171–196.

43. Lynn Sharp Paine and Mihnea Moldoveanu, "Royal Dutch/Shell in Nigeria," case study 9-399-126, Harvard Business School, Boston, MA, 1999.

44. Nicholas Schoon, "Greenpeace's Brent Spar Apology," *The Independent*, September 6, 1995, p. 3.

45. Roger Cowe, "Boardrooms Discover Corporate Ethics," *Guardian Weekly*, March 28, 1999, p. 27; Shell, *Profits and Principles—Does There Have To Be a Choice?* (London: Shell International, 1998).

46. Tom McCawley, "Racing to Improve Its Reputation: Nike Has Fought to Shed Its Image as an Exploiter of Third-World Labor Yet It Is Still a Target of Activists," *Financial Times*, December 21, 2000, p. 14; Philip Rosenzweig, "How Should Multinationals Set Global Workplace Standards?" *Financial Times*, March 27, 1998, p. 11 (surveys); <www.nikebiz.com/labor>. See Klein [op. cit.] for a more skeptical view of Nike's response to the sweatshop issue.

47. N. Craig Smith, *Morality and the Market: Consumer Pressure for Corporate Accountability* (London: Routledge, 1990).

48. <www.mori.com/polls/1999/millpoll>.

49. Tom J. Brown and Peter A. Dacin, "The Company and the Product: Corporate Associations and Consumer Product Responses," *Journal of Marketing*, 61 (January 1997): 69.

50. Sankar Sen and C.B. Bhattacharya, "Does Doing Good Always Lead to Doing Better? Consumer Reactions to Corporate Social Responsibility," *Journal of Marketing Research*, 38 (May 2001): 225–243.

51. Michael Skapinker, "The Problem with Ethical Shoppers," *Financial Times*, November 30, 2002, p. 10; Simon Caulkin, "Once a Minority Cause, Fairtrade Is Now Becoming Mainstream," *The Observer*, February 2, 2003, p. 6.

52. Ibid.

53. Quoted in Robert L. Gildea, "Consumer Survey Confirms Corporate Social Action Affects Buying Decisions," *Public Relations Quarterly* 39 (Winter 1994–1995): 21.

54. See <www.homedepot.com> and <www.diy.com/aboutbandq/sustainability/history/Timber>.

55. Minette E. Drumwright, "Socially Responsible Organizational Buying: Environmental Concern as a Noneconomic Buying Criterion," *Journal of Marketing*, 58/3 (July 1994): 1–19.

56. Sandra A. Waddock, Charles Bodwell, and Samuel B. Graves, "Responsibility: The New Business Imperative," *The Academy of Management Executive*, 16/2 (May 2002): 132–148.

57. WEF (2003), op. cit.

58. UK DTI, op. cit.

59. Assets in professionally managed, socially screened investment portfolios rose to $2.01 trillion in 2001, an increase of 35% on 1999. Altogether, over $2.3 trillion was in professionally managed portfolios utilizing one or more of the three dynamic strategies that together define socially responsible investing in the U.S.—screening ($1,421 billion), shareholder advocacy ($305 billion), and/or community investing ($7.6 billion) (a further $592 billion is in both screening and shareholder advocacy). See Social Investment Forum, *2001 Report on Socially Responsible Investing Trends in the United States* (Washington, D.C.: Social Investment Forum, 2001).

60. Steve Johnson, "The FTSE4Good Index: 'Lite' Index Is Accused over Quality Standards," *Financial Times*, May 11, 2002, p. 9 (Money section).

61. There is some survey evidence to suggest a reduction in expenditure on CSR in 2002 [see Jericho Communications, op. cit.]. John Elkington has also observed some belt-tightening, including closures of CSR departments, but he sees this as a potentially useful removal of "camouflage" rather than a diminution of substantive CSR activity [source: private communication].

62. Jean-Pierre Garnier's speech to GSK employees shortly after the merger of Glaxo Wellcome and SmithKline Beecham. Smith and Duncan, op. cit., p. 1.

63. David Henderson, *Misguided Virtue: False Notions of Corporate Social Responsibility* (Wellington, New Zealand: New Zealand Business Roundtable, 2001); Ethan B. Kapstein, "The Corporate Ethics Crusade," *Foreign Affairs*, 80/5 (2001): 105–119.

64. Kapstein, op. cit.

65. Milton Friedman, *Capitalism and Freedom* (Chicago, IL: University of Chicago Press, 1962), pp. 60–61.

66. Smith, op. cit., pp. 69–75.

67. Adam Smith, *The Wealth of Nations* (London: Everyman, 1971 [1776]), Vol. 1, p. 400.

68. Henry Mintzberg, "The Case for Corporate Social Responsibility," *The Journal of Business Strategy*, 4/2 (Fall 1983): 12.

69. SustainAbility, op. cit.

70. Philip Morris spent $100 million touting its $75 million in charitable donations in 1999. It spent $250 million in 2000. See Ronald Alsop, "Perils of Corporate Philanthropy," *Wall Street Journal*, January 16, 2002, p. B1.

71. Martin, op. cit., p. 70.

72. Joshua D. Margolis and James P. Walsh, *People and Profits* (Mahwah, NJ: Lawrence Erlbaum, 2001).

73. WBCSD, "Corporate Social Responsibility: Making Good Business Sense," report

from World Business Council for Sustainable Development, January 2000, p. 22, <www.wbcsd.ch>.

74. See Hess et al. [op. cit.] for some excellent examples of corporate community involvement.

75. SustainAbility, op. cit.

76. This is consistent with the approach recommended by Hess et al. [op. cit.] in the more specific case of CSR in the form of "corporate social initiatives."

77. Described as "materiality" by SustainAbility, op. cit., p. 2.

78. WBCSD (2000), op. cit., p. 7.

79. <www.shell.com>. It is one of the "Magnificent Seven" top reports in "Trust Us" [SustainAbility, op. cit.]. In 2000, for example, Shell reported that 60 people (55 contractors and 5 Shell employees) died in work activity, up from 47 in 1999, and described this as "unacceptable." Most of the deaths were in road accidents in developing countries and Shell said it was responding to the problem with road safety awareness and training programs.

80. <www.btplc.com/Betterworld>. BT is also in SustainAbility's "Magnificent Seven."

81. Westpac, *A Fresh Perspective: Our First Social Impact Report* (Sydney: Westpac Banking Corporation, 2002).

82. <www.btplc.com/Betterworld>.

83. <www.starbucks.com/aboutus/CSR_FY01_AR.pdf>.

84. <www.shell.com>; <www.bp.com>; <www.riotinto.com>.

85. WEF (2003), op. cit.; WBCSD (2000), op. cit.

86. WBCSD (2000), op. cit., p. 15.

87. <www.shell.com>.

88. WBCSD (2000), op. cit.

89. <www.shell.com>.

90. This industry perspective is questioned by WHO and UNAIDS (the Joint United Nations Programme on HIV/AIDS): "While far greater investments in health and social services infrastructure are needed to expand access to treatment on a massive scale, many countries have underutilized health system capacity that, but for the lack of financing and affordability, could be used to expand treatment today." See WHO and UNAIDS, "Accelerating Access Initiative: Widening Access to Care and Support for People Living with HIV/AIDS. Progress Report June 2002," (Geneva: WHO), p. 2.

91. Geoff Dyer, "Netherlands Acts Against Re-Sold AIDS Drugs," *Financial Times*, October 3, 2002, p. 8.

92. "U.S. Schools Reject Coke's Plan to Teach the World," *Australian Financial Review*, July 6, 2001, p. 27.

93. Duncan McLeod, "Suspicion over Microsoft Gift to Poor Schools," *Financial Times*, October 8, 2002, p. 12.

94. Royal Society for the Encouragement of Arts, Manufactures and Commerce (RSA), *Tomorrow's Company: The Role of Business in a Changing World* (London: RSA, 1995).

95. For discussion of the potential role of managers' personal preferences, see Spar and La Mure, op. cit.

96. Martin, op. cit. He refers to these projects as "structural CSR" and cites the promulgation of regulations requiring air bags in automobiles as one example.

THE CASE AGAINST CORPORATE SOCIAL RESPONSIBILITY

Aneel Karnani

Can companies do well by doing good? Yes—sometimes. But the idea that companies have a responsibility to act in the public interest and will profit from doing so is fundamentally flawed.

Large companies now routinely claim that they aren't in business just for the profits, that they're also intent on serving some larger social purpose. They trumpet their efforts to produce healthier foods or more fuel-efficient vehicles, conserve energy and other resources in their operations, or otherwise make the world a better place. Influential institutions like the Academy of Management and the United Nations, among many others, encourage companies to pursue such strategies.

It's not surprising that this idea has won over so many people—it's a very appealing proposition. You can have your cake and eat it too!

But it's an illusion, and a potentially dangerous one.

Very simply, in cases where private profits and public interests are aligned, the idea of corporate social responsibility is irrelevant: Companies that simply do everything they can to boost profits will end up increasing social welfare. In circumstances in which profits and social welfare are in direct opposition, an appeal to corporate social responsibility will almost always be ineffective, because executives are unlikely to act voluntarily in the public interest and against shareholder interests.

Irrelevant or ineffective, take your pick. But it's worse than that. The danger is that a focus on social responsibility will delay or discourage more effective measures to enhance social welfare in those cases where profits and the public good are at odds. As society looks to companies to address these problems, the real solutions may be ignored.

Well and Good

To get a better fix on the irrelevance or ineffectiveness of corporate social responsibility efforts, let's first look at situations where profits and social welfare are in synch.

Consider the market for healthier food. Fast-food outlets have profited by expanding their offerings to include salads and other options designed to appeal to health-conscious consumers. Other companies have found new sources of revenue in low-fat, whole-grain and other types of foods that have grown in popularity. Social welfare is improved. Everybody wins.

Similarly, auto makers have profited from responding to consumer demand for more fuel-efficient vehicles, a plus for the environment. And many companies have boosted profits while enhancing social welfare by reducing their energy consumption and thus their costs.

But social welfare isn't the driving force behind these trends. Healthier foods and more fuel-efficient vehicles didn't become so common until they became profitable for their makers. Energy conservation didn't become so important to many companies until energy became more costly. These companies are benefiting society while acting in their own interests; social activists urging them to change their ways had little impact. It is the relentless maximisation of profits, not a commitment to social responsibility that has proved to be a boon to the public in these cases.

Unfortunately, not all companies take advantage of such opportunities, and in those cases both social welfare and profits suffer. These companies have one of two problems: Their executives are either incompetent or are putting their own interests ahead of the company's long-term financial interests. For instance, an executive might be averse to any risk, including the development of new products that might jeopardize the short-term financial performance of the company and thereby affect his compensation, even if taking that risk would improve the company's longer-term prospects.

An appeal to social responsibility won't solve either of those problems. Pressure from shareholders for sustainable growth in profitability can. It can lead to incompetent managers being replaced and to a realignment of incentives for executives, so that their compensation is tied more directly to the company's long-term success.

When There's a Choice

Still, the fact is that while companies sometimes can do well by doing good, more often they can't. Because in most cases, doing what's best for society means sacrificing profits.

This is true for most of society's pervasive and persistent problems; if it weren't, those problems would have been solved long ago by companies seeking to maximize their profits. A prime example is the pollution caused by manufacturing. Reducing that pollution is costly to the manufacturers and that eats into profits. Poverty is another obvious example. Companies could pay their workers more and charge less for their products, but their profits would suffer.

So now what? Should executives in this situations heed the call for corporate social responsibility even without the allure of profiting from it?

You can argue that they should. But you shouldn't expect that they will.

Executives are hired to maximize profits; that is their responsibility to their company's shareholders. Even if executives wanted to forgo some profit to benefit society, they could expect to lose their jobs if they tried—and be replaced by managers who would restore profit as the top priority. The movement for corporate social responsibility is in direct opposition, in such cases, to the movement for better corporate governance, which demands that managers fulfill their fiduciary duty to act in the shareholders' interest or be relieved of their responsibilities. That's one reason so many companies talk a great deal about social responsibility but do nothing—a tactic known as green washing.

Managers who sacrifice profit for the common good also are in effect imposing a tax on their shareholders and arbitrarily deciding how that money should be spent. In that sense they are usurping the role of elected government officials, if only on a small scale.

Privately owned companies are a different story. If an owner-operated business chooses to accept diminished profit in order to enhance social welfare, that decision isn't being imposed on shareholders. And, of course, it is admirable and desirable for the leaders of successful public companies to use some of their personal fortune for charitable purposes, as many have throughout history and many do now. But those leaders shouldn't presume to pursue their philanthropic goals with shareholder money. Indeed, many shareholders themselves use significant amounts of the money they make from their investments to help fund charities or otherwise improve social welfare.

This is not to say, of course, that companies should be left free to pursue the greatest possible profits without regard for the social consequences. But, appeals to corporate social responsibility are not an effective way to strike a balance between profits and the public good.

The Power of Regulation

So how can that balance best be struck?

The ultimate solution is government regulation. Its greatest appeal is that it is binding. Government has the power to enforce regulation. No need to rely on anyone's best intentions.

But government regulation isn't perfect, and it can even end up *reducing* public welfare because of its cost or inefficiency. The government also may lack the resources and competence to design and administer appropriate regulations, particularly for complex industries requiring much specialized knowledge. And industry groups might find ways to influence regulation to the point where it is ineffective or even ends up benefiting the industry at the expense of the general population.

Outright corruption can make the situation even worse. What's more, all the problems of government failure are exacerbated in developing countries with weak and often corrupt governments.

Still, with all their faults, governments are a far more effective protector of the public good than any campaign for corporate social responsibility.

Watchdogs and Advocates

Civil society also plays a role in constraining corporate behavior that reduces social welfare, acting as a watchdog and advocate. Various nonprofit organizations and movements provide a voice for a wide variety of social, political, environmental, ethnic, cultural and community interests.

The Rainforest Action Network, for example, is an organization that agitates, often quite effectively, for environmental protection and sustainability.

Its website states, "Our campaigns leverage public opinion and consumer pressure to turn the public stigma of environmental destruction into a business nightmare for any American company that refuses to adopt responsible environmental policies." That's quite a different approach from trying to convince executives that they should do what's best for society because it's the right thing to do and won't hurt their bottom line.

Overall, though, such activism has a mixed track record, and it can't be relied on as the primary mechanism for imposing constraints on corporate behavior—especially in most developing countries, where civil society lacks adequate resources to exert much influence and there is insufficient awareness of public issues among the population.

Self-Control

Self-regulation is another alternative, but it suffers from the same drawback as the concept of corporate social responsibility: Companies are unlikely to voluntarily act in the public interest at the expense of shareholder interests.

But self-regulation can be useful. It tends to promote good practices and target specific problems within industries, impose lower compliance costs on businesses than government regulation, and offer quick, low-cost dispute-resolution procedures. Self-regulation can also be more flexible than government regulation, allowing it to respond more effectively to changing circumstances.

The challenge is to design self-regulation in a manner that emphasizes transparency and accountability, consistent with what the public expects from government regulation. It is up to the government to ensure that any self-regulation meets that standard. And the government must be prepared to step in and impose its own regulations if the industry fails to police itself effectively.

Financial Calculation

In the end, social responsibility is a financial calculation for executives, just like any other aspect of their business. The only sure way to influence corporate decision making is to impose an unacceptable cost—regulatory mandates, taxes, punitive fines, public embarrassment—on socially unacceptable behavior.

Pleas for corporate social responsibility will be truly embraced only by those executives who are smart enough to see that doing the right thing is a byproduct of their pursuit of profit. And that renders such pleas pointless.

Chapter 3

What is CSR?
Concepts and theories

IN THIS CHAPTER WE WILL:

- Establish some further basic understanding of the notion of CSR
- Examine the varied terminology applied to CSR
- Discuss the different levels and domains of the CSR concept
- Explore the variety of theoretical avenues and the diversity of theoretical concepts in CSR

Introduction

At this stage of our book some readers might no longer be able to shake the feeling of slight confusion. Not only is CSR vaguely defined and widely applied (Chapter 1), there is also still no common consensus that it should exist in the first place (Chapter 2). It is time then to lead the discussion to the substance of the CSR topic: what are the core ideas and schools of thought within the field of CSR?

In this chapter we will introduce those main concepts and theories of CSR. You might have noticed that already in Chapter 2, the two readings by Smith and Karnani not only differ in their assessment of CSR, but also have a fairly different understanding of what CSR essentially is. Indeed, as Pierre-Yves Néron (2010) has put it, CSR is still a field of 'conceptual anarchy'!

This state of 'anarchy' has mostly to do with the fact that CSR is still a relatively new and emerging practice that is largely defined and pragmatically developed by companies. However, even allowing for this a major fault line is visible. Table 3.1[1] provides an overview of this distinction. On the one side we have 'Traditional CSR', an approach by which a company generates its profits and creates value without

Table 3.1: Basic types of CSR

	Traditional CSR	Contemporary CSR
Focus	Risk	Reward
Drivers	Image, Brand, Public Acceptance	Performance, Markets, Products
Actors	Corporation, unilateral philanthropy	Corporation + Multi-stakeholder networks, collaborative value creation
Relation to the bottom-line	No direct contribution: CSR is value distribution	Integral goal: CSR is value creation
Orientation	Reactive	Proactive
Motto	'CSR is bolt-on'	'CSR is built-in'

much consideration for wider societal expectation beyond shareholders, and maybe, customers. Once the profit is generated, the company then spends the money (or in other words, distributes the value it has created) on a variety of CSR projects, activities and causes which are of value to important stakeholders. The driver here is that such donations will ultimately build up brand allegiance, enhance the wider image of the company, and provide for greater public acceptance. A good example for this approach is Deutsche Bank,[2] which lists under its CSR activities issues such as 'Education', 'Social Investments', 'Art & Music', and 'Employee Volunteering'. Most of these activities though have little relation to how Deutsche Bank actually generates its profits and creates value in their core operations as a financial service provider.

Companies that subscribe to 'Contemporary CSR', however, see responsible behaviour as an opportunity to generate profits, while at the same time living up to expectations of society. That is, rather than unilaterally donating money (through CSR projects) that they have generated from their 'normal' business, companies practising contemporary CSR make CSR part of their normal business. They work with stakeholders to understand their interests and expectations, and attempt to cater to them by offering business solutions to their needs. CSR for these companies is an integral, 'built-in' management practice, a part of their core value creating activity that is driven by attention to market trends, product development and performance throughout the entire value chain. A fitting example of this approach is the consumer goods multinational Unilever.[3] Their 'Sustainable Living Plan' lists a number of areas where product innovations, changes in manufacturing or shifts toward sustainable suppliers include activities that are directly related to their value chain and ultimately to the way Unilever generates its profits. Unlike Deutsche Bank, Unilever sees CSR as a way to generate profits, rather than as a way to share or 'give back' parts of their economic success.

The two examples here are already pointing to the fact that in the wider area of CSR companies frame their activities by using distinct concepts and approaches. In the following sections, we will highlight some of the most popular concepts that have dominated the debate in CSR over the last decades.

Corporate social responsibility

CWS 3.1

Visit the companion website for more links to companies with examples of both types of CSR

Corporate social responsibility can be considered as the most longstanding concept in the area and has been used by business and academia for more than 50 years (Carroll, 2008). The 'pyramid model' discussed in the reading in this chapter by Mark Schwartz and Archie Carroll probably provides the most widely known academic framework for understanding the concept. As such, the idea is a fundamentally American one and reflects strongly the Anglo-American business context. Interestingly, many companies globally have adopted this language, however often omitting the 'social' and just speaking about 'corporate responsibility'. This shift in language is partly due to the intention to include a broader set of responsibilities into the concept, such as to the environment, which in part is reflected in the academic literature on the topic as well (e.g. Cannon, 1994; Tully, 2005). Furthermore, it hints towards the fact that CSR needs to be contextualized in a specific context, and in many such contexts, for instance in Central and Eastern Europe, the attribute 'social' still evokes reminiscences of the term 'socialism' – something businesses try emphatically to avoid. Similar trends towards 'regional CSR jargon' are visible in most other parts of the world (Visser & Tolhurst, 2010).

Business ethics

Within academic research and teaching the term 'business ethics' has often been used as an umbrella label to discuss CSR (Carroll, 1999: 291). Historically, in most universities, CSR issues were taught by a professor of business ethics or in a business ethics course, and in many business schools this is still the case today. Therefore, many issues in the relationship between business and society have been studied initially from an ethical perspective and some of the leading academic voices in CSR today have a background in philosophy. Business ethics can be defined as 'the study of business situations, activities and decisions where issues of right and wrong are addressed' (Crane & Matten, 2010: 5) – and as such is concerned mainly with the rights and wrongs, or the morality, of different business practices. While this clearly forms part of the CSR agenda, there is also a whole set of CSR questions concerned more with how to manage, measure, and implement CSR. Similarly, with the recent growth in areas of CSR we arguably see a bifurcation of the traditional business ethics field: while traditional business ethicists look at specific dilemmas and decisions of an ethical nature, such as payment of bribes, discrimination, or ethical marketing, CSR is oriented towards the wider role of the corporation in the global economy. Today, we are just as likely to see CSR taught by a strategy or marketing professor – or even a politics or law professor, as we are a business ethics professor.

Sustainability

The concept of sustainability or sustainable development is another bracket under which CSR is discussed in business, politics and academia. Originating from forestry and environmental management, sustainability in a business context aims at mapping out how an organization can successfully survive without compromising the eco-logical, social, and economic survival of its current and future environment (for details see the reading by Garriga and Melé in this chapter). Again, the language and concept of sustainability reflects the influence of different regional contexts on the understanding of CSR. In particular in Continental Europe, corporations had been forced to think about their impact on and responsibility to wider society in the context of the rise of the green movement during the 1970s and 1980s. Consequently, some corporations became involved in CSR through ecological issues. Today, with issues such as climate change, food, water, and energy security at the top of the corporate agenda, many companies such as BMW, Daimler/Mercedes, Shell, and Unilever, now talk about their CSR in terms of sustainability – where sustainability refers to a broader set of social, economic and environmental imperatives.

This concern with sustainability is also reflected on the political level: for instance, the seminal paper on CSR by the Commission of the European Communities (2002) equates CSR with sustainable development. In a similar vein, the United Nations Global Compact as a crucial platform for CSR globally has moved towards the language of sustainability, as UN Secretary General Ban-Ki Moon put it in the ten-year anniversary report of the Compact:

> Some firms have saved money; others have minimized risks; still others have discovered new opportunities linked to the concept of sustainability. ... Expanding markets and advancing the economic and social well-being of people and societies can be two sides of the same coin.
> (United Nations Global Compact, 2012: 5)

As this quote neatly illustrates, sustainability appears to be the most common interpretation of what we referred to above as 'contemporary CSR'.

Corporate citizenship

As van Luijk (2001) has pointed out, the language of 'responsibility' or even 'ethics' has not always appealed to business since it might be seen as entailing a somewhat reproachful connotation. Since the early 1990s we can observe a significant turn in the language of CSR towards the label of corporate citizenship. In particular, companies that faced considerable public criticism and attacks in the past, such as Microsoft and ExxonMobil, have adopted this terminology, evoking a notion of corporations as a good neighbour, shoulder to shoulder with other fellow-citizens, filling their rightful place in society.

While this new terminology has primarily been business driven, and represents not much more than a re-labelling of CSR (Matten & Crane, 2005) the ongoing

CWS 3.2

Visit the companion website for more links to companies who use these different terms to refer to their CSR activities

academic debate on corporate citizenship has focused on highlighting the political nature of CSR. For instance, many CSR activities of companies today, such as the global fight against HIV/AIDS, or responsible forms of advertising, are carried out in close cooperation with political actors, such as government departments, non-government organizations, etc. This reveals the changing nature of the role of business in society towards some degree of participation in political governance (Crane et al, 2008). The debate about the political nature of CSR is still relatively young but represents one of the currently most dynamic discussions in the CSR literature (Néron, 2010; Scherer & Palazzo, 2011).

Introducing the readings

Both readings in this chapter cover seminal contributions in the CSR area, providing an in-depth explication of perhaps the most popular CSR concept in the extant literature as well as one of the most comprehensive overviews and analyses of the current academic debate on CSR.

Theoretical debates in CSR

Elisabet Garriga and Domènec Melé succeed in their rather ambitious attempt to map out the different theories used in CSR. Their analysis is an impressive overview of, foremost, the academic debate on CSR. While in the introduction to this chapter we have mapped out the core concepts of CSR predominantly used in business, this paper provides the various facets of the debate in academic research, regardless of their impact in the real world. The paper also helps in understanding why CSR is often referred to as an 'interdisciplinary' topic: the array of theories used include business studies, economics, sociology, politics, law, and philosophy. This is an indispensable read for any student of CSR, not least because it also provides references to most of the key contributions to the theoretical CSR literature over the past 50 odd years.

Levels and domains of CSR

One of the most long-standing and widely cited frameworks depicting CSR is Archie Carroll's four levels of CSR that was subsequently reformatted as a 'pyramid of CSR' (Carroll, 1991). The reading by Mark Schwartz and Carroll himself briefly introduces the CSR pyramid before discussing some of its limitations and proposing an alternative.

The core pyramid model has achieved renown because of its combination of simplicity, comprehensiveness, and plausibility. It starts with the economic responsibility of the firm to produce goods and services in a profitable manner. This 'foundation upon which all others rest' is pretty uncontroversial and fairly uncontested even by the harshest CSR critics. The next level of legal responsibilities also reflects this pragmatic approach – to abide by the law is a fairly uncontroversial business responsibility by any standards. The next two levels, the ethical and philanthropic responsibilities, go beyond these and represent the voluntary activities of corporations to live up to societal expectations.

Carroll's pyramid model has not been without its critics – for example, several authors have suggested that the model is less suitable for national contexts outside the US (e.g. Maignan, 2001; Visser, 2008). Therefore, together with Schwartz, Carroll develops in this more recent article a new framework based on 'three domains' of CSR rather than 'four levels'. Jettisoning the philanthropic responsibilities and acknowledging the critical overlaps between different types of responsibility, the new model develops a more sophisticated analysis of the different types of social responsibility that corporations may be faced with. While the article will probably never achieve the kind of lasting impact that Carroll's original formulation has, it represents an important update and advance on some of the rather simplistic assumptions of the initial framework. If even the original author of the pyramid of CSR is proposing an augmentation and amendment to his model, we should certainly take note!

Challenges for practice

While the topic of CSR theories and concepts may seem to be a primarily academic concern, there are a number of practical challenges that are also raised.

1. Should a company develop a 'traditional' or 'contemporary' CSR approach? This will depend on a number of factors, including:
   a) Why is the company engaging in CSR in the first place – to give something back, to improve its image, to develop new areas of business, to improve its competitiveness, or what?
   b) What are the key activities that are to be included in its CSR program?
   c) Does CSR relate primarily to value creation or value distribution in the company?
2. What is the best language to use in communicating about CSR to internal and external stakeholders?
   a) Which of the four main concepts – CSR, ethics, sustainability, or citizenship – should a company adopt?
   b) What are the reasons for the choice of this language?
3. Applying the Venn diagram in the Schwartz and Carroll reading to some of the main CSR decisions taken in practice by a company:
   a) Have these decisions been concerned with 'ethical', 'economic' or 'legal' responsibilities – or a combination of these?
   b) Do decision-makers actually evaluate decisions along these lines? If so, why? If not, why not?

Study questions

1. To what extent do you consider the plethora of terms and concepts in the CSR area a strength or a weakness for practitioners and researchers of CSR?
2. What are the key differences between traditional and contemporary CSR? Discuss in the context of companies from your home country, suggesting which of the approaches appears to be most dominant.
3. What are the main types of CSR theory as set out by Garriga and Melé? Why do you think these different theoretical approaches have emerged? Is it feasible or preferable to integrate them?
4. What are the core elements of CSR in Schwartz and Carroll's definition? Set out examples of companies that have upheld these specific levels of responsibility as well as companies that have violated them.
5. Think of Schwartz and Carroll's three domains model from the perspective of a small business. Does it apply equally as well as to a large corporation? Similarly, which theories of CSR as mapped out by Garriga and Melé would be most useful in a small business context?

Further reading

Spence, L. J. And Rutherfoord, R. (2001) 'Social responsibility, profit maximisation and the small firm owner-manager', *Small Business and Enterprise Development*, 8(2): 126–139.

This article applies the CSR concept to small- and medium sized enterprises. It discusses the main differences and highlights the reasons why CSR is also a topic for SMEs. The paper is particularly useful as most businesses globally are SMEs, yet face similar challenges to those that have led large companies to adopt CSR.

Matten, D. & Moon, J. (2008) '"Implicit" and "explicit" CSR: a conceptual framework for a comparative understanding of CSR', *Academy of Management Review*, 33(2): 404–424.

As outlined in Chapter 1, the recent rise of CSR and its move on to the agenda of business has mostly happened outside its original North American context. When CSR is adopted in a country where the idea of social responsibility as a management task is a novel idea, it does not mean that the expectation of society towards business and its obligations had not existed before. Often though, these expectations have been met in different ways. This paper provides a useful model of how we can understand and explain these differences.

Visser, W. (2008) 'CSR in developing countries', in A. Crane, A. McWilliams, D. Matten, J. Moon, & D. Siegel (eds) *The Oxford handbook of CSR*, Oxford: Oxford University Press, 473–499.

One of the areas of particular growth for CSR is in the developing world. This article maps out the specific demands on and characteristics of CSR in a developing country context. It resonates nicely with the readings in this chapter, in particular Schwartz & Carroll as it applies the 'pyramid of CSR' to a developing country context.

Endnotes

1   There is an abundance of literature arguing along the lines of this suggested dichotomy. In this volume, most readings in Section B take the 'contemporary' view, with Porter and Kramer in Chapter 7 probably being the most vocal critique of the 'traditional' view. Good reference points are also Porter and Kramer (2011) and Visser (2010). See also Grayson and Hodges (2004) from where we acknowledge taking the 'built-in versus bolt-on' metaphor.
2   www.db.com/csr/index_e.htm (Accessed 30 August, 2012).
3   http://unilever.com/sustainable-living/ (Accessed 30 August, 2012).

References

Cannon, T. (1994) *Corporate responsibility*, London: Pearson.
Carroll, A. B. (1991) 'The pyramid of corporate social responsibility: toward the moral management of organizational stakeholders', *Business Horizons*, July–August: 39–48.
Carroll, A. B. (1999) 'Corporate social responsibility – evolution of a definitional construct', *Business & Society*, 38(3): 268–295.
Carroll, A. B. (2008) 'A history of corporate social responsibility: concepts and practices', in A. Crane, A. McWilliams, D. Matten, J. Moon, & D. Siegel (eds) *The Oxford handbook of CSR*, Oxford: Oxford University Press, 19–46.
Commission of the European Communities (2002) *Communication from the Commission concerning corporate social responsibility: a business contribution to sustainable development*, Brussels: EU Commission.
Crane, A. & Matten, D. (2010) *Business ethics: managing corporate citizenship and sustainability in the age of globalization* (3rd edn), Oxford: Oxford University Press.
Crane, A., Matten, D., & Moon, J. (2008) *Corporations and citizenship*, Cambridge: Cambridge University Press.
Grayson, D. & Hodges, A. (2004) *Corporate social opportunity: seven steps to make corporate social responsibility work for your business*, Sheffield: Greenleaf.
Maignan, I. (2001) 'Consumers' perceptions of corporate social responsibilities: a cross-cultural comparison', *Journal of Business Ethics*, 30(1/1): 57–72.
Matten, D. & Crane, A. (2005) 'Corporate citizenship – toward an extended

theoretical conceptualisation', *Academy of Management Review*, 30(1): 166–179.

Néron, P. Y. (2010) 'Business and the polis: what does it mean to see corporations as political actors?' *Journal of Business Ethics*, 94: 333–352.

Porter, M. E. & Kramer, M. R. (2011) 'Creating shared value', *Harvard Business Review*, 89(January–February): 62–77.

Scherer, A. G. & Palazzo, G. (2011) 'The new political role of business in a globalized world: a review of a new perspective on CSR and its implications for the firm, governance, and democracy', *Journal of Management Studies*, 48(4): 899–931.

Tully, S. (2005) *International documents on corporate responsibility*, Cheltenham, UK and Northampton, MA: Edward Elgar.

United Nations Global Compact (2012) *United Nations global compact annual review – anniversary edition June 2010*, New York: United Nations.

van Luijk, H. J. L. (2001) 'Business ethics in Europe: a tale of two efforts', in R. Frederick (ed.) *A companion to business ethics*, Cambridge, MA and Oxford: Blackwell, 643–658.

Visser, W. (2008) 'CSR in developing countries', in A. Crane, A. McWilliams, D. Matten, J. Moon, & D. Siegel (eds) *The Oxford handbook of CSR*, Oxford: Oxford University Press, 473–499.

Visser, W. (2010) 'The age of responsibility: CSR 2.0 and the new DNA of business', *Journal of Business Systems, Governance and Ethics*, 5(3): 7–22.

Visser, W. & Tolhurst, N. (eds) (2010) *The world guide to CSR: a country-by-country analysis of corporate sustainability and responsibility*, Sheffield: Greenleaf.

CORPORATE SOCIAL RESPONSIBILITY THEORIES: MAPPING THE TERRITORY

Elisabet Garriga and Domènec Melé

Introduction

Since the second half of the 20th century a long debate on corporate social responsibility (CSR) has been taking place. In 1953, Bowen (1953) wrote the seminal book *Social Responsibilities of the Businessman*. Since then there has been a shift in terminology from the social responsibility of business to CSR. Additionally, this field has grown significantly and today contains a great proliferation of theories, approaches and terminologies. Society and business, social issues management, public policy and business, stakeholder management, corporate accountability are just some of the terms used to describe the phenomena related to corporate responsibility in society. Recently, renewed interest for corporate social responsibilities and new alternative concepts have been proposed, including corporate citizenship and corporate sustainability.

Some scholars have compared these new concepts with the classic notion of CSR (see van Marrewijk, 2003 for corporate sustainability; and Matten *et al.*, 2003 and Wood and Logsdon, 2002 for corporate citizenship).

Furthermore, some theories combine different approaches and use the same terminology with different meanings. This problem is an old one. It was 30 years ago that Votaw wrote: "corporate social responsibility means something, but not always the same thing to everybody. To some it conveys the idea of legal responsibility or liability; to others, it means socially responsible behavior in the ethical sense; to still others, the meaning transmitted is that of 'responsible for' in a causal mode; many simply equate it with a charitable contribution; some take it to mean socially conscious; many of those who embrace it most fervently see it as a mere synonym for legitimacy in the context of belonging or being proper or valid; a few see a sort of fiduciary duty imposing higher standards of behavior on businessmen than on citizens at large" (Votaw, 1972, p.25). Nowadays the panorama is not much better. Carroll, one of the most prestigious scholars in this discipline, characterized the situation as "an eclectic field with loose boundaries, multiple memberships, and differing training/perspectives; broadly rather than focused, multidisciplinary; wide breadth; brings in a wider range of literature; and interdisciplinary" (Carroll, 1994, p. 14). Actually, as Carroll added (1994, p. 6), the map of the overall field is quite poor.

However, some attempts have been made to address this deficiency. Frederick (1987, 1998) outlined a classification based on a conceptual transition from the ethical–philosophical concept of CSR (what he calls CSR1), to the action-orientated managerial concept of social responsiveness (CSR2). He then included a normative element based on ethics and values (CSR3) and finally he introduced the cosmos as the basic normative reference for social issues in management and considered the role of science and religion in these issues (CSR 4). In a more systematic way, Heald (1988) and Carroll (1999) have offered a historical sequence of the main developments in how the responsibilities of business in society have been understood.

Other classifications have been suggested based on matters related to CSR, such as Issues Management (Wartick and Rude, 1986; Wood, 1991a) or the concept of Corporate Citizenship (Altman, 1998). An alternative approach is presented by Brummer (1991) who proposes a classification in four groups of theories based on six criteria (motive, relation to profits, group affected by decisions, type of act, type of effect, expressed or ideal interest). These classifications, in spite of their valuable contribution, are quite limited in scope and, what is more, the nature of the relationship between business and society is rarely situated at the center of their discussion. This vision could be questioned as CSR seems to be a consequence of how this relationship is understood (Jones, 1983; McMahon, 1986; Preston, 1975; Wood, 1991b).

In order to contribute to a clarification of the field of business and society, our aim here is to map the territory in which most relevant CSR theories and related approaches are situated. We will do so by considering each theory from the perspective of how the interaction phenomena between business and society are focused.

As the starting point for a proper classification, we assume as hypothesis that the most relevant CSR theories and related approaches are focused on one of the following aspects of social reality: economics, politics, social integration and ethics. The inspiration for this hypothesis is rooted in four aspects that, according to Parsons (1961), can be observed in any social system: adaptation to the environment (related to resources and economics), goal attainment (related to politics), social integration and pattern maintenance or latency (related to culture and values).[1] This hypothesis permits us to classify these theories in four groups:

1   A first group in which it is assumed that the corporation is an instrument for wealth creation and that this is its sole social responsibility. Only the economic aspect of the interactions between business and society is considered. So any supposed social activity is accepted if, and only if, it is consistent with wealth creation. This group of theories could be called *instrumental theories* because they understand CSR as a mere means to the end of profits.

2   A second group in which the social power of corporation is emphasized, specifically in its relationship with society and its responsibility in the political arena associated with this power. This leads the corporation to accept social duties and rights or participate in certain social cooperation. We will call this group *political theories*.

3   A third group includes theories which consider that business ought to integrate social demands. They usually argue that business depends on society for its continuity and growth and even for the existence of business itself. We can term this group *integrative theories*.

4   A fourth group of theories understands that the relationship between business and society is embedded with ethical values. This leads to a vision of CSR from an ethical perspective and as a consequence, firms ought to accept social responsibilities as an ethical obligation above any other consideration. We can term this group *ethical theories*.

Throughout this paper we will present the most relevant theories on CSR and related matters, trying to prove that they are all focused on one of the aforementioned aspects. We will not explain each theory in detail, only what is necessary to verify our hypothesis and, if necessary, some complementary information to clarify what each is about. At the same time, we will attempt to situate these theories and approaches within a general map describing the current panorama regarding the role of business in society.

Instrumental theories

In this group of theories CSR is seen only as a strategic tool to achieve economic objectives and, ultimately, wealth creation. Representative of this approach is the well-known Friedman view that "the only one responsibility of business towards society is the maximization of profits to the shareholders within the legal framework and the ethical custom of the country" (1970).[2]

Instrumental theories have a long tradition and have enjoyed a wide acceptance in business so far. As Windsor (2001) has pointed out recently, "a leitmotiv of wealth creation progressively dominates the managerial conception of responsibility" (Windsor, 2001, p. 226).

Concern for profits does not exclude taking into account the interests of all who have a stake in the firm (stakeholders). It has been argued that in certain conditions the satisfaction of these interests can contribute to maximizing the shareholder value (Mitchell *et al.*, 1997; Ogden and Watson, 1999). An adequate level of investment in philanthropy and social activities is also acceptable for the sake of profits (McWilliams and Siegel, 2001). We will return to these points afterwards.

In practice, a number of studies have been carried out to determine the correlation between CSR and corporate financial performance. Of these, an increasing number show a positive correlation between the social responsibility and financial performance of corporations in most cases (Frooman, 1997; Griffin and Mahon, 1997; Key and Popkin, 1998; Roman *et al.*, 1999; Waddock and Graves, 1997). However, these findings have to be read with caution since such correlation is difficult to measure (Griffin, 2000; Rowley and Berman, 2000).

Three main groups of instrumental theories can be identified, depending on the economic objective proposed. In the first group the objective is the maximization of shareholder value, measured by the share price. Frequently, this leads to a short-term profits orientation. The second group of theories focuses on the strategic goal of achieving competitive advantages, which would produce long-term profits. In both cases, CSR is only a question of enlightened self-interest (Keim, 1978) since CSRs are a mere instrument for profits. The third is related to cause-related marketing and is very close to the second. Let us examine briefly the philosophy and some variants of these groups.

Maximising the shareholder value

A well-known approach is that which takes the straightforward contribution to maximizing the shareholder value as the supreme criterion to evaluate specific corporate social activity. Any investment in social demands that would produce an increase of the shareholder value should be made, acting without deception and fraud. In contrast, if the social demands only impose a cost on the company they should be rejected. Friedman (1970) is clear, giving an example about investment in the local community: "It will be in the long run interest of a corporation that is a major employer in a small community to devote resources to providing amenities to that community or to improving its government. That makes it easier to attract desirable employees, it may reduce the wage bill or lessen losses from pilferage and sabotage or have other worthwhile effects." So, the socio-economic objectives are completely separate from the economic objectives.

Currently, this approach usually takes the shareholder value maximization as the supreme reference for corporate decision-making. The Agency Theory (Jensen and Meckling, 1976; Ross, 1973) is the most popular way to articulate this reference. However, today it is quite readily accepted that shareholder value maximization is not incompatible with satisfying certain interests of people with a stake in the firm (stakeholders). In this respect, Jensen (2000) has proposed what he calls "enlightened value maximization". This concept specifies long-term value maximization or value-seeking as the firm's objective. At the same time, this objective is employed as the criterion for making the requisite tradeoffs among its stakeholders.

Strategies for achieving competitive advantages

A second group of theories are focused on how to allocate resources in order to achieve long-term social objectives and create a competitive advantage (Husted and Allen, 2000). In this group three approaches can be included: (a) social investments in competitive context, (b) natural resource-based view of the firm and its dynamic capabilities and (c) strategies for the bottom of the economic pyramid.

(a) Social investments in a competitive context. Porter and Kramer (2002) have recently applied the well-known Porter model on competitive advantage (Porter, 1980) to consider investment in areas of what they call competitive context.[3] The authors argue that investing in philanthropic activities may be the only way to improve the context of competitive advantage of a firm and usually creates greater social value than individual donors or government can. The reason presented – the opposite of Friedman's position – is that the firm has the knowledge and resources for a better understanding of how to solve some problems related to its mission. As Burke and Logsdon (1996) pointed out, when philanthropic activities are closer to the company's mission, they create greater wealth than other kinds of donations. That is what happens, e.g., when a telecommunications company is teaching computer network administration to students of the local community.

Porter and Kramer conclude, "philanthropic investments by members of a cluster, either individually or collectively, can have a powerful effect on the cluster competitiveness and the performance of all its constituent companies" (2002, pp. 60–61).

(b) Natural resource-based view of the firm and dynamic capabilities. The resource-based view of the firm (Barney, 1991; Wernerfelt, 1984) maintains that the ability of a firm to perform better than its competitors depends on the unique interplay of human, organizational, and physical resources over time. Traditionally, resources that are most likely to lead to competitive advantage are those that meet four criteria: they should be valuable, rare, and inimitable, and the organization must be organized to deploy these resources effectively.

The "dynamic capabilities" approach presents the dynamic aspect of the resources; it is focused on the drivers behind the creation, evolution and recombination of the resources into new sources of competitive advantage (Teece *et al.*, 1997). So dynamic capabilities are organizational and strategic routines, by which managers acquire resources, modify them, integrate them, and recombine them to generate new value-creating strategies. Based on this perspective, some authors have identified social and ethical resources and capabilities which can be a source of competitive advantage, such as the process of moral decision-making (Petrick and Quinn, 2001), the process of perception, deliberation and responsiveness or capacity of adaptation (Litz, 1996) and the development of proper relationships with the primary stakeholders: employees, customers, suppliers, and communities (Harrison and St. John, 1996; Hillman and Keim, 2001).

A more complete model of the 'Resource-Based View of the Firm' has been presented by Hart (1995). It includes aspects of dynamic capabilities and a link with the external environment. Hart argues that the most important drivers for new resource and capabilities development will be constraints and challenges posed by the natural biophysical environment. Hart has developed his conceptual framework with three main interconnected strategic capabilities: pollution prevention, product stewardship and sustainable development. He considers as critical resources continuous improvement, stakeholder integration and shared vision.

(c) Strategies for the bottom of the economic pyramid. Traditionally most business strategies are focused on targeting products at upper- and middle-class people, but most of the world's population is poor or lower-middle class. At the bottom of the economic pyramid there may be some 4000 million people. On reflection, certain strategies can serve the poor and simultaneously make profits. Prahalad (2002), analyzing the India experience, has suggested some mind-set changes for converting the poor into active consumers. The first of these is seeing the poor as an opportunity to innovate rather than as a problem.

A specific means for attending to the bottom of the economic pyramid is disruptive innovation. Disruptive innovations (Christensen and Overdorf, 2000; Christensen *et al.*, 2001) are products or services that do not have the same capabilities and conditions as those being used by customers in the mainstream markets; as a result they can be introduced only for new or less demanding applications among non-traditional customers, with a low-cost production and adapted to the necessities of the population. For example a telecommunications company inventing a small cellular telephone system with lower costs but also with less service adapted to the base of the economic pyramid.

Disruptive innovations can improve the social and economic conditions at the "base of the pyramid" and at the same time they create a competitive advantage for the firms in telecommunications, consumer electronics and energy production and many other industries, especially in developing countries (Hart and Christensen, 2002; Prahalad and Hammond, 2002).

Cause-related marketing

Cause-related marketing has been defined as "the process of formulating and implementing marketing activities that are characterized by an offer from the firm to contribute a specified amount to a designated cause when customers engage in revenue-providing exchanges that satisfy organizational and individual objectives" (Varadarajan and Menon, 1988, p. 60). Its goal then is to enhance company revenues and sales or customer relationship by building the brand through the acquisition of, and association with the ethical dimension or social responsibility dimension (Murray and Montanari, 1986; Varadarajan and Menon, 1988). In a way, it seeks product differentiation by creating socially responsible attributes that affect company reputation (Smith and Higgins, 2000). As McWilliams and Siegel (2001, p.120) have pointed out: "support of cause related marketing creates a reputation that a firm is reliable and honest. Consumers typically assume that the products of a reliable and honest firm will be of high quality". For example, a pesticide-free or non-animal-tested ingredient can be perceived by some buyers as preferable to other attributes of competitors' products.

Other activities, which typically exploit cause-related marketing, are classical musical concerts, art exhibitions, golf tournaments or literary campaigns. All of these are a form of enlightened self-interest and a win–win situation as both the company and the charitable cause receive benefits: "The brand manager uses consumer concern for business responsibility as a means for securing competitive advantage. At the same time a charitable cause receives substantial financial benefits" (Smith and Higgins, 2000, p. 309).

Political Theories

A group of CSR theories and approaches focus on interactions and connections between business and society and on the power and position of business and its inherent responsibility. They include both political considerations and political analysis in the CSR debate. Although there are a variety of approaches, two major theories can be distinguished: Corporate Constitutionalism and Corporate Citizenship.

Corporate constitutionalism

Davis (1960) was one of the first to explore the role of power that business has in society and the social impact of this power.[4] In doing so, he introduces business power as a new element in the debate of CSR. He held that business is a social institution and it must use power responsibly. Additionally, Davis noted that the causes that generate the social power of the firm are not solely internal of the firm but also external. Their locus is unstable and constantly shifting, from the economic to the social forum and from there to the political forum and vice versa.

Davis attacked the assumption of the classical economic theory of perfect competition that precludes the involvement of the firm in society besides the creation of wealth. The firm has power to influence the equilibrium of the market and therefore the price is not a Pareto optimum reflecting the free will of participants with perfect knowledge of the market.

Davis formulated two principles that express how social power has to be managed: "the social power equation" and "the iron law of responsibility". The social power equation principle states that "social responsibilities of businessmen arise from the amount of social power that they have" (Davis, 1967, p. 48). The iron law of responsibility refers to the negative consequences of the absence of use of power. In his own words: "Whoever does not use his social power responsibly will lose it. In the long run those who do not use power in a manner which society considers responsible will tend to lose it because other groups eventually will step in to assume those responsibilities" (1960, p. 63). So if a firm does not use its social power, it will lose its position in society because other groups will occupy it, especially when society demands responsibility from business (Davis, 1960).

According to Davis, the equation of social power-responsibility has to be understood through the functional role of business and managers. In this respect, Davis rejects the idea of total responsibility of business as he rejected the radical free-market ideology of no responsibility of business. The limits of functional power come from the pressures of different constituency groups. This "restricts organizational power in the same way that a governmental constitution does." The constituency groups do not destroy power. Rather they define conditions for its responsible use. They channel organizational power in a supportive way and to protect other interests against unreasonable organizational power (Davis, 1967, p. 68). As a consequence, his theory is called "Corporate Constitutionalism".

Integrative social contract theory

Donaldson (1982) considered the business and society relationship from the social contract tradition, mainly from the philosophical thought of Locke. He assumed that a sort of implicit social contract between business and society exists. This social contract implies some indirect obligations of business towards society. This approach would overcome some limitations of deontological and teleological theories applied to business.

Afterwards, Donaldson and Dunfee (1994, 1999) extended this approach and proposed an "Integrative Social Contract Theory" (ISCT) in order to take into account the socio-cultural context and also to integrate empirical and normative aspects of management. Social responsibilities come from consent. These scholars assumed two levels of consent. Firstly a theoretical macrosocial contract appealing to all rational contractors, and secondly, a real microsocial contract by members of numerous localized communities. According to these authors, this theory offers a process in which the contracts among industries, departments and economic systems can be legitimate. In this process the participants will agree upon the ground rules defining the foundation of economics that will be acceptable to them.

The macrosocial contract provides rules for any social contracting. These rules are called the "hyper-norms"; they ought to take precedence over other contracts. These hyper-norms are so fundamental and basic that they "are discernible in a convergence of religious, political and philosophical thought" (Donaldson and Dunfee, 2000, p. 441). The microsocial contracts show explicit or implicit agreements that are binding within an identified community, whatever this may be: industry, companies or economic systems. These microsocial contracts, which generate "authentic norms", are based on the attitudes and behaviors of the members of the norm-generating community and, in order to be legitimate, have to accord with the hyper-norms.

Corporate citizenship

Although the idea of the firm as citizen is not new (Davis, 1973) a renewed interest in this concept among practitioners has appeared recently due to certain factors that have had an impact on the business and society relationship. Among these factors, especially worthy of note are the crisis of the Welfare State and the globalization phenomenon. These, together with the deregulation process and decreasing costs with technological improvements, have meant that some large multinational companies have greater economical and social power than some governments. The corporate citizenship framework looks to give an account of this new reality, as we will try to explain here.

In the 1980s the term "corporate citizenship" was introduced into the business and society relationship mainly through practitioners (Altman and Vidaver-Cohen, 2000). Since the late 1990s and early 21st century this term has become more and more popular in business and increasing academic work has been carried out (Andriof and McIntosh, 2001; Matten and Crane, 2005).

Although the academic reflection on the concept of "corporation citizenship", and on a similar one called "the business citizen", is quite recent (Matten et al., 2003; Wood and Logsdon, 2002; among others), this notion has always connoted a sense of belonging to a community. Perhaps for this reason it has been so popular among managers and business people, because it is increasingly clear that business needs to take into account the community where it is operating.

The term "corporate citizenship" cannot have the same meaning for everybody. Matten et al. (2003) have distinguished three views of "corporate citizenship": (1) a limited view, (2) a view equivalent to CSR and (3) an extended view of corporate citizenship, which is held by them. In the limited view "corporate citizenship" is used in a sense quite close to corporate philanthropy, social investment or certain responsibilities assumed towards the local community. The equivalent to the CSR view is quite common. Carroll (1999) believes that "corporate citizenship" seems a new conceptualisation of the role of business in society and depending on which way it is defined, this notion largely overlaps with other theories on the responsibility of business in society. Finally, in the extended view of corporate citizenship (Matten et al., 2003; Matten and Crane, 2005), corporations enter the arena of citizenship at the point of government failure in the protection of citizenship. This view arises from the fact that some corporations have gradually come to replace the most powerful institution in the traditional concept of citizenship, namely government.

The term "citizenship", taken from political science, is at the core of the "corporate citizenship" notion. For Wood and Logsdon "business citizenship cannot be deemed equivalent to individual citizenship – instead it derives from and is secondary to individual citizenship" (2002, p. 86). Whether or not this view is accepted, theories and approaches on "corporate citizenship" are focused on rights, responsibilities and possible partnerships of business in society.

Some theories on corporate citizenship are based on a social contract theory (Dion, 2001) as developed by Donaldson and Dunfee (1994, 1999), although other approaches are also possible (Wood and Logsdon, 2002).

In spite of some noteworthy differences in corporate citizenship theories, most authors generally converge on some points, such as a strong sense of business responsibility towards the local community, partnerships, which are the specific ways of formalizing the willingness to improve the local community,[5] and for consideration for the environment.

The concern for local community has extended progressively to a global concern in great part due to the very intense protests against globalization, mainly since the end of the 1990s. This sense of global corporate citizenship led to the joint statement "Global Corporate Citizenship – the Leadership Challenge for CEOs and Boards", signed by 34 of the world's largest multinational corporations during the World Economic Forum in New York in January 2002. Subsequently, business with local responsibility and, at the same time, being a global actor that places emphasis on business responsibilities in a global context, have been considered as a key issue by some scholars (Tichy *et al.*, 1997; Wood and Logsdon, 2002).

Integrative Theories

This group of theories looks at how business integrates social demands, arguing that business depends on society for its existence, continuity and growth. Social demands are generally considered to be the way in which society interacts with business and gives it a certain legitimacy and prestige. As a consequence, corporate management should take into account social demands, and integrate them in such a way that the business operates in accordance with social values.

So, the content of business responsibility is limited to the space and time of each situation depending on the values of society at that moment, and comes through the company's functional roles (Preston and Post, 1975). In other words, there is no specific action that management is responsible for performing throughout time and in each industry. Basically, the theories of this group are focused on the detection and scanning of, and response to, the social demands that achieve social legitimacy, greater social acceptance and prestige.

Issues management

Social responsiveness, or responsiveness in the face of social issues, and processes to manage them within the organization (Sethi, 1975) was an approach which arose in the 1970s. In this approach it is crucial to consider the gap between what the organization's relevant publics expect its performance to be and the organization's actual performance. These gaps are usually located in the zone that Ackerman (1973, p. 92) calls the "zone of discretion" (neither regulated nor illegal nor sanctioned) where the company receives some unclear signals from the environment. The firm should perceive the gap and choose a response in order to close it (Ackerman and Bauer, 1976).

Ackerman (1973), among other scholars, analyzed the relevant factors regarding the internal structures of organizations and integration mechanisms to manage social issues within the organization. The way a social objective is spread and integrated across the organization, he termed "process of institutionalisation". According to Jones (1980, p. 65), "corporate behavior should not in most cases be judged by the decisions actually reached but by the process by which they are reached". Consequently, he emphasized the idea of process rather than principles as the appropriate approach to CSR issues.

Jones draws an analogy with the political process assessing that the appropriate process of CSR should be a fair process where all interests have had the opportunity to be heard. So Jones has shifted the criterion to the inputs in the decision-making process rather than the outcomes, and has focused more on the process of implementation of CSR activities than on the process of conceptualization.

The concept of "social responsiveness" was soon widened with the concept "Issues Management". The latter includes the former but emphasizes the process for making a corporate response to social issues. Issues management has been defined by Wartick and Rude (1986, p. 124) as the "processes by which the corporation can identify, evaluate and respond to those social and political issues which may impact significantly upon it". They add that issues management attempts to minimize "surprises" which accompany social and political change by serving as an early warning system for potential environmental threats and opportunities. Further, it prompts more systematic and effective responses to particular issues by serving as a coordinating and integrating force within the corporation. Issues management research has been influenced by the strategy field, since it has been seen as a special group of strategic issues (Greening and Gray, 1994), or a part of international studies (Brewer, 1992). That led to the study of topics related with issues (identification, evaluation and categorization), formalization of stages of social issues and management issue response. Other factors, which have been considered, include the corporate responses to media exposure, interest group pressures and business crises, as well as organizational size, top management commitment and other organizational factors.

The principle of public responsibility

Some authors have tried to give an appropriate content and substance to help and guide the firm's responsibility by limiting the scope of the corporate responsibility. Preston and Post (1975, 1981) criticized a responsiveness approach and the purely process approach (Jones, 1980) as insufficient. Instead, they proposed "the principle of public responsibility". They choose the term "public" rather than "social", to stress the importance of the public process, rather than personal-morality views of narrow interest groups defining the scope of responsibilities.

According to Preston and Post an appropriate guideline for a legitimate managerial behavior is found within the framework of relevant public policy. They added that "public policy includes not only the literal text of law and regulation but also the broad pattern of social direction reflected in public opinion, emerging issues, formal legal requirements and enforcement or implementation practices" (Preston and Post, 1981, p. 57). This is the essence of the principle of public responsibility.

Preston and Post analyzed the scope of managerial responsibility in terms of the "primary" and "secondary" involvement of the firm in its social environment. Primary involvement includes the essential economic task of the firm, such as locating and establishing its facilities, procuring suppliers, engaging employees, carrying out its production functions and marketing products. It also includes legal requirements. Secondary involvements come as a consequence of the primary. They are, e.g., career and earning opportunities for some individuals, which come from the primary activity of selection and advancement of employees.

At the same time, these authors are in favor of business intervention in the public policy process especially with respect to areas in which specific public policy is not yet clearly established or it is in transition: "It is legitimate – and may be essential – that affected firms participate openly in the policy formation" (Preston and Post, 1981, p. 61).

In practice, discovering the content of the principle of public responsibility is a complex and difficult task and requires substantial management attention. As Preston and Post recognized, "the content of public policy is not necessarily obvious or easy to discover, nor is it invariable over time" (1981, p. 57). According to this view, if business adhered to the standards of performance in law and the existing public policy process, then it would be judged acceptably responsive in terms of social expectations.

The development of this approach was parallel to the study of the scope regarding business–government relationship (Vogel, 1986). These studies focused on government regulations – their formulation and implementation – as well as corporate strategies to influence these regulations, including campaign contributions, lobbying, coalition building, grass-roots organization, corporate public affairs and the role of public interest and other advocacy groups.

Stakeholder management

Instead of focusing on generic responsiveness, specific issues or on the public responsibility principle, the approach called "stakeholder management" is oriented towards "stakeholders" or people who affect or are affected by corporate policies and practices. Although the practice of stakeholder management is long-established, its academic development started only at the end of the 1970s (see, e.g., Sturdivant, 1979). In a seminal paper, Emshoff and Freeman (1978) presented two basic principles, which underpin stakeholder management. The first is that the central goal is to achieve maximum overall cooperation between the entire system of stakeholder groups and the objectives of the corporation. The second states that the most efficient strategies for managing stakeholder relations involve efforts, which simultaneously deal with issues affecting multiple stakeholders.

Stakeholder management tries to integrate groups with a stake in the firm into managerial decision-making. A great deal of empirical research has been done, guided by a sense of pragmatism. It includes topics such as how to determine the best practice in corporate stakeholder relations (Bendheim *et al.*, 1998), stakeholder salience to managers (Agle and Mitchell, 1999; Mitchell *et al.*, 1997), the impact of stakeholder management on financial performance (Berman *et al.*, 1999), the influence of stakeholder network structural relations (Rowley, 1997) and how managers can successfully balance the competing demands of various stakeholder groups (Ogden and Watson, 1999).

In recent times, corporations have been pressured by non-governmental organizations (NGOs), activists, communities, governments, media and other institutional forces. These groups demand what they consider to be responsible corporate practices. Now some corporations are seeking corporate responses to social demands by establishing dialogue with a wide spectrum of stakeholders.

Stakeholder dialogue helps to address the question of responsiveness to the generally unclear signals received from the environment. In addition, this dialogue "not only enhances a company's sensitivity to its environment but also increases the environment's understanding of the dilemmas facing the organization" (Kaptein and Van Tulder, 2003, p. 208).

Corporate social performance

A set of theories attempts to integrate some of the previous theories. The corporate social performance (CSP) includes a search for social legitimacy, with processes for giving appropriate responses.

Carroll (1979), generally considered to have introduced this model, suggested a model of "corporate performance" with three elements: a basic definition of social responsibility, a listing of issues in which social responsibility exists and a specification of the philosophy of response to social issues. Carroll considered that a definition of social responsibility, which fully addresses the entire range of obligations business has to society, must embody the economic, legal, ethical, and discretionary categories of business performance. He later incorporated his four-part categorization into a "Pyramid of Corporate Social Responsibilities" (Carroll, 1991). Recently, Schwartz and Carroll (2003) have proposed an alternative approach based on three core domains (economic, legal and ethical responsibilities) and a Venn model framework. The Venn framework yields seven CSR categories resulting from the overlap of the three core domains.

Wartick and Cochran (1985) extended the Carroll approach suggesting that corporate social involvement rests on the principles of social responsibility, the process of social responsiveness and the policy of issues management.

A new development came with Wood (1991b) who presented a model of corporate social performance composed of principles of CSR, processes of corporate social responsiveness and outcomes of corporate behavior. The principles of CSR are understood to be analytical forms to be filled with value content that is operationalized. They include: principles of CSR, expressed on institutional, organizational and individual levels, processes of corporate social responsiveness, such as environmental assessment, stakeholder management and issues management, and outcomes of corporate behavior including social impacts, social programs and social policies.

Ethical Theories

A fourth group of theories or approaches focuses on the ethical requirements that cement the relationship between business and society. They are based on principles that express the right thing to do or the necessity to achieve a good society. As main approaches we can distinguish the following.

Normative stakeholder theory

Stakeholder management has been included within the integrative theories group because some authors consider that this form of management is a way to integrate social demands. However, stakeholder management has become an ethically based theory mainly since 1984 when Freeman wrote *Strategic Management: a Stakeholder Approach*. In this book, he took as starting point that "managers bear a fiduciary relationship to stakeholders" (Freeman, 1984, p. xx), instead of having exclusively fiduciary duties towards stockholders, as was held by the conventional view of the firm. He understood as stakeholders those groups who have a stake in or claim on the firm (suppliers, customers, employees, stockholders, and the local community). In a more precise way, Donaldson and Preston (1995, p. 67) held that the stakeholder theory has a normative core based on two major ideas: (1) stakeholders are persons or groups with legitimate interests in procedural and/or substantive aspects of corporate activity (stakeholders are identified by their interests in the corporation, whether or not the corporation has any corresponding functional interest in *them* and (2) the interests of all stakeholders are of *intrinsic value* (that is, each group of stakeholders merits consideration for its own sake and not merely because of its ability to further the interests of some other group, such as the shareowners).

Following this theory, a socially responsible firm requires simultaneous attention to the legitimate interests of all appropriate stakeholders and has to balance such a multiplicity of interests and not only the interests of the firm's stockholders. Supporters of normative stakeholder theory have attempted to justify it through arguments taken from Kantian capitalism (Bowie, 1991; Evan and Freeman, 1988), modern theories of property and distributive justice (Donaldson and Preston, 1995), and also Libertarian theories with its notions of freedom, rights and consent (Freeman and Philips, 2002).

A generic formulation of stakeholder theory is not sufficient. In order to point out how corporations have to be governed and how managers ought to act, a *normative core* of ethical principles is required (Freeman, 1994). To this end, different scholars have proposed differing normative ethical theories. Freeman and Evan (1990) introduced Rawlsian principles. Bowie (1998) proposed a combination of Kantian and Rawlsian grounds. Freeman (1994) proposed the doctrine of fair contracts and Phillips (1997, 2003) suggested introducing the fairness principle based on six of Rawls' characteristics of the principle of fair play: mutual benefit, justice, cooperation, sacrifice, free-rider possibility and voluntary acceptance of the benefits of cooperative schemes. Lately, Freeman and Phillips (2002) have presented six principles for the guidance of stakeholder theory by combining Libertarian concepts and the Fairness principle. Some scholars (Burton and Dunn, 1996; Wicks *et al.*, 1994) proposed instead using a "feminist ethics" approach. Donaldson and Dunfee (1999) hold their "Integrative Social Contract Theory". Argandoña (1998) suggested the common good notion and Wijnberg (2000) an Aristotelian approach. From a practical perspective, the normative core of which is risk management, The Clarkson Center for Business Ethics (1999) has published a set of *Principles of Stakeholder Management*.

Stakeholder normative theory has suffered critical distortions and friendly misinterpretations, which Freeman and co-workers are trying to clarify (Phillips *et al.*, 2003). In practice, this theory has been applied to a variety of business fields, including stakeholder management for the business and society relationship, in a number of textbooks. Some of these have been republished several times (Carroll and Buchholtz, 2002; Post *et al.*, 2002; Weiss, 2003; among others).

In short, stakeholder approach grounded in ethical theories presents a different perspective on CSR, in which ethics is central.

Universal rights

Human rights have been taken as a basis for CSR, especially in the global market place (Cassel, 2001). In recent years, some human-rights-based approaches for corporate responsibility have been proposed. One of them is the UN Global Compact, which includes nine principles in the areas of human rights, labor and the environment. It was first presented by the United Nations Secretary-General Kofi Annan in an address to The World Economic Forum in 1999. In 2000 the Global Compact's operational phase was launched at UN Headquarters in New York. Many companies have since adopted it. Another, previously presented and updated in 1999, is The Global Sullivan Principles, which has the objective of supporting economic, social and political justice by companies where they do business. The certification SA8000 (www.cepaa.org) for accreditation of social responsibility is also based on human and labor rights. Despite using different approaches, all are based on the Universal Declaration of Human Rights adopted by the United Nations general assembly in 1948 and on other intentional declarations of human rights, labor rights and environmental protection.

Although for many people universal rights are a question of mere consensus, they have a theoretical grounding, and some moral philosophy theories give them support (Donnelly, 1985). It is worth mentioning the Natural Law tradition (Simon, 1992), which defends the existence of natural human rights (Maritain, 1971).

Sustainable development

Another values-based concept, which has become popular, is "sustainable development". Although this approach was developed at macro level rather than corporate level, it demands a relevant corporate contribution. The term came into widespread use in 1987, when the World Commission on Environment and Development (United Nations) published a report known as "Brundtland Report". This report stated that "sustainable development" seeks to meet the needs of the present without compromising the ability to meet the future generation to meet their own needs (World Commission on Environment and Development, 1987, p. 8). Although this report originally only included the environmental factor, the concept of "sustainable development" has since expanded to include the consideration of the social dimension as being inseparable from development. In the words of the World Business Council for Sustainable Development (2000, p. 2), sustainable development "requires the integration of social, environmental, and economic considerations to make balanced judgments for the long term".

Numerous definitions have been proposed for sustainable development (see a review in Gladwin and Kennelly, 1995, p. 877). In spite of which, content analysis of the main definitions suggests that sustainable development is "a process of achieving human development in an inclusive, connected, equiparable, prudent and secure manner" (Gladwin and Kennelly, 1995, p. 876).

The problem comes when the corporation has to develop the processes and implement strategies to meet the corporate challenge of corporate sustainable development. As Wheeler et al. (2003, p. 17) have stated, sustainability is "an ideal toward which society and business can continually strive, the way we strive is by creating value, creating outcomes that are consistent with the ideal of sustainability along social environmental and economic dimensions".[6]

However, some suggestions have been proposed to achieve corporate ecological sustainability (Shrivastava, 1995; Stead and Stead, 2000; among others). A pragmatic proposal is to extend the traditional "bottom line" accounting, which shows overall net profitability, to a "triple bottom line" that would include economic, social and environmental aspects of corporation. Van Marrewijk and Werre (2003) maintain that corporate sustainability is a custom-made process and each organization should choose its own specific ambition and approach regarding corporate sustainability. This should meet the organization's aims and intentions, and be aligned with the organization strategy, as an appropriate response to the circumstances in which the organization operates.

The common good approach

This third group of approaches, less consolidated than the stakeholder approach but with potential, holds the common good of society as the referential value for CSR (Mahon and McGowan, 1991; Velasquez, 1992). The common good is a classical concept rooted in Aristotelian tradition (Smith, 1999), in Medieval Scholastics (Kempshall, 1999), developed philosophically (Maritain, 1966) and assumed into Catholic social thought (Carey, 2001) as a key reference for business ethics (Alford and Naughton, 2002; Melé, 2002; Pope John Paul II, 1991, #43). This approach maintains that business, as with any other social group or individual in society, has to contribute to the common good, because it is a part of society. In this respect, it has been argued that business is a mediating institution (Fort, 1996, 1999). Business should be neither harmful to nor a parasite on society, but purely a positive contributor to the well-being of the society.

Business contributes to the common good in different ways, such as creating wealth, providing goods and services in an efficient and fair way, at the same time respecting the dignity and the inalienable and fundamental rights of the individual. Furthermore, it contributes to social well-being and a harmonic way of living together in just, peaceful and friendly conditions, both in the present and in the future (Melé, 2002).

To some extent, this approach has a lot in common with both the stakeholder approach (Argandoña, 1998) and sustainable development, but the philosophical base is different. Although there are several ways of understanding the notion of common good (Sulmasy, 2001), the interpretation based on the knowledge of human nature and its fulfilment seems to us particularly convincing. It permits the circumnavigation of cultural relativism, which is frequently embedded in some definitions of sustainable development.

The common good notion is also very close to the Japanese concept of Kyosei (Goodpaster, 1999; Kaku, 1997; Yamaji, 1997), understood as "living and working together for the common good", which, together with the principle of human dignity, is one of the founding principles of the popular "The Caux Roundtable Principles for Business" (www.cauxroundtable.org).

Discussion

The preceding description, summed up on Table 3.2, leads to the conclusion that the hypothesis considered in the introduction about the four basic focal points employed by CSR theories and related approaches is adequate. Consequently, most of the current theories related to CSR could be broadly classified as instrumental, political, integrative and ethical theories.

Donati (1991), a contemporary sociologist, has reviewed many aspects of the work of Parsons. He suggests that adaptation, goal attainment, integration and latency presented by Parsons (1961) as rigid functions, have to be understood as four interconnected dimensions present in every social phenomenon. This suggests that the concept of business and society relationship must include these four aspects or dimensions and some connection among them must exist. This must be reflected in every theory. In some authors, such as Friedman, it is relatively easy to discover these dimensions and connections, in other theories it is not so easy.

In fact, although the main concern in the Friedman view (Friedman, 1970; Friedman and Friedman, 1962) is for wealth creation, as we have pointed out above, this concern is rooted in certain cultural values regarding the free market, private property and the fact that wealth creation is good for society. This shows us that certain values are present, even though they are frequently questioned. At the same time, he accepts the rules of the free market, laws and ethical customs in each place. Friedman and, above all, Jensen (2000) also accept the integration of some social demands into the company if it is profitable in the long-term. Regarding politics, underpinning the Friedman view there is a functional conception of the social with clear political consequences. Society is understood as a mechanism with mono-functional groups, each with a concrete purpose. Thus, the exclusive purpose of business organizations is the creation of wealth. It is held that business operating in a free market is the best way to allocate scarce resources because society can achieve an optimum situation in the sense of Pareto (Pareto Optimum). This means that the satisfaction of all people involved in the situation is the greatest possible or, at least, the situation satisfies most of them without being detrimental for others. However, in the presence of externalities, when decision-makers do not take into account secondary effects of their actions that burden or benefit others, the market is inefficient and the equilibrium is not a Pareto optimum. When externalities appear, another system of society, the political system, should act. The political system must confront these externalities through taxes, regulation and minimum package of rights. So, business contributes to the welfare of society through the market mechanism and in compliance with the law. Of course, outside business, the manager can spend any quantity of personal money on social activities according to his or her personal preferences. However, the social objectives and demands come under business consideration only through the law applied by the political system.

A contrasting theory, in which the four dimensions mentioned and their connections are not so easy to discover, is "the principle of public responsibility" of Preston and Post (1975). However, these dimensions are implicit. In fact, this theory presupposes a certain conception of society and values. The political dimension is clear, since public policy is assumed as a basic criterion. Regarding wealth creation, undoubtedly the application of this theory would have consequences for profit generation. Actually, these scholars recognize that what they call secondary relationships (related to secondary involvements) "as essential to effective management over the long term" (Preston and Post, 1981, p. 57).

It is not our aim to review all theories described, but what has been said regarding the four dimensions in the approaches of Friedman and Preston and Post, could probably be extended to other theories. If our intuition is correct, a proper concept of the business and society relationship should include these four aspects or dimensions, and some mode of integration of them. Although most theories studied do not make it explicit, one can appreciate a tendency to overcome this deficit.

In fact, in the last few years, some theories have been proposed in which two or even more of these dimensions and their interconnection have been considered. That is the case, e.g., of Wood's Corporate Social Performance model (1991b). This model basically focuses on integrating social demands, however, it also considers institutional legitimacy, accepting that "society grants legitimacy and power to business" (Davis, 1973, p. 314). In this manner, Wood introduces both political and integrative dimensions while economic and ethical dimensions are implicit. Regarding the latter, the stated principles of corporate responsibility assumed are based on social control rather than on prescriptive responsibility coming from ethics. This is precisely the criticism Swanson (1995) made of Wood's model. As an alternative, Swanson (1995, 1999) proposed a derived model in which she tried to include the ethical dimension explicitly, through a theory of values. Following Frederick (1992) she accepted that business organizations have responsibilities related to economizing and ecologizing. Furthermore executive decision-making should forgo power-seeking in favour of directing the firm to economize and ecologize.

More recently, Wood and Logsdon (2002), dealing with the corporate or business citizen model, have introduced the ethical dimension in their model. They focus on the political dimension but also incorporate universal rights into their vision of corporate behavior.

Theories on CSR, which take long-term profits as the main goal normally, use an empirical methodology and are descriptive, although explicitly they also present a conditional prescription. Their generic statement might take the form: "if you want to maximize profits you must assume CSR in the way proposed by this theory". In contrast, ethical theories are prescriptive and use a normative methodology. Integrating empirical and normative aspects of CSR, or economic and ethics, is a great challenge. Some authors (Brandy,

Table 3.2: Corporate social responsibilities theories and related approaches

Types of theory	Approaches	Short description	Some key references
Instrumental Theories (focusing on achieving economic objectives through social activities)	Maximization of shareholder value	Long-term value maximization	Friedman (1970), Jensen (2000)
	Strategies for competitive advantages	• Social investments in a competitive context	Porter and Kramer (2002)
		• Strategies based on the natural resource view of the firm and the dynamic capabilities of the firm	Hart (1995), Lizt (1996)
		• Strategies for the bottom of the economic pyramid	Prahalad and Hammond (2002), Hart and Christensen (2002), Prahalad (2003)
	Cause-related marketing	Altruistic activities socially recognized used as an instrument of marketing	Varadarajan and Menon (1988), Murray and Montanari (1986)
Political theories (focusing on a responsible use of business power in the political arena)	Corporate constitutionalism	Social responsibilities of businesses arise from the amount of social power that they have	Davis (1960, 1967)
	Integrative Social Contract Theory	Assumes that a social contract between business and society exists	Donaldson and Dunfee (1994, 1999)
	Corporate (or business) citizenship	The firm is understood as being like a citizen with certain involvement in the community	Wood and Logsdon (2002), Andriof and McIntosh (2001), Matten and Crane (2005)

Integrative theories (focusing on the integration of social demands)	Issues management	Corporate processes of response to those social and political issues which may impact significantly upon it	Sethi (1975), Ackerman (1973), Jones (1980), Vogel (1986), Wartick and Mahon (1994)
	Public responsibility	Law and the existing public policy process are taken as a reference for social performance	Preston and Post (1975, 1981)
	Stakeholder management	Balances the interests of the stakeholders of the firm	Mitchell *et al.* (1997), Agle and Mitchell (1999), Rowley (1997)
	Corporate social performance	Searches for social legitimacy and processes to give appropriate responses to social issues	Carroll (1979), Wartick and Cochran (1985), Wood (1991b), Swanson (1995)
Ethical theories (focusing on the right thing to achieve a good society)	Stakeholder normative theory	Considers fiduciary duties towards stakeholders of the firm. Its application requires reference to some moral theory (Kantian, Utilitarianism, theories of justice, etc.)	Freeman (1984, 1994), Evan and Freeman (1988), Donaldson and Preston (1995), Freeman and Phillips (2002), Phillips *et al.* (2003)
	Universal rights	Frameworks based on human rights, labor rights and respect for the environment	The Global Sullivan Principles (1999), UN Global Compact (1999)
	Sustainable development	Aimed at achieving human development considering present and future generations	World Commission on Environment and Development (Brundtland Report) (1987), Gladwin and Kennelly (1995)
	The common good	Oriented towards the common good of society	Alford and Naughton (2002), Melé (2002), Kaku (1997)

1990; Etzioni, 1988; Quinn and Jones, 1995; and Swanson, 1999; Treviño and Weaver, 1994; among others) have considered this problem, but it is far from being resolved. This lack of integration has been denounced as the cause of the lack of a paradigm for the business and society field (Swanson, 1999).

Finally, the current situation presents many competing ethical theories. This very often produces confusion and scepticism. The problem is especially serious in the case of ethical theories, and even within each group of theories. Considering, for instance, the stakeholder normative theory. As we have explained above, this can be developed using a great number of different ethical theories. Although each of these theories states universal principles, in practice, the global effect is one of unabashed relativism: "If you are Utilitarian, you'll do this, if you are Kantian you'll do that" (Solomon, 1992, p. 318).

Conclusion

We can conclude that most current CSR theories are focused on four main aspects: (1) meeting objectives that produce long-term profits, (2) using business power in a responsible way, (3) integrating social demands and (4) contributing to a good society by doing what is ethically correct. This permits us to classify the most relevant theories on CSR and related concepts into four groups, which we have called instrumental, political, integrative and value theories. Most of the theories considered do not make explicit the implications of each specific approach for the aspects considered in other groups of theories.

Further research could analyze these four dimensions and their connection in the most relevant theories and consider their contributions and limitations. What seems more challenging, however, is to develop a new theory, which would overcome these limitations. This would require an accurate knowledge of reality and a sound ethical foundation.

Notes

1   Parsons considers the existence of four interconnected problems in any action system: (1) the problem mobilizing of resources from the environment and then distributing them throughout the system, which requires adaptation to environment; (2) the problem of establishing priorities among system goals and mobilizing system resources for the attainment of the goals; (3) the problem of coordinating and maintaining viable relationships among system units and (4) the problem of assuring that the actors in the social system display the appropriate values. This entails motivation and other characteristics (pattern maintenance) and dealing with the internal tensions and strain of the actors in the social system (tension management). That means preserving the basic structure of the system and adjusting to changing conditions within the framework that the basic structure provides. According to Parsons these problems necessitate four requisites or imperatives for the maintenance

of a social system: adaptation (A), goal attainment (G), integration (I) and pattern maintenance or latency (L).

2   Some years before, T. Levitt, a Harvard Business School professor, expressed this approach in an even more radical way: "Corporate welfare makes good sense if it makes good economic sense – and not infrequently it does. But if something does not make economic sense, sentiment or idealism ought not to let it in the door" (Levitt, 1958, p. 42).

3   According to Porter and Kramer (2002), a competitive context consists of four interrelated elements of the local business environment that shape potential productivity. The first element is the factor condition, which involves employee education, natural resources, high quality technological institutions and physical infrastructure. The second element is related to demand conditions: that is to say, how the firm can influence the quality and the size of local market by, for example, developing educated and demanding customers. The third, the context for strategy and rivalry involves how the firm can invest in incentives and norms that rule competition as for example all the efforts for reducing corruption, preventing the formation of cartels and opening markets. The last is the firm's investment in related and supporting industries, for example, strengthening the relationship with suppliers of services, components and machinery.

4   According to Davis, "markets leave business theoretically without any social power and hence, no social responsibility (balanced zero equation). This zero equation of no power and no responsibility is a proper theoretical model for pure competition, but it is theory only and it's inconsistent with the power realities of modern organizations. They possess such a great initiative, economic assets, and power in their actions do have social effects" (Davis, 1967, p. 49).

5   In fact, different models have been constructed in order to explain how and why partnerships are built and how to determine, measure, evaluate partnerships (Andriof, 2001; Zadek, 2001).

6   That is not the only problem. According to Gladwin and Kennelly (1995, p. 876), the concept of sustainable development is "fuzzy, elusive, contestable and/or ideologically controversial" and with multiple objectives and ingredients, complex interdependencies and considerable moral thickness. But, in spite of everything, the concept is becoming more and more popular and has introduced an important element to the CSR debate.

References

Ackerman, R. (1973) 'How Companies Respond to Social Demands', *Harvard Business Review* 51(4): 88–98.

Ackerman, R. and Bauer, R. (1976) *Corporate Social Responsiveness*, Reston, Virginia.

Agle, B. and Mitchell, R. (1999) 'Who Matters to CEOs? An Investigation of Stakeholder Attributes and Salience, Corporate Performance and CEO Values', *Academy of Management Journal* 42(5): 507–526.

Alford, H. and Naughton, M. (2002) 'Beyond the Shareholder Model of the Firm: Working toward the Common Good of a Business', in S.A. Cortright and M. Naughton (eds) *Rethinking the Purpose of Business: Interdisciplinary Essays from the Catholic Social Tradition*, Notre Dame University Press, Notre Dame, pp. 27–47.

Altman, B. (1998) 'Corporate Community Relations in the 1990s: A Study in Transformation', *Business and Society* 37(2): 221–228.

Altman, B. and Vidaver-Cohen, D. (2000) 'Corporate Citizenship in the New Millennium: Foundation for an Architecture of Excellence', *Business and Society Review* 105(1): 145–169.

Andriof, J. and McIntosh, M. (eds) (2001) *Perspectives on Corporate Citizenship*, Greenleaf, Sheffield, UK.

Andriof, J. (2001) 'Patterns of Stakeholder Partnership Building', in J. Andriof and M. McIntosh, (eds) *Perspectives on Corporate Citizenship*, Greenleaf, Sheffield, UK, pp. 200–213.

Argandoña, A. (1998) 'The Stakeholder Theory and the Common Good', *Journal of Business Ethics* 17: 1093–1102.

Barney, J. (1991) 'Firm Resource and Sustained Competitive Advantage', *Journal of Management* 17: 99–120.

Bendheim, C., Waddock, S. and Graves, S. (1998) 'Determining Best Practice in Corporate-Stakeholder Relations Using Data Envelopment Analysis', *Business and Society* 37(3): 306–339.

Berman, S., Wicks, A., Kotha, S. and Jones, T. (1999) 'Does Stakeholder Orientation Matter? The Relationship between Stakeholder Management Models and Firm Financial Performance', *Academy of Management Journal* 42(5): 488–509.

Bowen, H. (1953) *Social Responsibilities of the Businessman*, Harper & Row, New York.

Bowie, N. (1991) 'New Directions in Corporate Social Responsibility', *Business Horizons* 34(4): 56–66.

Bowie, N. (1998) 'A Kantian Theory of Capitalism', *Business Ethics Quarterly*, Ruffin Series, Special Issue, No. 1: 37–60.

Brandy, F. (1990) *Ethical Managing: Rules and Results*, Macmillan, London.

Brewer, T. (1992) 'An Issue Area Approach to the Analysis of MNE–Government Relations', *Journal of International Business Studies* 23: 295–309.

Brummer, J. (1991) *Corporate Responsibility and Legitimacy*, Greenwood Press, New York.

Burke, L. and Logsdon, J. (1996) 'How Corporate Social Responsibility Pays Off', *Long Range Planning* 29(4): 495–503.

Burton, B. and Dunn, C. (1996) 'Feminist Ethics as Moral Grounding for Stakeholder Theory', *Business Ethics Quarterly* 6(2): 133–147.

Carey, J. (2001) 'The Common Good in Catholic Social Thought', *St. John's Law Review* 75(2): 311–313.

Carroll, A. (1979) 'A Three-Dimensional Conceptual Model of Corporate Performance', *Academy of Management Review* 4(4): 497–505.

Carroll, A. (1991) 'The Pyramid of Corporate Social Responsibility: Towards the Moral Management of Organizational Stakeholders', *Business Horizons* (July/August): 39–48.

Carroll, A. (1994) 'Social Issues in Management Research', *Business and Society* 33(1): 5–25.

Carroll, A. (1999) 'Corporate Social Responsibility: Evolution of Definitional Construct', *Business and Society* 38(3): 268–295.

Carroll, A. and Buchholtz, A. (2002) *Business and Society: Ethics and Stakeholder Management*, 5th edn, South-Western, Cincinnati.

Cassel, D. (2001) 'Human Rights and Business Responsibilities in the Global Marketplace', *Business Ethics Quarterly* 11(2): 261–274.

Christensen, C., Craig, T. and Hart, S. (2001) 'The Great Disruption', *Foreign Affairs* 80(2): 80–96.

Christensen, C. and Overdorf, M. (2000) 'Meeting the Challenge of Disruptive Change', *Harvard Business Review* 78(2): 66–75.

Davis, K. (1960) 'Can Business Afford to Ignore Corporate Social Responsibilities?', *California Management Review* 2: 70–76.

Davis, K. (1967) 'Understanding the Social Responsibility Puzzle', *Business Horizons* 10(4): 45–51.

Davis, K. (1973) 'The Case For and Against Business Assumption of Social Responsibilities', *Academy of Management Journal* 16: 312–322.

Dion, M. (2001) 'Corporate Citizenship and Ethics of Care: Corporate Values, Codes of Ethics and Global Governance', in J. Andriof and M. McIntosh (eds) *Perspectives on Corporate Citizenship* (Greenleaf, Sheffield, UK), pp. 118–138.

Donaldson, T. (1982) *Corporations and Morality*, Prentice Hall, Englewood Cliffs, NJ.

Donaldson, T. and Dunfee, T. (1994) 'Towards a Unified Conception of Business Ethics: Integrative Social Contracts Theory', *Academy of Management Review* 19: 252–284.

Donaldson, T. and Dunfee, T. (1999) *Ties That Bind: A Social Contracts Approach to Business Ethics*, Harvard Business School, Boston.

Donaldson, T. and Dunfee, T. (2000) 'Précis for Ties that Bind', *Business and Society* 105(Winter): 436–444.

Donaldson, T. and Preston, L. (1995) 'The Stakeholder Theory of the Corporation: Concepts, Evidence, and Implications', *Academy of Management Review* 20(1): 65–91.

Donati, P. (1991) *Teoria relazionale della società*, Franco Agnelli, Milano.

Donnelly, J. (1985) *The Concept of Human Rights*, Croom Helm, London.

Emshoff, J. and Freeman, R. (1978) 'Stakeholder Management', Working Paper from the Wharton Applied Research Center (July). Quoted by Sturdivant (1979).

Etzioni, A. (1988) *The Moral Dimension: Towards a New Economics*, The Free Press, New York.

Evan, W and Freeman, R. (1988) 'A Stakeholder Theory of the Modern Corporation: Kantian Capitalism', in T. Beauchamp and N. Bowie (eds) *Ethical Theory and Business*, Prentice Hall, Englewood Cliffs, pp. 75–93.

Fort, T. (1996) 'Business as Mediating Institutions', *Business Ethics Quarterly* 6(2): 149–164.

Fort, T. (1999) 'The First Man and the Company Man: The Common Good, Transcendence, and Mediating Institutions', *American Business Law Journal* 36(3): 391–435.

Frederick, W. (1987) 'Theories of Corporate Social Performance', in S. Sethi and C. Flabe (eds) *Business and Society: Dimensions of Conflict and Cooperation*, Lexington Books, New York, pp. 142–161.

Frederick, W. (1992) 'Anchoring Values in Nature: Towards a Theory of Business Values', *Business Ethics Quarterly* 2(3): 283–304.

Frederick, W. (1998) 'Moving to CSR 4', *Business and Society* 37(1): 40–60.

Freeman, R. (1984) *Strategic Management: A Stakeholder Approach*, Pitman, Boston.

Freeman, R. (1994) 'The Politics of Stakeholder Theory: Some Future Directions', *Business Ethics Quarterly* 4(4): 409–429.

Freeman, R. and Evan, W. (1990) 'Corporate Governance: A Stakeholder Interpretation', *Journal of Behavioral Economics* 19(4): 337–359.

Freeman, R. and Phillips, R. (2002) 'Stakeholder Theory: A Libertarian Defence', *Business Ethics Quarterly* 12(3): 331–349.

Friedman, M. (1970) 'The Social Responsibility of Business Is to Increase Its Profits', *New York Times Magazine*, September 13th: 32–33, 122, 126.

Friedman, M. and Friedman, R. (1962) *Capitalism and Freedom,* University of Chicago Press, Chicago.

Frooman, J. (1997) 'Socially Irresponsible and Illegal Behavior and Shareholder Wealth', *Business and Society* 36(3): 221–250.

Gladwin, T. and Kennelly, J. (1995) 'Shifting Paradigms for Sustainable Development: Implications for Management Theory and Research', *Academy of Management Review* 20(4): 874–904.

Global Sullivan Principles, The (1999) http://globalsullivanprinciples.org (September 2003).

Goodpaster, K. (1999) 'Bridging East and West in Management Ethics: Kyosei and the Moral Point of View', in G. Enderle (ed.) *International Business Ethics: Challenges and Approaches*, University of Notre Dame Press, Notre Dame, pp. 151–159.

Greening, D. and Gray, B. (1994) 'Testing a Model of Organizational Response to Social and Political Issues', *Academy of Management Journal* 37: 467–498.

Griffin, J. (2000) 'Corporate Social Performance: Research Directions for the 21st Century', *Business and Society* 39(4): 479–493.

Griffin, J. and Mahon, J. (1997) 'The Corporate Social Performance and Corporate Financial Performance Debate: Twenty-five Years of Incomparable Research', *Business and Society* 36(1): 5–31.

Harrison, J. and St. John, C. (1996) 'Managing and Partnering with External Stakeholders', *Academy of Management Executive* 10(2): 46–61.

Hart, S. (1995) 'A Natural-Resource-Based View of the Firm', *Academy of Management Review* 20(4): 986–1012.

Hart, S. and Christensen, C. (2002) 'The Great Leap: Driving Innovation from the Base of the Pyramid', *MIT Sloan Management Review* 44(1): 51–57.

Heald, M. (1988) *The Social Responsibilities of Business: Company and Community, 1900–1960,* Transaction Books, New Brunswick.

Hillman, A. and Keim, G. (2001) 'Shareholder Value, Stakeholder Management, and Social Issues: What's the Bottom Line', *Strategic Management Journal* 22(2): 125–140.

Husted, B. and Allen, D. (2000) 'Is It Ethical to Use Ethics as Strategy?', *Journal of Business Ethics* 27(1–2): 21–32.

Jensen, M. (2000) 'Value Maximization, Stakeholder Theory, and the Corporate Objective Function', in M. Beer and N. Nohria (eds) *Breaking the Code of Change*, Harvard Business School Press, Boston, pp. 37–58. Reprinted (2002) as 'Value Maximization, Stakeholder Theory, and the Corporate Objective Function', *Business Ethics Quarterly* 12(2): 235–256.

Jensen, M. and Meckling, W. (1976) 'Theory of the Firm: Managerial Behavior, Agency Cost and Capital Structure', *Journal of Financial Economics* 3 (October): 305–360.

Jones, T. (1980) 'Corporate Social Responsibility Revisited, Redefined', *California Management Review* 22(2): 59–67.

Jones, T. (1983) 'An Integrating Framework for Research in Business and Society: A Step Toward the Elusive Paradigm?' *Academy of Management Review* 8(4): 559–565.

Kaku, R. (1997) 'The Path of Kyosei', *Harvard Business Review* 75(4): 55–62.

Kaptein, M. and Van Tulder, R. (2003) 'Toward Effective Stakeholder Dialogue', *Business and Society Review* 108(Summer): 203–225.

Keim, G. (1978) 'Corporate Social Responsibility: An Assessment of the Enlightened Self-Interest Model', *Academy of Management Review* 3(1): 32–40.

Kempshall, M. (1999) *The Common Good in Late Medieval Political Thought*, Oxford University Press, Oxford.

Key, S. and Popkin, S. (1998) 'Integrating Ethics into the Strategic Management Process: Doing Well by Doing Good', *Management Decision* 36(5–6): 331–339.

Levitt, T. (1958) 'The Dangers of Social Responsibility', *Harvard Business Review* 36 (September–October): 41–50.

Litz, R. (1996) 'A Resource-Based View of the Socially Responsible Firm: Stakeholder Interdependence, Ethical Awareness, and Issue Responsiveness as Strategic Assets', *Journal of Business Ethics* 15: 1355–1363.

McMahon, T. (1986) 'Models of the Relationship of the Firm to Society', *Journal of Business Ethics* 5: 181–191.

McWilliams, A. and Siegel, D. (2001) 'Corporate Social Responsibility: A Theory of the Firm Perspective', *Academy of Management Review* 26(1): 117–127.

Mahon, J. and McGowan, R. (1991) 'Searching for the Common Good: A Process-Oriented Approach', *Business Horizons* 34(4): 79–87.

Maritain, J. (1966) *The Person and the Common Good*, Notre Dame University Press, Notre Dame.

Maritain, J. (1971 [c1943]) *The Rights of Man and Natural Law*, Gordian Press, New York.

Matten, D. and Crane, A. (2005) 'Corporate Citizenship: Toward an Extended Theoretical Conceptualization', *Academy of Management Review* 30(1): 166–179.

Matten, D., Crane, A. and Chapple, W. (2003) 'Behind the Mask: Revealing the True Face of Corporate Citizenship', *Journal of Business Ethics* 45(1–2): 109–120.

Melé, D. (2002) *Not Only Stakeholder Interests: The Firm Oriented toward the Common Good*, University of Notre Dame Press, Notre Dame.

Mitchell, R., Agle, B. and Wood, D. (1997) 'Toward a Theory of Stakeholder Identification and Salience: Defining the Principle of Who and What Really Counts', *Academy of Management Review* 22(4): 853–886.

Murray, K. and Montanari, J. (1986) 'Strategic Management of the Socially Responsible Firm: Integrating Management and Marketing Theory', *Academy of Management Review* 11(4): 815–828.

Ogden, S. and Watson, R. (1999) 'Corporate Performance and Stakeholder Management: Balancing Shareholder and Customer Interests in the U.K. Privatized Water Industry', *Academy of Management Journal* 42(5): 526–538.

Parsons, T. (1961) 'An Outline of the Social System', in T. Parsons, E. Shils, K. Naegle and J. Pitts (eds) *Theories of Society*, Free Press, New York.

Petrick, J. and Quinn, J. (2001) 'The Challenge of Leadership Accountability for Integrity Capacity as a Strategic Asset', *Journal of Business Ethics* 34: 331–343.

Phillips, R. (1997) 'Stakeholder Theory and a Principle of Fairness', *Business Ethics Quarterly* 7(1): 51–66.

Phillips, R. (2003) 'Stakeholder Legitimacy', *Business Ethics Quarterly* 13(1): 25–41.

Phillips, R., Freeman, E. and Wicks, A. (2003) 'What Stakeholder Theory Is Not', *Business Ethics Quarterly* 13(1): 479–502.

Pope John Paul II (1991) Encyclical *'Centesimus Annus'* (Catholic Truth Society, London) and www.vatican.va.

Porter, M. (1980) *Competitive Strategy: Techniques for Analyzing Industries and Competitors*, Free Press, New York.

Porter, M. and Kramer, M. (2002) 'The Competitive Advantage of Corporate Philanthropy', *Harvard Business Review* 80(12): 56–69.

Porter, M. and Van der Linde, C. (1995) 'Green and Competitive: Ending the Stalemate', *Harvard Business Review* 73(5): 120–133.

Post, J., Preston, L., Sauter-Sachs, S. and Sachs, S. (2002) *Redefining the Corporation: Stakeholder Management and Organizational Wealth*, Stanford University Press, Stanford.

Prahalad, C. (2002) 'Strategies for the Bottom of the Economic Pyramid: India as a Source of Innovation', *Reflections: The SOL Journal* 3(4): 6–18.

Prahalad, C. and Hammond, A. (2002) 'Serving the World's Poor, Profitably', *Harvard Business Review* 80(9): 48–58.

Preston, L. (1975) 'Corporation and Society: The Search for a Paradigm', *Journal of Economic Literature* 13(2): 434–454.

Preston, L. and Post, J. (1975) 'Private Management and Public Policy', *The Principle of Public Responsibility*, Prentice Hall, Englewood Cliffs, NJ.

Preston, L. and Post, J. (1981) 'Private Management and Public Policy', *California Management Review* 23(3): 56–63.

Quinn, D. and Jones, T. (1995) 'An Agent Morality View of Business Policy', *Academy of Management Review* 20(1): 22–42.

Roman, R., Hayibor, S. and Agle, B. (1999) 'The Relationship between Social Performance and Financial Performance', *Business and Society* 38(1): 109–125.

Ross, S. (1973) 'The Economy Theory of the Agency: The Principal's Problem', *American Economic Review* 63: 134–139.

Rowley, T. (1997) 'Moving Beyond Dyadic Ties: A Network Theory of Stakeholder Influences', *Academy of Management Review* 22(4): 887–911.

Rowley, T. and Berman, S. (2000) 'New Brand of Corporate Social Performance', *Business and Society* 39(4): 397–412.

Schwartz, M. and Carroll, A. (2003) 'Corporate Social Responsibility: A Three-Domain Approach', *Business Ethics Quarterly* 13(4): 503–530.

Sethi, S. (1975) 'Dimensions of Corporate Social Performance: An Analytical Framework', *California Management Review* 17(3): 58–65.

Shrivastava, P. (1995) 'The Role of Corporations in Achieving Ecological Sustainability', *Academy of Management Review* 20: 936–960.

Simon, Y. (1992) (1965), in V. Kuic (ed.), *The Tradition of Natural Law: A Philosopher's Reflections*, Fordham University Press, New York.

Smith, T. (1999) 'Aristotle on the Conditions for and Limits of the Common Good', *American Political Science Review* 93(3): 625–637.

Smith, W. and Higgins, M. (2000) 'Cause-Related Marketing: Ethics and the Ecstatic', *Business and Society* 39(3): 304–322.

Solomon, R. (1992) 'Corporate Roles, Personal Virtues: An Aristotelian Approach to Business Ethics', *Business Ethics Quarterly* 2(3): 317–340.

Stead, J. and Stead, E. (2000) 'Eco-enterprise Strategy: Standing for Sustainability', *Journal of Business Ethics* 24(4): 313–330.

Sturdivant, F. (1979) 'Executives and Activists: Test of Stakeholder Management', *California Management Review* 22(Fall): 53–59.

Sulmasy, D. (2001) 'Four Basic Notions of the Common Good', *St. John's Law Review* 75(2): 303–311.

Swanson, D. (1995) 'Addressing a Theoretical Problem by Reorienting the Corporate Social Performance Model', *Academy of Management Review* 20(1): 43–64.

Swanson, D. (1999) 'Toward an Integrative Theory of Business and Society: A Research Strategy for Corporate Social Performance', *Academy of Management Review* 24(3): 506–521.

Teece, D., Pisano, G. and Shuen, A. (1997) 'Dynamic Capabilities and Strategic Management', *Strategic Management Journal* 18(7): 509–533.

The Clarkson Center for Business Ethics (1999) *Principles of Stakeholder Management* (Joseph L. Rotman School of Management, Toronto, Canada). Reprinted (2002) in *Business Ethics Quarterly* 12(4): 257–264.

Tichy, N., McGill, A. and St. Clair, L. (1997) *Corporate Global Citizenship*, The New Lexington Press, San Francisco.

Treviño, L. and Weaver, G. (1994) 'Normative and Empirical Business Ethics', *Business Ethics Quarterly* 4(2): 129–143.

United Nations (1999) Global Compact (www.unglobalcompact.org).

Van Marrewijk, M. (2003) 'Concept and Definitions of CSR and Corporate Sustainability: Between Agency and Communion', *Journal of Business Ethics* 44: 95–105.

Van Marrewijk, M. and Werre, M. (2003) 'Multiple Levels of Corporate Sustainability', *Journal of Business Ethics* 44(2/3): 107–120.

Varadarajan, P. and Menon, A. (1988) 'Cause-Related Marketing: A Coalignment of Marketing Strategy and Corporate Philanthropy', *Journal of Marketing* 52(3): 58–74.

Velasquez, M. (1992) 'International Business, Morality and the Common Good', *Business Ethics Quarterly* 2(1): 27–40.

Vogel, D. (1986) 'The Study of Social Issues in Management: A Critical Appraisal', *California Management Review* 28(2): 142–152.

Votaw, D. (1972) 'Genius Became Rare: A Comment on the Doctrine of Social Responsibility Pt 1', *California Management Review* 15(2): 25–31.

Waddock, S. and Graves, S. (1997) 'The Corporate Social Performance–Financial Performance Link', *Strategic Management Journal* 18(4): 303–320.

Wartick, S. and Cochran, P. (1985) 'The Evolution of Corporate Social Performance Model', *Academy of Management Review* 10(4): 758–769.

Wartick, S. and Rude, R. (1986) 'Issues Management: Corporate Fad or Corporate Function?', *California Management Review* 29(1): 124–132.

Wartick, S. and Mahon, J. (1994) 'Towards a Substantive Definition of the Corporate Issue Construct: A Review and Synthesis of Literature', *Business and Society* 33(3): 293–311.

Weiss, J. (2003) *Business Ethics: A Stakeholder and Issues Management Approach*, 3rd edn, Thomson – South-Western. Ohio.

Wernerfelt, B. (1984) 'A Resource Based View of the Firm', *Strategic Management Review* 5: 171–180.

Wheeler, D., Colbert, B. and Freeman, R. (2003) 'Focusing on Value: Reconciling Corporate Social Responsibility, Sustainability and a Stakeholder Approach in a Network World', *Journal of General Management* 28(3): 1–29.

Wicks, A., Gilbert, Jr, D. and Freeman, R. (1994) 'A Feminist Reinterpretation of the Stakeholder Concept', *Business Ethics Quarterly* 4(4): 475–497.

Wijnberg, N. (2000) 'Normative Stakeholder Theory and Aristotle: The Link between Ethics and Politics', *Journal of Business Ethics* 25: 329–342.

Windsor, D. (2001) 'The Future of Corporate Social Responsibility', *International Journal of Organizational Analysis* 9(3): 225–256.

Wood, D. (1991a) 'Social Issues in Management: Theory and Research in Corporate Social Performance', *Journal of Management* 17(2): 383–406.

Wood, D. (1991b) 'Corporate Social Performance Revisited', *Academy of Management Review* 16(4): 691–718.

Wood, D. and Logsdon, J. (2002) 'Business Citizenship: From Individuals to Organizations', *Business Ethics Quarterly*, Ruffin Series, No. 3: 59–94.

World Business Council for Sustainable Development (2000) *Corporate Social Responsibility: Making Good Business Sense*, World Business Council for Sustainable Development, Geneva.

World Commission on Environment and Development (1987) *Our Common Future*, Oxford University Press, Oxford.

Yamaji, K. (1997) 'A Global Perspective of Ethics in Business', *Business Ethics Quarterly* 7(3): 55–71.

Zadek, S. (2001) 'Partnership Alchemy: Engagement, Innovation, and Governance', in J. Andriof and M. McIntosh (eds) *Perspectives on Corporate Citizenship*, Greenleaf, Sheffield, UK, pp. 200–212.

CORPORATE SOCIAL RESPONSIBILITY: A THREE-DOMAIN APPROACH

Mark S. Schwartz and Archie B. Carroll

For the past several decades, the debate over the proper relationship between business and society has focused on the topic of corporate social responsibility (CSR) (Klonoski 1991). In the modern era, the stage was set for this debate by Keith Davis, who posed two intriguing questions in the 1960s: "What does the businessperson owe society?" (Davis 1967) and "Can business afford to ignore its social responsibilities?" (Davis 1960). Although many have attempted to define CSR over the years, the concept has remained vague and ambiguous to some (Makower 1994: 12). Definitions of CSR fall into two general schools of thought, those that argue that business is obligated only to maximize profits within the boundaries of the law and minimal ethical constraints (Friedman 1970; Levitt 1958), and those that have suggested a broader range of obligations toward society (Andrews 1973; Carroll 1979; Davis and Blomstrom 1975; Epstein 1987; McGuire 1963).

An important attempt to bridge the gap between economics and other expectations was offered by Archie Carroll (1979). His efforts culminated in the following proposed definition of corporate social responsibility:

> The social responsibility of business encompasses the *economic, legal, ethical,* and *discretionary* expectations that society has of organizations at a given point in time. (1979: 500, emphasis added)

As a helpful way of graphically depicting the components of his CSR definition and expounding upon them, he later incorporated his four-part categorization into a "Pyramid of Corporate Social Responsibility" (1991, 1993). Carroll's Pyramid of CSR is presented in Figure 3.1.

Carroll's four categories or domains of CSR have been utilized by numerous theorists (Wartick and Cochran 1985; Wood 1991; Swanson 1995, 1999) and empirical researchers (Aupperle 1984; Aupperle, Carroll, and Hatfield 1985; Burton and Hegarty 1999; Clarkson 1995; Ibrahim and Angelidis 1993, 1994, 1995; Mallott 1993; O'Neill, Saunders, and McCarthy 1989; Pinkston and Carroll 1996; Smith, Wokutch, Harrington, and Dennis 2001; Spencer and Butler 1987; Strong and Meyer 1992). Several business and society and business ethics texts have incorporated Carroll's CSR domains (Boatright 1993; Buchholz 1995; Weiss 1994) or have depicted the CSR Pyramid (Carroll and Buchholtz 2000, 2003; Jackson, Miller, and Miller 1997; Sexty 1995; Trevino and Nelson 1995). According to Wood and Jones (1996: 45), Carroll's four domains have "enjoyed wide popularity among SIM (Social Issues in Management) scholars." Such use suggests that Carroll's CSR domains and pyramid framework remain a leading paradigm of CSR in the social issues in management field. Due to the acceptance and impact of Carroll's CSR contributions, it may be appropriate to re-examine his model to determine whether it can be modified or improved or if there is a possible alternative approach to conceptualizing corporate social responsibility.

In a quest to propose an alternative approach to CSR that strives to augment and amend the Carroll model, the following paper will consist of four parts: (1) a brief discussion of some issues or limitations of Carroll's model; (2) a presentation of the new alternative model, the "Three-Domain

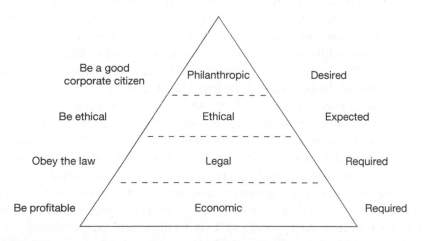

Figure 3.1: Carroll's (1991) Pyramid of Corporate Social Responsibility

Source: A. B. Carroll, "The Pyramid of Corporate Social Responsibility: Toward the Moral Management of Organizational Stakeholders," *Business Horizons* (July–August 1991): 39–48.

Model of CSR"; (3) a discussion of the limitations of the new model; and (4) future teaching and research implications of the new model.

Issues with Carroll's Model

Three issues with respect to the Carroll model are identified and discussed as they are items upon which the proposed three-domain model proposes changes. The three issues include: (1) the use of a pyramid to depict the relationships among the four components of the model; (2) the role of philanthropy as a separate component in the model; and (3) the incomplete theoretical development of the economic, legal, and ethical domains.

Use of a Pyramid Framework

Although there is considerable value in Carroll's four-part model, his use of a pyramid framework to depict his CSR domains may be confusing or inappropriate for some applications. First, to some, the pyramid framework suggests a hierarchy of CSR domains. One may be led to conclude that the domain at the top of the pyramid, philanthropic responsibilities, is the most important or highly valued domain, that should be strived for by all corporations, while the economic domain at the base of the pyramid is the least valued CSR domain. For example, Reidenbach and Robin (1991: 274) use a pyramid to depict their conceptual model of corporate moral development, and suggest that the top of the pyramid represents the highest or most advanced stage of moral development (i.e., the "ethical" corporation), while the base of the pyramid portrays the lowest or least advanced stage (i.e., the "amoral" corporation). This is clearly not the perspective of the pyramid's rankings of CSR priorities that Carroll intended, since he stipulates that the economic and legal domains are the most fundamental while philanthropic responsibilities are considered less important than the other three domains (1991: 42). However, the pyramid framework could lead one to misunderstand the priorities of the four CSR domains.

Second, a pyramid framework cannot fully capture the *overlapping* nature of the CSR domains, a disadvantage recognized by Carroll (1993: 34). Such mutuality is an integral characteristic of CSR (Clarkson 1991: 349) and of such fundamental importance that it must be included and clearly depicted in any proposed CSR model. Carroll's use of dotted lines separating the domains does not fully capture the non-mutually exclusive nature of the domains, nor does it denote two of the critical tension points among them, the tension between the economic and ethical and the economic and philanthropic domains (Carroll 1993: 34).

Use of a Separate Philanthropic Category

In addition to the possible misunderstandings inherent in using a pyramid, Carroll's use of a "philanthropic/discretionary" category can be confusing and may be seen as unnecessary to some. Carroll acknowledges that it may in fact be "inaccurate" (1979: 500) or a "misnomer" (1993: 33) to call such activities "responsibilities" due to their voluntary or discretionary nature. Others agree that philanthropy cannot be considered a responsibility in itself (L'Etang 1994; Stone 1975). In this respect, philanthropy is not considered a duty or social responsibility of business (i.e., an expected act based on what Kantians might refer to as a "perfect" duty), but something that is merely desirable or beyond what duty requires (e.g., a supererogatory act based on what Kantians might refer to as an "imperfect" duty).

The new model proposes that such a category, if it were believed to exist, would better be subsumed under ethical and/or economic responsibilities. The central reasons for this placement are that, first, it is sometimes difficult to distinguish between "philanthropic" and "ethical" activities on both a theoretical and practical level, and second, philanthropic activities might simply be based on economic interests.

At the theoretical level, the ethical principle of utilitarianism can be used to justify many philanthropic activities, including all of the examples Carroll (1993: 33) refers to (e.g., giving to charity, adopting a school, providing a day-care center for working mothers, conducting in-house programs for drug abusers). For example, Shaw and Post (1993: 746) argue that rule utilitarianism supports corporate philanthropy as a means of complying with a "rule" which maximizes the public welfare.

In this vein, it could be argued that philanthropic activities are simply an example of an ethically motivated activity. One formulation of Kant's categorical imperative is that one should treat people as an end in themselves and not merely as a means to an end. If a company provides a day-care center for working mothers or conducts in-house programs for drug abusers, is it not possible that they are treating their employees as ends in themselves and not merely as a means?

When Carroll says that the essence of these philanthropic activities is that they are "not generally *expected* of business in an ethical sense" (1993: 33, emphasis added), this raises the question of exactly when an activity can be considered ethical as opposed to philanthropic according to Carroll's treatment of these two domains. For example, is a corporation's contribution to a charitable organization an ethical activity (i.e., expected by society) or a philanthropic activity (i.e., merely desired by society)? Evidence currently indicates that the majority of companies donate to charitable organizations (Carroll 1993: 387), with a majority of the population expecting that companies make charitable donations (Sexty 1995: 274). Do these findings not suggest that society now *expects* corporate philanthropic contributions? According to Carroll's definitions, the paramount example of a philanthropic activity, giving to charitable organizations, could arguably fall under the ethical domain, rather than needing to be separated into a philanthropic domain as currently defined.

Even if one is able to make a theoretical distinction between ethical and philanthropic activities, there is still an issue as to whether such a distinction could be applied by empirical researchers in the field. Clarkson (1995: 95), for example, raises concerns over the ability to define and measure discretionary activities in the actual corporate world. Aupperle, Carroll, and Hatfield (1985: 455) state that Carroll's philanthropic domain is "difficult to ascertain and evaluate." Strong and Meyer conclude in their study that while there was strong support for the existence of the economic, legal, and ethical components of corporate social responsibility, it may be appropriate for the philanthropic category to be removed from Carroll's framework when attempting to measure managerial perceptions of responsibility. They state: "The results for discretionary (philanthropic) responsibility do not support the survey's use as a general measure of managerial perception of responsibility *of this component* of social responsibility" (1992: 92, emphasis added). Although many researchers have found support for a philanthropic component, the concerns raised by other researchers suggest that its use as a distinct component of CSR might be re-examined.

In addition to ethical reasons, corporate philanthropy might also be based primarily on economic motives (Shaw and Post 1993: 748), often referred to as "strategic giving" or "strategic philanthropy" (Yankee 1996: 9–10). Whether to increase sales, help improve public image, or to improve employee morale, corporate community involvement or corporate giving to charitable organizations can help sustain the bottom line for business in the long-term. When corporations engage in philanthropy for these reasons, they are simply acting out of economic motives, based on their economic responsibility, as opposed to a distinct philanthropic obligation.

Incomplete Development of Economic, Legal, and Ethical Domains

Another issue with Carroll's model is the incomplete discussion and inclusion of criteria for assessing corporate activities or motives as falling into each of the domains, especially the legal and ethical domains. Carroll provides little discussion of how corporations may engage in multiple domains other than by suggesting that a toy manufacturer making safe toys would be complying simultaneously with its economic, legal, and ethical responsibilities (1979: 501). Such a cursory discussion limits the theoretical foundation that is necessary to utilize the model for certain kinds of empirical study and for teaching purposes. The economic, legal, and ethical domains will now be expounded upon.

Economic domain

Carroll defines the economic domain of CSR as follows (1991: 40–42): "Perform in a manner consistent with maximizing earnings per share, being as profitable as possible, maintaining a strong competitive position and high level of operating efficiency." It may be that this definition fails to capture certain economic activities. The new model will clarify the economic domain below.

Legal domain

Carroll's category of legal responsibility is defined as obeying or complying with the law (1979: 500; 1993: 33). The legal responsibility is depicted as reflecting a view of "codified ethics" in the sense that law embodies basic notions of fairness as established by our lawmakers. It is stressed that it is business's responsibility to comply with these laws. A broader appreciation of the legal system and its influence on corporate activities indicates a much wider range of legally-based activities that ought to be discussed. For example, legality may be broken down into three general categories: (i) compliance; (ii) avoidance of civil litigation; and (iii) anticipation of the law. Each of these will be more fully discussed in the presentation of the new model.

Ethical domain

The ethical domain of CSR includes those activities that are based on their adherence to a set of ethical or moral standards or principles. Carroll's definition of the ethical domain is not broadly developed (1991: 41). He defines the ethical domain of CSR as any activities or practices that are expected or prohibited by society members although not codified into law. They are responsibilities which "embody those standards, norms or expectations that reflect a concern for what consumers, employees, shareholders, and the community regard as fair, just, or in keeping with the respect or protection of stakeholders' moral rights." Superimposed on such ethical expectations are the implied levels of ethical performance suggested by consideration "of the great ethical principles of . . . justice, rights, and utilitarianism" (1991: 40–42). Though Carroll names the various ethical postures, they are not completely discussed. In short, though Carroll appropriately identifies the legal and ethical categories of CSR, he does not flesh them out as broadly or as completely as they need to be articulated.

The Three-Domain Model of CSR

The three-domain model of CSR is composed of the three responsibility areas: economic, legal, and ethical. In general, these domain categories are defined in a manner consistent with Carroll's four-part model, with the exception that the philanthropic category is subsumed under the ethical and/or economic domains, reflecting the possible differing motivations for philanthropic activities. Further, in our discussion, the domains are developed more completely both in terms of what each means or implies and in terms of the overlapping categories that are identified when the three domains are depicted in a Venn diagram format. By using a Venn diagram, the model initially suggests that none of the three CSR domains (i.e., economic, legal, or ethical) is prima facie more important or significant relative to the others. Following a discussion of the model's components, a brief treatment of its limitations will be presented. Figure 3.2 presents the three-domain model of CSR.

Economic Domain

For the purposes of the three-domain model, the economic domain captures those activities which are intended to have either a direct or indirect positive economic impact on the corporation in question. In this sense, it is similar to the Carroll formulation of this component. The positive impact is based on two distinct but related criteria (Poitras 1994): (i) the maximization of profits and/or (ii) the maximization of share value. Examples of direct economic activities include actions intended to increase sales or avoid litigation. Examples of possible indirect economic activities include activities that are designed to improve employee morale or the company's public image. Any activity that is pursued with improving profits and/or share value in mind is deemed to be economically motivated.

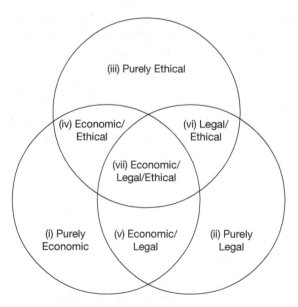

Figure 3.2: The Three-Domain Model of Corporate Social Responsibility

It is to be expected that the vast majority of corporate activities will be economic in nature. However, there may be some activities that would not be included. A corporation's actions would fall outside of the economic domain if (i) they are not intended to maximize profit (or minimize loss) when a more profitable alternative exists, or (ii) they are engaged in without any real consideration of the possible economic consequences to the firm. In terms of the outcome or results, if the activity produces a decline in profits or share value, this may be an indication of a non-economic motive, but may also merely represent a flawed business decision (and the action would still be considered to fall within the economic domain).

Legal Domain

The legal category of CSR pertains to the business firm's responsiveness to legal expectations mandated and expected by society in the form of federal, state, and local jurisdictions, or through legal principles as developed in case law. In this context, legality may be viewed in terms of three general categories: (1) compliance, (2) avoidance of civil litigation, and (3) anticipation of the law. The first legal category, compliance, can be further sub-divided into three types: *passive*, *restrictive*, and *opportunistic*. The first type of compliance is of a *passive* or accidental nature—the company is doing what it wants and just happens to be complying with the law. For example, if the speed limit is fifty-five miles per hour and one drives at or below fifty-five miles per hour because one believes it is safer to do so and not because of the speed limit, one is *passively* complying with the law. If there is a safety standard for a certain product that a company would have adhered to even if the legal requirement did not exist, the company is in a passive compliance mode. If the *motivations* of the corporation are being analyzed by the newly proposed model, passive compliance by the corporation, due to its unintentional nature, would place it outside of the legal domain. This would be the case despite such motives being potentially labeled as legal under Carroll's Pyramid Model. If *outcomes* were being analyzed, the corporation would fall within the legal domain even if it passively or accidentally complied with the law.

The second type of compliance, referred to as *restrictive* compliance, occurs when a corporation is legally compelled to do something that it would not otherwise want to do. If one is in a hurry and would like to drive sixty-five miles per hour but one does not do so because of the fifty-five miles per hour speed limit, one is *restrictively* or intentionally complying with the law. The payment of taxes, tariffs, or duties is often done reluctantly and, therefore, restrictively. Although a company may want to pollute at higher levels or sell goods with fewer safety warnings, the law may prohibit it from doing so, leading to restrictive compliance. The adjective *restrictive* is used to reflect the idea that the legal system is limiting, constraining, or modifying otherwise intended behavior in a restrictive fashion.

The third type of compliance is that of *opportunistic* compliance. There are two general modes of opportunistic compliance. First, a corporation may actively seek out and take advantage of loopholes in the legislation to be able to engage in certain activities. In such cases one typically finds that the corporation is abiding by the letter of the law but not the spirit of the law. Second, a corporation may choose to operate in a particular jurisdiction because of its weaker legal standards. In such a case, the corporation has based its decision on the legal system, and is still technically complying with the law. Corporations which decide to operate in developing nations because of less stringent environmental, employee-welfare, or consumer-protection legislation are opportunistically complying with the law. The decision to test drive one's new sports car on a highway because of its higher speed limit entails opportunistically complying with the law. The decision has been based in this case on a consideration of the legal system.

Carroll's treatment of the legal domain appears to embrace these types of legal motives although he does not distinguish between or elaborate upon them. There are, however, other legal dimensions as well. The second general legal category, *avoidance*, relates to corporate activities that are motivated by the desire to avoid possible current or future civil litigation for negligent conduct. In response to such fears, corporations may, for example, disengage in the manufacture of dangerous products, voluntarily recall products, or cease non-environmentally friendly activities. Companies that act in ways despite being aware that they will most likely be sued as a result (e.g., for negligent activity) would fall outside of the legal domain, despite being in compliance with laws and regulations. Often these companies engage in a legal defensive strategy whereby they attempt to settle all lawsuits.

The third legal category consists of the *anticipation* of changes to legislation. The legal process is often slow in nature, and corporations may wish to engage in activities that will result in immediate compliance upon the legislation's eventual enactment. Changes to legislation in other jurisdictions often serve as an indication of forthcoming similar legislation in one's own jurisdiction. If laws are anticipated, companies may engage in voluntary activities to help prevent, modify, or slow down the pace of new legislation being enacted, and are thus acting based on a consideration of the legal system.

Activities would fall outside of the legal domain when they take place despite (i) an awareness of non-compliance with the law, (ii) an awareness of actual or potential civil negligence, or (iii) merely passive compliance with the law. Table 3.3 indicates examples of the various types of legal motives and the typical responses one might hear from a corporation.

Table 3.3: Examples of legal motives and possible responses

Type of Legal Motive	Typical Corporate/Managerial Response
Passive Compliance (Outside Legal Domain)	"Well, looking back on it, we did happen to comply with the law."
Restrictive Compliance	"We wanted to do something else but the law prevented us." "We did it in order to comply with the law."
Opportunistic Compliance	"Well, the law allows us to do it." "We operate in that jurisdiction because of the less stringent legal standards."
Avoidance of Civil Litigation	"We did it because we might get sued otherwise." "Lawsuits will be dropped."
Anticipation of the Law	"The law is going to be changed soon." "We wanted to pre-empt the need for legislation."

Ethical Domain

The ethical domain of the three-domain model refers to the ethical responsibilities of business as expected by the general population and relevant stakeholders. This domain includes responsiveness to both domestic and global ethical imperatives. Based on this general definition, the three-domain model both broadens and refines Carroll's concept of the ethical domain by including only three general ethical standards: (a) conventional; (b) consequentialist; and (c) deontological.

(a) Conventional standard

The standard of conventions can be explained by the moral philosophy known as ethical relativism (Pojman 1995: 31). The manner by which Carroll defines the standard of conventions as noted above appears to limit it to a concern for justice or moral rights. For the purposes of the new model, the standard of conventions will be defined as those standards or norms which have been accepted by the organization, the industry, the profession, or society as necessary for the proper functioning of business. Society is defined as embodying the corporation's stakeholders, including shareholders, employees, consumers, competitors, suppliers, and the local community, in addition to general citizens. Societal norms can vary depending on one's reference point (i.e., different stakeholder groups). To minimize this limitation, and to enhance the standard's practical application, reference should be made to formal codes of conduct or ethics (e.g., organizational, industrial, professional, or international) to establish whether a company is acting ethically according to the conventional standard.

Many objections and concerns have been raised by philosophers to the use of relativism in providing a moral justification to the actions of an individual or organization. As a result, the conventional standard is relevant for the purposes of the ethical domain with respect to only those formal codes of conduct or ethics that remain grounded in (or at least do not directly conflict with) either or both of the ethical standards discussed below (i.e., consequentialist or deontological). This approach is similar to those who suggest that although "context matters when deciding what is right and what is wrong," actions must still comply with a set of "minimum ethical standards" (Donaldson 1996: 6–7). Personal standards are rejected as representing an ethical principle that is too relativistic and arbitrary to stand as an ethical standard (De George 1986; Freeman and Gilbert 1988; Pojman 1995).

(b) Consequentialist standard

The consequentialist standard (sometimes referred to as "teleological") focuses on ends or consequences. Although there are several types of consequentialism, the form that is relevant for the purposes of the ethical domain suggests that "the morally right thing to do is to promote the good of persons" (Hoffman, Frederick, and Schwartz 2001: 26). In this respect, consequentialism includes both egoism (promoting the good of an individual) and utilitarianism (promoting the good of society). Although egoism can be used as a moral justification for the economic domain, only utilitarianism is considered relevant for the purposes of the ethical domain under the consequentialist standard. As a result, an action is considered ethical according to consequentialism when it promotes the good of society, or more specifically, when the action is intended to produce the greatest net benefit (or lowest net cost) to society when compared to all of the other alternatives (Velasquez 2002: 75).

(c) Deontological standard

The deontological standard, as opposed to focusing on consequences, is defined as embodying those activities which reflect a consideration of one's duty or obligation (De George 1999: 80). This category would embrace two of Carroll's ethical principles, moral rights and justice. Rights are defined as an individual's "entitlement to something" (De George 1986: 79) and can be of a positive or negative nature (Feinberg 1973: 59–61). Justice can be of several different types, distributive (whether benefits and burdens have been distributed equitably), compensatory, or retributive (Velasquez 1992: 90). Instead of only relying on the principles of moral rights and justice, the three-domain model utilizes the category of deontological principles because it has the potential to more specifically capture a broader range of potential ethical justifications that have been suggested in the literature as duty-based in nature. Examples include: religious doctrine (see Herman 1997; De George 1999: 80); Kant's categorical imperative (Kant 1988); Ross's prima facie obligations (Ross 1930); or more specific core values such as trustworthiness (i.e., honesty, integrity, reliability, loyalty); responsibility (i.e., account-ability); caring (i.e., avoid unnecessary harm); and citizenship (i.e., assist the community, protect the environment) (Josephson 1997).

Activities would fall outside of the ethical domain when they (i) are amoral in nature (i.e., with an unawareness or indifference to the morality of the action), (ii) take place despite an awareness that the action conflicts with certain moral principles (i.e., are unethical), or (iii) are only intended to produce a net benefit for the corporation and not for the affected stakeholders (i.e., are only supported by egoism) (De George 1986: 45; Freeman and Gilbert 1988: 72).

Overlapping Domains

A major feature of the three-domain model is the depiction of economic, legal, and ethical domains of responsibility in a Venn diagram which highlights the overlapping nature of the domains and the resultant creation of seven categories in which CSR may be conceptualized, analyzed, and illustrated. The ideal overlap resides at the center of the model where economic, legal, and ethical responsibilities are simultaneously fulfilled, but other pure and overlapping segments of the model create situations which also must be explored and illustrated because they represent situations decision makers may face in the business world.

For purposes of better understanding the model and for illustration, several corporate examples entailing business ethics will be described and categorized as best falling within each of these seven CSR categories. The three-domain model is especially useful for analyses that focus on the forces that come into play in ethical decision making as opposed to more general discussions of CSR, where philanthropy might assume a more prominent role.

Each of the seven segments will be described and illustrated. It should be kept in mind that it is extremely difficult to identify examples that ideally and perfectly illustrate each theoretical segment of the model. In spite of this, it is helpful to suggest examples that may very well fit and illustrate the tensions inherent in the various model segments.

i) Purely Economic

Activities which are purely economic in nature must have a direct or indirect economic benefit, be illegal (criminally or civilly) or passively comply with the law, and be considered amoral or unethical (other than based on egoism, i.e., the corporation's best interests). Many of the most highly criticized corporate activities fall into this category. For example, Film Recovery Systems, a company involved in the extraction of silver from old x-ray film, failed to take legally required steps which would have prevented the death of an employee in the early 1980s. The employee died of cyanide toxicity despite the company having been previously warned of its gross violations of worker safety standards (Reidenbach and Robin 1991: 276). Other companies falling within this domain by intentionally breaking the law include General Electric, which engaged in illegal price fixing during the 1950s (Velasquez 1992: 199–206), and Lockheed Aircraft, which made secret payments to Japanese government officials from 1972–1975 in order to obtain business (Velasquez 1992: 207–209). One could well argue that the recently revealed actions and decisions of Enron—such as deceiving its stakeholders by shifting debt from its balance sheet—and Arthur Andersen—ordering the shredding of documents—illustrate business decision making which took only the economic domain of responsibility into consideration (Financial Times 2002).

Other corporations falling within this category are passively complying with the law, but are acting unethically for economic motives. For example, Nestle continued selling infant formula in the third world, despite knowledge that the use of the product was increasing infant mortality. Nestle was passively complying with the law and appeared to act based purely on economic motives (Velasquez 1992: 304). The Johns Manville Corporation appeared to be operating in this category when it "legally" allowed employees to continue working despite the company's knowledge of the health hazards of asbestos (Silverstein 1987). Chisso, a Japanese industrial corporation, discharged mercury into the ocean during the 1970s knowing it posed a danger to local residents, but remaining secure in the knowledge that its emission levels complied with Japanese government guidelines (Donaldson 1982: 1–2). The Ford Motor Company continued to manufacture its Pinto model car during the 1970s despite knowledge of its dangerous defect and knowing that it would be sued as a result (Velasquez 1992: 110–114).

More recently, Firestone, as well as Ford, appears to fall within the purely economic domain based on tire blowouts and rollovers involving Firestone tires placed on Ford Explorers (Naughton and Hosenball 2000). Tobacco companies may have fallen within this domain for decades, in knowingly producing and marketing a dangerous and addictive product without providing full disclosure to smokers. Another corporate example might include Dow Corning, which allegedly for economic gain "failed to fully apprise women of the known risks of breast implants," irrespective of the obligations stipulated in its own code of ethics (Byrne 1996: 10). This category could relate to what Reidenbach and Robin (1991: 275) call the "amoral" corporation, meaning a corporation unconcerned about the law or ethics, or what Carroll terms "amoral management" (Carroll 1987: 9).

ii) Purely Legal

Corporate actions that are not considered ethical and have no direct or indirect economic benefit fall into this category. The activity must take place because of the legal system and not in spite of it. A response that one of the reasons for the act was "because it's the law" might be enough to support a degree of consideration for the legal system. Very few activities can be considered purely legal as most activities that are considered legal are also considered ethical. In addition, most activities which are legally required also possess an economic incentive (Posner 1986). Companies that hesitantly place warnings on their products (e.g., tobacco manufacturers), or abide by holiday shopping legislation despite financial loss, could conceivably fall into this category.

The activities of Napster, at least in its early stages, may fall within this domain, in that its actions were legal, yet not intended to produce revenue and undertaken despite the ethical concerns raised. The founder, Shawn Fanning, established a website allowing users to share music files. The program was given away for free and users were not charged anything, and thus the initial actions of Napster fall outside of the economic domain. Fanning argued that Napster "was not doing anything illegal," and in this respect he appears to have opportunistically taken advantage of the law (although the service was later declared to be legally problematic). Fanning appeared to be acting despite an awareness of the ethical concerns, in that the service was providing its users with the opportunity to infringe copyright (a violation of moral rights) held by musicians and music companies (Velasquez 2002: 61–63).

iii) Purely Ethical

Any purely ethical activity that has no direct or indirect economic or legal implications would fall into this theoretical category. Such activities are performed because they are considered ethical based on at least one moral principle (e.g., conventions, deontological, consequential) despite their lack of positive economic impact. Other than corporate philanthropic activities that are not based on economic interests, few corporate activities currently fall into this category. The primary reason is that many activities that are considered ethical can somehow be linked to long term, indirect economic benefits.

A number of corporate examples falling within the purely ethical domain may be suggested, however. For example, 3M's decision to retire its pollution credits despite economic loss might be viewed as a purely ethical activity (Carroll 1993: 343). When Sir Cadbury decided to honour a contract to supply English soldiers in the Boer War with chocolates at cost (indicating a passive or neutral economic motive), despite his personal opposition to the war, he was making a purely ethical decision (Cadbury 1987; Reidenbach and Robin 1991). Restaurant chain Chick-fil-A, which does not operate on Sundays, is abiding by a religious deontological principle while forgoing additional revenue, and can be considered purely ethical (Zigarelli 2000). Although debatable, the act of immediately recalling millions of bottles of Tylenol in 1982 by Johnson & Johnson upon being informed of several deaths, despite facing significant economic loss, appears to have been based on ethical motives alone due to its corporate credo that placed the safety of the users of its products before stockholder interests (Davis and Frederick 1984: 549–560; Reidenbach and Robin 1991: 280). The decision by Levi Strauss and Timberland in 1993 to pull out of China in protest of human rights abuses, despite the loss of potential profits, appears to place these companies within this category (Kaltenheuser 1995: 21). Merck and Co. engaged in an ethical act during the 1980s by developing and distributing for free a pill curing millions of people living in developing nations of river blindness, despite an awareness that no sales revenue would be generated (Bollier and Weiss 1991). In the final analysis, it is difficult to find and defend corporate practices or decisions that illustrate purely ethical motives because it is impossible to fully know all the motives that went into a decision and the resulting consequences.

iv) Economic / Ethical

In this category the corporate activity is not based on legal considerations, but is ethical and economic simultaneously. This category would include many corporate activities motivated by the often repeated maxim, "good ethics is good business." To be considered ethical, the activity must go beyond rational egoistic concerns and be based on conventionalist, consequentialist, or deontological principles. Virtually all activities in this category will involve passive compliance with the law because almost all illegal activities would be considered unethical. Corporations which give to charity for both economic and ethical reasons (Carroll 1993: 382) would fall within this category. Corporations in the environmental sector (Smith 1990), the "social" or "environmental" mutual fund industry (Ellmen 1996; Lowry 1991), or involved in the sale of "green" products, such as The Body Shop (Shearer 1990), can be considered directly economic while simultaneously ethical. The decision by StarKist, a unit of H. J. Heinz, to use dolphin-safe nets (Rice 1990), or 3M's introduction of a waste-reduction program (Carroll 1993: 356), could be considered ethical while providing indirect economic benefits.

Following a severe fire destroying several of its factory buildings, textile manufacturer Malden Mills remained in Massachusetts and continued paying its employees their wages and health benefits until the factories were rebuilt, despite no legal obligation to do so. The CEO of Malden Mills appeared to be acting on the basis of both ethical (i.e., deontological) and indirect economic reasons (e.g., retaining quality employees, improving morale and productivity, etc.) (Teal 1996).

Many "social marketing" activities fall within this domain. For example, in describing Ben & Jerry's policy of giving away free ice cream, the former CEO describes the simultaneous ethical and economic motivations: "The motivation for giving back had always been genuine. At the same time, it was proving to be an effective marketing strategy. There was no doubt that our customers were more inclined to buy our ice cream and support our business because of how we, in turn, supported the community" (Lager 1994: 126).

This domain would probably contain a high level of corporate activity and might be equated with Reidenbach and Robin's (1991) "emergent ethical" corporation, which they describe as a corporation in which management "actively seeks a greater balance between profits and ethics" (1991: 279).

v) Economic/Legal

Very few activities which corporations engage in are both economic and legal, while also considered unethical. The reason is that activities which are based on a concern for the legal system (i.e., restrictive compliance, avoidance of civil litigation, or anticipation of the law) would most likely be considered ethical as well. The exception might be those companies that opportunistically comply with the law, searching for and using legislative and administrative loopholes for economic gain. Such opportunistic activities are often considered unethical. For example, although the use of bankruptcy laws is not inherently unethical, and can sometimes lead to the saving of jobs, some companies might try to use such laws in an opportunistic manner that can be considered ethically inappropriate. Dow Corning has been criticized for using protective bankruptcy laws to avoid massive litigation due to its breast implants (Reisch 1994). The Canadian retailing giant Eaton's was criticized for using bankruptcy protection in a manner which was not ethical (Brooks 1997: 1).

Other companies operate in third world countries because of lower environmental (i.e., "eco-dumping"), worker safety (i.e., "social dumping"), or product safety standards (Brooke 1995: B8; Nicholson 1997: 292). By doing so these companies are opportunistically taking advantage of the law. For example, Union Carbide acted opportunistically by operating a pesticide plant in Bhopal, India, according to India's relatively weak legal safety standards, despite operating a similar plant in the U.S. according to much more stringent standards. As a result, a poisonous leak in 1984 led to the deaths of over 2,500 people and the injuries of 300,000 others (Trevino and Nelson 1995:188).

An example of restrictive legal compliance would be a company abiding by a country's boycott for economic gain such as Pepsi's refusal to sell its product to Israel in order to maintain its sales in Arab countries (Reingold and Lansing 1994). Companies operating in China such as Chrysler Corporation are being asked to obey laws that often deny basic freedoms to Chinese citizens. Although such companies may prefer not to obey such laws, they do so because of their desire to continue doing business in the country (Freeman and Gilbert 1988: 37; Kaltenheuser 1995: 20–23).

All of the above activities might be considered unethical, economic, and legal in the opportunistic or restrictive compliance sense. This category is similar to Sethi's (1979: 65) "social obligation" corporation, in which corporate behavior is "in response to market forces or legal constraints," Reidenbach and Robin's (1991: 276) "legalistic" corporation, in which management is preoccupied with compliance with the letter of the law, or with Carroll's concept of "amoral management" (1987: 11). Unlike Reidenbach and Robin's approach however, the three-domain model would not consider a corporation which merely passively complied with the law to be a legalistic corporation.

vi) Legal/Ethical

Certain corporate activities occur not because of any economic benefit, but because they are both legally required and ethical. Activities that are both ethical and legal often provide indirect economic benefits meaning that few corporate activities will fall into this category. The activity of installing an anti-pollution device because it is legally required (i.e., restrictive compliance) and considered ethical even if there is no long term economic benefit would fall within this category.

The decision by General Electric to finally support the cost of dredging the Hudson River of PCBs that were released by the company decades ago (at a time when it was legal to do so) might indicate a shift from the purely economic domain to the legal/ethical domain. The company appears to be responding due to legal pressures, from both the U.S. government as well as civil lawsuits. The decision may also reflect a recognition by the company that the action is morally required based on a past injustice, regardless of the additional cost that is required (Hudsonvoice 2002). The pharmaceutical companies that are providing HIV/AIDS drugs at below cost (i.e., non-economic) to African countries might also be considered to be acting ethically (CNN 2000). At the same time their actions also appear to fall within the legal domain in that these companies are trying to avoid patent infringement legislation being enacted that would permit generic manufacturers to make the same drugs (DeYoung 2001: A13). The example of Smith & Wesson adding safety features to its handguns appears to have been based on ethical motives (i.e., the CEO argued that the decision was "the right thing to do") and legal motives (i.e., avoidance of government lawsuits). The decision was taken despite harsh criticism from the gun industry as well as consumers, placing it within the legal/ethical domain (Paulson 2000).

vii) Economic/Legal/Ethical

An activity which is motivated simultaneously by the bottom line, the legal system, and ethical principles would fall into this category. The decision by Procter & Gamble to pull its Rely tampons from the shelves due to the potential link with toxic shock syndrome may have been motivated by all three CSR domains (Reidenbach and Robin 1991: 278–279). Wal-Mart's decision to stop selling cigarettes in its Canadian stores appears to have been motivated by economic concerns (e.g., public relations), anticipation of changes to legislation, and ethical concerns (Heinzl 1994). This category conforms to Carroll's "moral management," according to which management desires "profitability, but only within the confines of obeying the law and being sensitive to ethical standards" (1987: 10). It also conforms to Lynn Sharp Paine's "integrity strategy" (Paine 1994). Paine's integrity strategy envisions ethics as the driving force in the organization although profits and legal obedience are obviously relevant factors. Carroll and Buchholtz argue that caution is needed in many of the overlapping segments of economics, law, and ethics, but in this central segment the management recommendation is to "go for it," because all three categories of responsibility are met (Carroll and Buchholtz 2003: 175). From a normative point of view, this central segment (economic/legal/ethical) is where firms should seek to operate whenever possible, or in the economic/ethical segment (as long as the company is passively complying with the law). Figure 3.3 provides a summary of a number of corporate examples discussed above and where they would be situated within the three-domain model.

Limitations of the Three-Domain Model

Though the proposed model addresses some of the issues raised with the Carroll four-part construct, there also are limitations with the three-domain

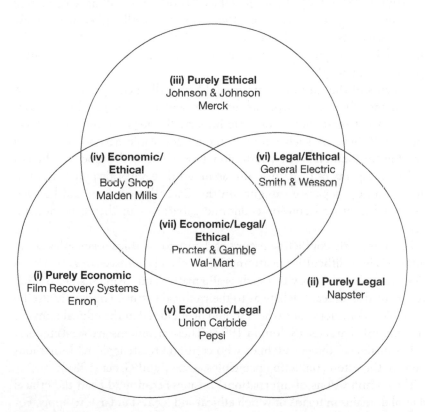

Figure 3.3: The Three-Domain Model of Corporate Social Responsibility: Corporate Examples

model that should be stated. The following reflects some of the important concerns.

The new model is based on several major assumptions. The model assumes that the three domains of CSR are somewhat distinct, and that they are all-encompassing. In terms of being somewhat distinct, some might question whether any action can be identified as "purely economic," "purely legal," or "purely ethical." In other words, one might argue that economic, legal, and ethical systems are all interwoven and inseparable. Although our model attempts to create distinctions through the establishment of the "pure" domains, it should be noted that each of these three domains is only "pure" in certain respects. There will still be an overlap with the other domains at least to some extent.

For example, a "purely economic" action can still be in accordance with the law (although not intended to) and could still be supported by the ethical standard of egoism (i.e., in the best financial interests of the corporation). A "purely legal" action, even if restrictive in nature, would still involve economic consequences (such as a loss to the corporation) and would still be supported by the ethical standard of cultural relativism. In fact, many argue that "businesses have a moral obligation to respect legitimate law" (Orts and Strudler 2002: 226). A "purely ethical" action will still have economic consequences (e.g., negative or break-even) and will still either be passively legal or illegal. As opposed to egoism or cultural relativism, however, the action will be supported by other conventional, consequentialist, or deonto-logical moral principles.

In terms of the three-domain model being all encompassing, it is not clear whether there are corporate activities which are engaged in without reference to at least their economic impact, the legal system, or ethical principles. If there are such activities, the model would have to be adjusted to account for them. It is our assumption, however, that the model embraces all relevant aspects of CSR. It is also assumed that philanthropic activities, assumed to be a separate category in the Carroll model, would be seen as part of the ethical and/or economic categories in the three-domain model.

The inherently conflicting nature of the various ethical principles could result in serious difficulties in attempting to classify motives or activities as ethical. For example, activities such as affirmative action and insider trading have received significant debate as to their ethical nature. There may also be other ethical considerations which should be included in the ethical domain, such as moral character (Solomon 1992). These problems are continuously faced by business ethics academics who continue to struggle with methods to resolve the often conflicting principles (Derry and Green 1989).

The complications of international business confound both the ethical and legal domains in terms of which ethical and legal standards to apply. For example, if the motivations of a multinational corporation are being evaluated, should the standards of the home country be considered, or the host country in which the corporation is operating? The use of the opportunistic legal compliance category and the conventions ethical category address most of these concerns. In such instances, the company is often operating within the legal domain by opportunistically complying with the law, and could be acting ethically based on national conventions. Other ethical principles, such as moral rights or utilitarianism, may be violated in such cases, however. The complexities of international business ethics continue to be addressed by numerous business ethicists (e.g., De George 1993; Donaldson 1989; Donaldson and Dunfee 1999).

Finally, it is expected that certain CSR categories (e.g., purely legal, purely ethical, and economic/legal) will rarely apply, thus limiting the conceptual or practical application of some segments of the model. The major reason for this is due to the presumably high correlation between activities that are both economic and legal, and those that are both legal and ethical. The fact that some reasonable examples can still be provided for each of the seven CSR categories, however, suggests that all of the categories should be included in the conceptual framework, even though several of them will be less important from a practical application point-of-view.

Implications for Teaching and Research

The three-domain model should be useful both for teaching and research in the business ethics and social issues in management fields. As a conceptual model, its primary usefulness will be in the realm of pedagogy—helping others to conceptualize the components of CSR and the nuances involved in their understanding and application. From a research standpoint, the model creates a definition and overlapping segments that may be further explored. Following is a brief discussion of each of these areas.

Teaching Social Issues in Management and Business Ethics

There is an ongoing debate as to appropriate methods for teaching business and society, social issues in management, and business ethics. It is proposed that the three-domain model of CSR provides a scheme for conceptualizing the major issues in one or more of these literatures. Once the model is described and discussed in some detail in a classroom setting, students can apply the model by engaging in practical exercises. Instructors can provide or ask students to find articles in the general or business media which discuss a certain corporate decision or activity. The activity can then be classified by the student or groups of students. This can lead to class discussions on whether students agree with the classification and the implications for the corporation acting in its chosen manner.

The model helps to classify many of the major case studies which have been presented in business ethics literature, for example, the Ford Pinto, Johns Manville and asbestos, Johnson & Johnson and Tylenol, Procter & Gamble and the Rely tampon, Union Carbide and Bhopal, and the activities of Ben & Jerry's and The Body Shop. Students can debate, for example, whether it is really the case that Johnson & Johnson should fall within the purely ethical domain. Were there not economic or legal motives as well for their actions? Has Ford shifted out of the purely economic domain following its Pinto disaster with respect to its actions involving Firestone tires? What activities of Ben & Jerry's or The Body Shop might be considered purely ethical, if any? The model can also be used as a measure of testing students' understanding of the different CSR domains by providing past or current examples of corporate activities and asking students to justify their classifications of the examples within the CSR framework.

In a related vein, the model should be valuable in the process of analyzing case studies in a classroom setting. The three-domain model assists the student in identifying and analyzing the competing forces at work in a business decision and in assessing the relative mix of economic, legal, and ethical forces and motivations that *are* at work and *ought* to be at work. In this context, the model helps the student to describe and understand *what is going on* and also from a normative perspective to suggest *what ought to be taking place*. Thus, the model has both diagnostic and normative properties.

Although it is not being proposed that the three-domain model provides definitive answers to the following questions, the model may provide a useful construct for beginning to engage in many of the major debates, such as: What is corporate social responsibility? Should it involve dimensions beyond economic, legal, and ethical responsibility? What is the relationship between economics, law, and ethics? Are they ever distinct? Why should corporations be socially responsible? How does one determine social responsibility? Should philanthropy be considered a distinct social obligation of business, or considered to be subsumed under ethical and/or economic responsibilities? What should be included in the ethical domain? Should companies avoid actions when they know they will be subjected to lawsuits as a result? What examples demonstrate that good business ethics is good business? Are there examples of good business ethics being bad business? What is more important, the motivations of companies or the results of their activities and practices?

The model might also be used to help analyze and discuss growing trends in the business and society field including: business ethics, corporate citizenship, social investment, social auditing, sustainability, triple bottom-line, social or cause-related marketing, strategic philanthropy, and stake-holder management. Each of these concepts involves, to some extent, aspects of economics, law, and ethics (including societal impact), such that the three-domain model might provide an initial framework to better understand these new developments and their relationship to each other.

Research Implications

In addition to teaching applications and implications, the three-domain model could be used in a variety of ways with respect to empirical research. Three future research uses of the model include: (1) the development of a research instrument for measurement of CSR and its component domains, (2) use of the model and instrument to develop CSR "portraits," and (3) use of the model and instrument to investigate future research questions.

Development of a Research Instrument. The three-domain CSR model, as presented, represents the conceptualization stage in the research process. In this stage, the meaning of the concepts to be studied was described. Two additional decisions needed in the research process include operationalization of the variables under consideration and choice of research method to be used (Babbie 1992: 104). The most logical next step in future research would be the operationalization of the variables and the creation of a valid and reliable data gathering instrument by which data regarding the model could be gathered. Then, this research instrument could be used primarily through survey research.

It is beyond the scope of this paper to present a research instrument that would enable the measurement of CSR in the three-domain model. This is a task for future research. In general terms, however, we can describe that it would be composed of several parts which operationalize the economic, legal, and ethical domains. These could then be used individually to pursue research questions concerning their particular role in CSR, their relationships with other variables, or collectively as an overall measurement of CSR. This procedure would follow the pattern established by Aupperle (1984) in his research instrument designed to collect data on Carroll's four categories of CSR. That instrument has been used in many empirical studies of CSR and it is anticipated that the research instrument patterned after the three-domain model would likewise be useful in exploring a number of interesting and important research questions.

Development of Corporate Social Responsibility (CSR) "Portraits." Once the research instrument is developed, one objective might be to establish the emphasis respondents place on each of the CSR domains (including overlapping domains). Once this takes place, "CSR Portraits" (i.e., graphical representations of one's CSR prioritizations) might be generated for whichever entity is being analyzed (e.g., individuals, stakeholders, corporations).

Individual employee CSR Portraits could be aggregated together to generate a CSR Portrait for a functional area or a company as a whole. CSR Portraits could also be established for stakeholder groups based on the domains they believe the corporation is currently emphasizing ("actual" CSR Portrait) or would prefer the corporation to operate within ("desired" CSR Portrait). Portraits could also be created for the corporation's Board of Directors, subsidiary corporations, or joint venture partners. If CSR Portraits are obtained from several firms in a specific industry, it may be

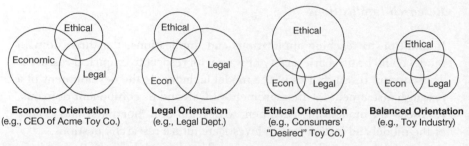

Figure 3.4: Corporate social responsibility "portraits"

possible to construct an industry CSR Portrait by weighting each firm's portrait by its market share or other financial measure, and then aggregating them together. For instance, a CSR portrait for the tobacco industry might look very different from a CSR portrait for the toy industry. Figure 3.4 provides a possible way to depict CSR Portraits of a hypothetical toy company. The greater the emphasis placed on a given domain, the larger the area which will be depicted in the CSR Portrait.

Investigating Future Research Questions

The three-domain model of CSR might be used to further answer a number of possible research questions. Some possible research questions include:

1. What aspects within each of the three domains are, or should be considered, more important relative to each other (e.g., profits vs. share value; legal compliance vs. avoid civil litigation vs. anticipate law; conventions vs. deontological vs. consequences)?
2. To what extent do corporate activities fall within each of the seven CSR categories?
3. Are corporate examples used in teaching business more prevalent within certain domains?
4. Is there a difference between those corporate examples used in business ethics courses as opposed to other business school courses with respect to the domains? If there is a difference, might this have an impact on students' perceptions of the responsibilities of business?
5. Do corporations tend to shift from one domain to another (i.e., change their emphasis) following a significant corporate scandal?
6. Do students tend to shift their preference from one domain to another after taking a business ethics or social issues in management course?
7. Do corporate employees tend to shift their preference from one domain to another following legal compliance or ethics training?
8. Is CSR performance (i.e., acting within certain CSR domains such as the economic/legal/ethical category) associated with firm financial performance? Does it lead or lag financial performance? (CSR performance is also referred to as CSP—corporate social performance).

Future research can be greatly facilitated following the three-domain model. One issue is the creation of an instrument designed to measure CSR and its component domains. A second issue is the possible creation of CSR Portraits using data gathered via the research instrument. A third issue is the exploration of existing and future research questions. With the creation and testing of a research instrument, the research process will be greatly advanced as a number of different populations and samples may be studied.

Conclusion

The proposed model, the "Three-Domain Model of CSR," extrapolated from the foundational work of Carroll, is proposed as an alternative means of describing CSR activity and orientations which pervade the business community. The proposed model eliminates the separate philanthropic category and subsumes it within the economic and/or ethical spheres. It is considered that this treatment more appropriately depicts the placement of philanthropy, particularly for business ethics applications. It is proposed that the new model more completely and accurately portrays the relationships between the three central CSR domains: economic, legal, and ethical. The three-domain model also helps eliminate the inherent assumption of a hierarchical relationship among the domains which some perceived in Carroll's pyramidal depiction of CSR. The broadening of the domains' descriptions provides a more complete construct by which to better classify corporate activities. One of the difficulties faced by researchers is the ability to properly classify corporations and their activities within a CSR construct (Clarkson 1995: 96). The new model is intended to provide a more appropriate means and theoretical framework by which to categorize CSR activities. It is anticipated that as corporate managers and business students reflect on corporate actions and where they should be classified within the three-domain model, an improved understanding of the relationship between business and society and more specifically between economics, law, and ethics, might take place.

References

Andrews, K. R. 1973. "Can The Best Corporations Be Made Moral?" *Harvard Business Review* (May–June): 57–64.

Aupperle, K. E. 1984. "An Empirical Measure of Corporate Social Orientation." In *Research in Corporate Social Performance and Policy* 6, ed. L. E. Preston (Greenwich, Conn.: JAI Press): 27–54.

Aupperle, K. E., A. B. Carroll, and J. D. Hatfield. 1985. "An Empirical Examination of the Relationship Between Corporate Social Responsibility and Profitability." *Academy of Management Review* 28(2): 446–463.

Babbie, Earl R. 1992. *The Practice of Social Research* (6th ed.) (Belmont, Calif.: Wadsworth Publishing Co.).

Boatright, J. R. 1993. *Ethics and the Conduct of Business* (Englewood Cliffs, N.J.: Prentice Hall).

Bollier, D., and S. Weiss, 1991. "Merck & Co. Inc." *The Business Enterprise Trust*.

Brooke, J. 1995. "Miners Strike Gold in Latin America." *The Globe and Mail* (July 13): B8.

Brooks, L. 1997. "Was Eaton's Legal and Ethical?" *The Corporate Ethics Monitor* 9(1): 1.

Buchholz, R. A. 1995. *Business, Environment, and Public Policy* (5th ed.) (Englewood Cliffs, N.J.: Prentice Hall).

Burton, B. K., and W. H. Hegarty. 1999. "Some Determinants of Student Corporate Social Responsibility Orientation." *Business and Society* 38(2): 188–205.

Byrne, J. A. 1996. *Informed Consent* (New York: McGraw-Hill).

Cadbury, A. 1987. "Ethical Managers Make Their Own Rules." *Harvard Business Review* (September/October): 69–73.

Carroll, A. B. 1979. "A Three-Dimensional Conceptual Model of Corporate Performance." *Academy of Management Review* 4(4): 497–505.

——. 1987. "In Search of the Moral Manager." *Business Horizons* (March/April): 7–15.

——. 1990. "Principles of Business Ethics: Their Role in Decision Making and an Initial Consensus." *Management Decisions* 28(8): 20–24.

——. 1991. "The Pyramid of Corporate Social Responsibility: Toward the Moral Management of Organizational Stakeholders." *Business Horizons* (July/August): 39–48.

——. 1993. *Business and Society: Ethics and Stakeholder Management* (2nd ed.) (Cincinnati: South-Western College Publishing).

——. 1994. "Social Issues in Management Research: Experts' Views, Analysis, and Commentary." *Business and Society* 33(1): 5–29.

——. 1999. "Corporate Social Responsibility: Evolution of a Definitional Construct." *Business and Society* 38(3) (September): 268–295.

Carroll, A. B., and A. K. Buchholtz. 2000. *Business and Society: Ethics and Stakeholder Management* (4th ed.) (Cincinnati: South-Western Publishing Co.).

——. 2003. *Business and Society: Ethics and Stakeholder Management* (5th ed.) (Cincinnati: Thomson-South-Western).

Clarkson, M. B. E. 1991. "Defining, Evaluating, and Managing Corporate Social Performance: The Stakeholder Management Model." In *Research in Corporate Social Performance and Policy* 12, ed. W. F. Frederick (Greenwich, Conn.: JAI Press): 331–358.

——. 1995. "A Stakeholder Framework for Analyzing and Evaluating Corporate Social Performance." *Academy of Management Review* 20(1): 92–117.

CNN. 2000. "Pharmaceutical Firms to Slash Cost of AIDS Costs in Africa." http://www.cnn.com/2000/WORLD/africa/05/11/aids.africa/index.html.

Cross, F. B., and R. L. Miller. 1995. *West's Legal Environment of Business* (2nd ed.) (St. Paul, Minn.: West Publishing).

Davis, K. 1960. "Can Business Afford to Ignore Social Responsibilities?" *California Management Review* 11(3) (Spring): 70–76.

——. 1967. "Understanding the Social Responsibility Puzzle: What Does the Businessman Owe to Society?" *Business Horizons* 10(4) (Winter): 45–50.

Davis, K., and R. L. Blomstrom. 1975. *Business and Society* (3rd ed.) (New York: McGraw-Hill).

Davis, K., and W. E. Frederick. 1984. *Business and Society: Management, Public Policy, Ethics* (5th ed.) (New York: McGraw-Hill).

De George, R. T. 1986. *Business Ethics* (2nd ed.) (New York: Macmillan Publishing).

——. 1993. *Competing With Integrity in International Business* (New York: Oxford University Press).

——. 1999. *Business Ethics* (5th ed.) (Upper Saddle River, N.J.: Prentice Hall).

Derry, R., and R. Green. 1989. "Ethical Theory in Business Ethics: A Critical Assessment." *Journal of Business Ethics* 8: 521–533.

DeYoung, K. 2001. "Makers of AIDS Drugs Drop S. Africa Suit." *Washington Post* (April 19): A13.

Donaldson, T. 1982. *Corporations and Morality* (Englewood Cliffs, N.J.: Prentice Hall).

——. 1989. *The Ethics of International Business* (New York: Oxford University Press).

——. 1996. "Values in Tension: Ethics Away From Home." *Harvard Business Review* (September/October): 5–12.

Donaldson, T., and T. Dunfee. 1999. "When Ethics Travel: The Promise and Peril of Global Business Ethics." *California Management Review* 41(4) (Summer): 48–49.

Ellmen, E. 1996. *The Canadian Ethical Money Guide* (Toronto: James Lorimer & Company).

Epstein, E. M. 1987. "The Corporate Social Policy Process: Beyond Business Ethics, Corporate Social Responsibility, and Corporate Social Responsiveness." *California Management Review* 29(3): 99–114.

Feinberg, J. 1973. *Social Philosophy* (Englewood Cliffs, N.J.: Prentice Hall).

Ferrell, O. C., and J. Fraedrich. 1991. *Business Ethics: Ethical Decision Making and Cases* (Boston, Mass.: Houghton Mifflin Company).

Financial Times. 2002. "Enron: The Collapse." http://specials.ft.com/enron/index.html.

Freeman, R. E., and D. R. Gilbert, Jr. 1988. *Corporate Strategy and the Search For Ethics* (Englewood Cliffs, N.J.: Prentice Hall).

Friedman, M. 1970. "The Social Responsibility of Business is to Increase its Profits." *The New York Times Magazine* 33: 122–126.

Heinzl, J. 1994. "Wal-Mart Canada To Stop Selling Tobacco Products." *The Globe and Mail* (November 5): B3.

Herman, S. W. 1997. "Enlarging the Conversation." *Business Ethics Quarterly* 7(2): 5–20.

Hoffman, W. M., R. E. Frederick, and M. S. Schwartz. 2001. *Business Ethics: Readings and Cases in Corporate Morality* (4th ed.) (New York: McGraw-Hill).

Hudsonvoice. 2002. "GE Presents Offer to EPA on Hudson Dredging Project" (April 9). http://www.hudsonwatch.com/.

Ibrahim, N. A., and J. A. Angelidis. 1993. "Corporate Social Responsibility: A Comparative Analysis of Perceptions of Top Executives and Business Students." *The Mid-Atlantic Journal of Business* 29(3): 303–314.

——. 1994. "Cross-National Differences in Social Responsiveness: A Study of American and Egyptian Business Students." *International Journal of Management* 11(3): 815–826.

——. 1995. "The Corporate Social Responsiveness Orientation of Board Members: Are There Differences Between Inside and Outside Directors?" *Journal of Business Ethics* 14: 405–410.

Jackson, J. H., R. L. Miller, and S. G. Miller. 1997. *Business and Society Today: Managing Social Issues* (Pacific Grove: West Publishing Company).

Josephson, M. 1997. *Ethics in the Workplace: Resource Reading Materials* (Marina del Rey, Calif.: Josephson Institute of Ethics).

Kaltenheuser, S. 1995. "China: Doing Business Under an Immoral Government." *Business Ethics* 9(3): 20–23.

Kant, I. 1988. "Fundamental Principles of the Metaphysics of Morals." In *Kant's Ethical Philosophy* (Indianapolis, Ind.: Hackett Publishing Company).

Klonoski, R. 1991. "Foundational Considerations in the Corporate Social Responsibility Debate." *Business Horizons* (July/August): 9–18.

Kohlberg, L. 1963. "The Development of Children's Orientations Toward a Moral Order: Sequence in the Development of Human Thought." *Vita Humana* 6: 11–33.

Lager, F. 1994. *Ben & Jerry's: The Inside Scoop* (New York: Crown Publishers).

L'Etang, J. 1994. "Public Relations and Corporate Social Responsibility: Some Issues Arising." *Journal of Business Ethics* 13: 111–123.

Levitt, T. 1958. "The Dangers of Social Responsibility." *Harvard Business Review* 36(5): 41–50.

Lowry, R. P. 1991. *Good Money* (New York: W. W. Norton & Company).

Makower, J. 1994. *Beyond the Bottom Line* (New York: Simon & Schuster).

Mallott, M. J. 1993. *Operationalizing Corporate Social Performance: Managerial Perceptions of Principles, Processes and Outcomes.* Unpublished doctoral dissertation, University of Pittsburgh.

McGuire, J. B., A. Sundgren, and T. Schneeweis. 1988. "Corporate Social Responsibility and Firm Financial Performance." *Academy of Management Journal* 31(4): 854–872.

McGuire, J. W. 1963. *Business and Society* (New York: McGraw-Hill).

Naughton, K., and M. Hosenball. 2000. "Ford vs. Firestone." *Newsweek* (September 18): 28–33.

Nicholson, M. J. 1997. *Legal Aspects of International Business: A Canadian Perspective* (Scarborough, Ont.: Prentice Hall).

O'Neill, H. M., C. B. Saunders, and A. D. McCarthy. 1989. "Board Members, Corporate Social Responsiveness and Profitability: Are Tradeoffs Necessary? *Journal of Business Ethics* 8: 353–357.

Orts, E., and A. Strudler. 2002. "The Ethical and Environmental Limits To Stakeholder Theory." *Business Ethics Quarterly* 12(2): 215–233.

Paine, L. S. 1994. "Managing for Organizational Integrity." *Harvard Business Review* (March/April): 106–117.

Paulson, A. 2000. "Smith and Wesson Agrees to Landmark Gun Safety Settlement." *CNN.com* (March 17) www.cnn.com/2000/allpolitics/stories/03/17/gun.lawsuit.

Pinkston, T. S., and A. B. Carroll. 1996. "A Retrospective Examination of CSR Orientations: Have They Changed?" *Journal of Business Ethics* 15: 199–206.

Poitras, G. 1994. "Shareholder Wealth Maximization, Business Ethics and Social Responsibility." *Journal of Business Ethics* 13: 125–134.

Pojman, L. P. 1995. *Ethics: Discovering Right and Wrong* (Belmont, Calif.: Wadsworth Publishing).

Posner, R. A. 1986. *Economic Analysis of Law* (3rd ed.) (Boston: Little, Brown and Company).

Reidenbach, R. E., and D. P. Robin. 1991. "A Conceptual Model of Corporate Moral Development." *Journal of Business Ethics* 10: 273–284.

Reingold, R. N., and P. Lansing. 1994. *Business Ethics Quarterly* 4(3): 335–353.

Reisch, M. 1994. "Dow Corning Mulls Over Filing For Bankruptcy." *Chemical & Engineering News* 75(25): 8.

Rice, F. 1990. "How To Deal With Tough Customers." *Fortune* (December 3): 38–48.

Ross, W. D. 1930. *The Right and the Good* (Oxford: Clarendon Press).

Sethi, S. P. 1979. "A Conceptual Framework For Environmental Analysis of Social Issues and Evaluation of Business Response Patterns." *Academy of Management Review* 4(1): 63–74.

Sexty, R. W. 1995. *Canadian Business and Society* (Scarborough, Ont.: Prentice Hall).

Shaw, B., and F. R. Post. 1993. "A Moral Basis for Corporate Philanthropy." *Journal of Business Ethics* 12: 745–751.

Shearer, J. W. 1990. "Business and the New Environmental Imperative." *Business Quarterly* (Winter): 49.

Silverstein, D. 1987. "Managing Corporate Social Responsibility in a Changing Legal Environment." *American Business Law Journal* 25: 528.

Smith, E. T. 1990. "The Greening of Corporate America." *Business Week* (April 23): 100.

Smith, W. J., R. E. Wokutch, K. V. Harrington, and B. S. Dennis. 2001. "An Examination of the Influence of Diversity and Stakeholder Role on Corporate Social Orientation." *Business and Society* 40(3): 266–294.

Solomon, R. C. 1992. "Corporate Roles, Personal Virtues: An Aristotelean Approach to Business Ethics." *Business Ethics Quarterly* 2(3): 317–339.

Spencer, B. A., and J. K. Butler, Jr. 1987. "Measuring the Relative Importance of Social Responsibility Components: A Decision Modeling Approach." *Journal of Business Ethics* 6: 573–577.

Stone, C. D. 1975. *Where The Law Ends* (New York: Harper and Row Publishers).

Strong, K. C., and G. D. Meyer. 1992. "An Integrative Descriptive Model of Ethical Decision Making." *Journal of Business Ethics* 11: 89–94.

Swanson, D. L. 1995. "Addressing a Theoretical Problem by Reorienting the Corporate Social Performance Model." *Academy of Management Review* 20(1): 43–64.

——. 1999. "Toward an Integrative Theory of Business and Society: A Research Strategy for Corporate Social Performance." *Academy of Management Review* 24(3): 521–596.

Teal, T. 1996. "Not a Fool, Not a Saint." *Fortune* (November 11): 201–204.

Treviño, L. K., and K. A. Nelson. 1995. *Managing Business Ethics* (New York: John Wiley and Sons).

Velasquez, M. G. 1992. *Business Ethics: Concepts and Cases* (3rd ed.) (New Jersey: Prentice Hall).

——. 2002. *Business Ethics: Concepts and Cases* (5th ed.) (Upper Saddle River, N.J.: Prentice Hall).

Wartick, S. L., and P. L. Cochran. 1985. "The Evolution of the Corporate Social Performance Model." *Academy of Management Review* 10(4): 758–769.

Weiss, J. W. 1994. *Business Ethics: A Managerial, Stakeholder Approach* (Belmont, Calif.: Wadsworth Publishing Co.).

Wood, D. J. 1991. "Corporate Social Performance Revisited." *Academy of Management Review* 16(4): 691–718.

Wood, D. J., and R. E. Jones. 1996. "Research in Corporate Social Performance: What Have We Learned?" In *Corporate Philanthropy at the Crossroads*, ed. D. R. Burlingame and D. R. Young (Bloomington, Ind.: Indiana University Press): 41–85.

Yankee, J. A. 1996. "Corporate Support of Nonprofit Organizations." In *Corporate Philanthropy at the Crossroads*, ed. D. R. Burlingame and D. R. Young (Bloomington, Ind.: Indiana University Press): 7–22.

Zigarelli, M. 2000. "Business By the Book Pays Off For Chick-fil-A Founder." http://www.connectionmagazine.org/archives_old/archives/2000/june/ChickFilA.htm.

Chapter 4

Responsibilities to stakeholders

IN THIS CHAPTER WE WILL:

- Define and conceptualize the idea of what a stakeholder is
- Understand the basic ideas of stakeholder theory
- Examine the multifaceted aspects of stakeholder theory
- Learn to distinguish between different levels of CSR
- Discuss the relevance of stakeholder theory for the broader understanding and practice of CSR

Introduction

At this stage of our journey into the world of CSR we have understood why CSR exists, what its basic features are and what the main ideas of explaining and managing CSR look like. Clearly, companies have an impact on society beyond just their economic role, and society has certain expectations toward them. As future practitioners of CSR, however, we might ask ourselves at this stage how we could possibly translate this fairly vague construct of 'society' into something concrete. How can we translate the 'social' in CSR into an object of managerial attention and action?

This is exactly the point where the notion of stakeholders enters the picture. If a manager would try and think what exactly his or her responsibilities are to this fairly abstract entity called 'society', considering them in terms of definable constituencies, i.e. 'stakeholders' is perhaps the answer. Probably the best known advocate of stakeholder theory, and one of its principal originators, R. Edward Freeman, puts it plainly and simply in the foreword of the book whose third chapter is our first reading in this section:

> A stakeholder is any group or individual who can affect, or is affected by, the achievement of a corporation's purpose.
>
> (Freeman, 2010: vi)

In essence then, stakeholder theory helps us to find a very pragmatic answer as to what the 'S' in CSR in a given situation actually is. As such, stakeholder theory is mainly a managerial tool: in a given situation, a company needs to work with selected individuals or groups in society to fulfil its aims and these 'stakeholders' that can have an influence on the company's goals have to be taken into account. This simple approach to make the broader, abstract entity of 'society' concrete and tangible for the company is one of the reasons why stakeholder theory today is a core element in most basic introductions to strategic management.

The moral aspect of stakeholder theory

One aspect that makes stakeholder theory particularly interesting in the CSR context is the fact that it is not just an analytical tool to identify and manage crucial constituencies of the company. As Freeman reiterates 'stakeholder theory is a theory of organizational management *and ethics*' (in Phillips et al, 2003: 480, emphasis added). Stakeholder theory has always been a core CSR theory as it argues that if the company affects individuals or groups to reach its goals, these groups also have a legitimate interest in the corporation. So, depending on how the company affects them, and their relative power and influence, they have a more or less higher 'stake' in the corporation, thereby putting them in a position where the company should consider their interests (see Mitchell, Agle, & Wood's reading later in this chapter).

There are different normative approaches in business ethics to make these claims legitimate (Phillips et al, 2003: 481) and there might be contestation about the degree of legitimacy of different stakes in a given situation. Think of British Petroleum in the aftermath of the Deepwater Horizon oil spill in the Gulf of Mexico in 2010. Among the constituencies who were affected by the spill we had actors as diverse as the local community, the local fishing industry, BP employees, BP's shareholders, the suppliers of the failed machinery, and the US government. A major challenge for BP here was to find out whose claims were the most legitimate, as it could not possibly fulfill every group's demands at the same time. The central message of stakeholder theory then is that corporations are not only strategically rational, but arguably also morally obligated, to consider the interests of the individuals or groups they affect and are affected by.

It is this normative element that sets the stakeholder model of the firm apart from the traditional managerial model of the firm (Donaldson & Preston, 1995) – such as that espoused by the CSR critics in Chapter 2 – where only the interests of the owners are considered as legitimate (see Table 4.1). This was clearly illustrated in the BP Deepwater Horizon case introduced above: the analysis of the disaster surfaced that pressures to cut costs (i.e. preserving the interests of shareholders) was probably the main reason for the spill in the first place.[1] In this sense then the

Table 4.1: Managerial model versus stakeholder model of the firm

	Managerial model of the firm	*Stakeholder model of the firm*
Main interest group	Owners (shareholders)	All groups that are affected by the firm's pursuit of its goals
Legitimacy of stake	Property rights	Broad set of all the rights of those groups which are affected by the firm
Role of stakeholders	Apart from owners, stakeholders are a means to maximize the firm's goal	All stakeholders are an end in themselves with legitimate interests in the firm
Goal of management	Maximizing value and return for the owners of the firm	Maximizing value for all groups that have a stake in the firm
Role of management	Agent of the owners	Balancing all interests of the firm's stakeholders
Social responsibility	Individual (owners)	Organizational

management of BP was acting according to the traditional managerial model of the firm. The case, however, shows that in today's business world this model is no longer fully fit for purpose. In order to manage the legitimate claims of all their stakeholders in the aftermath of the accident, BP not only suffered huge damage to its share price and reputation, but also had to put up a fund worth $20 billion to address their other stakeholders' interests.

The relevance of stakeholder theory

Stakeholder theory is arguably the single most influential theory in CSR. This is largely because, from a pragmatic point of view, the stakeholder model simply provides a more realistic picture of the business world today. Even former General Electric CEO Jack Welch, who is known as a long-standing staunch advocate of shareholder value maximization, told the *Financial Times* recently that shareholder value as a strategy 'is a dumb idea' and that 'your main constituencies are your employees, your customers and your products' (Guerrera, 2009).

In its various fashions stakeholder theory is used in most areas of CSR and has given rise to a large body of literature (see for an overview Freeman et al, 2010). But also beyond academia, corporations have adopted the language of stakeholders and even some governments frame their various relations in this language (Kelly et al, 1997). In a CSR context, the main implication of stakeholder thinking is a new role for management: rather than being 'agents' of shareholders only, managers find themselves in a role of assessing and balancing the interests of all stakeholders in running the firm. It has also therefore given rise to new approaches to corporate governance: if the stakes of multiple stakeholders are legitimate it is perhaps inappropriate if only the interests of shareholders are represented on the board. Thus,

CWS 4.2

Visit the companion website for links to some companies that have explicitly included responsibilities to wider stakeholder groups in their CSR approach

stakeholders should also, arguably, be allowed a fair share of influence on how 'their' corporation is run. In this context, there is an ongoing debate on how and to what degree such a 'stakeholder democracy' (Matten & Crane, 2005) is at all a desirable and realistic aspiration for the modern corporation.

Introducing the readings

The two readings in this chapter provide, first, an in-depth outline of the basic features of the theory, written by probably the single most influential author on the topic, and then we go on to an excellent in-depth analysis of how to apply stakeholder theory in a specific managerial situation.

Basic features of stakeholder theory

R. Edward Freeman is considered the main progenitor of stakeholder theory and this selection is the third chapter from his seminal 1984 book on the topic (Freeman, 2010). The chapter still very much breathes the initial context of stakeholder theory, which is also reflected by the main title of the book: rather than being a CSR theory, the approach was designed to be a new approach to strategic management. Consequently, Freeman draws stakeholder theory, first, as an analytical (or 'rational', as he puts it) tool: it helps us to design 'maps' of all relevant groups or individuals in the context of the achievement of the company's goals. Second, on the 'process' level, stakeholder thinking helps us to consider which players will actually be influential in the process of achieving the company's goals. Third, Freeman fleshes out the 'transactional' level of stakeholder theory by analysing how the company reaches different goals by successfully managing its relationships with customers, employees, the press or analysts, just to name a few of the examples he provides.

It is interesting to see that the normative or ethical side of stakeholder theory, which came out much more clearly in other (mostly later) writings by Freeman, is still relatively absent in this initial outline of the theory. The only slight hint to normative questions is given away in the concluding section where the author makes 'a plea for voluntarism' in the application of the framework. The reasons he gives are interesting as well: not only, he argues, is voluntarism the only philosophy compatible with the American social fabric, but all other approaches, in his view, are not cost-effective. One might discuss the extent to which this makes stakeholder thinking just another largely US-centric idea – a feature that we have already discussed in relation to CSR itself. Alternatively, some authors have argued that the principles of stakeholder theory, and sometimes even the label, have long been enshrined in management theory and practice in regions such as Northern Europe, Scandinavia and East Asia (Araki, 2005; Nasi, 1995).

How to apply stakeholder theory

Ronald Mitchell, Bradley Agle, and Donna Wood's reading is a classic in the CSR literature as it addresses the important question we briefly raised above: which stakeholder group should a firm pay attention to? In the real world, a company may have a large number of groups that would qualify as stakeholders; yet in a world of limited resources, the manager cannot deal with all of them in a given situation. The article presents an operational framework describing how managers can solve this problem by looking at three simple criteria: power, legitimacy, and urgency. Power relates to the stakeholder's ability to affect the company; typically, customers (e.g. by refusing to purchase the firm's products) or governments (by issuing laws that are binding for the firm) are considered powerful stakeholders. Legitimacy relates to the question of how justified the interest of the group in the firm is. It is here where, for instance, the rise of NGOs as corporate stakeholders can be understood. They may be perceived as raising issues such as environmental impacts or human rights of workers, which may have varying degrees of legitimacy – and the organizations themselves may also be perceived as a more or less legitimate representatives of those issues because of their membership or tactics. Urgency highlights the fact that in a given situation, not all interests of stakeholders ask for immediate attention. Typically, in a situation of crisis or accident (as in the BP case above) the stakeholders directly harmed receive the most prominent attention since their problems are considered to be the most urgent ones. Based on these three criteria the article develops a framework setting out how a firm can categorize different stakeholder groups and develop specific strategic approaches to manage them.

   Mitchell, Agle and Wood's article has been very widely cited in the CSR and stakeholder theory literature. It not only offers a very pragmatic and intuitively appealing framework, but also includes a very useful review of some of the key definitions and debates in stakeholder theory. In empirical testing, the model has been supported, with power being identified as the most important factor for gaining stakeholder salience (Parent & Deephouse, 2007). However, the approach also has a number of shortcomings. For example, there is an important question about who gets to assess stakeholder power, urgency and legitimacy, and whether such assessments are very objective or accurate. Similarly, by applying these criteria companies may easily ignore weak, minority, or fringe stakeholders despite them having important concerns that should be heard.

Challenges for practice

For managers, stakeholder theory represents a useful framework for developing CSR policy and practice. Some critical questions managers might ask through the lens of stakeholder theory are:

1. In whose interest is, or should, the company be managed?
2. What would a stakeholder map of the company's stakeholders look like?
   a) Which stakeholders should be included, and why?
   b) Which groups should be excluded, and why?
3. How would these stakeholders be prioritized?
   a) How much power, legitimacy and urgency does each of the stakeholders have?
   b) What approach should the company have to each of these groups?
4. What are the key challenges in managing all stakeholders' interests simultaneously, and how can they be overcome?

Study questions

1. What is a stakeholder of an organization? Why should even the most profit-driven manager bother about the firm's stakeholders?
2. Construct a normative (moral) and an instrumental (strategic) set of arguments suggesting why firms should or should not consider the interests of core stakeholders such as employees, consumers, suppliers and shareholders. Which is the most persuasive? Discuss using practical examples.
3. What are key practical implications for managers from stakeholder theory? What tools, structures, processes or strategies would stakeholder theory suggest for firms seeking to be socially responsible?
4. Using Mitchell, Agle, and Wood's stakeholder salience framework, describe how a firm would determine the relative importance of its various stakeholders. Using examples, set out the advantages and disadvantages of such an approach.
5. To what extent is stakeholder theory a uniquely US concept? Answer the question by drawing on examples of how key stakeholders, such as owners, employees, managers and local communities relate to companies in a Western European, Scandinavian, or Japanese context.

Further reading

Donaldson, T. & Preston, L. E. (1995) 'The stakeholder theory of the corporation: concepts, evidence, and implications', *Academy of Management Review*, 20(1): 65–91.
This article takes stock of the main developments in stakeholder theory and disentangles the various aspects and levels of the approach. This paper is important because it makes clear that, as with much of the CSR debate, different people mean different things when they discuss stakeholder theory, and the authors help us to understand the various ways that the theory can be interpreted.

Jensen, M. C. (2010) 'Value maximization, stakeholder theory, and the corporate objective function', *Journal of Applied Corporate Finance*, 22(1): 32–42.
Harvard professor Michael Jensen is probably one of the most vocal and prominent critics of stakeholder theory. This paper neatly summarizes his main concerns, which zoom in on the problem that stakeholder theory forces managers to address the expectations of multiple constituencies. Unlike the CSR critics discussed in Chapter 2, Jensen's critique is mostly fuelled by the pragmatic consideration that managers can only do their job efficiently and accountably if they are held to one specific and measurable goal.

Endnote

1   www.nytimes.com/2011/09/15/science/earth/15spill.html (Accessed 30 August, 2012).

References

Araki, T. (2005) 'Corporate governance reforms, labor law developments, and the future of Japan's practice-dependent stakeholder model', *Japan Labor Review*, 2(1): 26–57.
Donaldson, T. & Preston, L. E. (1995) 'The stakeholder theory of the corporation: concepts, evidence, and implications', *Academy of Management Review*, 20(1): 65–91.
Freeman, R. E. (2010) *Strategic management: a stakeholder approach* (reprint of the 1984 original), New York: Cambridge University Press.
Freeman, R. E., Harrison, J. S., Wicks, A. C., Parmar, B. L., & De Colle, S. (2010) *Stakeholder theory: the state of the art*, New York: Cambridge University Press.
Guerrera, F. (2009) 'Welch denounces corporate obsessions', *Financial Times*, 13 March.
Kelly, G., Kelly, D., & Gamble, A. (eds) (1997) *Stakeholder capitalism*, Basingstoke: Macmillan.
Matten, D. & Crane, A. (2005) 'What is stakeholder democracy? Perspectives and issues', *Business Ethics: A European Review*, 14(1): 6–13.
Nasi, J. (1995) 'A Scandinavian approach to stakeholder thinking: an analysis of its theoretical and practical uses, 1964–1980', in J. Nasi (ed.) *Understanding stakeholder thinking*, Helsinki: LSR-Julkaisut Oy, 97–115.
Parent, M. M. & Deephouse, D. L. (2007) 'A case study of stakeholder identification and prioritization by managers', *Journal of Business Ethics*, 75(Spring): 1–23.
Phillips, R., Freeman, R. E., & Wicks, A. C. (2003) 'What stakeholder theory is not', *Business Ethics Quarterly*, 13(4): 479–502.

STAKEHOLDER MANAGEMENT: FRAMEWORK AND PHILOSOPHY

R. Edward Freeman

Introduction

Organizations have stakeholders. That is, there are groups and individuals who can affect, or are affected by, the achievement of an organization's mission. I have shown that if business organizations are to be successful in the current and future environment then executives must take multiple stakeholder groups into account. The purpose of this chapter is to discuss how the stakeholder management framework can be used to better understand and manage both internal and external change, and how the management philosophy which accompanies this framework fits into our more customary way of thinking about organizations.[1]

The Stakeholder Framework

The literature yields a broad range of definitions of the stakeholder concept. From the standpoint of strategic management, or the achievement of organizational purpose, we need an inclusive definition. We must not leave out any group or individual who can affect or is affected by organizational purpose, because that group may prevent our accomplishments. Theoretically, therefore "stakeholder" must be able to capture a broad range of groups and individuals, even though when we put the concept to practical tests we must be willing to ignore certain groups who will have little or no impact on the corporation at this point in time. Such a broad notion of "stakeholders" will include a number of groups who may not be "legitimate" in the sense that they will have vastly different values and agendas for action from our own. Some groups may have as an objective simply to interfere with the smooth operations of our business. For instance, some corporations must count "terrorist groups" as stakeholders. As unsavoury as it is to admit that such "illegitimate" groups have a stake in our business, from the standpoint of strategic management, it must be done. Strategies must be put in place to deal with terrorists if they can substantially affect the operations of the business.

The stakeholder concept must capture specific groups and individuals as "stakeholders." As we move from a theory of strategic planning to a theory of strategic management, we must adopt an action orientation.[2] Therefore, if the stakeholder concept is to have practical significance, it must be capable of yielding concrete actions with specific groups and individuals. "Stakeholder

Management" as a concept, refers to the necessity for an organization to manage the relationships with its specific stakeholder groups in an action-oriented way.

The very definition of "stakeholder" as "any group or individual who can affect or is affected by the achievement of an organization's purpose" gives rise to the need for processes and techniques to enhance the strategic management capability of the organization. There are at least three levels at which we must understand the processes which an organization uses to manage the relationships with its stakeholders.[3]

First of all, we must understand from a rational perspective, who are the stakeholders in the organization and what are the perceived stakes. Second, we must understand the organizational processes used to either implicitly or explicitly manage the organization's relationships with its stakeholders, and whether these processes "fit" with the rational "stakeholder map" of the organization. Finally, we must understand the set of transactions or bargains among the organization and its stakeholders and deduce whether these negotiations "fit" with the stakeholder map and the organizational processes for stakeholders.

We might define an organization's "Stakeholder Management Capability" in terms of its ability to put these three levels of analysis together.[4] For instance, an organization which understands its stakeholder map and the stakes of each group, which has organizational processes to take these groups and their stakes into account routinely as part of the standard operating procedures of the organization and which implements a set of transactions or bargains to balance the interests of these stakeholders to achieve the organization's purpose, would be said to have high (or superior) stakeholder management capability. On the other hand, an organization which does not understand who its stakeholders are, has no processes for dealing with their concerns and has no set of transactions for negotiating with stakeholders would be said to have low (or inferior) stakeholder management capability. Each of these levels of analysis needs to be discussed in more detail, if the stakeholder management framework is to become a useful managerial tool.

The Rational Level: Stakeholder Maps

Any framework which seeks to enhance an organization's stakeholder management capability must begin with an application of the basic definition. Who are those groups and individuals who can affect and are affected by the achievement of an organization's purpose? How can we construct a "stakeholder map" of an organization? What are the problems in constructing such a map?

The traditional picture of the firm consisting of customers, suppliers, employees and owners has had to change to encompass the emergence of environmentalists, consumer advocates, media, governments, global competitors, etc. I base this argument on an analysis of the changes in the business environment of the last twenty years. The resulting generic stake-holder map can serve as a starting point for the construction of a stakeholder map of a typical firm. Ideally the starting point for constructing a map for a particular business is an historical analysis of the environment of that particular firm.[5] In the absence of such an historical document, Exhibit 1 can serve as a checkpoint for an initial generic stakeholder map.

Exhibit 1 depicts a stakeholder map around one major strategic issue for one very large organization, the XYZ Company, based primarily in the U.S. The executives in this organization, however, believed that Exhibit 1 could be used as a starting point for almost any issue of importance to the company. Unfortunately, most attempts at "stakeholder analysis" end with the construction of Exhibit 1. As the literature suggests, the primary use of the stakeholder concept has been as a tool for gathering information about generic stakeholders. "Generic stakeholders" refers to "those categories of groups who can affect. . . ." While "Government" is a category, it is EPA, OSHA, FTC, Congress, etc. who can take actions to affect the achievement of an organization's purpose. Therefore, for stakeholder analysis to be meaningful Exhibit 1 must be taken one step further. Specific stakeholder groups must be identified. Exhibit 2 is a chart of specific stakeholders to accompany Exhibit 1 for the XYZ Company. Even in Exhibit 2 some groups are aggregated, in order to disguise the identity of the company. Thus, "Investment Banks" would be replaced by the names of those investment banks actually used by XYZ.

Most very large organizations have a stakeholder map and accompanying stakeholder chart which is relatively similar to the above exhibits. There will be variations among industries, companies, and geographies at the specific stakeholder level, but the two exhibits can be used as a checklist of stake-holder groups. In the several industries analyzed in subsequent chapters there is little variation at the generic level.

Exhibit 3 is an analysis of the stakes of some of those specific stakeholder groups listed in the stakeholder chart (Exhibit 2). Thus the stake of Political Parties #1 and #2 is as a heavy user of XYZ's product, as being able to influence the regulatory process to mandate change in XYZ's operations and as being able to elevate XYZ to national attention via the political process. The stake of XYZ's owners varied among specific stakeholder groups. Those employees of XYZ, and the pension funds of XYZ's unions are concerned with long term growth of XYZ's stock, as their retirement income will depend on the ability of XYZ to earn returns during their retirement years. Other shareowner groups want current income, as XYZ has been known for steady though modest growth over time. Customer Segment #1 used a lot of XYZ's product and was interested in how the product could be improved over time for a small incremental cost. Customer Segment #2 used only a small amount of XYZ's product, but that small amount was a critical ingredient for Customer Segment #2, and there were no readily available

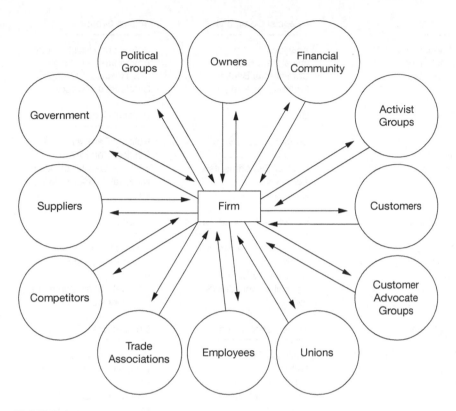

Exhibit 1 Stakeholder map of a very large organization

substitutes. Thus, the stakes of the different customer segment stakeholders differed. One customer advocate group was concerned about the effects of XYZ's product decisions on the elderly, who were for the most part highly dependent on XYZ's products. Another consumer advocate group was worried about other XYZ products in terms of safety.

As these three exhibits from the XYZ company show, the construction of a rational "stakeholder map" is not an easy task in terms of identifying specific groups and the stakes of each. The exhibits are enormously over-simplified, for they depict the stakeholders of XYZ as static, whereas in reality, they change over time, and their stakes change depending on the strategic issue under consideration. Similarly, the construction of an accurate portfolio is no easy task as the problems with measuring market share have shown.[6] The task becomes even harder when we consider several implications of these three exhibits.

The first implication is that just as Merton (1957) identified the role set for individuals in society, and Evan (1966) generalized this notion for organizations to the organization set, we might combine these notions into a "stakeholder role set," or the set of roles which an individual or group may play qua being a stakeholder in an organization. For example, an employee may be a customer for XYZ's products, may belong to a Union of

Owners	Financial Community	Activist Groups
Shareowners	Analysts	Safety and Health Groups
Bondholders	Investment Banks	Environmental Groups
Employees	Commercial Banks	"Big Business" Groups
	Federal Reserve	Single Issue Groups

Suppliers	Government	Political Groups
Firm #1	Congress	Political Party #1
Firm #2	Courts	Political Party #2
Firm #3	Cabinet Departments	National League of Cities
etc.	Agency #1	National Council of Mayors
	Agency #2	etc.

Customers	Customer Advocate Groups	Unions
Customer Segment #1	Consumer Federation of	Union of Workers #1
Customer Segment #2	America	Union of Workers #2
etc.	Consumer's Union	etc.
	Council of Consumers	Political Action Committees
	etc.	of Unions

Employees	Trade Associations	Competitors
Employee Segment #1	Business Roundtable	Domestic Competitor #1
Employee Segment #2	NAM	Domestic Competitor #2
etc.	Customer Trade Org. #1	etc.
	Customer Trade Org. #2	Foreign Competitor #1
	etc.	etc.

Exhibit 2 Specific stakeholders in a very large organization*

*The actual names of most stakeholder groups are disguised.

Customer Segment #1	Political Parties #1 and #2
High Users of Product	High Users of Product
Improvement of Product	Able to Influence Regulatory Process
	Able to Get Media Attention on a National Scale

Customer Segment #2	Customer Advocate #1
Low Users of Product	Effects of XYZ on the Elderly
No Available Substitute	

Employees	Consumer Advocate #2
Jobs and Job Security	Safety of XYZ's Products
Pension Benefits	

Owners	
Growth and Income	
Stability of Stock Price and Dividend	

Exhibit 3 'Stakes' of selected stakeholders in XYZ company

XYZ, may be an owner of XYZ, may be a member of Political Party #1 and may even be a member of a consumer advocate group. Many members of certain stakeholder groups are also members of other stakeholder groups, and *qua stakeholder in an organization* may have to balance (or not balance) conflicting and competing roles. Conflict within each person and among group members may result. The role set of a particular stakeholder may well generate different and conflicting expectations of corporate action. For certain organizations and stakeholder groups, a "stakeholder role set" analysis may be appropriate. Exhibit 4 is an example of the stakeholder role set of employees and a government official.

The second implication of Exhibits 1–3 is the interconnection of stakeholder groups, or the interorganizational relationships which exist, a

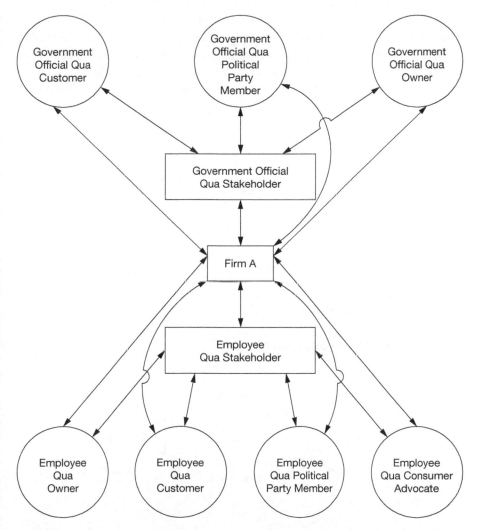

Exhibit 4 Possible stakeholder role set of employees and government officials

phenomenon well studied in organizational theory.[7] XYZ Company found that one of their Unions was also a large contributor to an adversarial consumer advocate group who was pressuring a key government agency to more closely regulate XYZ. Networks of stakeholder groups easily emerge on a particular issue and endure over time. Coalitions of groups form to help or oppose a company on a particular issue. Also, some firms are quite adept at working indirectly, i.e. at influencing Stakeholder A to influence Stakeholder B, to influence Stakeholder C.[8]

More traditional examples include the emergence of the courts as a key stakeholder in takeover bids. Marathon Oil successfully used the courts and the agencies involved in anti-trust to fend off a takeover bid from Mobil, while finding U.S. Steel to come to the rescue. AT&T recently marshalled the support of employees and stockholders to try and influence the Congress through a letter writing campaign. While there is some research on power and influence networks, little is known in the way of formulating strategies for utilizing such networks in a positive and proactive fashion. Little is known, prescriptively, about what range of alternatives is open to managers who want to utilize such an indirect approach to dealing with stakeholders. Exhibit 5 depicts several networks, and illustrates the necessity of thinking

Example #1: Marathon–U.S. Steel Merger

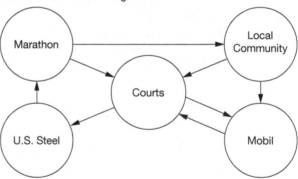

Example #2: AT&T and House Bill 5158

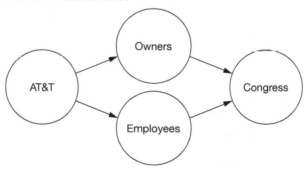

Exhibit 5 Typical indirect or coalition strategies

through the possible networks that can emerge or be created to accomplish organizational purposes.

The courts and some government agencies play a special role as part of the process by which groups interact. They have a special kind of "stake," one of formal power. While they usually do not initiate action, they can serve as resolver of conflicts, or as guarantor of due process. If we generalize this notion we see that another implication of Exhibits 1–3 is the phenomenon of the differing kinds of stakes and the differing perceptions of stakes that various groups have. "Stake" is obviously multi-dimensional, and not measured solely in dollar terms. However, exactly what the dimensions are of "stake" is a more difficult question. Exhibit 3 ranges across a broad spectrum of phenomena from more traditional dollar returns to stockholders to a call for "voice" in running the affairs of XYZ (Hirschman, 1970). Clearly we need to understand "stake" in more detail.

One analytical device depicts an organization's stakeholders on a two-dimensional grid.[9] The first dimension categorizes stakeholders by "interest" or "stake." The idea is to look at the range of perceived stakes of multiple stakeholders. While there are no hard and fast criteria to apply here, one typical categorization is to classify "stake" from "having an equity interest in the firm" to "being an influencer" or in Dill's (1975) terms, "being a kibbitzer, or someone who has an interest in what the firm does because it affects them in some way, even if not directly in marketplace terms." We might place a middle category between equity and kibbitzer and call it having a "market" stake. These three categories of a continuum are meant to represent the more traditional theory of the firm's differing stakes of owners (equity stake), customers and suppliers (market stake) and government (kibbitzer).

The second dimension of this classificatory grid can be understood in terms of power, or loosely speaking, the ability to use resources to make an event actually happen.[10] The three points of interest on this continuum are voting power, economic power and political power. Owners can expend resources in terms of voting power, by voting for directors or voting to support management, or even "voting" their shares in the marketplace in a takeover battle. Customers and suppliers can expend resources in terms of economic power, measured by dollars invested in R&D, switching to another firm, raising price or withholding supply. Government can expend resources in terms of political power by passing legislation, writing new regulations or bringing suit in the courts.

Exhibit 6 represents this two dimensional grid, with owners being the textbook case of an equity stake and voting power; customers and suppliers having a market stake and economic power; and government having an influencer stake and political power. The diagonal of Exhibit 6 represents the development of classical management thought, and the prevailing "world-view" of the modern business firm. Management concepts and principles have evolved to treat the stakeholders along this diagonal. Managers learn how to handle stockholders and boards of directors via their ability to vote

POWER \ STAKE	Formal or Voting	Economic	Political
Equity	Stockholders Directors Minority Interests		
Economic		Customers Competitors Suppliers Debt Holders Unions	Foreign Governments
Influencers			Consumer Advocates Government Nader's Raiders Sierra Club Trade Association

Exhibit 6 Classical stakeholder grid

on certain key decisions, and conflicts are resolved by the procedures and processes written into the corporate charter or by methods which involve former legal parameters. Strategic planners, marketing managers, financial analysts and operations executives base their decisions on marketplace variables and a long tradition of wisdom and research based on an economic analysis of marketplace forces. Public relations and public affairs managers and lobbyists learn to deal in the political arena, to curry the favor of politicians and to learn to strategically use PACs, "perks" and the regulatory process.

As long as the "real world" approximately fits this diagonal case of Exhibit 6 there are few problems. Each set of managerial problems and issues has an established body of knowledge upon which to draw in times of change. Another way of further supporting the argument of Chapter One is to say that the world can no longer be seen in terms of the diagonal of Exhibit 6.

For instance, in the auto industry one part of government has acquired formal power, the Chrysler Loan Guarantee Board, while in the steel industry some agencies have acquired economic power in terms of the imposition of import quotas or the trigger-price mechanism. The SEC might be viewed as a kibbitzer with formal power in terms of disclosure and accounting rules. Outside directors, now, do not necessarily have an equity stake. This is especially true of women, minority group members and academics who are becoming more normal for the boards of large corporations, even though it is far from certain that such directors are really effective and not merely symbolic. Some traditional kibbitzer groups are buying stock and acquiring an equity stake. While they also acquire formal power, the yearly demonstration at the stockholders' meeting or the proxy fight over social issues is built on their political power base. Witness the marshalling of the political process by church groups in bringing up issues such as selling infant formula in the third world or investing in South Africa at the annual stockholders' meeting. Unions are using political power as well as their equity stake in terms of pension fund investing, to influence management decisions. Customers are being organized by consumer advocates to exercise the voice option and to politicize the marketplace.

In short the nice neat orderly world of Exhibit 6 is no longer realistic. The real world looks more like Exhibit 7 which catalogs some of the differing stakes mentioned above. Of course, each individual organization will have its own separate grid, and given the complexity of the stakeholder role set, there may be groups which fall into more than one box on the grid. The "messiness" of Exhibit 7 lends credence to the search for alternative applications of more traditional management knowledge and processes. Getting the last two degrees of knowledge out of the diagonal of Exhibit 6 is simply no longer good enough. We must find innovative ways of understanding both the power and stakes of a variety of influential and interconnecting stakeholder groups. Thus MacMillan (1978) has argued that elements of strategic planning, traditionally reserved for market stakeholders with economic power, can be applied to the pure political case. While there is a long tradition of applying economic analysis to public policy questions, we are beginning to see the application of political concepts to economic questions, via recent discussions of co-determination and quality of work life. [11]

The second issue which a "power and stakes" analysis surfaces is the issue of congruent perceptions among the organization and its stakeholders. There may be differing perceptions of both power and stake depending on one's point of view. An organization may not understand that a particular union

POWER / STAKE	Formal or Voting	Economic	Political
Equity	Stockholders Directors Minority Interests		Dissident Stockholders
Economic		Suppliers Debt Holders Customers Unions	Local Governments Foreign Governments Consumer Groups Unions
Influencers	Government SEC Outside Directors	EPA OSHA	Nader's Raiders Government Trade Associations

Exhibit 7 'Real world' stakeholder grid

has political power, and may treat the union as a "purely economic entity," only to be surprised when the union gets a bill introduced in the legislature to prevent a proposed plant closing. The ABC Company completely misread the power and stake of a group of realtors who were upset over a proposed change in ABC's product. The legislature in the state where ABC operates was composed of a number of realtors, who easily introduced a bill to prevent the proposed product changes. It was only by some tough eleventh hour negotiations that ABC escaped some completely devastating legislation. The DEF Utility could not understand why a consumer advocate group was opposing them on a certain issue which had no economic effect on the group. Finally they spoke to a consumer leader who told them that the only reason that the group was opposing them was that they had not informed the group of the proposed rate change before the case was filed. In short the consumer group perceived that they had a different stake than that perceived by the management of DEF. DEF managers naturally believed that so long as the proposed rate change was in the economic interest of the consumer group and its constituency there would be no problem. The consumer group perceived things differently, that they had a vital role to play as influencer or kibbitzer.

Analyzing stakeholders in terms of the organization's perceptions of their power and stake is not enough. When these perceptions are out of line with the perceptions of the stakeholders, all the brilliant strategic thinking in the world will not work. The congruence problem is a real one in most companies for there are few organizational processes to check the assumptions that managers make every day about their stakeholders. The rational analysis proposed here in terms of stakeholder maps must be tempered by a thorough understanding of the workings of the organization through an analysis of its strategic and operational processes.

The "Process" Level: Environmental Scanning and the Like

Large complex organizations have many processes for accomplishing tasks. From routine applications of procedures and policies to the use of more sophisticated analytical tools, managers invent processes to accomplish routine tasks and to routinize complex tasks. To understand organizations and how they manage stakeholder relationships it is necessary to look at the "Standard Operating Procedures," "the way we do things around here," or the organizational processes that are used to achieve some kind of "fit" with the external environment. While there are many such processes, I shall concentrate on three well known and often used ones which purport to assist managers in the strategic management of corporations: Portfolio Analysis Processes, Strategic Review Processes and Environmental Scanning Processes. Variations of each of these strategic management processes are used in many large complex organizations. Each is usually inadequate in terms of taking complex stakeholder relationships into account and can be enriched by the stakeholder concept.

A good deal of research during the past twenty years has gone into understanding how a corporation can be seen as a set or portfolio of businesses.[12] Discrete business units are easier to manage and factors for success may well be easier to discern at the business level, than at the aggregated level of the corporation as a whole. The idea is to look at this set of businesses as stocks in a portfolio, with selection and nourishment given to winners and the door given to losers. Corporate planners and division managers (or Strategic Business Unit managers) plot the firm's set of businesses on a matrix which arrays an external against an internal dimension. The external dimension is usually labeled "Industry Attractiveness" and is usually measured by the growth rate of the industry under consideration. The internal dimension is usually labeled "Business Strengths" and is usually measured by market share. The corporate managers, after plotting the portfolio of businesses, seek to arrive at a balanced portfolio which maximizes returns (measured by Return on Equity or Earnings per Share or Return on Investment, etc.) and minimizes risks. Managers of particular businesses are then given a strategic mission based on their place in the portfolio and the potential of the business in question.

As an analytical tool and a management process, Portfolio Analysis can easily be out of touch with the stakeholder maps of most firms, as depicted in earlier exhibits. It simply looks at too narrow a range of stakeholders, and measures business performance on too narrow a dimension. While industry growth rate may be influenced by a number of non-marketplace stakeholders, to rely on it solely is to forgo opportunities to influence stakeholders which may determine the future growth rate of the industry. For example, in the auto industry foreign competitors and governments, U.S. government agencies, the Congress, the courts, Ralph Nader and the Center for Auto Safety, environmental groups, the United Auto Workers, etc. all have an influence on future growth rates in the industry. However, if market share is relied upon as the sole criterion to measure competitive strength, we will not necessarily invest resources to deal with all of the groups who can influence future market position. Market share is too broad a measure and an overreliance on it can be detrimental.

To illustrate, consider the fate of JKL Company after spending several million dollars in R&D to develop a new product which would serve as a substitute to a large established market. JKL believed that the product offered high growth potential, and in accordance with accepted theory, introduced the new product before getting approval from a key government agency which closely regulates the industry in which JKL would be competing. The product was later found to be carcinogenic and JKL took a large loss. Market share was not the sole indicator of success for JKL.

Or, consider Proctor and Gamble's experience with Rely tampons. P&G had entered a mature market with a new product and spent heavily to gain market share. When reports linking Rely with toxic shock syndrome surfaced, P&G voluntarily moved Rely from the market rather than jeopardize future products and its corporate reputation. Industry attractiveness was not the sole criterion for the success of Rely. The future attractiveness of the market together with the possibility of tarnishing P&G's excellent reputation, caused them to make a decision that was quite expensive. Even though it cannot be shown that use of Rely caused the disease, the mere possibility of a linkage was enough for P&G to recall the product.

Similarly, Johnson and Johnson acted quickly to recall the entire stock of Extra-Strength Tylenol after several deaths were reported as a result of criminal tampering with bottles of the product. Someone allegedly put cyanide capsules in bottles of the product after it was on retail store shelves. Johnson and Johnson's actions were lauded on "60 Minutes," a show sometimes critical of the actions of large corporations. They have reintroduced the product in "tamper proof" packages, and advertised heavily. Portfolio analysis simply cannot prepare the corporation to deal with issues such as those faced by these companies. Industry or market attractiveness analysis is not sophisticated enough to yield practical conclusions in areas where economics, social and political forces and new technologies combine.

The point of this critique of portfolio analysis is not that managers must be certain of success before taking action, nor that since market share and industry attractiveness do not yield certainty they must be rejected. But, rather, that *the strategic processes that we use must, as a minimum, raise the right questions*. Portfolio analysis processes are enormously useful in helping managers understand some of the factors for success in a business, yet for the most part they ignore non-marketplace stakeholders who can often, though not always, determine the success or failure of a business.

A related issue is that to view the corporation as a portfolio of businesses to be managed like stocks in an investment portfolio runs the risk that managerial processes will become overly concerned with the financial performance of the corporation.[13] While financial performance is vital to the health of a business, it is but one criterion used by external stakeholders to judge the viability of the corporation over time. When interpreted too narrowly, portfolio processes are asking for more regulation of "externalities," more social critics and ultimately less productive work.

A second strategic management process, made famous by Harold Geneen at ITT, is the strategic review process (Pascale and Athos, 1981; Charan, 1982). The idea of this process is for the top executives in a corporation to periodically meet with division or Strategic Business Unit (SBU) managers in a formal review session. Progress towards the planned goal is reviewed and new strategies are sometimes formulated. Top executives are usually accompanied by staff experts who have unearthed hard questions for the reviewee to answer. These reviews are usually built into the strategic planning cycle and are used as methods of communicating expectations and evaluating both personal and business performance.

The major problem with strategic reviews, in terms of being in synch with the stakeholder map of an organization, is that they do not encourage and reward an external orientation or stakeholder thinking. The emphasis from the point of view of the divisional manager under review is to "look good" to the senior executives who are reviewing performance. The formality of most strategic review processes and the mixing of personal and business evaluation make it difficult for the division manager to pay attention to multiple stakeholder concerns, which may contradict established corporate wisdom about the factors for success in a particular business. The nature of the organizational beast is such that it doesn't like and doesn't reward bad news and can hardly tolerate innovation. (How else can we explain the state of U.S. business?) It is much easier to play "Blame the Stakeholder" after the fact. "What senior executive in his right mind can hold a division manager accountable for a regulation which accounts for lost profits?" While responsibility for profits has been decentralized in most large multi-business firms, the responsibility for managing non-marketplace stakeholders (and some marketplace stakeholders) has not. Corporate Public Relations and Public Affairs are for the most part responsible for ensuring a stable business climate for all the corporation's businesses. Division managers naturally perceive that they have a lack of control over critical stakeholder variables. During one seminar on stakeholder analysis with division managers the predominant response was "Great stuff, too bad my boss isn't here to hear it." Upon giving the same seminar to the top levels in the corporation the predominant response was "Great stuff, too bad our people (the division managers) weren't here to hear it." While too much should not be made of an isolated case, processes like the strategic review process can exacerbate the inability of the organization to ask the right questions.

A third strategic management process which explicitly tries to focus the organization externally is Environmental Scanning.[14] Adopting a metaphor of the radar technology, the idea is for corporate managers to "put up their antennae" and to scan the business horizon for key events, trends, etc. which will affect the business in the future. There are several versions of environmental scanning, each of which has strengths and weakness. Scenario building, whereby several key events and trends are linked together to form a possible future for the organization, is a favorite technique of some corporate planners and a product of several consulting firms. Another technique is trend analysis, whereby key variables, usually demographic and economic are monitored for change. And, futures research, which predicts the future, is yet another technique for helping managers scan the external environment.

While all of these processes are useful, most of them do not yield concrete action steps. It is hard to see how a 10 year forecast can help the SBU manager worried about how to overcome the latest regulation. Consequently, most corporate plans have an environmental scan in the front section of the plan, which states the environmental assumptions on which the plan is based. These assumptions are usually stated in terms of an econometric forecast of macro-economic variables such as inflation, unemployment, interest rates, etc. If the assumptions have not been forgotten by the time the plan produces concrete strategic programs, they surely will be by the time the results are reviewed. Then, no one is held accountable for using the wrong assumptions.

Focusing the strategic management processes in a corporation is a necessary condition for success in the current business environment. However, this external focus must be pervasive, from "front-end" analysis to control processes. Our portfolio analysis, strategic review and environmental scanning processes must get better and more sophisticated, yet this is not the whole story.

Organizational processes serve multiple purposes. One purpose is as a vehicle for communication, and as symbols for what the corporation stands for.[15],[16] "The way we do things around here" depicts what activities are necessary for success in the organization. And, the activities necessary for success inside the organization must bear some relationship to the tasks that the external environment requires of the organization if it is to be a successful and ongoing concern. Therefore, if the external environment is a rich multi-stakeholder one, the strategic processes need not be baroque 25-step rigid analytical devices, but rather existing strategic processes which work reasonably well must be enriched with a concern for multiple stakeholders.

For instance, strategic management processes. . . . can easily be enriched by adding "who are our stakeholders" to a concern with corporate mission; "how do stakeholders affect each division, business and function, and its

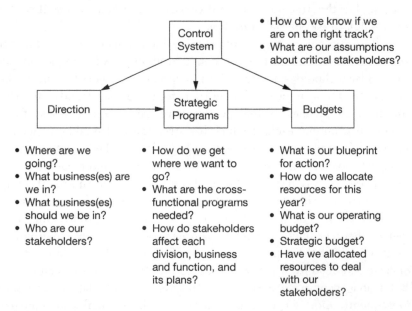

Exhibit 8 Typical strategic planning process schematic

Source: Lorange, 1980

plans" to the formulation of strategic programs; "have we allocated resources to deal with our stakeholders" in the budget cycle; and "what are our critical assumptions about key stakeholders" to the control process. Exhibit 8 depicts a revised version of Lorange's schema for strategic management processes. Each of these questions which are added will be discussed in more detail in subsequent chapters. The point is that relatively simple ideas can be used to encourage managers to think through the external environments of their businesses, and that such ideas must be added to organizational processes if they are to continue to be useful and to "fit" the stakeholder picture of the firm that is emerging.

The "Transactional" Level: Interacting with Stakeholders

The bottom line for stakeholder management has to be the set of transactions that managers in organizations have with stakeholders. How do the organization and its managers interact with stakeholders? What resources are allocated to interact with which groups? There has been a lot of research in social psychology about the so called "transactional environment" of individuals and organizations, and I shall not attempt to recapitulate that research here.[17] Suffice it to say that the nature of the behavior of organizational members and the nature of the goods and services being exchanged are key ingredients in successful organizational transactions with stakeholders.

Corporations have many daily transactions with stakeholder groups, such as selling things to customers and buying things from suppliers. Other transactions are also fairly ordinary and unexciting, such as paying dividends to stockholders or negotiating a new contract with the union. Yet when we move from this relatively comfortable zone of transactions to dealing with some of the changes that have occurred in traditional marketplace stakeholders and the emergence of new stakeholder groups there is little wonder that transactions break down. The lack of "fit" of an organization's transactions with its processes and its processes with its stakeholder map becomes a real source of discontent.

The XAB Company is an interesting study in how this lack of fit can be dysfunctional. XAB understood its stakeholder map and had some organizational processes to formulate and implement strategies with important non-traditional stakeholder groups. However, XAB sent some top executives out to talk with several of these groups who had little empathy with the causes of these groups. Needless to say the company has made little progress with them. Perhaps the strategy and the processes are inappropriate given the objectives of the company. However, another interpretation is that the transactions between company and stakeholders have not given the strategy and processes a fair test.

New England Telephone adopted a stakeholder approach to implementing a plan for charging for Directory Assistance in Massachusetts (Emshoff and Freeman, 1979). The rational analysis of the stakeholder environment was sound and the planning process used to chart out an implementation scenario was successful. However, its transactions with several key stakeholders, most notably and ironically, its own union, as well as the State Legislature, were not successful. The union got a piece of legislation prohibiting the company's plan passed in the state legislature, and even though the company was successful in persuading the Governor of Massachusetts to veto the legislation, as there was no public support, the state legislature overrode the Governor's veto, at the cost of $20 million to the customers of New England Telephone.

Consumer complaints are an area where there is usually a noticeable breakdown in the organization's Stakeholder Management Capability. Many large corporations simply ignore consumer complaints and dismiss them as that 5 percent of the market which they had rather someone else serve. Not only are there few successful processes for dealing with consumer complaints, but the transactions involved are material for every stand-up comic who ever walked. Nothing is more frustrating to the consumer than being told "sorry, I wish I could help you, but it's company policy to do things this way." One consumer leader commented that being told it was company policy may well finish the incident for the manager, but it begins the incident for the consumer advocate.[18] Several successful companies seem to "overspend" on handling consumer complaints. IBM's commitment to service, P&G's consumer complaint department and the Sears philosophy of taking merchandising back with no questions asked, yield valuable lessons in understanding the nature of transactions with customers. These companies act as if consumer complaints yield an opportunity for understanding customer needs which ultimately translates into a good bottom line and satisfied stakeholders.

Other sets of transactions, which often get out of line with process and rational analysis, include the firm's relationships with the media, shareholder meetings, meetings with financial analysts, encounters with government officials and day to day interactions with employees and unions.

Many managers actively perspire during "60 Minutes" in fear of being before the sharp tongues of the reporters and the skilful editing of the news show producers. Some organizations have become proactive and given their senior executives special training on "How to Meet the Press."

Shareholder meetings have become rituals for most corporations, except for the occasional meaningful proxy fight à la Rockwell-SCM. Rather than carry out meaningful transactions with shareholders in accordance with a clearly thought out strategy and process, executives now treat stockholders to lunch and speeches (with the stockholders' money) and a round of abuse from corporate critics who have bought one share of stock in order to be heard.

Meetings with financial analysts are another opportunity for transactions which can be made consistent with a firm's strategy and processes. Many executives understand that U.S. firms have underinvested in modern plant and equipment relative to foreign competition, and that they have lost sight of the marketing prowess of some of their competitors. How U.S. corporations can regain their competitive edge is a source of much debate in managerial and academic circles. Yet to regain competitive position will be neither easy nor inexpensive. Many U.S. firms will have to "take a hit on earnings" for several years in a row to be truly competitive. Most financial analysts are by their nature short-term focused. If executives use meetings with analysts to tout earnings per share, which may be inflated in real terms, then analysts will continue to expect short-term results. Talk of an investment strategy to regain competitive edge will be just talk. The transactions which executives make with analysts must square with the strategy of the organization regardless of the pain. By taking a leadership position in this area perhaps the thoughtful company can change the expectations of financial analysts. Of course, there is a vicious "chicken–egg" cycle here, that illustrates the dilemma of attempting to change stakeholder expectations. If we are measured on short-term performance results, and such a system is reinforced by expectations from the financial community, then to break the cycle involves additional pain. If strategic investments really are necessary then we must bite the bullet, and work to change the expectations of analysts, stockholders, and even board members, even at substantial personal risk.

Transactions with government officials often take place under adversarial conditions. Because government is a source of trouble for many companies, their transactions with government show their discontent. One company is reported to have rented a truck and dumped the requested documentation on the doorstep of the government agency which requested it. When stakeholder relationships are viewed on both sides as adversarial it is a small wonder that anyone ever changes. The Business Roundtable, as a transactional organization for large businesses with the government, published a study decrying the cost of regulation and calling for regulatory reform. While it is clear that the regulatory process has gotten out of control in some areas, a more helpful transaction would have been to try and gain some formal input into the regulatory process. To gain such input would mean that a firm's transactions with the government could be made congruent with its organizational processes, and the firm could formulate strategies for influencing government in a positive way, breaking down the adversarial barriers of so many years and so many hard-fought battles.

Perhaps the most fruitful area for transactional analysis is with the employee stakeholder group. One large company announced that it was committing to "Quality of Work Life," and set up national and local committees to form a partnership with its employees for the long term. However, shortly thereafter the company announced that many employees were in fact "surplus," and offered incentive programs for early retirement. Its transactions were simply inconsistent with its stated future direction for this stakeholder group. Much has been written lately about Japan and Theory

Z (Ouchi, 1981), and co-determination in Europe. However, before U.S. managers launch into different directions with employees, perhaps we should understand whether our current managerial principles can work. When processes are set up to treat employees one way, no matter how well-meaning or "humanistic" they may be, and day-to-day transactions treat them another, it is not lack of theory that is the problem. The real importance of the suggestion box in Japan, and Quality Circles that work, is the consistent message that they send to employees, that their ideas have some impact on the firm.

If corporate managers ignore certain stakeholder groups at the rational and process level, then there is little to be done at the transactional level. Encounters between corporation and stakeholder will be on the one hand brief, episodic and hostile, and on the other hand non-existent, if another firm can supply their needs. Successful transactions with stakeholders are built on understanding the "legitimacy" of the stakeholder and having processes to routinely surface their concerns. However the transactions themselves, must be executed by managers who understand the "currencies" in which the stakeholders are paid. There is simply no substitute for thinking through how a particular individual can "win" and how the organization can "win" at the same time.

Clearly, there must be some "fit" among the elements of an organization's Stakeholder Management Capability – defined as its understanding or conceptual map of its stakeholders, the processes for dealing with these

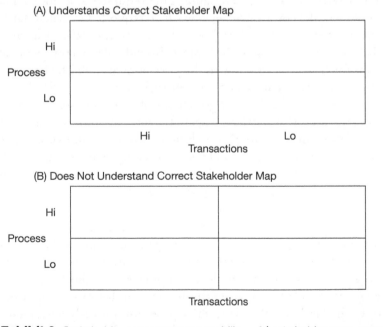

Exhibit 9 Stakeholder management capability = f (stakeholder map, organizational process, stakeholder transactions)

stakeholders, and the transactions which it uses to carry out the achievement of organization purpose with stakeholders. Exhibit 9 illustrates how some criteria might be used to measure the Stakeholder Management Capability of an organization. Whether an organization falls into the "Understands Correct Stakeholder Map" or "Does Not Understand Correct Stakeholder Map" is a relatively easy test. If, over time, an organization is continually surprised and continually plays "Blame the Stakeholder" then something is amiss. Whether an organization's processes and transactions are in line with that stakeholder map is a more difficult problem, for as I have shown, we do not have an adequate understanding as to what processes are appropriate for the multitude of stakeholders which firms now have. I shall return to the issue of defining a firm's Stakeholder Management Capability, by way of suggesting several processes to be used to understand and manage stakeholder relationships. However, before attempting such a task it is necessary to be more explicit about the underlying philosophy which accompanies the Stakeholder Management model. How can the multitude of charts, graphs, and maps be integrated into the current managerial wisdom of running a successful business?

The Stakeholder Philosophy: A Plea for Voluntarism

While the temptation to play "Blame the Stakeholder" is a strong one, the major problem facing U.S. managers is really not an external one, but an internal one. Pogo's saying is once again applicable, "we have met the enemy and he is us." The challenge for us is to reorient our thinking and our managerial processes externally, in order to be responsive to stakeholders. There are three levels of analysis which must be consistent, rational, process and transactional. However, there are several common themes, or philosophical propositions, which can serve as "intellectual glue" to hold these ideas together. Such a philosophy of management is necessary if we arc to undertake the rather considerable task of regaining managerial competence in the new business environment, without losing even more of our competitive position in the marketplace. We must learn to use our current knowledge and skill-base to respond quickly to the "stakeholder challenge" and to create some initial "win–win" situations, if meaningful change is to occur.

Such a philosophy of management must be based on the idea of voluntarism, if it is to be implemented in U.S. based companies. Not only is voluntarism the only philosophy which is consistent with our social fabric, but the costs of other approaches are simply too high. Voluntarism means that an organization must on its own will undertake to satisfy its key stakeholders. A situation where a solution to a stakeholder problem is imposed by a government agency or the courts must be seen as a managerial failure. Similarly, a situation where Firm A satisfies the needs of consumer advocates, government agency, etc. better than Firm B, must be seen as a competitive loss by Firm B. The driving force of an organization becomes, under a voluntarism philosophy of management, to satisfy the needs of as many stakeholders as possible.

Consider the current "Stakeholder Dilemma" in which many firms find themselves. The following story is a simplified illustration based on several real situations.

An Activist Group (AG) is worried about some aspect of the ABC Company's Product Y. AG believes that if ABC is allowed to continue to produce and sell the product as it now exists, harm will be done to the public and to some of AG's constituents. AG is a credible group in some circles, especially with a key government agency and the national media. While it has not always been successful in getting large corporations to be responsive to its claims, it has had some successes. AG does not have a large reservoir of resources, nevertheless, it can devote adequate resources to the pursual of this current case. ABC believes that there is nothing wrong with its product, and that they should be allowed to continue to sell it. ABC is a veteran of several campaigns against its products, and it has won some and lost some in the past, but each has been expensive to wage.

Let us assume that ABC has two major strategic responses. It can *Negotiate* with AG to reach a mutually agreeable solution with respect to Product Y by listening to the concerns of the leaders of AG, explaining the position of ABC on Product Y, exploring solutions to AG's concerns, voluntarily agreeing how AG and ABC are to proceed on this and future areas of mutual concern, involving other interested parties in the discussions, etc. Or, it can *Play Hard Ball*, by ignoring AG's concern, perhaps disparaging AG and the cause that it stands for, respond when AG files a formal complaint, try to delay AG through countersuits, etc.

Of course, AG also has two very similar strategies. It can *Negotiate* with ABC by attending meetings with ABC managers and presenting the concerns of AG, attempting to understand the needs of other interested parties in Product Y, working with ABC to find a mutually acceptable solution, or a mutually acceptable process for finding a solution to the issue in a timely fashion, etc. AG can also *Play Hard Ball* by trying to make a splash in the media, bringing formal action in the Courts against ABC, complaining to government agencies which regulate ABC, tying ABC up on other issues unrelated to Product Y, introducing legislation prohibiting the sale of Product Y, etc.

Clearly if both parties negotiate, then an agreement which both find mutually satisfactory is the result.[19] Both parties may have to compromise, or at least be willing to compromise, if negotiation is to proceed in good faith, else *Negotiate* is an identical strategy to *Play Hard Ball*. If ABC negotiates and AG decides to play hard ball (perhaps after the first session, AG decides to double cross ABC), then ABC will be embarrassed and vulnerable to AG's formal challenges by having admitted that there may be some legitimacy to AG's claims about Product Y. AG members will have the feeling of having "beaten" ABC and may well be successful in their challenge to Product Y. Managers in ABC will not trust AG, and will respond in a "win–lose" way to AG's initiatives. On the other hand if AG tries to negotiate and ABC responds by playing hard ball, the same sorts of feelings arise for AG members as in the case where AG double-crossed ABC. If both parties Play Hard Ball, then the outcome is a long drawn out process with a solution imposed by the courts, government agencies and legislation – plus the cost of doing battle.

The most preferred outcome for ABC, in a cold and calculating sense, is for AG to negotiate and for ABC to double cross, since ABC then "beats" AG. The most preferred outcome for AG is for ABC to negotiate and for AG to double cross, thereby "beating" ABC. Yet when each plays its preferred strategy, *Play Hard Ball*, the result is far inferior to the result of playing the *Negotiate* strategy. In a real sense, by following the dictates of self-interest, both lose.

Exhibit 10 sets out the form of this stakeholder problem. Of course, it is identical in form with the so called "Prisoners' Dilemma Game" which illustrates the difficulty of achieving cooperative solutions under communication constraints.[20] In the classical form of the game, two suspects to a crime (which they actually committed) are caught, and interrogated separately. Each is told that if they confess a light sentence will be passed depending on whether or not the other confesses. If one prisoner turns state's evidence and the other does not, the book is thrown at the non-confessing prisoner. If both confess, then each gets a medium-length sentence, while if neither confess they are convicted of a much lesser charge. Neither confessing yields a preferred outcome to both confessing, but self-interest dictates confessing. The payoff structure is identical to Exhibit 10 with "Negotiate" replacing "Don't Confess" and "Play Hard Ball" replacing "Confess." If the prisoners could communicate they would form an agreement not to confess, or agree to get revenge if the other double-crossed. The lack of communication and the ability to form binding agreements dooms the prisoners to a heavy sentence.

The striking fact about the Stakeholder Dilemma version of this game is that there are absolutely no such communication constraints upon ABC and AG, and there are no constraints which prevent binding agreements. The managerial processes of both groups simply do not include considering communication and responsiveness as normal managerial activities. The status quo imposes similar Prisoners' Dilemma-like constraints on ABC and AG.

The "Stakeholder Dilemma" game is one which is played out in some form in many organizations.[21] The only way out is to *voluntarily* adopt a posture of negotiation with stakeholder groups. Why negotiate voluntarily? Because, there is no other way to keep from having a solution imposed upon the organization from outside. And, to accept such an imposition of a solution to a problem is to give up the managerial role. Additionally, there seems to be no reason to pay the enforcement costs of adversarial proceedings. How

Outcomes

	ABC's Strategies	
	Negotiate	Hard Ball
Negotiate	Mutually acceptable solution	ABC "wins", does not give in
AG's Strategies	Each must compromise	AG "loses"
Hard Ball	AG "wins", does not give in	ABC & AG have solution imposed from outside
	ABC Loses	Cost of Adversarial proceedings

Payoff Table

		ABC		
		N	HB	
AG	N	(2, 2)	(4, 1)	1 = Most Preferred Outcome
	HB	(1, 4)	(3, 3)	4 = Least Preferred Outcome

Exhibit 10 The 'stakeholder dilemma' game

many managers, lawyers and other professionals in large organizations spend most of their time in some sort of adversarial proceedings with stakeholders? Could not these resources be put to work more productively?

Our managerial processes must make managers "Free to Cooperate," rather than forcing them to play the Stakeholder Dilemma Game. Negotiation must become accepted practice, rather than conflict escalation through formal channels. The "try it, fix it, do it" mentality (Peters and Waterman, 1982) which many companies have used successfully with customers, must be applied to other stakeholder groups. This implies that voluntarism as a basic managerial value must permeate the organization which is successful in managing its relationships with multiple stakeholders.

This philosophy of voluntarism can be summarized in several pre-scriptive propositions which build on successful managerial theories and techniques. These propositions should be taken as tentative statements of a theory which needs much more elaboration, but which are hopefully practical suggestions.

Organizations with high Stakeholder Management Capability design and implement communication processes with multiple stakeholders.

An example of a communication process is the recent formation by some utilities, of Consumer Advisory Panels, whereby the company brings issues which are usually settled in the formal regulatory process to the attention of leaders of consumer advocate groups well in advance of actually filing the rate case. Company executives and consumer leaders can negotiate on the issues of mutual concern and avoid the costly adversarial proceedings of the rate case on a number of issues.

Organizations with high Stakeholder Management Capability explicitly negotiate with stakeholders on critical issues and seek voluntary agreements.

An example of explicit negotiation is AT&T's convening an industry-wide conference of telecommunications executives, academics and consumer leaders over the issue of how to reprice local telephone service to bring it in line with its true costs. The outcomes of such a meeting are multiple and not all have been successful. However, the tenor of negotiation was set, and at least some of the local telephone companies have begun to explicitly follow up and negotiate on issues before the rate case proceedings.

Organizations with high Stakeholder Management Capability generalize the marketing approach to serve multiple stakeholders. Specifically, they overspend on understanding stakeholder needs, use marketing techniques to segment stakeholders to provide a better understanding of their individual needs and use marketing research tools to understand, viz., the multi-attribute nature of most stakeholder groups.

We might define "overspending" as paying extra attention, beyond that warranted by considerations of efficiency, to those groups who are critical for the long term success of the firm. Overspending on stakeholders without whose support the company would fail can make sense in a number of instances. For instance P&G overspends on customers, interviewing several thousand customers a year. AT&T overspends on the attention it pays to the regulatory process, which was for a long time, its major source of revenue. Oil companies should, likewise, consider adopting a conscious policy of overspending on OPEC and government and stakeholder who can convey a positive image to the public. Chemical companies have not overspent on environmentalists, for the most part, with the results being onerous regulations and reputations as "spoilers of the environment."

Organizations with high Stakeholder Management Capability integrate boundary spanners into the strategic formulation processes in the organization.

Many organizations have public relations and public affairs managers who have a good working knowledge of stakeholder concerns, and marketing and production managers who have expertise in the needs of customers and suppliers. However, these managers are not always a part of the strategic planning process. Hence, their expertise is lost. The assumption is that those managers who are rewarded to be sensitive to stakeholder needs are in the best position to represent their interests inside the organization. For this representation to occur successfully, those boundary spanners must have some credibility and some meaningful role to play in the organizational processes.

Organizations with high Stakeholder Management Capability are proactive. They anticipate stakeholder concerns and try to influence the stakeholder environment.

The micro-computer industry is full of firms who practice anticipation as a way of life. These firms, some of them quite small, spend resource trying to "guess" what will best serve the customer in the future and where the market will be. Similarly, large computer manufacturers, should be "guessing" that issues such as "privacy" and "individual freedom" and "computer literacy" will be major concerns as we move to technologies where "1984" is a distinct possibility. Several utilities try to anticipate the concerns of intervenors in their rate cases, and actively seek out those groups which will be critical to try and influence their views.

Organizations with high Stakeholder Management Capability allocate resources in a manner consistent with stakeholder concerns.

Emshoff (1980) tells of analyzing the stakeholders in a large international firm and ranking the stakeholders in order of importance. A rough check was also made of how the firm's resources were allocated to deal with those groups who would be most important in the future. The results of his investigation were that almost no resources were being allocated to deal with those groups felt to be absolutely critical to the future success of the company. Many executives are not reticent to play "Blame the Stakeholder," yet are not willing to devote resources to changing a particular stakeholder's point of view.

Managers in organizations with high Stakeholder Management Capability think in "stakeholder-serving" terms.

Just as many successful companies think in terms of "how to serve the customer" or "how to serve the employees," it is possible to generalize this philosophy to "how to serve my stakeholders." The "reason for being" for most organizations is that they serve some need in their external environment. When an organization loses its sense of purpose and mission, when it focuses itself internally on the needs of its managers, it is in danger of becoming irrelevant. Someone else (if competition is possible) will serve the environmental need better. The more we can begin to think in terms of how to better serve stakeholders, the more likely we will be to survive and prosper over time.

Summary

The purpose of this chapter has been to explicate the stakeholder management framework and philosophy in general terms. I have shown that the three levels of analysis, rational, process and transactional must be consistent if the stakeholder concept is to make a difference in the way that organizations are managed. I have offered a brief sketch of the principles of voluntarism which I believe must go hand in hand with the application of the stakeholder concept to strategic management processes.

Notes

1   The ideas presented in this chapter form part of a paper, "Managing Stakeholders: One Key to Successful Adaptation", presented to the Academy of Management National Meeting in August 1982. I wish to thank the participants in the symposium on managing adaptation, and its chairperson, Professor Bala Chakravarthy, for many helpful comments. In addition, several Faculty members at the University of Pittsburgh's Graduate School of Management and Rutgers University's Department of Management have made helpful comments. In particular Barry Mitnick and Aubrey Mendelow have been encouraging over the past year.

2   See Schendel and Hofer (1979) for a collection of essays that catalog the development of strategic management. Freeman (1983) is an overview of how the stakeholder concept fits into the development of strategic management theory, as well as a conceptual history of the term, "stakeholder."

3   My use of "rational," "process" and "transactional" parallels Graham Allison's (1971) three levels of organizational analysis. However, the three levels are not mutually exclusive as is often interpreted from Allison's account. Each level of analysis offers a different "lens" for viewing the organization and offers different kinds of explanation for some underlying phenomena broadly called "organization behavior." While the explanations at each level need not be identical, they do need to be consistent. Hence, the concept of "fit" among the three levels. The application of this three-leveled conceptual scheme is not unique to the stakeholder concept, as it is conceivable that we could define the process and transactional levels to complement a "portfolio approach" to strategic management.

4   Chakravarthy (1981) defines a similar concept of the adaptive capabilities of an organization using "management capability" and "organization capability."

5   For instance, as in a clinical case study, viz., Emshoff and Freeman's (1981) analysis of the brewing industry around the issue of beverage container legislation or an in-depth historical study as per Miles (1982) of tobacco companies.

6   The point here is that any theory must explicitly define the range of entities over which the propositions in the theory range. Sometimes it is convenient to speak of "stakeholders" as referring to categories, or sets, of specific groups. But, I insist that, strictly speaking, it is specific groups and individuals which are real, and hence, which can be strictly said to "hold stakes." For a philosophical treatment of the rather nominalistic position taken here see Nelson Goodman (1955).

7   The literature on interorganizational relations is quite enormous and is rich in insights for strategic management. Evan (1976), Negandhi (1975), Nystrom and Starbuck (1981) are excellent collections of articles, each of which contains review articles which summarize the state of the art.

8   See Miles' (1982) analysis of the tobacco industry, and Wilson (1981) for analyses of coalitions among interest groups.

9   For a discussion of this grid in the context of corporate governance see Freeman and Reed (1983).

10 The approach to "power" outlined here is quite simplistic, and should be viewed as illustrative rather than definitive. Pfeffer (1981) is suggestive of a more comprehensive analysis of the concept which could be applied to the "power and stakes" grid.

11 For an interesting distinction between economic and political explanations see the work of Hirschman (1970; 1981).

12 For a more complete discussion of portfolio theory see Abell (1980), Rothschild (1976), Lorange (1980), and the literature referenced in these works.

13 The critique of portfolio theory surfaced here is quite general in that it applies equally well to "misuses" of other processes. The point is that the processes must be capable of "fitting" with the other levels of analysis. They must describe the world as it is, and must prescribe transactions that are consistent with such a description.

14 See Schendel and Hofer (1979) for several review articles on the state of the art in environmental scanning.

15 Lorange (1980) explores the communications aspects of strategic management, and recommends a 3×3 matrix to diagram such processes.

16 See Freeman (1983) for an analysis of "what do we stand for" and the relationship of enterprise-level strategy to the stakeholder concept and managerial values.

17 Emery and Trist (1965), Pfeffer and Salancik (1978) and many others have looked at the transactional level of organizations. Van de Ven, Emmett and Koenig (1975) describe several different models of transactions.

18 Interview with Professor Currin Shields, University of Arizona, and past President of the Conference of Consumer Organizations, a national consortium of local consumer advocate organizations.

19 The structure of the payoffs of the game outlined here presupposes that the issue is vague enough for there not to be a "clearly optimal" solution, but that a solution which is mutually acceptable is possible, and further that this mutually acceptable solution is preferable by both parties to a solution which is imposed by external parties, such as government.

20 There is a vast literature on the Prisoners' Dilemma, however, a clear discussion of the game can be found in Luce and Raiffa (1957). The game described here is similar to the plight of wheat farmers that is taught in every introductory economics class and chronicled by Garrett Hardin in the "Tragedy of the Commons."

21 I am not claiming that every game that a corporation plays with stakeholders is a Prisoners' Dilemma game, but only that some interactions are Prisoners' Dilemmas. The use of game theory in strategic management, as an explanatory tool, is a long-neglected research issue. McDonald (1977) is one source. Recent work in applying game theory at the conceptual level can be found in Brams (1981) and Muzzio (1982). Both of these works by political scientists yield interesting insights into the workings of individuals in organizations.

References

Abell, D. (1980) *Defining the Business*, Englewood Cliffs: Prentice Hall, Inc.

Allison, G. (1971) *Essence of Decision*, Boston: Little Brown.

Brams, S. (1981) *Biblical Games*, Cambridge: MIT Press.

Chakravarthy, B. (1981) *Managing Coal*, Albany: SUNY Press.

Charan, R. (1982) 'The Strategic Review Process', *The Journal of Business Strategy* 2(4): 50–60.

Dill, W. (1975) 'Public Participation in Corporate Planning: Strategic Management in a Kibitzer's World', *Long Range Planning* 8(1): 57–63.

Emery, F. and Trist, E. (1965) 'The Causal Texture of Organizational Environments', *Human Relations* 18: 21–31.

Emshoff, J. (1980) *Managerial Breakthroughs*, New York: AMACOM.

Emshoff, J. and Freeman, E. (1979) 'Who's Butting Into Your Business', *The Wharton Magazine* 1: 44–48, 58–59.

Emshoff, J. and Freeman, E. (1981) 'Stakeholder Management: A Case Study of the U.S. Brewers and the Container Issue', *Applications of Management Science*, Volume 1, 57–90.

Evan, W. (1966) 'The Organization Set: Toward a Theory of Inter-Organizational Relations', in J. Thompson, (ed.) *Approaches to Organizational Design*, Pittsburgh: University of Pittsburgh Press, pp. 175–190; also in W. Evan (1976) *Organization Theory: Structures, Systems, and Environments*, New York: John Wiley & Sons.

Evan, W. (1976) *Organization Theory: Structures, Systems, and Environments*, New York: John Wiley & Sons.

Freeman, R. (1983) 'Strategic Management: A Stakeholder Approach', in R. Lamb (ed.) *Advances in Strategic Management*, Vol. 1, Greenwich: JAI Press, pp. 31–60.

Freeman, R. and Reed, D. (1983) 'Stockholders and Stakeholders: A New Perspective on Corporate Governance', in C. Huizinga (ed.) *Corporate Governance: A Definitive Exploration of the Issues*, Los Angeles: University Press.

Goodman, N. (1955) *Fact, Fiction, and Forecast*, New York: Bobbs Merrill Co.

Hirschman, A. (1970) *Exit, Voice and Loyalty*, Cambridge, MA: Harvard University Press.

Hirschman, A. (1981) *Essays in Trespassing*, Cambridge: Cambridge University Press.

Lorange, P. (1980) *Corporate Planning: An Executive Viewpoint*, Englewood Cliffs: Prentice Hall, Inc.

Luce, D. and Raiffa, H. (1957) *Games and Decisions*, New York: John Wiley & Sons.

McDonald, J. (1977) *The Game of Business*, New York: Anchor Press.

MacMillan, I. (1978) *Strategy Formulation: Political Concepts*, St Paul: West Publishing Co.

Merton, R. (1957) *Social Theory and Social Structure*, Glencoe: The Free Press.

Miles, R. (1982) *Coffin Nails and Corporate Strategies*, Englewood Cliffs: Prentice Hall Inc.

Muzzio, D. (1982) *Watergate Games*, New York: New York University Press.

Negandhi, A. (ed.) (1975) *Interorganization Theory*, Canton: The Kent State University Press.

Nystrom, P. and Starbuck, W. (eds) (1981) *Handbook of Organizational Design*, Volumes 1 and 2, New York: Oxford University Press.

Ouchi, W. (1981) *Theory Z*, Reading: Addison Wesley.

Pascale, R. and Athos, A. (1981) *The Art of Japanese Management*, New York: Simon & Schuster.

Peters, T. and Waterman, R. (1982) *Searching for Excellence*, New York: Harper & Row.

Pfeffer, J. (1981) *Power in Organizations*, Marshfield: Pitman Publishing Inc.

Pfeffer, J. and Salancik, G. (1978) *The External Control of Organizations*, New York: Harper & Row.

Rothschild, W. (1976) *Putting It All Together*, New York: AMACOM.

Schendel, D. and Hofer, C. (eds) (1979) *Strategic Management: A New View of Business Policy and Planning*, Boston: Little, Brown.

Van de Ven, A., Emmett, D. and Koenig, R. (1975) 'Frameworks for Interorganizational Analysis', in A. Negandhi, *Interorganization Theory*, pp. 19–38, Canton: The Kent State University Press.

Wilson, G. (1981) *Interest Groups in the United States*, New York: Oxford University Press.

TOWARD A THEORY OF STAKEHOLDER IDENTIFICATION AND SALIENCE: DEFINING THE PRINCIPLE OF WHO AND WHAT REALLY COUNTS

R. K. Mitchell, B. R. Agle and D. J. Wood

Since Freeman (1984) published his landmark book, *Strategic Management: A Stakeholder Approach*, the concept of "stakeholders" has become embedded in management scholarship and in managers' thinking. Yet, as popular as the term has become and as richly descriptive as it is, there is no agreement on what Freeman (1994) calls "The Principle of Who or What Really Counts." That is, who (or what) are the stakeholders of the firm? And to whom (or what) do managers pay attention? The first question calls for a *normative theory of stakeholder identification*, to explain logically why managers should consider certain classes of entities as stakeholders. The second question calls for a *descriptive theory of stakeholder salience*, to explain the conditions under which managers do consider certain classes of entities as stakeholders.

Stakeholder theory, reviewed in this article, offers a maddening variety of signals on how questions of stakeholder identification might be answered. We will see stakeholders identified as primary or secondary stakeholders; as owners and nonowners of the firm; as owners of capital or owners of less tangible assets; as actors or those acted upon; as those existing in a voluntary or an involuntary relationship with the firm; as rights-holders, contractors, or moral claimants; as resource providers to or dependents of the firm; as risk-takers or influencers; and as legal principals to whom agent-managers bear a fiduciary duty. In the stakeholder literature there are a few broad definitions that attempt to specify the empirical reality that virtually anyone can affect or be affected by an organization's actions. What is needed is a theory of stakeholder identification that can reliably separate stakeholders from nonstakeholders.

Also in the stakeholder literature are a number of narrow definitions that attempt to specify the pragmatic reality that managers simply cannot attend to all actual or potential claims, and that propose a variety of priorities for managerial attention. In this article we suggest that the question of stakeholder salience—the degree to which managers give priority to competing stakeholder claims—goes beyond the question of stakeholder identification, because the dynamics inherent in each relationship involve complex considerations that are not readily explained by the stakeholder framework as it currently stands. What is needed also is a theory of stakeholder salience that can explain to whom and to what managers actually pay attention.

Among the various ways of identifying stakeholders, as well as in the agency, behavioral, ecological, institutional, resource dependence, and transaction cost theories of the firm, we have found no single attribute within a given theory that can guide us reliably on these issues. However, we find that one can extract from these literatures the idea that just a few attributes can be used to identify different classes of stakeholders in a firm's environment. We begin our analysis with Freeman's definition of stakeholder—"any group or individual who can affect or is affected by the achievement of the organization's objectives" (1984: 46)—and develop a theory of stakeholder identification drawn from these various theoretical literatures. We start with a broad definition so that no stakeholders, potential or actual, are excluded from analysis arbitrarily or a priori. We then propose that classes of stakeholders can be identified by their possession or attributed possession of one, two, or all three of the following attributes: (1) the stakeholder's *power* to influence the firm, (2) the *legitimacy* of the stakeholder's relationship with the firm, and (3) the *urgency* of the stakeholder's claim on the firm. This theory produces a comprehensive typology of stakeholders based on the normative assumption that these variables define the field of stakeholders: those entities to whom managers should pay attention.

Building upon this typology, we further propose a theory of stakeholder salience. In this theory we suggest a dynamic model, based upon the identification typology, that permits the explicit recognition of situational uniqueness and managerial perception to explain how managers prioritize stakeholder relationships. We demonstrate how the identification typology allows predictions to be made about managerial behavior with respect to each class of stakeholder, as well as predictions about how stakeholders change from one class to another and what this means to managers. In the theory of stakeholder salience, we do not argue that managers should pay attention to this or that class of stakeholders. Rather, we argue that to achieve certain ends, or because of perceptual factors, managers do pay certain kinds of attention to certain kinds of stakeholders. Knowing what types of stakeholders actually exist, which our identification typology facilitates, and why managers respond to them the way they do, which our notion of salience clarifies, sets the stage for future work in stakeholder theory that specifies how and under what circumstances managers can and should respond to various stakeholder types.

The argument proceeds as follows. First, we review the stakeholder literature, laying out the various explicit and implicit positions on "The Principle of Who or What Really Counts." We then present our defense of the three key attributes—power, legitimacy, and urgency—as identifiers of stakeholder classes and briefly examine the major organizational theories to discern how they handle these three crucial variables. Next we introduce managers and salience into the discussion and present our analysis of the stakeholder classes that result from possession of one, two, or three of these attributes, giving special attention to the managerial implications of the existence and salience of each stakeholder class. Finally, we further illustrate the theory's dynamic qualities by showing how stakeholders can shift from one class to another, with important consequences for managers and the firm itself, and we explore the research questions and directions that emerge from the theory.

STAKEHOLDER THEORY—STATE OF THE ART

For more than a decade the stakeholder approach to understanding the firm in its environment has been a powerful heuristic device, intended to broaden management's vision of its roles and responsibilities beyond the profit maximization function to include interests and claims of nonstockholding groups. Stakeholder *theory*, in contrast, attempts to articulate a fundamental question in a systematic way: which groups are stakeholders deserving or requiring management attention, and which are not? In this section we examine how scholars have so far answered these central questions. Who is a stakeholder, and what is a stake? What does stakeholder theory offer that is not found in other theories of the firm?

Who Is a Stakeholder, and What Is a Stake?

There is not much disagreement on *what kind of entity* can be a stakeholder. Persons, groups, neighborhoods, organizations, institutions, societies, and even the natural environment are generally thought to qualify as actual or potential stakeholders. We find that it is the view taken about the existence and nature of the stake that presents an area of argument, because it is upon the basis of "stake" that "what counts" is ultimately decided.

Early vagueness in definition

In an early statement Jones defined corporate social responsibility as "the notion that corporations have an obligation to constituent groups in society other than stockholders and beyond that prescribed by law or union contract, indicating that a stake may go beyond mere ownership" (1980: 59–60). He then asked the pragmatic questions stakeholder theory still seeks to answer: "What are these groups? How many of these groups must be served? Which of their interests are most important? How can their interests be balanced? How much corporate money should be allotted to serve these interests?" (1980: 60).

These questions are still being explored in stakeholder literature and management thinking. Alkhafaji, for example, defines stakeholders as "groups to whom the corporation is responsible" (1989: 36). Thompson, Wartick, and Smith define stakeholders as groups "in relationship with an organization" (1991: 209). Most scholars, however, have attempted to specify a more concrete stakeholder definition, albeit with limited success.

Broad or narrow view?

Windsor (1992) correctly points out that stakeholder theorists differ considerably on whether they take a broad or narrow view of a firm's stakeholder universe. Freeman and Reed (1983) recognized early on that there would be serious differences of opinion about broad versus narrow definitions of "Who or What Really Counts." Their broad definition of a stakeholder as an individual or group who "can affect the achievement of an organization's objectives or who is affected by the achievement of an organization's objectives" (1983: 91) is virtually identical to Freeman's (1984) definition. And their narrow definition reverted to the language of the Stanford Research Institute (1963), defining stakeholders as those groups "on which the organization is dependent for its continued survival" (1983: 91).

Freeman's now-classic definition is this: "A stakeholder in an organization is (by definition) any group or individual who can affect or is affected by the achievement of the organization's objectives" (1984: 46). This is certainly one of the broadest definitions in the literature, for it leaves the notion of stake and the field of possible stakeholders unambiguously open to include virtually anyone. In this definition the basis of the stake can be unidirectional or bidirectional—"can affect or is affected by"—and there is no implication or necessity of reciprocal impact, as definitions involving relationships, transactions, or contracts require. Excluded from having a stake are only those who cannot affect the firm (have no power) and are not affected by it (have no claim or relationship).

In contrast, Clarkson offers one of the narrower definitions of stakeholders as voluntary or involuntary risk-bearers: "Voluntary stakeholders bear some form of risk as a result of having invested some form of capital, human or financial, something of value, in a firm. Involuntary stakeholders are placed at risk as a result of a firm's activities. But without the element of risk there is no stake" (1994: 5). A stake, in this sense, is only something that can be lost. The use of risk to denote stake appears to be a way to narrow the stakeholder field to those with *legitimate claims*, regardless of their power to influence the firm or the legitimacy of their relationship to the firm. This search for legitimacy, we argue later, is necessary to understand fully a firm's stakeholder environment, but it also can be a powerful blinder to the real impact of stakeholder power and claim urgency. We argue, in contrast to the position of all those who appear to focus primarily on legitimacy, that this narrower view captures only one key attribute of stakeholder salience to managers.

Between the broad and narrow are many other efforts to define what constitutes a stakeholder. The range of definitions as it has developed chronologically appears in Table 4.2.

Table 4.2: Who is a stakeholder? A chronology

Source	Stake
Stanford memo, 1963	"those groups without whose support the organization would cease to exist" (cited in Freeman & Reed, 1983, and Freeman, 1984)
Rhenman, 1964	"are depending on the firm in order to achieve their personal goals and on whom the firm is depending for its existence" (cited in Näsi, 1995)
Ahlstedt & Jahnukainen, 1971	"driven by their own interests and goals are participants in a firm, and thus depending on it and whom for its sake the firm is depending" (cited in Näsi, 1995)
Freeman & Reed, 1983: 91	Wide: "can affect the achievement of an organization's objectives or who is affected by the achievement of an organization's objectives" Narrow: "on which the organization is dependent for its continued survival"
Freeman, 1984: 46	"can affect or is affected by the achievement of the organization's objectives"
Freeman & Gilbert, 1987: 397	"can affect or is affected by a business"
Cornell & Shapiro, 1987: 5	"claimants" who have "contracts"
Evan & Freeman, 1988: 75–76	"have a stake in or claim on the firm"
Evan & Freeman, 1988: 79	"benefit from or are harmed by, and whose rights are violated or respected by, corporate actions"
Bowie, 1988: 112, n. 2	"without whose support the organization would cease to exist"
Alkhafaji, 1989: 36	"groups to whom the corporation is responsible"
Carroll, 1989: 57	"asserts to have one or more of these kinds of stakes"– "ranging from an interest to a right (legal or moral) to ownership or legal title to the company's assets or property"
Freeman & Evan, 1990	contract holders
Thompson et al., 1991: 209	in "relationship with an organization"
Savage et al., 1991: 61	"have an interest in the actions of an organization and . . . the ability to influence it"
Hill & Jones, 1992: 133	"constituents who have a legitimate claim on the firm . . . established through the existence of an exchange relationship" who supply "the firm with critical resources (contributions) and in exchange each expects its interests to be satisfied (by inducements)"
Brenner, 1993: 205	"having some legitimate, non-trivial relationship with an organization [such as] exchange transactions, action impacts, and moral responsibilities"

Table 4.2: Continued

Source	Stake
Carroll, 1993: 60	"asserts to have one or more of the kinds of stakes in business–may be affected or affect . . ."
Freeman, 1994: 415	participants in "the human process of joint value creation"
Wicks et al., 1994: 483	"interact with and give meaning and definition to the corporation"
Langtry, 1994: 433	the firm is significantly responsible for their well-being, or they hold a moral or legal claim on the firm
Starik, 1994: 90	"can and are making their actual stakes known"–"are or might be influenced by, or are or potentially are influencers of, some organization"
Clarkson, 1994: 5	"bear some form of risk as a result of having invested some form of capital, human or financial, something of value, in a firm" or "are placed at risk as a result of a firm's activities"
Clarkson, 1995: 106	"have, or claim, ownership, rights, or interests in a corporation and its activities"
Näsi, 1995: 19	"interact with the firm and thus make its operation possible"
Brenner, 1995: 76, n. I	"are or which could impact or be impacted by the firm/organization"
Donaldson & Preston, 1995: 85	"persons or groups with legitimate interests in procedural and/or substantive aspects of corporate activity"

Major differences between broad and narrow views

Narrow views of stakeholders are based on the practical reality of limited resources, limited time and attention, and limited patience of managers for dealing with external constraints. In general, narrow views of stakeholders attempt to define relevant groups in terms of their *direct relevance to the firm's core economic interests*. For example, several scholars define stakeholders in terms of their necessity for the firm's survival (Bowie, 1988; Freeman & Reed, 1983; Näsi, 1995); as noted, Clarkson (1995) defines stakeholders as those who have placed something at risk in relationship with the firm, whereas Freeman and Evan (1990), Hill and Jones (1992), and Cornell and Shapiro (1987) speak of stakeholders as contractors or participants in exchange relationships.

A few scholars narrow the field of relevant groups in terms of their *moral claims*, arguing that the essence of stakeholder management should be the firm's participation in creating and sustaining moral relationships (Freeman, 1994; Wicks, Gilbert, & Freeman, 1994), or the firm's fulfilling its affirmative duty to stakeholders in terms of fairly distributing the harms and benefits of the firm's actions (Donaldson & Preston, 1995; Evan & Freeman,

1988; Langtry, 1994). In any case, we see those favoring a narrow definition of stakeholders as searching for a "normative core" of legitimacy so that managers can be advised to focus on the claims of a few legitimate stakeholders.

The broad view of stakeholders, in contrast, is based on the empirical reality that companies can indeed be vitally affected by, or they can vitally affect, almost anyone. But it is bewilderingly complex for managers to apply. The idea of comprehensively identifying stakeholder types, then, is to equip managers with the ability to recognize and respond effectively to a disparate, yet systematically comprehensible, set of entities who may or may not have legitimate claims, but who may be able to affect or are affected by the firm nonetheless, and thus affect the interests of those who do have legitimate claims.

The ultimate aim of stakeholder management practices, according to this view, could be firm centered or system centered; that is, managers might want to know about all of their stakeholders for firm-centered purposes of survival, economic well-being, damage control, taking advantage of opportunities, "doing in" the competition, winning friends and influencing public policy, coalition building, and so forth. Or, in contrast, managers might want an exhaustive list of all stakeholders in order to participate in a fair balancing of various claims and interests within the firm's social system. Both the former public affairs approach and the latter social responsibility approach require broad knowledge of actual and potential actors and claimants in the firm's environment.

Claimants versus influencers

In order to clarify the term "stake," we need to differentiate between groups that have a legal, moral, or presumed claim on the firm and groups that have an ability to influence the firm's behavior, direction, process, or outcomes. Savage, Nix, Whitehead, and Blair (1991) consider two attributes to be necessary to identify a stakeholder: (1) a claim and (2) the ability to influence a firm. Brenner (1993) and Starik (1994), however, pose these attributes as either/or components of the definition of those with a stake.

In our view this is a muddled set, confusing and contrasting two of the three criteria we see as important. Influencers have power over the firm, whether or not they have valid claims or any claims at all and whether or not they wish to press their claims. Claimants may have legitimate claims or illegitimate ones, and they may or may not have any power to influence the firm. Power and legitimacy are different, sometimes overlapping dimensions, and each can exist without the other. A theory of stakeholder identification must accommodate these differences.

Actual versus potential relationship

Another crucial question leading to the comprehensibility of the term "stake" is whether an entity can be a stakeholder without being in actual relationship with the firm. Some scholars (e.g., Ring, 1994) emphatically answer, "No." We argue that, on the contrary, the *potential* relationship can be as relevant as the actual one. Clarkson's (1994) idea of involuntary stakeholders as those with something not willfully placed at risk addresses the potentiality issue somewhat. Starik quite clearly includes potential when he refers to stakeholders as those who "are or might be influenced by, or are or potentially are influencers of, some organization" (1994: 90). We suggest that a theory of stakeholder identification and salience must somehow account for *latent* stakeholders if it is to be both comprehensive and useful, because such identification can, at a minimum, help organizations avoid problems and perhaps even enhance effectiveness.

Power, dependence, and reciprocity in relationships

If the firm and a stakeholder have a relationship, what is the nature of that relationship? The literature offers a confusing jumble of answers to this question, but most answers use a power-dependence frame of some sort. As Table 4.3 shows, some definitions focus on the firm's dependency on stakeholders for its survival; some focus on the stakeholder's dependency on the firm for upholding its rights, minimizing harms, or achieving its interest; and some focus on the mutuality of power-dependence relations (although, interestingly, we found no definition that emphasized mutual power, and only two from Scandinavia that emphasized mutual dependence).

As shown, a broad-view sorting of stakeholders along previously defined dimensions is still somewhat overwhelming.

Sorting criteria

Thus, although Freeman's (1984) definition is widely cited in the literature, it is not accepted universally among scholars working in the stakeholder minefields. Narrowing the range of stakeholders requires applying some acceptable and justifiable sorting criteria to the field of possibilities. Some additional approaches are relationship based, built on acknowledged transactional conditions, such as the existence of a legal or implied contract, an exchange relationship, or an identifiable power-dependence relationship. Others are claim based, citing the existence or attribution of a legal or moral right, a real or attributed benefit or harm, or merely an interest.

Overall, the information in Table 4.3 suggests that scholars who attempt to narrow the definition of stakeholder emphasize the *claim's legitimacy* based upon contract, exchange, legal title, legal right, moral right, at-risk status, or moral interest in the harms and benefits generated by company actions and that, in contrast, scholars who favor a broad definition emphasize the *stakeholder's power* to influence the firm's behavior, whether or not there are legitimate claims. As a bridging concept, we argue that the broad concept of stakeholder management must be better defined in order to serve the narrower interests of legitimate stakeholders. Otherwise, influencing groups

Table 4.3: A sorting of rationales for stakeholder identification

---

A Relationship Exists

The firm and stakeholder are in relationship:
Thompson et al., 1991: 209–in "relationship with an organization"
Brenner, 1993: 205–"having some legitimate, non-trivial relationship with an organization [such as] exchange transactions, action impacts, and moral responsibilities"
Freeman, 1994: 415–participants in "the human process of joint value creation"
Wicks et al., 1994: 483–"interact with and give meaning and definition to the corporation"

The stakeholder exercises voice with respect to the firm:
Starik, 1994: 90–"can and are making their actual stakes known"–"are or might be influenced by, or are or potentially are influencers of, some organization"

Power Dependence: Stakeholder Dominant

The firm is dependent on the stakeholder:
Stanford memo, 1963–"those groups without whose support the organization would cease to exist" (cited in Freeman & Reed, 1983, and Freeman, 1984)
Freeman & Reed, 1983: 91–Narrow: "on which the organization is dependent for its continued survival"
Bowie, 1988: 112, n. 2–"without whose support the organization would cease to exist"
Näsi, 1995: 19–"interact with the firm and thus make its operation possible"

The stakeholder has power over the firm:
Freeman, 1984: 46–"can affect or is affected by the achievement of the organization's objectives"
Freeman & Gilbert, 1987: 397–"can affect or is affected by a business"
Savage et al., 1991: 61–"have an interest in the actions of an organization and . . . the ability to influence it"
Carroll, 1993: 60–"asserts to have one or more of the kinds of stakes in business"–may be affected or affect . . .
Starik, 1994: 90–"can and are making their actual stakes known"–"are or might be influenced by, or are or potentially are influencers of, some organization"
Brenner, 1995: 76, n. 1–"are or which could impact or be impacted by the firm/organization"

Power Dependence: Firm Dominant

The stakeholder is dependent on the firm:
Langtry, 1994: 433–the firm is significantly responsible for their well-being, or they hold a moral or legal claim on the firm

The firm has power over the stakeholder:
Freeman & Reed, 1983: 91–Wide: "can affect the achievement of an organization's objectives or who is affected by the achievement of an organization's objectives"
Freeman, 1984: 46–"can affect or is affected by the achievement of the organization's objectives"
Freeman & Gilbert, 1987: 397–"can affect or is affected by a business"
Carroll, 1993: 60–"asserts to have one or more of the kinds of stakes in business"–"may be affected or affect . . ."
Starik, 1994: 90–"can and are making their actual stakes known"–"are or might be influenced by, or are or potentially are influencers of, some organization"
Brenner, 1995: 76, n. 1.–"are or which could impact or be impacted by the firm/organization"

Table 4.3: Continued

Mutual Power-Dependence Relationship

The firm and stakeholder are mutually dependent:
Rhenman, 1964–"are depending on the firm in order to achieve their personal goals and on whom the firm is depending for its existence" (cited in Näsi, 1995)
Ahlstedt & Jahnukainen, 1971–"driven by their own interests and goals are participants in a firm, and thus depending on it and whom for its sake the firm is depending" (cited in Näsi, 1995)

Basis for Legitimacy of Relationship

The firm and stakeholder are in contractual relationship:
Cornell & Shapiro, 1987: 5–"claimants" who have "contracts"
Carroll, 1989: 57–"asserts to have one or more of these kinds of stakes"–"ranging from an interest to a right (legal or moral) to ownership or legal title to the company's assets or property"
Freeman & Evan, 1990–contract holders
Hill & Jones, 1992: 133–"constituents who have a legitimate claim on the firm . . . established through the existence of an exchange relationship" who supply "the firm with critical resources (contributions) and in exchange each expects its interests to be satisfied (by inducements)"

The stakeholder has a claim on the firm:
Evan & Freeman, 1988: 75–76–"have a stake in or claim on the firm"
Alkhafaji, 1989: 36–"groups to whom the corporation is responsible"
Carroll, 1989: 57–"asserts to have one or more of these kinds of stakes"–"ranging from an interest to a right (legal or moral) to ownership or legal title to the company's assets or property"
Hill & Jones, 1992: 133–"constituents who have a legitimate claim on the firm . . . established through the existence of an exchange relationship" who supply "the firm with critical resources (contributions) and in exchange each expects its interests to be satisfied (by inducements)"
Langtry, 1994: 433–the firm is significantly responsible for their well-being, or they hold a moral or legal claim on the firm
Clarkson, 1995: 106–"have, or claim, ownership, rights, or interests in a corporation and its activities"

The stakeholder has something at risk:
Clarkson, 1994: 5–"bear some form of risk as a result of having invested some form of capital, human or financial, something of value, in a firm" or "are placed at risk as a result of a firm's activities"

The stakeholder has a moral claim on the firm:
Evan & Freeman, 1988: 79–"benefit from or are harmed by, and whose rights are violated or respected by, corporate actions"
Carroll, 1989: 57–"asserts to have one or more of these kinds of stakes"–"ranging from an interest to a right (legal or moral) to ownership or legal title to the company's assets or property"
Langtry, 1994: 433–the firm is significantly responsible for their well-being, or they hold a moral or legal claim on the firm
Clarkson, 1995: 106–"have, or claim, ownership, rights, or interests in a corporation and its activities"

Table 4.3: Continued

Donaldson & Preston, 1995: 85–"identified through the actual or potential harms and benefits that they experience or anticipate experiencing as a result of the firm's actions or inactions"

Stakeholder Interests–Legitimacy Not Implied

The stakeholder has an interest in the firm:
Carroll, 1989: 57–"asserts to have one or more of these kinds of stakes"–"ranging from an interest to a right (legal or moral) to ownership or legal title to the company's assets or property"
Savage et al., 1991: 61–"have an interest in the actions of an organization and . . . have the ability to influence it"
Carroll, 1993: 60–"asserts to have one or more of the kinds of stakes in business"–may be affected or affect . . .
Clarkson, 1995: 106–"have, or claim, ownership, rights, or interests in a corporation and its activities"

with power over the firm can disrupt operations so severely that legitimate claims cannot be met and the firm may not survive. Yet, at the same time, it is important to recognize the legitimacy of some claims over others. Power and legitimacy, then, are necessarily core attributes of a comprehensive stakeholder identification model. We argue that when these attributes are evaluated in light of the compelling demands of urgency, a systematic, comprehensible, and dynamic model is the result.

What Added Value Does a Theory of Stakeholder Identification Offer?

As we see from the preceding discussion of the stakeholder literature, one can extract just a few attributes to identify different classes of stakeholders that are salient to managers in certain respects. We also can see that stakeholder power and legitimacy of the claim frequently are treated as competing explanations of stakeholder status, when instead they are partially intersecting variables. Interestingly, this conceptual competition between power and legitimacy is reflected in virtually every major theory of the firm – particularly in agency, behavioral, institutional, population ecology, resource dependence, and transaction cost theories. This state-of-the-field provides an opportunity for a theory of stakeholder identification to move us forward by showing how power and legitimacy interact and, when combined with urgency, create different types of stakeholders with different expected behavioral patterns regarding the firm.

Agency, resource dependence, and transaction cost theories are particularly helpful in explaining why power plays such an important role in the attention managers give to stakeholders. The central problem agency theory addresses is how principals can control the behavior of their agents to achieve their, rather than the agents', interests. The power of agents to act in ways divergent from the interests of principals may be limited by use of incentives or monitoring (Jensen & Meckling, 1976), so that managers are expected to attend to those stakeholders having the power to reward and/or punish them. Resource dependence theory suggests that power accrues to those who control resources needed by the organization, creating power differentials among parties (Pfeffer, 1981), and it confirms that the possession of resource power makes a stakeholder important to managers. Transaction cost theory proposes that the power accruing to economic actors with small numbers bargaining advantages will affect the nature of firm governance and structure (Williamson, 1975, 1985). That is, stakeholders outside the firm boundary who participate in a very small competitive set can increase transaction costs to levels that justify their absorption into the firm, where the costs of hierarchy are lower than the transaction costs of market failure—a clear indication of their significance to managers (Jones & Hill, 1988).

These three organizational theories teach us why power is a crucial variable in a theory of stakeholder-manager relations. But, as previously noted, power alone does not help us to fully understand salience in the stakeholder-manager relationship. There remain stakeholders who do not have power, but who nevertheless matter to firms and managers. Other means to identify "Who or What Really Counts" are needed.

Organizational theories with an open-system orientation (Scott, 1987), including institutional and population ecology theories, help us to understand the crucial effects of the environment upon organizations, but they are less helpful when it comes to understanding power in stakeholder-manager relationships. In both theories organizational legitimacy is linked closely with survival (see Meyer & Rowan, 1977, and Carroll & Hannan, 1989, respectively). In the socially constructed world within which managers engage stakeholders, these two theories suggest that "legitimate" stakeholders are the ones who "really count." Under institutional theory, "illegitimacy" results in isomorphic pressures on organizations that operate outside of accepted norms (DiMaggio & Powell, 1983). Under population ecology theory, lack of legitimacy results in organizational mortality (Carroll & Hannan, 1989). According to these two theories, legitimacy figures heavily in helping us to identify stakeholders that merit managerial attention. However, emphasizing legitimacy and ignoring power leave major gaps in a stakeholder identification scheme, because some legitimate stakeholders have no influence.

A final attribute that profoundly influences managerial perception and attention, although not the primary feature of any particular organizational theory, is implicit in each. Agency theory treats this attribute in terms of its contribution to cost, as does transaction cost theory. Behavioral theory (Cyert & March, 1963) treats it as a consequence of unmet "aspirations." Institutional, resource dependence, and population ecology theories treat it in terms of outside pressures on the firm. This attribute is *urgency*, the degree to which stakeholder claims call for immediate attention. Whether dealing with the prevention of losses, the pursuit of goals, or selection pressures, one constant in the stakeholder-manager relationship is the attention-getting capacity of the urgent claim. Urgency, as we discuss below, adds a catalytic component to a theory of stakeholder identification, for urgency demands attention.

In summary, it is clear that no individual organizational theory offers systematic answers to questions about stakeholder identification and salience, although most such theories have much to tell us about the role of power or legitimacy (but not both) in stakeholder-manager relations. Urgency, in contrast, is not a main focus of any organizational theory, but it is critical nonetheless to any theory that purports to identify stakeholders and to explain the degree of attention paid to them by managers. Therefore, we suggest that to better understand "The Principle of Who and What Really Counts," we need to evaluate stakeholder-manager relationships systematically, both actual and potential, in terms of the relative absence or presence of all or some of the attributes: power, legitimacy, and/or urgency.

Defining Stakeholder Attributes

Power

Most current definitions of power derive, at least in part, from the early Weberian idea that power is "the probability that one actor within a social relationship would be in a position to carry out his own will despite resistance" (Weber, 1947). Pfeffer rephrases Dahl's (1957) definition of power as "a relationship among social actors in which one social actor, A, can get another social actor, B, to do something that B would not otherwise have done" (1981: 3). Like Pfeffer and Weber, we concur that "power may be tricky to define, but it is not that difficult to recognize: '[it is] the ability of those who possess power to bring about the outcomes they desire'" (Salancik & Pfeffer, 1974: 3). This leads to the following question: How is power exercized, or, alternatively, what are the bases of power?

French and Raven's (1960) typology of power bases is one framework commonly cited in the organizational literature in answer to this question, but from a sociological perspective it is messy, for there is not a sorting logic at work to create the mutually exclusive and exhaustive categories a true typology requires. Etzioni (1964) suggests a logic for the more precise categorization of power in the organizational setting, based on the type of resource used to exercise power: *coercive* power, based on the physical resources of force, violence, or restraint; *utilitarian* power, based on material or financial resources; and *normative* power, based on symbolic resources.[1]

Therefore, a party to a relationship has power, to the extent it has or can gain access to coercive, utilitarian, or normative means, to impose its will in the relationship. We note, however, that this access to means is a variable, not a steady state, which is one reason why power is transitory: it can be acquired as well as lost.

Legitimacy

It is apparent from our analysis in Table 4.3 that narrow-definition scholars, particularly those seeking a "normative core" for stakeholder theory, are focused almost exclusively on defining the basis of stakeholder legitimacy. Whether or not that core of legitimacy is to be found in something "at risk," or in property rights, in moral claims, or in some other construct, articulations of "The Principle of Who or What Really Counts" generally are legitimacy based.

However, the notion of "legitimacy," loosely referring to socially accepted and expected structures or behaviors, often is coupled implicitly with that of power when people attempt to evaluate the nature of relationships in society. Davis, for example, distinguishes legitimate from illegitimate use of power by declaring, "In the long run, those who do not use power in a manner which society considers responsible will tend to lose it" (1973: 314). Many scholars seeking to define a firm's stakeholders narrowly also make an implicit assumption that legitimate stakeholders are necessarily powerful, when this is not always the case (e.g., minority stockholders in a closely held company), and that powerful stakeholders are necessarily legitimate (e.g., corporate raiders in the eyes of current managers).

Despite this common linkage, we accept Weber's (1947) proposal that legitimacy and power are distinct attributes that can combine to create *authority* (defined by Weber as the legitimate use of power) but that can exist independently as well. An entity may have legitimate standing in society, or it may have a legitimate claim on the firm, but unless it has either power to enforce its will in the relationship or a perception that its claim is urgent, it will not achieve salience for the firm's managers. For this reason we argue that a comprehensive theory of stakeholder salience requires that separate attention be paid to legitimacy as an attribute of stakeholder-manager relations.

Recently, Suchman (1995) has worked to strengthen the conceptual moorings of the notion of legitimacy, building upon Weber's functionalism (1947), Parsons' structural-functional theory (1960), "open systems" theory (Scott, 1987), and institutional theory (DiMaggio & Powell, 1983). The definition that Suchman suggests is broad based and recognizes the evaluative, cognitive, and socially constructed nature of legitimacy. He defines legitimacy as "a generalized perception or assumption that the actions of an entity are desirable, proper, or appropriate within some socially constructed system of norms, values, beliefs, and definitions" (1995: 574).

Although this definition is imprecise and difficult to operationalize, it is representative of sociologically based definitions of legitimacy and contains several descriptions that are useful in our approach to stakeholder identification. Therefore, we accept and utilize Suchman's definition of legitimacy, recognizing that the social system within which legitimacy is attained is a system with multiple levels of analysis, the most common of which are the individual, organizational, and societal (Wood, 1991). This definition implies that legitimacy is a desirable social good, that it is something larger and more shared than a mere self-perception, and that it may be defined and negotiated differently at various levels of social organization.

Urgency

Viewing power and legitimacy as independent variables in stakeholder-manager relationships takes us some distance toward a theory of stakeholder identification and salience, but it does not capture the dynamics of stakeholder-manager interactions. We propose that adding the stakeholder attribute of urgency helps move the model from static to dynamic. "Urgency" is defined by the Merriam-Webster Dictionary as "calling for immediate attention" or "pressing." We believe that urgency, with synonyms including "compelling," "driving," and "imperative," exists only when two conditions are met: (1) when a relationship or claim is of a time-sensitive nature and (2) when that relationship or claim is important or critical to the stakeholder. Thus, similar to Jones' (1993) description of moral intensity as a multidimensional construct, we argue that urgency is based on the following two attributes: (1) time sensitivity—the degree to which managerial delay in attending to the claim or relationship is unacceptable to the stakeholder, and (2) criticality—the importance of the claim or the relationship to the stakeholder. We define urgency as the degree to which stakeholder claims call for immediate attention.

Although it was virtually ignored until now in any explicit sense in the stakeholder literature, the idea of paying attention to various stakeholder relationships in a timely fashion has been a focus of issues management (Wartick & Mahon, 1994) and crisis management scholars for decades. Eyestone (1978) highlighted the speed with which an issue can become salient to a firm, and Cobb and Elder discussed the important role symbols play in creating time urgency: "Symbols such as 'Freedom Now' have an advantage because they connote a specific time commitment to action. If one is attempting to mobilize a public against some outside threat, one must emphasize the rapidity with which the opponent is gaining strength" (1972: 139).

However, although time sensitivity is necessary, it is not sufficient to identify a stakeholder's claim or "manager relationship" as urgent. In addition, the stakeholder must view its claim on the firm or its relationship with the firm as critical or highly important. Some examples of why a stakeholder would view its relationship with the firm as critical include the following:

● ownership—the stakeholder's possession of firm-specific assets, or those assets tied to a firm that cannot be used in a different way without loss of value (Hill & Jones, 1992; Williamson, 1985), making it very costly for the stakeholder to exit the relationship;

- sentiment—as in the case of easily traded stock that is held by generations of owners within a family, regardless of the stock's performance;
- expectation—the stakeholder's anticipation that the firm will continue providing it with something of great value (e.g., compensation and benefits in the case of employees); or
- exposure—the importance the stakeholder attaches to that which is at risk in the relationship with the firm (Clarkson, 1994).

Our theory does not specify why stakeholders assess their relationships with firms as critical. Furthermore, our theory does not attempt to predict the circumstances under which "time will be of the essence." Rather, when both factors are present, our theory captures the resulting multidimensional attribute as *urgency*, juxtaposes it with the attributes of power and legitimacy, and proposes dynamism in the systematic identification of stakeholders.

Additional Features of Stakeholder Attributes

Table 4.4 summarizes the constructs, definitions, and origins of the concepts discussed thus far in the article. To support a dynamic theory of stakeholder identification and salience, however, we need to consider several additional implications of power, legitimacy, and urgency. First, each attribute is a variable, not a steady state, and can change for any particular entity or stakeholder-manager relationship. Second, the existence (or degree present) of each attribute is a matter of multiple perceptions and is a constructed reality rather than an "objective" one. Third, an individual or entity may not be "conscious" of possessing the attribute or, if conscious of possession, may not choose to enact any implied behaviors. These features of stakeholder attributes, summarized below, are important to the theory's dynamism; that is, they provide a preliminary framework for understanding how stakeholders can gain or lose salience to a firm's managers:

1. Stakeholder attributes are variable, not steady state.
2. Stakeholder attributes are socially constructed, not objective, reality.
3. Consciousness and willful exercise may or may not be present.

Thus, with respect to power, for example, access to the means of influencing another entity's behavior is a variable, with both discrete and continuous features. As we argued earlier, power may be coercive, utilitarian, or normative—qualitatively different types that may exist independently or in combination. Each type of power may range from nonexistent to complete. Power is transitory—it can be acquired as well as lost. Further, possession of power does not necessarily imply its actual or intended use, nor does

Table 4.4: Key constructs in the theory of stakeholder indentification and salience

Construct	Definition	Sources
Stakeholder	Any group or individual who can affect or is affected by the achievement of the organization's objectives	Freeman, 1984; Jones, 1995; Kreiner & Bhambri, 1988
Power	A relationship among social actors in which one social actor, A, can get another social actor, B, to do something that B would not have otherwise done	Dahl, 1957; Pfeffer, 1981; Weber, 1947
Bases	Coercive–force/threat Utilitarian–material/incentives Normative–symbolic influences	Etzioni, 1964
Legitimacy	A generalized perception or assumption that the actions of an entity are desirable, proper, or appropriate within some socially constructed system of norms, values, beliefs, definitions	Suchman, 1995; Weber, 1947
Bases	Individual Organizational Societal	Wood, 1991
Urgency	The degree to which stakeholder claims call for immediate attention	Original–builds on the definition from the Merriam-Webster Dictionary
Bases	Time sensitivity–the degree to which managerial delay in attending to the claim or relationship is unacceptable to the stakeholder	Eyestone, 1978; Wartick & Mahon, 1994
	Criticality–the importance of the claim or the relationship to the stakeholder	Original–asset specificity from Hill & Jones, 1992; Williamson, 1985
Salience	The degree to which managers give priority to competing stakeholder claims	Original–builds on the definition from the Merriam-Webster Dictionary

possession of power imply consciousness of such possession by the possessor or "correct" perception of objective reality by the perceivers. An entity may possess power to impose its will upon a firm, but unless it is aware of its power and willing to exercise it on the firm, it is not a stakeholder with high salience for managers. Rather, latent power exists in stakeholder relationships, and the exercise of stakeholder power is triggered by conditions that are manifest in the other two attributes of the relationship: legitimacy and urgency. That is, power by itself does not guarantee high salience in a stakeholder-manager relationship. Power gains authority through legitimacy, and it gains exercise through urgency.

Legitimacy, like power, is a variable rather than a steady state—a dynamic attribute of the stakeholder-manager relationship. It may be present or absent. If it is present, it is based upon a generalized virtue that is perceived for or attributed to a stakeholder at one or more social levels of analysis. Claimants may or may not correctly perceive the legitimacy of their claims; likewise, managers may have perceptions of stakeholder legitimacy that are at variance with the stakeholder's own perception. Also, like the power attribute, legitimacy's contribution to stakeholder salience depends upon interaction with the other two attributes: power and urgency. Legitimacy gains rights through power and voice through urgency.

Finally, urgency is not a steady-state attribute but can vary across stakeholder-manager relationships or within a single relationship across time. As is true of power and legitimacy, urgency is a socially constructed perceptual phenomenon and may be perceived correctly or falsely by the stakeholder, the managers, or others in the firm's environment. For example, neighbors of a nuclear power plant that is about to melt down have a serious claim on that plant, but they may not be aware of the time pressure and criticality and, thus, may not act on their claim. Urgency by itself is not sufficient to guarantee high salience in the stakeholder manager relationship. However, when it is combined with at least one of the other attributes, urgency will change the relationship and cause it to increase in salience to the firm's managers. Specifically, in combination with legitimacy, urgency promotes access to decision-making channels, and in combination with power, it encourages one-sided stakeholder action. In combination with both, urgency triggers reciprocal acknowledgment and action between stakeholders and managers.

These three features of stakeholder attributes—variable status, perceptual quality, and variable consciousness and will—lay the groundwork for a future analysis of the dynamic nature of stakeholder-manager relations. The common "bicycle-wheel" model of a firm's stakeholder environment does not begin to capture the ebb and flow of changes in stakeholder-manager relations or the fact that these relations are multilateral and often coalitional, not bilateral and independent. We explore the dynamic possibilities of the theory of stakeholder salience briefly in the concluding section, but it seems clear that a great deal more paradigmatic development is now possible because of our ability to recognize theoretically that stakeholder-manager relations are not static but, rather, are in constant flux.

Managers' Role in the Theory

Cyert and March (1963) contributed to the management literature the notion of organizations as coalitions of individuals and organized "sub coalitions" (1963: 27), with "disparate demands, changing foci of attention, and limited ability to attend to all problems simultaneously" (1963: 43), which, under uncertainty, must seek feedback from the environment (1963: 12). Pfeffer & Salancik (1978) picked up the idea of organizations as coalitions of varying interests and contributed the notion that organizations are "other-directed" (1978: 257), being influenced by actors that control critical resources and have the attention of managers (1978: 259–260). In developing their stakeholder-agency model, Hill and Jones (1992) employed the agency theory view of the firm as a nexus of contracts between stakeholders and managers at a central node, where managers have the responsibility to reconcile divergent interests by making strategic decisions and allocating strategic resources in a manner that is most consistent with the claims of the other stakeholder groups (1992: 134). They write:

> Whatever the magnitude of their stake, each stakeholder is a part of the nexus of implicit and explicit contracts that constitutes the firm. However, as a group, managers are unique in this respect because of their position at the centre of the nexus of contracts. Managers are the only group of stakeholders who enter into a contractual relationship with all other stakeholders. Managers are also the only group of stakeholders with *direct* control over the decision-making apparatus of the firm. (Hill & Jones, 1992: 134; emphasis in original)

The idea that the organization is an environmentally dependent coalition of divergent interests, which depends upon gaining the attention of (making claims upon) managers at the center of the nexus to effect reconciliations among stakeholders, suggests that the perspective of managers might be vital. We propose that, although groups can be identified reliably as stakeholders based on their possession of power, legitimacy, and urgency in relationship to the firm, it is the firm's managers who determine which stakeholders are *salient* and therefore will receive management attention. In short, one can identify a firm's stakeholders based on attributes, but managers may or may not perceive the stakeholder field correctly. The stakeholders winning management's attention will be only those the managers perceive to be highly salient.[2]

Therefore, if managers are central to this theory, what role do their own characteristics play? The propositions we present later suggest that the manager's *perception* of a stakeholder's attributes is critical to the manager's view of stakeholder salience. Therefore, we suggest, although space constraints prohibit systematic development here, that managerial characteristics are a moderator of the relationships presented in this article. For example, managers vary greatly in their environmental scanning practices (Daft, Sormunen, & Parks, 1988) and in their values (Hambrick & Mason, 1984). Differences in managerial values are illustrative of the moderating effects of management characteristics (Frederick, 1995). Greer and Downey (1982) have found that managers' values relative to social regulation have a strong effect on how they react to stakeholders covered by these statutes. Another value theorists suggest as important in this relationship is management's sense of self-interest or self-sacrifice. Although some theorists have suggested that all behavior ultimately is self-interested (Dawkins, 1976; Wilson, 1974), several social scientists have questioned the common assumption of self-interest and have suggested that people often act in ways that benefit others, even to their own detriment (see Etzioni, 1988; Granovetter, 1985; Perrow, 1986). Like Perrow (1986) and Brenner and Cochran (1991), we treat managerial characteristics as a variable and suggest that it will be an important moderator of the stakeholder-manager relationship.

STAKEHOLDER CLASSES

Up to this point in the article, we have argued that a definition of "The Principle of Who or What Really Counts" rests upon the assumptions, first, that managers who want to achieve certain ends pay particular kinds of attention to various classes of stakeholders; second, that managers' perceptions dictate stakeholder salience; and third, that the various classes of stakeholders might be identified based upon the possession, or the attributed possession, of one, two, or all three of the attributes: power, legitimacy, and urgency. We now proceed to our analysis of the stakeholder classes that result from the various combinations of these attributes, as shown in Figure 4.1.

We first lay out the stakeholder types that emerge from various combinations of the attributes: power, legitimacy, and urgency. Logically and conceptually, seven types are examined—three possessing only one attribute, three possessing two attributes, and one possessing all three attributes. We

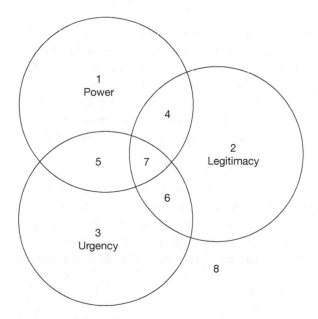

Figure 4.1: Qualitative classes of stakeholders

propose that stakeholders' possession of these attributes, upon further methodological and empirical work, can be measured reliably. This analysis allows and justifies identification of entities that should be considered stakeholders of the firm, and it also constitutes the set from which managers select those entities they perceive as salient. According to this model, then, entities with no power, legitimacy, or urgency in relation to the firm are not stakeholders and will be perceived as having no salience by the firm's managers.

In conjunction with the analysis of stakeholder types, and based on the assumption that managers' perceptions of stakeholders form the crucial variable in determining organizational resource allocation in response to stakeholder claims, we also present several propositions leading to a theory of stakeholder salience.

Therefore:

Proposition 1: Stakeholder salience will be positively related to the cumulative number of stakeholder attributes—power, legitimacy, and urgency—perceived by managers to be present.

The low salience classes (areas 1, 2, and 3), which we term "latent" stakeholders, are identified by their possession or attributed possession of only one of the attributes. The moderately salient stakeholders (areas 4, 5, and 6) are identified by their possession or attributed possession of two of the attributes, and because they are stakeholders who "expect something," we call them "expectant" stakeholders. The combination of all three attributes (including the dynamic relations among them) is the defining feature of highly salient stakeholders (area 7).

In this section we present our analysis of the stakeholder classes that the theory identifies, paying special attention to the managerial implications of the existence of each stakeholder class. We have given each class a descriptive name to facilitate discussion, recognizing that the names are less important than the theoretical types they represent. We invite the indulgence of the reader as we alliterate these descriptive names as a mnemonic device to promote recall and as a further means to suggest a starting point for future dialogue.

As Figure 4.2 illustrates, latent stakeholders are those possessing only one of the three attributes, and include dormant, discretionary, and demanding stakeholders. Expectant stakeholders are those possessing two attributes, and include dominant, dependent, and dangerous stakeholders. Definitive stakeholders are those possessing all three attributes. Finally, individuals or entities possessing none of the attributes are nonstakeholders or potential stakeholders.

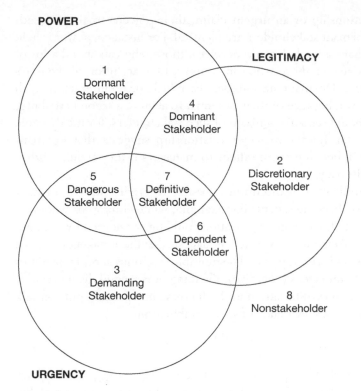

POWER

LEGITIMACY

1
Dormant
Stakeholder

4
Dominant
Stakeholder

2
Discretionary
Stakeholder

5
Dangerous
Stakeholder

7
Definitive
Stakeholder

6
Dependent
Stakeholder

3
Demanding
Stakeholder

8
Nonstakeholder

URGENCY

Figure 4.2: Stakeholder typology: One, two, or three attributes present

Latent Stakeholders

With limited time, energy, and other resources to track stakeholder behavior and to manage relationships, managers may well do nothing about stakeholders they believe possess only one of the identifying attributes, and managers may not even go so far as to recognize those stakeholders' existence. Similarly, latent stakeholders are not likely to give any attention or acknowledgment to the firm. Hence:

> *Proposition la: Stakeholder salience will be low where only one of the stakeholder attributes—power, legitimacy, and urgency—is perceived by managers to be present.*

In the next few paragraphs we discuss the reasoning behind this expectation as it applies to each class of latent stakeholder, and we also discuss the implications for managers.

Dormant stakeholders

The relevant attribute of a dormant stakeholder is power. Dormant stakeholders possess power to impose their will on a firm, but by not having a legitimate relationship or an urgent claim, their power remains unused. Examples of dormant stakeholders are plentiful. For instance, power is held by those who have a loaded gun (coercive), those who can spend a lot of money (utilitarian), or those who can command the attention of the news media (symbolic). Dormant stakeholders have little or no interaction with the firm. However, because of their potential to acquire a second attribute, management should remain cognizant of such stakeholders, for the dynamic nature of the stakeholder manager relationship suggests that dormant stakeholders will become more salient to managers if they acquire either urgency or legitimacy.

Although difficult, it is oftentimes possible to predict which dormant stakeholders may become salient. For example, while employees who have been fired or laid off from an organization could be considered by the firm to be dormant stakeholders, experience suggests that these stakeholders can seek to exercise their latent power. The multiple shootings at postal facilities by ex-U.S. mail employees (coercive), the filing of wrongful dismissal suits in the court system (utilitarian), and the increase in "speaking out" on talk radio (symbolic) all are evidence of such combinations.

Discretionary stakeholders

Discretionary stakeholders possess the attribute of legitimacy, but they have no power to influence the firm and no urgent claims. Discretionary stakeholders are a particularly interesting group for scholars of corporate social responsibility and performance (see Wood, 1991), for they are most likely to be recipients of what Carroll (1979) calls discretionary corporate social responsibility, which he later redefined as corporate philanthropy (Carroll, 1991). The key point regarding discretionary stakeholders is that, absent power and urgent claims, there is absolutely no pressure on managers to engage in an active relationship with such a stakeholder, although managers can choose to do so.

Not all recipients of corporate philanthropy are discretionary stakeholders—only those with neither power over nor urgent claims on the firm. Examples of discretionary stakeholders include beneficiaries of the Take-A-Taxi program in the Twin Cities, in which the Fingerhut company picks up the tab for anyone who feels they have consumed too much alcohol to drive, and nonprofit organizations, such as schools, soup kitchens, and hospitals, who receive donations and volunteer labor from such companies as Rhino Records, Timberland, Honeywell, Just Desserts, and Levi Strauss.

Demanding stakeholders

Where the sole relevant attribute of the stakeholder-manager relationship is urgency, the stakeholder is described as "demanding." Demanding stakeholders, those with urgent claims but having neither power nor legitimacy, are the "mosquitoes buzzing in the ears" of managers: irksome but not dangerous, bothersome but not warranting more than passing management attention, if any at all. Where stakeholders are unable or unwilling to acquire either the power or the legitimacy necessary to move their claim into a more salient status, the "noise" of urgency is insufficient to project a stakeholder claim beyond latency. For example, a lone millenarian picketer who marches outside the headquarters with a sign that says, "The end of the world is coming! Acme chemical is the cause!" might be extremely irritating to Acme's managers, but the claims of the picketer remain largely unconsidered.

Expectant Stakeholders

As we consider the potential relationship between managers and the group of stakeholders with two of the three identifying stakeholder attributes, we observe a qualitatively different zone of salience. In analyzing the situations in which any two of the three attributes—power, legitimacy, and urgency— are present, we cannot help but notice the change in momentum that characterizes this condition. Whereas one-attribute low salience stakeholders are anticipated to have a latent relationship with managers, two-attribute moderate-salience stakeholders are seen as "expecting something," because the combination of two attributes leads the stakeholder to an active versus a passive stance, with a corresponding increase in firm responsiveness to the stakeholder's interests. Thus, the level of engagement between managers and these expectant stakeholders is likely to be higher. Accordingly:

> Proposition 1b: Stakeholder salience will be moderate where two of the stakeholder attributes—power, legitimacy, and urgency—are perceived by managers to be present.

We describe the three expectant stakeholder classes (dominant, dependent, and dangerous) in the following paragraphs.

Dominant stakeholders

In the situation where stakeholders are both powerful and legitimate, their influence in the firm is assured, since by possessing power with legitimacy, they form the "dominant coalition" in the enterprise (Cyert & March, 1963). We characterize these stakeholders as "dominant," in deference to the legitimate claims they have upon the firm and their ability to act on these claims (rather than as a forecast of their intentions with respect to the firm— they may or may not ever choose to act on their claims). It seems clear to us, at least, that the expectations of any stakeholders perceived by managers to have power and legitimacy will "matter" to managers.

Thus, we might expect that dominant stakeholders will have some formal mechanism in place that acknowledges the importance of their relationship with the firm. For example, corporate boards of directors generally include representatives of owners, significant creditors, and community leaders, and there is normally an investor relations office to handle ongoing relationships with investors. Most corporations have a human resources department that acknowledges the importance of the firm-employee relationship. Public affairs offices are common in firms that depend on maintaining good relationships with government. In addition, corporations produce reports to legitimate, powerful stakeholders, including annual reports, proxy statements, and, increasingly, environmental and social responsibility reports. Dominant stakeholders, in fact, are those stakeholders that so many scholars are trying to establish as the *only* stakeholders of the firm. In our typology dominant stakeholders expect and receive much of managers' attention, but they are by no means the full set of stakeholders to whom managers should or do relate.

Dependent stakeholders

We characterize stakeholders who lack power but who have urgent legitimate claims as "dependent," because these stakeholders depend upon others (other stakeholders or the firm's managers) for the power necessary to carry out their will. Because power in this relationship is not reciprocal, its exercise is governed either through the advocacy or guardianship of other stakeholders, or through the guidance of internal management values.

Using the case of the giant oil spill from the Exxon Valdez in Prince William Sound as an example, we can show that several stakeholder groups had urgent and legitimate claims, but they had little or no power to enforce their will in the relationship. To satisfy their claims these stakeholders had to rely on the advocacy of other, powerful stakeholders or on the benevolence and voluntarism of the firm's management. Included in this category were local residents, marine mammals and birds, and even the natural environment itself (Starik, 1993). For the claims of these dependent stakeholders to be satisfied, it was necessary for dominant stakeholders—the Alaska state government and the court system—to provide guardianship of the region's citizens, animals, and ecosystems. Here a dependent stakeholder moved into the most salient stakeholder class by having its urgent claims adopted by dominant stakeholders, illustrating the dynamism that can be modeled effectively using the theory and principles of stakeholder identification and salience suggested here.

Dangerous stakeholders

We suggest that where urgency and power characterize a stakeholder who lacks legitimacy, that stakeholder will be coercive and possibly violent, making the stakeholder "dangerous," literally, to the firm. "Coercion" is suggested as a descriptor because the use of coercive power often accompanies illegitimate status.

Examples of unlawful, yet common, attempts at using coercive means to advance stakeholder claims (which may or may not be legitimate) include wildcat strikes, employee sabotage, and terrorism. For example, in the 1970s General Motors' employees in Lordstown, Ohio, welded pop cans to engine blocks to protest certain company policies. Other examples of stakeholders using coercive tactics include environmentalists spiking trees in areas to be logged and religious or political terrorists using bombings, shootings, or kidnappings to call attention to their claims. The actions of these stakeholders not only are outside the bounds of legitimacy but are dangerous, both to the stakeholder-manager relationship and to the individuals and entities involved.

It is important for us to note that we, along with other responsible individuals, are very uncomfortable with the notion that those whose actions are dangerous, both to stakeholder-manager relationships as well as to life and well-being, might be accorded some measure of legitimacy by virtue of the typology proposed in this analysis. Notwithstanding our discomfort, however, we are even more concerned that failure to identify dangerous stakeholders would result in missed opportunities for mitigating the dangers and in lower levels of preparedness, where no accommodation is possible. Further, to maintain the integrity of our approach to better define stakeholders, we feel bound to "identify" dangerous stakeholders without "acknowledging" them, for, like most of our colleagues, we abhor their practices. We are fully aware that society's "refusal to acknowledge" after identification of a dangerous stakeholder, by counteracting terror in all its forms, is an effective counteragent in the battle to maintain civility and civilization. The identification of this class of stakeholder is undertaken with the support of this tactic in mind.

Definitive Stakeholders

Previously, we defined "salience" as the degree to which managers give priority to competing stakeholder claims. Thus:

> *Proposition lc: Stakeholder salience will be high where all three of the stakeholder attributes—power, legitimacy, and urgency—are perceived by managers to be present.*

By definition, a stakeholder exhibiting both power and legitimacy already will be a member of a firm's dominant coalition. When such a stakeholder's claim is urgent, managers have a clear and immediate mandate to attend to and give priority to that stakeholder's claim. The most common occurrence is likely to be the movement of a dominant stakeholder into the "definitive" category.

For example, in 1993 stockholders (dominant stakeholders) of IBM, General Motors, Kodak, Westinghouse, and American Express became active when they felt that their legitimate interests were not being served by the managers of these companies. A sense of urgency was engendered when these powerful, legitimate stakeholders saw their stock values plummet. Because top managers did not respond sufficiently or appropriately to these definitive stakeholders, they were removed, thus demonstrating in a general way the importance of an accurate perception of power, legitimacy, and urgency; the necessity of acknowledgment and action that salience implies; and, more specifically, the consequences of the misperception of or inattention to the claims of definitive stakeholders.

Any expectant stakeholder can become a definitive stakeholder by acquiring the missing attribute. As we saw earlier, dependent Alaskan citizens became definitive stakeholders of Exxon by acquiring a powerful ally in government. Likewise, the "dangerous" African National Congress became a definitive stakeholder of South African companies when it acquired legitimacy by winning free national elections.

RESEARCH AND MANAGEMENT CONSEQUENCES OF A DYNAMIC THEORY OF STAKEHOLDER IDENTIFICATION

In our analysis we have proposed that stakeholders possess some combination of three critical attributes: power, legitimacy, and urgency. We predict that the salience of a particular stakeholder to the firm's management is low if only one attribute is present, moderate if two attributes are present, and high if all three attributes are present.

Dynamism in Stakeholder–Manager Relations

As our earlier discussion demonstrates, latent stakeholders can increase their salience to managers and move into the "expectant stakeholder" category by acquiring just one of the missing attributes. If the stakeholder is particularly clever, for example, at coalition building, political action, or social construction of reality, that stakeholder can move into the "definitive stakeholder" category (characterized by high salience to managers), starting from any position—latent, expectant, or potential.

Static maps of a firm's stakeholder environment are heuristically useful if the intent is to raise consciousness about "Who or What Really Counts" to managers or to specify the stakeholder configuration at a particular time point. But even though most theorists might try for static clarity, managers should never forget that stakeholders change in salience, requiring different degrees and types of attention depending on their attributed possession of power, legitimacy, and/or urgency, and that levels of these attributes (and thereby salience) can vary from issue to issue and from time to time.

We can observe an example of stakeholder dynamism in recent events in South Africa. The African National Congress (ANC) began as a group with an urgent claim but not a legitimate one, given the ruling South African culture and government, and it had no power. At first it was a latent, demanding stakeholder. The ANC next moved into the "dangerous category" by using coercive power. However, this did not lead to definitive status. It was only by acquiring legitimacy while relinquishing the use of coercive power, and thus becoming a dependent stakeholder, that the ANC was able to achieve definitive status, high salience, and eventual success.

Thus, when the ANC moved its urgent claim into the world environment, the claim's legitimacy was established, and the ANC, as well as the South Africans it represented, became an expectant, dependent stakeholder of the multinational enterprises (MNEs) located in South Africa. As a dependent stakeholder, the ANC was able to acquire the protection, advocacy, and guardianship of more salient stakeholders (especially investors). With the powerful advocacy of these stakeholders, the ANC moved into the "definitive" zone of the stakeholder attribute model for South African MNEs. In fact, it is now widely acknowledged that the worldwide divestment/disinvestment movement, led by MNE stockholders, was a major force in the transformation of the South African system of government and the rise to political power of the ANC (e.g., see Paul, 1992).

Another example of dynamism in stakeholder attributes is offered by Näsi, Näsi, and Savage (1994). This case, involving a business owner, workers, and the courts, illustrates how a dependent stakeholder worker group (one with a legitimate and urgent claim) can increase its salience to a firm's managers by aligning itself with other stakeholders (in this case, a union and the courts) who have the power to impose their will upon a stubborn business owner.

Thus, using our identification typology, we are able to explain stakeholder salience and dynamism systematically. This new capability has implications for management, research, and for the future of the stakeholder framework.

Implications for Management, Research, and Future Directions

On the basis of the model we develop in this article, we can envision refinements in long-standing management techniques designed to assist managers in dealing with multiple stakeholders' interests. Presently, management techniques based on the stakeholder heuristic are being utilized to help managers deal effectively with multiple stakeholder relationships. Current methods include identification of stakeholder roles (e.g., employees, owners, communities, suppliers, and customers), analysis of stakeholder interests, and evaluation of the type and level of stakeholder power (e.g., see current textbooks by Carroll, 1993; Frederick, Post, Lawrence, & Weber, 1996; and Wood, 1994).

The approach introduced in this paper has the potential to improve upon current practice. To current techniques that emphasize power and interests, the model we suggest adds the vital dimensions of legitimacy and urgency. Further, this model enables a more systematic sorting by managers of stakeholder-manager relationships as these relationships attain and relinquish salience in the dynamics of ongoing business. In addition, our three-attribute model permits managers to map the legitimacy of stakeholders and therefore to become sensitized to the moral implications of their actions with respect to each stakeholder. In this sense, our model supports and initiates normative thought in the managerial context. Thus, these refinements contribute to the potential effectiveness of managers as they deal with multiple stakeholder interests. And, as these refinements find their way into accepted practice, we can further envision subsequent rounds of inquiry, which test whether "new maps" result in "new methods."

Stakeholder theory, we believe, holds the key to more effective management and to a more useful, comprehensive theory of the firm in society. Focusing attention on salience in the manager-stakeholder relationships existing in a firm's environment appears to be a productive strategy for researchers and managers alike in realizing these aspirations. The stakeholder identification typology we have developed here is amenable to empirical operationalization and to the generation of testable hypotheses concerning, for example, predictions about the circumstances under which a stakeholder in one category might attempt to acquire a missing attribute and thus enhance its salience to a firm's managers. We have not developed such operational definitions and hypotheses here, for lack of space, but we believe that such development is the next logical step in articulating completely "The Principle of Who or What Really Counts."

Specifically, we call for empirical research that answers these questions: Are present descriptions of stakeholder attributes adequate? Do the inferences we make herein hold when examining real stakeholder-manager relationships? Are there models of interrelationships among the variables identified here (and possible others) that reveal more subtle, but perhaps more basic, systematics? We realize that for these and other such questions to be addressed, item and scale development, demographic calibration, and second-order model building, among other things, are necessary.

In the process we hope that additional clarity can be achieved at the conceptual level as well. We ask, what are the implications of this model and its subsequent tests for additional research on power, legitimacy, and urgency? More importantly, are power, legitimacy, and urgency really the correct and parsimonious set of variables in understanding stakeholdermanager relationships? We acknowledge that despite their level of emphasis in the second Toronto conference, and despite our logical and theoretical justification of their importance in developing a more inferential and empirically based stakeholder theory, other stakeholder attributes also may be well suited to stakeholder analysis—and we call for the critical evaluation of our choices.

Finally, in attempting to build momentum in the development of stakeholder theory, we are acutely aware that we have necessarily made sweeping assumptions that, for the sake of clarity in a preliminary articulation, are passed over, with the implicit understanding that for the theory to hold, these must be revisited and assessed. For example, we assume and argue that power and legitimacy are distinct attributes. But some might cast one as a subset of the other. To build our identification typology, we treat each attribute as "present or absent," when it is clear that each operates on a continuum or series of continua. Each of these issues, and others like them, point toward additional inquiry that can enrich the theory and add to its usefulness.

Conclusion: The Search for Legitimacy in Stakeholder Theory

Many stakeholder scholars, in attempting to narrow the range of "Who or What Really Counts" in a firm's stakeholder environment, are searching for the bases of legitimacy in stakeholder-manager relationships. When scholars such as Freeman, Clarkson, Donaldson, Preston, and Dunfee argue that stakeholder theory must articulate a "normative core," they are looking for a compelling reason why some claims and some relationships are legitimate and worthy of management attention and why others are not. They discount the importance of power in stakeholder-manager relations, arguing that the important thing is whether the stakeholder has legitimate (e.g., moral, legal, and property-based) claims.

The theory of stakeholder identification and salience developed in this article in no way discredits this search for a legitimate normative core for stakeholder theory. It makes sense to articulate theoretically why certain groups will hold legitimate, possibly stable claims on managers and firm; these are the stakeholders who should really count. Our aim, however, is to expand scholarly and management understanding beyond legitimacy to incorporate stakeholder power and urgency of a claim, because these attributes of entities in a firm's environment—and their dynamism over periods of time or variation in issues—will make a critical difference in managers' ability to meet legitimate claims and protect legitimate interests. We offer this preliminary theory as a way of understanding which stakeholders do really count.

In 1978 William C. Frederick (in a paper subsequently published in 1994) observed that business and society scholarship was in a transition from a moral focus on social responsibility (CSR_1) to an amoral focus on social responsiveness (CSR_2). When stakeholder theory focuses only on issues of legitimacy, it acquires the fuzzy moral flavor of CSR_1. Focusing only on stakeholder power, however, as several major organizational theories would lead us to do, yields the amorality and self-interested action focus of CSR_2. Instead, we propose a merger.

In sum, we argue that stakeholder theory must account for power and urgency as well as legitimacy, no matter how distasteful or unsettling the results. Managers *must* know about entities in their environment that hold power and have the intent to impose their will upon the firm. *Power and urgency must be attended to if managers are to serve the legal and moral interests of legitimate stakeholders.*

Notes

*We thank the members of the Second Toronto Conference on Stakeholder Theory, sponsored by the Clarkson Centre for Business Ethics at the University of Toronto, where the centrality of these three attributes to a theory of stakeholder-manager relationships was first noted. We also recognize the contribution of various working groups in SIM and IABS and are grateful for the comments provided by A. R. Elangoven and Barry Mitnick, the intellectual and financial support of Fritz Faulhaber, and the valuable insights of the consulting editor and the anonymous reviewers.

1   Etzioni explains these types of power as follows:

The use of a gun, a whip, or a lock is physical since it affects the body; the threat to use physical sanctions is viewed as physical because the effect on the subject is similar in kind, though not in intensity, to the actual use. Control based on application of physical means is ascribed as *coercive power*.

Material rewards consist of goods and services. The granting of symbols (e.g. money) which allow one to acquire goods and services is classified as material because the effect on the recipient is similar to that of material means. The use of material means for control purposes constitutes *utilitarian power*.

Pure symbols are those whose use does not constitute a physical threat or a claim on material rewards. These include normative symbols, those of prestige and esteem; and social symbols, those of love and acceptance. When physical contact is used to symbolize love, or material objects to symbolize prestige, such contacts or objects are viewed as symbols because their effect on the recipient is similar to that of "pure" symbols. The use of symbols for control purposes is referred to as *normative, normative-social, or social power.* (1964: 59)

2   We note, however, that Freeman and Evan view the firm "as a series of multilateral contracts among stakeholders" (1990: 342), with no central role for managers. This implies a network theory solution to the problem of systematic description, in comparison with the cognitive approach that we take. We make no representations about a fully networked, nonnexus approach. We merely suggest the sociology-organization theory approach as a logically developed "sorting system" for improving the descriptive capability of the stakeholder approach.

References

Ahlstedt, L., & Jahnukainen, I. 1971. *Yritysorganisaatio yhteistoiminnan ohjausjaerjestel-maenae.* Helsinki: Weilin + Goeoes.

Alkhafaji, A. F. 1989. *A stakeholder approach to corporate governance. Managing in a dynamic environment.* Westport, CT: Quorum Books.

Bowie, N. 1988. The moral obligations of multinational corporations. In S. Luper-Foy (Ed.), *Problems of international justice:* 97–113. Boulder, CO: Westview Press.

Brenner, S. N. 1993. The stakeholder theory of the firm and organizational decision making: Some propositions and a model. In J. Pasquero & D. Collins (Eds.), *Proceedings of the Fourth Annual Meeting of the International Association for Business and Society:* 205–210. San Diego.

Brenner, S. N. 1995. Stakeholder theory of the firm: Its consistency with current management techniques. In J. Näsi (Ed.), *Understanding stakeholder thinking:* 75–96. Helsinki: LSR–Julkaisut Oy.

Brenner, S. N., & Cochran, P. L. 1991. The stakeholder model of the firm: Implications for business and society research. In J. F. Mahon (Ed.), *Proceedings of the Second Annual Meeting of the International Association for Business and Society:* 449–467. Sundance, UT.

Carroll, A. B. 1979. A three-dimensional model of corporate performance. *Academy of Management Review*, 4: 497–505.

Carroll, A. B. 1989. *Business and society: Ethics and stakeholder management.* Cincinnati: South-Western.

Caroll, A. B. 1991. The pyramid of corporate social responsibility: Toward the moral management of organizational stakeholders. *Business Horizons,* July–August: 30–48.

Carroll, A. B. 1993. *Business and society: Ethics and stakeholder management* (2nd ed.). Cincinnati: South-Western.

Carroll, G. R., & Hannan, M. T. 1989. Density delay in the evolution of organizational populations: A model and five empirical tests. *Administrative Science Quarterly,* 34: 411–430.

Clarkson, M. 1994. A risk based model of stakeholder theory. *Proceedings of the Second Toronto Conference on Stakeholder Theory.* Toronto: Centre for Corporate Social Performance & Ethics, University of Toronto.

Clarkson, M. B. E. 1995. A stakeholder framework for analyzing and evaluating corporate social performance. *Academy of Management Review,* 20: 92–117.

Cobb, R. W., & Elder, C. D. 1972. *Participation in American politics: The dynamics of agenda building.* Baltimore: Johns Hopkins University Press.

Cornell, B., & Shapiro, A. C. 1987. Corporate stakeholders and corporate finance. *Financial Management,* 16: 5–14.

Cyert, R. M., & March, J. G. 1963. *The behavioral theory of the firm.* Englewood Cliffs, NJ: Prentice-Hall.

Daft, R. L., Sormunen, J., & Parks, D. 1988. Chief executive scanning, environmental characteristics, and company performance: An empirical study. *Strategic Management Journal*, 9: 123–139.

Dahl, R. A. 1957. The concept of power. *Behavioral Science*, 2: 201–215.

Davis, K. 1973. The case for and against business assumption of social responsibility. *Academy of Management Journal,* 16: 312–322.

Dawkins, R. 1976. *The selfish gene.* New York: Oxford University Press.

Dimaggio, P. J., & Powell, W. W. 1983. The iron cage revisited: Institutional isomorphism and collective rationality in organization fields. *American Sociological Review,* 46: 147–160.

Dimaggio, P. J., & Powell, W. W. 1991. Introduction. In W. W. Powell & P. J. DiMaggio (Eds.), *The new institutionalism in organizational analysis:* 1–38. Chicago: University of Chicago Press.

Donaldson, T., & Preston, L. E. 1995. The stakeholder theory of the corporation: Concepts, evidence, and implications. *Academy of Management Review,* 20: 65–91.

Etzioni, A. 1964. *Modern organizations.* Englewood Cliffs, NJ: Prentice-Hall.

Etzioni, A. 1988. *The moral dimension.* New York: Basic Books.

Evan, W. M., & Freeman, R. E. 1988. A stakeholder theory of the modern corporation: Kantian capitalism. In T. L. Beauchamp & N. Bowie (Eds.), *Ethical theory and business:* 75–84. Englewood Cliffs, NJ: Prentice-Hall.

Eyestone, R. 1978. *From social issue to public policy*. New York: Wiley.

Frederick, W. C. 1994. From CSR₁ to CSR₂. The maturing of business-and-society thought. *Business & Society*, 33: 150–164.

Frederick, W. C. 1995. *Values, nature and culture in the American corporation*. New York: Oxford University Press.

Frederick, W. C., Post, J. E., Lawrence, A., & Weber, J. 1996. *Business and society: Corporate strategy, public policy, ethics* (8th. ed.). New York: McGraw-Hill.

Freeman, R. E. 1984. *Strategic management: A stakeholder approach*. Boston: Pitman.

Freeman, R. E. 1994. The politics of stakeholder theory: Some future directions. *Business Ethics Quarterly* 4: 409–421.

Freeman, R. E., & Evan, W. M. 1990. Corporate governance: A stakeholder interpretation. *Journal of Behavioral Economics*, 19: 337–359.

Freeman, R. E., & Gilbert, D. R. 1987. Managing stakeholder relationships. In S. P. Sethi & C. M. Falbe (Eds.), *Business and society: Dimensions of conflict and cooperation*, 397–423. Lexington, MA: Lexington Books.

Freeman, R. E., & Reed, D. L. 1983. Stockholders and stakeholders: A new perspective on corporate governance. *California Management Review*, 25(3): 93–94.

French, J. R. P., & Raven, B. 1960. The base of social power. In D. Cartwright & A. F. Zander (Eds.), *Group dynamics* (2nd ed.): 607–623. Evanston, IL: Row, Peterson.

Granovetter, M. 1985. Economic action and social structure: A theory of embeddedness. *American Journal of Sociology*, 91: 481–510.

Greer, C. R., & Downey, H. K. 1982. Industrial compliance with social legislation: Investigations of decision rationales. *Academy of Management Review*, 7: 488–498.

Hambrick, D. C., & Mason, P. A. 1984. Upper echelons: The organization as a reflection of its top managers. *Academy of Management Review*, 9: 193–206.

Hill, C. W. L., & Jones, T. M. 1992. Stakeholder-agency theory. *Journal of Management Studies*, 29(2): 131–154.

Jensen, M. C., & Meckling, W. H. 1976. Theory of the firm: Managerial behavior, agency costs, and ownership structure. *Journal of Financial Economics*, 3: 305–360.

Jones, G. R., & Hill, C. W. L. 1988. Transaction cost analysis of strategy–structure choice. *Strategic Management Journal*, 9: 159–172.

Jones, T. M. 1980. Corporate social responsibility revisited, redefined. *California Management Review*, 22(2): 59–67.

Jones, T. M. 1993 Ethical decision-making by individuals in organizations: An issue-contingent model. *Academy of Management Review* 16: 366–395.

Jones, T. M. 1995. Instrumental stakeholder theory: A synthesis of ethics and economics. *Academy of Management Review*, 20: 404–437.

Kreiner, P., & Bhambri, A. 1988. Influence and information in organization-stakeholder relationships. *Academy of Management Best Paper Proceedings:* 319–323. Anaheim, CA.

Langtry, B. 1994. Stakeholders and the moral responsibilities of business. *Business Ethics Quarterly*, 4: 431–443.

Meyer, J. W., & Rowan, B. 1977. Institutional organizations: Formal structures as myth and ceremony. *American Journal of Sociology*, 80: 340–363.

Näsi, J. 1995. What is stakeholder thinking? A snapshot of a social theory of the firm. In J. Näsi (Ed.), *Understanding stakeholder thinking:* 19–32. Helsinki: LSR-Julkaisut Oy.

Näsi, J., Näsi, S., & Savage, G. T. 1994. A stubborn entrepreneur under pressure of a union and the courts: An analysis of stakeholder strategies in a conflict process. In S. Wartick & D. Collins (Eds.), *Proceedings of the Fifth Annual Meeting of the International Association for Business and Society:* 228–234. Hilton Head, SC.

Parsons, T. 1960. *Structure and process in modern societies.* New York: Free Press.

Paul, K. 1992. The impact of U.S. sanctions on Japanese business in South Africa: Further developments in the internationalization of social activism. *Business & Society,* 31: 51–58.

Perrow, C. 1986. *Complex organizations: A critical essay.* New York: Random House.

Pfeffer, J. 1981. *Power in organizations.* Marshfield, MA: Pitman.

Pfeffer, I., & Salancik, G. 1978. *The external control of organizations: A resource dependence perspective.* New York: Harper & Row.

Rhenman, E. 1964. *Foeretagsdemokrati och foeretagsorganisation.* Stockholm: Thule.

Ring, P. S. 1994. Fragile and resilient trust and their roles in cooperative inter-organizational relationships. In J. Pasquero & D. Collins (Eds.), *Proceedings of the Fourth Annual Meeting of the International Association for Business and Society:* 107–113. San Diego.

Salancik, G. R., & Pfeffer, J. 1974. The bases and use of power in organizational decision making: The case of universities. *Administrative Science Quarterly,* 19: 453–473.

Savage, G. T., Nix, T. H., Whitehead, C. J., & Blair, J. D. 1991. Strategies for assessing and managing organizational stakeholders. *Academy of Management Executive,* 5: 61–75.

Scott, W. R. 1987. *Organizations: Rational, natural, and open systems.* Englewood Cliffs, NJ: Prentice-Hall.

Starik, M. 1993. Is the environment an organizational stakeholder? Naturally! In J. Pasquero & D. Collins (Eds.), *Proceedings of the Fourth Annual Meeting of the International Association for Business and Society:* 466–471. San Diego.

Starik, M. 1994. Essay by Mark Starik. pp. 89–95 of The Toronto conference: Reflections on stakeholder theory. *Business & Society,* 33: 82–131.

Suchman, M. C. 1995. Managing legitimacy: Strategic and institutional approaches. *Academy of Management Review,* 20: 571–610.

Thompson, J. K., Wartick, S. L., & Smith, H. L. 1991. Integrating corporate social performance and stakeholder management: Implications for a research agenda in small business. *Research in Corporate Social Performance and Policy,* 12: 207–230.

Wartick, S. L., & Mahon, J. M. 1994. Toward a substantive definition of the corporate issue construct: A review and synthesis of the literature. *Business & Society,* 33: 293–311.

Weber, M. 1947. *The theory of social and economic organization.* New York: Free Press.

Wicks, A. C., Gilbert, D. R., Jr., & Freeman, R. E. 1994. A feminist reinterpretation of the stakeholder concept. *Business Ethics Quarterly,* 4(4): 475–497.

Williamson, O. 1975. *Markets and hierarchies.* New York: Free Press.

Williamson, O. 1985. *The economic institutions of capitalism.* New York: Free Press.

Wilson, E. O. 1974. *Ecology, evolution and population biology, readings from Scientific American.* San Francisco: W. H. Freeman.

Windsor, D. 1992. Stakeholder management in multinational enterprises. In S. N. Brenner & S. A. Waddock (Eds.), *Proceedings of the Third Annual Meeting of the International Association for Business and Society:* 121–128. Leuven, Belgium.

Wood, D. J. 1991. Corporate social performance revisited. *Academy of Management Review* 16: 691–718.

Wood, D. J. 1994. *Business and Society* (2nd ed.). New York: HarperCollins.

Vodafone: Africa calling

The Vodafone Group started as a small mobile phone operator in the UK and in 25 years has grown into a global business giant and the one of the most valued brands in the world. With almost 400 million customers across Europe, Asia, Africa, North America, and the Middle East it is now the world's largest mobile telecommunications company by revenue.[1]

CSR at Vodafone

Vodafone has generally been regarded as one of the CSR leaders in a sector that faces a number of CSR opportunities and threats. On the one hand, mobile telecommunications companies have been criticized for high mobile phone tariffs, including excessive roaming charges and opaque pricing structures. Similarly, critics have raised concerns over potential health threats from the radiofrequency fields emitted by handsets and base stations. Mobile companies have also had to manage the risks faced by their young consumers in terms of access to adult content, phone bullying, and other forms of potential abuse. On the positive side, providing access to mobile telecommunications can be a boon to social and economic development in emerging economies, it promotes digital inclusion, and can provide the basis for a raft of socially beneficial services to a wide range of customers across the globe.

Vodafone has taken a two-pronged approach to these CSR opportunities and challenges. Its for-profit businesses and subsidiaries deal with CSR through the lens of the Vodafone sustainability strategy that emphasizes three themes, namely 'responsible, ethical, and honest behaviour", "eco-efficiency" and "creating sustainable societies'. These themes take on a different complexion in the different areas in which the company operates. With around two thirds of its customers now in emerging markets, the group sees significant opportunities to develop its business in lower income countries while also creating a positive social impact. Therefore, in these markets, the company has focused significant energy in building CSR-related initiatives in health, food distribution, financial services, and agriculture, often with a view to growing new revenue streams. In more mature markets, however, needs are different, and hence CSR initiatives there tend to target issues such as privacy, health concerns, tax avoidance, and energy efficiency. In New Zealand, for example, the company intends to use its network for developing services in remote monitoring of electricity, gas and water, thereby enabling its consumers to save energy and reduce carbon emissions.

The second way that Vodafone approaches CSR is through its charitable wing, the Vodafone Foundation, along with some 26 country-level Vodafone foundations. According to its website, the Foundation is based on 'the belief that our mobile communications technologies can address some of the world's most pressing humanitarian challenges and our responsibility is to utilise our innovative mobile technology in mobilising social change and improving people's lives'. The Foundation provides funding of around US $30 million annually through social investments to communities in need across the world. This includes donations to disaster relief, projects that use mobile telecommunications to address humanitarian problems, and its World of Difference programme, which mobilizes people to take time out from their jobs and pays them to work for a charity of their choice.[2]

Vodafone in Africa

Africa represents an important frontier for Vodafone's CSR practice. The company has two major holdings within the continent: a 40 per cent stake in Safaricom[3] and a 65 per cent stake in the Vodacom group.[4] Through these two companies, Vodafone offers its services in South Africa, Mozambique, Lesotho, Tanzania, Kenya, and the Democratic Republic of Congo.

Across Africa the group's business strategy aligns well with its social goals since it looks to expand its operations into underdeveloped communities and leverage its infrastructure to offer innovative products for medical, financial, and agricultural services. The company believes that by providing access to telecommunication and making connectivity affordable, it can create better living standards and help communities flourish. Vodafone's mHealth solutions and its M-Pesa initiative are two examples of how the company is simultaneously seeking to build new business and meet its CSR objectives in Africa.

mHealth

mHealth is the application of mobile communications and network technologies for healthcare.[5] With the intent to bring hospitals to home, Vodafone's mHealth solutions represent the company's attempt to use its information and communication technology (ICT) infrastructure to provide remote medical assistance in 26 of the countries where it operates, including many in Africa.

Vodafone's mHealth services include the tracking and supply of medicines in remote health centres, with an aim to transfer data in real time. In Tanzania during a pilot run of this service, the number of health facilities running out of medicines dropped from 90 per cent to 6 per cent.[6] mHealth projects also look at facilitating clinical research and prescription adherence. In terms of research, patients can feed in their responses to questions prepared by medical researchers and submit them using a standard mobile handset. For prescription adherence, mHealth solutions utilize mobile handsets to send out regular reminders to patients by SMS thereby automating dispensary follow-up.[7] Finally, the company's mHealth initiatives also enable the transfer of medical expertise and data remotely. For example, with the company's Nompilo project in South Africa, Vodafone works with the Department of Health and local NGOs to enable community care workers in remote communities to register, record and recall patient data securely on their handsets, while giving healthcare managers realtime information to ensure better integrated care.[8]

M-Pesa

M-Pesa, a payment service for the unbanked, was pioneered by Vodafone through Safaricom, its Kenya-based business which is managed and 40 per cent owned by Vodafone.[9] First launched in 2007, M-Pesa enables a range of financial services to be conducted by those without access to formal banks or bank accounts simply by using their mobile phones. The range of services includes money transfer, disbursement and repayment of microloans, merchant payments, airtime purchases, and disbursement and receipt of salaries.[10]

Today, M-Pesa allows Vodafone customers in Kenya, Tanzania, Afghanistan, South Africa, and India to use a variety of financial services on his or her handset without needing to visit a bank or start a formal bank account. The impact of the service has been enormous both socially and financially. M-Pesa has almost become the gold standard of money transfer for citizens of Tanzania and Kenya. In Kenya, it is used by one third of the 41 millon population,[11] whilst in Tanzania it generates transactions worth US $10 million per month.[12] The financial benefits of the service are highlighted in Safaricom's annual reports, which shows that almost 75 per cent of the revenue earned by Vodafone through its Kenyan subsidiary come from M-Pesa in license fees.[13]

Meeting the diverse needs of African stakeholders

Moving away from the technological innovations such as mHealth and M-Pesa that are employed to generate social and economic good in Africa, the company's South Africa-based subsidiary, Vodacom, provides some further insight into how Vodafone is seeking to respond to the diverse needs of its African stakeholders.

With respect to customers, the mobile services provider has launched handsets for the less privileged, people with disabilities, and the elderly. For instance, their range of Ultra Low Cost (ULC) handsets are aimed at 'democratizing communications' by enabling even those on low incomes to purchase an entry level phone. The company has also launched two new-model speaking phones for the visually impaired, three products for the hearing impaired and a specially designed phone for the elderly.[14]

In terms of employees, Vodacom is working in line with South Africa's Broad Based Black Economic Empowerment (BBBEE) Codes of Good Practice, which are aimed at overturning the decades of injustice created by the apartheid regime. The company is South Africa's leading telecommunications company in terms of its BBBEE performance, but challenges remain in securing greater black empowerment within the company. For example, in 2010, 70 per cent of Vodacom's workforce was black, yet only 27 per cent of management positions were held by black Africans.[15] Moves to increase black equity ownership are managed through YeboYethu Limited, a minority (3.4 per cent) equity holder of Vodacom South Africa. YeboYethu Limited in turn is held by Vodacom SA employees (45 per cent) and by black South African citizens (55 per cent), meaning that Vodacom at least earmarks some proportion of its shareholding to the black population.[16] The group also engages in preferential procurement since influencing the supply chain to embrace black empowerment is another way in which it can expedite transformation in the South African economy. Procurement from BBBEE-accredited suppliers amounts to about one half of the company's total procurement spend.[17]

Vodafone's African foundations

As with its CSR practice elsewhere, Vodafone also looks to meet its social obligations through charitable foundations. In Africa, the group has two dominant foundations – the Vodacom Foundation and the Safaricom Foundation. The Vodacom Foundation allocates its resources in a 5:3:2 ratio between long term (multi-year), medium term (three years) and short term projects. Acting essentially as a funding agency, the foundation evaluates programs/NGOs on the grounds of social change sought, expected degree of impact, sustainability, governance, track record, and solvency. Broadly both foundations offer funding for poverty alleviation, environment, healthcare, arts and culture, and community sports. The Foundations also respond to disasters and humanitarian emergencies.[18]

Vodafone have also funded economic and policy research on the impact of mobile phones in Africa. One report funded by Vodafone found that mobile phones can have a positive and significant impact on economic growth and social stability, emphasizing that:

- A developing country with an extra ten phones per 100 people would have had GDP growth 0.59 per cent higher than an otherwise identical country.

- Fixed and mobile communications networks have a positive effect on the size of foreign direct investment.
- Mobiles aid in economic development and transformation of the economy. Many of the small businesses surveyed used mobiles as their only means of communication, with the highest proportion of all among black-owned businesses.
- A majority of small businesses reported an increase in profits as a result of mobile phones, in spite of call costs.
- More than three quarters of respondents said they had more contact and better relationships with family and friends as a result of mobile phones, especially in rural areas that are often not served by fixed-line telecommunication services.[19]

Changing political contexts

The CSR challenges in a continent as diverse and complex as Africa are ever changing. The Arab Spring of 2011, where citizen revolts across much of North Africa and the Middle East precipitated insurgencies, military action, and political upheaval in much of the region, brought Vodafone a new challenge in terms of how to manage its role in political unrest.

Vodafone Egypt, in particular, came under severe criticism for its stance during the 2011 civic revolt against the Mubarak regime. The critical juncture was the Mubarak government's request to Vodafone and other mobile operators to temporarily shut down their services in some parts of the nation to inhibit the protestors' ability to organize. Not only did Vodafone comply with the directive, it also sent out specific pro-government messages by SMS as demanded by the regime. Only towards the end of the revolt did the company take on a stronger stand, by refusing to send the last pro-Mubarak message under its brand name and limiting its circulation.

According to media reports, 'some sections of the Egyptian society considered Vodafone's protocol to be cowardly and despite the company's clarification that the move was to protect the well being of its employees (physical danger and of being arrested), people blamed the organization'.[20] Many were unconvinced that a company of Vodafone's size and influence could not have resisted the government and sided with the Egyptian people, suggesting that the firm was 'complicit in dictatorship'.[21]

As a mark of retaliation, Vodafone Egypt's Facebook page was hacked, and a message left by the hackers on the page received hundreds of comments and likes before the page disappeared.[22] The website ihatevodafoneegypt.com also acted as a forum for virulent criticism. Subsequently, the organization received further rebuke when a television commercial made by the firm's advertising agency JWT (allegedly without Vodafone Egypt's knowledge) was made public, provoking widespread anger on social media sites for its suggestion that Vodafone played a role in the ousting of the Mubarak regime. The advertisement featured Vodafone's 'power to you' slogan over images of the revolution, seemingly rewriting history by showing Vodafone's posters on Tahrir Square, the centre of the protests, and alluding to the power of social media in starting the revolution.[23] While these events took place far from the heartland of Vodafone's African businesses in South and East Africa, they demonstrated well that along with the CSR opportunities, business in Africa also brings with it significant CSR risks.

Study questions

1. To what extent does Vodafone in Africa demonstrate the seven core characteristics of CSR as set out in Chapter 1?
2. Using the example of Vodafone in Africa, describe the main ways that CSR will differ for Vodafone in developing countries compared with in more mature or developed economies.
3. Consider the case for CSR as illustrated by Vodafone. Is Aneel Karnani right in suggesting that managers will focus attention on CSR only where it aligns with profit maximization – and that governments should regulate in cases where the two are not aligned?
4. In Chapter 2, N. Craig Smith suggests that there may be ethical and/or strategic reasons for engaging in CSR, but that commitment to CSR must be assessed relative to the specific vulnerabilities and opportunities of a particular company. What are these vulnerabilities and opportunities with respect to Vodafone in Africa, and should it develop an ethical or strategic approach to CSR?
5. Consider the four types of CSR theories discussed by Garriga and Melé in Chapter 3. How would each of them apply to the case of Vodafone in Africa and what contribution, if any, do the theories have to understanding CSR practice?

Endnotes

1   www.vodafone.com/content/index/about/about_us.html
2   www.vodafone.com/content/index/about/foundation/about_foundation.html
3   www.safaricom.co.ke/fileadmin/M-PESA/Documents/Press_release/MONEY-TRANSFER-SERVICE-Launch.pdf
4   Vodacom Sustainability Report Page 6
5   http://mhealth.vodafone.com/discover_mhealth/
6   http://mhealth.vodafone.com/solutions/access_to_medicine/supply_logistics_safety/
7   http://mhealth.vodafone.com/solutions/clinical_research/patient_reporting_outcomes/
8   http://mhealth.vodafone.com/global/solutions/mobile_flexible_working/field_force_enablement/community_care/index.jsp

9   http://webarchive.nationalarchives.gov.uk/+/http://www.dfid.gov.uk/media-room/news-stories/2007/M-PESA-1-million-kenyans-bank-by-phone/

10 www.roshan.af/Roshan/M-Paisa.aspx

11 www.thinkm-pesa.com/2011/08/water-delivery-through-payment-platform.html

12 http://thecitizen.co.tz/magazines/31-business-week/3032-money-transfervodacom-m-pesa-takes-financial-sector-by-storm

13 http://online.wsj.com/article/BT-CO-20110815-708880.html

14 Vodacom 2010 Group Sustainability Report: www.vodacom.com/pdf/sustainability_reports/sus_report_2010.pdf

15 Ibid.

16 Ibid.

17 Ibid.

18 http://safaricom.co.ke/foundation/index.php?id=25

19 Vodafone (2005) Africa: The Impact of Mobile Phones, Moving the Debate Forward, The Vodafone Policy Paper Series, No. 2, March 2005: http://info.worldbank.org/etools/docs/library/152872/Vodafone%20Survey.pdf

20 www.channel4.com/news/vodafone-egypt-faces-hashtag-backlash

21 www.guardian.co.uk/world/2011/jun/03/vodafone-egypt-advert-claims-revolution

22 www.egypt-business.com/Web/details/Vodafone-Egypts-Facebook-page-hacked-then-disappeared/781

23 www.ft.com/intl/cms/s/0/34c9b2f2-8de7-11e0-a0c4-00144feab49a.html#axzz1YWyJRdUN

SECTION B

Applying CSR

Having now discussed what CSR is, elaborated on some of its basic underlying principles and key theories, and considered the arguments for and against the adoption of responsible business practices above and beyond the legal minimum, we now move onto the issue of how these issues can be applied to specific business activities. This is an incredibly important aspect of the debate around CSR, most notably because, whether we agree or not about the significance or relevance of CSR for the modern corporation, it is, in essence, a real management process that takes place in thousands of businesses across the globe.

Let us make no mistake about it: CSR – or something that goes under the banner of CSR or one of its many counterparts – is now practised in most large corporations in Europe and the US, as well as parts of Asia, and has been taken up by corporations from many major developing countries such as Brazil, India, and increasingly China. The CSR practices of huge multinationals such as BP, Carrefour, McDonalds, Microsoft, Nestlé, Shell, Toyota, Unilever, and Walmart affect millions, perhaps billions, of people across the world, whether through the products they supply, the people they employ, the communities they locate in, or the natural environments they affect.

Therefore, the question of *how* corporations actually implement their social responsibilities could not be a more important one. It is one thing to talk in the abstract about the social role and responsibilities of the corporation, but it is quite another to consider how the corporation can apply those responsibilities to tangible business activities.

In this section, we consider the responsibilities of the corporation in four key arenas,[1] followed by an integrative case study that deals with all four:

- CSR in the marketplace
- CSR in the workplace

- CSR in the community
- CSR in the ecological environment
- Integrative case study *HSBC: banking on CSR?*

These four areas, we would suggest, capture the main areas of business where the philosophy and practice of CSR can be meaningfully applied. They also represent specific arenas of practice where the interests of particular stakeholder groups can be usefully considered, i.e. under CSR in the marketplace we will consider consumers and (to a lesser extent) suppliers, under CSR in the workplace we will consider employees, and so on.

The purpose of breaking the application of CSR down to four specific arenas is twofold. First, it helps to provide some issue-specific focus for some of the key debates in the CSR literature. For instance, when we ask whether CSR pays off for the firm, we might consider this question in more detail by asking, does CSR involvement in the community pay off, or do customers respond positively to CSR initiatives? In this sense, the distinct arenas provide greater *specificity* and *simplification* – i.e. sometimes CSR is too broad and overarching to be able to address important questions meaningfully. Second, it makes sense from the perspective of business practice. While many firms will seek to integrate their CSR initiatives, they also need to consider how to suffuse responsibility throughout the different functions. If a responsible firm must know how to market its products responsibly, manage its environmental impacts, and protect the human rights of its employees, it will need to engender responsibility in its marketing team, its production units, and in its human resource department. Therefore, by breaking the subject down in this way, we are providing an *applied perspective* that offers greater potential for understanding CSR practice.

At the end of Section B, we extend this applied perspective to consider the different arenas of CSR in the context of the real-world experiences of the global banking giant, HSBC. This case study explores the challenges posed to the bank in designing an integrated CSR strategy in the developing world.

Endnote

1   This categorization was inspired by the core CSR areas distinguished by the UK's leading CSR member organization, Business in the Community. See www.bitc.org.uk.

Chapter 5

CSR in the marketplace

IN THIS CHAPTER WE WILL:

- Explain some of the core corporate responsibilities in the marketplace
- Evaluate the argument that market demands offer a substantial imperative for corporations to engage in social responsibility
- Distinguish between different marketplaces in which corporations might encounter CSR
- Examine how companies might enhance social welfare by developing products for consumers at the bottom of the pyramid
- Explore how corporations might respond to demands from consumers for greater responsibility
- Examine the meaning of key concepts such as ethical branding, cause-related marketing, and reputational risk management

Introduction

The marketplace is frequently portrayed as one of the most important arenas for considering CSR. Firms that develop socially responsible products and practices will often seek to be rewarded for doing so by attracting consumers, earning a premium, or building a brand that customers evaluate more favourably. Success in the marketplace is often touted as a key indicator that CSR genuinely matters and can be commercially viable. For example, the social responsibility of an automotive company is heavily dependent on the market success of environmentally friendly models such as electric vehicles and hybrids.

For many, the marketplace is also one of the main areas where business irresponsibility is exposed. For example, in controversial industries such as alcohol, tobacco, or fast food, the impact of firms' products and marketing on consumers dominates the CSR agenda. Should KFC provide only 'unhealthy' food or should it also offer salads, fruit, and other healthier alternatives? Should Carlsberg help problem drinkers to reduce consumption of their products? Is British American Tobacco being responsible if they advertise their products in some countries, despite being banned from doing so in others due to public health concerns? These are just some of the marketplace responsibility issues facing controversial industries, but similar considerations confront all corporations in some way or other, whether they sell cars, chewing gum, or financial services. The responsible design and marketing of products and services is one of the core responsibilities of the corporation.

The marketplace is crucial for another reason too – demands from consumers and other stakeholders of products and services are said to act as a key driver for CSR activities more generally. The basic argument here is that CSR is essentially a market preference expressed by consumers. In one of the most well known expressions of this view, McWilliams and Siegel state:

> One way to assess investment in CSR is as a mechanism for product differentiation. In this context, there are CSR 'resources' and 'outputs'. A firm can create a certain level of CSR by embodying its products with CSR attributes (such as pesticide-free fruit) or by using CSR-related resources in its production process (such as naturally occurring insect inhibitors and organic fertilizers). As such, it seems natural to consider the nature of the markets for CSR attributes and CSR-related resources.
>
> (McWilliams and Siegel, 2001: 119)

Another way of looking at this is to say that the market can act as a social control of business (Smith, 1990) – namely, that consumers can use the market to ensure that corporations act responsibly. If firms do not, consumers can retract their purchase dollars or even boycott the company; if, however, firms do act responsibly, they will gain the approval of consumers with 'ethical' preferences and (at least in theory) flourish in the marketplace. Of course, this also means that if sufficient numbers of consumers do not express any market preferences for CSR, or they are not willing to pay for them, then it may well be rational for firms to desist from additional investment in CSR.

What we have then are two main types of responsibility in the marketplace: on the one hand we have what Garriga and Melé (Chapter 3) might call an *ethical* type, namely that firms have a social responsibility to ensure that their marketplace activities offer appropriate benefits to consumers. On the other hand, we have a more *instrumental* type, which suggests that firms should offer social responsibility to the extent that it is demanded by consumers.

The market for CSR

The instrumental argument regarding the market imperatives for responsible business is widely prevalent in the CSR world, especially among practitioners. This is typically presented as part of the business case for CSR – namely does CSR really pay off in the marketplace? This question is at the heart of the instrumental perspective on CSR that, as we saw in Chapter 2, suggests that firms should invest in social responsibility when it is in their own 'enlightened' self-interest. While we saw there that Aneel Karnani regarded this as the only context in which firms would invest in CSR, N. Craig Smith countered that firms might have multiple motivations for engaging in responsible practices.

The empirical evidence regarding this relationship between social responsibility and business success is quite mixed. On the one hand, there is a large swathe of studies that provide support for an overall positive relationship between CSR and financial performance (see for example Orlitzky et al, 2003). On the other hand, the evidence for a substantial market for CSR is probably less convincing than many advocates of the business case suggest. David Vogel's conclusions following an expansive examination of the evidence are unusually candid regarding the limited significance of this market:

> Unfortunately, there is no evidence that behaving more virtuously makes firms more profitable. This finding is important because, unless there is a clear business case for CSR, firms will have fewer incentives to act more responsibly. Conversely, the fact that CSR also does not make firms less profitable means that it is possible for a firm to commit resources to CSR without becoming less competitive. In brief, there is a place in the business system for responsible firms, but the market for virtue is not sufficiently important to make it in the interest of all firms to behave more responsibly.
>
> (Vogel, 2005: 20)

Vogel's case is persuasive, in that it suggests that some companies can potentially derive market rewards for CSR, but many will not. Consider the markets for typical student purchases such as computers, books, apartment rentals, music downloads, or beer: are customers' decisions in these markets significantly influenced by social performance of the products or their producers? Probably not. Vogel is correct in insisting that market imperatives for CSR are present only for some firms in some instances, and should not be regarded as a generalized feature of all markets.

Understanding the marketplaces of CSR

So what are the different types of marketplaces that we need to consider? When considering CSR in the marketplace, we are referring to a range of business practices including sourcing, buying, marketing, advertising, pricing, and selling of products and services. This occurs in a range of different marketplaces, the most important of which are:

Consumer markets

These are markets where firms will be marketing directly to end-consumers. Here, issues such as responsible marketing and the development of CSR brands and communications to consumers are some of the main considerations. Some consumer markets, such as those concentrated on food and beverages or apparel, seem to gain a disproportionate amount of CSR attention, either because they directly affect the end-consumer (such as health and nutrition issues in the food sector) or they are targeted by activists and the media (such as child labour issues in apparel).

Financial markets

These are markets for stocks, shares, bonds, and other financial products. Here, customers may still be individual end-consumers who, for example, invest their money in shares of companies they regard as socially responsible. More importantly, though, the customer here may be another company, such as a pension fund or other institutional investors, that screens out irresponsible firms (or screens in responsible ones) as part of its investment portfolio. This is a particular case of the market preference for CSR discussed above known as socially responsible investment (SRI).

Business-to-business markets

These are markets that operate between firms for the supply of goods and services. Here the 'customer' is essentially another firm. This usually means that the corporate customer has significantly more power than an individual customer has to influence the behaviour of the firms it is sourcing from. For example, a company such as Nike can leverage its buying power in global supply chains to improve the conditions of workers in its contractors' factories in developing countries (Zadek, 2004). A huge retailer such as Walmart can influence thousands of suppliers to develop more sustainable practices through its immense buying power coupled with a commitment to reducing waste, enhancing environmental efficiencies and developing more organic products (Ganesan et al, 2009). The controversy surrounding Apple and its suppliers' factories in China which has hit the headlines a number of times due to poor labour conditions, accidents and even suicides at Foxconn manufacturing plants,[1] goes to show that this is an ongoing area of concern for global companies.

In this chapter, we mainly focus on the first category, with some discussion of the latter two – but most of the issues raised can be applied to any type of market. We also will deal in more detail with supply chain issues in Section C of the book when we discuss the management and implementation of CSR.

Introducing the readings

The two readings that follow offer a good introduction to marketplace issues, dealing in turn with the questions of how markets can be harnessed for improving the lives of the poor in developing countries, and then how firms should respond to specific market preferences for CSR.

Marketing to the 'bottom of the pyramid' (BOP)

The spirit of a 'win-win' approach to CSR in the marketplace is striking in the first reading by the late management guru C.K. Prahalad and his co-author Allen Hammond. The paper is one in a series of publications by Prahalad setting out the bottom of the pyramid concept, or just BOP for short. The BOP refers to those at the very bottom of the world's earnings league, the poorest of the poor. Prahalad and Hammond's contention is that the world's poor have been neglected by business. However, in developing products and services specifically for these neglected consumers, firms can not only improve the lives of the most disadvantaged in our societies, but that great profits can be reaped in doing so.

BOP thinking offers a seductive promise to executives and it is no surprise that it has revolutionized how many people in the business world view low-income markets. Food companies such as Danone have developed low cost, high nutrition, products for poor consumers, car companies such as Tata Motors have developed automotives such as the Tata Nano specifically for low-income consumers, while microcredit is now widely available to those with limited financial means who were previously unable to access the formal banking sector.

The BOP concept is not, however, without its critics. For example Aneel Karnani (2007) – the author of one of the readings in Chapter 2 – argues that the BOP proposition is 'too good to be true' and 'riddled with fallacies' (Karnani, 2007: 90). He contends that because the costs of marketing to the poor are typically high (because of geographic dispersion, weak infrastructure, and small transaction values), the BOP market is actually 'quite small . . . [and] unlikely to be very profitable, especially for a large company' (2007: 91). Critically, he also raises the very real prospect that low-income consumers face potential exploitation from multinationals, raising the prospect that BOP initiatives may actually reduce rather than increase the social welfare of those being targeted. These criticisms represent an important flip-side to the exciting opportunities for win-win successes in BOP markets that Prahalad and Hammond articulate. The challenge this poses for companies is to find the markets where win-wins are genuinely feasible, and to structure BOP initiatives in these markets to ensure success for all, such as by partnering with NGOs and community groups to look after the interests of consumers.

CWS 5.1

Visit the companion website for links and clips of real-life CSR issues in these three types of marketplaces

CWS 5.2

Visit the companion website for up-to-date examples of companies marketing to the bottom of the pyramid

RESPONDING TO MARKET PREFERENCES FOR CSR

Many companies invest in CSR because they believe their customers demand it. Andrew Crane's reading seeks to address the question of what firms can or should do when faced with a supposed market preference for CSR. Focusing his attention on the response of firms to 'ethical consumers', Crane considers in particular the strategies that firms may implement to appeal to ethical consumers, both in the well-defined 'ethical niches' targeted by companies such as Ecover and the Co-operative Bank, and in mainstream markets targeted by major multinationals. In so doing, he discusses various marketing strategies such as 'ethical branding', cause-related marketing, CSR labelling, and reputational risk management.

In examining these strategies in practice, Crane proposes that many niche companies have increasingly moved to mainstream positioning in order to gain market share. Conversely, more mainstream approaches to CSR have increasingly focused on risk management rather than explicit ethical branding. Indeed, evidence suggests that given heterogeneity in firm strategies and consumer responses, there is no 'one size fits all' with respect to how firms should respond to consumer preferences for CSR (Sen & Bhattacharya, 2001). It is also worth remembering that although many consumers express a commitment to rewarding socially responsible firms, their actual market place behaviour does not always reinforce this very strongly (Devinney et al, 2010; Öberseder et al, 2011).

Crane talks mainly about consumer markets, but his analysis can also be applied to financial markets, where evidence suggests that SRI has been undergoing similar processes of mainstreaming and risk management in recent years (Friedman & Miles, 2001; Sparkes & Cowton, 2004). Notably, the labels 'ethical investment' and even 'socially responsible investment' are increasingly being dropped in favour of simply 'responsible investment', with considerable attention being paid to the potential financial risk issues associated with such issues. For example, the UN-backed Principles for Responsible Investment (UNPRI) is predicated on the idea that 'environmental, social and corporate governance (ESG) issues can affect the performance of investment portfolios and therefore must be given appropriate consideration by investors if they are to fulfil their fiduciary (or equivalent) duty.'[2] Again, the win-win perspective that typically dominates CSR issues in the marketplace is present here. Referring back to our core elements of CSR in Chapter 1, in financial markets, as with consumer markets, the emphasis is typically on CSR as a 'built-in', 'beyond philanthropy' approach rather than one bolted-on as an extension or alternative to existing business concerns.

Challenges for practice

Take a close look at a company you work for or with which you are familiar.

1. Are there any market signals that suggest that the company will be either rewarded or punished in the marketplace for socially responsible behaviour?
    a) What form do these signals take?
    b) How have they changed over time or across different contexts (e.g. different countries)?
2. To what extent do you think these market imperatives drive actual CSR practice at the company?
    a) Will the company engage in CSR without positive encouragement from the market?
    b) How much CSR is 'enough' according to the market, and does this match with other stakeholders' expectations?
3. How does or could the company reach out to low income consumers at the bottom of the pyramid, either locally or internationally?
    a) Do poorer consumers represent a viable market opportunity?
    b) If not, what else would need to be in place to make the bottom of the pyramid attractive to the company?

Study questions

1. Do firms have responsibility for their products and services over and above ensuring that they comply with safety legislation and are promoted honestly?
2. To what extent can consumers act as a social control of corporations? In which of the three marketplace contexts – consumer, financial and business-to-business markets – is this control likely to be the most extensive?
3. Should companies be concerned with providing products for the poor? If so, under what conditions should they enter bottom of the pyramid markets?
4. What is an ethical brand, and what are the advantages and disadvantages of developing one? Nominate a firm that you would say has developed an ethical brand, giving reasons for your nomination.
5. 'Reputational risk management is not about CSR – it's simply good management'. Discuss.

Further reading

Karnani, A. (2007) 'The mirage of marketing to the bottom of the pyramid: how
the private sector can help alleviate poverty', *California Management
Review*, 49(4): 90–111.
This article provides an important critique of the bottom of the pyramid concept
advanced by Prahalad and Hammond in their article. Reading this will give you
an alternative perspective on how to use (or not use) markets to eradicate
poverty.

Sparkes, R. & Cowton, C. J. (2004) 'The maturing of socially responsible investment: a review of the developing link with corporate social responsibility',
Journal of Business Ethics, 52(1): 45–57.
CSR in the marketplace is not only about consumer markets. This article
discusses the relationship between SRI and CSR, providing a useful introduction to the issues involved in financial markets potentially acting as a force
for social responsibility.

Vogel, D. (2005) 'Is there a market for virtue? The business case for corporate
social responsibility', *California Management Review*, 47(4): 19–45.
This is a good overview of the business case for CSR, and how the market
can act as a driver for CSR. Vogel's conclusions are interesting in that he
regards the 'market for virtue' as actually quite limited.

Endnotes

1   See the series of articles in the *New York Times* in January–April 2012,
    www.nytimes.com.
2   UN Principles for Responsible Investment website, www.unpri.org/about
    (Accessed 30 August, 2012).

References

Devinney, T. M., Auger, P., & Eckhardt, G. M. (2010) *The myth of the ethical
consumer*, Cambridge: Cambridge University Press.
Friedman, A. L. & Miles, S. (2001) 'Socially responsible investment and corporate
social and environmental reporting in the UK: an exploratory study', *The British
Accounting Review*, 33: 523–548.
Ganesan, S., George, M., Jap, S., Palmatier, R. W., & Weitz, B. (2009) 'Supply chain
management and retailer performance: emerging trends, issues, and
implications for research and practice', *Journal of Retailing*, 85(1): 84–94.
Karnani, A. (2007) 'The mirage of marketing to the bottom of the pyramid: how the

private sector can help alleviate poverty', *California Management Review*, 49(4): 90–111.

McWilliams, A. & Siegel, D. (2001) 'Corporate social responsibility: a theory of the firm perspective', *Academy of Management Review*, 26(1): 117–127.

Öberseder, M., Schlegelmilch, B. B., & Gruber, V. (2011) 'Why don't consumers care about CSR? A qualitative study exploring the role of CSR in consumption decisions', *Journal of Business Ethics*, 104(4): 449–460.

Orlitzky, M., Schmidt, F. L., & Rynes, S. L. (2003) 'Corporate social and financial performance: a meta-analysis', *Organization Studies*, 24(3): 403–411.

Sen, S. & Bhattacharya, C. B. (2001) 'Does doing good always lead to doing better? Consumer reactions to corporate social responsibility', *Journal of Marketing Research*, 38(May): 225–243.

Smith, N. C. (1990) *Morality and the market: consumer pressure for corporate accountability*, London: Routledge.

Sparkes, R. & Cowton, C. J. (2004) 'The maturing of socially responsible investment: a review of the developing link with corporate social responsibility', *Journal of Business Ethics*, 52(1): 45–57.

Vogel, D. J. (2005) 'Is there a market for virtue? The business case for corporate social responsibility', *California Management Review*, 47(4): 19–45.

Zadek, S. (2004) 'The path to corporate responsibility', *Harvard Business Review*, 82(December): 125–132.

SERVING THE WORLD'S POOR, *PROFITABLY*

C.K. Prahalad and Allen Hammond

Consider this bleak vision of the world 15 years from now: The global economy recovers from its current stagnation but growth remains anemic. Deflation continues to threaten, the gap between rich and poor keeps widening, and incidents of economic chaos, governmental collapse, and civil war plague developing regions. Terrorism remains a constant threat, diverting significant public and private resources to security concerns. Opposition to the global market system intensifies. Multinational companies find it difficult to expand, and many become risk averse, slowing investment and pulling back from emerging markets.

Now consider this much brighter scenario: Driven by private investment and widespread entrepreneurial activity, the economies of developing regions grow vigorously, creating jobs and wealth and bringing hundreds of millions of new consumers into the global marketplace every year. China, India, Brazil, and, gradually, South Africa become new engines of global economic growth, promoting prosperity around the world. The resulting decrease in poverty produces a range of social benefits, helping to stabilize many developing regions and reduce civil and cross-border conflicts. The threat of terrorism and war recedes. Multinational companies expand rapidly in an era of intense innovation and competition.

Both of these scenarios are possible. Which one comes to pass will be determined primarily by one factor: the willingness of big, multinational companies to enter and invest in the world's poorest markets. By stimulating commerce and development at the bottom of the economic pyramid, MNCs could radically improve the lives of billions of people and help bring into being a more stable, less dangerous world. Achieving this goal does not require multinationals to spearhead global social development initiatives for charitable purposes. They need only act in their own self-interest, for there are enormous business benefits to be gained by entering developing markets. In fact, many innovative companies – entrepreneurial outfits and large, established enterprises alike – are already serving the world's poor in ways that generate strong revenues, lead to greater operating efficiencies, and uncover new sources of innovation. For these companies – and those that follow their lead – building businesses aimed at the bottom of the pyramid promises to provide important competitive advantages as the twenty-first century unfolds.

Big companies are not going to solve the economic ills of developing countries by themselves, of course. It will also take targeted financial aid from the developed world and improvements in the governance of the developing nations themselves. But it's clear to us that prosperity can come to the poorest regions only through the direct and sustained involvement of multinational companies. And it's equally clear that the multinationals can enhance their own prosperity in the process.

Untapped Potential

Everyone knows that the world's poor are distressingly plentiful. Fully 65% of the world's population earns less than $2,000 each per year – that's 4 billion people. But despite the vastness of this market, it remains largely untapped by multinational companies. The reluctance to invest is easy to understand. Companies assume that people with such low incomes have little to spend on goods and services and that what they do spend goes to basic needs like food and shelter. They also assume that various barriers to commerce – corruption, illiteracy, inadequate infrastructure, currency fluctuations, bureaucratic red tape – make it impossible to do business profitably in these regions.

But such assumptions reflect a narrow and largely outdated view of the developing world. The fact is, many multinationals already successfully do business in developing countries (although most currently focus on selling to the small upper-middle-class segments of these markets), and their experience shows that the barriers to commerce – although real – are much lower than is typically thought. Moreover, several positive trends in developing countries – from political reform, to a growing openness to investment, to the development of low-cost wireless communication networks – are reducing the barriers further while also providing businesses with greater access to even the poorest city slums and rural areas. Indeed, once the misperceptions are wiped away, the enormous economic potential that lies at the bottom of the pyramid becomes clear.

Take the assumption that the poor have no money. It sounds obvious on the surface, but it's wrong. While individual incomes may be low, the aggregate buying power of poor communities is actually quite large. The average per capita income of villagers in rural Bangladesh, for instance, is less than $200 per year, but as a group they are avid consumers of tele-communications services. Grameen Telecom's village phones, which are owned by a single entrepreneur but used by the entire community, generate an average revenue of roughly $90 a month – and as much as $1,000 a month in some large villages. Customers of these village phones, who pay cash for each use, spend an average of 7% of their income on phone services – a far higher percentage than consumers in traditional markets do.

It's also incorrect to assume that the poor are too concerned with fulfilling their basic needs to "waste" money on nonessential goods. In fact, the poor often do buy "luxury" items. In the Mumbai shantytown of Dharavi, for example, 85% of households own a television set, 75% own a pressure cooker and a mixer, 56% own a gas stove, and 21% have telephones. That's because buying a house in Mumbai, for most people at the bottom of the pyramid, is not a realistic option. Neither is getting access to running water. They accept that reality, and rather than saving for a rainy day, they spend their income on things they can get now that improve the quality of their lives.

Another big misperception about developing markets is that the goods sold there are incredibly cheap and, hence, there's no room for a new competitor to come in and turn a profit. In reality, consumers at the bottom of the pyramid pay much higher prices for most things than middle-class consumers do, which means that there's a real opportunity for companies, particularly big corporations with economies of scale and efficient supply chains, to capture market share by offering higher quality goods at lower prices while maintaining attractive margins. In fact, throughout the developing world, urban slum dwellers pay, for instance, between four and 100 times as much for drinking water as middle- and upper-class families. Food also costs 20% to 30% more in the poorest communities since there is no access to bulk discount stores. On the service side of the economy, local money-lenders charge interest of 10% to 15% *per day,* with annual rates running as high as 2,000%. Even the lucky small-scale entrepreneurs who get loans from nonprofit microfinance institutions pay between 40% and 70% interest per year – rates that are illegal in most developed countries. (For a closer look at how the prices of goods compare in rich and poor areas, see the exhibit "The High-Cost Economy of the Poor.")

It can also be surprisingly cheap to market and deliver products and services to the world's poor. That's because many of them live in cities that are densely populated today and will be even more so in the years to come. Figures from the UN and the World Resources Institute indicate that by 2015, in Africa, 225 cities will each have populations of more than 1 million; in Latin America, another 225; and in Asia, 903. The population of at least 27 cities will reach or exceed 8 million. Collectively, the 1,300 largest cities will account for some 1.5 billion to 2 billion people, roughly half of whom will be bottom-of-the-pyramid (BOP) consumers now served primarily by informal economies. Companies that operate in these areas will have access to millions of potential new customers, who together have billions of dollars to spend. The poor in Rio de Janeiro, for instance, have a total purchasing power of $1.2 billion ($600 per person). Shantytowns in Johannesburg or Mumbai are no different.

The slums of these cities already have distinct ecosystems, with retail shops, small businesses, schools, clinics, and moneylenders. Although there are few reliable estimates of the value of commercial transactions in slums, business activity appears to be thriving. Dharavi—covering an area of just 435 acres—boasts scores of businesses ranging from leather, textiles, plastic recycling, and surgical sutures to gold jewelry, illicit liquor, detergents, and groceries. The scale of the businesses varies from one-person operations to bigger, well-recognized producers of brand-name products. Dharavi generates an estimated $450 million in manufacturing revenues, or about $1 million per acre of land. Established shantytowns in São Paulo, Rio, and Mexico City are equally productive. The seeds of a vibrant commercial sector have been sown.

While the rural poor are naturally harder to reach than the urban poor, they also represent a large untapped opportunity for companies. Indeed, 60% of India's GDP is generated in rural areas. The critical barrier to doing business in rural regions is distribution access, not a lack of buying power. But new information technology and communications infrastructures – especially wireless – promise to become an inexpensive way to establish marketing and distribution channels in these communities.

Conventional wisdom says that people in BOP markets cannot use such advanced technologies, but that's just another misconception. Poor rural women in Bangladesh have had no difficulty using GSM cell phones, despite never before using phones of any type. In Kenya, teenagers from slums are being successfully trained as Web page designers. Poor farmers in El Salvador use telecenters to negotiate the sale of their crops over the Internet. And women in Indian coastal villages have in less than a week learned to use PCs to interpret real-time satellite images showing concentrations of schools of fish in the Arabian Sea so they can direct their husbands to the best fishing areas. Clearly, poor communities are ready to adopt new technologies that improve their economic opportunities or their quality of life. The lesson for multinationals: Don't hesitate to deploy advanced technologies at the bottom of the pyramid while, or even before, deploying them in advanced countries.

A final misperception concerns the highly charged issue of exploitation of the poor by MNCs. The informal economies that now serve poor communities are full of inefficiencies and exploitive intermediaries. So if a microfinance institution charges 50% annual interest when the alternative is either 1,000% interest or no loan at all, is that exploiting or helping the poor? If a large financial company such as Citigroup were to use its scale to offer microloans at 20%, is that exploiting or helping the poor? The issue is not just cost but also quality – quality in the range and fairness of financial services, quality of food, quality of water. We argue that when MNCs provide basic goods and services that reduce costs to the poor and help improve their standard of living – while generating an acceptable return on investment – the results benefit everyone.

The Business Case

The business opportunities at the bottom of the pyramid have not gone unnoticed. Over the last five years, we have seen nongovernmental organizations (NGOs), entrepreneurial start-ups, and a handful of forward-thinking multinationals conduct vigorous commercial experiments in poor communities. Their experience is a proof of concept: Businesses can gain three important advantages by serving the poor – a new source of revenue growth, greater efficiency, and access to innovation. Let's look at examples of each.

Top-Line Growth

Growth is an important challenge for every company, but today it is especially critical for very large companies many of which appear to have nearly saturated their existing markets. That's why BOP markets represent such an opportunity for MNCs: They are fundamentally new sources of growth. And because these markets are in the earliest stages of economic development, growth can be extremely rapid.

Latent demand for low-priced, high-quality goods is enormous. Consider the reaction when Hindustan Lever, the Indian subsidiary of Unilever, recently introduced what was for it a new product category – candy – aimed at the bottom of the pyramid. A high-quality confection made with real sugar and fruit, the candy sells for only about a penny a serving. At such a price, it may seem like a marginal business opportunity, but in just six months it became the fastest-growing category in the company's portfolio. Not only is it profitable, but the company estimates it has the potential to generate revenues of $200 million per year in India and comparable markets in five years. Hindustan Lever has had similar successes in India with low-priced detergent and iodized salt. Beyond generating new sales, the company is establishing its business and its brand in a vast new market.

There is equally strong demand for affordable services. TARAhaat, a start-up focused on rural India, has introduced a range of computer-enabled education services ranging from basic IT training to English proficiency to vocational skills. The products are expected to be the largest single revenue generator for the company and its franchisees over the next several years.[1] Credit and financial services are also in high demand among the poor. Citibank's ATM-based banking experiment in India, called Suvidha, for instance, which requires a minimum deposit of just $25, enlisted 150,000 customers in one year in the city of Bangalore alone.

Small-business services are also popular in BOP markets. Centers run in Uganda by the Women's Information Resource Electronic Service (WIRES) provide female entrepreneurs with information on markets and prices, as well as credit and trade support services, packaged in simple, ready-to-use formats in local languages. The centers are planning to offer other small-business services such as printing, faxing, and copying, along with access to accounting, spreadsheet, and other software. In Bolivia, a start-up has partnered with the Bolivian Association of Ecological Producers Organizations to offer business information and communications services to more than 25,000 small producers of ecoagricultural products.

Most companies target consumers at the upper tiers of the economic pyramid, completely overlooking the business potential at its base. But though they may each be earning the equivalent of less than $2,000 a year, the people at the bottom of the pyramid make up a colossal market – 4 billion strong – the vast majority of the world's population.

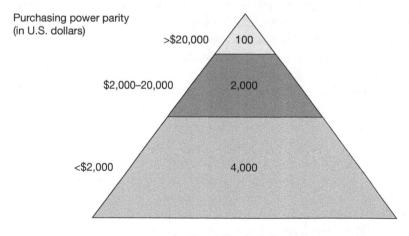

Figure 5.1: The world pyramid

It's true that some services simply cannot be offered at a low-enough cost to be profitable, at least not with traditional technologies or business models. Most mobile telecommunications providers, for example, cannot yet profitably operate their networks at affordable prices in the developing world. One answer is to find alternative technology. A microfinance organization in Bolivia named PRODEM, for example, uses multilingual smart-card ATMs to substantially reduce its marginal cost per customer. Smart cards store a customer's personal details, account numbers, transaction records, and a fingerprint, allowing cash dispensers to operate without permanent network connections – which is key in remote areas. What's more, the machines offer voice commands in Spanish and several local dialects and are equipped with touch screens so that PRODEM's customer base can be extended to illiterate and semiliterate people.

Another answer is to aggregate demand, making the community – not the individual–the network customer. Gyandoot, a start-up in the Dhar district of central India, where 60% of the population falls below the poverty level, illustrates the benefits of a shared access model. The company has a network of 39 Internet-enabled kiosks that provide local entrepreneurs with Internet and telecommunications access, as well as with governmental, educational, and other services. Each kiosk serves 25 to 30 surrounding villages; the entire network reaches more than 600 villages and over half a million people.

Networks like these can be useful channels for marketing and distributing many kinds of low-cost products and services. Aptech's Computer Education division, for example, has built its own network of 1,000 learning centers in India to market and distribute Vidya, a computer-training course specially designed for BOP consumers and available in seven Indian languages. Pioneer HiBred, a DuPont company, uses Internet kiosks in Latin America to deliver agricultural information and to interact with customers. Farmers can report different crop diseases or weather conditions, receive advice over the wire, and order seeds, fertilizers, and pesticides. This network strategy increases both sales and customer loyalty.

Reduced Costs

No less important than top-line growth are cost-saving opportunities. Outsourcing operations to low-cost labor markets has, of course, long been a popular way to contain costs, and it has led to the increasing prominence of China in manufacturing and India in software. Now, thanks to the rapid expansion of high-speed digital networks, companies are realizing even greater savings by locating such labor-intensive service functions as call centers, marketing services, and back-office transaction processing in developing areas. For example, the nearly 20 companies that use OrphanIT. com's affiliate-marketing services, provided via its telecenters in India and the Philippines, pay one-tenth the going rate for similar services in the United States or Australia. Venture capitalist Vinod Khosla describes

the remote-services opportunity this way: "I suspect that by 2010, we will be talking about [remote services] as the fastest-growing part of the world economy, with many trillions of dollars of new markets created." Besides keeping costs down, outsourcing jobs to BOP markets can enhance growth, since job creation ultimately increases local consumers' purchasing power.

But tapping into cheap labor pools is not the only way MNCs can enhance their efficiency by operating in developing regions. The competitive necessity of maintaining a low cost structure in these areas can push companies to discover creative ways to configure their products, finances, and supply chains to enhance productivity. And these discoveries can often be incorporated back into their existing operations in developed markets.

For instance, companies targeting the BOP market are finding that the shared access model, which disaggregates access from ownership, not only widens their customer base but increases asset productivity as well. Poor people, rather than buying their own computers, Internet connections, cell phones, refrigerators, and even cars, can use such equipment on a pay-per-use basis. Typically, the providers of such services get considerably more revenue per dollar of investment in the underlying assets. One shared Internet line, for example, can serve as many as 50 people, generating more revenue per day than if it were dedicated to a single customer at a flat fee. Shared access creates the opportunity to gain far greater returns from all sorts of infrastructure investments.

When we compare the costs of essentials in Dharavi, a shantytown of more than 1 million people in the heart of Mumbai, India, with those of Warden Road, an upper-class community in a nice Mumbai suburb, a disturbing picture emerges. Clearly, costs could be dramatically reduced if the poor could benefit from the scope, scale, and supply-chain efficiencies of large enterprises, as their middle-class counterparts do. This pattern is common around the world, even in developed countries. For instance, a similar, if less exaggerated, disparity exists between the inner-city poor and the suburban rich in the United States.

Table 5.1: The high cost economy of the poor

Cost	Dharavi	Warden Road	Poverty premium
credit (annual interest)	600%–1,000%	12%–18%	53x
municipal-grade water (per cubic meter)	$1.12	$0.03	37x
phone call (per minute)	$0.04–$0.05	$0.025	1.8x
diarrhea medication	$20	$2	10x
rice (per kilogram)	$0.28	$0.24	1.2x

In terms of finances, to operate successfully in BOP markets, managers must also rethink their business metrics – specifically, the traditional focus on high gross margins. In developing markets, the profit margin on individual units will always be low. What really counts is capital efficiency – getting the highest possible returns on capital employed (ROCE). Hindustan Lever, for instance, operates a \$2.6 billion business portfolio with zero working capital. The key is constant efforts to reduce capital investments by extensively outsourcing manufacturing, streamlining supply chains, actively managing receivables, and paying close attention to distributors' performance. Very low capital needs, focused distribution and technology investments, and very large volumes at low margins lead to very high ROCE businesses, creating great economic value for shareholders. It's a model that can be equally attractive in developed and developing markets.

Streamlining supply chains often involves replacing assets with information. Consider, for example, the experience of ITC, one of India's largest companies. Its agribusiness division has deployed a total of 970 kiosks serving 600,000 farmers who supply it with soy, coffee, shrimp, and wheat from 5,000 villages spread across India. This kiosk program, called e-Choupal, helps increase the farmers' productivity by disseminating the latest information on weather and best practices in farming, and by supporting other services like soil and water testing, thus facilitating the supply of quality inputs to both the farmers and ITC. The kiosks also serve as an e-procurement system, helping farmers earn higher prices by minimizing transaction costs involved in marketing farm produce. The head of ITC's agribusiness reports that the company's procurement costs have fallen since e-Choupal was implemented. And that's despite paying higher prices to its farmers: The program has enabled the company to eliminate multiple transportation, bagging, and handling steps – from farm to local market, from market to broker, from broker to processor – that did not add value in the chain.

Innovation

BOP markets are hot-beds of commercial and technological experimentation. The Swedish wireless company Ericsson, for instance, has developed a small cellular telephone system, called a MiniGSM, that local operators in BOP markets can use to offer cell phone service to a small area at a radically lower cost than conventional equipment entails. Packaged for easy shipment and deployment, it provides stand-alone or networked voice and data communications for up to 5,000 users within a 35-kilometer radius. Capital costs to the operator can be as low as \$4 per user, assuming a shared-use model with individual phones operated by local entrepreneurs. The MIT Media Lab, in collaboration with the Indian government, is developing low-cost devices that allow people to use voice commands to communicate –

without keyboards – with various Internet sites in multiple languages. These new access devices promise to be far less complex than traditional computers but would perform many of the same basic functions.[2]

As we have seen, connectivity is a big issue for BOP consumers. Companies that can find ways to dramatically lower connection costs, therefore, will have a very strong market position. And that is exactly what the Indian company n-Logue is trying to do. It connects hundreds of franchised village kiosks containing both a computer and a phone with centralized nodes that are, in turn, connected to the national phone network and the Internet. Each node, also a franchise, can serve between 30,000 and 50,000 customers, providing phone, e-mail, Internet services, and relevant local information at affordable prices to villagers in rural India. Capital costs for the n-Logue system are now about $400 per wireless "line" and are projected to decline to $100 – at least ten times lower than conventional telecom costs. On a per-customer basis, the cost may amount to as little as $1.[3] This appears to be a powerful model for ending rural isolation and linking untapped rural markets to the global economy.

New wireless technologies are likely to spur further business model innovations and lower costs even more. Ultrawideband, for example, is currently licensed in the United States only for limited, very low-power applications, in part because it spreads a signal across already-crowded portions of the broadcast spectrum. In many developing countries, however, the spectrum is less congested. In fact, the U.S.-based Dandin Group is already building an ultrawideband communications system for the Kingdom of Tonga, whose population of about 100,000 is spread over dozens of islands, making it a test bed for a next-generation technology that could transform the economics of Internet access.

E-commerce systems that run over the phone or the Internet are enormously important in BOP markets because they eliminate the need for layers of intermediaries. Consider how the U.S. start-up Voxiva has changed the way information is shared and business is transacted in Peru. The company partners with Telefonica, the dominant local carrier, to offer automated business applications over the phone. The inexpensive services include voice mail, data entry, and order placement; customers can check account balances, monitor delivery status, and access prerecorded information directories. According to the Boston Consulting Group, the Peruvian Ministry of Health uses Voxiva to disseminate information, take pharmaceutical orders, and link healthcare workers spread across 6,000 offices and clinics. Microfinance institutions use Voxiva to process loan applications and communicate with borrowers. Voxiva offers Web-based services, too, but far more of its potential customers in Latin America have access to a phone.

E-commerce companies are not the only ones turning the limitations of BOP markets to strategic advantage. A lack of dependable electric power stimulated the UK-based start-up Free-play Group to introduce hand-cranked radios in South Africa that subsequently became popular with hikers in the United States. Similar breakthroughs are being pioneered in the use of solar-powered devices such as battery chargers and water pumps. In China, where pesticide costs have often limited the use of modern agricultural techniques, there are now 13,000 small farmers – more than in the rest of the world combined – growing cotton that has been genetically engineered to be pest resistant.

Strategies for Serving BOP Markets

Certainly, succeeding in BOP markets requires multinationals to think creatively. The biggest change, though, has to come in the attitudes and practices of executives. Unless CEOs and other business leaders confront their own preconceptions, companies are unlikely to master the challenges of BOP markets. The traditional workforce is so rigidly conditioned to operate in higher-margin markets that, without formal training, it is unlikely to see the vast potential of the BOP market. The most pressing need, then, is education. Perhaps MNCs should create the equivalent of the Peace Corps: Having young managers spend a couple of formative years in BOP markets would open their eyes to the promise and the realities of doing business there.

To date, few multinationals have developed a cadre of people who are comfortable with these markets. Hindustan Lever is one of the exceptions. The company expects executive recruits to spend at least eight weeks in the villages of India to get a gut-level experience of Indian BOP markets. The new executives must become involved in some community project – building a road, cleaning up a water catchment area, teaching in a school, improving a health clinic. The goal is to engage with the local population. To buttress this effort, Hindustan Lever is initiating a massive program for managers at all levels – from the CEO down – to reconnect with their poorest customers. They'll talk with the poor in both rural and urban areas, visit the shops these customers frequent, and ask them about their experience with the company's products and those of its competitors.

In addition to expanding managers' understanding of BOP markets, companies will need to make structural changes. To capitalize on the innovation potential of these markets, for example, they might set up R&D units in developing countries that are specifically focused on local opportunities. When Hewlett-Packard launched its e-Inclusion division, which concentrates on rural markets, it established a branch of its famed HP Labs in India charged with developing products and services explicitly for this market. Hindustan Lever maintains a significant R&D effort in India, as well.

Companies might also create venture groups and internal investment funds aimed at seeding entrepreneurial efforts in BOP markets. Such investments reap direct benefits in terms of business experience and market development. They can also play an indirect but vital role in growing the overall BOP market in sectors that will ultimately benefit the multinational.

At least one major U.S. corporation is planning to launch such a fund, and the G8's Digital Opportunity Task Force is proposing a similar one focused on digital ventures.

MNCs should also consider creating a business development task force aimed at these markets. Assembling a diverse group of people from across the corporation and empowering it to function as a skunk works team that ignores conventional dogma will likely lead to greater innovation. Companies that have tried this approach have been surprised by the amount of interest such a task force generates. Many employees want to work on projects that have the potential to make a real difference in improving the lives of the poor. When Hewlett-Packard announced its e-Inclusion division, for example, it was overwhelmed by far more volunteers than it could accommodate.

Making internal changes is important, but so is reaching out to external partners. Joining with businesses that are already established in these markets can be an effective entry strategy, since these companies will naturally understand the market dynamics better. In addition to limiting the risks for each player, partnerships also maximize the existing infrastructure – both physical and social. MNCs seeking partners should look beyond businesses to NGOs and community groups. They are key sources of knowledge about customers' behavior, and they often experiment the most with new services and new delivery models. In fact, of the social enterprises experimenting with creative uses of digital technology that the Digital Dividend Project Clearinghouse tracked, nearly 80% are NGOs. In Namibia, for instance, an organization called SchoolNet is providing low-cost, alternative technology solutions – such as solar power and wireless approaches – to schools and community-based groups throughout the country. SchoolNet is currently linking as many as 35 new schools every month.

Entrepreneurs also will be critical partners. According to an analysis by McKinsey & Company, the rapid growth of cable TV in India – there are 50 million connections a decade after introduction – is largely due to small entrepreneurs. These individuals have been building the last mile of the network, typically by putting a satellite dish on their own houses and laying cable to connect their neighbors. A note of caution, however. Entrepreneurs in BOP markets lack access to the advice, technical help, seed funding, and business support services available in the industrial world. So MNCs may need to take on mentoring roles or partner with local business development organizations that can help entrepreneurs create investment and partnering opportunities.

It's worth noting that, contrary to popular opinion, women play a significant role in the economic development of these regions. MNCs, therefore, should pay particular attention to women entrepreneurs. Women are also likely to play the most critical role in product acceptance not only because of their childcare and household management activities but also because of the social capital that they have built up in their communities. Listening to and educating such customers is essential for success.

Sharing Intelligence

What creative new approaches to serving the bottom-of-the-pyramid markets have digital technologies made possible? Which sectors or countries show the most economic activity or the fastest growth? What new business models show promise? What kinds of partnerships – for funding, distribution, public relations – have been most successful?

The Digital Dividend Project Clearinghouse (digitaldividend.org) helps answer those types of questions. The Web site tracks the activities of organizations that use digital tools to provide connectivity and deliver services to underserved populations in developing countries. Currently, it contains information on 700 active projects around the world. Maintained under the auspices of the nonprofit World Resources Institute, the site lets participants in different projects share experiences and swap knowledge with one another. Moreover, the site provides data for trend analyses and other specialized studies that facilitate market analyses, local partnerships, and rapid, low-cost learning.

Regardless of the opportunities, many companies will consider the bottom of the pyramid to be too risky. We've shown how partnerships can limit risk; another option is to enter into consortia. Imagine sharing the costs of building a rural network with the communications company that would operate it, a consumer goods company seeking channels to expand its sales, and a bank that is financing the construction and wants to make loans to and collect deposits from rural customers.

Investing where powerful synergies exist will also mitigate risk. The Global Digital Opportunity Initiative, a partnership of the Markle Foundation and the UN Development Programme, will help a small number of countries implement a strategy to harness the power of information and communications technologies to increase development. The countries will be chosen in part based on their interest and their willingness to make supportive regulatory and market reforms. To concentrate resources and create reinforcing effects, the initiative will encourage international aid agencies and global companies to assist with implementation.

All of the strategies we've outlined here will be of little use, however, unless the external barriers we've touched on – poor infrastructure, inadequate connectivity, corrupt intermediaries, and the like – are removed. Here's where technology holds the most promise. Information and communications technologies can grant access to otherwise isolated communities, provide marketing and distribution channels, bypass intermediaries, drive down transaction costs, and help aggregate demand and buying power. Smart cards and other emerging technologies are inexpensive ways to give poor customers a secure identity, a transaction or credit history, and even a virtual address — prerequisites for interacting with the formal economy. That's why high-tech companies aren't the only ones that should be interested in closing the global digital divide; encouraging the spread of low-cost digital networks at the bottom of the pyramid is a priority for virtually all companies that want to enter and engage with these markets. Improved connectivity is an important catalyst for more effective markets, which are critical to boosting income levels and accelerating economic growth.

Moreover, global companies stand to gain from the effects of network expansion in these markets. According to Metcalfe's Law, the usefulness of a network equals the square of the number of users. By the same logic, the value and vigor of the economic activity that will be generated when hundreds of thousands of previously isolated rural communities can buy and sell from one another and from urban markets will increase dramatically — to the benefit of all participants.

***

Since BOP markets require significant rethinking of managerial practices, it is legitimate for managers to ask: Is it worth the effort?

We think the answer is yes. For one thing, big corporations should solve big problems — and what is a more pressing concern than alleviating the poverty that 4 billion people are currently mired in? It is hard to argue that the wealth of technology and talent within leading multinationals is better allocated to producing incremental variations of existing products than to addressing the real needs — and real opportunities — at the bottom of the pyramid. Moreover, through competition, multinationals are likely to bring to BOP markets a level of accountability for performance and resources that neither international development agencies nor national governments have demonstrated during the last 50 years. Participation by MNCs could set a new standard, as well as a new market-driven paradigm, for addressing poverty.

But ethical concerns aside, we've shown that the potential for expanding the bottom of the market is just too great to ignore. Big companies need to focus on big market opportunities if they want to generate real growth. It is simply good business strategy to be involved in large, untapped markets that offer new customers, cost-saving opportunities, and access to radical innovation. The business opportunities at the bottom of the pyramid are real, and they are open to any MNC willing to engage and learn.

Notes

1.   Andrew Lawlor, Caitlin Peterson, and Vivek Sandell, "Catalyzing Rural Development: TARAhaat.com" (World Resources Institute, July 2001).
2.   Michael Best and Colin M. Maclay, "Community Internet Access in Rural Areas: Solving the Economic Sustainability Puzzle," *The Global Information Technology Report 2001–2002: Readiness for the Networked World,* ed., Geoffrey Kirkman (Oxford

University Press, 2002), available on-line at http://www.cid.harvard.edu/cr/gitrr_O3O2O2.html.
3.   Joy Howard, Erik Simanis, and Charis Simms, "Sustainable Deployment for Rural Connectivity: The n-Logue Model" (World Resources Institute, July 2001).

ETHICAL CONSUMERS AND THE CSR MARKETPLACE

Andrew Crane

Introduction

It is now commonplace to assert that consumers want firms to be more socially responsible. All things being equal, who would not want to buy from a responsible company rather than an irresponsible one? Who would not choose the fairly traded, organic, eco-friendly product over the exploitative, pesticide-ridden, polluting one — assuming of course that you do not have to compromise on quality, taste or design . . . — or pay more for the privilege. But things are rarely that simple. Often it is far from easy to distinguish the responsible from the irresponsible. And even when there are clear socially responsible attributes, they rarely come without a trade-off or two. For all their avowed commitment to rewarding socially responsible firms, customers are not always willing to back up their promises with their wallets. So although the message has now gotten through to many companies that their consumers increasingly have social, ethical and environmental expectations that they wish to see addressed in one way or another, the big question is *how* should firms respond to these expectations?

In this article, I shall explore this question in the context of marketing strategy, focusing in particular on how companies might engage in CSR to appeal to the ethical demands of consumers. This is an important area to consider, not least because it starts us thinking about how (or even whether) ethical concerns might be translated into tangible practices, products and services. But perhaps more importantly, it also starts to focus our attentions on the myriad challenges that ethical consumers might pose for companies, and in particular on the difficulties inherent in turning their demands into a viable and sustainable business proposition.

I will begin by establishing the types and range of companies that might be within the field of vision for socially or ethically concerned consumers — and put this into the context of the other non-consumer stakeholders likely to also be interested in the company's CSR practices. Then I will go on to look at specific strategic positions that might be adopted by the firm, primarily with a view to delineating strategies appropriate to 'ethical niche' and 'mainstream' orientations, before proceeding to outline the challenges and tensions that these postures typically raise. Once I have set out these broad strategic orientations, I will look a little closer at the types of CSR products, brands, images, and programmes that organizations might produce to appeal to consumers, and how we might conceptualize them as 'augmentations' to the basic value proposition. Crucially, these types of augmentations typically have implications well beyond the purview of the marketing department, and so we will finish with some consideration of the deeper issues around corporate-wide commitment to CSR necessary to develop appropriate market responses to CSR. I will conclude with a summary of the main points and a few brief comments on the state of current theory and practice and prospects for the future.

Companies in the CSR Marketplace

Responding to the social, ethical and environmental demands of consumers is something that all sorts of companies might need to do at some stage – from companies that have been expressly established to pursue particular social goals, such as those in the co-operative or fair trade movements, all the way up to huge multinational corporations dedicated to maximising shareholder value, such as Monsanto or BP. For example, in the confectionary industry, some companies such as the US-based Endangered Species Chocolate are specifically dedicated to sustainable farming and ethical trade, producing all-natural organic chocolate products and donating 10% of net profits to conservation efforts. Others, such as Kraft, the global market leader, have a much larger target market (currently around 15% of the global confectionary market) which means that whilst they commit to a range of social and environmental practices across their span of operations, fair trade principles are limited only to specific products (e.g. its Cadbury Dairy Milk bars) and organic products are largely the restricted to its Green & Blacks brand, which is just one of the firm's many chocolate brands including Cadbury, Cote d'Or, Marabou, Milka, and Toblerone.

So in examining how companies seek to appeal positively to consumers through CSR, it is not unusual to think primarily of those companies at either extreme of the spectrum – i.e. those most in the 'firing line' of boycotters (at one end), or those seeking to capitalise on an explicitly 'ethical' selling proposition (at the other). But even a good deal of those occupying more of a middle ground will need to exercise some kind of strategic decision making, perhaps because they recognize that the firing line is going to reach them too at some time, or because they cherish a reputation for being a 'good citizen'.

Now, although certain companies might wish to respond to the social concerns consumers, it needs to be said that there are many companies that do not, and probably even *need* not, consider these concerns of their consumers at all. Although I am not going to discuss these companies here, it is worth remembering that the ones that do seek to respond to 'ethical' or 'responsible' consumers are by no means necessarily in the majority. And, as we shall see, even for many of these, CSR considerations are not always at the heart of their operations.

The first substantive issue to note here is that it is almost impossible to separate out the impact of ethically concerned consumers on organizations from the host of other CSR forces that might confront them. This includes pressure from the media, government, civil society, competitors, or any other relevant constituency. In part, this inability to separate out the impact of consumers is due to lack of research. But there is also a largely unexamined assumption prevalent in much of the debate around marketing and CSR that firms will automatically respond to the demands of consumers – the 'accepted sequence' (Galbraith, 1974) of *consumer sovereignty* – i.e. an assumption that consumers drive the decisions of companies through their purchase 'votes' rather than the other way round. Notwithstanding the theoretical limitations of this assumption, there are also a number of conditions that might influence this purported cause-and-effect relationship, such as the amount of concentrated power wielded by consumers, and the vulnerability and visibility of the corporate brand in the marketplace.

The relative influence of ethically concerned consumers on firms compared with other CSR forces is not, however, just a matter of establishing empirical fact. There is an extremely important normative question here that is frequently eclipsed by the assumption that firms *will* respond to consumers – namely, whether firms *should* respond to the social and ethical demands of consumers. Now to many advocates of CSR, this probably sounds perverse. But from a normative standpoint, there seems to be no *prima facie* reason why a firm – even supposing it wanted to act in the best interests of society – should privilege the views of one particular group of consumers, or one particular preference expressed by consumers, however well meaning those consumers might appear to be. Although marketers often assume the primacy of consumer interests, a multi-stakeholder view of the firm would typically regard this as problematic (Jackson, 2001). Moreover, who is to say that answering the demands of one set of ethical consumers is really in the best interests of society?

Of course, it *may* be, but then again, it may not. Indeed, determining the right thing to do is inevitably fraught with complexity and uncertainty, especially when firms have a whole range of stakeholders to satisfy. Often the issues are too complex and global for consumers to really know what the best solutions are. Listening to, and attempting to appeal to concerned consumers is one possible approach for companies to take, but there are clearly other, perhaps preferable, approaches that can also be considered (see Crane and Desmond, 2002). Indeed, should we even have consumers making *choices* about whether firms should harm employees in the supply chain, use slaves in the production process, or pollute the environment? Shouldn't these be fundamental requirements?

Many firms often held up as exemplars of successful social responsibility, such as Ben & Jerry's, Tom's of Maine, and the Body Shop have claimed to have followed the instincts and drives of their leaders in determining their ethical stance rather than taking a customer-led approach (see Chappell, 1993; Lager, 1994; Roddick, 1992). This kind of internal drive could be seen as a more stable (though arguably less 'democratic') foundation for responsible business than one that relies on changing market preferences. Similarly, it could be argued that government and civil society organizations have a more legitimate mandate to act in society's best interests than individual consumers, and so companies should primarily determine their CSR priorities in consultation with these parties rather than conducting customer opinion surveys. These propositions are most certainly contestable, but that does not deflect from the issue that the appropriate status of consumers' CSR demands is an often-overlooked issue that almost certainly warrants further debate in the literature. At the very least, I think it is worth considering consumers as just one part of the CSR landscape confronting corporations, albeit one that may well be influential in how firms orient themselves to the CSR marketplace. Let us now turn our attention to the types of strategies that firms may adopt in establishing this orientation.

Strategies for orienting towards the CSR marketplace: mainstreaming or ethical niche?

In recent years, there has been a growing number of commentators extolling firms to listen to and respond to the social, ethical and environmental demands of consumers, to 'sell corporate social responsibility' (Cobb, 2002), to build 'ethical brands' (Mitchell, 1997), and to capitalise on the growing CSR market. The notion of a CSR or 'ethical' market is perhaps a rather nebulous one, but what I mean by it here is essentially a demand, either implicit or explicit, for corporate actions, communications, or other artefacts that have a positive and identifiable CSR component to those outside the company. This can mean products with social, ethical or environmental features of one kind or another, such as fair trade or recycled products; it can mean cause-related marketing programmes, employee welfare programmes, or the development of an ethical code; in fact, it can mean a whole host of corporate endeavours that consumers and other stakeholders might demand from corporations for supposedly socially responsible reasons.

Probably the most straightforward way of thinking about how firms orient towards this CSR marketplace is to conceive of a continuum of focus, from a narrow specialization in an 'ethical niche' towards an attempt to address CSR within a more 'mainstream' market. Basically, all I'm saying here is that some firms focus exclusively or mainly on promoting their CSR credentials (ethical niche), whilst others primarily stress other factors, yet still articulate their CSR credentials as a secondary or additional factor (mainstreaming).

One obvious way of conceptualising this distinction is to consider niche and mainstreaming strategies as the two main manifestations of Porter's

(1985) 'differentiation' strategies, whereby firms seek to position themselves as offering superior qualities either across the whole market or in a specific market niche (see Figure 5.2 for a simple depiction). Why should we consider CSR as a 'differentiation'? Well, this is a slightly tricky one, since for many people, the whole idea of using social responsibility to strategically promote firms and products is in fact questionable in itself (for a discussion, see Husted and Allen, 2000). Again, such thinking starts to raise another of the fundamental paradoxes in much of our thinking about firms in relation to CSR and consumers. On the one hand, we want firms to *genuinely* and *actively* embrace social responsibility, but at the same time, we extol them to listen to and respond to ethical consumers. The former represents taking a stand on what you as a firm believe in – the latter represents a more *instrumental* and *reactive* approach based in what you think others believe in.

Putting such tensions aside for one moment though (we will return to them later), the mere fact that some, perhaps many consumers, are likely to be attracted to firms they perceive to be socially responsible suggests that such considerations are a means by which consumers differentiate between firms and their offerings. In this sense, firms promoting their CSR credentials may be seen as offering 'augmentations' to the basic product offering (Crane, 2001). It is not just a bank account, but a bank account from a 'caring' bank; not just a bar of chocolate, but a bar of chocolate that ensures growers a decent standard of living; not just a trip to the supermarket, but one to a supermarket that gives some of the money you spend back to local schools. There will certainly be other augmentations too, but CSR qualities are part of the bundle of benefits through which firms seek to differentiate themselves in the mind of the consumer.

There are, I should add, considerable limitations to the usefulness of Porter's (1985) model for understanding strategic positioning (e.g. Miller and Dess, 1993). However, as long as we use this model simply to identify the basic approaches evident in the CSR marketplace, it seems to be a reasonable conceptualisation, and in so far as it is widely understood and used in strategy theory and practice, it seems to be a useful starting point for thinking about how firms respond to the CSR concerns of their consumers. Let us then now look in a little more detail at these main differentiating orientations.

	Low cost	Differentiation
Broad	*CSR cost leadership*	*Mainstream CSR orientation*
Narrow	*CSR cost focus*	*Ethical niche*

Figure 5.2: Orientations to the CSR marketplace

ETHICAL NICHE ORIENTATION

Firms targeting the ethical niche will see their customers as having strong ethical preferences which drive their product selections, and other consumer decisions, such as where and how to shop. Hence, such companies will typically position their products as socially responsible alternatives to conventional competitive offerings. According to marketing logic, these companies' products should therefore offer unique CSR features above and beyond industry standards, and communications should generally concentrate on emphasising these benefits rather than other attributes of the product or the firm. Again, conventional marketing logic would tend to dictate that this type of differentiation should provide added value to consumers, and so should command a premium price. Firms occupying the ethical niche might also ordinarily have social, ethical, or environmental goals as an integral part of their espoused mission, coupled with a public commitment to certain principles or practices.

Consider the example of Triodos, the Dutch 'ethical bank', whose mission is 'to make money work for positive change', and which markets its corporate banking services to a niche of charities and 'social businesses'. Similarly, the Canada-based Me to We Style is an apparel company 'committed to providing ethically manufactured, quality apparel for the socially-conscious consumer'. Given their commitment to ensuring growers a premium price, many companies marketing certified fair trade products (such as Max Havelaar products in the Netherlands or TransFair in the US) have also typically targeted a niche of concerned consumers, as have 'green' firms offering more environmentally benign products, such as the Belgium cleaning products company Ecover, or the US toiletries firm Tom's of Maine. The key point is that ethical niche firms see their aims best achieved by satisfying a relatively small group of concerned customers, and as a result, are mainly small specialist firms.

MAINSTREAM CSR ORIENTATION

In contrast, a mainstreaming orientation towards the CSR marketplace includes a range of different types of firm, with potentially very different values. The ethical considerations of consumers are still important here, and mainstreaming firms may well have ethical codes, or use labels such as eco-labels to certify their credentials. But these will not be the *main* selling proposition of the products and services on offer, the primary focus of differentiation. This means that it could be that CSR credentials are seen as a fundamental part of doing business, or simply an 'added extra', or even a passing fad, but either way, these firms will not principally position their products on this basis.

The reasons why these firms do not seek to invoke CSR issues as the main selling proposition for their products might stem from a range of factors, including a concern that consumers might judge them as simply 'greenwashers', doubts over consumers' willingness to pay a premium for CSR attributes, or a fear that such promoting such attributes might even have a negative or distracting effect on the consumer's evaluation of the product's quality. Recycled materials for example are often perceived to be lower quality than virgin, and so companies may elect not to actively promote this CSR feature to their main customer base. I think it is reasonable to assume that the basic underlying assumption here is that firms believe that most of their consumers' CSR concerns are secondary to other considerations such as price, quality, and convenience – or at least are secondary for more of the time than they are primary. Mainstream firms typically target a larger market than niche firms, and it would appear that there are few if any markets where differentiation *primarily* on the basis of CSR is a sustainable business proposition beyond a narrow niche. This is not to say that firms will ignore the ethical considerations of their consumers in this context, since we are very much concerned with those firms that do attempt to differentiate at least partly on the basis of CSR. Such differentiation though is typically just one element in a portfolio of differentiating factors that is necessary to gain significant market share in mainstream markets.

This is a relatively broad definition, so naturally there are numerous examples of firms in this category, from companies such as the UK home improvements company B&Q, which pioneered the use of the Forest Stewardship Council sustainable timber accreditation programme in the UK, to the US clothing company American Apparel which typically makes little mention of its industry-leading labor conditions when promoting its high street fashions. The key point is that mainstream firms see their aims best achieved by satisfying a relatively large group of customers who are concerned about CSR issues, but are unwilling to sacrifice the other aspects they value for those concerns.

A LOW-COST CSR ORIENTATION?

If then it seems reasonable to suggest that firms orienting towards the CSR marketplace have adopted some form of differentiating strategy, we might also consider whether firms adopting Porter's (1985) other main strategic posture – a *low cost strategy* – could seek to orient towards the CSR market. Given that attention to CSR and the concomitant needs to certify and communicate CSR credentials is inevitably a costly business, it might seem on the face of it fairly unlikely that a firm seeking to maintain a strong cost advantage over its competitors would desire, or be able, to appeal very successfully to responsible consumers.

However, in the specific area of sustainability, a low cost strategy is a very plausible alternative. This is because firms have opportunities for reducing resource inputs, operating more efficiently and/or establishing cost leadership by pre-empting legislative burdens. A good example of a main-stream low cost orientation is Wal-Mart, which in recent years has sought to position itself as a sustainability leader whilst still achieving low cost leadership – and hence low prices for customers. In the ethical niche, the UK energy supplier Ecotricity offers to match its competitors' prices (or as it puts it 'green for the price of brown') at the same time as claiming to have the 'greenest outcome' due to being the provider with the greatest propor-tion of investment in renewable energy[1].

Whilst issues such as eco-efficiency are specific to environmental considerations, there is also cost leadership potential for some other non-environmental CSR issues. Consider the case of CSR issues potentially subject to new stricter legislation, such as employee rights or social report-ing. Here, firms can gain cost advantages by pre-empting legislation and developing appropriate competences sooner than their competitors (Porter and van der Linde, 1995). For instance, moves to implement mandatory social reporting in countries such as Denmark and France has conferred cost advantages on companies that were already well advanced along the learning curve and had established efficient procedures for auditing and reporting on CSR prior to the introduction of the legislation. Still, in the main it is in the sustainability area of CSR where much of the cost reductions can be realized so whilst a low cost orientation to the CSR marketplace is certainly a possibility, it is far more difficult to realize across a broad range of CSR issues. Wal-Mart, for instance, has been far more successful in reconciling its cost minimisation strategy with eco-efficiencies than with other CSR issues such as employee rights and welfare.

OPPORTUNITIES AND TENSIONS IN CSR MARKETPLACE ORIENTATIONS

Returning to the question of differentiation strategies, both the mainstream and ethical niche approaches offer certain opportunities as well as raising significant tensions for firms. In the case of niche firms, it might be said to be reasonably straightforward to maintain a CSR focus whilst marketing to a fairly committed group of consumers. However, there are often intense competitive pressures from mainstream firms who see opportunities in these niches, and who may be able enjoy cost advantages and superior marketing budgets in targeting them. For instance, many niche firms focusing on organic products now face intense competitive threats from powerful retail multiples that have rapidly expanded their ranges in recent years. Wal-Mart, for one, has explicitly set out to bring down the cost of organic food so that it no longer remains just a luxury item for a select niche but also becomes accessible for typical Wal-Mart customers (Hockerts and Wüstenhagen, 2010).

In other instances, ethical niche firms may actually find themselves dissatisfied with miniscule market shares, and effectively 'preaching to the converted'. The drive for more mass-market success, firm growth, and a larger audience for the socially responsible message have therefore led many ethical niche firms to seek opportunities for expansion beyond their existing niche. As Meyer (1999) suggests, this often requires firms to think more in terms of Hamel and Prahalad's (1991) 'expeditionary marketing' approach and 'envision' appropriate mass markets. This means looking towards shaping future markets and going beyond typical niche assumptions and practices that may restrict growth – such as depending on specialist distribution channels and relying on conventional 'ethical' marketing practices.

For instance, many fair trade companies in the UK such as Cafédirect, Day Chocolate, and Traidcraft have shifted from the movement's traditional 'solidarity' approach towards a more market-oriented model in a bid to appeal to a more mainstream market (Davies and Crane, 2003; Nicholls, 2002). This has led to a change in emphasis in product advertising towards product quality and other aspects of consumer self-interest rather than the typical fair trade message that emphasizes producer poverty. As Wright (2003) argues, Cafédirect's groundbreaking success in seizing market share in the UK coffee coincided with a shift in communications strategy, from a 'bleeding hearts' message to one reinforcing the 'pleasures of consumerism.' Thus, 'emphasis is placed on the gratification available to the consumers, who can realize their self-worth and display their distinction through treating themselves to a superior coffee' (Wright, 2003: 21).

Such moves, as one might imagine, almost inevitably raises tensions between the need to increase competitiveness and attract more customers whilst at the same time honouring corporate values and maintaining ethical integrity (Hockerts and Wüstenhagen, 2010). For example, some ethical nichers seeking to go mainstream may have to face the thorny question of whether they should risk dilution of their ethical values and reputation by sourcing from, or supplying to, large multinationals. Major retailers might open the doors to larger markets, but potentially not share the same values as an ethical niche company. Research at the UK fair trade company Day Chocolate, for instance, has suggested that the acceptability of various types of relationships with mass market companies such as Sainsbury's, Shell, Body Shop and McDonald's is a matter of quite complex rationalisation and renegotiation amongst managers about who is 'acceptable' or not to work with (Davies and Crane, 2003). Similarly, ethical nichers risk alienating existing customers and staff alike if a move to the mainstream marks too much of a break with established traditions (Dey, 2002).

At the most extreme, ethical nichers may even be purchased by mainstream firms, as was the case with Ben & Jerry's ice cream, which was bought by Unilever, the Body Shop, which was taken over by L'Oreal, and Burt's Bees which is now part of Clorox. This offers opportunities to change mainstream companies from within, but also represents a major risk in mission dilution as the niche company disappears into the corporate giant, and has to accept a new set of operating principles and performance metrics.

Subsequent efforts to target the mass market with a CSR message has considerable potential to engender strategic confusion.

Building CSR campaigns and brands

CSR differentiation or augmentation is essentially about a process of creating an 'ethical image', a 'good reputation' or what marketers typically refer to as a socially responsible or ethical *brand*. The challenge of creating such a brand has given rise to considerable discussion across the business and research communities, especially given growing concerns about falling levels of trust in corporations to behave in a responsible manner (Porter and Kramer, 2011) coupled with efforts by corporations to use their social responsibility programmes more strategically in order to enhance brand value (Middlemiss, 2003; Mitchell, 1997).

Many brands actually communicate social or ethical elements of one sort or another, especially values such as trust and honesty, but also increasingly qualities such as 'good citizenship', 'social responsibility' and 'environmental concern' (Lane Keller, 2000). Of course, most firms would like to build brands that customers trust; however, for the most part, what we mean by trust here is typically conceptualized in fairly limited terms, such as trusting the brand to be truthful about its ingredients, deliver consistent quality, or offer value-for-money. Trusting a company to be socially responsible goes considerably further than this, and it is evident that many brands are facing something of a trust deficit in terms of the public's faith in their commitment to doing the right thing. Perceived brand authenticity thus becomes a critical factor in the success of CSR communications efforts.

Such problems in the ethical image of corporations are of course something mainly faced by large multinationals, especially as it is typically multinationals that have borne the brunt of the major scandals, media exposés, and boycotts that have accelerated the public's loss of trust. To some extent, the ethical nichers identified in the previous section may have found themselves somewhat insulated from (and possibly even benefiting from) this growing trust deficit of big business. However, it has to be said that the more people distrust business – whether large or small, 'ethical' or otherwise – the more scrutiny business is subjected to, and the harder it becomes for *any* firm to maintain trust and legitimacy.

In fact, this is likely to impact upon firms seeking to respond in a positive way to the CSR marketplace perhaps even more than many others. After all, differentiating on the basis of ethics or social responsibility, even when this is only a minor element in the overall bundle of attributes offered, is somewhat different to many other forms of differentiation. Most notably, in order to be credible, 'ethical' differentiation requires a whole company effort (Crane, 2001). Compare for example the difference involved in backing up a claim that a company is more 'socially responsible' than a competitor or a product 'more ethical', with the rather more straightforward task of claiming that a sofa is more comfortable, a drink better tasting, or a manufacturer better at designing stylish automotives. Whilst the latter claims can be ascertained by consumers simply by sitting on, tasting, or looking at the products on offer, the former are far more difficult to determine since such claims assume numerous contingencies deep within the operations of the firm and even beyond its boundaries to include the operations of suppliers, advertisers, investors, etc.

In part, this is because most evaluations of CSR claims, even when very product specific, are likely to involve some evaluation of the reputation of the company more broadly. After all, any attempt to differentiate a product as a socially responsible alternative may be assessed by consumers against a backdrop of knowledge about how the company treats its workforce, its environmental record, which companies it has bought from or sold to in the past, and all kinds of other possible factors. Consumers may not always be very consistent themselves in their purchasing, but they are often quick to denounce a 'cynical' or 'hypocritical' corporation for any observable gap between the socially responsible image projected in advertising campaigns and the 'reality' perceived in the stores and through the media.

Probably the key issue here is one of consistency. I am not sure how realistic it is for firms to really be completely consistent in all they do, not least because they often have such conflicting demands, and will project different impressions, identities, even different 'realities' to their various stakeholders (Crane and Livesey, 2003). Nonetheless, marketers often seek to emphasize that in the marketing game 'perception *is* reality' so it is not so much whether firms *are* consistent that matters, but whether they *appear* to be. Such a view is popular with brand managers and other advocates of corporate branding, since much of their raison d'être is to find and deliver a stable and consistent image of the firm. However, as Cheney and Christensen (2000) argue, there is great potential for self-delusion and self-seduction in such beliefs.

This means that in a fragmented and volatile business environment, where corporations are ever more complex, and where some degree of consumer cynicism can be almost taken for granted, the search for a shared understanding about a corporation's values may often be a hopelessly idealistic one. Indeed, many of the high profile campaigns waged by pressure groups against corporations have involved a hijacking of the carefully nurtured brand image of companies such as Exxon, McDonald's and Nike, in order to take advantage of the brands' immense global leverage to promulgate a radically different message to the ones intended by the companies. The corporate image, insofar as it is a response to, or reflection of, the ethical concerns of consumers, is open to contestation by those same consumers.

A new approach to CSR branding?

So what can corporations do when faced with such a business environment, where many consumers and other stakeholders seem to be demanding more in CSR terms, but at the same time, are extremely quick to contest the brand image and denounce any efforts they deem to be hypocritical or insufficient? One way to respond could be through better communication to stakeholders that avoids the overly glossy and sometimes deliberately misleading attempts to create a positive CSR image without the necessary substance. I think it is fair to say that the most risible attempts at corporate 'greenwash' are probably behind us now – the late 1980s and early 1990s were often characterized by critics as a time when the communications environment was awash with misleading and over-hyped claims (Davis, 1992; National Consumer Council, 1996). However, still companies continue to commit many of the 'sins of greenwashing' such as vagueness, irrelevance, and lack of substantiation (Terrachoice, 2010).

Despite the continued problem of greenwashing, many firms appear to have backed away from an approach based primarily on communicating a responsible image, not least because of the cynicism and 'backlash' that it has engendered amongst consumers and other stakeholders in the past (Crane, 2000). Although there are of course exceptions, corporations now seem to be more reserved and cautious about the type of claims that they make. As Robert Wilson, the former Chair of Rio Tinto (a company no stranger to criticism) said on the dangers of not 'walking the talk': 'It's pretty important to get the policies and implementation right before you start spending too much time on the external communications' (Middlemiss, 2003: 358).

For some this has meant taking a more defensive or 'muted' approach (Crane, 2000), whereby specific CSR claims are relegated behind other brand attributes. Labels and certifications that confirm to customers that products have certain socially responsible qualities (such as sustainably sourced or fairly traded) are now commonplace but rarely represent a major component of the brand image. As we saw earlier, this is consistent with a more mainstream approach to the CSR marketplace, but it also means that social responsibility becomes more of a background quality that isn't necessarily vigorously promoted, but is embedded as part of a broader programme of *corporate marketing* (Hildebrand et al., 2011) and *reputational risk management* (Middlemiss, 2003). Increasingly, it would appear, the key factor for many companies when orienting towards the mainstream CSR market is not so very much the lure of increasing sales, but rather an attempt to develop a distinctive identity and prevent the brand from being attacked.

Companies such as these are now all too aware of the dangers inherent in attempting to maintain legitimacy in the face of the critical attention of consumers, NGOs, and other potential critics. Therefore, it is perhaps not too surprising that many firms have invested in more defensive approaches to communicating their responsibility, such as third party certifications and social and sustainability reports. Similarly, many such companies have also increasingly claimed to have moved from a one-way model of communicating their social responsibility towards a dialoguing model that actually consults with stakeholders to determine their expectations and priorities (Crane and Livesey, 2003).

It is debateable how many multinationals have actually succeeded in this endeavour, or how far they have actually progressed (or intend to progress) down this path. However, it is fairly clear that the conventional wisdom now is that rather than just undertaking a 'charm offensive' in the foreground of the marketplace through advertising and PR, the most effective way to build a CSR brand is to adopt a more holistic, long term, and some might say conservative approach that focuses more on communicating with key reality definers in the relative background of the CSR industry and being more transparent about products, their sourcing, and their impacts. Some leading multinationals such as Unilever and Marks and Spencer have set out ambitious but specific long term targets as part of major strategic CSR initiatives. Many others have increasingly provided greater information about the social, ethical and environmental dimensions of their products without necessarily putting such information directly in the face of consumers.

Of course, this is not to deny that many firms are actively promoting a growing range of ostensibly 'ethical' products to consumers, such as fair trade or organic produce, energy efficient washing machines, and the like. But as we have seen, the CSR claims have decreased in emphasis, whilst the whole bureaucratic process of backing up and certifying claims as well as the emphasis on reputational risk management has rapidly escalated in importance. Similarly, other popular ways of appealing directly to ethical consumers, such as *cause-related marketing,* tend to be rather conservative in their approach to brand building. By cause-related marketing, I mean where consumer purchases are linked to corporate contributions to good causes – essentially a co-alignment of marketing goals with corporate philanthropy (Varadarajan and Menon, 1988). For examples, in the Tesco for School and Clubs Campaign in the UK customers collect vouchers for every £10 they spend in Tesco supermarkets and then local schools and clubs can redeem the vouchers for computer and sports equipment.

Such programmes have become increasingly popular with corporations and charities alike (Cobb, 2002; Lewis, 2003). And as far as CSR branding is concerned, although cause-related marketing is one of the most visible aspects of a company's social responsibility programme (Lewis, 2003) it has a relatively narrow remit that tends to focus attention on the specific project rather than the company's broader social role and impacts. As a result, such campaigns are likely to contribute only gradually to the CSR brand image (and for some consumers, arguably not at all) given that the motivations for such 'win-win' initiatives will always be questioned to some extent. Perhaps though, as Cobb (2002: 26) argues, 'even the disillusioned will concede that actions which benefit society are still worthy, whatever the motive.' Hence, providing the project and the partnering are right, cause-related marketing is probably a relatively safe option for companies seeking to look good in the CSR marketplace.

The question of motive that has arisen here in relation to cause-related marketing is something that I raised earlier in the chapter. This is an important issue that in many ways goes to the heart of what exactly consumers expect from corporations in CSR terms – do they just want action that benefits society, or do they also desire firms to be ethical in a deeper sense, perhaps to be motivated by some degree of altruism, or guided by a mission to do good? I will not seek to provide a definitive answer to this question, since my aim in this chapter is not to examine consumers' preferences but to explore how firms respond to them. Therefore, in the final section, I will look a little more closely at how ethical preferences from consumers are interpreted, and made meaningful inside companies – and in so doing, start to unpack the whole motives issue a little more.

What do companies know about the CSR concerns of their consumers?

So far in this article I have spoken of companies as if they were essentially 'black boxes' that responded in certain ways to certain kinds of stimulus from consumers and other stakeholders. This is helpful in some ways, but also somewhat limiting in others. In particular, it begs certain questions about the motives of corporations, and about what we might call the 'ethical essence' of the company – is its commitment to social responsibility genuine, do its managers really believe in what they are doing, is it in the final analysis an 'ethical company'? These are not really questions that it is particularly easy to answer, and many of them rest on fairly shaky anthropomorphic assumptions that a company 'thinks', 'feels', or 'believes' in anything in the first place. But at the very least, they start us thinking about organizational processes that translates the actions or commitments of consumers into tangible CSR products, campaigns, and other corporate artefacts.

I think the first thing to say here is that most companies probably don't have a very clear idea of their consumers' ethical beliefs and values in the first place. Companies such as the UK's Cooperative Bank and the Co-operative Group may have preceded their ethical branding initiatives back in the mid 1990s with extensive customer surveys ascertaining views on various issues such as animal welfare, the environment, fair trade, and the supply of weapons (CWS, 1995; Kitson, 1996), but these remain the exception. Certainly many ethical niche companies don't tend to go in for (or cannot afford) formal market research. And amongst mainstream firms, the whole idea of canvassing the ethical opinions of the customer base has still not received a wide uptake. Most companies would appear to rely on evidence from more general surveys and market intelligence such as that provided by polling organizations such as MORI, Globescan or Edelman as well as the occasional question or two that might make it onto their usual market research instruments.

Regardless though of the factuality of customers' CSR opinions and demands, there is little doubt that some sense of consumer pressure towards CSR is felt within companies. Of course, this doesn't necessarily mean that the pressure experienced inside corporations is necessarily recognisable as the same thing that the customer expresses (or intends to express) outside. The corporate decision making process itself often obscures or reconstructs the ethical concerns of consumers. For a start, most organizations interface with consumers at something of a distance – they canvass opinions through agencies, and with mail-shot questionnaires; if they interact with consumers, it is often only at the point of sale; and those making decisions in production or marketing or finance remain physically and psychologically distant from the end consumer.

Similarly, because of the bureaucratic nature of most organizations, customers' ethical thoughts and feelings often need to be labelled, aggregated, quantified, and fed into the productive process as inputs and outputs, targets and projections, as objects or units to be plotted onto a chart (Desmond and Crane, 2004). Consumers' social considerations are largely relevant only to the extent that they drive sales, not because they are intrinsically important in themselves from an ethical point of view. Ethical consumers therefore can enter this process as moral persons but leave it as a series of abstract preferences, variables, and averages (Desmond and Crane, 2004). You and I, the thinking, feeling moral person becomes simply a preference on a questionnaire, a number in a database.

Perhaps the most intriguing situation in this respect is when the whole idea of there being ethical consumers 'out there' is surfaced within a firm in order to drive the development of some kind of ethical policy or social responsibility programme. Customer-focused firms consistently invoke 'consumer pressure' as one of the main drivers behind their attention to social responsibility. Regardless of the truth of this claim, or the beneficial outcomes this may ultimately have, the point is that it essentially instrumentalizes the consumer to construct a convincing motive of corporate self interest. In most cases, I would suggest that there are a whole host of reasons and motives used by managers to explain and rationalize social programmes, but the potency of the concept of the responsible consumer is in its power to suggest that failure to act in an ethical manner may bring upon the firm dire reputational consequences. Perhaps in the long run this instrumentalization doesn't really matter, providing of course that the firm does good deeds and contributes positively to society. But it does give us a clearer conception of the fascinating and at times bewildering paradoxes that surround the whole notion of ethical consumerism when it comes to seeing how exactly it might actually impact upon corporations and managers in the CSR marketplace.

Summary and conclusions

The purpose of this article was to provide an overview of the issues and challenges for organizations involved in responding to the CSR marketplace, specifically in regard to 'ethical' consumers. I first discussed the range of different companies likely to be confronted by such pressures, as well as the strategic postures they might choose to adopt in the face of them – primarily focusing on differentiation strategies of ethical niche versus mainstream orientations. A predominant trend identified here was a move to the mainstream by ethical niche firms, although as we saw, such a re-orientation raised a number of challenges and tensions. I then reviewed current thinking about CSR 'branding', and in particular, the apparent shift away from explicit ethical branding towards a more conservative approach, as well as narrower, and safer, cause-related marketing initiatives. I then finished with a brief discussion of how the CSR concerns of consumers might be interpreted inside the company.

Overall, I would say that there is evidence of growing interest in the corporate response to consumers' social, ethical and environmental concerns, particularly in terms of how social responsibility issues can be incorporated into organizational practices such as branding, cause-related marketing, and reputational risk management. Of course, consumers are not the only reason that researchers and practitioners are interested in such things, but they are certainly implicated in various ways. That said, there is still a lot of scope for much closer attention to the specific influence of consumers' preferences and values on corporations; it seems to me that too often a simplistic cause-and-effect relation between the two is just automatically assumed rather than rigorously examined. More in-depth, in-company research would probably surface some extremely valuable insights that may well challenge some of our conventional thinking on the subject.

It is also important to recognize that this is very much an area in transition, with new knowledge and new practices emerging all the time. For example, in the area of labelling and certification, some are calling now for a new model that sees these as 'pre-competitive' – i.e. something that firms do in collaboration and at a standardized level rather than trying to outdo one another (Watanatada and Mak, 2011). What this could mean for CSR and marketing is that the whole practice of backing up claims to be socially responsible could be something that entire industries or groups of companies seek to achieve together. These would be the basic standards necessary to enter a market, not ones where firms might seek to offer differentiation with respect to their competitors. So CSR branding and other marketplace practices will no doubt continue to shift and evolve. Expectations are on the rise and consumers are becoming more demanding, but companies too are gradually becoming more astute about how to turn responsible practice into marketplace success.

Note

1   Sourced from Ecotricity website: www.ecotricity.co.uk. Accessed 6 June, 2012.

References

Chappell, T. 1993. *The Soul of a Business: Managing for Profit and the Common Good*. New York: Bantam Books.

Cheney, G. and Christensen, L.T. 2000. Self-absorption and self-seduction in the corporate identity game. In Schultz, M., M.J. Hatch, and M. Holten Larsen (eds), *The expressive organization: linking identity, reputation, and the corporate brand*. Oxford: Oxford University Press: 246–70.

Cobb, R. 2002. Selling responsibility. *Marketing Business*, June 2002: 25–27.

Crane, A. 2000. Facing the backlash: green marketing and strategic re-orientation in the 1990s. *Journal of Strategic Marketing*, 8 (3): 277–96.

Crane, A. 2001. Unpacking the Ethical Product. *Journal of Business Ethics*, 30: 361–73.

Crane, A. and Desmond, J. 2002. Societal Marketing and Morality. *European Journal of Marketing*, 36 (5/6): 548–69.

Crane, A. and Livesey, S. 2003. Are you talking to me? Stakeholder communication and the risks and rewards of dialogue. In Andriof, J. S. et al. (eds), *Unfolding stakeholder thinking 2: relationships, communication, reporting and performance*. Sheffield: Greenleaf: 39–52.

CWS. 1995. *Responsible Retailing*. Manchester: CWS Ltd.

Davies, I.A and Crane, A. 2003. Ethical decision-making in fair trade companies. *Journal of Business Ethics*, 45 (1/2): 79–92.

Davis, J. J. 1992. Ethics and Environmental Marketing. *Journal of Business Ethics*, 11: 81–87.

Desmond, J. and Crane, A. 2004. Morality and the consequences of marketing action. *Journal of Business Research*, forthcoming.

Dey, C.R. 2002. Social bookkeeping at Traidcraft plc: an ethnographic study of a struggle for the meaning of fair trade. Paper presented at 12th CSEAR Research Summer School, Dundee.

Galbraith, J.K. 1974. *The new industrial state*. 2nd ed. Harmondsworth: Penguin.

Hamel, G. and Prahalad, C.K. 1991. Corporate imagination and expeditionary marketing. *Harvard Business Review*, 69 (Jul/Aug): 81–92.

Hildebrand, D., Sen, S., and Bhattacharya, C. B. 2011. Corporate social responsibility: a corporate marketing perspective. *European Journal of Marketing*, 45 (9/10): 1353–64.

Hockerts, K. and Wüstenhagen, R. 2010. Greening Goliaths versus emerging Davids—Theorizing about the role of incumbents and new entrants in sustainable entrepreneurship. *Journal of Business Venturing*, 25(5): 481–92.

Husted, B.W and Allen, D.B. 2000. Is it ethical to use ethics as strategy? *Journal of Business Ethics*, 27 (1/2): 21–31.

Jackson, J. 2001. Prioritising customers and other stakeholders using the AHP. *European Journal of Marketing*, 35 (7/8): 858–71.

Kitson, A. 1996. Taking the pulse: ethics and the British Co-operative Bank. *Journal of Business Ethics*, 15 (9): 1021–31.

Lager, F. 1994. *Ben and Jerry's: the inside scoop*. New York: Crown Publishers Inc.

Lane Keller, K. 2000. Building and managing corporate brand equity. In Schultz, M., Hatch, M.J. and Holten Larsen, M. (eds), *The expressive organization: linking identity, reputation, and the corporate brand*. Oxford: Oxford University Press: 115–37.

Lewis, E. 2003. Why giving is good for you. *Brand Strategy*, 170 (Apr): 26–8.

Meyer, A. 1999. Green and competitive beyond the niche: reflections on green positioning strategies. Paper presented at Business Strategy and the Environment Conference, University of Leeds.

Middlemiss, N. 2003. Authentic not cosmetic: CSR as brand enhancement. *Journal of Brand Management*, 10 (4/5): 353–61.

Miller, A and Dess, G.G. 1993. Assessing Porter's (1980) model in terms of its generalizability, accuracy and simplicity. *Journal of Management Studies*, 30 (4): 553–85.

Mitchell, A. 1997. The Power of Ethical Branding. *Marketing Week*, May 22: 26–27.

National Consumer Council. 1996. *Green Claims: A Consumer Investigation into Marketing Claims About the Environment*. London: National Consumer Council.

Nicholls, A. J. 2002. Strategic options in fair trade retailing. *International Journal of Retail and Distribution Management*, 30 (1): 6–17.

Porter, M. E. 1985. *Competitive advantage: creating and sustaining superior performance*. New York: Free Press.

Porter, M. E. and van der Linde, C. 1995. Green and competitive. *Harvard Business Review*, September–October: 120–34.

Porter, M. E. and Kramer, M. R. 2011. Creating shared value. *Harvard Business Review*, 89 (January–February): 62–77.

Roddick, A. 1992. *Body and soul*. London: Vermillion.

Smith, N. C. 1990. *Morality and the market: consumer pressure for corporate accountability*. London: Routledge.

Terrachoice. 2010. *The sins of greenwashing: home and family edition*: www.sinsofgreenwashing.org.

Varadarajan, P. R. and Menon, A. 1988. Cause-related marketing: a coalignment of marketing strategy and corporate philanthropy. *Journal of Marketing*, 52 (July): 58–74.

Watantada, P. and Mak, H. 2011. *Signed, Sealed . . . Delivered? Behind Certifications and Beyond Labels*: Sustainability: http://www.sustainability.com/library/signed-sealed-delivered-1#.T9eZ7BdDy88.

Wright, C. 2003. Consuming lives, consuming landscapes: interpreting advertisements for Cafedirect coffees. Paper presented at British Sociological Association Annual Conference, University of York, UK.

Chapter 6

CSR in the workplace

IN THIS CHAPTER WE WILL:

- Introduce some of the core corporate responsibilities in the workplace
- Explain the different types of workplace where CSR might be relevant
- Examine the meaning of key concepts such as human rights, working environment, and labour standards.
- Consider the link between CSR and labour and human rights in terms of workplace equality
- Explore the role that CSR can play in recruitment and retention of employees

Introduction

Employees are in many respects at the centre of a company's CSR. First, corporate reputation frequently appears to rest on the treatment of employees. Major brands such as McDonald's, Walmart, Air Canada, and others have been threatened by accusations of poor labour relations at home, while there is pervasive media scrutiny of working conditions in developing countries, including accusations of child labour, forced overtime, and abuse of human rights. Second, as we see in the reading by Bhattacharya, Sen, and Korschun in this chapter, a reputation for social responsibility can, in some circumstances, help to attract skilled knowledge workers to firms, and thereby boost their performance (Greening & Turban, 2000). Third, companies seeking to engage with CSR need their employees to buy-in to the concept in order to implement the service levels it requires. If employees feel they are not treated well themselves, transferring a culture of socially responsible behaviour towards other stakeholders will be problematic to say the least. Fourth, provision of employment is often seen as the most fundamental social – and economic – role of business, not least for small- and medium-sized enterprises. Whichever way we look at it, if we want to understand and apply CSR better, we are bound to undertake a thorough examination of workplace issues (Graafland & van de Ven, 2006).

Responsibilities in the workplace were in fact among the first elements of social responsibility recognized and taken up by corporations. Enlightened industrialists of the nineteenth century, such as the Ford, Lever, and Cadbury families recognized that the working and housing conditions of their employees needed improving – and that attention to employee welfare could in turn bring benefits to the firm (Cannon, 1994). Model communities built at Port Sunlight and Bournville in the late nineteenth century in the UK, or homes for Ford employees in Dearborn, Michigan, in the US, for example, offered factory workers decent affordable housing near to their place of work. Such schemes were, of course, what we would now refer to as enlightened self-interest and paternalistic in that the founding fathers expected the workers living in the model villages to lead lives of piety and sobriety, and to repay the debt to their benefactors with high commitment, reliability, and hard work. Nevertheless, such approaches to CSR clearly offered benefits to workers and employers alike, and can be observed in various ways in countries across the globe. The focus of the intervention changes with the local needs, of course, with companies such as Mercedes-Benz focusing their efforts within their South African subsidiary on HIV/AIDS prevention[1] (see also the example of Vodafone in Africa in Integrative case 1).

Over time, expectations of corporate responsibilities towards employees have seen significant shifts, especially with the rise and fall of unionization over the past 100 years or so in some countries, and the institutionalization of labour laws in most parts of the world. Trade unions as stakeholders in CSR seem nevertheless to lack visibility. The nature of their role is unclear, with some unions considering CSR to be a threat because of a perceived increase in management control, and others claiming CSR as their natural territory (Preuss et al, 2006).

The role of human resource management professionals is similarly unclear, with tensions between representing the employee voice and seeking to maximize efficiency and returns from the workforce as with any other resource input (Greenwood & Simmons, 2004). In much of continental Europe, for instance, corporations have tended not to consider workplace issues as a major facet of CSR because the legal protection of employees is so well developed and comprehensive, and because labour unions have traditionally been strong (Matten & Moon, 2008). This leaves little scope for 'voluntary' CSR initiatives in the workplace beyond the legal minimum. In other countries, however, corporations may at times have been expected to take on responsibility for providing good working conditions, equality of opportunity, health and safety in the workplace, and so on, due to the absence of effective legal protection or enforcement.

Today, with aging and diversifying populations in many Western countries, wide scale restructuring in industry, the rise of the multinational, and the mounting significance of outsourcing through global supply chains, CSR in the workplace has become a major issue for companies everywhere. The need to deal with concrete issues for workers remains, covering areas such as occupational health and safety,

CWS 6.1

See the companion website for recent initiatives by trade unions and the human resources profession with respect to CSR both physical and psychological (sometimes called the working environment), fair pay and conditions, equal opportunities, fair process, and free association. Whether this pertains to the provision of employee pension schemes in the US, the off-shoring of the workforce to low-cost countries such as China and Vietnam, or the problems of protecting employees from HIV/AIDS in Africa, workplace issues are now central to CSR. Employers are expected to show a duty of care to their workers. The point is that the relevant social responsibilities will vary according to the particular workplace, not least in terms of sector, local conditions, and institutional context.

Understanding the workplaces of CSR

Workplace issues in CSR will vary according to parameters such as highly regulated or unregulated workplaces, or in-house or outsourced workplaces.

Regulated workplaces

These are typically found in developed countries where legislation largely takes care of most of the main problems of employee protection. Here, then, CSR is likely to focus on ensuring that the firm lives up to the spirit as well as the letter of the law, and goes beyond legislation by attending to issues of diversity, work-life balance, training and employability, pension provision, anti-harassment, etc. Highly regulated sectors include the chemical industry, where there is tight EU regulation such as Registration, Evaluation, Authorisation and Restriction of Chemical substances, known as REACH introduced in 2006.

Less regulated workplaces

These are typically found in developing countries, either because employee protection legislation is absent or it is poorly enforced. Hence, CSR issues here will tend to include such concerns as working conditions, pay, unionization, health and safety, equal opportunities, etc. It is important to note that less regulated workplaces can also occur in developed countries, for example, when the workplace is part of the informal economy, or in industries characterized by seasonal work and low levels of collective organization such as agriculture (particularly around harvesting) and tourism. Some national or regional governments have sought to close these regulatory gaps. For example, California, which has a large agricultural sector dominated by seasonal labourers from Latin America, introduced new legislation on human trafficking in the past decade, while Canada introduced its first National Action Plan to Combat Human Trafficking in 2012.[2]

In-house workplaces

Corporations are obviously directly responsible for their own in-house workers. Nevertheless there is sometimes a difference in how full-time, core employees and part-time, peripheral employees are treated. Where the willingness or the ability to provide responsible workplace practices is limited, other actors such as major customers, trade unions or NGOs might become involved in CSR programmes aimed at improving practices.

Outsourced workplaces

Producers of branded products with media profiles have also at times been expected to take on some responsibility for the workplaces of their suppliers, suggesting an 'extended responsibility' for working conditions in the supply chain (van Tulder et al, 2009). This is not to say that the supplier is absolved from responsibility for managing conditions in their own workplace, but the nature of its responsibilities may change, for example, because the purchasing company begins to act as a quasi-regulator imposing codes of conduct as soft law and acting as a corporate social watchdog (Spence & Bourlakis, 2009). Some outsourced workplaces can go beyond immediate first-tier suppliers to encompass a network of responsibility that stretches throughout the supply chain, both upstream and downstream.

CSR workplace codes and standards

What we can see then is that CSR in the workplace is quite a complex arena, with different contexts, issues, and responsibilities arising for the corporation in diverse situations. However, corporations can be guided as to their responsibilities by a variety of codes and guidelines. Some of the most important of these include the OECD guidelines for multinationals, the ILO global labour standards and decent work agenda, SA 8000 standard on decent workplaces, ISO 26000 social responsibility standard and the UN Global Compact.

Another high-profile initiative that is likely to gain in importance in workplace CSR focuses specifically on human rights. Led by John Ruggie the UN Secretary-General's Special Representative on Business and Human Rights, the 'Protect, Respect and Remedy framework' or more formally the Guiding Principles on Business and Human Rights, rests on three pillars:[3]

1.   The state's duty to *protect* against human rights abuses by third parties, including business;
2.   Corporate responsibility to *respect* human rights; and
3.   Greater access by victims to effective *remedy*, both judicial and non-judicial.

There are also a range of different CSR tools that have been developed to tackle workplace responsibility issues, such as codes of conduct and social and ethical auditing systems. These are intended to enable companies to manage their workplace responsibilities more effectively and create an appropriate set of standards and metrics for demonstrating accountability to core labour standards. We will discuss these in Section C of the book.

Introducing the readings

The two readings offer a closer look at two different aspects of CSR in the workplace. The first reading by Peter Utting is on equality and CSR, the second reading by Bhattacharya and colleagues on the advantages CSR can bring for recruitment and retention. The readings take quite contrasting starting positions, being critical of CSR, in the first case and seeking instrumental advantage through it in the second. Perhaps unsurprisingly the two readings have somewhat different audiences in mind. Utting's critique is published in the *Third World Quarterly*, so can be expected to have a scholarly orientation, particularly with an interest in development and social justice. In contrast, Bhattacharya, Sen and Korschun write for the *MIT Sloan Review*, a journal for business executives. The contrast shows how different audiences can be drawn into a similar issue, that of workplace CSR, from the basis of quite contrasting entry points.

Equality in the workplace

In Utting's paper we see the advantage that can be gained by looking at CSR through a different lens. His focus on equality – an issue relating to moral justice and practical fairness – enables a fresh look at workplace practices and highlights the failings of the evolving concept and practice of CSR. Utting considers four central components of equality, defined as social protection, rights, empowerment and redistribution. He argues that social (and environmental) protection have to date received much attention from a CSR perspective. He notes an emerging CSR discourse relating to human rights, but argues that empowerment of weaker groups in society and redistribution of income within enterprises and value chains is given very limited attention.

Utting's work highlights an important context that much of the literature on CSR overlooks, specifically that MNCs which commonly promote CSR with glossy reports and communications (see Chapter 9), simultaneously lobby aggressively for labour market flexibility, deregulation and the weakening of institutions designed for social protection. He also notes that the standards and principles available to support equality in the workplace, such as the ILO standard and the UN Global Compact are selectively used by large corporations, which cherry-pick some aspects and overlook – without explanation – those that do not suit their agenda. He cites the inclusion of reference to human rights being unmatched, for example by attention to gender equality. Hence, Utting alleges that corporations just use CSR where it is

CWS 6.2

See the companion website for more information, links and examples of global labour standards, including the Protect, Respect and Remedy framework to their own advantage. Indeed in the second reading in this chapter, the instrumental value of CSR is actively promoted to business executives.

CSR as an employee recruitment and retention tool

At the beginning of the chapter we noted the various ways in which CSR in the workplace is an important issue. Despite the economic crisis, and some would argue because of it, potential employees include the reputation of the firm beyond financial success as an aspect of employment decisions. In short, people want to work for organizations that they can be proud to be associated with and whose actions are in keeping with their personal values. Bhattacharya, Sen and Korschun, who have backgrounds in marketing, take this point seriously, and suggest that companies can capitalize on their CSR investments by using CSR as a form of internal marketing to employees as internal customers. They base their claims on research on employees specifically, which in itself is an unusual approach, with executives and managers being the more common organizational targets. Like the Utting article, this different lens gives a fresh view on CSR.

Bhattacharya and colleagues propose that there are four barriers to using CSR as an internal marketing lever: lack of awareness of CSR by employees; limited understanding of the potential of CSR to fulfil employee needs; a poor understanding of returns to CSR, particularly in turns of motivation of employees and identification with the firm; and a tendency to take a top-down approach to CSR. We might reflect that Utting would be opposed to this stance because it is an example of 'cherry-picking' aspects of CSR that are seen to have organizational advantages. This puts the two readings in the wider context of whether the motives for CSR matter, or whether we should simply seek to motivate organizations to act socially responsibly wherever possible, and maximize the social – and other – returns associated (see the reading by N. Craig Smith in Chapter 2 for a more detailed discussion on strategic and moral motivations for CSR.

Challenges for practice

Take a close look at a company you work for or with which you are familiar.

1. Is the organization an example of a regulated/unregulated context?
   a) What legislative or regulative conditions apply to working conditions?
   b) Are there examples of 'soft law' in this case?
   c) How does the regulatory context influence your experience of the business in practice from an employee's perspective?
2. Are there issues of employee working conditions external to the core business?

a) Describe any differences you can observe between internal and external workplace practices.
b) How can you explain these differences?
3. Can you identify which (if any) codes or standards are primarily drawn upon in this business?
a) How familiar are organizational employees with the content of the primary standard?
b) Who in the organization if anyone is responsible for the implementation of the workplace code or standard?

Study questions

1. What social responsibilities does a firm have in the workplace? Outline a business case for these responsibilities.
2. To what extent can firms be expected to extend their workplace responsibilities to employees in their supply chain?
3. Which stakeholders have a role to play in workplace CSR and how do they influence practice? Justify your choices and illustrate with examples.
4. In what way is the integrity of the organization in question if externally orientated CSR practices are not matched by internally orientated CSR?
5. How does a critical approach to workplace CSR contrast with an instrumental perspective?

Further reading

Dawkins, C. (2012) 'Labored relations: corporate citizenship, labor unions, and freedom of association', *Business Ethics Quarterly* 22(3): 473–500.
This article takes a new look at the issue of free association, i.e. the possibility to form a collective and operate as a trade union. This is a much overlooked area within CSR research, but Dawkins argues – in alignment with the Universal Declaration of Human Rights – that freedom of association is a fundamental human right and that labour rights and human rights should be synonymous.

Rupp, D. E., Ganapathi, J., Aguilera, R. V., & Williams, C. A. (2006) 'Employee reactions to corporate social responsibility: an organizational justice framework', *Journal of Organizational Behavior* 27(4): 537–543.
This article is a useful one to help draw together the two readings in this chapter. It uses organizational justice theory to link organizational drivers and motives with employee attitudes, behaviours and emotions.

Endnotes

1   www.mercedes-benzsa.co.za/sustainable-development/corporate-social-responsibility/hiv-aids/ (accessed 30 August, 2012).
2   http://oag.ca.gov/human-trafficking (accessed 30 August, 2012); www.public safety.gc.ca/media/nr/2012/nr20120606-eng.aspx (accessed 30 August, 2012).
3   www.business-humanrights.org/SpecialRepPortal/Home/Protect-Respect-Remedy-Framework (accessed 30 August, 2012).

References

Cannon, T. (1994) *Corporate responsibility*, London: Pearson.
Graafland, J. J. & van de Ven, B. W. (2006) 'Strategic and moral motivation for corporate social responsibility', *Journal of Corporate Citizenship*, 22(Summer): 111–123.
Greening, D. W. & Turban, D. B. (2000) 'Corporate social performance as a competitive advantage in attracting a quality workforce', *Business & Society*, 39(3): 254–280.
Greenwood, M. & Simmons, J. (2004) 'A stakeholder approach to ethical human resource management', *Business & Professional Ethics Journal*, 23(3): 3–23.
Matten, D. & Moon, J. (2008) '"Implicit" and "explicit" CSR: a conceptual framework for a comparative understanding of corporate social responsibility', *Academy of Management Review*, 33(2): 404–424.
Preuss, L., Haunschild, A., & Matten, D. (2006) 'Trade unions and CSR: a European research agenda', *Journal of Public Affairs*, 6(3–4): 256–268.
Spence, L. & Bourlakis, M. (2009) 'From CSR to SCR: the evolution of supply chain responsibility', *Supply Chain Management: An International Journal*, 14(4): 291–302.
van Tulder, R., van Wijk, J., & Kolk, A. (2009) 'From chain liability to chain responsibility: MNE approaches to implement safety and health codes in international supply chains', *Journal of Business Ethics*, 85(Supp.2): 399–412.

CSR AND EQUALITY

Peter Utting

Background

A key debate within academia and civil society relates to whether CSR is simply a palliative for a model of capitalism that generates perverse social and environmental effects, and an instrument for reinforcing corporate control over developmental processes and institutions,[1] or a crucial element of 'embedded liberalism'. The latter is characterized by markets that facilitate the mobilization and allocation of resources for the benefit of humanity, and by the presence of institutions that correct for the imbalances in corporate rights and obligations that have been a feature of economic globalization and liberalization.[2]

Assessments of CSR generally focus on discrete aspects such as environmental management, working conditions, labour rights, business – community relations, the so-called business case for CSR, and corporate accountability structures and mechanisms. Increasing attention is now being focused on sets of indicators that provide a more comprehensive framework for assessment. Such frameworks often take as their point of departure the economic, social and environmental components recognized in the concept of 'sustainable development'. Some emphasize labour and human rights dimensions. More recently attempts to examine the relationship of CSR to poverty reduction have focused on various 'micro' and 'macro' impacts of both individual firms and the global value chains with which they are associated.[3]

This paper suggests that assessments of the social and developmental implications of CSR could usefully consider another angle or set of issues related to both equality, which involves levelling or minimizing disparities, and equity, with its implications of fairness and social justice. Equity and equality have recently re-emerged as central concerns of the international development community.[4] Greater equality is both a goal in itself and a means to economic and social development.[5] The 'intrinsic' and 'instrumental' reasons for addressing inequality include innate concerns in society for justice, the fact that principles of equality and equity are often integral to legal traditions, including international human rights law, and the negative impacts of inequality on efficiency, growth, poverty reduction and social cohesion.[6]

Examining the connections between CSR and equality is not meant to imply that corporations, or the private sector more generally, have a primary responsibility for promoting equality. Historically, as today, the state and multilateral institutions have played the key role in this regard. Nevertheless, the CSR agenda,[7] with its emphasis on improvements in working and supply chain conditions, community assistance and development, labour and human rights, and stakeholder dialogue and participation, has obvious implications for equality and equity. While conceptualisations and definitions of these terms, or points of emphasis regarding what elements are important from a policy perspective, vary considerably, here attention is focused on how CSR relates to four crucial aspects of equality and equity: social protection, rights, empowerment and redistribution.

Social protection

What has been the contribution of CSR to social protection, defined here broadly in terms of the welfare and well-being of workers and other groups, or 'stakeholders'. Much of the CSR agenda has been directly concerned with these aspects, focusing, for example, on improvements in working conditions, assistance to communities where company operations are located or support for international development and relief programmes. Considerable attention has also been focused on specific social issues such as HIV/AIDS and post-conflict rehabilitation. Recently there has been an attempt to connect CSR more directly with the contemporary global poverty reduction agenda, through what has been labelled the 'bottom of the pyramid' approach.[8]

While the range of CSR issues addressed by companies that are more proactive in this field has tended to expand, many firms continue to concentrate their CSR activities in arenas external to the company, via philanthropy or corporate social investment in community initiatives. In the USA it is estimated that large corporations allocate 77% of funding for corporate charitable activities to local metropolitan areas which host the corporation.[9] These charitable grants averaged US$3.5 million per large corporation in 2002 but could reach levels of $100 million per annum in the case of companies like Wal-Mart.[10] In the USA the number of corporate foundations doubled from 1295 to 2549 between 1987 and 2003, and their level of grant giving reached $3.5 billion. In real terms this represented a doubling of the value of grants over the same period. Much of this spending was channelled to traditional philanthropic outlets such as educational, health, cultural, sporting and environmental activities and institutions.

Relatively little went abroad. The World Economic Forum (WEF) estimates that the Fortune Global 500 companies provide, annually, cash donations in the region of $12 billion and roughly an equivalent amount ($10–15 billion) in kind. Approximately 10%–15% of this amount is thought to support activities related to low-income countries.[11] Such figures need to be put in context. This level of corporate 'aid' in support of developing countries (roughly $3 billion) represents about 4% of Overseas Development Assistance, which amounted to $80 billion in 2004. Corporate philanthropy associated with developing countries is, however, increasing, causing *Business Week* to declare in 2004, 'global philanthropy is one of the hottest US exports these days'.[12] Such a development reflects not only the mega-grant giving of a few billionaires such as Bill Gates and Warren Buffet, particularly for global health programmes, but also the ways in which corporations are adjusting to the geographical and social realities of global value chains. The WEF notes that total private philanthropic giving may exceed foreign direct investment (FDI) inflows in the case of some poor countries,[13] although this says as much about the skewed nature of FDI inflows to developing countries – flows that are heavily concentrated in just a few countries – as it does about corporate generosity.

While the CSR movement and agenda have evolved and developed in more socially inclusive ways, CSR discourse still runs well ahead of reality. From the perspective of social protection the downside to CSR centres on three main aspects. First, while the rhetoric surrounding CSR gives the impression that much of big business has turned over a new leaf as regards social responsibility, and that its supply chains are following suit, the reality is that only a small percentage of the world's 70 000 TNCs, 700 000 affiliates and millions of suppliers have seriously embraced CSR. This is evident from the numbers of companies that engage actively with leading multi-stakeholder initiatives, such as the UN Global Compact, Global Reporting Initiative (GRI) and the Ethical Trading Initiative (ETI).

Second, the quality of CSR interventions is often weak in the sense that there is often a considerable gap between stated intentions and actual implementation. This has been well documented in relation to certain basic CSR tools. While the range of issues addressed under company codes of conduct, for example, has expanded, procedures related to implementation are often under-developed.[14] This is also apparent in the case of international codes or sets of principles, such as the Organisation for Economic Co-operation and Development (OECD) Guidelines for Multinational Enterprises, the UN Global Compact Principles, and the Equator Principles, which have all expanded while implementation and compliance mechanisms remain weak.[15]

An assessment of social auditing by the Clean Clothes Campaign (CCC) noted some progress in relation to a few brand name companies, but major limitations in the dominant approach, particularly in the retail sector.[16] Company reports and audits are often short on meaningful indicators to measure performance and impacts, and they are not particularly useful for assessing how positive CSR initiatives are faring in relation to negative social and environmental performance. Furthermore, far more attention is likely to be focused on improvements in occupational health and safety as opposed to industrial relations and labour rights.[17] Other concerns about reporting and social auditing systems relate to their cost and complexity, as well as to the proliferation of different methods and institutions. Given the tremendous size of global corporations, their geographical reach, their value chains that may involve thousands of suppliers, and the increasing range of CSR issues, it seems improbable that a third party can keep a tab on all this, and do so in a meaningful way. Commercial auditors often have neither sufficient time, autonomy nor skills to adequately assess the situation of workers and industrial relations.[18]

A third basic weakness of the CSR agenda from the perspective of social protection relates to issues that are marginalized or remain off-limits. Until recently there was relatively little discussion within mainstream CSR circles of negative trends associated with employers' contributions to social insurance and employee health schemes. While the range of CSR concerns related to developing countries has broadened, priority issues are often those of particular concern to activists and others in the North, for example child labour, 'sweatshops' and environmental degradation associated with mining and deforestation. Issues relevant to particular stakeholders in developing countries, such as women workers, sometimes get short shrift. Potentially CSR has a crucial role to play in relation to women workers, not only because of the state of their working conditions, but also because the rise in female employment has, in contrast to the historical experience of male employment in some sectors, often not been accompanied by access to work-related welfare entitlements associated with social policy.[19]

Much of the literature and learning associated with CSR, particularly within the field of business management, has also marginalized certain developmental concerns of poorer countries related to issues like the cost and impact of CSR initiatives and instruments on smaller enterprises, the situation of informal sector workers, and whether TNCs or large retailers cut and run when their suppliers come under the CSR spotlight.[20] Many companies that are proactive in the field of CSR have improved the working conditions of their core workforce but simultaneously have laid off workers and relied increasingly on sub-contracting, which often implies a deterioration of labour standards. UNRISD studies in South Africa, India and Brazil, and the study by Oxfam and Unilever of the national development impact of Unilever-Indonesia, have highlighted this situation.[21] The analysis of corporate social spending in Brazil, carried out by the Instituto Brasileiro de Análises Sociais e Econômicas, reveals the apparently contradictory situation where companies are spending more per worker on health and safety in their core enterprises, yet the number of workplace accidents and injuries per 1000 workers is increasing. A possible explanation relates to the increasing reliance on sub-contracting.[22]

Many of the world's largest corporations and business associations actively promote CSR while simultaneously lobbying forcefully for macroeconomic, labour market and other social policies associated with forms of labour market flexibilisation, deregulation, and fiscal 'reform' that can result in the weakening of institutions and systems of social protection.[23] Others are actively involved in privatization schemes related to basic services, which in some developing countries have had negative implications in terms of affordability for low-income groups.[24] In short, CSR generally attempts to curb specific types of malpractice and improve selected aspects of social performance without questioning various contradictory policies and practices that can have perverse consequences in terms of equality and equity.

Rights

Equality depends crucially on the recognition and realization of the rights of workers, women, children, indigenous peoples and other groups that have historically been oppressed, exploited and marginalized. To what extent does the CSR agenda address these aspects?

The evolution or broadening of the CSR agenda through time has seen 'rights' emerge as an important component. The early emphasis within codes of conduct and voluntary initiatives on improvements in working conditions was later complemented by a focus on labour rights, particularly those enshrined in the International Labour Organisation's core conventions associated with discrimination, forced labour, freedom of association and collective bargaining. Such standards now figure in numerous codes of conduct and form a sub-set of the 10 principles of the UN Global Compact. There have emerged a number of high profile non-governmental and multi-stakeholder initiatives that actively promote labour rights, particularly in the supply chains of certain industries, notably apparel and footwear.

Converting the emerging labour rights discourse into meaningful interventions has been more difficult. Companies often pick and choose which labour rights they include in their codes of conduct. Large TNCs that project themselves as CSR leaders often ignore standards related to freedom of association and collective bargaining in their policy statements.[25] Even some of the more high profile CSR initiatives, such as the Global Compact, which have emphasized issues of human rights appear to pay limited attention to key aspects of rights, such as those relating to women and gender equality.[26]

Where companies have collaborated with NGOs and multi-stakeholder standard-setting initiatives that promote labour rights, the results have been mixed. A recent evaluation of the ETI notes progress in relation to labour rights as the weakest aspect of this scheme, which aims to promote and improve the implementation of corporate codes of practice covering supply chain activities.[27] A study of labour rights in the sportswear industry notes limited progress, even in the context where the World Federation of Sporting Goods Industries and several leading companies are collaborating with the Play Fair Alliance, a network of civil society organizations that promotes labour rights. Some advances were apparent in relation to transparency, cooperation with trade unions and NGOs, workers' training and the prevention of discrimination in certain factories. The report also notes, however, that 'business practices frequently undermine and contradict their stated commitment to respect trade union rights'. Such practices include cutting contracts of suppliers that have respected labour rights, sourcing from Export Processing Zones or China, where certain basic labour rights are not respected, and turning a blind eye when suppliers employ workers on short-term contracts, which act as a disincentive to unionisation.[28]

Several non-governmental or multi-stakeholder institutions promoting labour rights dimensions of CSR have also adopted fairly weak procedures for assessing compliance with agreed standards. Indeed, some of the most vibrant certification activity, notably that associated with schemes such as SA8000, takes place in China, where labour rights, such as freedom of association and collective bargaining, are not even recognized. Schemes that have adopted fairly rigorous assessment methods, such as the CCC and the Worker Rights Consortium (WRC), tend to be limited in their capacity to scale up their activities. Several Global Union Federations have promoted their own variant of codes of conduct and CSR implementation accords with TNCs via Global Framework Agreements. Such agreements commit signature corporations to uphold an agreed set of labour standards throughout their global corporate structure. This is potentially an important development, in that it extends the arena of union-management negotiation from the national to the global level. In practice, however, the quality of implementation and review procedures can vary considerably, and in the absence of international arbitration and mediation institutions, as well as human and financial resources, Global Union Federations have limited options for seeking redress in cases of non-compliance.[29]

Through time the CSR agenda has expanded to embrace more explicitly the broader set of rights enshrined in the Universal Declaration of Human Rights. This has been in response to exposés of corporate complicity in human rights abuses, particularly in the extractive industries and to related pressures from activists and consumers. It is also a reaction to new CSR institutions such as World Bank/International Finance Corporation (IFC) guidelines related to indigenous peoples, the UN Global Compact, the Financial Times/London Stock Exchange's (FTSE) ethical indices (FTSE4Good), the Voluntary Principles on Security and Human Rights,[30] and the draft UN Norms on the Responsibilities of TNCs and other Business Enterprises with Regard to Human Rights (hereafter referred to as the UN Norms). The guidelines of the GRI have also been revised to strengthen, *inter alia*, indicators related to human rights.

The incorporation of human rights in the CSR agenda is important not only for socio-legal reasons but also because it can provide a framework for operationalizing CSR by invoking a range of issues that require action. Potentially this can act as a corrective to the more piecemeal and fragmented approach that is common among companies engaging with CSR. Furthermore, since the human rights agenda is only deemed to be relevant to companies when it applies to their 'sphere of influence' or 'complicity' in human rights abuses, it necessarily focuses attention on a company's relations with, and its impacts on, multiple stakeholders, including governments, consumers, workers, communities and future generations.

An increasing number of companies are incorporating references to human rights in their policy statements. A recent survey of the *Fortune* Global 500 corporations found that 91% of the 102 companies that responded had an explicit set of principles or management practices related to human rights, and concluded that 'no survey conducted a mere five years ago would have yielded comparable results'.[31] The survey also found that some rights figure more prominently in official company policy than others. The right to health and to an adequate standard of living generally received less attention, especially among US firms.[32]

Policy statements, of course, do not necessarily translate into concrete advances in relation to the realization of human rights. The case of the oil industry is a clear example of this, with most of the oil majors referencing human rights in their principles and codes of conduct. At the same time several corporations, such as BP, Unocal and Total, continue to be on the receiving end of bad practice 'awards' (or nominations) for human and labour rights abuses, while others, such as Shell and Chevron, figure prominently in awards for environmental malpractice.[33]

The apparent gap between rhetoric and reality suggests the need for periodic monitoring of corporate activities. In the case of the oil industry this is extremely difficult given the remote and often dangerous locations where companies operate, and the highly limited capacities of both NGO watchdog organizations and state inspection units in developing countries. The alternative of corporate self-evaluation and reporting, which appears to be on the increase, has obvious limitations, while the design and use of new tools such as human rights impact assessments are still in their infancy.[34]

The process of ratcheting up the responsibilities of TNCs *vis-à-vis* human rights is politically sensitive and provides a good example of the ongoing tensions between voluntary and legal approaches to improving corporate social and environmental performance. This is clearly seen in the case of the UN Norms. These were drafted in an attempt to address some of the weaknesses that characterize the UN Global Compact and voluntary initiatives more generally, namely picking and choosing among standards, weak compliance with agreed standards, and free-riding. Six of the Global Compact's 10 principles, which participating companies agree to adhere to, relate directly to labour and human rights. While the Global Compact has been successful in internationalizing CSR discourse, relatively few of the over 2500 participating companies provide comprehensive evidence of compliance with the 10 principles. Furthermore, a study conducted in 2004 found that only 9% of participating companies were taking actions that they would not otherwise have taken had they remained outside the initiative.[35]

The UN Norms pull together a wide range of standards derived from international law that applies to states, but which are commonly found in multi-stakeholder initiatives related to CSR. They state that all TNCs and related companies have an obligation to uphold such standards, and propose an implementation and monitoring mechanism. They push the envelope even further by calling for 'adequate reparation' in cases where stakeholders are affected by non-compliance. Some of these harder aspects were anathema to certain business interests and governments, and the interim report of the UN Secretary-General's Special Representative on Business and Human Rights suggested that the UN Norms were 'a distraction' and that the route forward lay with 'principled pragmatism'.[36] A few large TNCs did, however, take a proactive stance by joining the Business Leaders Initiative on Human Rights which is trial testing the UN Norms.

Empowerment

Some interpretations of equality emphasize not only equality of opportunity but also equality of outcomes. To achieve this it is necessary to challenge structural dimensions of development that result in highly skewed patterns of distribution of both resources and power.[37] An important aspect in this regard, which is emphasized by certain rights-based approaches to development, is not only the recognition and realization of rights, but also the idea that inclusive and equitable development depends on the capacity of the disempowered and disadvantaged to exert claims on the powerful. The struggle for equity, therefore, is fundamentally a political struggle which involves increasing the voice and influence of weaker groups in society and reconfiguring the balance of social forces through accountability and other mechanisms that keep corporate power in check. To what extent has CSR facilitated these aspects?

One of the most significant developments in relation to empowerment relates to the fact that CSR has been a useful mobilizing tool, particularly in the North but also increasingly in the South. As Shamir points out 'the more the public domain is privatized, the more the private is politicised and becomes a matter of public concern'.[38] Activism associated with CSR issues has rallied numerous civil society groups and organizations around a common concern related to the negative impacts of large corporations in relation to social and sustainable development, and the growing imbalances between corporate rights and obligations under globalization and liberalization. CSR instruments and institutions are being used to defend and enhance the interests of workers, communities and other groups and stakeholders. This is apparent, for example, in relation to new social movements and forms of transnational activism centred on such issues as 'sweatshops', fair trade, corruption and environmental pollution,[39] as well as in broad-based groupings of civil society organizations that test and apply CSR instruments. An example of the latter is OECD Watch, an international network of 47 NGOs, that monitors the application of the OECD Guidelines on Multinational Enterprises.

Various multi-stakeholder initiatives such as the ETI and SA8000 have also opened up some spaces for dialogue and negotiation where trade unions and NGOs can speak on behalf of workers and communities. Concerns have arisen regarding the question of who speaks for whom, with trade union organizations, in particular, concerned that some NGOs that are unaccountable to workers claim to speak on their behalf.[40] Civil society organizations that join such initiatives sometimes have to walk a tightrope, given the fine line that exists between promoting subaltern interests and legitimising institutions that may reinforce corporate power.

Some of the more effective institutional initiatives involving standard setting, monitoring and/or certification appear to be those that are organically linked to social movement activism,[41] such as the WRC, the CCC and the Forest Stewardship Council. Transnational links that enable northern-based NGOs and trade union organizations to act as a conduit for channelling grievances and negotiating solutions through CSR and other institutions for groups engaged in struggles at the grassroots play a crucial role in what has been called 'counter-hegemonic globalization'.[42] From the perspective of participation and empowerment, however, a major weakness of the CSR 'movement' has been the limited participation of stakeholders from developing countries in consultation and decision-making processes associated with CSR and in the design of CSR instruments and institutions.[43]

Some initiatives, such as the CCC, the WRC and national monitoring schemes like the Grupo de Monitoreo Independiente de El Salvador, attempt to promote monitoring and verification methods that not only gather information from workers but use the auditing process to channel information to workers and encourage social dialogue. In the main what predominates, however, are fairly conventional social auditing techniques that, at best, can only scratch the surface and, at worst, constitute policing mechanisms.[44] A study carried out in Costa Rica among banana plantation workers, which examined the potential contribution of certification or multi-stakeholder initiatives such as SA8000 and the ETI to workers' empowerment, found serious limitations with 'rapid social auditing'. It proposed replicating the methods of certain organizations that promote 'participatory workplace appraisal', under which social auditing would not only check that spaces for empowerment exist but also attempt to create such spaces.[45]

One of the areas of greatest weakness in relation to both social protection and empowerment relates to the extremely limited attention within the CSR agenda to the vast majority of workers, producers and enterprises in developing countries that are associated with micro- and small enterprises, small-scale agriculture and the so-called informal sector. As the Oxfam/Unilever report referred to above points out, the question is how to use CSR practices to strengthen the position of weaker stakeholders throughout the value chain.[46] While some large global corporations have responded to civil society and consumer pressures to improve conditions in their supply chains, such attention has yet to penetrate significantly beyond upper-tier suppliers. As noted above, the CSR agenda has tended to ignore processes of subcontracting that involve more precarious forms of employment and the casualization of labour. Another concern is that conventional approaches to CSR may be consolidating a 'labour aristocracy' and restricting the capacity of firms in developing countries to absorb labour from the informal sector.[47]

When considering the issue of CSR and empowerment, it is also important to examine the counter-side of the power equation, namely the power of TNCs and corporate elites. Theoretically there are strong grounds for assuming that CSR reinforces corporate power. This is implicit in the so-called business case for CSR and the fact that it is many of the world's largest TNCs that have engaged more proactively with this agenda. It is explicit in a body of political economy analysis that draws on Gramscian theory. The latter suggests that the CSR agenda is an important feature of a mode of domination that has enabled large corporations and business elites to fend off criticism and regulatory threats, and to reinforce their power and influence by actually accommodating certain oppositional demands, intervening proactively in the CSR arena, and attempting to lead the CSR movement.[48] It has also been suggested that CSR is an important feature of 'new ethicalism', that is, the turn to morals and ethical norms as a means of shoring up the neoliberal agenda in a context where legal and other institutional arrangements have proved insufficient.[49] This type of analysis also points to the considerable spaces that exist for social movements and some marginalized social groups to advance in terms of articulating and realizing specific demands, or in relation to so-called 'counter-hegemonic' struggles.[50] CSR is an important terrain of struggle, one where organized business interests have proven to be extremely adept and savvy.

While the CSR agenda is concerned with some aspects of corporate accountability, it does not fundamentally question the economic power and political influence of TNCs. While both aspects of power are difficult to measure,[51] attempts to do so indicate the tremendous size of the largest CSRs, which make up between 20 and 30 of the world's largest 100 economic units (national economies and corporations).[52] According to UNCTAD, the value-added of the top 100 non-financials increased as a percentage of global GDP from 3.5% to 4.3% between 1990 and 2000.[53] What is more significant is the increasing control exercised by the largest corporations over global value chains as a result of sub-contracting and other arrangements. According to one estimate, the top 800 non-financial corporations (measured by stock market capitalisation) may, in effect, directly and indirectly control up to 50% of global GDP, if one takes into account both upstream and downstream activities of the company.[54] From the perspective of CSR and equality the worrying aspect of this analysis is that such issues remain largely off-limits in the mainstream CSR agenda.

Redistribution

Perhaps the weakest aspect of both CSR discourse and practice relates to redistribution. Before considering this aspect, it is important to identify what the elements of a redistributive CSR agenda might be. Presumably they would relate to progressive shifts in the distribution of income within enterprises and value chains that favour labour, small producers and other low-income stakeholders, and poorer countries; they would include fair and transparent fiscal policies and practices conducive to progressive taxation, and lobbying for redistributive policies or at least not lobbying for regressive policies that have perverse social, environmental and developmental impacts.

While aggregate data on CSR spending are hard to come by, there is little to suggest that it alters in any meaningful way the relative returns to capital and labour. Indeed, the rise of CSR coincides with a phase of capitalist development where returns to capital have generally outpaced returns to labour, with the share of profits in the national income of many countries having increased and that of wages and salaries having declined. Data on income distribution in the US indicate the dramatic changes that have occurred in recent decades. The share of national income in the USA accounted for by the top 1% of income earners, which had remained stable at around 8% from the mid-1950s to the mid-1980s, increased to 15% by 1998.[55] In a similar vein, 'the ratio of the median compensation of workers to the salaries of CEOs [in the USA] increased from just over thirty to one in 1970 to more than four hundred to one by 2000'.[56] Even the significant increase in the dollar value of corporate giving noted earlier, which occurred in the USA during the 1990s, appears less impressive when compared to the performance of profits. Whereas corporate charitable contributions increased by 4.2% a year, the annual increase in corporate profits was 5.6%. Furthermore, in relation to pre-tax income there was a decline from a peak of 2% in 1986 to 1% in 1996.[57]

In the USA, in particular, corporate contributions to social insurance and healthcare have declined, and employers have transferred more of the burden of pension costs and health insurance to employees.[58] Such contributions are particularly low in the retail sector, where less than half of employees receive health benefits and part-time workers are usually ineligible. High-profile companies like Wal-Mart and Starbucks have come under fire for their practices, given the fact that only 47% and 42% of workers receive health benefits, respectively,[59] as well as the fact that many of their workers must continue to rely on public assistance programmes, which imply large costs for taxpayers.[60]

Two of the most explicit CSR initiatives related to redistribution within the enterprise or the value chain involve 'living wages' and 'fair trade', both of which pay, in effect, premium (above-market) prices to labour and small producers, respectively. While there has been much discussion about living wages within CSR circles since the late 1990s, particularly in connection with CSR reforms in the apparel and footwear sectors, there has been little progress in practice, beyond compliance with minimum wage legislation.

The involvement of large companies in fair trade schemes has sparked a heated debate regarding their developmental implications. Proponents see this as, potentially, a crucial mechanism to ensure that fair-trade markets break out of their very niche status. Critics see it as a dilution of fair-trade standards and a means by which large companies can position themselves competitively in a relatively small but growing market. In relation to redistribution a key question is the premium price received by producers. When the fair-trade system was introduced for products like coffee, the premium price was nearly double the market price. This meant that the increased prices paid by northern consumers, and the restructuring of the value chain (both in terms of fewer intermediaries and improved margins for small producers), potentially had significant redistributive implications. Leaving aside the question as to how much of the premium price is actually received by producers, it is important to note that the involvement of large companies in sectors such as fair-trade coffee has occurred at a time when the gap between the market and fair-trade price has narrowed considerably. This suggests that large firms may in effect be free-riding on a brand created under very different circumstances and that their involvement has few, if any, redistributive implications. Other benefits of fair trade, notably its role in empowering small producers and their organizations, are also marginalized by the larger firms that enter this arena.

Another key redistributive element relates to taxation and corporate fiscal practices. Here there has been some positive movement via the growing attention to issues of corruption and greater transparency as regards corporate payments to governments. Anti-corruption is a core element of the OECD Guidelines for Multinational Corporations, and was added as a 10th principle to the UN Global Compact in 2004. It is also a central concern of activist campaigns such as Publish What You Pay, and the Extractive Industries Transparency Initiative. While corruption has emerged as a CSR issue, progressive taxation has not. There is little to suggest that the position of the corporate CSR community is very different from that of organized business interests that lobby for ongoing reductions in corporate taxation and a lowering of tax rates for the highest income brackets in which CEOs find themselves. CSR takes place against a backdrop where fiscal policy is becoming increasingly regressive: as tax structures shift in favour of consumption taxes, the contribution of corporate taxation to total tax has remained fairly stable at the relatively low level of 8% to 9% in the OECD area, and corporate income tax rates continue to decline.[61]

Furthermore, transfer pricing and other mechanisms that result in the under-reporting of profits and tax avoidance are not only rife but are reportedly practised by companies projecting themselves as CSR leaders.[62] The leading auditing and certification firm, KPMG, has several executives facing prosecution for actively promoting tax evasion. Even more recently, in September 2006, another proactive CSR company, GlaxoSmithKline, had to pay the US Internal Revenue Service (IRS) a $3.4 billion fine for transfer pricing, the largest ever single payment made to the IRS to resolve a tax dispute.[63]

Conclusion

While states must assume primary responsibility for crafting institutions that can deal with inequality, CSR discourse positions large corporations as actors concerned with a variety of issues that have obvious implications for equality. The above discussion suggests that the CSR agenda has focused mainly on aspects of equality that have to do with social (and environmental) protection. More recently it has broadened to embrace labour rights and other human rights. Progress in terms of realising rights, however, lags well behind the rhetoric. Aspects related to empowerment remain weak, while redistribution still figures only marginally on the CSR radar.

Should we expect more progress in this regard? If CSR is to complement the efforts of state institutions in promoting equality, there appear to be two central challenges. The first involves filling major gaps that characterize the CSR agenda, in particular the gulf that continues to exist between words and deeds, and the fact that crucial components of equality related to empowerment and redistribution still remain marginal. Second, if CSR, even in its truncated form, complemented the efforts of government, civil society and multilateral actors in areas of social protection and rights, then it could play a constructive role in relation to equality. Where the CSR agenda is particularly problematic, however, relates not only to limits regarding the scale, scope and quality of CSR interventions and institutions, but the fact that it is part and parcel of a broader 'reform' agenda that promotes both market liberalization and self-regulation, often at the cost of labour rights, decent wages, employment security, corporate social welfare, universal social provisioning, and both state and trade union regulatory capacity. Unless these aspects are addressed, piecemeal additions and adjustments to the CSR agenda are unlikely to do much to further its contribution to equality.

Notes

The author would like to thank Kate Ives, Anders Rafn, José Carlos Marques and Anita Tombez for research and editorial assistance; Peter Newell, Jedrzej George Frynas, Rhys Jenkins, Shahra Razavi and two anonymous reviewers for comments, as well as various participants at the conference 'Beyond CSR: Business, Poverty and Social Justice' (London, 22 May 2006), where a draft of this paper was originally presented.

1. Judith Richter, *Holding Corporations Accountable: Corporate Conduct, International Codes and Citizen Action*, London: Zed Books, 2001; and Ann Zammit, *Development at Risk: Rethinking UN – Business Partnerships*, Geneva: South Centre/UNRISD, 2003.
2. John G Ruggie, 'Taking embedded liberalism global: the corporate connection', in David Held & Mathias Koenig-Archibugi (eds), *Taming Globalization: Frontiers of Governance*, Cambridge: Polity Press, 2003; Charles Holliday, Stephan Schmidheiny & Philip Watts, *Walking the Talk: The Business Case for Sustainable Development*, Sheffield: Greenleaf Publishing, 2002; and Michael Hopkins, *The Planetary Bargain: Corporate Social Responsibility Matters*, London: Earthscan, 2003.
3. Jason Clay *et al*, *Exploring the Links between International Business and Poverty Reduction: A Case Study of Unilever in Indonesia*, an Oxfam GB, Novib, Unilever, and Unilever-Indonesia joint research project, Oxford: Oxfam GB, Novib Oxfam Netherlands and Unilever, 2005; and Ans Kolk & Rob Van Tulder, 'Poverty alleviation as a business strategy? Evaluating commitments of frontrunner multinational corporations', *World Development*, 34 (5), 2006, pp 789–801.
4. See UNRISD, *Gender Equality: Striving for Justice in an Unequal World*, Geneva: UNRISD, 2005; UNDP, *Human Development Report 2005: International Cooperation at a Crossroads: Aid, Trade and Security in an Unequal World*, New York: UNDP, 2005; UNDESA, *Report*

on the World Social Situation: the Inequality Predicament, New York: United Nations, 2005; World Bank, World Development Report 2006: Equity and Development, New York: Oxford University Press, 2005..

5. Edward Anderson & Tammie O'Neil, A New Equity Agenda? Reflections on the 2006 World Development Report, the 2005 Human Development Report and the 2005 Report on the World Social Situation, Working Paper 265, London: ODI, 2006.

6. Ibid.

7. Given the expanding range of issues being addressed under the umbrella of CSR, and the fact that different companies, business associations, civil society and other organizations promoting CSR emphasize different aspects, it is often pointed out that there is not a uniform 'CSR agenda'. Nevertheless, there is 'an agenda' in the sense that a) there is growing consensus about the range of issues that companies should be concerned with, and b) CSR represents a particular approach to corporate regulation – one that emphasizes voluntary initiatives and self-regulation.

8. This involves firms stimulating productive activity and consumer markets at the 'bottom of the pyramid', a term used to refer to the two-thirds of the world's population that live at or below the US$2 a day level. CK Prahalad, The Fortune at the Bottom of the Pyramid: Eradicating Poverty through Profits, Upper Saddle River, NJ: Wharton School Publishing, 2005. See also UNDP, Commission on the Private Sector and Development, Unleashing Entrepreneurship: Making Business Work for the Poor, Report to the Secretary-General of the United Nations, New York: UNDP, 2004; and Kolk & Van Tulder, 'Poverty alleviation as a business strategy?'.

9. Doug Guthrie, Survey on Corporate – Community Relations, 2004, at www. ssrc.org/programs/ business_institutions/publications/CCR_Selected_Results_ of_the_Survey.pdf.

10. Ibid.

11. WEF, 'Building on the Monterrey Consensus: the growing role of public – private partnerships in mobilizing resources for development', United Nations High-Level Plenary Meeting on Financing for Development, September, Geneva, 2005, p 5.

12. Jessi Hempel & Lauren Gard, with Michelle Conlin, David Polek and Joshua Tanzer, 'The corporate givers', Business Week, 29 November 2004.

13. WEF, 'Building on the Monterey Consensus'.

14. Rhys Jenkins, Ruth Pearson & Gill Seyfang (eds), Corporate Responsibility and Labour Rights: Codes of Conduct in the Global Economy, London: Earthscan, 2002; Stephanie Barrientos, Catherine Dolan & Anne Tallontire, 'A gendered value chain approach to codes of conduct in African horticulture', World Development, 31 (9), 2003, pp 1511–1526; Stephanie Barrientos & Sally Smith, The ETI Code of Labour Practice: Do Workers Really Benefit?, Brighton: Institute of Development Studies, 2006; and Marina Prieto-Carrón, 'Corporate social responsibility in Latin America: Chiquita, women banana workers and structural inequalities', Journal of Corporate Citizenship, 21, 2006, pp 85 –94.

15. OECD Watch, Five Years On: A review of the OECD Guidelines and National Contact Points, Amsterdam: Centre for Research on Multinational Corporations (SOMO), 2005; Peter Utting & Ann Zammit, Beyond Pragmatism: Appraising UN – Business Partnerships, Programme on Markets, Business and Regulation, Paper No 1, Geneva: UNRISD, 2006.

16. CCC, Looking for a Quick Fix: How Social Auditing is Keeping Workers in Sweatshops, Amsterdam, 2005.

17. Barrientos & Smith, The EIT Code of Labour Practice; and Kolk & Van Tulder, 'Poverty alleviation as a business strategy?'.

18. Dara O'Rourke, Monitoring the Monitors: A Critique of PricewaterhouseCoopers (PwC) Labor Monitoring, 2000, at http://Web.mit.edu/dorourke/www/index.html; and CCC, Looking for a Quick Fix.

19. S Razavi & R Pearson, 'Globalization, export-oriented employment and social policy: gendered connections', in S Razavi, R Pearson & C Danloy (eds), Globalization,

Export-Oriented Employment and Social Policy: Gendered Connections, Basingstoke: Palgrave Macmillan/UNRISD, 2004.

20. UNRISD, *Corporate Social Responsibility and Development: Towards a New Agenda?*, Report of the UNRISD Conference, Geneva, 17–18 November 2003, Geneva: UNRISD, 2004; and Zammit, *Development at Risk.*

21. See David Fig *et al, The Political Economy of Corporate Responsibility in South Africa* (provisional title), Geneva: UNRISD, forthcoming; Atul Sood & Bimal Arora, *The Political Economy of Corporate Responsibility in India*, Programme on Technology, Business and Society, Paper No 18, Geneva: UNRISD, 2006; Paola Cappellin & Gian Mario Giuliani, *The Political Economy of Corporate Responsibility in Brazil: Social and Environmental Dimensions*, Programme on Technology, Business and Society, Paper No 14, Geneva: UNRISD, 2004; and Clay *et al, Exploring the Links between International Business and Poverty Reduction.*

22. Joao Sucupira, 'Balanço social: diversidade, participacão, e segurança do trabalho', *Democracia Viva*, 20, 2004, pp 58–63, at www.premiobalancosocial.org.br/artigos.asp.

23. Kevin Farnsworth, 'Promoting business-centred welfare: international and European business perspectives on social policy', *Journal of European Social Policy*, 15 (1), 2005, pp 65–80; and Belén Balanyá , Ann Doherty, Olivier Hoedeman, Adam Ma'anit & Erik Wesselius, *Europe Inc: Regional and Global Restructuring and the Rise of Corporate Power*, London: Pluto Press, 2000.

24. Naren Prasad, 'Privatization results: private sector participation in water services after 15 years', *Development Policy Review*, 24 (6), 2006, pp 669–692.

25. Kolk & Van Tulder, 'Poverty alleviation as a business strategy?'.

26. See Maureen Kilgour, 'The UN Global Compact and substantive equality for women', in this issue.

27. Barrientos & Smith, *The ETI Code of Labour Practice.*

28. Oxfam International, *Offside! Labour Rights and Sportswear Production in Asia*, Oxford: Oxfam International, 2006, p 3.

29. Peter Utting, 'Regulating business via multistakeholder initiatives: a preliminary assessment', in NGLS/UNRISD, *Voluntary Approaches to Corporate Responsibility: Reading and a Resource Guide*, Geneva: NGLS, 2002.

30. With the participation of the US and the UK governments, oil, mining and energy companies, and human rights, labour and corporate responsibility organizations, the Voluntary Principles were established in 2000 with the goal of maintaining the safety and security of extractive operations while ensuring that human rights and fundamental freedoms are respected.

31. John G Ruggie, *Human Rights Policies and Management Practices of Fortune Global 500 Firms: Results of a Survey*, Cambridge, MA: John F Kennedy School of Government, Harvard University, 2006, p 7.

32. *Ibid.*

33. See, for example, the Public Eye on Davos Awards for 2005. See also Peter Utting & Kate Ives, 'The politics of corporate responsibility and the oil industry', *St Antony's International Review*, 2 (1), 2006, pp 11 –34.

34. At the time of writing, the IFC, in collaboration with the International Business Leaders Forum, is developing one such tool. For a discussion on human rights impact assessments, see Special Representative of the Secretary-General, Interim Report of the Special Representative of the Secretary-General on the issue of human rights and transnational corporations and other business enterprises, UN document E/CN.4/2006/97, Commission on Human Rights, Geneva, 2006.

35. McKinsey & Company, *Assessing the Global Compact's Impact*, 2004.

36. Special Representative of the Secretary-General, Interim Report.

37. Anne Phillips, '"Really" equal: opportunities and autonomy,' *Journal of Political Philosophy*, 14 (1), 2006, p 30.

38. Ronen Shamir, 'Corporate social responsibility: a case of hegemony and counter-hegemony', in Santos & Rodgrıguez-Garavito, *Law and Globalization from Below,* p 93.

39. Jem Bendell, *Barricades and Boardrooms: A Contemporary History of the Corporate Accountability Movement*, Programme on Technology, Business and Society, Paper No 13, Geneva: UNRISD, 2004; Robin Broad, *Global Backlash: Citizen Initatives for a Just World Economy*, New York: Rowman and Littlefield, 2002; and Peter Utting, 'Corporate responsibility and the movement of business', *Development in Practice*, 15, 2005, pp 375–388.

40. UNRISD, *Corporate Social Responsibility and Development*.

41. Michael Conroy, 'Can advocacy-led certification systems transform global corporate practices?', in Broad, *Global Backlash*.

42. Peter Evans, 'Counter-hegemonic globalization: transnational social movements in the contemporary global political economy', in Janoski *et al, Handbook of Political Sociology*, Cambridge: Cambridge University Press, 2005; Boaventura de Sousa Santos & César Rodriguez-Garavito, 'Law, politics and the subaltern in counter-hegemonic globalization', in Santos & Rodrıguez-Garavito, *Law and Globalization from Below*; and Niamh Garvey & Peter Newell, 'Corporate accountability to the poor? Assessing the effectiveness of community-based strategies', *Development in Practice*, 15 (3–4), pp 389–404.

43. Bendell, *Barricades and Boardrooms*.

44. CCC, *Looking for a Quick Fix*.

45. Jem Bendell, *Towards Workplace Participatory Rural Appraisal: Report from a Focus Group of Women Banana Workers*, New Academy of Business, Occasional Paper, Bristol: New Academy of Business, September 2001.

46. Clay *et al, Exploring the Links between International Business and Poverty Reduction*.

47. Naila Kabeer, 'Globalization, labor standards, and women's rights: dilemmas of collective (in)action in an interdependent world', *Feminist Economics*, 10 (1), 2004, pp 3–35; and Zammit, *Development at Risk*.

48. See David Levy & Peter Newell, 'Business strategy and international environmental governance: toward a neo-Gramscian synthesis', *Global Environmental Politics*, 2 (4), 2002, pp 84–101; Jem Bendell & David Murphy, 'Towards civil regulation: NGOs and the politics of corporate environmentalism', in Peter Utting (ed), *The Greening of Business in Developing Countries: Rhetoric, Reality and Prospects*, London: Zed Books/UNRISD, 2002; and Peter Utting, *Business Responsibility for Sustainable Development*, Occasional Paper No 2, Geneva: UNRISD, 2000.

49. Ngai-Ling Sum, 'From ''new constitutionalism'' to ''new ethicalism'': global business governance and the discourses and practices of corporate social responsibility', paper prepared for the European Consortium for Political Research Joint Sessions, Workshop 24: Transnational Private Governance in the Global Political Economy, Granada, 14–19 April 2005.

50. See, in particular, Shamir, 'Corporate social responsibility'; Santos & Rodrıguez-Garavito, 'Law, politics and the subaltern in counter-hegemonic globalization'; and Peter Utting, *Rethinking Business Regulation: From Self-Regulation to Social Control*, Programme on Technology, Business and Society, Paper No 15, Geneva: UNRISD, 2005.

51. Rob Van Tulder, 'The power of core companies', *European Business Forum*, 10, 2002.

52. UNCTAD, *World Investment Report: Transnational Corporations and Export Competitiveness*, Geneva: UNCTAD, 2002.

53. *Ibid*, p 91.

54. Paul Dembinsky, 'Economic power and social responsibility of very big enterprises-facts and challenges', *Finance & The Common Good/Bien Commun*, 15, 2003, pp 27–34.

55. Thomas Piketty & Emmanuel Saez, 'Income inequality in the United States 1913–1998', *Quarterly Journal of Economics*, CXVIII (1), 2003, pp 8–10; and David Harvey, 'Neo-liberalism as creative destruction', *Geografiska Annaler: Series B, Human Geography*, 88 (2), 2006, p 148.

56. Harvey, 'Neo-liberalism as creative destruction', p 149.

57. Christopher Schmitt, 'Corporate charity: why it's slowing', *Business Week*, 18 December 2000, at www.businessweek.com.

58. Dan Roberts, 'America's dilemma: as business retreats from its welfare role, who will take up the burden?', *Financial Times*, 13 January 2005.

59. Carol Hymowitz, 'Big companies become big targets unless they guard images carefully', *Wall Street Journal*, 12 December 2005.

60. Arindrajit Dub & Ken Jacobs, *Hidden Cost of Wal-Mart Jobs: Use of Safety Net Programs by Wal-Mart Workers in California*, Briefing Paper Series, University of California Berkeley Labor Center, 2 August, Berkeley: Center for Labor Research and Education, 2004.

61. OECD, *Recent Tax Policy Trends and Reforms in OECD Countries*, OECD Tax Policy Studies, No 9, Paris: OECD, 2004.

62. Manuel Riesco, 'Pay your taxes! Corporate social responsibility and the mining industry in Chile', in Riesco *et al, The 'Pay Your Taxes' Debate: Perspectives on Corporate Taxation and Social Responsibility in the Chilean Mining Industry*, Programme on Technology, Business and Society, Paper No 16, Geneva: UNRISD, 2005.

63. See www.irs.gov/newsroom/article/0,,id=162359,00.html. [2]

USING CORPORATE SOCIAL RESPONSIBILITY TO WIN THE WAR FOR TALENT

C.B. Bhattacharya, Sankar Sen and Daniel Korschun

It is by now an article of faith that employees who are skilled, creative and driven to satisfy customers are essential for differentiating a company from its competitors. Increasingly, success comes from being able to attract, motivate and retain a talented pool of workers. However, with a finite number of extraordinary employees to go around, the competition for them is fierce.[1]

There is growing evidence that a company's corporate social responsibility activities comprise a legitimate, compelling and increasingly important way to attract and retain good employees. For example, in a bid to burnish their images as socially responsible companies and thereby attract and retain talent, CEOs of high-profile companies such as Home Depot, Delta Air Lines and SAP recently pledged to deploy millions of employee volunteers to work on various community projects.[2] Their efforts appear to make sense: Jim Copeland, Jr., former CEO of Deloitte Touche Tohmatsu, puts it this way: "The best professionals in the world want to work in organizations in which they can thrive, and they want to work for companies that exhibit good corporate citizenship."[3]

In general, CSR initiatives reveal the values of a company and thus can be part of the "employee value proposition" that recent studies indicate is the lens through which managers must view talent management today. CSR also humanizes the company in ways that other facets of the job cannot; it depicts the company as a contributor to society rather than as an entity concerned solely with maximizing profits. As other researchers explain it, "a paycheck may keep a person on the job physically, but it alone will not keep a person on the job emotionally."[4] Moreover, because of the many forms that it can take, CSR often serves as a genuine point of differentiation for the company. It is not surprising, then, that so many companies engage in so many CSR initiatives. Indeed, many companies big and small, including blue-chip names such as Cisco Systems, General Electric and IBM, view employee engagement in CSR as a "strategic imperative."[5] Yet few if any companies have figured out how best to reap the returns of such CSR engagement. We consider "internal marketing" to be the most apt rubric under which CSR can be used to acquire and retain employees. Such a perspective holds that just as companies succeed by fulfilling the needs of their customers, they can manage their employees best by viewing them as internal customers, fulfilling their needs through a compelling menu of "job-products" whose features include salary, benefits packages and job responsibilities.[6] Designed properly, the job-products can contribute dramatically to job satisfaction, employee retention and productivity.

A key task for managers, then, is to incorporate CSR into job-products that are tailored to the often diverse needs of employees. However, few managers are clear about how to identify and understand the needs of different employee segments and subsequently configure their CSR efforts to address the unique needs of each segment. Researchers Michael Porter and Mark Kramer observed that "[m]ost companies feel compelled to give to charity. Few have figured out how to do it well."[7] That is not to suggest that companies do not engage in any strategic CSR thinking. But it is evident that much of the thinking has been restricted thus far to approaches intended to engage external stakeholders such as consumers, regulators and watchdog groups.[8]

There are further challenges with the range of ways in which businesses approach CSR. Although there is convergence on the concept that CSR refers essentially to a company's commitment to improving societal well-being through discretionary business practices and contributions of corporate resources, there is great divergence in how it is executed and therefore in how effective CSR can be for managing talent.[9]

As a rule, senior executives are content with CSR engagement at broad levels ("We support recycling"). However, most have not yet grasped that the specificity with which a company supports or engages in a social initiative makes a big difference to how it is perceived by employees.[10] For instance, a company that supports dental health can engage in corporate philanthropy — donating money to the American Dental Association, say — or in cause marketing (a percentage of toothpaste purchases goes to the American Dental Association) or to corporate social marketing programs that promote actual behavior change, such as clinics in inner cities to train children to have better dental health practices. Different groups of employees will view those approaches in very different ways — and value them quite differently.

About the Research

To understand better when, how and why employees react to CSR, we devised a two-part study. The first part involved a series of in-depth interviews and eight focus groups with employees of a major consumer-goods company, followed by a global employee survey (10,000-plus responses) administered by the company itself. Each focus group comprised five to eight participants at various locations, including the company's U.S. headquarters, a manufacturing plant, a regional sales office and one non-U.S. location. The second part featured a series of interviews followed by two online surveys of employees (yielding 481 responses) from more than 10 companies in the manufacturing, retail and service sectors. (Details of the study methodology are available from the authors on request.) The data from these primary research studies, viewed through the clarifying lens of our general research program, provided valuable insights into the challenges and opportunities facing companies that want to deploy their CSR efforts strategically in the war for talent.

With that in mind, we sought to understand the barriers that managers face in using their CSR initiatives to attract and retain the best employees and the ways in which these barriers might be overcome. The research grew out of a larger program examining the impact of CSR on company stakeholders. (See "About the Research.") Our prior work suggests that stakeholders' responses to CSR are generally favorable, yet highly dependent upon the perceptions and characteristics of the individual, the company and, to some extent, the broader industry and macro-environmental context.

The Challenges of Using CSR As An Internal Marketing Lever

Our research indicates that CSR's opportunity to serve as an effective internal marketing lever is limited by four related issues. First, companies often keep their employees at arm's length, not communicating the extent and details of their CSR efforts in a clear and consistent manner. Second, companies formulate their CSR programs without explicitly considering the diverse set of employee needs that can be fulfilled by such programs. Third, companies do not fully understand the psychological mechanisms that link their CSR programs to anticipated positive returns from their employees (for example, pro-company behaviors, higher productivity, longer tenures and so on). Finally, we find that companies take a decidedly top-down approach in the formulation, execution and maintenance of their CSR programs, often mandating participation rather than involving employees on their own terms. We discuss each of these barriers in more detail next.

1. Employees' Lack of Awareness and Involvement in CSR

An employee's proximity to CSR spans a continuum: from a complete lack of awareness to direct involvement. Our research suggests that most employees are not close to their employers' CSR efforts; while many have a vague notion that their employer is socially responsible, they know little to nothing about the specific activities the company engages in. Proximity is also program-specific: An employee can be highly engaged with one initiative yet completely unaware of the company's other CSR activities. Moreover, while many employees are eager to know more about such initiatives, they frequently find it difficult to discover more about them. Companies often miss prime opportunities to connect with employees by tucking away news about CSR on remote pages of the intranet.

We find that even companies that are spending millions of dollars to support compelling social initiatives fail to seize opportunities to inform employees fully about their good works, let alone involve them in such initiatives. Consider this suggestion from one of our retail sector interviewees:

> There is maybe one [announcement] at the end of the year — 'By the way, [the company] donated $12 million last year to nonprofit educational organizations' — but it's a small blurb. I think you could increase the impact on associates if they were to publicize it more throughout the year. Just bring it to the attention of the associates more.
> — Male, Headquarters Office of Specialty Retailer

The quantitative studies confirmed our hypotheses. In the follow-up global survey conducted by the U.S. consumer goods company — an organization that works hard to articulate and communicate its CSR internally — 90% of respondents agreed it was important for the company to be engaged in CSR, but only about 50% agreed that they had a clear understanding of the nature of this engagement. Moreover, in the two online surveys conducted later, only 37% of the employees were aware of their respective companies' CSR. Clearly, a major challenge for managers is to increase their employees' proximity to their CSR initiatives, taking them from unawareness to active involvement.

2. Limited Understanding of Employee Needs Fulfilled by CSR

The internal marketing literature shows that, not surprisingly, the success of a specific job-product stems largely from the extent to which it fulfills key employee needs. As with the basic facets of job-product such as pay, benefits, advancement opportunities and job role, a company's CSR programs can satisfy one or more higher-order psychosocial needs. In fact, it could be argued that CSR's power as an internal marketing lever rests largely on its ability to satisfy those needs meaningfully.

However, companies are mostly oblivious to such issues. That is not entirely surprising, given that the task of unearthing employees' needs is anything but straightforward. The task is further complicated by our finding that one size does not necessarily fit all: The needs vary in their relative importance across employee segments. The primary research uncovered at least four fundamental needs that employees seek to fulfill through their proximity to their employers' CSR activities. These are detailed next.

Creating opportunities for self-enhancement

We found that some employees like to work for socially responsible companies because it gives them opportunities for personal growth. The results can be emotionally rewarding when employees use such opportunities to express their own sense of responsibility to their immediate or even larger community. The research also reveals that when employees work on CSR projects that involve tasks outside of their daily routine, they learn specific skills that can help them advance in their careers. For example, Green Mountain Coffee Roasters Inc. of Waterbury, Vermont, has sent more than 20% of its full-time employees to coffee farms in an effort to educate them about sourcing issues. The employees subsequently use this knowledge in their daily work. Similarly, organizational or marketing skills developed in a community outreach program may give employees the tools necessary for greater job effectiveness.

Improving work-personal life integration

Employees' work and personal lives are inextricably intertwined, and they often look to integrate these two spheres so they can transition more smoothly between them.[11] Interestingly, the research shows that CSR can help employees feel less stressed when they feel they are effectively balancing the needs of work and family. Integration between the two parts of employees' lives is enhanced when they interpret their employers' socially responsible behavior as an indication that the company places the same importance on personal values that they do themselves. More concretely, the CSR initiatives that achieve this integration often involve the employees' own social communities (for instance, schools that their children attend).

Building a bridge to the company

Employees who work in remote locations often feel isolated from (and to some extent underappreciated by) what they perceive to be the literal as well as psychosocial center of the company — the headquarters or a major regional office hub. Naturally, these employees have a need to feel more connected or "plugged in" to the company's social and professional networks, so they often look for opportunities to connect with others around the company. The far-flung employees viewed CSR initiatives as a means for the company to demonstrate a commitment to them and as a potential bond between employees regardless of location. Listen to this woman who works in a regional sales office far from HQ:

> *The power of [the company] supporting what we want to do here in this community ... wow, that makes me feel more connected to the company.*
> — *Female, Regional Office of Consumer-Goods Company*

CSR often provides a bridge to colleagues scattered across multiple locations — programs where employees work closely with others whom they may not have met or with whom they would not normally work. It also provides a benefit on a more abstract level, where individuals feel that they are part of a collective effort to make a difference in the world. A pertinent example: Satellite office employees of one company that helped the victims of the 2004 Asian tsunami said they felt more connected to distant colleagues regardless of their jobs and assignments.

Creating a "reputation shield."

Employees often find themselves having to defend their companies' reputations to hostile external stakeholders. This is particularly germane for global companies that have operations in locations where the local population and media have negative or even hostile feelings toward the company. For example, Wal-Mart Stores Inc. has received considerable criticism from many communities because they view the retailing giant as a threat to small-business owners. These pockets of ill will obviously can be harmful to the company, but they also can hurt employees' self-esteem. As one focus group individual stated:

> *You get outside . . . and it is either no knowledge or a lot of negative knowledge, and it is a very painful thing, because we all know better inside the company.*
> — *Male, Overseas Office of Consumer-Goods Company*

The research indicates that a company's CSR activity helps employees combat such negative external images by educating external audiences, and sometimes even themselves, about the company's core values and ethics.

In this way, CSR provides a "reputation shield" that deflects negative sentiment.

Companies now need to shift their approaches to CSR management if they are to realize fully the returns that CSR promises. Here are seven factors that merit particular attention.

3. Poor Understanding of Employee Returns to CSR

For companies truly to leverage their CSR in the quest for talent, it's crucial to understand the key outcomes that CSR produces for the company, the psychological drivers of those outcomes and the many contingencies that moderate the links between CSR initiatives and outcomes. The need is underscored by a recent PricewaterhouseCoopers LLP study that points to employee motivation as one of the top two factors helping chief executive officers make the business case for CSR activities (58% of respondents rated CSR so, second only to reputation/brand at 79%).[12] However, most companies devote few if any resources to gaining insights into the employee-specific processes and outcomes that stem from their CSR inputs.

When personal needs are fulfilled at work, employees are likely to identify with the company. Identification is a psychological concept that reflects the extent to which employees feel that their sense of self overlaps with their sense of their employer. Employees who identify strongly with the company view its successes as their own, and they incorporate its characteristics into their own self-concepts.[13] For example, employees at The Timberland Co. are known to have a near cultlike sense of belonging due, in part, to the company's CSR efforts. CSR has already been pinpointed

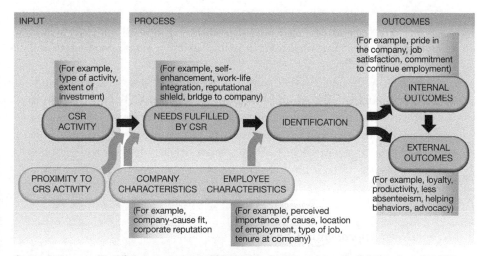

Companies now need to shift their approaches to CSR management if they are to realize fully the returns that CSR promises. Here are seven factors that merit particular attention.

Figure 6.1: Recommended shifts in CSR management approach

as a key factor in such identification among consumers and job applicants in a variety of contexts.[14] Our research adds considerable evidence to support the idea that employees identify with a company when they believe it is socially responsible.

The importance of such CSR-induced identification stems from the slew of pro-company outcomes it engenders. These outcomes can be thought of in terms of two basic and related categories: internal and external. Internal to the employee (residing in his or her mind) are outcomes such as high level of commitment, greater morale and a dedication to excellence in work tasks. CSR-based identification by employees can cause them to feel satisfaction in their job, a sense of pride and a feeling of well-being. Said one focus group participant:

> It makes you feel good that [the company] is out there helping others and helping the environment. We do a lot of things for volunteer work outside that represent [the company] and I'm proud of that.
> — Male, Manufacturing Plant of Consumer-Goods Company

These primarily psychological outcomes lead to external (behavioral) outcomes: They cause employees to contribute resources toward the achievement of their employers' goals.[15] External outcomes, evident in both the focus group findings and interviews with executives, include a reduction in absenteeism and employee retention, as described by this employee:

> One of the things that keeps me here is some of the positive things that we do in the community and being able to be part of that as a result.
> — Female, Headquarters Office of Consumer-Goods Company

Employees also noted that their employer's commitment to socially responsible behavior inspires them to work harder, be more productive and focus more on quality.

The follow-up quantitative survey conducted by the consumer-goods organization confirmed that employee engagement in CSR led to pride in the company, which in turn was positively related to employee performance and negatively to intention to quit. Similarly, our online survey results show that employee engagement in CSR is positively related to customer focus and pro-company citizenship behaviors and it runs counter to employees' intentions to leave.

4. Top-Down Approach to CSR

Finally, there is a huge chasm between executive teams and their employees regarding the appropriate sources and ownership of CSR initiatives. In a recent study of CSR ownership by the United Nations Global Compact (the world's largest global corporate citizenship initiative) and the Wharton School of the University of Pennsylvania, 71% of the 400 companies surveyed indicated that their CSR policies and practices were developed/managed at the CEO level, 57% at the board of directors level and 56% at the senior management level. The findings of our research are no different: Most companies see CSR development, implementation and management as top-down processes. In other words, it is senior management that decides what to support — and how. As one of our interview respondents put it:

> *Every CEO we've had for the past couple of years has had a focus in the community and has made the company sort of take it on. The two CEOs and the one before that were into blood drives. So what is one of the things that we had to do on every one of our sites? Blood drives!*
> — *Female, Headquarters Office, Toys and Sporting Goods Company*

Clearly, a more strategic approach to CSR warrants greater ownership of the initiatives by employees. They yearn to play greater roles — in effect, to become co-creators of CSR value. In the words of a focus group respondent:

> *If we are looking to energize employees . . . there's going to be a natural tendency to say, 'We're going to empower you through charitable giving in some capacity.' I have half a dozen organizations that I work with, and I'd love to be able to extend that reach through [the company].*
> — *Female, Regional Office of Consumer-Goods Company*

Opportunities Through Optimal CSR Strategies

As CSR becomes more widespread, it also is changing rapidly. What was once ancillary to business practice quickly is becoming an essential element of corporate strategy. Companies now need to shift their approaches to CSR management if they are to realize fully the returns that CSR promises. (See "Recommended Shifts in CSR Management Approach.")

Based on the barriers identified above, we recommend that managers take the following five steps:

Increase Employee Proximity to CSR

The most straightforward implication of our research is that companies must bring employees closer to their CSR activities. The most specific and important aspect of this is communication; companies need to inform employees about their CSR programs in a concrete, coherent and consistent manner. Such communication has to include both the rationale behind the CSR involvement and the specifics of the programs, their operations, the company resources allocated and the challenges faced, and most importantly, the successes of the programs.

Many companies are starting to do a good job of communicating their CSR commitments to their external publics; the same lessons can be applied to internal communication. At the same time, companies need to realize that employees, like consumers, can learn about a company's involvement in specific CSR (and the lack thereof) and its motivations for doing so from multiple sources (for example, blogs, online chat rooms and other media), many of which are external to the company and therefore cannot be controlled by its marketing department. External sources can be highly credible because they are seen to be more "objective" than corporate press releases. Thus, companies must aim for high credibility in their communications to offset employee cynicism. This can be achieved by involving credible and influential internal sources (for example, corporate online communities such as IBM's On Demand Community) and with a bias toward objective information rather than feel-good rhetoric. While the latter is undoubtedly important in inspiring employees to get involved and to feel part of a greater cause, by itself it can come across as empty PR.

Managers who want to be strategic about CSR's leverage have to understand how their CSR "inputs" translate into employee "outputs" that benefit the company. This framework helps managers see the connections between inputs — specific CSR initiatives — and outputs in terms of employees' thoughts and behaviors.

Bringing employees closer to CSR obviously does not end with communication: Companies must encourage active participation. This is not just a matter of exhorting employees to get involved; companies need to provide specific opportunities for involvement in ways that do not take away from employees' ability to fulfill their regular responsibilities. Better yet, companies can consider making CSR participation integral to those professional responsibilities: activities such as Green Mountain Coffee's sending full-time employees to coffee farms, for instance.

Finally, as in other aspects of their employees' jobs, companies need to provide objective and constructive feedback about performance in CSR-related activities in ways that encourage and allow employees to make the most personally and professionally significant contributions possible. This can take the form of 360-degree evaluations as well as awards.

Use a Contingent Input-Output Approach to Make CSR Decisions

In general, the research suggests that if companies truly are to be strategic about their CSR deployments, they have to rely on their understanding of how their CSR inputs translate to pro-company outputs. A framework

CSR MANAGEMENT FACTOR	TRADITIONAL APPROACH	OPTIMAL ENGAGEMENT
MEASUREMENT AND CONTROL	Not clearly defined	Contingent input-output approach
INTERNAL MARKETING OBJECTIVE	Change employee attitudes	Fulfill employee needs
IMPLEMENTATION	Uniform across company	Tailored to employee segments
KEY INDICATOR	Job satisfaction	Identification
VALUE CREATION	Top-down	Co-created
EMPLOYEE ROLE	Enabler	Enactor
COMPANY ROLE	Enactor	Enabler

Managers who want to be strategic about CSR's leverage have to understand how their CSR "inputs" translate into employee "outputs" that benefit the company. This framework helps managers see the connections between inputs – specific CSR initiatives – and outputs in terms of employees' thoughts and behaviors.

Figure 6.2: Employee Reactions to CSR

is presented. (See "Employee Reactions to CSR.") It adopts a contingent approach to seeing how employees benefit from a company's CSR initiatives and whether and how the benefits translate to favorable company outcomes.

We advise managers to begin CSR planning by adapting such an input-output model for their own unique contexts, using research to identify the inputs in terms of the issues or causes the company ought to support, the processes and, most importantly, the desired employeecentric outputs of each CSR program. Once the programs are implemented, the outputs can be monitored through internal surveys to determine which programs are delivering the most value to employees and, ultimately, to the company. There should be metrics for internal outcomes (for example, attitude toward the company, well-being and commitment to continued employment) and external outcomes (such as absenteeism, retention, work effort, productivity) as well as for the underlying processes (identification).

Finally, in trying to assess the returns from CSR initiatives, managers should consider the many multipliers (that is, the contingencies) that may amplify or dampen the initiatives' effects. Programs that make a huge impact for some employees may have little effect on others, depending on a variety of employee and company characteristics.[16] Thus, the key to constructing effective CSR programs lies in understanding not just the extent to which these programs can satisfy key employee needs, engendering identification, but also the employee- and company-specific factors that can magnify or dilute the effects of CSR. Employee factors include tenure at the company, the nature of their jobs, age, gender and their perceived importance of the cause at the center of a particular CSR program.[17] For example, while most people will respond favorably to programs that support breast cancer research, female employees in the high-risk age bracket are likely to feel greater affinity for such a program.

Understand and Fulfill Employee Needs

Companies need to segment their employees based on the relative importance of their CSR-related needs and then design and target segment-specific CSR programs to meet those diverse needs. Employee segments can be identified in the same way that companies use "benefit segmentation" among customers and look for demographic or psychographic correlations for these segments to identify and target them more easily. In our research, for example, a key segment seems to be employees who live where their companies are viewed unfavorably by the local population; there, it may be necessary to run CSR programs that not only have great social impact in those particular markets but also have high external visibility.

Clearly it's not easy to create a CSR "offering" for each benefit segment. As is typical with customer segmentation, companies may want to articulate the relative attractiveness of different employee segments and target their CSR programs to the segments with the greatest present or future value. The success of the programs can be gauged in terms of the extent to which the targeted employee needs were actually met.

Strengthen Employee Identification

Our research indicates that CSR can dramatically strengthen identification because it reveals more unequivocally than most other corporate endeavors the values or "soul" of the company. Thus, the basic objective in devising effective CSR strategies should be to increase employee identification rather than other, more commonly monitored indicators such as job satisfaction.

Measures of identification range from the anecdotal to the formal. For instance, identification is easily recognizable anecdotally through "we" statements that employees use when describing the organization; employees who identify strongly will frequently make a distinction between "we insiders" and people "outside" the company. The organizational behavior and marketing literatures can be tapped for more formal measures of identification.[18]

Involve Employees in Co-Creating CSR Value

Managers must seek to involve their employees in the planning, design and implementation of CSR programs, making them participants rather than onlookers. Since employees know their own needs best, those who co-produce CSR programs can be expected to develop programs that give them the most meaning and purpose. Involving employees in such ways can greatly assist managers in fulfilling needs that might otherwise be difficult to identify.

Another way to view this is to think of employees as the primary enactors of social responsibility programs rather than the enablers. In this view, the company and its employees essentially switch roles. Employees see themselves as closer to their communities than company executives and therefore more qualified to take the lead in designing and implementing CSR programs. For example, rather than matching employee donations at a charity of the company's choice, employees prefer it when the company matches their donations to charities of their choice.

Importantly, shifting the primary responsibility for CSR programs to employees does not absolve the company of its responsibility to be an effective enabler. The company must maintain clear, open, continuous two-way communication about CSR, providing the requisite guidance and resources so employees can effectively implement their CSR plans. That includes going beyond merely allowing CSR involvement on company time to working, ideally, with employee groups to help them fully integrate their CSR efforts into coherent and compelling job-products.

Conclusion

Now that many global companies are investing millions of dollars in CSR initiatives, it has never been more worthwhile to assess the returns in terms of improved connections with employees. Still, plenty of challenges remain. Our research suggests that successful CSR strategies must be based on a clearly articulated and contingent input-output perspective. They must also satisfy varying employee needs, encourage employee identification and be co-created with employees. In particular, CSR is most effective when employees are the actual enactors, with the company acting as an enabler. Corporate social responsibility is an especially complex strategic endeavor. It is clear that it now calls for considerably more attention and commitment from business leaders if it is to produce tangible results in terms of improved employee attraction, motivation and retention.

Notes

1. E. Michaels, H. Handfield-Jones and B. Axelrod, "The War for Talent" (Boston: Harvard Business School Press, 2001); and C.A. Bartlett and S. Ghoshal, "Building Competitive Advantage Through People," MIT Sloan Management Review 43, no. 2 (winter 2002): 34–41.
2. B. Grow, S. Hamm and L. Lee, "The Debate Over Doing Good," BusinessWeek, Aug. 15, 2005, 76–78.
3. Quotation from "Responding to the Leadership Challenge: Findings of a CEO Survey on Global Corporate Citizenship," white paper, World Economic Forum, Geneva, Switzerland, 2003.

4.   L. Berry and A. Parasuraman, "Services Marketing Starts From Within," *Marketing Management* 1, no. 1 (winter 1992): 24–34.

5.   Grow, "Debate Over Doing Good," 76–78.

6.   E. Gummesson, "Using Internal Marketing to Develop a New Culture: The Case of Ericsson," *Journal of Business and Industrial Marketing* 2, no. 3 (summer 1987): 23–28; W.R. George, "Internal Marketing and Organizational Behavior: A Partnership in Developing Customer-Conscious Employees at Every Level," *Journal of Business Research* 20, no. 1 (January 1990): 63–70; and P.K. Ahmed and M. Rafiq, "Internal Marketing Issues and Challenges," *European Journal of Marketing* 37, no. 9 (2003): 1177–1186.

7.   M. Porter and M.R. Kramer, "Strategy & Society: The Link Between Competitive Advantage and Corporate Social Responsibility," *Harvard Business Review* 84, no. 12 (December 2006): 78–92.

8.   "2004 Cone Corporate Citizenship Study," December 8, 2004, www. coneinc.com; and P. Ellen, D.J. Webb and L.A. Mohr, "Building Corporate Associations: Consumer Attributions for Corporate Socially Responsible Programs," *Journal of the Academy of Marketing Science* 34, no. 2 (spring 2006): 147–157.

9.   P. Kotler and N. Lee, "Corporate Social Responsibility: Doing the Most Good for Your Company and Your Cause" (Hoboken, New Jersey: Wiley & Sons, 2004).

10. For example, for the past several years Wal-Mart has been a top corporate donor, but research revealed that because of its fragmented giving, few people could recall what or whom Wal-Mart supports. Now it is giving its CSR a sharper focus. From Grow, "Debate Over Doing Good," 76–78.

11. S.C. Clark, "Work/Family Border Theory: A New Theory of Work/ Family Balance," *Human Relations* 53, no. 6 (2002): 747–770.

12. World Economic Forum, "Responding to the Leadership Challenge."

13. B.E. Ashforth and F. Mael, "Social Identity Theory and the Organization," *Academy of Management Review* 14, no. 1 (January 1989): 20–39; and C.B. Bhattacharya and S. Sen, "Consumer-Company Identification: A Framework for Understanding Consumers' Relationships with Companies," *Journal of Marketing* 67, no. 2 (April 2003): 76–88.

14. S. Sen, C.B. Bhattacharya and D. Korschun, "The Role of Corporate Social Responsibility in Strengthening Multiple Stakeholder Relationships: A Field Experiment," *Journal of the Academy of Marketing Science* 34, no. 2 (spring 2006): 158–166; and D.B. Turban and D.W. Greening, "Corporate Social Performance and Organizational Attractiveness to Prospective Employees," *Academy of Management Journal* 40, no. 3 (June 1997): 658–672.

15. I. Maignan and O.C. Ferrell, "Corporate Social Responsibility and Marketing: An Integrative Framework," *Journal of the Academy of Marketing Science* 32, no. 1 (winter 2004): 3–19.

16. C.B. Bhattacharya and S. Sen, "Doing Better at Doing Good: When, Why, and How Consumers Respond to Corporate Social Initiatives," *California Management Review* 47, no. 1 (fall 2004): 9–24.

17. Sen, "Role of Corporate Social Responsibility," 158–166.

18. M. Bergami and R. Bagozzi, "Self-Categorization, Affective Commitment and Group Self-Esteem as Distinct Aspects of Social Identity in the Organization," *British Journal of Social Psychology* 39, no. 4 (December 2000): 555–577.

Chapter 7

CSR in the community

IN THIS CHAPTER WE WILL:

- Explain some of the core corporate responsibilities in the community
- Show how community responsibilities vary according to different cultural and temporal contexts
- Examine the meaning of key concepts such as corporate philanthropy, strategic philanthropy, and corporate community involvement
- Understand different strategic approaches used by corporations in fulfilling their community responsibilities
- Examine how social and economic objectives can potentially be aligned through community investments in the firm's competitive context

Introduction

Some years ago, it would have been quite common for many people to equate CSR with community responsibilities such as donations to good causes and involvement in local development initiatives. While we would argue that this is too narrow a perspective to capture the full possibilities of the CSR concept, there are good reasons for such a view. To begin with, philanthropic donations to local community initiatives were among the first corporate activities to go under the banner of CSR, especially in the US where the term was first coined (Carroll, 1999). Second, even today, community initiatives are typically the first manifestation of CSR to become evident in countries and cultures relatively new to CSR. For example, Chapple and Moon (2005) show that firms in Asian countries including India, Thailand, Singapore,

Malaysia, and the Philippines have reported far more on their community initiatives than they have on marketplace and workplace CSR issues. Finally, community programmes are probably the most obvious manifestation of the voluntary and discretionary elements that are often seen to be central to CSR. While treating your employees or customers well can very readily be seen as simply good business (or even a matter of legal compliance), donating money to charity or helping out in the local community is more often seen to be a matter of corporate largesse.

It is then perhaps no surprise that it was exactly this kind of CSR – donating to local community causes – that early protagonists in the field tended to focus on, whether to argue against CSR (Friedman, 1970) or elevate it as a desirable form of corporate citizenship at the top of the CSR pyramid (Carroll, 1999). While the debate has moved on and the focus shifted away from community and philanthropy, they remain core aspects and have helped to form the CSR field, and in particular 'traditional CSR' as discussed in Chapter 3.

But there is another side to CSR in relation to the community. Communities are literally the neighbours of business. Community issues are far from being just of relevance to large corporations with CSR programmes in developed countries. Community issues are perhaps even more critical for small- and medium-sized enterprises (Spence, 2007), where firms lack the individual power of large organizations, and in developing countries where there is a very real need for 'on the ground' support and development (see Muthuri et al, 2009). Newell (2005) argues that this makes communities key players in holding businesses to account, although this may be different in developing countries versus developed ones, since the resources of the community to mobilize any objection to corporate activities may be less.

In fact, if we reflect on Mitchell, Agle, and Wood's framework of stakeholder salience in Chapter 4, communities have relatively high legitimacy as corporate neighbours, low power, and usually low urgency (unless in pressing cases such as a dramatic pollution spill that needs immediate response). Once established, companies are unlikely to relocate or move overnight, and so the community is tied to the corporation but has little influence or control over it compared to other stakeholders.

Why then are communities nevertheless on the corporate radar? The explanation seems likely to be linked to the practical issues of being neighbours, since this makes the local community the obvious first point of focus for CSR efforts. Moreover, sometimes the well-being of the local community has significant implications for the success of the company – as the UK CSR charity Business in the Community puts it, 'healthy back streets make for healthy high streets'.[1] Firms also need to consider the importance of building good relations with the local community because it may be the main source of potential employees. Finally, local community problems are hard to miss, and close physical proximity can heighten the perceived moral intensity of community issues (see Jones, 1991)

Types of community responsibility

Community responsibilities may come in many shapes and forms. The most obvious and well-known would be philanthropic donations from the firm to local deserving causes, including community groups, educational initiatives, sporting associations, youth groups, health programmes, the arts, and so on. For example, the Japanese car-maker Toyota has the ambitious goal of 'creating a harmonious, self-sustaining society where a diverse range of people respect one another and work together, by assisting with local social contribution projects, supporting welfare services, encouraging self-reliance and other initiatives'.[2] Such philanthropy might be in the form of financial donations as well as contributions in terms of free products and employee time.

Often such philanthropy takes place at companies that rely particularly on their embeddedness in their local communities. In the US the largest corporate donors in 2010 were the retailers Safeway ($77m), Kroger ($64m), and Macy's ($41m).[3] In South Africa, the largest donors in 2010 were the mining company Anglo American ($62m) and the retailer Woolworths ($36m).[4]

Such corporate giving is particularly prevalent in the US (although this is in decline, as the reading in this chapter by Porter and Kramer notes), while in much of Europe the traditional assumption is that such funds would be provided by public bodies out of tax revenues (Brammer & Pavelin, 2005). There is, however, a long tradition of corporate foundations such as the German publishing giant Bertelsmann Foundation, or the FC Barcelona Foundation, part of the Spanish football club with a strong local identity. In parts of Asia, such as India or Pakistan, corporate giving is arguably less widespread than personal giving from wealthy industrialist patrons, although companies such as the Indian conglomerate Tata (see Integrative case 3) have long invested a substantial proportion of their profits in community programmes. Africa has for many years been a recipient of foreign aid creating an ingrained culture of philanthropy that, coupled with unusually high socio-economic needs, means that giving is an 'expected norm' in business (Visser, 2006).

Philanthropy towards the communities where corporations operate clearly remains a significant element of CSR in some contexts. However, the last few decades have also seen various important criticisms raised against straightforward corporate giving, either because it is seen as too paternalistic, an instrumental attempt to buy local compliance to corporate plans, or merely a public relations device that raises cynicism because it adds little of value to the cause, or even because it provides little real benefit to the firm (Hess et al, 2002). What we have seen then is a shift towards more 'built-in' responsibilities rather than simple 'bolt-on' approaches that leave most of the firm largely unaffected (Grayson & Hodges, 2004). These new approaches to community responsibility typically go under the label of 'strategic philanthropy' or 'corporate community investment' or 'involvement'.

CWS 7.1

See the companion website for links to information on corporate charitable giving globally

The shift to strategic philanthropy

Since the 1980s, corporate philanthropy has undergone a major makeover. What was once seen as a simple act of charity has now evolved into a strategic corporate process that, at least in principle, seeks to add value both to the cause and to the corporation. Such strategic philanthropy has seen a whole host of innovations in the area of community relations. This includes:

- **Linking employee volunteering to human resource development strategies.** Increasingly employees are extolled to go beyond simply donating their time and effort to local community projects, and are encouraged to select projects that will enhance their transferable skills and competences in ways that are of benefit to themselves and their employers. For example a participant in Pfizer's Global Health Fellow Program reports returning to her job in Michigan with enhanced consensus building and negotiation skills, problem solving and mentoring aptitude after working with a healthcare access project in Rwanda.[5]

- **Linking charitable giving to marketing strategies through cause-related marketing and sponsorship**. Donations are increasingly expected to provide tangible benefits to the firm in terms of increased sales, brand recognition, or brand identification among consumers. For instance in 2012 the Unilever Foundation and one of Unilever's leading toilet hygiene brands, Domestos, formed a partnership with the children's charity UNICEF on a sanitation programme in South Sudan and Vietnam.[6] This provided for 5 per cent of the proceeds of sales of bottles of Domestos to be donated to the charity's programme.

- **Establishing cross-sector partnerships with community groups.** More broadly, deeper partnerships beyond simply cause marketing can help companies build reputation and legitimacy with the public, as well as specific competence in managing social issues. Working with non-government organizations is widely touted to be a 'win-win' strategy for businesses facing a trust deficit in the community and charities facing a skills or resource deficit.

CWS 7.2

See the companion website for links to information on corporate volunteering, cause related marketing

This transformation of community responsibility into a more strategic approach suggests that firms can readily 'do well by doing good' – a philosophy that has many advocates (although not always such convincing evidence). Nonetheless, it is clear that in a broader sense, enlightened companies probably realize that they cannot succeed in communities that fail. Many firms in just about every nation of the globe engage in some form of community initiatives that seek to build contexts in which their business can thrive – whether it is for access to clean water in Malawi, education programmes in Brazilian favelas, or accommodation for displaced communities after the Great East Japan Earthquake.

Introducing the readings

The two readings in this chapter both address the more strategic approach to community responsibility, dealing first with understanding different strategic approaches to business' public and community responsibilities – and second, with the links between philanthropic projects and improvements in the competitive context of business – i.e. how to create the 'healthy backstreets' in ways that provide a strategic advantage to the firm.

Understanding the public responsibilities of business in developing countries

Our first reading starts with reflections on the public responsibility deficit, that is, a gap of health and welfare support among other things, experienced particularly by citizens in developing country contexts. Reflecting a perspective that has gained considerable traction in CSR in recent years, they note the increasingly quasi-governmental role of large private enterprises (Matten & Crane, 2005).

    Mike Valente and Andrew Crane draw on empirical data to categorize these 'public responsibility' strategies adopted by private enterprises in dealing with communities in need. These strategies can be understood as supplemental to government and civil society activity, in support of them, a substitute to such interventions or as a means to stimulate them. The paper seeks to move beyond the debate around the rights or wrongs of the blurring between government and corporate roles, to focus on how companies can 'add value' to the communities in which they exist.

CWS 7.3

See the companion website for a video of Dirk Matten talking about the quasi-governmental role of privately owned corporations

Enhancing the competitive context through community involvement

The second article is concerned with how to make philanthropy more strategically purposeful for the firm while also ensuring that tangible benefits are provided for the community – in the authors' words, 'bringing social and economic goals into alignment'. Michael Porter and Mark Kramer focus their attention on improvements in the *competitive context* in which firms operate. This reflects a long-standing emphasis in Porter's work on industry structure and firm positioning within the competitive environment, as demonstrated for example, by his widely cited works on the 'five forces' and 'generic strategies' (Porter, 1980, 1985).

    For many people, the original publishing of this reading in 2002 in the *Harvard Business Review* (HBR) signalled the start of the increasing attention to CSR among mainstream business academics. Indeed, this was followed by the once unlikely spectacle of Porter appearing as a keynote speaker in CSR conferences and two subsequent HBR publications on CSR (Porter & Kramer, 2006, 2011). Although many therefore saw this development as a further sign that CSR was now much more central to core strategy thinking, others also pointed to the way that Porter and other strategy theorists were as much wedging CSR into their existing ideas as they were expanding our understanding of it. Certainly it is clear from the two articles collated here that community responsibilities are no longer seen as simply minor add-ons to the 'real' business of corporations. It is also important to realize that this has mainly happened by finding ways of making community relationships pay off for the firm in a manner that even Milton Friedman might applaud.

Challenges for practice

A small school in a large village is offered a donation of sports equipment from a fast-food outlet (the only one in town). The equipment would be clearly branded with the fast-food outlet's logo.

1. How would you characterize this initiative according to Valente and Crane's typology of public responsibility strategies?
2. Identify the positive and negative aspects of the initiative for all stake-holders.
   a) Who would benefit most from such an arrangement and why? Be sure to consider all relevant stakeholders including the wider community.
3. Would your analysis differ if:
   a) The school is focusing on healthy eating at the time of the donation?
   b) The town is a deprived area?
   c) A relatively high proportion of the children are obese?
   d) The owner-manager was previously a prize-winning pupil at the school and is still friendly with the headteacher, working together on another local community initiative?
4. What could you do to ensure the best outcome for your organization if you were:
   a) The headteacher?
   b) The owner-manager of the fast-food outlet?

Study questions

1. 'Corporate responsibilities to the community are the least important of the firm's social responsibilities. Marketplace and workplace responsibilities are much more important because they relate to core stakeholders for the firm.' Critically evaluate this statement.
2. To what extent are corporate community initiatives likely to vary across national contexts? Support your answer with examples of community programmes from a multinational operating in several different continents.

3.   What is the difference between philanthropy and strategic philanthropy? Provide examples of each from current business practice.
4.   Why have firms sought to make their community programmes more strategic? What are the main advantages and disadvantages of such a development?
5.   Explain the differing strategic approaches to companies seeking to respond to public responsibilities not fulfilled by governments.

Further reading

Besser, T., Miller, N., & Perkins, R. (2006) 'For the greater good: business networks and business social responsibility to communities', *Entrepreneurship & Regional Development*, 18(4): 321–339.
This article offers a complementary approach to those discussed in this chapter by looking at the influence of business networks on CSR in relation to communities. As we noted earlier in the chapter, the community as a stakeholder is of particular relevance to small- and medium-sized enterprises, and this paper draws on this perspective, in addition to asking whether smaller firms can act collectively to scale-up their activities. They find that business networking contributes positively to local economic prosperity. Terry Besser and Nancy Miller have published a range of articles on community involvement that are well worth taking a look at, particularly if you are interested in the small business perspective.

Muthuri, J., Chapple, W., & Moon, J. (2009) 'An integrated approach to implementing "community participation" in corporate community involvement: lessons from Magadi Soda Company in Kenya', *Journal of Business Ethics*, 85(2): 431–444.
This article is a fascinating case example of community involvement in practice in a developing country. Muthuri and colleagues focus on the practice of community participation, which they argue can help to alleviate common criticisms of corporate community involvement, such as corporate patronage and insensitivity to context and local priorities. The paper draws theory and practice together to offer an illustration of the key processes and principles of community participation.

Spence, L. J., Schmidpeter, R., & Habisch, A. (2003) 'Assessing social capital: small and medium sized enterprises in Germany and the UK', *Journal of Business Ethics*, 47(1): 17–29.
This article uses the conceptual lens of social capital to help us understand the role of relationships – particularly local community-based ones such as customers, neighbours, and employees – in the running of smaller firms. The cultural comparative perspective, which includes interviews from Germany and the UK, adds some indication of national and cultural differences in developing and sustaining community relationships, although the article notes that industrial sector differences are equally as important in explaining difference.

Endnotes

1 www.bitc.org.uk/about_bitc/our_history/at_the_start.html (accessed 30 August, 2012).
2 www.toyota-global.com/sustainability/corporate_citizenship/society_ and_culture/ (accessed 30 August, 2012).
3 http://finance.yahoo.com/news/the-10-most-charitable-companies-in-america.html (accessed 30 August, 2012).
4 www.tradeinvestsa.co.za/feature_articles/485003.htm (accessed 30 August, 2012).
5 www.pfizer.com/files/philanthropy/globalhrnews.pdf (accessed 30 August, 2012).
6 www.domestosforunicef.com (accessed 30 August, 2012).

References

Brammer, S. & Pavelin, S. (2005) 'Corporate community contributions in the United Kingdom and the United States', *Journal of Business Ethics*, 56(1): 15–26.
Carroll, A. B. (1999) 'Corporate social responsibility – evolution of a definitional construct', *Business & Society*, 38(3): 268–295.
Chapple, W. & Moon, J. (2005) 'Corporate social responsibility in Asia: a seven country study of CSR website reporting', *Business and Society*, 44(4): 415–441.
Friedman, M. (1970) 'The social responsibility of business is to increase its profits', *New York Times Magazine*, 13 September: 13, 32–33, 122–126.
Grayson, D. & Hodges, A. (2004) *Corporate social opportunity: seven steps to make corporate social responsibility work for your business*, Sheffield: Greenleaf.
Hess, D., Rogovsky, N., & Dunfee, T. (2002) 'The next wave of corporate community involvement', *California Management Review*, 44(2): 110–125.
Jones, T. (1991) 'Ethical decision making by individuals in organizations: an issue-contingent model', *Academy of Management Review*, 16(2): 366–395.
Matten, D. & Crane, A. (2005) 'Corporate citizenship: toward an extended theoretical conceptualization', *Academy of Management Review*, 30(1): 166–179.
Muthuri, J., Chapple, W., & Moon, J. (2009) 'An integrated approach to implementing "community participation" in corporate community involvement: lessons from Magadi Soda Company in Kenya', *Journal of Business Ethics*, 85(2): 431–444.
Newell, P. (2005) 'Citizenship, accountability and community: the limits of the CSR agenda', *International Affairs*, 81: 541–557.
Porter, M. E. (1980) *Competitive strategy: techniques for analysing industries and competitors*, New York: Free Press.

Porter, M. E. (1985) *Competitive advantage: creating and sustaining superior performance*, New York: Free Press.

Porter, M. E. & Kramer, M. R. (2006) 'Strategy and society: the link between competitive advantage and corporate social responsibility', *Harvard Business Review*, 84 (December): 78–92.

Porter, M. E. & Kramer, M. R. (2011) 'Creating shared value', *Harvard Business Review*, 89(January–February): 62–77.

Spence, L. J. (2007) 'CSR and small business in a European policy context: the five "C"s of CSR and small business research agenda 2007', *Business and Society Review*, 112(4): 533–552.

Visser, W. (2006) 'Revisiting Carroll's CSR pyramid: an African perspective', in E. R. Pedersen & M. Huniche (eds) *Corporate citizenship in developing countries: new partnership perspectives*, Copenhagen: Copenhagen Business School Press, 29–56.

PUBLIC RESPONSIBILITY AND PRIVATE ENTERPRISE IN DEVELOPING COUNTRIES

Mike Valente and Andrew Crane

In recent decades, the trend towards greater involvement of private enterprise in achieving public goals is unmistakable. Nowhere is this more evident than in developing countries. From national security to health, and from human rights to education, business has increasingly been seen as a major player in addressing public problems in countries lacking basic infrastructure and services. On the one hand, business can provide an important contribution to public sector resource deficits and inefficiencies. On the other, firms can face a whole host of problems if their strategies backfire. Consider the experience of Blackwater Worldwide, the private security company, now renamed Xe. Blackwater was one of the largest companies providing essential security services in Iraq and other conflict zones. Yet, following a series of contentious incidents, the Iraqi government has revoked the company's license to operate in the country, forcing it to completely abandon its operations in Iraq.

In developing country contexts, firms encounter distinct challenges that place them in situations where they do more than simply go about the business of business. Faced with government incapacity to fulfill many basic human needs, it is private enterprises that increasingly fill the void. As former UN Secretary General Kofi Annan famously said at the launch of the UN Global Compact, "At a time when more than 1 billion people are denied the very minimum requirements of human dignity, business cannot afford to be seen as the problem." Firms have become involved in public activities as diverse as building schools and hospitals, enabling economic development, contributing to public health programs, building capacity for trade, bankrolling basic infrastructure, and providing security solutions.

In many cases, these activities go beyond traditional philanthropy or corporate social responsibility (CSR) programs in that they place firms in quasi-governmental roles where major decisions about public welfare and social provision have to be made. This then brings private enterprise into uncertain territory as firms struggle to navigate a new set of responsibilities that catapult them into a space more usually occupied by governments and non-government organizations in developed regions. With boundaries increasingly blurring between these once distinct sectors, we pinpoint the new challenges faced by private enterprise in addressing public responsibility in developing countries. We identify four strategic pathways taken by firms, and highlight the strategies for success that firms adopt in dealing with the distinct challenges that they face.

A Public Responsibility Deficit

As Bill Gates said at the World Economic Forum in January 2008, "The world is getting better, but it's not getting better fast enough, and it's not getting better for everyone." Infant mortality rates remain staggeringly high; a majority of the world's children continue to miss out on access to education and basic health care; and over 2 billion people live on less than $2 a day.[1]

To date, a range of actors appear to have failed to effectively address some of these most basic of citizen needs in developing countries. Developing country governments frequently lack the resources to tackle such over-whelming social problems. And, even where resources are available, corruption typically results in the remittance of only 30% of financial aid to citizens, handicapping the entrepreneurial will of many developing countries.[2] Industrialized nations have been criticized for creating an uneven playing field in international trade by imposing hypocritical subsidies that disallow developing nation access to the global marketplace.[3] Furthermore, international institutions such as the International Monetary Fund (IMF), the World Bank, and the World Trade Organization (WTO) have undergone detailed scrutiny by leading economists who suggest that their imposed macro-economic policies foster an inequitable globalization system that further cripples developing nations and compromises access to public services.[4] With the proliferation of international economic activity, the ability of nation states to protect public welfare is waning, particularly in developing countries. The lack of international governing bodies to keep up with this economic activity has resulted in a shift in power to large multinational corporations employing practices that lack sufficient government oversight.[5] Finally, non-governmental organizations, while effective in attending to many basic needs, also have only limited capacity to deal with the broader development challenges facing the developing world.

In light of this public responsibility deficit and the growing power and dominance of the private sector, we see increasing attention focusing on the role of companies in public service provision and the broader advancement of public welfare.[6] On the one hand, though, private enterprise has done little better than other institutional actors. Motivated by efficiency, shareholder value, and by limited enforcement of regulation, corporations have been accused of reckless business practices that disregard the social and environmental costs of doing business.[7] From oil to pharmaceuticals, water, information technology, and apparel, companies have been in the spotlight for failing to meet the needs of the most vulnerable and needy in society.

On the other hand, a burst of activity from multinationals, domestic firms and social enterprises over the past decade has unleashed a range of public solutions from the private sector in developing countries. One development here has been the emergence of innovations targeted at solving the needs of those at the bottom of the economic pyramid.[8] For example, Aravind's revolutionary eye care service model has provided once inaccessible health services for India's poor. Another strand has seen large firms extending their corporate responsibility programs to tackle deep-rooted social problems in developing countries.[9] For example, Heineken has demonstrated that corporations can play a key role in HIV/AIDS prevention and treatment in South Africa. Still another strand has seen small social entrepreneurial firms employ business models that aim to improve the livelihoods of the poor.[10] Turiya Group is a company that aims to build a more sustainable supply chain for a number of agricultural products in the Brazilian Rainforest (such as the açaí "superfruit") by facilitating the fair and equitable treatment of rural suppliers and acting as an intermediary for the international fair trade market.

These activities have led business into uncertain territory. While approaches such as bottom of the pyramid strategies and corporate responsibility programs tend to presume a distinction between the public and private sector, company executives in developing countries have increasingly seen their firms called upon to play a role more akin to government than business. Despite intensifying demands to deliver shareholder value, private enterprise has had to show how it can simultaneously contribute to the public good when the usual apparatus and infrastructure of government may be lacking. This requires attention not only to effective delivery of social goods, but also to broader expectations for accountability, inclusion, and democracy that traditionally lie with public bodies.[11] Attending to public responsibilities is therefore fraught with unknown obstacles for private enterprise managers, however valuable the participation of their companies in this realm might be. What is more, the problems vary according to the type of strategic orientation that firms adopt. Therefore, in order to address these challenges more effectively, we have researched how companies in developing countries orient their businesses to cope with these challenges and have developed a way of mapping the different types of public responsibility strategies that private enterprises engage in. In this way, we provide senior executives with clear insight on the types of challenges that they will face and offer straight-forward guidance on how to overcome them.

Public Responsibility Strategies

We refer to public responsibility strategies as strategies that firms develop to address public problems in the absence of effective governmental infra-structure or processes. In this respect, we are specifically concerned with gaps in public welfare and voids in public service provision in developing countries, typically as a result of deficits in public resources and capabilities, poor governance, or corruption.[12]

Public responsibility strategies may include some activities that might more typically be thought of as CSR or corporate philanthropy[13] but only those encapsulated by activities aimed at filling in for government absence— or what some have referred to as "political CSR" or "extended" corporate citizenship.[14] That is, we are concerned with how the basic entitlements of citizens are met through private enterprise rather than, say, with corporate efforts to "give something back" through discretionary social investments. For instance, donating money to an existing, functioning medical facility would simply be philanthropy whereas financing the building of a new medical facility in a district bereft of any medical services at all is more akin to a public responsibility. So this means that many CSR activities do not necessarily represent public responsibilities, and vice versa. For instance, utility firms involved in the direct provision of public services do not necessarily need to do so as a matter of "social responsibility" but out of simple self-interest in serving a new market—nonetheless, public respon-sibilities may be unavoidable. Specifically, by focusing our analysis on developing countries, we move away from the assumption implicit in much of the CSR literature that the "rules of the game" are set through a process of effective public policy and regulation towards a view of private enterprise operating in an arena of institutional incapacity.

To best understand the different strategies through which companies engage in public responsibility, we investigated 30 companies operating in developing regions of the world. Each company was qualitatively examined as a case study to understand how and why they engaged in public respon-sibility in the absence of effective public bodies. All companies were profit-based organizations operating in the manufacturing, services, or agriculture sectors and ranged in size from large subsidiaries of multi-national cor-porations to small social enterprises (see Table 7.1). Preliminary exploration of firm public responsibilities indicated that this phenomenon is not specific to a particular firm size. Commercial microfinance enterprises have been popularized as a private sector approach to poverty alleviation while the direct provision of public services by multinational corporations (e.g., health care facilities) has escalated in developing country contexts. Thus, to best capture the full range of public responsibility strategies and their challenges, we chose to study a range of firm sizes. We provide detailed descriptions of two of these cases in Appendix A. For the first 16 companies, 150 interviews were conducted with senior and middle-level employees of firms and relevant public actors such as communities, non-governmental organizations, and government. Secondary data were collected and analyzed for the remaining 14 cases, which were chosen to expand the dataset to additional developing country contexts. By examining company response to public welfare and service gaps across these cases, important similarities and differences emerged that helped conceptualize the strategies used, the associated challenges faced, and the tactics managers employed to overcome these challenges. For a full description of the methodology, see Appendix B.[15]

According to our research, public responsibility strategies can be categorized along two dimensions. The first dimension differentiates between strategies that focus on the firm's *core operations* and those that focus on the firm's *non-core operations*.

Firms targeting the former tackle social welfare issues as part of their basic business model, such as in the case of private sector providers of

Table 7.1: Case sampling

Sector	Africa	Latin America	Asia	Total by Sector	Subsectors Included
Agriculture	5	1	1	7	Tea Honey Cotton Vegetables Fruit Sugarcane
Manufacturing	7	2	2	11	Cement Oil and gas Gold Pulp and paper Aluminum Forestry Chemicals Steel
Services	6	2	4	12	Financial Health Energy Waste Tourism
Telecommunications					
Total by Region	**18**	**5**	**7**	**30**	

utilities, health services, education, and security. In this case, there may be little or no intention on the part of the firm to play the role of government but it may have to do so in the process of fulfilling its regular business operations where necessary governmental oversight is lacking. Core operations could encompass a firm's products and services and/or the value chain activities associated with the provision of those products and services.[16]

Firms that focus their public activities on non-core operations differ in that their core business may be largely unrelated to public goals, but they see value in enhancing the social and political environments in which they do business and over which they have influence to further these public goals. Non-core operations could encompass dimensions of a firm's competitive context, such as contributing to the basic services needed to operate the business, or they can encompass generic political issues that are beyond the firm's competitive context yet reside within the firm's broader sphere of influence.[17] For instance, at the second Forum of the United Nations Alliance of Civilizations in 2009, the United Nations Global Compact co-organized a working session meant to examine the specific actions companies can take to foster cross-cultural understanding and tolerance. In his address, Secretary General Ban Ki-Moon emphasized the role of business in bridging cultural divides to "help keep the peace."[18] In the absence of powerful transnational governing bodies, companies are increasingly expected to exert leverage within their sphere of influence for, in this case, international public welfare.

The second dimension highlights the difference between firm activities that provide specific *public services* versus those that aim to shape *political/ economic infrastructure* to achieve public goals. A distinction typically exists between governmental activities that administer citizenship through the provision of public services and activities that define citizenship through the development of policy and laws that determine "at which level and in which intensity certain entitlements and processes of participation should be guaranteed."[19] We draw on this distinction here when describing the two ways in which private enterprise can engage in public responsibilities. Public services are those services considered to be essential to modern life that, for moral reasons, are meant to be universally provided to all citizens, regardless of income. Examples include education, health care, water services, policing services, waste management, telecommunications, social housing, public transportation, and security. Firms' decisions to build schools or health care facilities represent a direct fulfillment of public services associated with the absence of child education or proper medical treatment.

In contrast, firm activities that develop political and/or economic infra-structure influence the broader political and economic landscape through which public policy is determined and public goals are achieved. Shell's human rights training for judges in Nigeria or MNC efforts to build capacity among local community governing bodies represent examples of public responsibility that lay the foundation for the achievement of public goals without any delivery of a particular service direct to the public. The point here is that companies initiate changes in public policy by altering the political landscape or economic context through which public goals are achieved. In some cases, building this infrastructure enhances the public's ability to access public services and/or spawns the emergence of third-party organizations to deliver these services. For instance, training judges on human rights enhances the ability of the Nigerian justice system to incorporate criteria related to universal definitions of human rights in its service to citizens. Thus, whereas the provision of public services represents an administrative role by the firm, the development of infrastructure influences the political and economic landscape through which public goals are achieved.

For companies to manage their public responsibilities effectively, they must first understand these dimensions and the relationships between them. Exhibit 1 "Public Responsibility Strategies" is a matrix that highlights the four different approaches identified in our research using a number of broad characteristics. Each is associated with a distinct set of challenges and strategies for success, as we discuss below.

Supplement Strategy

Companies frequently fill gaps left by the public sector by directly taking on public service roles through their corporate citizenship programs, even when these have little relationship with the core operations of the firm.[20] Companies may supplement existing government activity in geographical or functional areas where it is lacking, for example by building schools, health care facilities, or physical infrastructure. These strategies may be essential for augmenting inadequate governmental provision of public services in developing countries facing significant deficits in key social services.

Consider Magadi Soda Ash, the Kenyan-based mining company and subsidiary of parent firm Tata Group. With almost all government funded public programs in the region centered on the city of Nairobi, the firm's immediate physical environment outside the city limits faced a deficit of public infrastructure. As a result, the firm, as the only major corporation in the region, faced an increased expectation on the part of the surrounding Masai communities to provide necessary social services—for example, by constructing water treatment plants and extending water and power distribution to the community. The company also built, operated and maintained the community health clinic and several schools. They extended the 120-kilometer road from the southern edges of Nairobi to Magadi and built and operated an extension of the Kenyan railway line to transport the soda ash to the Mombasa port. These road and railway lines are now used for transportation by Kenyan citizens with little relationship to the company:

> "There were no roads. There was no water. There were no medical
> facilities. So even for the business to start, you needed to have a few

of those basic facilities. The government said, 'you guys want to extract deposits at Magadi, it's really up to you to provide all the amenities that you need—water, electricity, you name it'. We built the road that you just travelled on to get here."—Managing Director, Magadi Soda Ash

In the face of governmental absence, companies may respond in this manner as a means of preserving or enhancing their competitive context or giving back to their communities to earn a license to operate and to offset any negative impact of their operations. In other situations, a crisis such as a drought, disease, or extreme poverty can create a sense of urgency for the company to respond with public responsibility due to the absence of efficient governmental responses. There may also be situations where governmental capacity is limited and companies supplement public service roles alongside their public counterparts. Other companies take a more philanthropic approach and take on gaps in public service that lie within their broader sphere of influence, regardless of the benefit to their competitive context. Following the post-election conflict and subsequent famine in Kenya, Mabati Rolling Mills, an Indian-based steel company, rebuilt a primary school that had been burnt down as a result of the conflict in a distant region of Kenya. Yet while the use of private sector power and resources to fill institutional gaps may in the right circumstances lead to benefits for both enterprises and their communities, important challenges exist.

Addressing Democracy and Accountability

The first main challenge of a supplement strategy is public resistance to the firm's quasi-political role. Well-meaning programs may be derailed when activists question why companies are acting like governments with little, if any, democratic measures in place to ensure accountability. In supplementing government provision, companies are inevitably making public welfare choices on the basis of their own strategic orientation, and financial and operational constraints, rather than necessarily on the needs of the community. This strategic orientation may be based on developing an appropriate context with basic services that allow for or support core operations for competitive maximization; or it may be part of a public relations strategy that is conveyed to the general public to soften pressures, particularly from developed country stakeholders. Either way, the question remains of whether the services chosen are in the best interests of the public. This typically results in understandable skepticism on the part of the public and social activist groups. In many cases, companies can face a backlash should they be forced to retrench such investments as a result of difficult financial times, shifts in market prices, or pressure from shareholders or a parent firm.

Supplement strategies are most suitable in situations where they extend or augment already existing governmental public services. When they are targeted at complete institutional voids, the approach is best employed where the lack of public services represents an immediate threat to either the surrounding community or the company. Even then, successful companies will conduct rigorous analyses of potential impacts and make thorough investigations of alternative providers before making social commitments. Forward thinking managers will also involve the community in their decision making as early as possible by developing an open decision-making process around the social initiative. In the aftermath of a severe drought, Magadi Soda worked closely with respected leaders of the community to develop and implement an emergency food drop and water provision plan that drew upon the available human capital of the Masai and their invaluable knowledge of the surrounding landscape. The goal here is to build in an inclusive decision-making process and balance accountability appropriately so that the relationship with the community is tightly intertwined, and where ownership is shared across the development, management, and implementation of the project. This ensures that any provision of public service by the firm is perceived as legitimate by affected parties while guaranteeing efficiency gains due to the incorporation of external expertise and knowledge.

Averting Public Dependency and Futile Sustained Costs

Another important challenge of a supplement approach is the dependency created in the local community. Once made, public commitments may escalate and be difficult to reverse. Firms therefore face significant reputational threats, especially if they cease involvement in particular public initiatives further down the line. Moreover, because this approach is typically implemented by the firm in isolation, the company can become locked into a continuous commitment of scarce resources that generate little value for the surrounding areas. Frequently, community stakeholders in poverty-stricken areas will fabricate answers based on what they think the company wants to hear, resulting in projects that are not in the best interests of the community. This results in "white elephants" where new facilities are left abandoned and unused. A steel company in East Africa spent thousands of dollars building a bus shelter for a poor rural community outside of Mombasa, Kenya. In retrospect, it was learned that access to shelter while waiting for transportation was not an urgent need of the community especially given that buses pick up passengers at different locations depending on the time of day.

Companies can overcome this challenge by tapping into existing institutional structures in the community or among NGOs so that social initiatives can more easily become embedded in existing routines and behaviors, can draw on the insight of those most impacted, and can gain greater commitment for operational longevity. Facing an increasing HIV / AIDS crisis within the surrounding community, Bamburi Cement, a subsidiary of the French conglomerate Lafarge, looked to a well-institutionalized yet informal women's group to help develop and disseminate an HIV / AIDS program. The hiring of a clinician with experience in the community and knowledge of the women's groups was instrumental in this process, leading to a substantial increase in educational awareness of the disease:

Exhibit 1: Public responsibility strategies

	Provision of Public Services	*Infrastructure for Public Goals*
Non-Core Operations	**1–Supplement**	**2–Support**
	Scope	*Scope*
	Direct public service provision	Government capacity building
		Intervention on government activity/policy
	Examples	
	Building schools and hospitals	*Examples*
	Laying physical infrastructure	Building municipal government capacity
		Influencing international labor regulations
	Impact	
	Provision of key public services	
	Enabling competitive environment	*Impact*
	Addressing urgent public crises	Bolstering institutions
		Influencing public policy
	Key Challenges	Influencing decisions related to public goals
	Addressing democracy & accountability	
	Averting public dependency	*Key Challenges*
	Avoiding futile sustained costs	Overcoming mistrust/superficial relationships
		Motivated to report on inappropriate measures
	Benefits for Private Enterprise	
	License to operate	
	Supportive competitive context	*Benefits for Private Enterprise*
	Public relations	Relinquishes public service role
		Costs diverted to public bodies
	Ideal Scenario to Use Strategy	Gain local capabilities
	Situations of urgency or crisis	
	Threat to competitive context	*Ideal Scenario to Use Strategy*
	Where existing services can be augmented	Governmental/institutional incapacity
		Inadequate public goals and policies
	Strategies to Overcome Challenges	
	Shared ownership of projects	*Strategies to Overcome Challenges*
	Tap into existing institutional/social structures	Reciprocal understanding and collaboration
		Shift measures from output to impact

"HIV/AIDS was a problem for us and our employees. But you can't tackle this in house without involving the community. So we brought in a local clinician who worked with the community before and I think even led one of these women's groups. So she knew how decisions were made by the community and the types of programs that would work. That was important for us."—Managing Director, Bamburi Cement

Consequently, while the urgency of the social issue may require immediate attention by the company, researching and leveraging existing institutional and social structures among communities and NGOs dramatically

Exhibit 1: Continued

	Provision of Public Services	Infrastructure for Public Goals
Core Operations	**3–Substitute**	**4–Stimulate**
	Scope Privatization of government services	*Scope* Alternative economic model Market knowledge to influence government
	Examples Provision of military service Policing of labor practices	*Examples* Alternative agricultural system Commercial microfinance Lobby against Internet censorship
	Impact Commercial provision of public services Private bodies enforcing regulation	*Impact* Alters means by which to achieve public goals
	Key Challenges Accommodating a public service agenda Legitimizing privatized governance	*Key Challenges* Access to resources and support Overcoming institutional norms and biases
	Benefits for Private Enterprise Market/revenue opportunities Critical step in the value chain	*Benefits for Private Enterprise* Taps into entrepreneurial spirit of poor Ensures full diffusion of alternative approach
	Ideal Scenario to Use Strategy Value proposition around public services Stakeholder pressure to replace government	*Ideal Scenario to Use Strategy* Economic/political infrastructure needs change
	Strategies to Overcome Challenges Sanity check through outsourcing One piece of the puzzle of actors	*Strategies to Overcome Challenges* Gaining critical mass through partnerships Persistence and creativity through small steps

increases the effectiveness of the initiative while reducing public dependence on the firm. This reduces the possibility of white elephants.

Support Strategy

The second way that private enterprise may leverage its sphere of influence and/or enhance its competitive context in a way that is non-core to operations involves the use of its power and influence to support the achievement of broader public goals. Here, public responsibility does not entail the provision of public services such as education, health care, or physical infrastructure as much as it involves supporting the development of political infrastructure and will to assist in closing public welfare gaps such as social injustice, violence, and cultural intolerance. Support implies that the company leverages its position to facilitate action or affect change in those actors responsible for fulfilling public gaps. This may involve building capacity of governmental and civil society organizations to take on the fulfillment of public responsibility gaps or it may involve intervening in particular actions, taken by governmental organizations, that may or may not be in the best interests of pubic citizens. Critics of Royal Dutch Shell's hands-off approach to the Nigerian Ogoni conflict in 1995 called for increased intervention from the company to enforce fair and equitable treatment of captured activists.[21] Here, Shell was called on to exercise its influence to facilitate changes in governmental action but was instead complicit in ignoring human rights violations by those within its sphere of influence. Upon reflection, Shell's former Chairman remarked, "The biggest change . . . for an international corporation is this extension of responsibility . . . beyond just paying your taxes and beyond just relating effectively to communities around your factory fence."[22] Ultimately, under a support strategy, companies focus on supporting the establishment of an appropriate intermediary body, or encouraging shifts in the behavior of existing bodies, to make decisions for public welfare by developing social and political capacity to enable more effective social provision.

Consider Siberian-Urals Aluminum Company (Sual), a once independent vertically integrated aluminum producer located in Russia. When faced with deteriorating public health and education and limited small business capacity, Sual's approach to public responsibility included the development and creation of local self-governing bodies in and around the regions in which it operated. The company helped to create a public council for local self-governance reform in a region near its operations. The council identifies priority areas of public service provision while building a sense of ownership and accountability among elected officials around the development and implementation of specific projects. The company was also instrumental in facilitating the development of independent NGOs and helped create community foundations with a mandate to prioritize areas facing the most severe public deficits as defined by their respective communities. In

Tanzania, a subsidiary of a South African sugarcane company supported the launch of an independent community-based trust in collaboration with the World Bank to spearhead the identification and implementation of projects that would enhance the livelihoods of independent sugarcane farmers on whom the firm relied for harvest. The trust sources its revenue from sugarcane using a plot of land that it leases from the company and uses this revenue for social projects, including a mobile health unit and physical infrastructure development for the community.

What we see then in the support approach is that while the company may continue to demonstrate a concerted effort to ensure the enhancement of its competitive context and the welfare of its broader sphere of influence, it achieves this through non-core operations that bolster institutions and the required political and social infrastructure to achieve public goals. Responsibility and accountability of specific public services largely remains in the control of independent third parties, leaving the enterprise to focus on management and facilitation. So whereas the supplement approach is more suitable for immediate social problems, the support approach is more effective in building up institutional capacity over the long term. Again though, a number of challenges face firms adopting this strategy.

Overcoming Mistrust and Superficial Relationships

While the company may have good intentions by committing to a support strategy, success is very much dependent on overcoming the mistrust communities typically have for the private sector, and in particular for large domestic and multinational organizations. To effectively facilitate the development of governance structures, companies must be able to move beyond the often superficial relationships that typically persist in these situations.

In our research in Africa, CEOs of companies employing a support approach commented on the importance of regularly visiting communities and senior chiefs to gain sensitivity to their ways of life. Some CEOs waited several hours before being allowed to see the senior chief—an important signal that the CEO was genuinely committed to learning about the community. Other CEOs lived in the rural community contexts to fully understand the needs of the surrounding community:

> "We all learned rather quickly that we really didn't know them. I've had to learn the hard way that these people move slowly and they are pretty wise people who've been around for a long time. They know what they want and they'll take a longer-term view than we will. So understanding these needs and their way of life was critical."—CEO, Multinational Ecotourism Company

In the same way that the company learns about the community, the community begins to understand the needs and motivations of the company through their relationship with company officials. Over time, as trust develops, both sides can begin to see the genuine nature of their commitments and, more importantly, understand their respective needs and responsibilities. The CEO of a large mining company effectively brought together 35 representatives of a community to develop a community relations policy that would set out the process of engagement while identifying public priority areas. The community presented the policy to the company's parent board of directors for approval. This example highlights the importance of creating conditions of mutual dependency that begin to spark conversations about self-governance and collective ownership, because the community begins to see its role in conjunction with, rather than in isolation from or in opposition to, the company. Without this mutual dependency, mistrust proliferates and relationships remain superficial.

Pressure for Short-Term Contributions

Unlike the supplement strategy, which demonstrates immediate results, a support strategy requires a greater investment of resources over time for results that do not garner immediate approval in the public eye. Companies seeking a license to operate in the face of substantial pressure from communities, customers, NGOs, or shareholders may struggle to justify investing such time and effort that, while potentially more sustainable in the long term, may fail to demonstrate any immediate, visible impacts. This is particularly acute for companies facing consumer or media pressure where managers typically experience a need to demonstrate that they have "solved" the problem to protect their brands. A senior manager of a forestry company in South Africa discussed the pressures associated with demonstrating visible commitments to the community in the form of physical infrastructure development, schools, and hospitals. Although he recognized the limitations of this supplement approach over the long term, he garnered very little support for a long-term institutional capacity building approach:

> "We see better public relations benefits in philanthropy. Giving him the fish carries more clout for customers in the West than teaching him how to fish." —Senior Executive, Global Forestry Products

To overcome this perception, companies should work to educate their stakeholders and put more emphasis on process rather than content—or, put another way, impact metrics rather than evaluative metrics. More specifically, a support strategy calls for a shift in focus away from the number of schools or hospitals built as the measurable outcome (evaluative) to a focus on the degree to which capacity has been built within local communities (impact). This means that companies should report less about financial expenditures and philanthropic contributions and more on qualitative issues around the process of engagement, community achievements of self-governance, and the operationalization of community leadership. Because of the time required to achieve these outcomes, engaging in a support approach is more appropriate when the firm is not facing any urgent gaps in public services. Ultimately, the firm's responsibility is based on the creation of legitimate, sustainable, and effective bodies that take accountability for the development, operation, and maintenance of public services.

Substitute Strategy

In a substitute strategy, the firm takes over direct delivery of public services, but in contrast to the supplement approach, here it does so as part of its core operations either through its core product/service or in the chain of activities responsible for delivering that product/service. In many cases, politically based public sector provision is substituted by market-based private sector provision, for example, in the case of privatized utilities or military security. This approach typically centers on the alignment of company strategy with new market opportunities, often as a result of institutional voids in the public sphere. Companies taking this route may or may not want to engage in the political dimensions of their business, but such elements are intrinsically linked to their business model.

Many of the most prominent examples of this strategy are in private utilities where governments privatize particular public services or contract them out to companies. However, in developing countries, a wide range of business models require effective private substitution of public services in the product/service itself as well as part of the activities meant to deliver the product/service. Consider &Beyond (formerly Conservation Corporation Africa), an ecotourism company based in Johannesburg with lodges throughout Sub-Saharan Africa. &Beyond targets consumers seeking a luxury adventure vacation with a company that demonstrates sustainable practices. However, a lack of community public services such as education, health care, and physical infrastructure surrounding game reserves resulted in substantial local resistance to the firm and consequential disruptions to tourism and conservation operations throughout the various regions in which it operated. As a result, &Beyond could not even hope to implement its private business without attending to the urgency of these wider public problems. To implement its model, &Beyond had to build schools and hospitals in the communities surrounding its game reserves. However, unlike Magadi Soda Ash where these provisions were unrelated to core operations, &Beyond incorporated the provision of these services into its broader value proposition to the consumer. As part of the holiday experience with &Beyond, consumers are exposed to the community development projects they indirectly fund through their service fees. Unlike traditional game reserves that exclude the community, &Beyond incorporates the provision of public services into the value preposition to the consumer allowing them to tap into a niche market of eco- and social-conscious developed country consumers:

> "We started to get signals from customers that community projects were something they wanted to see in their ecotourism experience. There is a growing niche market out there right now. The traveler wants to know where they're going and what's being done for the surrounding communities. It really confirmed that this stuff is not philanthropic but really a strategic benefit."—Senior Manager, &Beyond

&Beyond also fills public responsibility gaps by providing environmental education to the local community. This has led to a decrease in clearcutting of trees for firewood and poaching of fauna. So although the firm had a direct role to play in providing public services, it has done so as a value-creating activity and ultimately as part of the core value proposition to the customer, not simply as a philanthropic add-on.

In other cases, however, a substitute approach can exist in isolated parts of a firm's supply chain where the substitution is not a result of market opportunities as much as governmental incapacity to administer public services such as regulatory enforcement. With labor representing a substantial part of the apparel sector's chain of value-creating activities, the monitoring and enforcement of labor practices undertaken by various players in the industry effectively substitutes for the ineffective enforcement practices of developing country governments.[23] Companies such as Nike and Puma (and, increasingly, companies in other sectors) are faced with the task of policing labor practices throughout their supply chin by auditing factories, working with factory managers to improve conditions, and punishing behavior through the termination of contracts. Yet while private sector supplanting of governmental activities may represent an opportunity or a necessity, this approach poses challenges to executives.

Accommodating a Public Service Agenda

Companies substituting the public sector with a for-profit model carry substantial risks, especially in sectors that provide basic human needs such as food, water, safety, and human rights. The first challenge is related to the company's ability to remain committed to the interests of the public. Unlike a public sector organization whose ultimate purpose is satisfying public interests,[24] a private sector organization has, as its root, the creation of profit and shareholder value.[25] While the company may have the best of intentions, the private-based model carries with it a number of institutional constraints that could very well run counter to the needs of the community and subsequently derail the firm's public agenda. This derailment could occur when firms pursue traditional tactics of the private organization such as reducing costs, seeking to capitalize on new market opportunities or developing new business models. Such shifts in strategy could compromise the stability of public services created by the company, representing an important obstacle for strategic change if and when the firm is expected to adjust its strategy in the face of market changes. Ultimately, in its quest for complying with traditional responsibilities of the private organization, the firm may struggle to maintain its commitment to these public services.

To address this challenge, companies must separate those public elements that are most relevant for their strategic mission from those that can be outsourced to other actors, even if the development of actor competencies to conduct these activities requires support from the company. These additional actors are not mere peripheral service providers in the supply chain as much as they are equal partners in the execution of the business model. The inclusion of public actors as partners in the execution of this model creates a sanity check around whether the actions of the company are in the best interests of the public in which it serves. Successful managers shift the strategic frame of the firm to a state where competitive advantage originates from being adept at aligning complementary competencies across a number of actors by drawing on their specific institutional capability and knowledge. For instance, rather than employing its own private security, &Beyond worked with local partners to develop a community security service that polices poaching activity in and around the game reserves:

> "It was unusual in the tourism industry to have the community as a partner. But they knew the behavior of the poachers and they were best suited to police this problem, not us. I'm sure they were also weary of being in bed with the big mean company."—Senior Manager, &Beyond

This has resulted in an important edge over other game reserves in the area without attracting hostility from the local community. This same challenge exists with companies substituting governments in particular parts of their supply chain. Apparel companies have often expressed difficulty in monitoring and enforcing activities in their factories and have subsequently engaged in close dialogue with NGOs to assist in the independent monitoring process. NGOs, such as the Fair Labor Association (FLA) whose mandate is to protect workers worldwide, also represent important sanity checks on whether the firm's existing labor enforcement approaches are in the best interests of the workers.[26] This positions the company among public partners (available or new) so that public needs are constantly presented alongside the traditional interests of shareholders, forcing the firm to reconcile any tension as a regular part of its value-creating and public responsibilities.

Legitimizing Privatized Governance

The second challenge is related to stakeholder resistance to a strategy that effectively introduces an element of privatized governance into the provision of public goods. Fabio Rosa, a social entrepreneur in Brazil, developed a business model that provides inexpensive power to the rural poor in Brazil at a fraction of the cost of traditional power alternatives. Because the business model challenged the government's central power service, Rosa spent years gaining official buy-in from the Brazilian government. Only when the media got hold of the story did government acceptance start to develop. Yet resistance may also originate from below when existing public services are privatized. When the World Bank required Bolivia to privatize the water service of its third-largest city, U.S.-based Bechtel Corporation gained control of the city's water. This led to a public outcry as compromises needed to be made around access to food, education, and health care given that water commanded more than a quarter of many citizens' income levels.[27] Although the government was in full support of Bechtel, citizen revolt led to one of the most well-known resistance movements to privatization.

Our research indicated that effective substitute strategies occurred when companies recognized that they were merely one piece in a larger constellation of actors with interests in creating sustainable value. In the Bechtel example, there was very little in the way of a democratic process that incorporated citizens in the decision making around water privatization. Impressions that present the firm as the dominant actor in the provision of these services result in substantial backlash and resistance by local and international communities. Apparel companies now sit alongside universities, human rights groups, labor and religious organizations, and consumer advocates as one actor on the FLA. Successful companies use this position to ensure that the enforcement of fair labor practices is a joint effort rather than a company-specific initiative. Companies are thus advised to cut through the red tape and engage directly with communities and informal groups most affected by the privatized governance as early as possible including them in the process as a partner rather than just as consumer or critic. Successful companies thus build coalitions to establish effective systems of governance before they enter developing country markets. Playing this more "civil" role also provides an ongoing and very essential tension between the public and private sectors that assists in strategy refinement and also creates reciprocal ownership among public actors of the business model employed.[28] While Bechtel's partnership with the government was important, it lacked essential relationships with critical community and NGO groups at an early enough stage to gain their buy-in and input on what such a model, if permitted, would look like. Identifying the key points of leverage in the public debate and positioning the firm appropriately are crucial in managing the public relations threats that face private firms in delivering public goods.

Stimulate Strategy

In contrast to substitute strategies where firms provide public services directly, firms adopting a stimulate strategy drive new models of social provision through the development of political or economic infrastructure that addresses gaps in public welfare. Here, unlike the support strategy where public responsibility bears no relation to the company's core operations, working towards the achievement of public goals represents a pivotal component of the company's core operations. Under this strategy, firms leverage their products and services or their set of value chain activities to stimulate different forms of economic activity or regulatory behavior that directly or indirectly contributes to the achievement of public goals. For instance, information technology companies in the Global Network Initiative have made commitments to lobby governments against censorship of the Internet in order to better serve their developing country consumers.[29] Commercial microfinance organizations, on the other hand, represent a form of business that leverages its core service of financial loans as a means to build the economic infrastructure for the achievement of public goals, such as poverty alleviation. In these two examples, the firm's efforts are not related to the direct provision of public services as much they are meant to change the existing political and economic infrastructure through which public goals are achieved.

The stimulate strategy, however, can extend beyond one or two isolated parts of a firm's value chain and be manifested in the entire set of activities defining its business model. Consider SEKEM, an Egyptian-based company that developed a supply chain based on organic agriculture. SEKEM's business model is unlike a typical entrepreneurial venture that builds its business within the boundaries of the existing economic infrastructure of a given national context. Instead, the SEKEM model stimulated a parallel agriculture system that shaped the socio-economic infrastructure of Egypt by incorporating broader public goals related to social equity and ecological preservation. The business gained commitment from over 800 rural Egyptian farmers to transition their land to organic soil while securing a market with large customers in Europe. The business model also spawned the creation of the Egyptian Biodynamic Association (EBDA), an NGO established to promote organic agriculture in Egypt and to provide cultivation support for farmers. In executing this business model, SEKEM gained the support of new and existing players operating vertically and horizontally along this alternative agricultural supply chain. In effect, the transformative nature of SEKEM's model challenged the existing economic infrastructure solidified by governmental bodies in a way that incorporated, to a more inclusive and comprehensive extent, the public goals of the nation. When asked what instigated the business model, the founder, Dr. Ibrahim Abouleish explained:

> "On my last journey through Egypt I had experienced a deep sense of hopelessness caused by the way of life of the Egyptian population. This had deeply moved me . . . I felt compassion for these people who could not be made responsible for their situation, but were forced to bear it and had learnt to carry it. Through SEKEM, I felt I would be able to change this situation of hopelessness and liberate them from their misery."—Ibrahim Abouleish, Founder, SEKEM

A stimulate strategy, then, sees firms introduce products and services (such as microfinance loans), initiatives related to the supply chain (such as global network initiatives), or comprehensive business models (such as alternative agricultural models) that lay the foundation for shifts in political and/or economic infrastructure and inevitably lead to a systemic contribution to broader public goals. Yet, while impactful, there are important challenges to consider.

Access to Resources and Support

Disruptive innovations of this kind require careful nurturing. The development of path-breaking business models, for instance, requires access to critical financial, social, and human capital along with stakeholder support to help legitimize the enterprise.[30] Success in accessing these resources requires a portfolio of capabilities, but critical amongst them is the need for agility and flexibility in the face of competing expectations from funders, clients, and others in the course of testing and refining the approach. This implies that while the entrepreneur may have predefined notions of what the business model will look like, success will likely be a function of incorporating a wide range of inputs due to the entrepreneur's dependence on these stakeholders. While access to resources is especially relevant for the entrepreneur, large companies working to stimulate changes in developing country regulation require political support from a range of actors including NGOs, competitors, industry associations, and human rights groups. This flexibility and input is especially important so that the business is able to generate the critical mass required to challenge existing economic and political infrastructure.

Honey Care Africa, a small farmer-centered enterprise based out of Nairobi Kenya, worked closely with Africa Now, a local Kenyan NGO, to develop a tripartite model linking the public and private sectors with rural farmers. While the founder of the business had original ideas for its design, his engagement with this NGO early on was instrumental in refining the approach to ensure that the model stimulated interest from communities to adopt an alternative approach to agriculture:

> "The NGOs, who have been here for a long time, have done a lot of work at the cross streets and thus have developed the capacities

of very many communities through a myriad of projects. And so we felt that the easiest way to actually reach the communities effectively is to go partner with these stakeholders." —Co-Founder, Honey Care Africa

Similar to the SEKEM model, Honey Care Africa set out to challenge existing agricultural practices in Kenya by building an alternative supply chain that was built on broader public goals of poverty alleviation, small farmer access to markets, fair and equitable treatment of farmers, and environmental conservation. Because the NGO, Africa Now, already had offices located throughout Kenya, Honey Care targeted these regions to develop its supplier base of farmers. This provided Africa Now's recipients with a much needed continual stream of income for access to public services while providing Honey Care with the social capital it required to build its supplier base. So the extent to which disruptive business models can challenge existing agricultural models and create the trickle-down effects for the achievement of broader public goals will depend on collaborative partnerships with those organizations that have the resource and institutional capacity to make it happen.

Overcoming Institutional Norms and Biases

Related to the resource challenge is the difficulty in overcoming existing norms and biases to which existing stakeholders have grown accustomed. SEKEM's founder, Ibrahim Abouleish, recalls visiting farmers around Egypt to encourage their transition to biodynamic cultivation and facing substantial resistance due to the 2–3 year conversion time required, not to mention the unknown potential of organic produce in the late 1970s. Successful managers are persistent and creative in helping stakeholders visualize how new approaches to business will better achieve their objectives compared with traditional approaches.

More importantly, however, firms are advised to seed multiple small-scale changes and to create islands of innovation rather than going straight for direct institutional change. The establishment of a microfinance bank was certainly not the original intention of Muhammad Yunus, founder of Grameen Bank. Grameen Bank arose through a series of steps whereby Yunus slowly began to realize that the most sustainable means of reaching large numbers of poor people would be to employ a banking model, but in a way that would provide loans to those most in need. Grameen Bank represents an example of a business that leverages its core service of financial loans as a means to build the economic infrastructure for the achievement of public goals. He explained:

"The whole Grameen story started with a blank sheet of paper. I never knew ahead of time that I was going to have a bank. All I was doing was trying to demonstrate that poverty alleviation can be achieved. It eventually became clear that a banking model was best. But with more than half of the population of the world unable to take out loans from existing financial institutions, I had to turn the existing banking system around so that the poorest people were receiving loans."—Muhammad Yunus, Founder of Grameen Bank.[31]

Getting the Strategy Right

Choosing the right strategy in responding to public service deficits is becoming a key management task in developing country contexts. However, there is no one-size-fits-all solution. Industrial sector, regional context, national factors such as economic and legal infrastructure, as well as company values and resources will all play a part in determining the most effective course of action. Crucially though, the role of the private sector in the provision of public services is growing in light of the increasing power of business and the lack of existing alternatives in developing country contexts. If private enterprise is to take this role seriously, managers need to be aware of the different approaches to public responsibility and their associated challenges.

In terms of public service provision, the supplement approach is recommended in situations of urgency or in situations where firm activity merely augments existing governmental efforts. The substitute approach should be pursued cautiously and only when the firm considers itself as one piece of a larger puzzle of actors working towards broader public goals and has the appropriate structures and measures in place to effectively and without compromise combine its commitment to profitability with the public agenda. In terms of developing infrastructure for public goals, the support approach is highly recommended for those firms operating in sectors unrelated to public services yet in contexts where the potential exists to develop a local governing body or improve the political capacity of one that is already present. On the other hand, the stimulate approach is best for those businesses that can leverage their core product and service or their broader chain of activities to foster change in the political or economic landscapes that determine how public goals are achieved.

It is also clear that successful firms need to remain agile in the face of changing internal and external circumstances. This may require a shift from one strategic approach to another or ambidexterity in executing multiple strategies concurrently. For instance, consider the case when a firm gets locked into a supplement strategy but its leaders want to reduce the burden of their political role. Magadi Soda Ash, for example, initially employed a supplement strategy, but then over time transitioned to a more indirect support approach:

"As the community got more involved, we started to question our role as a company in terms of doing all this philanthropic stuff. Maybe they should be the ones to manage this. In fact, they were having the same thoughts."—Former Managing Director, Magadi Soda Ash

Realizing that they were ill-suited to make decisions on public welfare and uncomfortable with the government-like role the company was playing, senior executives worked with the local community to build a municipal council made up of locally elected officials. Magadi Soda Ash then formalized a committee that encompassed elected chiefs and company executives to identify priority areas for the firm's public programs. As a result, whereas the company was initially responsible for overseeing the community health unit, for example, responsibility was eventually shifted to the community. This reduced the company's costs, minimized its obligation to operate activities for which it had little expertise, and enabled the local community to develop its own effective health care services.

Firms may also transition away from non-core forms of public responsibility to initiatives that are more central to strategy. BancoReal's establishment of a microfinance arm is an example of a transition from a supplement to a stimulate approach, while CEMEX's market expansion to the slums of Mexico represents a substitution for governmental public housing initiatives. Mining and extractive companies may transition to a stimulate approach by supporting the development of local small businesses to build capacity in their respective supply chains.

The conditions under which these changes should be made are largely based on the specific gaps in public service or welfare surrounding the firm along with the commitment level of the organization. Clearly, pursuing public responsibilities that address broader gaps in public goals represents a more comprehensive and complex approach than limiting commitment to the provision of specific services such as health care, policing, water distribution, or education. Companies should seek out information related to the underlying causes of public welfare gaps not only in their immediate competitive context but in their broader sphere of influence to determine whether the gaps are merely caused by missing public services or more comprehensively by the underlying political and economic infrastructure meant to achieve public goals. For instance, companies operating exclusively in the substitute strategy may be providing public services that represent remedies for symptoms of an underlying issue related to how public goals are achieved. The company may subsequently fall victim to community backlash regardless of the approach employed. While shifting to a stimulate strategy may represent too radical a shift for the firm, it may be worthwhile engaging in the support approach to bolster institutions that can effectively and democratically make decisions related to public service provision. In contrast, firms may need to complement their substitute approach with a supplement model where they take on other public services not related to their business to augment existing governmental efforts in situations of urgency. For instance, a water distribution company may assist in the development of housing services or partner with housing developers for those clients who face freak weather events.

Consequently, the four strategies introduced here are not mutually exclusive. Companies may find the need to tread different strategies. For instance, SEKEM complements its stimulate approach with the direct provision of education and health care on its mother farm just outside Cairo, while a mining company may need to commit to a supplement and support strategy concurrently especially when operating in conditions where the provision of public services is urgently required. The apparel sector's self-regulation of fair labor practices may tread both substitute and stimulate strategies. On the one hand, as already discussed, apparel companies adopt a substitute approach by replacing governmental policing of factory working conditions. On the other hand, companies have engaged in a stimulate approach in Kazakhstan by boycotting the sourcing of Kazak cotton in an effort to promote government action on forced and child labor. The economic carrot associated with foreign direct investment has encouraged many developing country governments to comply with MNC investment conditions, including the institutionalization of laws banning child labor and other unfair labor practices.[32] Thus, to effectively fill gaps left by government, many companies may need to develop a portfolio of strategies that caters to their specific operating context.

Conclusion

We have outlined the different types of strategies—supplement, support, substitute, and stimulate—firms adopt as they seek to discharge public responsibilities left underserved by government actors.

The message for managers of private enterprise in developing countries is clear. The burden of public responsibility is real, and only by effectively developing an appropriate strategic orientation can programs be developed in ways that add value both to the business and to the communities in which they operate. While researchers and practitioners may have voiced anxieties about the blurring of the lines between the economic and political spheres, such definitional debates overlook the very real problems of management in developing countries.[33] Companies must be ready to face challenges not commonly experienced in industrialized countries, where public infra-structure is typically already in place. Present research and management best practice tends to presume that public policy exists to guide firms in their social responsibilities. However, increasingly companies are forced to blur the lines between private and public activities by taking on roles typically undertaken by government bodies. This presents new and frequently unforeseen challenges not typically faced by companies. These challenges require carefully crafted solutions that are tailored to the specific strategic context in which firms are located.

APPENDIX A

Case Illustrations

Case in Point #1 Magadi Soda Ash: Supplementing Public Services

A subsidiary of the India-based Tata Group, Magadi Soda Ash is located 120km south of Kenya's capital, Nairobi. The company is situated adjacent to Lake Magadi, a body of water with a high concentration of various minerals resulting in a crusty surface of trona. Magadi breaks up the trona and crushes it at its processing plant into a fine powder known as soda ash. The soda ash is an ingredient in common detergents and glass. The remote location of Lake Magadi affords it very little governmental public services. At the time of the company's founding, there was no running water, educational facilities, health facilities or roads. Close to 30,000 Masai people live within a large geographic region surrounding the plant. In light of government incapacity, Magadi Soda has been responsible for developing the public services required to effectively operate its factories and operations. This public responsibility extends beyond the physical boundaries of the firm as the company installed and maintains the main highway that links Nairobi to Magadi in addition to the rail line that connects Magadi to the main Nairobi-Mombasa highway. While both transportation arteries are necessary to assist in company operations, they are available to the public.

Magadi Soda built and staffed the community hospital which sees over 10,000 patients annually, a secondary school in the region which includes over 15 buildings equipped with renewable sources of energy, running water, and other basic services for the school, which is located 20 km from the main town of Magadi. After a major drought in 1999 that led to greater pressure on the company to assist the surrounding Masai, the company began to question its supplement approach and initiated a more inclusive support approach that shifted its focus from the direct provision of public services to the gradual building of capacity of a central governing body. This governing body is made up of community senior chiefs, elected officials, NGOs, and company representatives and is charged with the broader responsibility of community welfare. This shifted the responsibility of public service provision from the company to this central body. Today, any issues related to public services are dealt with through this central mechanism with each actor providing important resources and capabilities.

Case in Point #2 SEKEM: Stimulating Alternative Approaches to Agriculture

With only $150,000 and a network of friends and supporters, Ibrahim Abouleish, the founder of SEKEM, launched a "mother farm" in the Egyptian desert, 60 km outside of Cairo. Abouleish founded SEKEM in response to a "deep sense of hopelessness caused by the way of life of the Egyptian population" and a determination to "liberate them from their misery." His goal was to heal the people and the land, and to build an organization for the comprehensive development of society in Egypt. Abouleish and SEKEM won the Right Livelihood Award (also known as the Alternative Nobel Prize) for integrating commercial goals with the promotion of social and cultural development of society. Over 120,000 trees were planted to create a shield from desert storms and a habitat for insects and animals. Wells were drilled at depths of more than 100 meters. Despite only 4% of the land in Egypt being suitable for agriculture, SEKEM built up soil fertility gradually using the dung of 40 cows donated by friends in Germany.

The 2004 Schwab Foundation "Outstanding Social Entrepreneur" went door to door educating farmers about the benefits of organic crops and the potential of the growing European market for organic produce. He guaranteed a market for all produce, at fair prices, using a supplier network that ran alongside the socially and ecologically detrimental effects of the existing agricultural system in Egypt. SEKEM founded the Egyptian Biodynamic Association, a knowledge and learning institution, to build the organic agricultural capacity of the Egyptian farmers, stimulating an alternative agricultural model that is based on fair prices, ecological preservation, sustainable livelihoods, and cultural development. SEKEM is now working closely with over 800 farmers across a group of six companies ranging in operations from the processing of herbs, spices, and fresh fruit and vegetables to textile manufacturing and pharmaceuticals.

APPENDIX B

Methodology

To best examine public responsibility strategies, we employed an inductive, qualitative research design, which involves exploring new phenomenon without preconceived hypotheses or expected theoretical outcomes.[34] We used 30 company case studies in three broad sectors of agriculture, manufacturing, and services across a range of developing country contexts (see Table 7.1). All 30 companies were profit-based, ranging in size from large subsidiaries of multinational corporations to profit-based social enterprises. The sample was structured into two parts. The first group of 16 cases was selected based on interviews conducted with International Finance

Corporation (IFC), the private-sector arm of the World Bank Group. IFC investment officers were helpful in identifying companies perceived to have a positive social impact on their surrounding communities, and that operated in contexts with substantial governmental voids related to the provision of public services and the achievement of public welfare. A second set of 14 cases was then identified in order to replicate and extend our emerging theory by adding further diversity within the three sectors and extending the context to other developing countries.

The data collection took place from November 2004 to February 2008. An average of 10 interviews was conducted for the first 16 cases across various levels inside the organization and with external stakeholders including senior community leaders, NGOs, farmers, government, and other relevant stakeholders. Several observations were documented during extended company visits of three to five days and archival data were collected to triangulate findings emerging from the primary data. Eight of the first 16 cases were visited and examined more than once to help uncover mobility across public responsibility strategies.

Data analysis followed best practice grounded theory methods and began as soon as data collection commenced to create overlap between data collection and data analysis.[35] This overlap was important because it assisted in theoretically sampling the second phase of cases to validate emerging conceptualizations of public responsibility by extending the study to additional business models, sectors, and regions. Manual coding of the 150 interview transcripts, observation notes, and archival data was used to understand the nature of the interface between the companies and their political role. Common themes were identified across the data sources for each case to compile 16 separate within-case analyses. From there, cross-case analyses were conducted to identify common themes across cases. This involved looking for differences in public service provision in seemingly similar cases and looking for similarities in public responsibility in seemingly different cases.[36]

Based on the cross-case analysis of these 16 cases, a preliminary typology of private enterprise public responsibility strategies emerged using two relevant dimensions. Moreover, a number of different challenges associated with each approach were identified in addition to approaches to overcome these challenges. The 14 additional cases were helpful in refining the typology and ensuring that the challenges introduced were indeed representative of the four approaches. While the 14 cases added in the second phase did not include primary data, coding of available archival data was sufficient to conduct within-case analyses and more importantly cross-case comparisons with the other cases. Ultimately, we were very confident having examined 30 cases across multiple sectors and contexts that the four public responsibility strategies identified were representative of firm political responsibility in developing country contexts.

Notes

1. United Nations Development Program, *Beyond Scarcity: Power, Poverty and the Global Water Crisis* (New York, NY: Human Development Report, 2006).
2. J. Sachs, *The End of Poverty* (New York, NY: Penguin Books, 2005).
3. S. Lewis, *Race Against Time* (Toronto: House of Anansi Press, 2005); J. Stiglitz, *Globalization and Its Discontents* (New York, NY: W.W. Norton & Co., 2002); J. Stiglitz, *Making Globalization Work* (New York, NY: W.W. Norton & Co., 2006).
4. E.g., Stiglitz, (2002), op. cit.; Stiglitz, (2006), op. cit.
5. D. Matten and A. Crane, "Corporate Citizenship: Towards an Extended Theoretical Conceptualization," *Academy of Management Review*, 30/1 (January 2005): 166–179; G. Palazzo and A. Scherer, "Corporate Social Responsibility, Democracy, and the Politicization of the Corporation," *Academy of Management Review*, 33/3 (July 2008): 773–775; J. Moon, A. Crane, and D. Matten, "Can Corporations be Citizens? Corporate Citizenship as a Metaphor for Business Participation in Society," *Business Ethics Quarterly*, 15/3 (July 2005): 429–453.
6. See for example, S. Hart, *Capitalism at the Crossroads: The Unlimited Business Opportunities in Solving the World's Most Difficult Problems* (Upper Saddle River, NJ: Wharton School Publishing, 2005); A. Scherer and G. Palazzo, "Toward a Political Conception of Corporate Responsibility: Business and Society Seen from a Habermasian Perspective," *Academy of Management Review*, 32/4 (October 2007): 1096–1120; Matten and Crane, op. cit.; G. Palazzo and A. Scherer, "Corporate Legitimacy as Deliberation: A Communicative Framework," *Journal of Business Ethics*, 66/1 (June 2006): 71–88.
7. J. Bakan, *The Corporation: The Pathological Pursuit of Profit and Power* (Toronto: Viking Canada, 2004).
8. Hart, op. cit.; C. Prahalad, *The Fortune at the Bottom of the Pyramid: Eradicating Poverty Through Profits* (Upper Saddle River, NJ: Wharton School Publishing, 2005); C. Prahalad and S. Hart, "The Fortune at the Bottom of the Pyramid," *strategy+business*, 26 (first quarter 2002): 1–14.
9. T. Dunfee, "Do firms with unique competencies for rescuing victims of human catastrophes have special obligations? Corporate Responsibility and the AIDS Catastrophe in Sub-Saharan Africa," *Business Ethics Quarterly*, 16/2 (April 2006): 185–210; Matten and Crane, op. cit.; S. Elankumaran, R. Seal, and A. Hashmi "Transcending Transformation: Enlightening Endeavors at Tata Steel," *Journal of Business Ethics*, 59/1–2 (June 2005): 109–119.
10. J. Elkington and P. Hartigan, *The Power of Unreasonable People* (Boston, MA: Harvard School Publishing, 2008); C. Seelos and J. Mair, "Social Entrepreneurship: Creating New Business Models to Serve the Poor" *Business Horizons*, 48/3 (May/June 2005): 241–246; D. Wheeler, K. McKague, J. Thomson, R. Davies, J. Medalye, and M. Prada, "Creating Sustainable Local Enterprise Networks," *Sloan Management Review*, 47 (Fall 2005): 33–40.
11. Scherer and Palazzo (2007), op. cit. For a perspective specifically focusing on the USA, see S. Barley, "Corporations, Democracy, and the Public Good," *Journal of Management Inquiry*, 16/3 (September 2007): 201–215.
12. For an earlier discussion of public responsibility in a developed country context, see L. Preston and J. Post, *Private Management and Public Policy: The Principle of Public Responsibility* (Englewood Cliffs, NJ: Prentice Hall, 1975). For a review of its subsequent incorporation into models of corporate social performance, see D. Wood, "Corporate Social Performance Revisited," *Academy of Management Review*, 16/4 (October 1991): 691–718. In these accounts, public responsibility is defined as "functions of organizational management within the specific context of public policy," where the assumption is that an effective, well-functioning public-policy process defines a regulative environment that sets the criteria for effective management of corporate responsibilities. In contrast, we consider contexts where such an environment is either largely absent or incapacitated in some way. We

recognize the diversity across developing countries when considering aspects such as governmental corruption and capacity, legal infrastructure, and social issues. Although the strategies we identify here span different contexts, firms should be aware of the variation in country level characteristics.

13. Although there are several definitions of Corporate Social Responsibility, we consider CSR to encompass corporate actions "that appear to further some social good beyond the interest of the firm and that which is required by law." A. McWilliams and D. Siegel, "Corporate Social Responsibility: A Theory of the Firm Perspective," *Academy of Management Review,* 26/1 (January 2001): 117–127, at p. 117.

14. For a discussion of "political CSR" see Scherer and Palazzo (2007), op. cit. An "extended" view of corporate citizenship is provided by Matten and Crane, op. cit.

15. Some of the companies mentioned as illustrative examples in the presentation of our findings are not included in the sample.

16. A firm's activities "that are performed to design, produce, market, deliver, and support its product" or service is called its value chain. M. Porter, *Competitive Advantage* (New York, NY: The Free Press, 1985), p. 34. Porter also suggests that each firm's value chain "is embedded in a larger stream of activities" (p. 34) that he calls the "value system." The value system could consist of upstream raw material suppliers' value chains, the focal firm's value chain, downstream distributor and retailer value chains, and the ultimate buyer's value chain. Both value chain and value systems are considered here.

17. Porter and Kramer prioritized social issues faced by a firm in a similar manner. M. Porter and M. Kramer, "Strategy and Society: The Link Between Competitive Advantage and Corporate Social Responsibility," *Harvard Business Review,* 84/12 (December 2006): 77–92.

18. United Nations Global Compact: "Business has Important Role in Bridging Cultural Divides," April 7, 2009, New York, NY, accessed September 5, 2009, <www.unglobalcompact.org/ NewsAndEvents/news_archives/2009_04_07.html>.

19. A. Crane, D. Matten, and J. Moon, *Corporations and Citizenship* (Cambridge: Cambridge University Press, 2008), p. 53.

20. Matten and Crane, op. cit.

21. D. Wheeler and P. Moszynski, "Blood on British Business Hands," *New Statesman & Society,* 8/379 (November 17, 1995): 14; BBC News, "Nigeria's Removal of Shell Hailed," BBC News, June 5, 2008, accessed September 10, 2008, <http://news.bbc.co.uk/go/pr/fr/-/2/hi/ africa/7437247.stm>.

22. Sir Mark Moody-Stuart, referenced from Bakan, op. cit.

23. S. Waddock, C. Bodwell, and S. Graves "Responsibility: The New Business Imperative," *Academy of Management Executive,* 16/2 (May 2002): 132–148.

24. These derailments are not limited to the private sector. There is indeed reference made to such derailments befalling public bodies where governments abuse public sectors. For example, see A. Kruger, "Government Failures in Development," *The Journal of Economic Perspectives,* 4/3 (Summer 1990): 9–23; M. Datta-Chaudhuri, "Market Failure and Government Failure," *The Journal of Economic Perspectives,* 4/3 (Summer 1990): 25–39.

25. J. Margolis and J. Walsh, "Misery Loves Companies: Rethinking Social Initiatives by Business," *Administrative Science Quarterly,* 48/2 (June 2003): 268–305.

26. D. Murphy and D. Mathew, "Nike and Global Labor Practices," a case study prepared for the new academy of business innovation network for socially responsible business, 2001, accessed September 10, 2009, <http://docs.google.com/gview?a=v&q=cache:kB2yrI7_IAgJ: www.newacademy.ac.uk/publications/keypublications/documents/nikereport.pdf+nike+ngos&hl=en&gl=ca&sig=AFQjCNEHQZafRLUIUS_AlvE8_PEzlIhiOA>.

27. Bakan, op. cit.

28. S. Zadek, "The Path to Corporate Responsibility," *Harvard Business Review,* 82/12 (December 2004): 125–132.

29. For more information on the Global Network Initiative, see <www.global networkinitiative. org>.

30.   J. Elkington and P. Hartigan, *The Power of Unreasonable People* (Boston, MA: Harvard School Publishing, 2008).
31.   Skoll Foundation, "The New Heroes," Portland, Oregon Public Broadcasting, 2005.
32.   Organization for Economic Co-operation and Development (OECD), "The Social Impact of Foreign Direct Investment", Policy Brief, July 2008.
33.   P. Edwards and H. Willmott, "Corporate Citizenship: Rise or Demise of a Myth?" *Academy of Management Review*, 33/3 (July 2008): 771–773; Palazzo and Scherer, "Corporate Social Responsibility, Democracy, and the Politicization of the Corporation," *Academy of Management Review*, 33/3 (July 2008): 773–775; C. Crook, "The Future of the State," *Economist*, 344/8035 (1997): 5–7.
34.   B. Glaser and A. Strauss, *The Discovery of Grounded Theory: Strategies for Qualitative Research* (Chicago, IL: Aldine Publishers Co., 1967); K. Eisenhardt, "Building Theories from Case Study Research," *Academy of Management Review*, 14/4 (October 1989): 532–540; A. Strauss and J. Corbin, *Basics of Qualitative Research* (Thousand Oaks, CA: Sage Publications, 1990).
35.   Eisenhardt, op. cit.; Glaser and Strauss, op. cit.
36.   Strauss and Corbin, op. cit.; Eisenhardt, op. cit.

THE COMPETITIVE ADVANTAGE OF
CORPORATE PHILANTHROPY

Michael E. Porter and Mark R. Kramer

Corporate philanthropy is in decline. Charitable contributions by U.S. companies fell 14.5% in real dollars last year, and over the last 15 years, corporate giving as a percentage of profits has dropped by 50%. The reasons are not hard to understand. Executives increasingly see themselves in a no-win situation, caught between critics demanding ever higher levels of "cor-porate social responsibility" and investors applying relentless pressure to maximize short-term profits. Giving more does not satisfy the critics – the more companies donate, the more is expected of them. And executives find it hard, if not impossible, to justify charitable expenditures in terms of bottom-line benefit.

This dilemma has led many companies to seek to be more strategic in their philanthropy. But what passes for "strategic philanthropy" today is almost never truly strategic, and often isn't even particularly effective as philanthropy. Increasingly, philanthropy is used as a form of public relations or advertising, promoting a company's image or brand through cause-related marketing or other high-profile sponsorships. Although it still represents only a small proportion of overall corporate charitable expenditures, U.S. corporate spending on cause-related marketing jumped from $125 million in 1990 to an estimated $828 million in 2002. Arts sponsorships are growing, too – they accounted for an additional $589 million in 2001. While these campaigns do provide much-needed support to worthy causes, they are intended as much to increase company visibility and improve employee morale as to create social impact. Tobacco giant Philip Morris, for example, spent $75 million on its charitable contributions in 1999 and then launched a $100 million advertising campaign to publicize them. Not surprisingly, there are genuine doubts about whether such approaches actually work or just breed public cynicism about company motives. (See the box "The Myth of Strategic Philanthropy.")

Given the current haziness surrounding corporate philanthropy, this seems an appropriate time to revisit the most basic of questions: Should corporations engage in philanthropy at all? The economist Milton Friedman laid down the gauntlet decades ago, arguing in a 1970 *New York Times Magazine* article that the only "social responsibility of business" is to "increase its profits." "The corporation," he wrote in his book *Capitalism and Freedom*, "is an instrument of the stockholders who own it. If the corporation makes a contribution, it prevents the individual stockholder from himself deciding how he should dispose of his funds." If charitable contributions are to be made, Friedman concluded, they should be made by individual stockholders – or, by extension, individual employees – and not by the corporation.

The way most corporate philanthropy is practiced today, Friedman is right. The majority of corporate contribution programs are diffuse and unfocused. Most consist of numerous small cash donations given to aid local civic causes or provide general operating support to universities and national charities in the hope of generating goodwill among employees, customers, and the local community. Rather than being tied to well-thought-out social or business objectives, the contributions often reflect the personal beliefs and values of executives or employees. Indeed, one of the most popular approaches – employee matching grants – explicitly leaves the choice of charity to the individual worker. Although aimed at enhancing morale, the same effect might be gained from an equal increase in wages that employees could then choose to donate to charity on a tax-deductible basis. It does indeed seem that many of the giving decisions companies make today would be better made by individuals donating their own money.

What about the programs that are at least superficially tied to business goals, such as cause-related marketing? Even the successful ones are hard to justify as charitable initiatives. Since all reasonable corporate expenditures are deductible, companies get no special tax advantage for spending on phil-anthropy as opposed to other corporate purposes. If cause-related marketing is good marketing, it is already deductible and does not benefit from being designated as charitable.

But does Friedman's argument always hold? Underlying it are two implicit assumptions. The first is that social and economic objectives are separate and distinct, so that a corporation's social spending comes at the expense of its economic results. The second is the assumption that corpo-rations, when they address social objectives, provide no greater benefit than is provided by individual donors.

These assumptions hold true when corporate contributions are unfo-cused and piecemeal, as is typically the case today. But there is another, more truly strategic way to think about philanthropy. Corporations can use their charitable efforts to improve their *competitive context* – the quality of the business environment in the location or locations where they operate. Using philanthropy to enhance context brings social and economic goals in to alignment and improves a company's long-term business prospects – thus contradicting Friedman's first assumption. In addition, addressing context enables a company not only to give money but also to leverage its capabilities and relationships in support of charitable causes. That produces social benefits far exceeding those provided by individual donors, foundations, or even governments. Context-focused giving thus contradicts Friedman's second assumption as well.

The Myth of Strategic Philanthropy

Few phrases are as overused and poorly defined as "strategic philanthropy." The term is used to cover virtually any kind of charitable activity that has some definable theme, goal, approach, or focus. In the corporate context, it generally means that there is some connection, however vague or tenuous, between the charitable contribution and the company's business. Often this connection is only semantic, enabling the company to rationalize its contributions in public reports and press releases. In fact, most corporate giving programs have nothing to do with a company's strategy. They are primarily aimed at generating goodwill and positive publicity and boosting employee morale.

Cause-related marketing, through which a company concentrates its giving on a single cause or admired organization, was one of the earliest practices cited as "strategic philanthropy," and it is a step above diffuse corporate contributions. At its most sophisticated, cause-related marketing can improve the reputation of a company by linking its identity with the admired qualities of a chosen non-profit partner or a popular cause. Companies that sponsor the Olympics, for example, gain not only wide exposure but also an association with the pursuit of excellence. And by concentrating funding through a deliberate selection process, cause-related marketing has the potential to create more impact than unfocused giving would provide.

However, cause-related marketing falls far short of truly strategic philanthropy. Its emphasis remains on publicity rather than social impact. The desired benefit is enhanced goodwill, not improvement in a company's ability to compete. True strategic giving, by contrast, addresses important social and economic goals simultaneously, targeting areas of competitive context where the company and society both benefit because the firm brings unique assets and expertise.

A handful of companies have begun to use context-focused philanthropy to achieve both social and economic gains. Cisco Systems, to take one example, has invested in an ambitious educational program – the Cisco Networking Academy – to train computer network administrators, thus alleviating a potential constraint on its growth while providing attractive job opportunities to high school graduates. By focusing on social needs that affect its corporate context and utilizing its unique attributes as a corporation to address them, Cisco has begun to demonstrate the unrealized potential of corporate philanthropy. Taking this new direction, however, requires fundamental changes in the way companies approach their contribution programs. Corporations need to rethink both *where* they focus their philanthropy and *how* they go about their giving.

Where to Focus

It is true that economic and social objectives have long been seen as distinct and often competing. But this is a false dichotomy; it represents an increasingly obsolete perspective in a world of open, knowledge-based competition. Companies do not function in isolation from the society around them. In fact, their ability to compete depends heavily on the circumstances of the locations where they operate. Improving education, for example, is generally seen as a social issue, but the educational level of the local workforce substantially affects a company's potential competitiveness. The more a social improvement relates to a company's business, the more it leads to economic benefits as well. In establishing its Networking Academy, for example, Cisco focused not on the educational system overall, but on the training needed to produce network administrators – the particular kind of education that made the most difference to Cisco's competitive context. (For a more detailed look at that program, see the box "The Cisco Networking Academy.")

In the long run, then, social and economic goals are not inherently conflicting but integrally connected. Competitiveness today depends on the productivity with which companies can use labor, capital, and natural resources to produce high-quality goods and services. Productivity depends on having workers who are educated, safe, healthy, decently housed, and motivated by a sense of opportunity. Preserving the environment benefits not only society but companies too, because reducing pollution and waste can lead to a more productive use of resources and help produce goods that consumers value. Boosting social and economic conditions in developing countries can create more productive locations for a company's operations as well as new markets for its products. Indeed, we are learning that the most effective method of addressing many of the world's pressing problems is often to mobilize the corporate sector in ways that benefit both society and companies.

That does not mean that every corporate expenditure will bring a social benefit or that every social benefit will improve competitiveness. Most corporate expenditures produce benefits only for the business, and charitable contributions unrelated to the business generate only social benefits. It is only where corporate expenditures produce simultaneous social and economic gains that corporate philanthropy and shareholder interests converge, as illustrated in Exhibit 2, "A Convergence of Interests." The highlighted area shows where corporate philanthropy has an important influence on a company's competitive context. It is here that philanthropy is truly strategic.

Competitive context has always been important to strategy. The availability of skilled and motivated employees; the efficiency of the local infrastructure, including roads and telecommunications; the size and sophistication of the local market; the extent of governmental regulations — such contextual variables have always influenced companies' ability to compete. But competitive context has become even more critical as the basis of competition has moved from cheap inputs to superior productivity. For one thing, modern knowledge- and technology-based competition hinges more and more on worker capabilities. For another, companies today depend more on local partnerships: They rely on outsourcing and collaboration with local suppliers and institutions rather than on vertical integration; they work more closely with customers; and they draw more on local universities and research institutes to conduct research and development. Finally, navigating increasingly complex local regulations and reducing approval times for new projects and products are becoming increasingly important to competition. As a result of these trends, companies' success has become more tightly

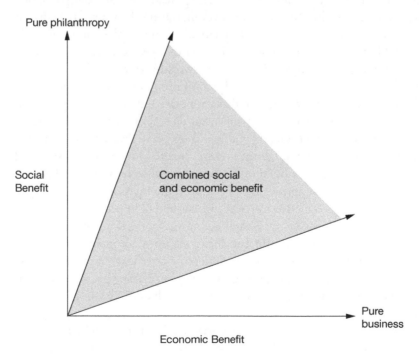

Exhibit 2 A convergence of interests

intertwined with local institutions and other contextual conditions. And the globalization of production and marketing means that context is often more important for a company not just in its home market but in multiple countries.

A company's competitive context consists of four interrelated elements of the local business environment that shape potential productivity: factor conditions, or the available inputs of production; demand conditions; the context for strategy and rivalry; and related and supporting industries. This framework is summarized in Exhibit 3, "The Four Elements of Competitive Context", and described in detail in Michael E. Porter's *The Competitive Advantage of Nations*. Weakness in any part of this context can erode the competitiveness of a nation or region as a business location.

Some aspects of the business environment, such as road systems, corporate tax rates, and corporate laws, have effects that cut across all industries. These general conditions can be crucial to competitiveness in developing countries, and improving them through corporate philanthropy can bring enormous social gains to the world's poorest nations. But often just as decisive, if not more, are aspects of context that are specific to a particular *cluster* – a geographic concentration of interconnected companies, suppliers, related industries, and specialized institutions in a particular field, such as high-performance cars in Germany or software in India. Clusters arise through the combined influence of all four elements of context. They are often prominent features of a region's economic landscape, and building them is essential to its development, allowing constituent firms to be more

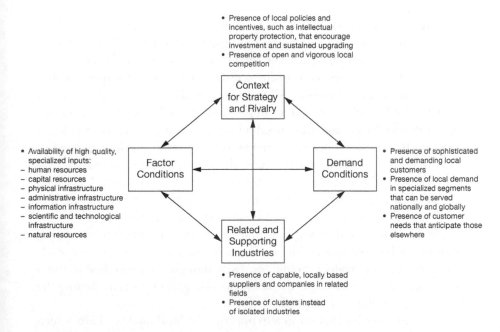

Exhibit 3 The four elements of competitive context

productive, making innovation easier, and fostering the formation of new businesses.

Philanthropic investments by members of a cluster, either individually or collectively, can have a powerful effect on the cluster's competitiveness and the performance of all of its constituent companies. Philanthropy can often be the most cost-effective way – and sometimes the only way – to improve competitive context. It enables companies to leverage not only their own resources but also the existing efforts and infrastructure of nonprofits and other institutions. Contributing to a university, for example, may be a far less expensive way to strengthen a local base of advanced skills in a company's field than developing training in-house. And philanthropy is amenable to collective corporate action, enabling costs to be spread over multiple companies. Finally, because of philanthropy's wide social benefits, companies are often able to forge partnerships with nonprofit organizations and governments that would be wary of collaborating on efforts that solely benefited a particular company.

Influencing Competitive Context

By carefully analyzing the elements of competitive context, a company can identify the areas of overlap between social and economic value that will most enhance its own and its cluster's competitiveness. Consider each of the four elements of context and how companies have influenced them through philanthropy in ways that have improved their long-term economic prospects.

Factor Conditions. Achieving high levels of productivity depends on the presence of trained workers, high-quality scientific and technological institutions, adequate physical infrastructure, transparent and efficient administrative processes (such as company registration or permit requirements), and available natural resources. All are areas that philanthropy can influence.

Charitable giving can, for example, improve education and training. DreamWorks SKG, the film production company, recently created a program to train low-income students in Los Angeles in skills needed to work in the entertainment industry. Each of the company's six divisions is working with the Los Angeles Community College District, local high schools, and after-school programs to create a specialized curriculum that combines classroom instruction with internships and mentoring. The social benefit is an improved educational system and better employment opportunities for low-income residents. The economic benefit is greater availability of specially trained graduates. Even though relatively few of them will join DreamWorks itself, the company also gains by strengthening the entertainment cluster it depends on.

Philanthropic initiatives can also improve the local quality of life, which benefits all citizens but is increasingly necessary to attract mobile employees with specialized talents. In 1996, SC Johnson, a manufacturer of cleaning and home-storage products, launched "Sustainable Racine," a project to make its home city in Wisconsin a better place in which to live and work. In partnership with local organizations, government, and residents, the company created a communitywide coalition focused on enhancing the local economy and the environment. One project, an agreement among four municipalities to coordinate water and sewer treatment, resulted in savings for residents and businesses while reducing pollution. Another project involved opening the community's first charter school, targeting at-risk students. Other efforts focused on economic revitalization: Commercial vacancy rates in downtown Racine have fallen from 46% to 18% as polluted sites have been reclaimed and jobs have returned for local residents.

Philanthropy can also improve inputs other than labor, through enhancements in, say, the quality of local research and development institutions, the effectiveness of administrative institutions such as the legal system, the quality of the physical infrastructure, or the sustainable development of natural resources. Exxon Mobil, for example, has devoted substantial resources to improving basic conditions such as roads and the rule of law in the developing countries where it operates.

Demand Conditions. Demand conditions in a nation or region include the size of the local market, the appropriateness of product standards, and the sophistication of local customers. Sophisticated local customers enhance the region's competitiveness by providing companies with insight into emerging customer needs and applying pressure for innovation. For example, the advanced state of medical practice in Boston has triggered a stream of innovation in Boston-based medical device companies.

Philanthropy can influence both the size and quality of the local market. The Cisco Networking Academy, for instance, improved demand conditions by helping customers obtain well-trained network administrators. In doing so, it increased the size of the market and the sophistication of users — and hence users' interest in more advanced solutions. Apple Computer has long donated computers to schools as a means of introducing its products to young people. This provides a clear social benefit to the schools while expanding Apple's potential market and turning students and teachers into more sophisticated purchasers. Safeco, an insurance and financial services firm, is working in partnership with nonprofits to expand affordable housing and enhance public safety. As home ownership and public safety increased in its four test markets, insurance sales did too, in some cases by up to 40%.

Context for Strategy and Rivalry. The rules, incentives, and norms governing competition in a nation or region have a fundamental influence on productivity. Policies that encourage investment, protect intellectual property, open local markets to trade, break up or prevent the formation of cartels and monopolies, and reduce corruption make a location a more attractive place to do business.

Philanthropy can have a strong influence on creating a more productive and transparent environment for competition. For example, 26 U.S. corporations and 38 corporations from other countries have joined to support Transparency International in its work to disclose and deter corruption around the world. By measuring and focusing public attention on corruption, the organization helps to create an environment that rewards fair competition and enhances productivity. This benefits local citizens while providing sponsoring companies improved access to markets.

Another example is the International Corporate Governance Network (ICGN), a nonprofit organization formed by major institutional investors, including the College Retirement Equities Fund (TIAA-CREF) and the California Public Employees Retirement System, known as CalPERS, to promote improved standards of corporate governance and disclosures, especially in developing countries. ICGN encourages uniform global accounting standards and equitable shareholder voting procedures. Developing countries and their citizens benefit as improved governance and disclosure enhance local corporate practices, expose unscrupulous local competitors, and make regions more attractive for foreign investment. The institutional investors that support this project also gain better and fairer capital markets in which to invest.

Related and Supporting Industries. A company's productivity can be greatly enhanced by having high-quality supporting industries and services nearby. While outsourcing from distant suppliers is possible, it is not as efficient as using capable local suppliers of services, components, and machinery. Proximity enhances responsiveness, exchange of information, and innovation, in addition to lowering transportation and inventory costs.

Philanthropy can foster the development of clusters and strengthen supporting industries. American Express, for example, depends on travel-related spending for a large share of its credit card and travel agency revenues. Hence, it is part of the travel cluster in each of the countries in which it operates, and it depends on the success of these clusters in improving the quality of tourism and attracting travelers. Since 1986, American Express has funded Travel and Tourism Academies in secondary schools, training students not for the credit card business, its core business, nor for its own travel services, but for careers in other travel agencies as well as airlines, hotels, and restaurants. The program, which includes teacher training, curriculum support, summer internships, and industry mentors, now operates in ten countries and more than 3,000 schools, with more than 120,000 students enrolled. It provides the major social benefits of improved educational and job opportunities for local citizens. Within the United States, 80% of students in the program go on to college, and 25% take jobs in the travel industry after graduation. The economic gains are also substantial, as local travel clusters become more competitive and better able to grow. That translates into important benefits for American Express.

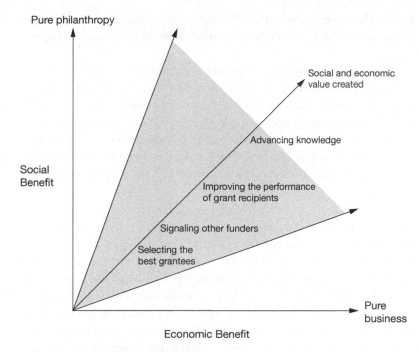

Exhibit 4 Maximizing philanthropy's value

The Free Rider Problem

When corporate philanthropy improves competitive context, other companies in the cluster or region, including direct competitors, often share the benefits. That raises an important question: Does the ability of other companies to be free riders negate the strategic value of context-focused philanthropy? The answer is *no*. The competitive benefits reaped by the donor company remain substantial, for five reasons:

- Improving context mainly benefits companies based in a given location. Not all competitors will be based in the same area, so the company will still gain an edge over the competition in general.
- Corporate philanthropy is ripe for collective activity. By sharing the costs with other companies in its cluster, including competitors, a company can greatly diminish the free rider problem.
- Leading companies will be best positioned to make substantial contributions and will in turn reap a major share of the benefits. Cisco, for example, with a leading market share in networking equipment, will benefit most from a larger, more rapidly growing market.
- Not all contextual advantages are of equal value to all competitors. The more tightly corporate philanthropy is aligned with a company's unique strategy — increasing skills, technology, or infrastructure on which the firm is especially reliant, say, or increasing demand within

a specialized segment where the company is strongest – the more disproportionately the company will benefit through enhancing the context.

- The company that initiates corporate philanthropy in a particular area will often get disproportionate benefits because of the superior reputation and relationships it builds. In its campaign to fight malaria in African countries, for example, Exxon Mobil not only improves public health. It also improves the health of its workers and contractors and builds strong relationships with local governments and nonprofits, advancing its goal of becoming the preferred resource-development partner.

A good example of how a company can gain an edge even when its contributions also benefit competitors is provided by Grand Circle Travel. Grand Circle, the leading direct marketer of international travel for older Americans, has a strategy based on offering rich cultural and educational experiences for its customers. Since 1992, its corporate foundation has given more than $12 million to historical preservation projects in locations that its customers like to visit, such as the Foundation of Friends of the Museum and Ruins of Ephesus in Turkey and the State Museum of Auschwitz-Birkenau in Poland. Other tours travel the same routes and so benefit from Grand Circle's donations. Through its philanthropy, however, Grand Circle has built close relationships with the organizations that maintain these sites and can provide its travelers with special opportunities to visit and learn about them. Grand Circle thus gains a unique competitive advantage that distinguishes it from other travel providers.

How to Contribute

Understanding the links between philanthropy and competitive context helps companies identify *where* they should focus their corporate giving. Understanding the ways in which philanthropy creates value highlights *how* they can achieve the greatest social and economic impact through their contributions. As we will see, the where and the how are mutually re-inforcing.

In "Philanthropy's New Agenda: Creating Value" (HBR November–December 1999), we outlined four ways in which charitable foundations can create social value: selecting the best grantees, signalling other funders, improving the performance of grant recipients, and advancing knowledge and practice in the field. These efforts build on one another: Increasingly greater value is generated as a donor moves up the ladder from selecting the right grantees to advancing knowledge. (See Exhibit 4, "Maximizing Philanthropy's Value.") The same principles apply to corporate giving, pointing the way to how corporate philanthropy can be most effective in enhancing competitive context. Focusing on the four principles also ensures that corporate donations have greater impact than donations of the same magnitude by individuals.

Selecting the Best Grantees. Most philanthropic activity involves giving money to other organizations that actually deliver the social benefits. The impact achieved by a donor, then, is largely determined by the effectiveness of the recipient. Selecting a more effective grantee or partner organization will lead to more social impact per dollar expended.

Selecting the most effective grantees in a given field is never easy. It may be obvious which nonprofit organizations raise the most money, have the greatest prestige, or manage the best development campaigns, but such factors may have little to do with how well the grantees use contributions. Extensive and disciplined research is usually required to select those recipients that will achieve the greatest social impact.

Individual donors rarely have the time or expertise to undertake such serious due diligence. Foundations are far more expert than individuals, but they have limited staff. Corporations, on the other hand, are well positioned to undertake such research if their philanthropy is connected to their business and they can tap into their internal capabilities, particularly the financial, managerial, and technical expertise of employees. Whether through their own operations or those of their suppliers and customers, corporations also often have a presence in many communities across a country or around the world. This can provide significant local knowledge and the ability to examine and compare the operation of nonprofits firsthand.

In some cases, a company can introduce and support a particularly effective nonprofit organization or program in many of the locations in which it operates. Grand Circle Travel, for example, uses its 15 overseas offices to identify historical preservation projects to fund. FleetBoston Financial assembles teams of employees with diverse management and financial skills to examine the inner-city economic development organizations that its foundation supports. The teams visit each nonprofit, interview management, review policies and procedures, and report to the corporate foundation on whether support should be continued and, if so, where it should be directed. This level of attention and expertise is substantially greater than most individual donors, foundations, or even government agencies can muster.

Signaling Other Funders. A donor can publicize the most effective nonprofit organizations and promote them to other donors, attracting greater funding and thus creating a more effective allocation of overall philanthropic spending.

Corporations bring uniquely valuable assets to this task. First, their reputations often command respect, becoming imprimaturs of credibility for grantees. Second, they are often able to influence a vast network of entities in their cluster, including customers, suppliers, and other partners. This gives them far greater reach than individual donors or even most nonprofits and foundations. Third, they often have access to communication channels and expertise that can be used to disseminate information widely, swiftly, and persuasively to other donors.

Signaling other funders is especially important in corporate philanthropy because it mitigates the free rider problem. Collective social investment by participants in a cluster can improve the context for all players, while reducing the cost borne by each one. By leveraging its relationships and brand identity to initiate social projects that are also funded by others, a corporation improves the cost–benefit ratio. The Cisco Networking Academy draws support from numerous technology companies in Cisco's cluster as well as educational systems and governments throughout the world, all of which benefit from the graduates' success. American Express's Travel and Tourism Academies depend on the help of more than 750 travel cluster partners who bear part of the cost and reap part of the benefit. Different companies will bring different strengths to a given philanthropic initiative. By tapping each company's distinctive expertise, the collective investment can be far more effective than a donation by any one company.

Improving the Performance of Grant Recipients. By improving the effectiveness of nonprofits, corporations create value for society, increasing the social impact achieved per dollar expended. While selecting the right grantee improves society's return on a single contribution, and signalling other funders improves the return on multiple contributions, improving grantee performance can increase the return on the grantee's total budget.

Unlike many other donors, corporations have the ability to work directly with nonprofits and other partners to help them become more effective. They bring unique assets and expertise that individuals and foundations lack, enabling them to provide a wide range of nonmonetary assistance that is less costly and more sophisticated than the services most grantees could purchase for themselves. And because they typically make long-term commitments to the communities in which they operate, corporations can work closely with local nonprofits over the extended periods of time needed for meaningful organizational improvement. By operating in multiple geographical areas, moreover, companies are able to facilitate the transfer of knowledge and operational improvements among nonprofits in different regions or countries. Contextual issues within a particular industry or cluster will often be similar across different locations, increasing a company's ability to add and derive value in multiple regions.

By tying corporate philanthropy to its business and strategy, a company can create even greater social value in improving grantee performance than other donors. Its specialized assets and expertise, after all, will be most useful in addressing problems related to its particular field. DreamWorks' film production expertise helped it design the educational curriculum necessary to help inner-city students in Los Angeles get jobs in the entertainment industry. The Cisco Networking Academy utilized the special expertise of Cisco employees.

The Cisco Networking Academy

Cisco Systems' Networking Academy exemplifies the powerful links that exist between a company's philanthropic strategy, its competitive context, and social benefits. Cisco, the leading producer of networking equipment and routers used to connect computers to the Internet, grew rapidly over the past decade. But as Internet use expanded, customers around the world encountered a chronic shortage of qualified network administrators, which became a limiting factor in Cisco's – and the entire IT industry's – continued growth. By one estimate, well over 1 million information technology jobs remained unfilled worldwide in the late 1990s. While Cisco was well aware of this constraint in its competitive context, it was only through philanthropy that the company found a way to address it.

The project began as a typical example of goodwill-based giving: Cisco contributed networking equipment to a high school near its headquarters, then expanded the program to other schools in the region. A Cisco engineer working with the schools realized, however, that the teachers and administrators lacked the training to manage the networks once they were installed. He and several other Cisco engineers volunteered to develop a program that would not only donate equipment but also train teachers how to build, design, and maintain computer networks. Students began attending these courses and were able to absorb the information successfully. As Cisco expanded the program, company executives began to realize that they could develop a Web-based distance-learning curriculum to train and certify secondary- and postsecondary-school students in network administration, a program that might have a much broader social and economic impact. The Networking Academy was born.

Because the social goal of the program was tightly linked to Cisco's specialized expertise, the company was able to create a high-quality curriculum rapidly and cost-effectively, creating far more social and economic value than if it had merely contributed cash and equipment to a worthy cause. At the suggestion of the U.S. Department of Education, the company began to target schools in "empowerment zones," designated by the federal government as among the most economically challenged communities in the country. The company also began to include community colleges and mid-career training in the program. More recently, it has worked with the United Nations to expand the effort to developing countries, where job opportunities are particularly scarce and networking skills particularly limited. Cisco has also organized a worldwide database of employment opportunities for academy graduates, creating a more efficient job market that benefits its cluster as well as the graduates and the regions in which they live.

Cisco has used its unique assets and expertise, along with its worldwide presence, to create a program that no other educational institution, government agency, foundation or corporate donor could have designed as well or expanded as rapidly. And it has amplified the impact by signalling other corporations on its cluster. Other companies supplemented Cisco's contributions by donating or discounting products and services of their own, such as Internet access and computer hardware and software. Several leading technology companies also began to recognize the value of the global infrastructure Cisco had created, and, rather than create their own Web-based learning programs, they partnered with Cisco. Companies such as Sun Microsystems, Hewlett-Packard, Adobe Systems, and Panduit expanded the academy curriculum by sponsoring courses in programming, IT essentials, Web design, and cabling. Because the project was linked to Cisco's business, it could gain the support of other companies in its cluster and use their contributions effectively.

Although the program is only five years old, it now operates 9,900 academies in secondary schools, community colleges, and community-based organizations in all 50 states and in 147 countries. The social and economic value that has been created is enormous. Cisco estimates that it has invested a total of $150 million since the program began. With that investment, it has brought the possibility of technology careers, and the technology itself, to men and women in some of the most economically depressed regions in the United States and around the world. More than 115,000 students have already graduated from the two-year program, and 263,000 students are currently enrolled, half of them outside the United States. The program continues to expand rapidly, with 50 to 100 new academies opening every week. Cisco estimates that 50% of academy graduates have found jobs in the IT industry, where the average salary for a network administrator in the United States is $67,000. Over the span of their careers, the incremental earnings potential of those who have already joined the workforce may approach several billion dollars.

To be sure, the program has benefited many free riders – employers around the world who gain access to highly skilled academy graduates and even direct competitors. But as the market-leading provider of routers, Cisco stands to benefit the most from this improvement in the competitive context. Through actively engaging others, Cisco has not had to bear the full cost of the program. Not only has Cisco enlarged its market and strengthened its cluster, but it has increased the sophistication of its customers. Through these tangible improvements in competitive context, and not just by the act of giving, Cisco has attracted international recognition for this program, generating justified pride and enthusiasm among company employees, goodwill among its partners, and a reputation for leadership in philanthropy.

FleetBoston Financial took similar advantage of its corporate expertise in launching its Community Renaissance Initiative. Recognizing that its major markets were in older East Coast cities, Fleet decided to focus on inner-city economic revitalization as perhaps the most important way to improve its context. Fleet combined its philanthropic contributions with its expertise in financial services, such as small business services, inner-city lending, home mortgages, and venture capital. The bank's foundation identified six communities where the bank had a presence, the economic need was great, and strong community-based organizations could be identified as reliable partners: Brooklyn and Buffalo, New York; Lawrence, Massachusetts; New Haven, Connecticut; and Camden and Jersey City, New Jersey. The foundation committed $725,000 to each city, building a coalition of local community, business, and government organizations to work on a set of issues identified by the community as central to its revitalization. Bank personnel provided technical advice and small business financing packages to local companies as well as home mortgages and home-buyer education programs. The foundation also attracted $6 million from private and municipal sources, greatly amplifying its own $4.5 million investment.

Another example is America Online, which has unique capabilities in managing Internet access and content. Working closely with educators, AOL developed AOL@School, a free, easy-to-use, non-commercial site tailored by grade level to students, administrators, and teachers. This service improves the classroom experience for hundreds of thousands of students nationally by giving them access to enrichment and reference tools while providing lesson plans and reference materials for teachers. Through this program, AOL has been able to leverage its specialized expertise, more than just its donations, to assist in improving secondary school performance more rapidly and cost-effectively than could most other organizations. In the process, it has improved both the long-term demand for its services and the talent needed to provide them.

Advancing Knowledge and Practice. Innovation drives productivity in the nonprofit sector as well as in the commercial sector. The greatest advances come not from incremental improvements in efficiency but from new and better approaches. The most powerful way to create social value, therefore, is by developing new means to address social problems and putting them into widespread practice.

The expertise, research capacity, and reach that companies bring to philanthropy can help nonprofits create new solutions that they could never afford to develop on their own. Since 1994, IBM has committed a total of $70 million to its Reinventing Education program, which now reaches 65,000 teachers and 6 million students. Working in partnership with urban school districts, state education departments, and colleges of education, IBM researched and developed a Web-based platform to support new instructional practices and strategies. The new curriculum is intended to redefine how teachers master their profession; it bridges the gap between teacher preparation and the classroom experience by providing a common platform that is used in the teachers' college courses and also supports their first years of teaching. Neither the colleges of education nor the school districts had the expertise or financial resources to develop such a program on their own. An independent evaluation in 2001 found that teachers in the Reinventing Education program were registering substantial gains in student performance.

Pfizer developed a cost-effective treatment for the prevention of trachoma, the leading cause of preventable blindness in developing countries. In addition to donating the drugs, Pfizer worked with the Edna McConnell Clark Foundation and world health organizations to create the infrastructure needed to prescribe and distribute them to populations that previously had little access to health care, much less modern pharmaceuticals. Within one year, the incidence of trachoma was reduced by 50% among target populations in Morocco and Tanzania. The program has since expanded aggressively, adding the Bill & Melinda Gates Foundation and the British government as partners, with the aim of reaching 30 million people worldwide. In addition to providing an important social benefit, Pfizer has enhanced its own long-term business prospects by helping build the infrastructure required to expand its markets.

Just as important as the creation of new knowledge is its adoption in practice. The know-how of corporate leaders, their clout and connections, and their presence in communities around the world create powerful networks for the dissemination of new ideas for addressing social problems. Corporations can facilitate global knowledge transfer and coordinated multisite implementation of new social initiatives with a proficiency that is unequaled by most other donors.

A Whole New Approach

When corporations support the right causes in the right ways – when they get the *where* and the *how* right – they set in motion a virtuous cycle. By focusing on the contextual conditions most important to their industries and strategies, companies ensure that their corporate capabilities will be particularly well suited to helping grantees create greater value. And by enhancing the value produced by philanthropic efforts in their fields, the companies gain a greater improvement in competitive context. Both the corporations and the causes they support reap important benefits.

Adopting a context-focused approach, however, goes against the grain of current philanthropic practice. Many companies actively distance their philanthropy from the business, believing this will lead to greater goodwill in local communities. While it is true that a growing number of companies aim to make their giving "strategic," few have connected giving to areas that improve their long-term competitive potential. And even fewer systematically apply their distinctive strengths to maximize the social and economic value created by their philanthropy. Instead, companies are often distracted by the desire to publicize how much money and effort they are contributing in order to foster an image of social responsibility and caring. Avon Products, for example, recently mobilized its 400,000 independent sales representatives in a high-profile door-to-door campaign to raise more than $32 million to fund breast cancer prevention. Fighting breast cancer is a worthy cause and one that is very meaningful to Avon's target market of female consumers. It is not, however, a material factor in Avon's competitive context or an area in which Avon has any inherent expertise. As a result, Avon may have greatly augmented its own cash contribution through effective fund-raising – and generated favorable publicity – but it failed to realize the full potential of its philanthropy to create social and economic value. Avon has done much good, but it could do even better. As long as companies remain focused on the public relations benefit of their contributions instead of the impact achieved, they will sacrifice opportunities to create social value.

This does not mean that corporations cannot also gain goodwill and enhance their reputations through philanthropy. But goodwill alone is not a sufficient motivation. Given public scepticism about the ethics of business – scepticism that has intensified in the wake of the string of corporate scandals this year – corporations that can demonstrate a significant impact on a social problem will gain more credibility than those that are merely big givers. The acid test of good corporate philanthropy is whether the desired social change is so beneficial to the company that the organization would pursue the change even if no one ever knew about it. Cisco, for example, has achieved wide recognition for its good works, but it would have had sufficient reason to develop the Networking Academy even if no goodwill had been created.

Moving to context-focused philanthropy will require a far more rigorous approach than is prevalent today. It will mean tightly integrating the management of philanthropy with other company activities. Rather than delegating philanthropy entirely to a public relations department or the staff of a corporate foundation, the CEO must lead the entire management team through a disciplined process to identify and implement a corporate giving strategy focused on improving context. Business units, in particular, must play central roles in identifying areas for contextual investments.

The new process would involve five steps:

Examine the competitive context in each of the company's important geographic locations. Where could social investment improve the company's or cluster's competitive potential? What are the key constraints that limit productivity, innovation, growth, and competitiveness? A company should pay special attention to the particular constraints that have a disproportionate effect on its strategy relative to competitors; improvements in these areas of context will potentially reinforce competitive advantage. The more specifically a contextual initiative is defined, the more likely the company is to create value and achieve its objectives. A broad initiative such as Avon's efforts to improve the health of all women will not necessarily deliver contextual benefits, even if it helps some employees or customers. And a tightly targeted objective does not necessarily diminish the scale of impact. Narrowly focused initiatives, like Pfizer's trachoma program, IBM's Reinventing Education, or Cisco's Networking Academy, can potentially benefit millions of people or strengthen the global market for an entire industry.

Review the existing philanthropic portfolio to see how it fits this new paradigm. Current programs will likely fall into three categories:

- Communal obligation: support of civic, welfare and educational organizations, motivated by the company's desire to be a good citizen.
- Goodwill building: contributions to support causes favored by employees, customers, or community leaders, often necessitated by the quid pro quo of business and the desire to improve the company's relationships.
- Strategic giving: philanthropy focused on enhancing competitive context, as outlined here.

Most corporate giving falls into the first two categories. While a certain percentage of giving in these categories may be necessary and desirable, the goal is to shift, as much as possible, a company's philanthropy into the third category. As for cause-related marketing, it is marketing, not philanthropy, and it must stand on its own merits.

Assess existing and potential corporate giving initiatives against the four forms of value creation. How can the company leverage its assets and expertise to select the most effective grantees, signal other funders, improve grantees' performance, and advance knowledge and practice? Given its strategy, where can the company create the greatest value through giving in ways that no other company could match?

Seek opportunities for collective action within a cluster and with other partners. Collective action will often be more effective than a solo effort in addressing context and enhancing the value created, and it helps mitigate the free rider problem by distributing costs broadly. Few companies today work together to achieve social objectives. This may be the result of a general reluctance to work with competitors, but clusters encompass many related partners and industries that do not compete directly. More likely, the tendency to view philanthropy as a form of public relations leads companies to invent their own contributions campaigns, which are branded with their own identities and therefore discourage partners. Focusing on the social change to be achieved, rather than the publicity to be gained, will expand the potential for partnerships and collective action.

Once a company has identified opportunities to improve the competitive context and determined the ways in which it can contribute by adding unique value, the search for partners becomes straightforward: Who else stands to benefit from this change in competitive context? And who has complementary expertise or resources? Conversely, what philanthropic initiatives by others are worth joining? Where can the company be a good partner to others by contributing in ways that will enhance value?

Rigorously track and evaluate results. Monitoring achievements is essential to continually improving the philanthropic strategy and its implementation. As with any other corporate activity, consistent improvement over time brings the greatest value. The most successful programs will not be short-term campaigns but long-term commitments that continue to grow in scale and sophistication.

The context-focused approach to philanthropy is not simple. One size does not fit all. Companies will differ in their comfort levels and time horizons for philanthropic activity, and individual firms will make different choices about how to implement our ideas. Philanthropy will never become an exact science — it is inherently an act of judgment and faith in the pursuit of long-term goals. However, the perspective and tools presented here will help any company make its philanthropic activities far more effective.

Were this approach to be widely adopted, the pattern of corporate contributions would shift significantly. The overall level of contributions would likely increase, and the social and economic value would go up even more sharply. Companies would be more confident about the value of their philanthropy and more committed to it. They would be able to communicate their philanthropic strategies more effectively to the communities in which they operate. Their choices of areas to support would be clearly understandable and would not seem unpredictable or idiosyncratic. Finally, there would be a better division of labor between corporate givers and other types of funders, with corporations tackling the areas where they are uniquely able to create value.

Charities too would benefit. They would see an increased and more predictable flow of corporate resources into the nonprofit sector. Just as important, they would develop close, long-term corporate partnerships that would better apply the expertise and assets of the for-profit sector to achieve social objectives. Just as companies can build on the nonprofit infrastructure to achieve their objectives more cost-effectively, nonprofits can benefit from using the commercial infrastructure.

To some corporate leaders, this new approach might seem too self-serving. They might argue that philanthropy is purely a matter of conscience and should not be adulterated by business objectives. In some industries, particularly those like petrochemicals and pharmaceuticals that are prone to public controversy, this view is so entrenched that many companies establish independent charitable foundations and entirely segregate giving from the business. In doing so, however, they give up tremendous opportunities to create greater value for society and themselves. Context-focused philanthropy does not just address a company's self-interest, it benefits many through broad social change. If a company's philanthropy only involved its own interests, after all, it would not qualify as a charitable deduction, and it might well threaten the company's reputation.

There is no inherent contradiction between improving competitive context and making a sincere commitment to bettering society. Indeed, as we've seen, the more closely a company's philanthropy is linked to its competitive context, the greater the company's contribution to society will be. Other areas, where the company neither creates added value nor derives benefit, should appropriately be left – as Friedman asserts – to individual donors following their own charitable impulses. If systematically pursued in a way that maximizes the value created, context-focused philanthropy can offer companies a new set of competitive tools that well justifies the investment or resources. At the same time, it can unlock a vastly more powerful way to make the world a better place.

Chapter 8

CSR in the ecological environment

IN THIS CHAPTER WE WILL:

- Discuss the growing attention to the ecological responsibilities of corporations
- Understand the broad implications of climate change
- Examine the meaning of sustainability in relation to CSR
- Explain some of the core corporate responsibilities in the ecological environment
- Examine how ecological responsibilities can be integrated into corporate strategy

Introduction

To some degree, the current wave of interest in CSR emerged from growing attention to ecological issues in business in the late 1980s and early 1990s. This transformation of ecological responsibilities 'from heresy to dogma' (Hoffman, 2001) brought with it a growing recognition among corporations that effective management of their ecological environment was a necessary part of doing business. To begin with, such responsibilities were mainly couched in terms of pollution prevention, waste minimisation, energy conservation, and recycling. They have since grown to incorporate deeper elements of sustainability, including addressing major global phenomenon such as climate change, biodiversity, and resource scarcity and security.

There are a number of factors driving the increasing attention to ecological problems, including population growth (from the present day 7 billion to an expected 9 billion by 2050), spiralling consumption and resource use in developed countries, major growth in industrialization in Asia and Latin America, the increasing power of

CWS 8.1

See the
companion
website
for more
information
on the cradle-
to-cradle
approach
to product
design, which
seeks to
upcycle rather
than recycle or
downcycle

non-governmental organizations to galvanize public opinion around the issues, sustained attention from regulators, and gathering evidence of the extent and cost to the economy and society of climate change. As a result, while firms now have a range of environmental management tools and techniques at their disposal to deal with ecological responsibilities – such as environmental management systems, the design phenomenon cradle-to-cradle lifecycle analysis (sometimes called C2C), ISO standards, etc. – they also have to face increasing expectations that require them to go beyond their existing technologies.

It is clear then that not only are the ecological responsibilities facing corporations not going away, but they are becoming ever larger, more complex, and challenging to solve.

It is one thing to institute a recycling programme into the office, or introduce 'end-of-pipe' technologies to reduce pollution from the manufacturing plant; it is quite another to consider how to change an entire industrial model to end a reliance on fossil fuels or to innovate a sustainable system of product recapture and reuse that prevents the need for endless supplies of non-renewable resources in the first place. Respected economist Nicholas Stern (2006) argues that the problems associated with climate change are particularly intractable because:

● Climate change is global in its causes and consequences;
● The impacts of climate change are long-term and persistent;
● Uncertainties and risks in the economic impacts are pervasive;
● There is a serious risk of major, irreversible change with non-marginal economic effects.

Concurring with the mainstream scientific perspective, Stern notes that climate change is linked to a failure of economic activity, particularly focusing on key areas that have become completely synonymous with our ideas of progress and development, such as energy, industry, transport, and land use. Yet the effects of climate change,[1] not least access to water, food, health, and use of land and the environment, have profound impacts on economic as well as life, health, and social welfare in the future, and possibly already via the extreme weather events such as the 2004 Indian ocean earthquake and tsunami (230,000 people killed in 14 countries), the 2010 Haiti earthquake (316,000 people died), 2010 Pakistan floods (the worst monsoons in the country's history), and the 2011 Great East Japan Earthquake which is considered to have been the most expensive natural disaster in world history with an economic cost of $US235 billion.

CWS 8.2

See the
companion
website for
more
information on
the causes and
impacts of
climate change
as they relate
to business

Given these economic impacts of climate change-related natural disasters, it is conspicuously the insurance industry that has been among the first corporate players to take climate change seriously. For example, global risk management and insurance company Munich Re states that such extreme weather events are 'a strong indicator' of climate change and critical to their future plans.[2]

From a CSR perspective, ecological issues can either be seen as a separate arena of responsibility from workplace, marketplace, and community issues – or as an issue that cuts through these and other areas. Indeed, there are few CSR issues that do not have some kind of ecological dimension, especially when considering the types of trade-offs between social, ecological, and economic factors that are captured in the notion of sustainability. As we saw in Chapter 3, the label of sustainability is even sometimes used synonymously with CSR in business circles, making clear-cut distinctions between areas of responsibility rather difficult to make. For the purposes of our discussion, however, responsibilities for the ecological environment are concerned with business impacts specifically on the sustainability of the natural environment, the main elements of which we will now introduce.

Core features of ecological responsibility

Sustainability of the natural environment is essentially about the long-term maintenance of the Earth's natural ability to sustain itself. Human progress, and industrialization in particular, are widely thought to pose a severe challenge for the continued sustainability of our society given expectations about increasing resource demands and limits to carrying capacity. For corporations, this presents a number of critical responsibilities in that it is business as much as any other institution that extracts resources, creates pollution through its processes and products, and generates waste that has to be absorbed by the Earth in some way.

To implement these responsibilities, various authors have suggested a number of actions that firms can take including (Bradbury & Clair, 1999; Hart, 1997; Menon & Menon, 1997; Stead & Stead, 2004):

Using natural resources efficiently and minimizing waste

The Earth has limited resources and finite capacity for absorbing waste. Corporations have a role to play in ensuring that non-renewable resources such as fossil fuels are preserved and renewable resources such as soft woods are managed sustainably. Certification bodies such as the Forest Stewardship Council have a role to play here, and companies are realizing that resource input reduction saves costs. This is probably the easiest example of environmental and economic 'win-win' situations. Many companies capitalize on this – for instance innovations in detergent formulations such as Proctor and Gamble's Ariel brand, have led to reduced size packaging, lower energy manufacturing processes, less transportation costs, and lower temperature washing, which in turn saves energy for consumers.[3]

Pollution prevention

Corporations, especially those in manufacturing, can be major polluters, giving rise to responsibilities to minimize pollution (end of pipe technologies) and the causes of pollution (clean technologies). A good example for these technologies is the car industry: in the 1970s, initially in the US and then later in most other parts of the world, the exhausts of cars were first treated by catalytic 'filters' that significantly reduced the emission of air pollutants. In recent years, however, new technologies such as hybrid and electric cars represent an attempt to prevent pollutants to come into existence in the first place.

Establishing product stewardship

Adopting a 'cradle to cradle' approach to product management means that corporations can take responsibility for a product's ecological impacts from resource extraction right through to the end of the life-cycle and reuse. This philosophy has been taken up quite radically by the EU commission in its directives on automobile, white goods, and electronics recycling. As a result, car companies are now obliged in many European countries to take back old cars at their end of life and recycle them into new raw materials (Kanari et al, 2003).

Innovating in products, processes, and services

CWS 8.3

See the companion website for links to Interface's 'Mission Zero' commitment and progress to date

Progress to sustainability will require radical transformations in the kinds of things that corporations do and produce. In order to achieve these changes, they need to innovate for the future. One of the most successful exemplars of a company that has put innovation of products, processes and services at the heart of its sustainability vision is Interface Carpets. Interface has radically redesigned its carpet products, their production processes, and its product delivery model in its quest to achieve what it calls 'Mission Zero' – a promise 'to eliminate any negative impact our company may have on the environment by the year 2020'. To date, Interface has reduced water use per unit by 80 per cent, reduced greenhouse gases by 40 per cent, and reduced energy use per unit by 43 per cent.[4]

Managing climate change

The production of greenhouse gases by industrial processes and products poses a serious challenge to the livelihood of the planet. It is increasingly recognized that firms have a responsibility to manage their carbon footprint by steadily reducing their reliance on fossil fuels and moving to carbon-neutral products and processes. In some countries this has been substantially helped along the way by regulation. The UK Climate Change Act 2008, for example requires that the country's greenhouse gas emissions for 2050 are at least 80 per cent lower than 1990 levels. The global political initiative, the United Nations Framework Convention on Climate Change, established in 1992, seeks to generate global consensus in annual meetings, but their achievements have to date been severely hampered by regional differences, particularly between developed and developing countries, and the rapidly developing BRIC economies (Brazil, Russia, India, and China). For example, the Rio+20 summit in 2012 agreed on the setting of Sustainable Development Goals, but failed to define their content.

Responding to natural disasters

Given the kind of extreme weather disasters mentioned earlier in the chapter, there are growing expectations for companies to respond to such events with substantial investments of time and resources. For example, 15 Toyota Group companies enabled employees to volunteer for recovery support after the Great East Japan Earthquake of 2011, while logistics company Deutsche Post DHL has institutionalized their support function with a Disaster Response Team network comprising 400 specially trained volunteer employees covering nearly all parts of the world prone to natural disasters.[5]

Ensuring resource security and resource justice

Finally, sustainability is not just about whether there are sufficient natural resources, but who owns them and who is able to access them. Corporations may be expected to increasingly play a role in ensuring that scarce, essential resources such as water, oil, and food are available to those who need them. Resource security is a critical strategy for companies taking a longer-term view. Not only is this a global issue related to poverty and potential conflict, but the self-interest of companies also prompts them to consider the problem of ensuring an ongoing supply of the scarce resources they need to stay in business. Hence supermarkets such as Sainsbury's work with farmers to improve efficiency and survival prospects of their food suppliers (Spence & Rinaldi, 2010). Coca-Cola, which experienced major problems relating to its water use in India in the mid-2000s (Rappeport, 2012), has instigated a far-reaching water stewardship programme, pledging to 'work to safely return to nature and communities an amount of water equivalent to what we use in our beverages and their production'.[6]

In all of these areas, corporations can play a significant role. However, because of their nature, the ecological responsibilities of corporations (like so many social responsibilities) are not necessarily individualized responsibilities that firms have to take on alone, but may also sometimes be collective responsibilities that they share with others. In the ecological arena, industry-wide initiatives, partnerships with NGOs and participation in regulatory initiatives with governments have been common forms of CSR for corporations (Bendell, 2000; Jamali & Keshishian, 2009), and many initiatives require collaboration with other firms in the product supply chain. We will explore some of these types of relationships with other actors in more detail in Chapter 11.

Introducing the readings

The two readings both speak to the prevailing discourse around ecological issues and business, that is, how can a phenomenon with such clear externalities for the firm be integrated into the organizations strategy and structures. They show the progression in this topic, with Stuart Hart's reading being first published in the late 1990s, while Pinkse and Kolk's piece first appeared in 2009. At one level, it is intriguing that the two readings, with a gap of more than a decade between them, make broadly the same argument, indicating that business people and those studying business are not yet fully persuaded that environmental issues *should* be embedded in corporate strategy. As with the previous chapters in Section B, seeking to embed CSR issues in the extant business philosophy and practice is still an argument being made and apparently not yet fully won. Indeed in Section C: Managing CSR we develop this perspective further, looking at how CSR might be implemented and managed in organizations through reporting and auditing, strategy and partnership, and self-regulation.

Integrating ecological responsibilities into corporate strategy

The first reading in this chapter is a classic, and indeed one of the first readings in *Harvard Business Review* to deal with environmental issues in business. Written by Stuart Hart, a business school professor now at Cornell University, the paper focuses on describing the ecological problems faced by business and society today, and then spelling out how management of these problems can successfully be integrated within the core strategy of the firm. As such, this very much reflects an instrumental view of CSR, which sees the solution of social or ecological problems as an opportunity for business to make money rather than just as a problem that needs to be avoided or fixed. As Hart makes clear in the final sentence of the reading: 'in the final analysis, it makes good business sense to pursue strategies for a sustainable world.'

Despite this avowedly instrumental stance, Hart also suggests other reasons why corporations should be involved in solving environmental problems – basically, that they are the only ones that can. As he puts it: 'corporations are the only organizations with the resources, the technology, the global reach, and ultimately, the motivation to achieve sustainability' and therefore, 'like it or not, the responsibility for ensuring a sustainable world falls largely on the shoulders of the world's enterprises'. So, in urging corporations to 'lead the way' in solving ecological problems by influencing governments and consumers, we see some echoes of the more political role that corporations can take by engaging in CSR.

Beyond responsiveness to climate change

The second reading narrows the focus somewhat by considering climate change challenges in particular. Thus Pinkse and Kolk reflect on strategic approaches to reducing greenhouse gas (GHG) emissions. They start from the assumption that different strategies are available to companies in dealing with climate change and then go about identifying the main factors that might explain the adoption of a particular strategy. This is important because it rejects a one-size-fits-all approach to climate change, but instead explains variation in corporate response according to various external issues, industry environment, and company specific factors.

The reading then goes on to describe a typology of climate change strategies. In so doing Pinkse and Kolk distinguish between innovation-led strategies (whether via process improvements, product development, or market development), and what they call compensation-led strategies, which focus on carbon trading. This attention to carbon markets is timely, as there is an emerging tradable commodity in the form of CO_2 emissions. The idea behind carbon markets is that since emitters of GHGs do not meet the costs of their actions, such external costs should be priced and then traded. Trading schemes such as this play a key role in climate policies to meet national and global emissions reduction targets. Some companies of course both reduce their own emissions internally, and buy credit on a more or less open market. There remains, however, an ongoing debate about the fairness of an emissions trading scheme wherein cash-rich organizations can buy carbon credits from the less wealthy or can participate in external carbon offsetting projects, while increasing their own emissions still further.

Ultimately, the discussion in this chapter suggests that there may be very good strategic reasons why voluntary corporate responses to ecological problems such as climate change make sense. However, some would argue that continuing within the rules of the current game will at best only mitigate the extremes of the challenge, and will not result in any fundamental change in how business operates in relation to the environment.

Challenges for practice

Take a close look at a company you work for or with which you are familiar.

1.   What regimes must the organization comply with in terms of environmental issues?
     a)   What national and supranational regulation is relevant?
     b)   What industry specific regulations or agreements apply?
     c)   What organizational codes and commitments around the environment are relevant in this case?
     d)   Which of the above has the most material impact on the business' operations?

2. How would you categorize the company's approach to environmental strategy:
   a) According to Hart?
   b) According to Pinkse and Kolk?
   c) Can you discern how the strategy has evolved over time?
3. Imagine you are commissioned with identifying the lessons to learn from the BP Deepwater Horizon oil spill for your company. What would be your key recommendations?

Study questions

1. 'To be responsible, corporations have to be sustainable.' Critically evaluate this statement in the light of current business approaches to the ecological environment.
2. What are the core features of corporate ecological responsibility? To what extent have these responsibilities changed over time?
3. Do ecological problems such as climate change present threats or opportunities to corporations? Provide a critical review based on the readings in this chapter.
4. How can a firm integrate its ecological responsibilities into its core strategies?
5. What are the differences between 'innovation' climate change strategies and 'compensation' strategies? Which, if either, is most likely to lead to climate-friendly corporate impacts?

Further reading

Dyllick, T. & Hockerts, K. (2002) 'Beyond the business case for corporate sustainability', *Business Strategy and the Environment*, 11(2): 130–141. Sustainable business attempts the simultaneous attainment of social, ecological and economic goals. This reading breaks this thinking down in different ways by conceptualizing – next to economic capital – 'natural' and 'social' capital, and then develops a set of criteria along which these different forms of capital can be managed by the firm.

Revell, A., Stokes, D., & Chen, H. (2010) 'Small businesses and the environment: turning over a new leaf?' *Business Strategy and the Environment*, 19: 273–288. This reading develops previous studies on the response of small business to environmental issues where they are often identified as laggards in attending to environmental challenges. The authors find that a high percentage of owner-managers are actively involved in recycling, energy efficiency, responsible buying and selling, and efforts to reduce their carbon emissions. This has resonance with the Stern Review's (2006) conclusions that the benefits of strong early action on climate change outweigh the costs, and that a transition to a low-carbon economy will bring opportunities for business growth.

Endnotes

1   If temperatures continue to rise, an increase of 2–3°C is predicted for around 2050, which would cause glacier melt, crop yield reduction, ocean acidification, rising sea levels, spreading of malnutrition, heat-stress and disease, ecosystem damage, and species extinction (Stern, 2006).

2   www.munichre.com/en/media_relations/company_news/2010/2010-11-08_company_news.aspx (Accessed 30 August, 2012).

3   www.pg.com/en_US/brands/household_care/ariel.shtml (Accessed 30 August, 2012).

4   www.interfaceglobal.com/Sustainability.aspx (Accessed 30 August, 2012).

5   www.toyota-global.com/sustainability/corporate_citizenship/society_and_culture/volunteer_activities/v_reconstruction/; www.dp-dhl.com/en/responsibility/disaster-management/disaster_response_drt.html (Accessed 30 August, 2012).

6   www.thecoca-colacompany.com/citizenship/water_main.html (Accessed 30 August, 2012).

References

Bendell, J. (ed.) (2000) *Terms for endearment: business, NGOs and sustainable development*, Sheffield: Greenleaf.

Bradbury, H. & Clair, J. A. (1999) 'Promoting sustainable organizations with Sweden's Natural Step', *Academy of Management Executive*, 13(4): 63–74.

Braungard, M. & McDonough, W. (2009) *Cradle to cradle: re-making the way we make things*, London: Random House.

Hart, S. L. (1997) 'Beyond greening: strategies for a sustainable world', *Harvard Business Review*, (January–February): 67–76.

Hoffman, A. J. (2001) *From heresy to dogma: an institutional history of corporate environmentalism* (expanded edn), Palo Alto, CA: Stanford University Press.

Jamali, D. & Keshishian, T. (2009) 'Uneasy alliances: lessons learned from partnerships between businesses and NGOs in the context of CSR', *Journal of Business Ethics*, 84(2): 277–295.

Kanari, N., Pineau, J. L., & Shallari, S. (2003) 'End-of-life vehicle recycling in the European Union', *JOM Journal of the Minerals, Metals and Materials Society*, 55(8): 15–19.

Menon, A. & Menon, A. (1997) 'Enviropreneurial marketing strategy: the emergence of corporate environmentalism as market strategy', *Journal of Marketing*, 61(1): 51–67.

Rappeport, A. (2012) 'Coke's $3bn to add fizz to India presence', *Financial Times*, June 26.

Smith, L. C., Murphy Smith, L., & Ashcroft, P. A. (2011) 'Analysis of environmental and economic damages from British Petroleum's Deepwater Horizon oil spill', *Albany Law Review*, 75(2): 563–585.

Spence, L. J. & Rinaldi, L. (2010) 'Sainsbury's: embedding sustainability in the supermarket supply chain', in A. Hopwood, J. Unerman and J. Fries (eds) *Accounting for sustainability: practical insights*, London: Earthscan, 47–71.

Stead, W. E. & Stead, J. G. (2004) *Sustainable strategic management*, London: M. E. Sharpe.

Stern, N. (2006) *The economics of climate change: the Stern Review*, Cambridge: Cambridge University Press.

BEYOND GREENING:
STRATEGIES FOR A SUSTAINABLE WORLD

Stuart Hart

The environmental revolution has been almost three decades in the making, and it has changed forever how companies do business. In the 1960s and 1970s, corporations were in a state of denial regarding their impact on the environment. Then a series of highly visible ecological problems created a groundswell of support for strict government regulation. In the United States, Lake Erie was dead. In Europe, the Rhine was on fire. In Japan, people were dying of mercury poisoning.

Today many companies have accepted their responsibility to do no harm to the environment. Products and production processes are becoming cleaner, and where such change is under way, the environment is on the mend. In the industrialized nations, more and more companies are "going green" as they realize that they can reduce pollution and increase profits simultaneously. We have come a long way.

But the distance we've traveled will seem small when, in 30 years, we look back at the 1990s. Beyond greening lies an enormous challenge – and an enormous opportunity. The challenge is to develop a *sustainable global economy*: an economy that the planet is capable of supporting indefinitely. Although we may be approaching ecological recovery in the developed world, the planet as a whole remains on an unsustainable course. Those who think that sustainability is only a matter of pollution control are missing the bigger picture. Even if all the companies in the developed world were to achieve zero emissions by the year 2000, the earth would still be stressed beyond what biologists refer to as its carrying capacity. Increasingly, the scourges of the late twentieth century – depleted farmland, fisheries, and forests; choking urban pollution; poverty; infectious disease; and migration – are spilling over geopolitical borders. The simple fact is this: in meeting our needs, we are destroying the ability of future generations to meet theirs.

The roots of the problem – explosive population growth and rapid economic development in the emerging economies – are political and social issues that exceed the mandate and the capabilities of any corporation. At the same time, corporations are the only organizations with the resources, the technology, the global reach, and, ultimately, the motivation to achieve sustainability.

It is easy to state the case in the negative: faced with impoverished customers, degraded environments, failing political systems, and unraveling societies, it will be increasingly difficult for corporations to do business. But the positive case is even more powerful. The more we learn about the challenges of sustainability, the clearer it is that we are poised at the threshold of a historic moment in which many of the world's industries may be transformed.

To date, the business logic for greening has been largely operational or technical: bottom-up pollution-prevention programs have saved companies billions of dollars. However, few executives realize that environmental opportunities might actually become a major source of *revenue growth*. Greening has been framed in terms of risk reduction, reengineering, or cost cutting. Rarely is greening linked to strategy or technology development, and as a result, most companies fail to recognize opportunities of potentially staggering proportions.

Worlds in Collision

The achievement of sustainability will mean billions of dollars in products, services, and technologies that barely exist today. Whereas yesterday's businesses were often oblivious to their negative impact on the environment and today's responsible businesses strive for zero impact, tomorrow's businesses must learn to make a positive impact. Increasingly, companies will be selling solutions to the world's environmental problems.

Envisioning tomorrow's businesses, therefore, requires a clear understanding of those problems. To move beyond greening to sustainability, we must first unravel a complex set of global interdependencies. In fact, the global economy is really three different, overlapping economies.

The *market economy* is the familiar world of commerce comprising both the developed nations and the emerging economies.[1] About a billion people – one-sixth of the world's population – live in the developed countries of the market economy. Those affluent societies account for more than 75 percent of the world's energy and resource consumption and create the bulk of industrial, toxic, and consumer waste. The developed economies thus leave large ecological *footprints* – defined as the amount of land required to meet a typical consumer's needs. (See Exhibit 1, "Ecological footprints.")

Despite such intense use of energy and materials, however, levels of pollution are relatively low in the developed economies. Three factors account for this seeming paradox: stringent environmental regulations, the greening of industry, and the relocation of the most polluting activities (such as commodity processing and heavy manufacturing) to the emerging market economies. Thus to some extent the greening of the developed world has been at the expense of the environments in emerging economies. Given the much larger population base in those countries, their rapid industrialization could easily offset the environmental gains made in the developed economies. Consider, for example, that the emerging economies in Asia and Latin America (and now Eastern Europe and the former Soviet Union) have added nearly 2 billion people to the market economy over the past 40 years.

With economic growth comes urbanization. Today one of every three people in the world lives in a city. By 2025, it will be two out of three. Demographers predict that by that year there will be well over 30 megacities with populations exceeding 8 million and more than 500 cities with populations exceeding 1 million. Urbanization on this scale presents enormous infrastructural and environmental challenges.

Because industrialization has focused initially on commodities and heavy manufacturing, cities in many emerging economies suffer from oppressive levels of pollution. Acid rain is a growing problem, especially in places where coal combustion is unregulated. The World Bank estimates that by 2010 there will be more than 1 billion motor vehicles in the world. Concentrated in cities, they will double current levels of energy use, smog precursors, and emissions of greenhouse gas.

The second economy is the *survival economy*: the traditional, village-based way of life found in the rural parts of most developing countries. It is

United States

The Netherlands

India

In the United States, it takes 12.2 acres to supply the average person's basic needs; in the Netherlands, 8 acres; in India, 1 acre. The Dutch ecological footprint covers 15 times the area of the Netherlands, whereas India's footprint exceeds its area by only about 35 percent. Most strikingly, if the entire world lived like North Americans, it would take three planet Earths to support the present world population

Source: Donella Meadows, "Our 'Footprints' Are Treading Too Much Earth," *Charleston (S.C.) Gazette*, April 1, 1996.

Exhibit 1 Ecological footprints

made up of 3 billion people, mainly Africans, Indians, and Chinese who are subsistence oriented and meet their basic needs directly from nature. Demographers generally agree that the world's population, currently growing by about 90 million people per year, will roughly double over the next 40 years. The developing nations will account for 90 percent of that growth, and most of it will occur in the survival economy.

Owing in part to the rapid expansion of the market economy, existence in the survival economy is becoming increasingly precarious. Extractive industries and infrastructure development have, in many cases, degraded the ecosystems upon which the survival economy depends. Rural populations are driven further into poverty as they compete for scarce natural resources. Women and children now spend on average four to six hours per day searching for fuelwood and four to six hours per day drawing and carrying water. Ironically, those conditions encourage high fertility rates because, in the short run, children help the family to garner needed resources. But in the long run, population growth in the survival economy only reinforces a vicious cycle of resource depletion and poverty.

Short-term survival pressures often force these rapidly growing rural populations into practices that cause long-term damage to forests, soil, and water. When wood becomes scarce, people burn dung for fuel, one of the greatest – and least well-known – environmental hazards in the world today. Contaminated drinking water is an equally grave problem. The World Health Organization estimates that burning dung and drinking contaminated water together cause 8 million deaths per year.

As it becomes more and more difficult to live off the land, millions of desperate people migrate to already overcrowded cities. In China, for example, an estimated 120 million people now roam from city to city, landless and jobless, driven from their villages by deforestation, soil erosion, floods, or droughts. Worldwide, the number of such "environmental refugees" from the survival economy may be as high as 500 million people, and the figure is growing.

The third economy is *nature's economy*, which consists of the natural systems and resources that support the market and the survival economies. Nonrenewable resources, such as oil, metals, and other minerals, are finite. Renewable resources, such as soils and forests, will replenish themselves – as long as their use does not exceed critical thresholds.

Technological innovations have created substitutes for many commonly used non-renewable resources, for example, optical fiber now replaces copper wire. And in the developed economies, demand for some virgin materials may actually diminish in the decades ahead because of reuse and recycling. Ironically, the greatest threat to sustainable development today is depletion of the world's *renewable* resources.

Forests, soils, water, and fisheries are all being pushed beyond their limits by human population growth and rapid industrial development. Insufficient fresh water may prove to be the most vexing problem in the developing world over the next decade, as agricultural, commercial, and residential uses increase. Water tables are being drawn down at an alarming rate, especially in the most heavily populated nations, such as China and India.

Soil is another resource at risk. More than 10 percent of the world's topsoil has been seriously eroded. Available cropland and rangeland are shrinking. Existing crop varieties are no longer responding to increased use of fertilizer. As a consequence, per capita world production of both grain and meat peaked and began to decline during the 1980s. Meanwhile, the world's 18 major oceanic fisheries have now reached or actually exceeded their maximum sustainable yields.

By some estimates, humankind now uses more than 40 percent of the planet's net primary productivity. If, as projected, the population doubles over the next 40 years, we may outcompete most other animal species for food, driving many to extinction. In short, human activity now exceeds sustainability on a global scale. (See Exhibit 2, "Major challenges to sustainability.")

As we approach the twenty-first century, the interdependence of the three economic spheres is increasingly evident. In fact, the three economies have become worlds in collision, creating the major social and environmental challenges facing the planet: climate change, pollution, resource depletion, poverty, and inequality.

Consider, for example, that the average American today consumes 17 times more than his or her Mexican counterpart (emerging economy) and hundreds of times more than the average Ethiopian (survival economy). The levels of material and energy consumption in the United States require large quantities of raw materials and commodities, sourced increasingly from the survival economy and produced in emerging economies.

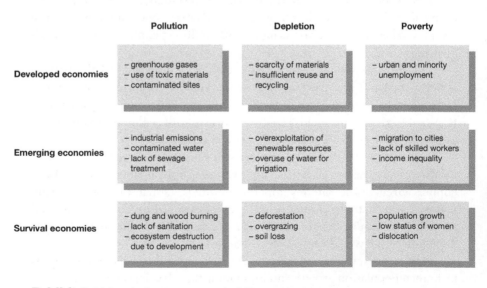

	Pollution	Depletion	Poverty
Developed economies	– greenhouse gases – use of toxic materials – contaminated sites	– scarcity of materials – insufficient reuse and recycling	– urban and minority unemployment
Emerging economies	– industrial emissions – contaminated water – lack of sewage treatment	– overexploitation of renewable resources – overuse of water for irrigation	– migration to cities – lack of skilled workers – income inequality
Survival economies	– dung and wood burning – lack of sanitation – ecosystem destruction due to development	– deforestation – overgrazing – soil loss	– population growth – low status of women – dislocation

Exhibit 2 Major challenges to sustainability

In the survival economy, massive infrastructure development (for example, dams, irrigation projects, highways, mining operations, and power generation projects), often aided by agencies, banks, and corporations in the developed countries, has provided access to raw materials. Unfortunately, such development has often had devastating consequences for nature's economy and has tended to strengthen existing political and economic elites, with little benefit to those in the survival economy.

At the same time, infrastructure development projects have contributed to a global glut of raw materials and hence to a long-term fall in commodity prices. And as commodity prices have fallen relative to the prices of manufactured goods, the currencies of developing countries have weakened and their terms of trade have become less favorable. Their purchasing power declines while their already substantial debt load becomes even larger. The net effect of this dynamic has been the transfer of vast amounts of wealth (estimated at $40 billion per year since 1985) from developing to developed countries, producing a vicious cycle of resource exploitation and pollution to service mounting debt. Today developing nations have a combined debt of more than $1.2 trillion, equal to nearly half of their collective gross national product.

Strategies for a Sustainable World

Nearly three decades ago, environmentalists such as Paul Ehrlich and Barry Commoner made this simple but powerful observation about sustainable development: the total environmental burden (EB) created by human activity is a function of three factors. They are population (P); affluence (A), which is a proxy for consumption; and technology (T), which is how wealth is created. The product of these three factors determines the total environmental burden. It can be expressed as a formula: $EB = P \times A \times T$.

Achieving sustainability will require stabilizing or reducing the environmental burden. That can be done by decreasing the human population, lowering the level of affluence (consumption), or changing fundamentally the technology used to create wealth. The first option, lowering the human population, does not appear feasible short of draconian political measures or the occurrence of a major public-health crisis that causes mass mortality.

The second option, decreasing the level of affluence, would only make the problem worse, because poverty and population growth go hand in hand: demographers have long known that birth rates are inversely correlated with level of education and standard of living. Thus stabilizing the human population will require improving the education and economic standing of the world's poor, particularly women of childbearing age. That can be accomplished only by creating wealth on a massive scale. Indeed, it may be necessary to grow the world economy as much as tenfold just to provide basic amenities to a population of 8 billion to 10 billion.

That leaves the third option: changing the technology used to create the goods and services that constitute the world's wealth. Although population and consumption may be societal issues, technology is the business of business.

If economic activity must increase tenfold over what it is today just to provide the bare essentials to a population double its current size, then technology will have to improve twentyfold merely to keep the planet at its current levels of environmental burden. Those who believe that ecological disaster will somehow be averted must also appreciate the commercial implications of such a belief: over the next decade or so, sustainable development will constitute one of the biggest opportunities in the history of commerce.

Nevertheless, as of today few companies have incorporated sustainability into their strategic thinking. Instead, environmental strategy consists largely of piecemeal projects aimed at controlling or preventing pollution. Focusing on sustainability requires putting business strategies to a new test. Taking the entire planet as the context in which they do business, companies must ask whether they are part of the solution to social and environmental problems or part of the problem. Only when a company thinks in those terms can it begin to develop a vision of sustainability – a shaping logic that goes beyond today's internal, operational focus on greening to a more external, strategic focus on sustainable development. Such a vision is needed to guide companies through three stages of environmental strategy.

Stage One: Pollution Prevention. The first step for most companies is to make the shift from pollution control to pollution prevention. Pollution control means cleaning up waste after it has been created. Pollution prevention focuses on minimizing or eliminating waste before it is created. Much like total quality management, pollution prevention strategies depend on continuous improvement efforts to reduce waste and energy use. This transformation is driven by a compelling logic: pollution prevention pays. Emerging global standards for environmental management systems (ISO 14000, for example) also have created strong incentives for companies to develop such capabilities.

Over the past decade, companies have sought to avoid colliding with nature's economy (and incurring the associated added costs) through greening and prevention strategies. Aeroquip Corporation, a $2.5 billion manufacturer of hoses, fittings, and couplings, saw an opportunity here. Like most industrial suppliers, Aeroquip never thought of itself as a provider of environmental solutions. But in 1990, its executives realized that the company's products might be especially valuable in meeting the need to reduce waste and prevent pollution. Aeroquip has generated a $250 million business by focusing its attention on developing products that reduce emissions. As companies in emerging economies realize the competitive benefits of using raw materials and resources more productively, businesses like Aeroquip's will continue to grow.

The emerging economies cannot afford to repeat all the environmental mistakes of Western development. With the sustainability imperative in mind, BASF, the German chemical giant, is helping to design and build chemical industries in China, India, Indonesia, and Malaysia that are less polluting than in the past. By colocating facilities that in the West have been geographically dispersed, BASF is able to create industrial ecosystems in which the waste from one process becomes the raw material for another. Colocation solves a problem common in the West, where recycling waste is often infeasible because transporting it from one site to another is dangerous and costly.

Stage Two: Product Stewardship. Product stewardship focuses on minimizing not only pollution from manufacturing but also all environmental impacts associated with the full life cycle of a product. As companies in stage one move closer to zero emissions, reducing the use of materials and production of waste requires fundamental changes in underlying product and process design.

Design for environment (DFE), a tool for creating products that are easier to recover, reuse, or recycle, is becoming increasingly important. With DFE, all the effects that a product could have on the environment are examined during its design phase. Cradle-to-grave analysis begins and ends outside the boundaries of a company's operations – it includes a full assessment of all inputs to the product and examines how customers use and dispose of it. DFE thus captures a broad range of external perspectives by including technical staff, environmental experts, end customers, and even community representatives in the process. Dow Chemical Company has pioneered the use of a board-level advisory panel of environmental experts and external representatives to aid its product-stewardship efforts.

By reducing materials and energy consumption, DFE can be highly profitable. Consider Xerox Corporation's Asset Recycle Management (ARM) program, which uses leased Xerox copiers as sources of high-quality, low-cost parts and components for new machines. A well-developed infrastructure for taking back leased copiers combined with a sophisticated remanufacturing process allows parts and components to be reconditioned, tested, and then reassembled into "new" machines. Xerox estimates that ARM savings in raw materials, labor, and waste disposal in 1995 alone were in the $300-million to $400-million range. In taking recycling to this level, Xerox has reconceptualized its business. By redefining the product-in-use as part of the company's asset base, Xerox has discovered a way to add value and lower costs. It can continually provide its lease customers with the latest product upgrades, giving them state-of-the-art functionality with minimal environmental impact.

Product stewardship is thus one way to reduce consumption in the developed economies. It may also aid the quest for sustainability because developing nations often try to emulate what they see happening in the developed nations. Properly executed, product stewardship also offers the potential for revenue growth through product differentiation. For example, Dunlop Tire Corporation and Akzo Nobel recently announced a new radial

Aracruz Celulose: A Strategy for the Survival Economy

"Poverty is one of the world's leading polluters," notes Erling Lorentzen, founder and chairman of Aracruz Celulose. The $2 billion Brazilian company is the world's largest producer of eucalyptus pulp. "You can't expect people who don't eat a proper meal to be concerned about the environment."[1]

From the very start, Aracruz has been built around a vision of sustainable development. Lorentzen understood that building a viable forest-products business in Brazil's impoverished and deforested state of Espirito Santo would require the simultaneous improvement of nature's economy and the survival economy.

First, to restore nature's economy, the company took advantage of a tax incentive for tree planting in the late 1960s and began buying and reforesting cut-over land. By 1992, the company had acquired over 200,000 hectares and planted 130,000 hectares with managed eucalyptus; the rest was restored as conservation land. By reforesting what had become highly degraded land, unsuitable for agriculture, the company addressed a fundamental environmental problem. At the same time, it created a first-rate source of fiber for its pulping operations. Aracruz's forest practices and its ability to clone seedlings have given the company advantages in both cost and quality.

Aracruz has tackled the problem of poverty head-on. Every year, the company gives away millions of eucalyptus seedlings to local farmers. It is a preemptive strategy, aimed at reducing the farmers' need to deplete the natural forests for fuel or lumber. Aracruz also has a long-term commitment to capability building. In the early years, Aracruz was able to hire local people for very low wages because of their desperate situation. But instead of simply exploiting the abundant supply of cheap labor, the company embarked on an aggressive social-investment strategy, spending $125 million to support the creation of hospitals, schools, housing, and a training center for employees. In fact, until recently, Aracruz spent more on its social investments than it did on wages (about $1.20 for every $1 in wages). Since that time, the standard of living has improved dramatically, as has productivity. The company no longer needs to invest so heavily in social infrastructure.

1 Marguerite Rigoglioso, "Stewards of the Seventh Generation," *Harvard Business School Bulletin*, April 1996, p. 55.

tire that makes use of an aramid fiber belt rather than the conventional steel belt. The new design makes recycling easier because it eliminates the expensive cryogenic crushing required to separate the steel belts from the tire's other materials. Because the new fiber-belt tire is 30 percent lighter, it dramatically improves gas mileage. Moreover, it is a safer tire because it improves the traction control of antilock braking systems.

The evolution from pollution prevention to product stewardship is now happening in multinational companies such as Dow, DuPont, Monsanto, Xerox, ABB, Philips, and Sony. For example, as part of a larger sustainability strategy dubbed A Growing Partnership with Nature, DuPont's agricultural products business developed a new type of herbicide that has helped farmers around the world reduce their annual use of chemicals by more than 45 million pounds. The new Sulfonylurea herbicides have also led to a 1-billion-pound reduction in the amount of chemical waste produced in the manufacture of agricultural chemicals. These herbicides are effective at 1 percent to 5 percent of the application rates of traditional chemicals, are non-toxic to animals and nontarget species, and biodegrade in the soil, leaving virtually no residue on crops. Because they require so much less material in their manufacture, they are also highly profitable.

Stage Three: Clean Technology. Companies with their eye on the future can begin to plan for and invest in tomorrow's technologies. The simple fact is that the existing technology base in many industries is not environmentally sustainable. The chemical industry, for example, while having made substantial headway over the past decade in pollution prevention and product stewardship, is still limited by its dependence on the chlorine molecule. (Many organochlorides are toxic or persistent or bioaccumulative.) As long as the industry relies on its historical competencies in chlorine chemistry, it will have trouble making major progress toward sustainability.

Monsanto is one company that is consciously developing new competencies. It is shifting the technology base for its agriculture business from bulk chemicals to biotechnology. It is betting that the bioengineering of crops rather than the application of chemical pesticides or fertilizers represents a sustainable path to increased agricultural yields.

Clean technologies are desperately needed in the emerging economies of Asia. Urban pollution there has reached oppressive levels. But precisely because manufacturing growth is so high – capital stock doubles every six years – there is an unprecedented opportunity to replace current product and process technologies with new, cleaner ones.

Japan's Research Institute for Innovative Technology for the Earth is one of several new research and technology consortia focusing on the development and commercialisation of clean technologies for the developing world. Having been provided with funding and staff by the Japanese government and more than 40 corporations, RITE has set forth an ambitious

100-year plan to create the next generation of power technology, which will eliminate or neutralize greenhouse gas emissions.

Sustainability Vision

Pollution prevention, product stewardship, and clean technology all move a company toward sustainability. But without a framework to give direction to those activities, their impact will dissipate. A vision of sustainability for an industry or a company is like a road map to the future, showing the way products and services must evolve and what new competencies will be needed to get there. Few companies today have such a road map. Ironically, chemical companies, regarded only a decade ago as the worst environmental villains, are among the few large corporations to have engaged the challenge of sustainable development seriously.

Companies can begin by taking stock of each component of what I call their *sustainability portfolio*. (See Exhibit 3, "The Sustainability Portfolio.") Is there an overarching vision of sustainability that gives direction to the company's activities? To what extent has the company progressed through the three stages of environmental strategy – from pollution prevention to product stewardship to clean technology?

Consider the auto industry. During the 1970s, government regulation of tailpipe emissions forced the industry to focus on pollution control. In the 1980s, the industry began to tackle pollution prevention. Initiatives such as the Corporate Average Fuel Efficiency requirement and the Toxic Release Inventory led auto companies to examine their product designs and manufacturing processes in order to improve fuel economy and lower emissions from their plants.

The 1990s are witnessing the first signs of product stewardship. In Germany, the 1990 "take-back" law required auto manufacturers to take responsibility for their vehicles at the end of their useful lives. Innovators such as BMW have influenced the design of new cars with their *design for disassembly* efforts. Industry-level consortia such as the Partnership for a New Generation of Vehicles are driven largely by the product stewardship logic of lowering the environmental impact of automobiles throughout their life cycle.

Early attempts to promote clean technology include such initiatives as California's zero-emission vehicle law and the U.N. Climate Change Convention, which ultimately will limit greenhouse gases on a global scale. But early efforts by industry incumbents have been either incremental – for example, natural-gas vehicles – or defensive in nature. Electric-vehicle programs, for instance, have been used to demonstrate the infeasibility of this technology rather than to lead the industry to a fundamentally cleaner technology.

tomorrow	**Clean technology** Is the environmental performance of our products limited by our existing competency base? Is there potential to realize major improvements through new technology?	**Sustainability vision** Does our corporate vision direct us toward the solution of social and environmental problems? Does our vision guide the development of new technologies, markets, products, and processes?
today	**Pollution prevention** Where are the most significant waste and emission streams from our current operations? Can we lower costs and risks by eliminating waste of the source or by using it as useful input?	**Product stewardship** What are the implications for product design and development if we assume responsibility for a product's entire life cycle? Can we add value or lower costs while simultaneously reducing the impact of our products?
	internal	**external**

This simple diagnostic tool can help any company determine whether its strategy is consistent with sustainability. First, assess your company's capability in each of the four quadrants by answering the questions in each box. Then rate yourself on the following scale for each quadrant: 1–nonexistent; 2–emerging; 3–established; or 4–institutionalized.

Most companies will be heavily skewed toward the lower left-hand quadrant, reflecting investment in pollution prevention. However, without investments in future technologies and markets (the upper half of the portfolio), the company's environmental strategy will not meet evolving needs.

Unbalanced portfolios spell trouble: a bottom-heavy portfolio suggests a good position today but future vulnerability. A top-heavy portfolio indicates a vision of sustainability without the operational or analytical skills needed to implement it. A portfolio skewed to the left side of the chart indicates a preoccupation with handling the environmental challenge through internal process improvements and technology-development initiatives. Finally, a portfolio skewed to the right side, although highly open and public, runs the risk of being labeled a "greenwash" because the underlying plant operations and core technology still cause significant environmental harm.

Exhibit 3 The sustainability portfolio

Although the auto industry has made progress, it falls far short of sustainability. For the vast majority of auto companies, pollution prevention and product stewardship are the end of the road. Most auto executives assume that if they close the loop in both production and design, they will have accomplished all the necessary environmental objectives.

But step back and try to imagine a sustainable vision for the industry. Growth in the emerging markets will generate massive transportation needs in the coming decades. Already the rush is on to stake out positions in China, India, and Latin America. But what form will this opportunity take?

Consider the potential impact of automobiles on China alone. Today there are fewer than 1 million cars on the road in China. However, with a population of more than 1 billion, it would take less than 30 percent market penetration to equal the current size of the U.S. car market (12 million to 15 million units sold per year). Ultimately, China might demand 50 million or more units annually. Because China's energy and transportation infrastructures are still being defined, there is an opportunity to develop a clean technology yielding important environmental and competitive benefits.

Amory Lovins of the Rocky Mountain Institute has demonstrated the feasibility of building *hypercars* – vehicles that are fully recyclable, 20 times more energy efficient, 100 times cleaner, and cheaper than existing cars. These vehicles retain the safety and performance of conventional cars but achieve radical simplification through the use of lightweight, composite materials, fewer parts, virtual prototyping, regenerative braking, and very small, hybrid engines. Hypercars, which are more akin to computers on wheels than to cars with microchips, may render obsolete most of the competencies associated with today's auto manufacturing – for example, metal stamping, tool and die making, and the internal combustion engine.

Assume for a minute that clean technology like the hypercar or Mazda's soon-to-be-released hydrogen rotary engine can be developed for a market such as China's. Now try to envision a transportation infrastructure capable of accommodating so many cars. How long will it take before gridlock and traffic jams force the auto industry to a halt? Sustainability will require new transportation solutions for the needs of emerging economies with huge populations. Will the giants in the auto industry be prepared for such radical change, or will they leave the field to new ventures that are not encumbered by the competencies of the past?

A clear and fully integrated environmental strategy should not only guide competency development, it should also shape the company's relationship to customers, suppliers, other companies, policymakers, and all its stakeholders. Companies can and must change the way customers think by creating preferences for products and services consistent with sustainability. Companies must become educators rather than mere marketers of products. (See Exhibit 4, "Building sustainable business strategies.")

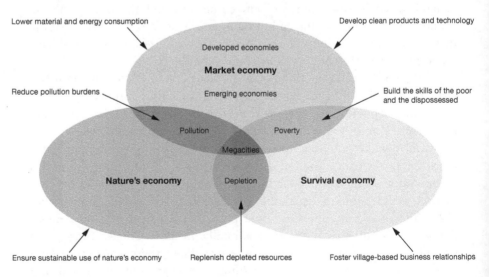

Exhibit 4 Building sustainable business strategies

For senior executives, embracing the quest for sustainability may well require a leap of faith. Some may feel that the risks associated with investing in unstable and unfamiliar markets outweigh the potential benefits. Others will recognize the power of such a positive mission to galvanize people in their organizations.

Regardless of their opinions on sustainability, executives will not be able to keep their heads in the sand for long. Since 1980, foreign direct investment by multinational corporations has increased from $500 billion to nearly $3 trillion per year. In fact, it now exceeds official development-assistance aid in developing countries. With free trade on the rise, the next decade may see the figure increase by another order of magnitude. The challenges presented by emerging markets in Asia and Latin America demand a new way of conceptualizing business opportunities. The rapid growth in emerging economies cannot be sustained in the face of mounting environmental deterioration, poverty, and resource depletion. In the coming decade, companies will be challenged to develop clean technologies and to implement strategies that drastically reduce the environmental burden in the developing world while simultaneously increasing its wealth and standard of living.

Like it or not, the responsibility for ensuring a sustainable world falls largely on the shoulders of the world's enterprises, the economic engines of the future. Clearly, public policy innovations (at both the national and international levels) and changes in individual consumption patterns will be needed to move toward sustainability. But corporations can and should lead the way, helping to shape public policy and driving change in consumers' behavior. In the final analysis, it makes good business sense to pursue strategies for a sustainable world.

Note

1   The terms *market economy, survival economy*, and *nature's economy* were suggested to me by Vandana Shiva, *Ecology and the Policies of Survival* (New Delhi: United Nations University Press, 1991).

BUSINESS STRATEGIES FOR CLIMATE CHANGE

Jonathan Pinkse and Ans Kolk

Emissions measurement, target setting and reporting, as discussed in the previous chapter, are generally considered to be the initial activities in a company's response to climate change. A common next step is evaluating and implementing options for the reduction of greenhouse gas (GHG) emissions in order to reach the aspirations expressed by the climate change targets. For most companies this means deploying a range of relatively 'easy-to-implement' activities that involve some basic technological and behavioural changes (Hoffman, 2006). Examples of such technological changes include measures to improve energy efficiency and reduce energy consumption such as improving insulation of company properties, introducing energy management systems aimed at a better management of lighting and heating of buildings, and replacing outdated, energy-inefficient production installations. Options for behavioural changes comprise improving employee awareness of the implications of their use of office equipment such as printers and computers for a company's energy consumption and reducing the carbon impact of business travel (Okereke, 2007). Particularly when climate change functions as an eye-opener by showing that there are previously untapped low-cost options to reduce energy use, reduction activities of this kind form the 'low-hanging fruit' of climate change mitigation (Hoffman, 2006). Overall, such activities are largely operational, and concern the integration of climate change in corporate day-to-day practices.

However, although for many companies becoming responsive to climate change does not go much further than operational improvements, this does not fully reveal the current state of companies' business practices. Corporate activities on climate change are not only a way of becoming more efficient operationally, but are also starting to play a role on a more strategic level (Porter and Reinhardt, 2007). Climate change can have a considerable influence on the value proposition of a company (Porter and Kramer, 2006), inducing it to fundamentally reconfigure business activities to simultaneously reduce climatic impact and enhance the competitive position (Kolk and Pinkse, 2008). At present, a range of strategic responses is emerging to address climate change and reduce GHG emissions through product and process improvements and emissions trading with the aim of creating and/or retaining value. The exact composition of such strategic options is company-specific, depending on the (perceived) risks and opportunities related to climate change, the competitive dynamic of the markets in which a company is active, and the type of regulation and stakeholder pressure relevant for the industry and countries in which it operates (Kolk and Levy, 2004).

This chapter examines GHG emissions-reduction options available to companies, focusing on the strategic responses that have emerged most recently, and identifies the actual patterns of market-oriented actions currently being taken. These business strategies for climate change consist of different combinations of the market components available to managers. We present a typology that shows that under current, rather flexible regulatory regimes (see Chapter 2), managers have the possibility to choose between a greater emphasis on improvements in their business activities through innovation on the one hand and compensatory approaches granted by the emerging carbon market on the other. An innovation strategy can improve a company's assets and competencies as a result of the development of new climate-friendly technologies or services that reduce emissions. Compensation involves the transfer of emissions or emissions-generating activities. Companies can follow these approaches merely on their own or by interacting with external actors, be it other companies in the supply chain or industry, non-governmental organizations (NGOs) or government agencies. Before explaining this typology (in section 2), however, we will first give some more background as to the factors that have influenced corporate activities on climate change.

1 FACTORS THAT INFLUENCE CORPORATE POSITIONS ON CLIMATE CHANGE

As with many other sustainability issues, developing strategies to reduce the negative impact on climate change and create a lasting impact on competitiveness is a joint influence of external and company-specific factors (Aragón-Correa and Sharma, 2003; Bansal, 2005; Delmas and Toffel, 2004; Kolk and Levy, 2004; Porter and Reinhardt, 2007) (see Table 8.1). The impact of sustainability issues in general and climate change in particular on companies depends to a large extent on external influences including physical effects, such as extreme weather events, rising sea levels, floods, droughts, etc. (Lash and Wellington, 2007), government policy (Rugman and Verbeke, 1998), and pressure from activists, NGOs, local communities and the media (Bansal, 2005; Buysse and Verbeke, 2003; Eesley and Lenox, 2006). As a consequence, an effective response to climate change relies on the way in which a company is able to anticipate critical incidents such as hurricanes, and, more important in the short term, to integrate the interests of the different stakeholders involved with the issue (Hart, 1995; Sharma and Vredenburg, 1998).

In the longer run, strategically adjusting to climate change is essentially a response to the physical effects of climate change. For example, sectors such as agriculture, food processing, fishery and forestry all depend on raw materials that are vulnerable to changing weather patterns (Lash and Wellington, 2007). For a food company such as Unilever this means that there is an increased risk of a faltering supply of agricultural products from parts of the world that are hit more often by increased occurrences of drought or storms that lower crop yields. Therefore, Unilever pursues a strategy of manufacturing a range of products that diversifies the risks of extreme weather conditions, and it keeps track of emissions related to energy use by taking the type of energy source into account. Likewise, Coca-Cola has started to study potential problems in water availability in parts of the world that may get less precipitation in coming decades (Lash and Wellington, 2007). Physical risks also affect firms that have operations in vulnerable areas (e.g. coastal regions), such as oil and gas companies with oil rigs in hurricane-prone areas such as the Caribbean. Ultimately, increased physical risks of climate change will have an adverse effect on the insurance industry, because they will be called upon when companies incur damages from extreme weather. It will come as no surprise, then, that the world's largest reinsurance companies – Swiss Re and Munich Re – were amongst the first to acknowledge the strategic risks of climate change (Dlugolecki and Keykhah, 2002).

However, in the shorter run, a corporate strategic response is not confined to adjustments in anticipation of the physical impact of climate change, but particularly a reaction to social, economic and political pressures (Kolk and Pinkse, 2004). Most notably, climate change has incited considerable political and regulatory machinery, with the Kyoto Protocol and the EU emissions trading scheme as the main outcomes so far. Climate change regulation is both viewed as a business risk and an opportunity. Which perspective a company holds depends on a wide variety of factors, including the industries and countries in which it operates. Typical industries that perceive it as a risk are the oil and gas industry, the automotive sector, and utilities (Ernst & Young, 2008). This is not surprising in view of the fact that emissions reduction regulation is mainly directed at these industries. In the current design of the European Union emissions trading scheme (EU ETS), for example, energy activities, the production and processing of metals, the mineral industry, and the pulp and paper sector are subject to a cap on greenhouse gas emissions (see Chapter 6).

Still, government regulation is sometimes also viewed as an opportunity. Strict regulation favours companies that have already started to take account

Table 8.1: Factors that influence corporate positions on climate change

Factor	Some components
External, issue-related factors	• Physical impact relevant to types and location of operations • Government policies and regulation • Stakeholder pressures and perceptions (including investors, consumers, NGOs, society at large)
Industry-related factors	• Industry structure (technological and competitive situation) • Industry growth • Concentration level
Company-specific factors	• Position within the supply chain • Economic situation and market positioning • History of involvement with (technological) alternatives • Degree of (de)centralisation • Degree of internationalisation of top management • Availability and type of internal climate expertise
Corporate	• Capacity to anticipate risks, spread vulnerabilities, and • Corporate culture and managerial perceptions • Capacity to anticipate risks, spread vulnerabilities, and manage stakeholders

of climate change in a relatively early phase and potentially crowd out companies that show a poor record with regard to emissions reductions (Levy, 1997). It might also be an opportunity for financial companies, which can assist customers that are affected by such regulation through facilitating their emissions trading activities or financing carbon offset projects for them. Another factor that influences regulatory impact is the geographic spread of a company. While it is quite clear for companies located in the EU what the regulatory impact is, in other countries where climate change regulation is still in a developmental state, such as the US, Canada and Japan, the regulatory impact is more uncertain. Since current investment decisions in installations such as coal-fired power plants will become very costly if regulations are implemented in the near future, regulations will already influence corporate strategy even before they have actually been implemented (Lash and Wellington, 2007).

Climate change has also become a social issue in the sense that people are starting to worry more about the impact on their living conditions. The worldwide box-office success of Al Gore's movie 'An Inconvenient Truth' is the clearest example of this. Correspondingly, NGOs and activists have also stepped up their pressure on companies to deal with the issue of climate change (Boiral, 2006). Not acting on climate change could therefore very well constitute a reputational risk (Hoffman, 2005); or, particularly in the US, a litigation risk (Lash and Wellington, 2007). In the past few years, public opinion in many countries has tilted towards a feeling that companies really should do something about climate change (for more details see the overview of public opinion polls in Chapter 1). Many activities in the field of climate change are therefore initiated to prevent loss of face vis-à-vis the public at large.

However, if maintaining reputation is the main driver, this could lead to climate change activities that reflect legitimacy-seeking behaviour only. The consequence may be that no structural changes will occur (Meyer and Rowan, 1977; Suchman, 1995). If this is the case companies merely pursue measures that satisfy stakeholder requests in the short run, but do not lead to emissions reductions in the long run. To illustrate, while 87 per cent of the companies that answered the Carbon Disclosure Project (CDP) claimed that they take climate change seriously, only 48 per cent had also implemented an emissions reduction programme (CDP, 2006). In other words, there are apparently quite a number of companies that have used the issue to 'greenwash' their public image by taking some small-scale symbolic actions which are broadly communicated (Ramus and Montiel, 2005). Without a doubt several multi-stakeholder partnerships on climate change that we identified in Chapter 3, are used for greenwashing purposes as well, as it is relatively easy to free-ride on the green credentials of some of the front-running companies that take part in a partnership as well (King and Lenox, 2000) or use the brand of renowned NGOs for marketing purposes (Van Huijstee et al, 2007). In the Netherlands, for example, electricity producer

Essent has a partnership with WWF, and uses their Panda label in marketing campaigns, but proposed to build new coal-fired power plants against the will of this NGO anyway.

While social and political pressures are important for companies in drawing their attention to the issue, climate change has, unlike many other environmental issues, a more dominant strategic impact, because it is also driven by market pressures (Hoffman, 2005). Increased attention for climate change makes consumers more aware of the climatic impact of their purchasing behaviour (Bonini *et al*, 2008), which sets in motion a market transition towards the production of less carbon-intensive products and services. A backlash from consumers against companies that have a negative impact on the climate is particularly risky for environmentally sensitive markets or markets where brand value plays an important role in retaining customers (Lash and Wellington, 2007).

In addition, investors fear that if companies in which they invest are not taking action this could lead to unmanageable financial risks. They thus put pressure on companies to minimize these risks, which means that companies which are lagging behind in their carbon management may be excluded from certain sources of capital. At first only oil and gas and electricity companies were hit by climate change-related shareholders' resolutions in this way (Monks *et al*, 2004). However, the *Financial Times* reported in March 2008 that institutional investors are broadening their scope and now also target airlines (e.g. US Airways and Southwest Airlines) and major banks (e.g. Citigroup) that finance carbon-intensive activities such as coal mining (Birchall, 2008).

Besides, the rise of the carbon market has put a price on CO_2 emissions, thus creating a new commodity. This new commodity in turn affects trading patterns in closely related commodities such as coal and natural gas, as it has an impact on the operation costs of power plants (Paolella and Taschini, 2006). Finally, there is market pressure from technological change and innovations by competitors or other companies with products within the same value chain (Okereke, 2007). For example, the development of new (bio)fuels means that car and aeroplane producers need to modify their designs accordingly; or vice-versa, when automotive companies induce technological change, for example by planning to use hydrogen as a fuel, this has implications for fuel suppliers.

It is also important to note that managerial perceptions play a role in companies' responses as well (Levy and Kolk, 2002). In other words, for the type of activities that companies pursue, it matters whether climate change is viewed as the physical impact of weather-related events, forthcoming climate change regulation, or an issue that attracts considerable societal concern (Kolk and Pinkse, 2004). What further complicates an understanding of corporate strategic responses is the fact that climate change does not form an isolated driver for organisational change (Berkhout *et al*, 2006); many other 'internal' drivers play a role as well, such as firms' objective to increase profits, and the particular industry setting should be reckoned with as well. Reducing the impact of or vulnerability to climate change may not always be the primary objective of firms to adjust to climate change.

For example, while in the case of the insurance industry, business responses will be linked to management of weather-related risks (Dlugolecki and Keykhah, 2002), for energy-related industries – e.g. the oil and gas industry, automotives, and electric utilities – it is more likely in anticipation of new government regulation (e.g. the EU ETS) or market pressure from competitors who already follow a more climate-friendly course (Levy and Kolk, 2002). For various other low-carbon industries, the main reason for adapting business practices to climate change may well lie in the fact that it attracts considerable attention from the public and media. Moreover, what further strengthens market transitions towards less carbon-intensive activities is the fact that worry about climate change is also closely entwined with rising energy prices (Okereke, 2007). A 2008 Ernst & Young report of the 10 most important strategic business risks did include climate change in position nine, but the strategic risk from energy shocks ranked even higher in position six (Ernst & Young, 2008).

So type of industry and industry structure play a role in the process of developing a competitive climate change strategy. Whether there are opportunities to create a market for new technologies depends, for example, on industry growth (Russo and Fouts, 1997), and the concentration level of an industry. The industry dynamic, in which companies are involved in the interaction with their competitors, also affects their behaviour vis-à-vis climate change. Companies compete for external funding on the best conditions, and want to increase market share, attract new customers and talented staff, and maintain good relations with investors. This leads to continuous efforts to be more 'attractive' and agile than competitors. Companies closely watch the behaviour of competitors, with a tendency to 'follow the leader' (cf. Knickerbocker, 1973) or to jump on the bandwagon (cf. Abrahamson and Rosenkopf, 1993), regardless or even despite of the fact that this may imply inefficiencies or losses. The clearest example is the automobile industry, where major companies are following Toyota's (first) move towards hybrid vehicles, even when they are not sure whether this will become more than a niche market only. This behaviour is particularly pervasive in highly concentrated markets, dominated by a few large multinationals (Kolk and Levy, 2004). However, there may also be a simple lack of knowledge about what the 'winning' approach will be. This is notable in the oil industry where companies follow different routes regarding (future) energy sources that they all seem to be exploring (Sæverud and Skjærseth, 2007).

Besides the industry, the position of a company in the supply chain stipulates the nature of the core products and services and the responsiveness of customers to the climate change issue. Rethinking product design or developing new products or services is particularly valuable for companies that operate closer to markets for the end-consumer, where differentiation pays off. Companies that are positioned higher up in the supply chain generally produce commodities instead of consumer products and do not have the same opportunity to differentiate their products. It is the dependency on environmentally-conscious consumers and the possibility of changing a product that will have a bearing on the climate strategy in consumer-oriented industries. Whether the customer is an individual or another business will also affect the decision on developing a climate strategy. Whereas business customers are less known for demanding environmentally friendly products, when they choose to do so, their demand will create more leverage, as they are more powerful as a customer. In recent years, for example, companies like Wal-Mart and McDonalds, which used to have rather bad track records on sustainability, have started to demand more sustainable products, thus creating immense pressure on companies supplying the goods that these two companies sell to the end-consumer. If a company directly sells to end-consumers instead, this used to lead to a niche strategy, because the willingness to pay for environmentally sound products was limited to a group of environmentally conscious consumers (Reinhardt, 1998). However, the increased consumer awareness of climate change in recent years may start to lead to a change in this respect, now creating the opportunity to service mass-markets with climate-friendly products as well (Bonini *et al*, 2008).

There are other company-specific factors that shape the specific approach taken. This includes, for example, top management commitment and the degree of internationalisation of top management (Levy and Kolk, 2002). The fact that BP became climate change 'front runner' in the oil industry was for a large part on account of the leadership role taken by John Browne, BP's CEO until May 2007. Similarly, the shift in leadership of ExxonMobil in January 2006 from Lee Raymond to Rex Tillerson appears to have led to a softening stance of this company. Also organizational structure plays a role as this determines for a large part how the strategic planning process takes shape and to what extent addressing an issue like climate change is a centralized or decentralized decision. In addition, organizational culture and a company's specific history shape the perception of climate change. One of the reasons that ExxonMobil has been rather reluctant to invest in renewable energy sources was because it made huge losses on such investments in the 1980s when the Reagan administration suddenly stopped granting large subsidies instigated by the preceding president, Carter. This, combined with the fact that decision authority had been highly centralised as well, left hardly any room for local initiatives that went against the reactive stance of the top of the company at all (Kolk and Levy, 2004).

Whether or not climate change becomes a strategic issue depends in the end on how it is perceived to affect the main value proposition of a company (Porter and Reinhardt, 2007). Even though companies typically emphasize the business opportunities related to climate change rather than the risks

(Kolk and Pinkse, 2004), it is not always the case that climate change is necessarily an issue of strategic importance to a company as well (Porter and Kramer, 2006). Nevertheless, the corporate emphasis on the business opportunities in relation to climate change is not that surprising as it reflects the overall trend that 'win-win' views have started to prevail (Kolk, 2000; Porter and Van der Linde, 1995; Walley and Whitehead, 1994). Of course not all companies have adopted this win-win mentality in the same way. On the one hand, the approach may be that the climate change is evaluated just as any other business issue, which means that it has to compete (at some stage) with other investment opportunities on the same financial criteria. On the other hand, the moral case for climate change may prevail, which means that climate-related activities are pursued, preferably but not necessarily to make a profit (Berger *et al*, 2007).

Typical examples of business opportunities from climate change are benefits from changes in (energy) costs, a potential for creating new markets and the development of new technologies (Hoffman, 2005). Perspectives on the kind of opportunities of climate change are obviously mixed, and depend upon company-specific attributes (Levy and Kolk, 2002). If the effect of emissions trading is that energy prices rise even further than they had already done due to other geopolitical developments, this firstly poses a risk for companies that are energy intensive. Only when companies have the technologies available to actually reduce emissions, will it be associated with savings from less energy use, and thus seen as a potential opportunity instead. A creation of new markets for low-carbon products and services is also seen as an opportunity by many as it pushes sales of products and services that have the potential to lower GHG emissions. However, it is not always easy to tap new markets for energy-efficient products because it may very well require large investments in innovative and new technologies, when no 'easy-to-implement' technologies are available. Likewise, higher demand for green electricity helps utilities that have an energy portfolio with a relatively large share of natural gas, renewable energy sources, and, more controversially, nuclear power (e.g. Electricité de France). But a fundamental switch in the portfolio of energy sources is a very slow and costly process, because historical investments have to be depreciated first, which usually takes around 30 years (Grubb, 2004).

To summarize, then, there are so many external, industry and company-specific factors that have a bearing on the way in which a climate change strategy evolves, that it is very difficult to predict the specific approach that companies will follow. What is more, there is not only a great diversity in drivers for climate strategy development, but companies also have a host of strategic options to choose from; to these we will pay more attention in the second half of this chapter.

2 STRATEGIC OPTIONS FOR ADDRESSING CLIMATE CHANGE

2.1 A typology of climate change strategies

To understand the kind of climate change strategies that have emerged in recent years, in this section we will examine the range of strategic GHG reduction options available to companies. Basically, corporate strategies for climate change consist of different combinations of market components, where companies not only have the option to deal with climate change by changing internal processes, but also involve external actors in the organisational environment in their strategies. The fact that external influences are often significant in first drawing companies' attention to climate change is clearly reflected in the emerging strategies as well. For example, the relatively flexible policies on climate change across the world give companies the opportunity to comply with the goals set by the government in co-operation with third parties. Such co-operative efforts can take place within a company's own supply chain, but can also move beyond the supply chain. This is seen in the formation of partnerships among competitors, and between companies and NGOs to develop and market low-emissions technologies (see Chapter 3).

In addition, emissions trading schemes play a key role in current climate policy, which opens up a whole new array of ways to comply with the regulatory or voluntary targets set for emissions reduction (see Chapters 4 and 6). Consequently, companies have a choice between on the one hand pursuing product- or process-oriented improvements and on the other hand emissions trading. To some extent, this could be seen as a corporate decision related to 'make' or 'buy' emissions reductions. Peculiar to the issue of climate change is, however, that companies can also do both: they can achieve some reductions internally and buy the balance; moreover, it is also possible that companies 'make and sell'. Such a 'make and sell' strategy particularly fits those companies that can reduce emissions at a relatively low cost and sell the ensuing surplus of emissions credits at a profit.

Corporate strategic responses to climate change can be captured by considering the make and/or buy/sell decision on the one hand, and the degree to which this involves interaction with other companies, on the other. When these two aspects are combined, the strategic options can be set out in a matrix with two dimensions: the main aim (strategic intent) and the form of organisation (degree of interaction). In the resulting typology (see Figure 8.1), six strategic options surface that can be part of a more comprehensive strategy for climate change (in which companies combine several options). The vertical axis of the typology is relatively straightforward, since it differentiates the degree to which companies choose interaction with others to reach their objectives. The typology distinguishes three organizational levels: the individual company (internal), companies' own supply chain (vertical), and interaction with companies outside the supply chain (competitors or companies in different sectors – horizontal).

	Main aim	
Organization	Innovation	Compensation
Internal (company)	Process improvement (1)	Internal transfer of emissions credits (2)
Vertical (supply chain)	Product development (3)	Supply chain measures (4)
Horizontal (beyond the supply chain)	New product/market combinations (5)	Acquisition of emissions credits (6)

Figure 8.1: Strategic options for climate change

The horizontal axis deals with differences regarding the main aim of corporate climate strategies. Companies can focus merely on innovation with regard to their own business activities or on compensation. Innovation involves the development of new environmental technologies or services to reduce emissions. The main difference with compensation lies in the fact that innovation fundamentally improves a company's technological capabilities (see also Chapter 7). For example, oil company Royal Dutch/Shell develops solar energy not only to reduce emissions, but also to secure its competitive position in the long run by acquiring new capabilities. Compensation leaves a company's own technological capabilities unaltered; companies use low-emissions and emissions-reduction technologies developed by others.

A company that takes action with regard to climate change does not necessarily adopt all measures identified in the typology, but it is likely that they will use combinations of the different cells. Which of the options will become part of a more comprehensive climate change strategy is likely to depend on managerial perceptions of the issue, as outlined above. Managers that perceive climate change as a business risk may have a tendency to rely on compensatory options. Compensation does not require processes of organisational change to the same extent as the implementation of innovative measures because it does not fundamentally change current process and product technology. It may therefore fit companies that want to avert possible risks in a less strenuous way. Focusing on improvements in business activities may be more apt for those companies that have a clearer view of the opportunities of climate policy. These companies are willing to take the risk of large-scale investments for the development of new environmental technologies, partly because they believe that their long-term survival depends on it.

2.2 Innovation

Innovation is a prime orientation on business activities that are directed at the production process (cell 1 in Figure 8.1) or at products (cell 3). Process improvements frequently encompass energy reduction (and/or higher energy efficiency), as most process improvements are aimed at the reduction of CO_2; generally seen as the main greenhouse gas. For low energy users, such as telecommunications, electronics, insurance and the financial sector, which do not generate large amounts of CO_2 emissions, the most important measure is the implementation of management programmes for energy conservation (for example, good housekeeping systems that control heating and reduce electricity use). This is often combined with a programme to increase staff awareness of energy conservation and restrictions on business travel. However, the relatively low energy-intensity of production activities also means that their potential to mitigate climate change is more limited. A moderate user of energy like the IT industry has more possibilities. Companies like Google and IBM, for example, have announced they will significantly increase energy efficiency of their data centres.

By contrast, energy-intensive industries have more options, but also experience greater external pressure to reduce CO_2 emissions. In industries such as chemicals, mining, metals, utilities, and oil and gas, new energy-efficient technologies are developed and implemented to achieve reductions. Process improvements can also involve measures to diminish the use of other GHGs. For example, semi-conductor producers take initiatives to optimise their production process in order to reduce the emission of perfluorinated compounds (PFCs), a greenhouse gas with a high climatic impact. In agriculture, waste management, and the oil and gas industry the release of methane (CH_4) is an important aspect of climate change strategies. The oil and gas industry can prevent CH_4 emissions by not using gas venting, and either switch to gas flaring (which is not optimal as it causes CO_2 emissions instead) or capture CH_4 and transform it to more productive uses with gas-to-liquid (GTL) technologies.

A supply-chain orientation to innovation is frequently taken by companies in automotives, chemicals, mining and electronics. They can focus on realising emissions reductions of existing products and/or developing new (energy-efficient) products. Many companies in these industries stress that, even though they can sufficiently reduce their own emissions, the impact of their products and services is much larger, and that this therefore seems a better way to reduce GHG emissions. Taking responsibility for emissions caused by the use of products is, for example, done through life-cycle analysis of major products. Companies such as BMW, General Electric, IBM and Unilever use such life-cycle programmes to integrate GHG emissions in the design phase of their products. For Unilever, the climatic impact of its home products strongly depends on household behaviour (e.g. the temperature at which laundry is washed). As a result, the company uses product design based on life-cycle analysis to enable a decrease of household energy consumption. In addition, it has programmes to increase consumer awareness. Computer hardware and electronic companies also follow an approach of improving their products' energy efficiency to help customers reduce emissions. An example is Dell's advertisements regarding the energy-reducing impact of its computer systems, thus enabling customers to diminish their energy use.

Still, as we have seen in Chapter 4, the vast majority of companies do not take into account emissions from the use of products or services, as this depends on uncontrollable factors like consumer behaviour. The main argument purported is that use of products and services does not lead to any significant emissions. This used to be specifically pervasive in service-oriented companies such as finance and insurance, but it has proven to be contestable. That is to say, this trend has been tilting in recent years as more and more reports have been published on the responsibility of the finance and insurance sectors to consider the climatic consequences of asset management (see Allianz/WWF, 2005, 2006). These studies show that there are considerable opportunities for financial companies for product innovation, for example, by developing products to hedge or insure against carbon risks.

In addition to these internal and supply-chain approaches, companies may use the option of drawing upon organisational capabilities as well, by exploring new product/market combinations (Figure 8.1, cell 5). A possible way to enter new markets is by becoming involved in a strategic alliance or another form of co-operation with other companies. The co-operation between many of the major oil and automobile companies in the California Fuel Cell Partnership (including Ford, GM, Toyota, Chevron, BP, Shell and many others) to develop fuel cells is a case in point of developing a whole new market based on hydrogen as a major fuel. Another example is Stora Enso, a Finnish paper, packaging and forest products company, which is using by-products of its core business to enter a new market for biofuels. In the production process of paper and forest products, Stora Enso also produces large amounts of sawmill and logging residues, which are used for the production of biodiesel in a demonstration plant as part of a joint venture with Finnish oil company Neste Oil. In this way, what used to be a waste product is now actively harvested to serve the purpose of entering new markets. Climate policy in the form of emissions trading may also induce companies to position their products and services outside traditional markets. For example, Barclays has become a broker in the carbon market, thus helping to arrange the sale of emissions credits from companies that have a surplus to those that are short on credits.

2.3 Compensation

Different from innovation, compensation includes internal transfer of emissions (Figure 8.1, cell 2), supply chain measures (cell 4), or acquisition of emissions credits through emissions trading or participation in offset projects (cell 6). Compensation means that companies do not primarily aim to reduce GHG emissions, but merely focus on transferring emissions or emissions-generating activities within the company or to other companies.

With regard to emissions-reducing technologies, companies that pursue compensatory approaches act as a passive, arm's length actor because they do not participate in the innovation process themselves. The option to offset emissions is mainly the result of the fact that emissions trading has emerged as the main policy instrument to combat climate change.

Internally oriented compensation particularly fits large companies that operate across borders. These companies can alleviate government pressure to mitigate climate change by transferring high-emissions activities to locations where stringent reduction plans are not (yet) in place. To what extent companies actually pursue this route depends a lot on the capital intensity of an industry. For example, the European steel industry has consistently complained about the regulatory burden of the EU ETS, and threatened to relocate steel mills to countries like China and India. However, in response to environmental regulation, relocation is used more regularly as a threat that is not carried out subsequently (Jaffe *et al*, 1995). What is more likely is that companies use internal or external carbon markets to carry out internal trades, transferring emissions credits between business units. BP and Shell have pioneered this option by setting up internal trading schemes, but this was not without problems (see Chapter 4; Victor and House, 2006). With its maturation and extending spread, it is now much easier to use the external carbon market and follow a policy of considering other business units as preferred trading partners. Integrating targets for emissions into investment decisions for new projects is also a form of internal compensation that fits companies active in a single country only. Another way of internal compensation is maintaining a diversified portfolio of products and services. This is particularly manifest in the car industry where one way of complying with stricter emissions standards is to introduce lighter vehicles to compensate for the excess emissions of the heavier vehicles in a company's product portfolio. To illustrate, for German company Daimler, known for producing large-sized cars under the Mercedes brand, the lightweight Smart helps in easing the regulatory pressure from the forthcoming mandatory European automobile emissions standards.

Supply chain measures for compensation aim to avoid the need for emissions cuts within the company. A company instead seeks to find solutions to ensure that activities and sources of high emissions are carried out elsewhere in the supply chain or that emissions are reduced further up the supply chain. The most common supply-chain measure is monitoring the carbon-intensity of supplied materials or suppliers. For example, Dell requires its most important suppliers to disclose information on their carbon emissions, because if they fail to do so Dell will no longer do business with them. However, the intensity by which suppliers are engaged in a company's own climate change strategy differs considerably. Some companies perform sampled monitoring of a limited number of large suppliers only, while others have detailed emissions targets and guidelines for all their suppliers. It must be noted that GHG emissions are not always that prominent in supplier selection; a number of companies select their suppliers based on more general grounds such as environmental programmes and ISO 14001 certification. For example, BMW expects suppliers to maintain the same environmental standards; UK-based utility Centrica has formed partnerships with suppliers to increase understanding of the complete supply chain.

Another supply chain measure is replacing inputs with a high potential for emissions by those with lower emissions. One way of doing this is substituting fossil fuels with carbon-free renewable energy sources. In non-carbon-intensive sectors, such as telecommunications and service-oriented sectors, this requires procurement of electricity and heating generated from clean energy sources. An example is the 2004 commitment by British Telecom to only purchase electricity that is generated by renewable sources and combined heat and power plants. More recently, in 2007, Google put pressure on electricity producers in a similar way, requiring them to generate at least one-fifth of electricity from renewable energy sources. For companies that use fuels directly for combustion purposes, fuel switching has a much larger impact, however, because it requires a radical change in the production process (for example, through the installation of combined heat and power generators). For utilities and chemical companies, for example, fuel switching means that coal-fired plants have to be replaced by gas-fired plants or divested altogether, which is often merely viewed as a measure of last resort. It should be noted, though, that since substitution of raw materials in many instances requires an adjustment in existing production facilities, this involves some innovation as well. Companies can also subcontract or outsource certain high-emissions activities such as transportation and distribution to reduce emissions internally while increasing those of business partners. In terms of environmental effectiveness, outsourcing has no benefit on an economy-wide scale, unless the subcontractor has specific capabilities, for example in logistics, that makes the whole distribution process more efficient than would be the case had the outsourcing company done it internally.

Finally, companies can also move beyond the supply chain and achieve reductions by interacting with others, either by buying emissions credits or by other forms of offsets, for example through the Clean Development Mechanism (CDM) or Joint Implementation (JI). By acting as a buyer on the carbon market, a company can balance its excess emissions. Similarly, offset projects designed under the Kyoto Protocol enable a company to attain and transfer credits by partnering with companies or governments in locations (for example, developing countries) where reductions can be achieved with less effort. It must be noted that alongside the regulatory-driven carbon market, a voluntary carbon market has developed (Gillenwater *et al*, 2007; see Chapter 6). Even though this does not have the same size, the voluntary market (consisting of the Chicago Climate Exchange (CCX) and the Over the Counter (OTC) offset market) had reached a US$91 million volume in 2007. Not surprisingly, the majority of companies active in this voluntary market are based in the US, as a regulatory carbon market is still lacking there (Hamilton *et al*, 2007). In the classification of Figure 8.1, offset projects are not considered to be innovative because they usually merely rely on the transfer of existing technologies instead of on the development of new ones.

2.4 Combining innovation and compensation: a carbon-neutral strategy

A recent trend that nicely illustrates the interaction between innovation and compensation as a means to reduce GHG emissions is the carbon-neutral concept. According to the Carbon Trust (2006: 15), 'carbon neutrality is achieved when emissions from a product, activity or a whole organisation are netted off, either through the purchase of an equivalent number of offsets or through a combination of emissions reduction and offsetting'. Carbon neutrality has become rather popular amongst service-oriented companies, such as financial institutions, media and IT companies. One of the first multinationals that announced its plans to become carbon neutral was Swiss Re, in 2003. At the end of 2004, it was followed by HSBC, a pledge which received critical acclaim and led many banks, including Barclays, Credit Suisse, Goldman Sachs, National Australia Bank and Toronto-Dominion Bank, to follow suit (Wright, 2006). Companies in the other sectors – for example, BSkyB, News Corp, PwC, Marks and Spencer, Reckitt Benckiser, Yahoo, Google, and TNT – have formulated similar programmes to become carbon neutral as well.

Carbon neutrality is appealing because it is a concept which is easy to understand and therefore also good to use for communication purposes. In other words, it can be an effective strategy to attract customers without having to explain the technical details of specific CO_2 targets. However, in actual practice it runs into many of the same problems as any other emissions target, such as determining the corporate carbon footprint, a baseline and a business-as-usual scenario (see Chapter 4). Moreover, it only seems fit for companies with relatively low direct emissions – it is hard to imagine an oil company becoming carbon neutral. Carbon neutrality is rather difficult because it is near to impossible to cut back on all energy consumption with internal measures. The Carbon Trust, for example, advises companies to first reduce direct internal emissions, which is equivalent to an innovative approach aimed at process improvements (Figure 8.1, cell 1). However, as it seems improbable to trim down such internal emissions to zero, companies are also recommended to resort to some form of compensation. The 'recommended' subsequent step is a supply-chain approach where companies aim at a cutback in indirect emissions (cell 4). For HSBC, for example, this meant the implementation of a scheme to purchase green power (Wright, 2006). Still, as not all emissions come from energy consumption, e.g. business travel, after these two stages companies typically still have a positive emissions balance. Completely netting off emissions therefore often also involves acquiring some type of emissions credits (cell 6) in the (voluntary) carbon market (Harvey, 2007).

However, the whole idea of carbon neutrality has been fiercely criticised (see Gillenwater *et al*, 2007; Revkin, 2007). Opponents do not really disapprove of internal and supply-chain measures, but rather the fact that the concept generally relies on buying offsets. The problem is that, particularly in the voluntary carbon market, there are many different types of compensation schemes available, which are not all that reliable. Moreover, the main type of compensation that offset retailers such as the CarbonNeutral Company have on offer is via investments in tree-planting programmes. The climatic impact of such programmes has been debated because tree plantations may come in the place of primary forest, thereby leading to a net increase in GHG emissions instead of a reduction. Moreover, it is not always clear whether the carbon offset projects lead to additional reductions from what would have been achieved otherwise. In the voluntary carbon market, monitoring to verify that claimed reductions are really achieved is often lacking. And even if projects are monitored, there is still no agreed-upon monitoring method. Furthermore, if property rights are not well-defined, emissions credits might be sold more than once (Gillenwater *et al*, 2007). Besides all these potential failures of the voluntary carbon market in delivering actual emissions reductions, there is also the issue of which emissions will be netted off. Most banks that become carbon neutral compensate their internal emissions, but do not go one step further in also neutralising the climatic impact of their financial investments, where their impact is much higher. This has been acknowledged by HSBC, which, although it does not take their investment into account in becoming carbon neutral, creates awareness among clients and requires disclosure of GHG emissions in their project finance activities (Wright, 2006).

Hence, despite the attractiveness of carbon neutrality for marketing purposes, companies that claim to be carbon neutral run a reputation risk as it could be seen as greenwashing. A potential 'solution' to this risk is by only acquiring offsets in the UN-led carbon market, for example by investing in emissions-reducing projects that live up to an NGO-endorsed monitoring standard such as the WWF Gold Standard for CDM and JI projects.

3 CONCLUDING REMARKS

This chapter analyzed the kind of options available to companies in developing their climate change strategy. The typology that we presented shows that there are various strategic options from which managers can choose in addressing the market components related to the issue of climate change, and that current strategies consist of different combinations of these market possibilities. Existing managerial discretion, resulting from perceptions of the risks and/or opportunities related to climate change, leads companies, also those active in one and the same sector, to choose different approaches. Further development can be expected in the next few years, since ongoing government, stakeholder and shareholder pressure will encourage companies to explore the full range of options, and adapt their climate change strategy in response to changes in external and company-specific factors. In the next two chapters we will explain the two main aims of climate change strategies identified in the typology. Chapter 6 first elaborates on compensation and discusses emissions trading, while Chapter 7 examines which capabilities companies might develop in response to climate change and how far-reaching the influence of climate change is on core business strategies.

References

Abrahamson, E, and Rosenkopf, L, 1993, 'Institutional and competitive bandwagons: using mathematical modeling as a tool to explore innovation diffusion', *Academy of Management Review*, 18(3): 487–517.

Allianz/WWF, 2005, *Climate Change and the Financial Sector: an Agenda for Action*, London: Allianz Group and WWF.

Allianz/WWF, 2006, *Climate Change and Insurance: an Agenda for Action in the United States*, New York: Allianz Group and WWF.

Aragón–Correa, J A, and Sharma, S, 2003, 'A contingent resource-based view of proactive corporate environmental strategy', *Academy of Management Review*, 28(1): 71–88.

Bansal, P, 2005, 'Evolving sustainably: a longitudinal study of corporate sustainable development', *Strategic Management Journal*, 26: 197–218.

Berger, I E, Cunningham, P H, and Drumwright, M E, 2007, 'Mainstreaming corporate social responsibility: developing markets for virtue', *California Management Review*, 49(4): 132–157.

Berkhout, F, Hertin, J, and Gann, D M, 2006, 'Learning to adapt: organizational adaptation to climate change impacts', *Climate Change*, 78: 135–156.

Birchall, J, 2008, 'US airlines pressed on climate change', *Financial Times*, 10 March.

Boiral, O, 2006, 'Global warming: should companies adopt a proactive strategy?' *Long Range Planning*, 39: 315–330.

Bonini, S M J, Hintz, G, and Mendonca, L T, 2008, 'Addressing consumer concerns about climate change', *McKinsey Quarterly*, March 2008.

Buysse, K, and Verbeke, A, 2003, 'Proactive environmental strategies: a stakeholder management perspective', *Strategic Management Journal*, 24: 453–470.

Carbon Trust, 2006, *The Carbon Trust Three Stage Approach to Developing a Robust Offset Strategy*, London: The Carbon Trust.

CDP, 2006, *Carbon Disclosure Project 2006 – Global FT500*, London: Innovest.

Delmas, M A, and Toffel, M W, 2004, 'Stakeholders and environmental management practices: an institutional framework', *Business Strategy and the Environment*, 13: 209–222.

Dlugolecki, A, and Keykhah, M, 2002, 'Climate change and the insurance sector: its role in adaptation and mitigation', *Greener Management International*, 39 (Autumn): 83–98.

Eesley, C, and Lenox, M J, 2006, 'Firm responses to secondary stakeholder action', *Strategic Management Journal*, 27: 765–781.

Ernst & Young, 2008, *Strategic Business Risk 2008 – The Top 10 Risks for Business*, London: Ernst & Young with Oxford Analytica.

Gillenwater, M, Broekhoff, D, Trexler, M, Hyman J, and Fowler, R, 2007, 'Policing the voluntary carbon market', *Nature Reports Climate Change*, 6: 85–87.

Grubb, M, 2004, 'Technology innovation and climate change policy: an overview of issues and options', *Keio Economic Studies*, 41(2): 103–132.

Hamilton, K, Bayon, R, Turner, G, and Higgins, D, 2007, *State of the Voluntary Carbon Markets 2007: Picking up Steam*, London/Washington: New Carbon Finance and The Ecosystem Marketplace.

Hart, S L, 1995, 'A natural-resource-based view of the firm', *Academy of Management Review*, 20(4): 986–1014.

Harvey, F, 2007, 'Next step is "positive" carbon neutrality', *Financial Times*, 7 June.

Hoffman, A J, 2005, 'Climate change strategy: the business logic behind voluntary greenhouse gas reductions', *California Management Review*, 47(3): 21–46.

Hoffman, A J, 2006, *Getting Ahead of the Curve: Corporate Strategies that Address Climate Change*, Arlington, VA: Pew Center on Global Climate Change.

Jaffe, A B, Peterson, S R, Portnoy, P R, and Stavins, R N, 1995, 'Environmental regulation and the competitiveness of U.S. manufacturing: what does the evidence tell us?' *Journal of Economic Literature*, 33: 132–163.

King, A A, and Lenox, M J, 2000, 'Industry self-regulation without sanctions: the chemical industry's responsible care program', *Academy of Management Journal*, 43(4): 698–716.

Knickerbocker, F T, 1973, *Oligopolistic Reaction and Multinational Enterprise*, Boston: Harvard University.

Kolk, A, 2000, *Economics of Environmental Management*, Harlow: Financial Times Prentice Hall.

Kolk, A, and Levy, D, 2004, 'Multinationals and global climate change: issue for the automotive and oil industries', in S M Lundan (ed), *Multinationals, Environment and Global Competition*, Vol. 9: 171–193, Amsterdam: Elsevier.

Kolk, A, and Pinkse, J, 2004, 'Market strategies for climate change', *European Management Journal*, 22(3): 304–314.

Kolk, A, and Pinkse, J, 2008, 'A perspective on multinational enterprises and climate change: learning from "an inconvenient truth". *Journal of International Business Studies*, forthcoming.

Lash, J, and Wellington, F, 2007, 'Competitive advantage on a warming planet', *Harvard Business Review*, 85(3): 94–102.

Levy, D L, 1997, 'Business and international environmental treaties: ozone depletion and climate change', *California Management Review*, 39(3): 54–71.

Levy, D L, and Kolk, A, 2002, 'Strategic responses to global climate change: conflicting pressures on multinationals in the oil industry', *Business and Politics*, 4(3): 275–300.

Meyer, J W, and Rowan, B, 1977, 'Institutionalized organizations: formal structure as myth and ceremony', *American Journal of Sociology*, 83(2): 340–363.

Monks, R, Miller, A, and Cook, J, 2004, 'Shareholder activism on environmental issues: a study of proposals at large US corporations (2000–2003)', *Natural Resources Forum*, 28: 317–330.

Okereke, C, 2007, 'An exploration of motivations, drivers and barriers to carbon management: the UK FTSE 100', *European Management Journal*, 25(6): 475–486.

Paolella, M S, and Taschini, L, 2006, 'An econometric analysis of emission trading allowances', *Swiss Finance Institute Research Paper Series*, 6(26): 1–42.

Porter, M E, and van der Linde, G, 1995, 'Green and competitive – Ending the stalemate', *Harvard Business Review*, 73(5): 120–138.

Porter, M E, and Kramer, M R, 2006, 'Strategy and society: the link between competitive advantage and corporate social responsibility', *Harvard Business Review*, 84(12): 78–92.

Porter, M E, and Reinhardt, F L, 2007, 'A strategic approach to climate', *Harvard Business Review*, 85(10): 22–26.

Ramus, C A, and Montiel, I, 2005, 'When are corporate environmental policies a form of greenwashing?' *Business and Society*, 44(4): 377–414.

Reinhardt, F L, 1998, 'Environmental product differentiation: implications for corporate strategy', *California Management Review*, 40(4): 43–73.

Revkin, A C, 2007, 'Carbon-neutral is hip, but is it green?' *The New York Times*, 29 April.

Rugman, A M, and Verbeke, A, 1998, 'Corporate strategies and environmental regulations: an organizing framework', *Strategic Management Journal*, 19: 363–375.

Russo, M V, and Fouts, P A, 1997, 'A resource-based perspective on corporate environmental performance and profitability', *Academy of Management Journal*, 40(3): 534–559.

Sæverud, I A, and Skjærseth, J B, 2007, 'Oil companies and climate change: inconsistencies between strategy formulation and implementation?' *Global Environmental Politics*, 7(3): 42–62.

Sharma, S, and Vredenburg, H, 1998, 'Proactive corporate environmental strategy and the development of competitively valuable organizational capabilities', *Strategic Management Journal*, 19: 729–753.

Suchman, M C, 1995, 'Managing legitimacy: strategic and institutional approaches', *Academy of Management Review*, 20(3): 571–610.

Van Huijstee, M M, Francken, M, and Leroy, P, 2007, 'Partnerships for sustainable development: a review of current literature', *Environmental Sciences*, 4(2): 75–89.

Victor, D G, and House, J C, 2006, 'BP's emissions trading system', *Energy Policy*, 34(15): 2100–2112.

Walley, N, and Whitehead, B, 1994, 'It's not easy being green', *Harvard Business Review*, 72(3): 46–52.

Wright, C, 2006, 'Carbon neutrality draws praise, raises expectations for HSBC', *Ecosystem Marketplace*, 1 August.

HSBC: banking on CSR?

Founded in 1865, the HSBC Group is one of the world's largest banking and financial services organizations. Serving 100 million customers through personal financial services and commercial banking, the group employs more than 300,000 people and has an asset base of US $2.5 trillion.[1] With a network spanning more than 80 countries and territories, and listings on the London, Hong Kong, New York, Paris, and Bermuda stock exchanges, little wonder it proclaims to be 'the world's local bank'.

CSR at HSBC

With the recent global meltdown, and protests such as the Occupy movement heavily targeting the failings of the financial sector, the issue of 'responsible banking' is high on the public agenda. As a result, the financial services industry has increasingly found itself trying to manage renewed regulatory pressures and regain a sense of credibility with customers, politicians, and the general public. Under the glare of constant media attention, the need for banks to be (or be seen to be) more responsible and enhance their positive contribution to society has gained unprecedented importance since the onset of the 2008 financial crisis. And with banks being critical to the flow of global finance, many pressing concerns are related to the very core of their business practices. As HSBC said in its 2011 Annual Report:

> At HSBC, we know how important it is that banks play a positive role in the economy and society at large. The fundamental role that banks play in intermediating between savings and lending is essential to economic growth. Throughout the world, access to financial services helps

businesses to flourish and economies to develop. Those services help individuals provide for their families; put a roof over their heads; and live a comfortable retirement. We also help companies to grow and prosper by enabling them to access debt and equity, as well as providing them with a wide range of products that facilitate trade. In this way, we connect our customers to the opportunities that will help them realise their ambitions.

(HSBC, 2011)

As one of the largest global financial institutions, HSBC is heavily exposed to the challenge of developing a responsible approach to banking, and it faces a range of potential social responsibility issues across its span of operations. These range from questions of where it invests its money, all the way up to how it manages its environmental footprint, and what it is doing to promote financial inclusion.

At the group level HSBC frames its CSR practices in the context of 'sustainability'. This is in contrast to some of its competitors, such as Citibank, which talks primarily about 'responsible finance'; Barclays, which focuses on 'citizenship'; and Deutsche Bank, which uses the heading of 'corporate social responsibility'. But regardless of the terminology, the issues faced by the global banking industry are broadly similar. 'Sustainability' at HSBC is presented in terms of 'managing our business across the world for the long term' and involves the main business stakeholders: 'that means achieving sustainable profits for our shareholders, building long-lasting relationships with customers, valuing our highly committed employees, respecting environmental limits and investing in communities'.[2]

Responsible lending and investment practices

Probably the main area where banks such as HSBC impact on society is through their lending and investment practices. A company such as HSBC lends billions of dollars every year to individuals, companies, and projects, which can have huge social and environmental consequences, both positive and negative. For example, HSBC was one of the big players in the subprime mortgage market in the US that ultimately led to the financial crisis of the late 2000s. The bank bet heavily on mortgage loans to high risk (or 'subprime') borrowers but when the housing bubble burst, many of those borrowers defaulted, leaving the company with huge amounts of bad debt. HSBC lost billions of dollars in the crisis, subsequently labelling its subprime business a 'catastrophic investment' (Treanor, 2009). It closed down its subprime lending arm, and continued to suffer losses of some US$2 billion annually in its US business right into the 2010s as it gradually wound down its operations (HSBC, 2011). Even so, by dint of its size and asset base, HSBC remained one of the more secure international banks during the crisis (Menon, 2009).

Beyond the social and ethical risks posed by individual lending, HSBC – like all major banks – also lends to businesses and makes huge capital investments in major projects, which of course may also pose significant social and environmental risks.

HSBC uses two main frameworks for evaluating these risks, which it captures under the banner of 'sustainable finance', namely the Equator Principles and the bank's own sector policies.

Equator Principles

The Equator Principles are 'a credit risk management framework used for determining, assessing and managing environmental and social risk in project finance transactions'.[3] They are intended to be a minimum standard under which project financing is provided – that is, borrowers who are unable or unwilling to comply with the standards set out under the Principles are not able to secure financing from Equator Principles signatories.

The Principles were launched in 2003 by several of HSBC's global competitors under a collaborative project with the International Finance Corporation (IFC), a part of the World Bank Group. HSBC signed up to the principles a few months after the launch and has remained a member since 2003. Altogether there are currently 77 adopting financial institutions, including most of the world's biggest banks.

The Principles provide HSBC with an internationally agreed way of ensuring that the projects they finance are developed in a socially responsible manner and reflect sound environmental management practices. Under the principles, any potential funding projects with capital costs exceeding $10 million are rated depending on their degree of potential social and environmental risks. In high- or medium-risk projects, action plans are devised to address the potential risks; if these plans are deemed adequate, an agreement to lend money may be made, on the condition that the action plan is followed. Independent monitoring is then implemented to ensure compliance with the standards over the period of the loan. In 2010, transactions worth US$6.7 billion were approved by HSBC using the Equator Principles framework. Of this, almost one quarter of the total amount (US$1.6 million) was accounted for high-risk category A projects, while about 60 per cent of transaction value was accounted for by category B, medium-risk projects.[4]

Sector policies

While the Equator Principles represent an internally agreed and rigorous framework for assessing and managing the social and environmental risks of bank lending, they only apply to large projects. However, HSBC's sector policies are both more specific (in that they only apply to HSBC, not any other financial institutions) and more encompassing (since they are applicable to all projects, regardless of size).[5] These policies currently cover eight broad sectors ranging from defence to forestry, and chemicals to mining. The policies specify what areas the bank will or will not provide financial services in. For example, the chemicals sector policy specifies that HSBC will not provide any forms of financial assistance to companies involved in chemical weapons, or those participating in the manufacture, storage or transportation of persistent organic pollutants (POPs).[6] Meanwhile the mining sector policy states both the activities that the bank will not provide financial services for (such as artisanal mining or the mining of diamonds not certified as conflict-free) as well as those it has a 'restricted appetite' for (such as mines that have 'no credible closure plan').[7]

Financial inclusion

In recent years, the extension of access to financial services to people otherwise unable to participate in the formal banking sector has become a major area of growth in financial services. Microfinance, where small sums are loaned to those excluded from conventional loans using innovative community-based borrowing systems, is probably the best known form of such financial inclusion. HSBC entered the microfinance business with pilot projects in the mid 2000s and currently operates commercial microfinance business in several emerging economies, most notably India, Mexico, and Russia. Some of the bank's global diversity as the world's local bank is played out in these businesses, featuring as they do some innovative variations such as an Islamic microfinance project in Pakistan, and an employee volunteer programme with Bankers Without Borders to support microfinance institutions in the Middle East.[8] The bank was also the first foreign bank to establish a banking business, HSBC Rural Bank, in China's rural areas, offering services specifically tailored to the needs of people and farmers in the many remote rural regions of the country.

HSBC and environmental protection

As with other banks, HSBC has two main areas of environmental impact – its own business operations and that of its customers. Over the past decade, climate change has become a central theme of HSBC's environmental programme as the bank has sought to take a leadership position on climate in the sector. In 2005, it was the first bank to be recognized as carbon neutral in its own operations, while in terms of its clients' business, the bank has sought to position itself to capitalize on potential opportunities emerging from the drive to meet climate goals. In 2007, HSBC established the Climate Change Centre of Excellence as a central source of climate knowledge. The centre aims to translate a wide range of expert inputs – from academic studies, think tanks and government regulations – into business opportunities for the bank and its clients.[9] As a result, the bank claims to have identified four main areas of opportunity in its emerging 'climate business': low carbon energy production (such as renewables), energy efficiency measures, climate adaption (especially in agriculture, infrastructure, and water), and providing climate finance, including environmental markets, debt and equity investment and insurance.[10] These are all areas that the bank sees as growing areas for investment as the transition to a low carbon economy is gradually effected.

Another major HSBC investment in climate change was the flagship US$100 million, HSBC Climate Partnership, which ran from 2007–2012. This five-year programme was a collaboration with the environmental NGOs, The Climate Group, Earthwatch, the Smithsonian Tropical Research Institute, and WWF. It aimed at delivering pioneering climate research, developing new methodologies and test projects, and creating new solutions to climate problems. HSBC's contribution was not only in terms of financial resources and expertise, but also the participation of more than 2000 employees who volunteered their time to take part in the partnership. According to the project's review and final report, the partnership succeeded in, among other things, delivering the largest ever forest research project; it enabled 32 million more people to have access to cleaner water; and protected an additional three million hectares of forestland.[11]

Responsibility in the workplace

The HSBC Climate Partnership is not only an example of how the company has sought to address environmental issues, but also demonstrates something of its approach to engaging employees on social issues. The project as a whole involved 63,000 days of volunteering time, and perhaps more critically, created a cadre of 'climate champions' within the company who had worked on major climate chal-lenges along with HSBC's partners in the project. These projects varied from wildlife conservation to energy management within the workplace. The partnership simulta-neously offered online courses and training to help employees further the cause of climate change. Back in HSBC, the climate champions subsequently integrated some of their new knowledge into efforts to make the workplace more sustainable. One such project saw the introduction of automatic shutting down of PCs overnight, which saved around 13 million kw/h of electricity and 2600 tonnes of CO_2 in North America alone before being rolled out across the entire group during the 2010s.[12]

Beyond employee engagement, one area where the HSBC workplace has received rather more negative media attention has been its remuneration policy. In the early 2010s, when income equality and executive pay became major touchstones of protests such as the Occupy movement, HSBC was criticized for paying out high salaries to executives while simultaneously recording falling profits and cutting back staff. For example, in 2011, while profits slipped 6 per cent, the bank's bonus pool remained steady at £2.7 billion, and more than 192 HSBC executives received pay in excess of £1 million, including £8.1 million for its highest paid employee and £7.2 million for its chief executive, Stuart Gulliver (Treanor, 2012a). Although union leaders denounced the situation as 'astonishing', the revelations were only made possible by the bank being the first UK bank to adopt new transparency measures over executive pay (Wilson, 2012).

Community initiatives

The 'community' takes on many facets in a 'glocal' (i.e. locally tailored, global in scope) business such as HSBC. Programmes such as those discussed above on financial inclusion, for example, seek to benefit underserved communities within the bank's span of operations. Beyond these commercial initiatives intended to generate new revenue streams, the bank also seeks to make a contribution to the communities in which it operates through charitable donations and support, as well as its more basic responsibilities to pay tax and thereby ensure that governments are suitably resourced to provide for their citizens.

HSBC's philanthropic work is largely focused around two main themes: the environment and education. As described above, major programmes such as the Climate Partnership have been developed to coordinate the firm's corporate giving to environmental initiatives. Meanwhile its educational giving includes projects such as Future First, a flagship project running in 49 of the 86 countries in which the company operates. The programme was established in 2006 as a partnership between HSBC, SOS Children's Villages, and local non-profit organizations, offering education and life skills training to orphans, homeless children, and children in care. The company's $25 million commitment is directed towards scholarships, teacher training, supporting school equipment, family support programmes and vocational training.[13]

Working within the same theme of education, HSBC also has a global financial education programme, 'JA More than Money', which teaches students about earning, spending, sharing, and saving money, as well as potential careers. The programme is run in partnership with Junior Achievement (JA) Worldwide (known as Young Enterprise in the UK) and is facilitated by HSBC volunteers. The programme currently runs in 32 countries and is targeted towards teaching financial literacy and skills to 7–11-year-olds.[14]

For all the impressive community development programmes established by HSBC, it has not been immune to criticism regarding its overall contribution to the communities in which it operates. Probably the main focus of negative attention has been its approach to taxation. In the UK, the company joined the 'least desirable club in the business world' in 2010 when it became the latest in a line of targets of tax justice demonstrators. A number of the bank's high street branches were occupied by campaigners critical of the bank's attempt to lower its tax burden by more than $3 billion through 'behind closed doors' negotiations with the UK tax authorities (Macalister & Clark, 2010). The following year, HSBC was investigated by the US Inland Revenue Service for purportedly selling tax evasion services to some of its wealthy American customers of Indian origin (Browning, 2011). Investigators claimed that a division of the bank had been encouraging its clients to set up undeclared offshore accounts in India, which led to the bank severing ties with hundreds of its clients (Fitzpatrick et al, 2011). A similar investigation followed in the UK regarding offshore accounts held at HSBC's private Swiss bank (Houlder, 2011). Again in 2012, the company was involved in a dispute with the UK tax authorities over a potential $5 billion tax bill for allegedly avoiding UK tax on dividends earned by some of its overseas subsidiaries (Treanor, 2012b).

Clearly, for all its positive contributions to those in need in its many local communities, HSBC faces the risk of major reputational risk if it is seen as evading its more basic responsibilities as a good citizen for paying, and ensuring its customers pay, an appropriate amount of tax. Coupled with further scandals in its core banking functions in the 2010s, including what it acknowledged as 'shameful' system failures that allowed terrorists and drug barons to launder money through its US and Mexico operations (Treanor, 2012c), only served to underline the very real problems of putting in place genuinely responsible banking in the world's local bank.

Study questions

1.   What should constitute 'responsible banking' for a company such as HSBC and how does it differ, if at all, from normal banking practice? Does HSBC live up to expectations as a responsible banker?
2.   What are the market incentives and disincentives faced by HSBC in developing more responsible banking? How do you think this will change in the future?
3.   Using Utting's four components of equality – social protection, rights, empowerment, and redistribution – explain how HSBC's approach to responsible banking contributes to greater equality and suggest how it could realistically be enhanced.
4.   To what extent do HSBC's charitable and environmental activities contribute to the company's competitive advantage? From the perspective of competitive advantage, are there any programmes that you think should be phased out or new programmes that you think should be developed?
5.   What are the main impacts of HSBC on climate change and what is it doing to address these impacts? What strategies might the bank have to develop in the future to move to a more sustainable business model?

Endnotes

1   www.hsbcpb.com/aboutus/about-hsbc-private-bank.html
2   www.hsbc.com/1/2//sustainability
3   www.equator-principles.com
4   www.hsbc.com/1/2/sustainability/sustainable-finance/
5   www.hsbc.com/1/2/sustainability/sustainable-finance/sector-policies
6   www.hsbc.com/1/PA_esf-ca-app-content/content/assets/csr/chemicals.pdf
7   www.hsbc.com/1/PA_esf-ca-app-content/content/assets/csr/070810_mining_policy.pdf
8   http://microfinanceafrica.net/tag/grameen-jameel-microfinance; www.cpifinancial.net/news/post/1043/hsbc-amanah-to-launch-pilot-islamic-microfinance-programme-
9   www.hsbc.com/1/2/newsroom/news/2007/hsbc-hires-specialist-to-head-up-new-climate-change-centre-of-excellence#top

10   www.hsbc.com/1/2/sustainability/sustainable-finance
11   www.hsbc.com/1/2/sustainability/hcp-2010
12   www.hsbc.com/1/2/sustainability/climate-partnership
13   www.hsbc.com/1/2/sustainability/future-first-achievements-aspirations
14   www.hsbc.com/1/2/sustainability/investing-in-communities

References

Browning, L. (2011) 'HSBC is said to be the focus of a tax-evasion investigation', *The New York Times*, 26 January.

Fitzpatrick, D., Perez, E., & Saunders, L. (2011) 'HSBC acts on offshore cash', *The Wall Street Journal*, 20 July.

HSBC (2011) 'Connecting customers to opportunities', www.hsbc.com/1/PA_esf-ca-app-content/content/assets/investor_relations/120420_hsbc_corporate_brochure.pdf.

Houlder, V. (2011) 'Tax evasion suspects given chance to come clean', *Financial Times*, 13 October.

Macalister, T. & Clark, A. (2010) 'Big business goes on the defensive as tax protesters win the propaganda war', *The Guardian*, 19 December.

Menon, J. (2009) 'HSBC to raise $17.7 billion as subprime cuts profit', www.bloomberg.com/apps/news?pid=newsarchive&sid=aGiiBHDGHLHY.

Treanor, J. (2009) 'HSBC's record £12.5bn cash call sends its shares tumbling', *The Guardian*, 2 March.

Treanor, J. (2012a) 'HSBC paid 192 staff more than £1m', *The Guardian*, 27 February.

Treanor, J. (2012b) 'HSBC faces potential £36bn UK tax bill if it loses HM Revenue and Customs case', *The Guardian*, 28 February.

Treanor, J. (2012c) 'HSBC sets aside $700m for money-laundering fines', *The Guardian*, 30 July.

Wilson, H. (2012) 'HSBC chief executive Stuart Gulliver paid £8m as profits rise', *The Telegraph*, 27 February.

SECTION C

Managing CSR

This last section of the book seeks to examine in more depth the management issues associated with CSR. Of course, this is not, by any means, the first time that we have come across CSR management issues in the text. Each of the four CSR contexts discussed in Section B posed their own unique management challenges, and even basic CSR theory often includes management considerations, such as how to effectively balance stakeholder responsibilities. However, in Section C we will focus much more closely on the practical management side of CSR. After all, discussing CSR in the abstract is not really much use unless it is put into practice by real managers, in real companies, and with real effects on societies.

A focus in this final part on managing CSR does not, however, mean that we will be providing a 'how to' guide for CSR managers. The purpose of an academic investigation into managing CSR in a global context is more to explore the challenges associated with putting CSR into practice, and enabling a more informed assessment of the different ways in which CSR can be managed and implemented. In so doing, we will certainly cast some light on the strengths and weaknesses of particular CSR management tools and techniques, but we will also be exploring the broader social and political significance of CSR management.

To this end, the chapters in this last part focus on three key aspects, followed by an integrative case study that provides us with the opportunity to explore these issues in a real-life situation:

- CSR reporting and auditing
- Developing CSR strategy
- CSR, partnerships, and self-regulation
- Integrative case study *CSR masala at the Tata Group*

In covering these different aspects of CSR management, we do not hope to cover every single aspect of management practice that might pertain to CSR. After all, as we will make clear in this chapter, social responsibility is not something that can be easily disentangled from the rest of a company's operations, nor can it be neatly tucked away into a CSR department so that people in other parts of the organization never need to go near it. While many large companies do indeed now have CSR managers or departments, these cannot ever expect to manage every aspect of responsibility in the firm since CSR issues pervade the organization from top to bottom and right across the global span of operations.

That said, we do hope to introduce the key issues that matter in terms of CSR management in the chapters that follow, such as what makes for a good CSR strategy, how to develop social partnerships with non-governmental organizations, and how CSR audits, reports, and codes of conduct can contribute to the effective management of CSR. Significantly, we also seek to show that even such 'practical' tools have significant social and political ramifications in terms of social accountability, international governance, and global justice and poverty. By concluding with the Tata case study, we take the opportunity to explore these issues in one of Asia's best known CSR practitioners, demonstrating that whatever else it is, CSR management is a huge challenge for companies in a global context.

Chapter 9

CSR reporting and auditing

IN THIS CHAPTER WE WILL:

- Explain the basic features of CSR reporting
- Understand the main reasons why companies become involved in CSR reporting
- Explore the role of CSR reporting in the broader accounting process
- Discuss key features of good CSR reporting and auditing
- Understand the role of stakeholder dialogue in CSR reporting

Introduction

It might be anticipated that a socially responsible company would respond to the expectations of society – and we have discussed in Section B various ways that managers can address these demands with regard to key stakeholders and issues. A crucial step in this process, however, is how stakeholders actually find out whether the company has acted responsibly or not. Somehow, a socially responsible company has to prove to its stakeholders that it is 'doing the right thing'. This is the point at which CSR reporting and auditing enters the picture.

Companies have long been required to audit and report on their performance, albeit with regard to a very limited range of issues and to just one main stakeholder. The annual report – mandatory for large businesses in most industrialized countries – reports on the financial performance of the firm, and is primarily prepared for the purposes of shareholders and, to a lesser degree, governments (for tax purposes). With the growth of CSR, however, we have seen a rise in *non-financial reporting* by many companies throughout the world, informing various stakeholders about their performance with regard to social and environmental issues, and often alluded to as the 'triple bottom line' (Brown et al, 2009). Shell, for example, state in their 2011 report that 'Our aim is to help meet the energy needs of society in ways that are economically, environmentally and socially responsible'.[1] Some go so far as to claim that CSR reporting has become the *de facto* law for business (KPMG, 2011).

In a recent survey of 3,400 companies globally across 16 sectors it was found that 95 per cent of the 250 largest companies in the world report on CSR activities, and that two-thirds of non-reporters are based in the US. In Europe, 71 per cent of companies in the survey provide CSR reports, compared with 69 per cent in the Americas, 61 per cent in the Middle East and Africa and just under a half of companies in Asia Pacific. It was found that organizational ownership influenced reporting, with 69 per cent of companies listed on the stock exchange reporting on CSR, and 57 per cent of state-owned companies also reporting. In contrast only 36 per cent of family-owned businesses reported on CSR (KPMG, 2011). Reporting seems to continuously grow, but this is not always matched by successful implementation of CSR.

CSR reporting and auditing: reasons and types

If we look at why companies audit and report on their social performance we can use the typology presented by Garriga and Melé in Chapter 3:

Instrumental/economic reasons

Social and environmental issues might pose a threat to the company's financial performance. In order to manage these risks, companies need to know about them and monitor them over time. If a company wants to avoid boycotts from consumers because of their employment practices in the developing world, it has to establish a system that keeps track of employment conditions across their global operations. For example, many companies in the clothing and retail industries such as Nike and Gap conduct *social audits* of their suppliers' factories, in part to mitigate previous exposure of unethical practices.

Political reasons

Large multinational corporations are perceived as increasingly powerful institutions in society. This increased power might call for more transparency and accountability to the public in terms of how the corporation has impacted on society (in the same way that a government might report on its social impacts).

Integrating demand from stakeholders

CSR reporting helps companies to improve their interaction with stakeholders. If a company wants to live up to the demands of stakeholders, they have to communicate in detail to these groups about their expectations and the company's respective performance. CSR auditing and reporting might then, ideally, be part of a broader process of dialogue and engagement with stakeholders. Global financial services group Nomura Holdings, for example, report that they are seeking to revitalize communities across Japan through stakeholder dialogue.[2]

Ethical reasons/responding to external pressure

Companies face growing pressures from governments, investors, customers, and competitors to live up to ethical standards. CSR reporting is a tool by which a company can communicate about its ethical values and how well they have performed against these goals. For example, introducing a recent non-financial report, the Ford Motor Company president and chief executive officer professes that corporate objectives are underpinned by the common good: 'Our goal is to create an exciting, viable, profitably growing company for the good of all of us.'[3] Typical situations where external pressure is applied are the interactions with large pension funds who increasingly want to know how well a company performs on the social and ethical indicators the fund uses in deciding which shares to add to its portfolio. In a relatively new development known as 'shareholder activism', shareholders are also acting as objectors to corporate policy, with CEO salaries coming under particular scrutiny and shareholder protests being felt by advertising giant WPP, Barclays Bank, the insurers AVIVA and Citigroup alike.

CSR reporting is currently still voluntary in most countries. There is, therefore, a wide variety in its language and content. Most companies that publish a CSR report (or 'corporate responsibility', 'sustainability', or 'corporate citizenship' report – we will regard these as synonymous) tend to inform their readers rather generally about the social performance of the company.

CSR reports are normally a result of a larger process of 'social accounting' within the company. A key element of this process is the 'social audit', which normally describes the actual measurement or checking exercise of the various indicators of social performance, such as pollution levels or number of injuries. Good CSR reports – analogous to financial reports – would also include some form of 'verification' resulting in an 'assurance' statement providing the addressees of the report with some indication about how accurate the CSR report actually is (Owen & O'Dwyer, 2007).

CWS 9.1

Visit the companion website for links to up-to-date examples of CSR reports from a range of companies

Current trends in CSR reporting

CSR reporting has often been criticized as nothing more than glossy public relations statements that make the company look good but have nothing do to with the actual social performance of the organization (Laufer, 2003). Being a voluntary exercise, the main problem seems to be that it is mainly up to the individual company to decide what to put into the report, how to measure social performance, and how to verify and audit the report. This heterogeneity in approach makes it not only rather difficult for stakeholders to assess the actual quality of a company's CSR, it also prevents the reader from comparing different companies with regard to their CSR performance. These problems have led to a number of initiatives to standardize CSR reporting and to provide mechanisms for enhancing the credibility of CSR reports.

Standardizing CSR reports

The most prominent effort to standardize CSR reporting is the guidelines of the 'Global Reporting Initiative' (GRI), published for the first time in 2000.[4] The GRI is a multi-stakeholder initiative of NGOs, industry associations, and many large (and some small) businesses, working together to develop a framework for sustainability reports. The GRI guidelines are developed for different sectors and are continually updated, the most recent set being released in 2011. While the GRI is an extremely important effort to harmonize CSR reporting, some critics argue that in attempting to be inclusive and consultative, its requisites tend to be negotiated down to facilitate compromise (Laufer, 2003).

Assurance

Another problem of CSR reports is the lack of assurance with, for instance, only three out of the top 100 US companies using external assurance for their CSR report (Context, 2006). To address this credibility gap, in 2002 AccountAbility established the 'AA1000S Assurance Standard', which aims to provide a coherent framework for assessing the processes underlying a CSR report. This is also associated with partner standards for principles and stakeholder engagement.[5] A more recent development is the International Standard Organization's ISO 26000 Social Responsibility standard, which was launched in 2010 after a long and sometimes controversial multi-stakeholder development process (Henriques, 2010). Defined as a management system standard rather than a reporting tool or a certification, ISO 26000 covers human rights, labour practices, the environment, fair operating practices, consumer issues, and community involvement and development. It is too early to assess the extent of its uptake, but as a formal, global initiative, it clearly has a role to play in the context of CSR reporting.

Regulation

The voluntary nature of CSR reporting is starting to be challenged in some contexts, with Denmark, France, Japan, Malaysia, and the UK all having some requirements for certain companies to report on non-financial issues. The Danish Parliament for example requires their largest businesses to publish reports on: i) CSR policies; ii) how these policies are translated into actions; and iii) what the business has achieved as a result of working with CSR and expectations for the future (if any). If the business has no CSR policy, this must be explicitly disclosed. Analysis of the success of this initiative shows that, while there are degrees of compliance with the requirements, 97 per cent of the companies are now reporting on CSR, though only 37 per cent report on their achievements (Danish Commerce and Companies Agency, 2010).

Integrated reporting

Finally, the establishment of the International Integrated Reporting Committee (IIRC) in 2010 marked a potential shift in CSR reporting for the future. The idea in short is to replace the annual report and separate CSR report with a single document that integrates the two aspects. The aim is to overcome the disconnect between social and financial reporting and to help embed CSR in strategic management and enable stakeholders to appreciate the non-financial impacts of social initiatives (Hopwood et al, 2010). The outcome should be a clear and concise representation of how an organization demonstrates stewardship and how it creates and sustains value (IIRC, 2011). In 2012 the integrated reporting concept was piloted across a wide range of companies.[6] With global backing from the leading accounting professions, the integrated reporting initiative looks likely to lead CSR reporting into a new era, and since an integrated report is intended to be the organization's primary reporting vehicle, bring CSR reporting firmly into the mainstream.

CWS 9.2
Visit the companion website for links to a range of CSR reporting standards and initiatives

Introducing the readings

Research on CSR reporting has tended to be conducted by those who understand financial reporting in organizations, namely accounting researchers. This is interesting in its own right, since within corporations the CSR department – not the accounting department – is usually focused primarily on the annual round of producing CSR reports. Nevertheless, the process of identifying material issues, establishing metrics, and monitoring and auditing performance is very much the territory of accountants. The readings in this chapter emerge from an influential group of CSR accounting scholars and practitioners who have been instrumental in pioneering CSR auditing and reporting particularly in Europe. They provide some concrete insights into the actual process of generating a CSR report, and some detail on the important aspect of stakeholder dialogue in social and environmental reporting. Social and ethical accounting, auditing, and reporting has developed into somewhat of a subfield within

CWS 9.3

Visit the
companion
website for
links to
professional
accounting
ethics
standards

the accounting literature, but also has a considerable degree of traction within the accounting profession, speaking directly to the ethical standards inherent with professional bodies.

What makes for successful CSR reporting?

The paper by Simon Zadek, Peter Pruzan, and Richard Evans provides insight into the practicalities of what they refer to as 'social and ethical accounting, auditing and reporting (SEAAR)'. The reading provides a brief overview of the history of the field, demonstrating that it was foremost a European initiative developed in Denmark and the UK. The 'quality principles' put together on the basis of their practical work and theoretical analysis represent an essential guide to the key criteria for good CSR reporting and auditing. These include inclusivity, comparability, completeness, evolution, management policies and systems, disclosure, external verification, and continuous improvement. There is a wider debate around the link between quality reporting and CSR implementation within the firm, but this reading deals specifically with what constitutes a robust CSR report. The authors importantly also identify two possible reasons for poor practice – namely, i) a lack of skill and experience in the accounting, auditing and reporting processes used; and ii) a deliberate attempt to avoid specificity. The first reason in particular points to the authors' concern that this arena should be led by individuals skilled in accounting techniques. This is an ongoing area of debate, but the basic point is clear, that a professionalization of reporting is needed to enhance the quality of reports. The wider argument, however, is what meaning a report has in relation to CSR practice in the business.

The importance of stakeholder dialogue in constructing the CSR report

The second reading in this chapter seeks to focus more closely on business practice in relation to reporting. Jeffrey Unerman does this by arguing that stakeholder dialogue is a vital aspect of non-financial reporting. He understands stakeholder engagement and dialogue to encompass structured approaches to engaging with actual and potential stakeholders. Unerman argues that dialogue is needed in order to ensure that the CSR report provides the needed information and discharges its accountability appropriately. Hence his implicit suggestion is that the CSR report should serve the needs of stakeholders. This is an interesting point since the industry that has grown up around reporting tends not to be explicit necessarily on the purpose and intended – or actual – audience of the report.

In focusing on stakeholder dialogue Unerman notes the challenges to the perfect dialogue. Drawing on appropriate social theory in the form of the work of Jürgen Habermas, he identifies these barriers as: the impossibility of direct dialogue and engagement with some stakeholders; addressing heterogeneous stakeholder views and expectations; prioritizing stakeholder needs on the basis of maximum negative consequences; and negotiating a consensus among mutually exclusive stakeholder views through discourse ethics. Thus we are drawn again to the question of the skills necessary to achieve a quality social report. Unerman's work suggests that skills of dialogue and consensus building are key, Zadek and colleagues that accounting skills are crucial. Future work might reflect on the capabilities needed for successful reporting and the role reporting plays in the organization's wider CSR commitment.

Challenges for practice

For practitioners of CSR, reporting is often a core area of activity. Some of the most important questions that arise in terms of CSR reporting practice are:

1. What should be included in a CSR report?
    a) What is of material importance in CSR?
    b) Which metrics should be used and how should they be applied?
    c) What are the main goals and objectives of the report?
    d) What quality principles should be applied?
2. How should the CSR report be compiled?
    a) Who should have an input (both internally and externally)?
    b) What disciplines and stakes should contributors represent?
    c) What type of input – informing, consultation or dialogue – should the participants have?
3. How should the report be communicated?
    a) Should the CSR report be stand-alone or integrated with financial reporting?
    b) What is the right balance of online and hard-copy reporting?
    c) Should ongoing, real-time reporting also be used to supplement the annual report?
    d) Who should be informed of the report and how?

Study questions

1. What is a CSR report and how is it related to stakeholder dialogue?
2. Identify two CSR reports from different organizations. Critically contrast them and identify their relative strengths and weaknesses. Can you relate these to the regulatory or sector contexts?
3. What are the processes involved in preparing for the development of a CSR report? How important are these processes in determining the quality of the final report?
4. What do you think are the main reasons that the standardization efforts of CSR reporting are still more or less in their infancy? What are the main drawbacks for such initiatives and how could they be addressed?

5.   Who, within an organization, is best placed to compile a CSR report? What skills do you think are necessary?

Further reading

Gray, R., Dey, C., Owen, D., Evans, R., & Zadek, S. (1997) 'Struggling with the praxis of social accounting: stakeholders, accountability, audits and procedures', *Accounting, Auditing and Accountability Journal*, 10(3): 325–364.
This reading gives an in depth and nevertheless broad overview of the early history of non-financial reporting.

Hess, D. (2008) 'The three pillars of corporate social reporting as new governance regulation: disclosure, dialogue, and development', *Business Ethics Quarterly*, 18(4): 447–482.
This reading takes a US perspective on CSR reporting and puts it in a framework of governance and regulatory mechanisms. With a particular focus on the GRI, Hess investigates the suggestion that CSR, and CSR reporting in particular, leads to a focus on process with no substantive change in corporate behaviour.

Endnotes

1   http://reports.shell.com/sustainability-report/2011/introduction/aboutshell.html?cat=m (Accessed 30 August, 2012).
2   www.nomuraholdings.com/csr/dialogue/revitalization.html (Accessed 30 August, 2012).
3   www.corporate.ford.com/microsites/sustainability-report-2011-12/review-message-mulally (Accessed 30 August, 2012).
4   www.globalreporting.org (Accessed 30 August, 2012).
5   www.accountability.org/standards/index.html (Accessed 30 August, 2012).
6   www.theiirc.org (Accessed 30 August, 2012).

References

Brown, D., Dillard, J., & Marshall, S. (2009) 'Triple bottom line: a business metaphor for a social construct', in J. F. Dillard, V. Dujon, & M. C. King (eds), *Understanding the social dimension of sustainability*, New York: Routledge: 211–230.
Context (2006) *Global corporate responsibility reporting trends 2006*, London: Context Consulting.

Danish Commerce and Companies Agency (in collaboration with Copenhagen Business School and The Institute of State Authorized Public Accountants in Denmark) (2010) *Corporate social responsibility and reporting in Denmark – impact of the legal requirement for reporting on CSR in the Danish Financial Statements Act*, Copenhagen: Danish Commerce and Companies Agency.

Henriques, A. (2010) 'ISO 26000: a standard for human rights?', *Sustainability Accounting, Management and Policy Journal*, 1(1): 103–105.

Hopwood, A., Unerman, J., & Fries, J. (eds) (2010) *Accounting for sustainability: practical insights*, London: Earthscan.

IIRC (2011) 'Towards integrated reporting: communicating value in the 21st century: summary of responses to the September 2011 discussion paper and next steps, 2012 by the International Integrated Reporting Council', www.theiirc. org/the-integrated-reporting-discussion-paper/discussion-paper-summary (Accessed 30 August, 2012).

KPMG (2011) 'KPMG international survey of corporate responsibility reporting 2011', KPMG International Cooperative, www.kpmg.com/Global/en/IssuesAnd Insights/ReadingsPublications/corporate-responsibility/Documents/2011-survey.pdf (Accessed 30 August, 2012).

Laufer, W. S. (2003) 'Social accountability and corporate greenwashing', *Journal of Business Ethics*, 43(3): 253–261.

Owen, D. L. & O'Dwyer, B. (2007) 'Corporate social responsibility: the reporting and assurance dimension', in A. Crane, D. Matten, A. McWilliams, J. Moon, & D. Siegel (eds) *The Oxford handbook of corporate social responsibility*, Oxford: Oxford University Press: 384–409.

SOCIAL AND ETHICAL ACCOUNTING, AUDITING AND REPORTING: HOW TO DO IT

Simon Zadek, Peter Pruzan and Richard Evans

There is a growing body of experiences in corporate SEAAR, particularly across Europe and North America.[1] Associated with this development has been the emergence of varied terminology and differing approaches. There are ethical accounts, social audits, ethical audits, social performance reports, and social reviews, just to name a few. In some cases these methodologies appear very similar. The ethical audit advocated by the European Institute for Business Ethics and the Nijenrode Business School,[2] for example, is similar in many respects to the social accounts method developed, adopted, and applied by Traidcraft plc and the New Economics Foundation.[3] The Body Shop International's ethical audit is, on the other hand, quite different since it represents a combination of social, environmental and animal testing audits.[4] This in turn is only comparable in parts to the 'ethical accounting' developed at the Copenhagen Business School and adopted by Sbn Bank and other companies and public sector organizations across Scandinavia.[5]

Much of the diversity in practice can be attributed to at least four significant differences in:

- interests on the part of those initiating the process;
- types of organizations;
- contexts; and
- theoretical and philosophical roots.

Many of these differences are entirely acceptable in that they reflect varied needs for which different methods are required. For example, organizations such as Sbn Bank in Denmark and Wøyen Mølle in Norway start with an emphasis on the evolution of shared values through ethical accounting. Not surprisingly, they focus on dialogue with key stakeholders rather than third-party verification. On the other hand, a company concerned with meeting the challenge of public accountability may well place far greater emphasis on securing adequate comparison with other companies or accepted social norms and benchmarks. For example, the move by companies in the textile, sportswear and toy sectors to adopt and comply with labour codes of conduct in their production in, and purchases from, the South, will focus on external verification precisely because the pressure comes from public consumer campaigns.[6] Similarly, a company principally concerned with public accountability may focus exclusively on the production of a report for external publication, whereas a company with an interest in SEAAR as a tool to facilitate internal change may have little or no interest in the published document, but may instead focus on the process of accounting, and the reports generated for internal use.

Identifying the right approach to SEAAR is therefore intimately related to *why* the particular organization engages in the exercise. This implies that there is no single approach that is correct for all situations: there is strength in diversity for diverse needs.

At the same time, there are variations between methods and practices that are not justified by any objective difference in circumstance and need. These are variations that may be rooted in two possible reasons for poor practices:

- an underspecification of the accounting, auditing and reporting process because of insufficient knowledge, skills, experience and/or resources applied in the process; and/or
- a deliberate attempt to underspecify the accounts and/or the verification process in order to report in a less than accurate, incomplete or unintelligible, manner.

For example, a company may undertake an externally verified exploration of the social impact of one area of its operations knowing full well that there is a critical problem associated with an area of work that they have chosen to omit from the assessment. An SEAAR exercise undertaken by a bank that did not deal with the nature of its investment portfolio, or an exercise by an advertising company that did not consider with care the nature of the images they were promoting and their effect, could not really be seen as being of adequate quality. Similarly, a company may forgo a dialogue with staff to determine key issues of concern because of inadequate resources, and as a result develop a survey that omits a range of critical issues that would profile the company in a negative light, or that are important for the staff and therefore for their prosperity to be responsible, committed and creative employees. It would not be appropriate, for example, for a fair trade organization (eg one seeking to offer a better deal to community suppliers in the South by offering such added benefits as a better price) to carry out an SEAAR exercise without adequate consultation with Southern suppliers.[7]

The challenge is to be able to distinguish between acceptable and unacceptable reasons for methodological (and terminological) differences. The failure to meet this challenge effectively will allow the 'bad to chase out the good', as companies and consultants alike find good reason to cut corners to save costs and to omit difficult areas from accounting, auditing and reporting. The ability to distinguish good from bad practice therefore provides a foundation on which standards can be set.

A Brief History of 'How'

An extensive array of methods has been offered up over the years for assessing and reporting on corporate social and ethical performance. This is not the place to attempt a scholarly exposition of this history, which has been achieved more effectively elsewhere.[8] Of interest here is not so much the history of how social and ethical accounting and auditing have been talked about and practised for their own sake. Rather, the intention is to show how today's emerging practice is informed by both the theoretical literature and earlier practical experience.

One of earliest proposed approaches to social auditing was that of the *cost* or *outlay audit*.[9] The basic idea, as the name suggests, was to specify the financial costs associated with social activities, and to set these out as an account of the social contribution made by the organization. The major disadvantage of this approach is that financial costs give little idea of the outcome's value. As one assessment of this method concluded: 'since the cost approach makes no effort to measure benefits to the corporation and others associated with the expenditures, it provides little evaluative information to the public.'[10]

Despite this very real limitation, the ready availability of financial data from conventional financial accounts and management systems has made this approach a durable one over the years. Many companies, for example, report on the amount of money that they donate to charitable causes, often expressed both as an absolute amount and as a percentage of pretax profits or gross earnings.[11] The cost or outlay approach has been formalized into a method also known as the *social balance*, effectively a record of financial costs based on a reanalysis of the audited financial accounts associated with actions that can be attributed to the company's social rather than its financial mission. This approach, for example, is currently being used by the Italian retail co-operative movement as the core of its *social balance* accounting, as in the case of Coop Italia.

A second methodological strand that has found its way into modern usage is *constituency accounting*, named by Grey in 1973.[12] Grey argued that traditional financial accounting could simply not accommodate the needs of SEAAR. Instead, an entirely new calculus was required. What he proposed was that companies should examine and report against the demands of key constituencies, whether inside or outside of the company concerned.[13]

There is little evidence of this 'constituency-based' approach having been taken up at the time that it was established at a theoretical level. As the US Department of Commerce commented at the time:

> While this approach attempts to assess benefits as well as costs, some critics believe that it does not state benefits in terms that are meaningful to constituencies outside the corporation. It has not been widely used in corporate social reporting.[14]

The concern raised about the accuracy and usefulness of benefits defined by constituents is one that warrants careful examination. However, such concerns have not prevented this form of consultation becoming a core part of many of the contemporary approaches to SEAAR in the guise of 'stakeholder consultation and dialogue'. As one senior corporate executive remarked at the time: 'All . . . [corporations] . . . must . . . be visibly attentive to public interest – to the public interest as the *public* views it.'[15] Consultation has not only become a vital means by which the views of key stakeholders can be elicited, it has also become a way of legitimizing a company's social and ethical accounting process. Very recently, for example, the financial services company Allied Dunbar produced a publicly available report covering some of its philanthropic activities. Rather than report the financial costs of its contribution following the *outlay approach* described above, Allied Dunbar chose to follow more closely the *constituency* or *stakeholder approach*. In its summary of its *Stakeholder Accountability Report* for 1996, the company declares:

> 1996 marks the twenty-first anniversary of the Staff Charity Fund [SCF]. What better time to study the views of those with most interest in its work. The future will hold new challenges and the way the SCF develops the relationship it enjoys with its stakeholders lies at the heart of what happens next.[16]

Stakeholders' views have been increasingly seen as a critical part of any thorough accounting, auditing and reporting process. However, it has also been clear from an early stage that even the most accurate reporting of these perceptions may not be adequate. For example, in one social accounting and auditing exercise with a British company, staff repeatedly highlighted the view that they were being paid too little. In considering the wage data, it became clear to the auditors that they were in fact being paid just as much as people working for other companies that required broadly the same 'job of work' in the same region of the country. Eventually, the external auditor understood that since the company declared itself to have unusually high moral and ethical codes and values, staff expected to be paid what they saw as a *decent* rather than a *comparable* wage. What needed to be highlighted in this case was the tension revealed by examining the relationship between normal comparative financial indicators and staff perceptions. To omit either would have been to miss the point (or at least *this* point).

The limitations of using financial data are not therefore seen as a reason for rejecting all manner of quantification. Similarly, the limitations in working with people's subjective views are not a reason to ignore or marginalize them.

Financial data, furthermore, has only been one element of the quantified information about social and ethical performance that has been publicly available. What has emerged from the early 1970s has been the practice of *corporate rating* against key social and ethical performance criteria. While many different approaches to this have been adopted, the essence of the practice has been to rate companies in one or both of two possible ways: against predetermined 'binary' criteria that seek the answer to the question: 'Is this company doing this?'; and against scaled criteria that seek to answer the question: 'How is the company doing in this area?'

One of the earliest documented users of this approach was the Interfaith Centre on Corporate Responsibility (ICCR), which took a particular interest, for example, in the practices of companies doing business in South Africa. Probably the most well-known contemporary practitioner in this area is the Council on Economic Priorities (CEP), a public-interest organization based in New York. CEP has been producing corporate ratings against social and environmental criteria for over 25 years, with a particular focus on retail companies and the education of consumers in their purchasing decisions through its annually produced *Shopping for a Better World*.[17] Corporate rating has developed rapidly since the mid 1980s, with a host of public interest NGOs entering the field with their own rating systems aimed at feeding the consumer public, and/or the growing number of ethical investment funds, with information.[18] Most recently, a group of these organizations from North America and Europe have come together in an effort to share information and to move towards some level of convergence in the manner in which screening is being undertaken.

A related development emerged in the 1970s on the back of the so-called *social indicators* movement.[19] Whereas *corporate rating* was an exclusively external activity undertaken by public interest, non-profit organizations and researchers, companies became more involved in the development and application of social performance indicators. The drive towards defining social indicators was closely intertwined with the growing interest in what we would now call stakeholder dialogue. For example, the US Department of Commerce saw some form of community consultation process as initiating the development or selection of relevant social indicators.

> For example, in establishing annual objectives for a corporate community affairs program, a firm would first attempt to develop a quality of life profile for the community, using social indicators regarding unemployment, environmental quality, education, health, and so on. Thereafter a firm could establish performance indicators for some or all of its own activities in relation to these indicators, establish priorities in relation to each other and then measure performance in relation to objectives and their assigned importance.[20]

Community-based approaches to selecting indicators of social and environmental development have emerged as a major theme of community development in the 1990s, particularly following the historic signing of the so-called Local Agenda 21 at the Earth Summit in Rio in 1992.[21] While certainly intended as an empowering process, these approaches can equally suffer from identifying what is important and how best to measure it. As Kim Davenport comments:

> [An] objection is that the catalogue of social indicators is not truly comprehensive, but simply reflects the concerns of the most active or organized constituencies. Also, establishing a fixed catalogue of social indicators might give corporations permission to ignore those issues outside of the catalogue. Moreover, the fixed catalogue could also prove a hindrance to the development and adoption of new, more effective, indicators.[22]

These perceived shortfalls of the pure constituency-based approach to selecting social indicators have opened the door to a complementary approach to the selection process: through identifying best practice or conventionally used indicators and benchmarks. For example, any report on the issue of gender within an organization would today be quickly ridiculed and dismissed if it omitted to report the number of men and women in different positions within the organization, or failed to provide data regarding wages and salaries to allow the proposition 'equal pay for equal work' to be tested. Similarly, any corporate environmental report found to have omitted information on the company's failure to comply with statutory regulations of self-imposed standards would be challenged in today's environmental-compliance sensitized world. At any time there are key issues for which there exist performance indicators that are widely acknowledged as an appropriate and essential part of any performance assessment and disclosure process.

Contemporary forms of SEAAR have drawn inspiration from many earlier approaches and initiatives, such as those highlighted in this section. For example, the Ethical Accounting Statement approach that emerged in Denmark in the late 1980s, through the work of Peter Pruzan and Ole Thyssen at the Copenhagen Business School, has focused exclusively on what might in earlier times have been called constituency accounting, rather than stakeholder dialogue.[23] Similarly, the approach developed by Traidcraft and the New Economics Foundation has drawn on the inspiration and calculus of the social indicators movement, as well as the lessons gained through the development of environmental auditing in the 1980s.[24] More generally, the analytic framework offered in the following paragraphs, certainly arises from the rich and complex history of SEAAR.[25]

Understanding Quality

This historical thumbnail sketch of how SEAAR has evolved highlights some of the key methodological strands, and their possible relationships with differing reasons for the implementation of specific practices. However, despite the need for continued sensitivity towards the needs of diversity, there are also good reasons for establishing methods to compare different approaches.

In short, we need to find ways to be able to tell if a specific exercise in social and ethical accounting, auditing and reporting is worth the candle.

We have developed for this purpose an analytic framework for exploring the quality of a particular experience or initiative in SEAAR. In doing so, we have been painfully aware of the sheer scale of experimentation in this area, and of its increasing quality across many different contexts. In this light, we offer the tool not as a finished product, but as a first stab at what needs to be continued over the coming period. The framework is a means of categorizing experiences or initiatives through:

- *principles* of 'good practice' in SEAAR,
- the *elements* into which the principles can be subdivided to enable more detailed analysis, and
- the *level and quality* of reporting.

Each of these elements of the framework are discussed below. The aim here has not been to judge the relative quality of the cases. At any rate each has been chosen for inclusion on the basis of representing good practice. Rather, the aim has been to use the case studies to demonstrate how the tool can be employed in assessing the relative merits of different approaches.

Table 9.1: *Typology*

Type	Name	Cases	Description
A	Corporate-Led Reporting	Glaxo Holdings plc	Statutory disclosure plus additional internally generated, non-verified discretionary disclosure
B	Ethical accounting	Aarhus Municipality Sbn Bank Wøyen Mølle	Non-statutory disclosure of unverified stakeholder perceptions based on stakeholder-selected issues and questions
C	Social evaluation	Ben & Jerry's Homemade, Inc.	Non-statutory disclosure of stakeholder views and social indicators based on exploration and views of external assessor
D	Social accounting & auditing	The Body Shop International plc Traidcraft plc	Statutory and non-statutory disclosure of stakeholder views, indicators and benchmarks with external verification of process
E	Outlay audit (social balance)	Coop Italia	Non-statutory disclosure of reanalysis of audited financial data to reveal social costs
F	Disclosure ranking	VanCity Savings and Credit Union	Non-statutory disclosure by external body of extent of public disclosure

---

BOX 9.1 The eight principles of quality

- Inclusivity
- Comparability
- Completeness
- Evolution

- Management Policies and Systems
- Disclosure
- Externally Verified
- Continuous Improvement

An initial typology of cases

We begin by offering a simple typology for the nine cases. The six different types (A to F) set out in Table 9.1 are not intended to be exhaustive, but rather to illustrate some of the key dimensions of the cases in their respective clusters.

The 'quality' principles

By voicing the history of different approaches to SEAAR, we are provided with a ready list of hints as to what are some of the key dimensions against which quality needs to be assessed. These have been formalized into eight key principles of quality.

Inclusivity

The principle of *inclusivity* means that the social and ethical accounting and auditing must reflect the views and accounts of all principal stakeholders, not only the particular stakeholders who have historically had the most influence over the evolution of the organization's formal mission statement. What this means, furthermore, is that the assessment cannot be based on a single set of values or a single set of objectives. While over time the various stakeholder groups *may* come to agree on many things, the assessment process cannot assume this to be the case and must therefore accommodate such diversity.[26] It is important to distinguish between consultation in the form of one-way surveying – ie essentially market research – and dialogue, which can be understood as a two-way process that brings the views and interests of all parties to the table.[27]

Comparability

The principle of *comparability* is quite simply that SEAAR enables the performance of the organization to be compared as a basis of assessment. Comparison may be based on the organization's performance in different periods, or on external benchmarks drawn from the experience of other organizations, statutory regulations or non-statutory norms. It is important that external benchmarks are selected for their relevance and legitimacy, not only for their accuracy. For example, comparisons of wage rates with outside organizations need to select the appropriate types of organizations, and also need to draw the comparative data from sources that would be considered legitimate (such as government statistics, or labour-research bodies).[28]

Completeness

The principle of *completeness* means that no area of the company's activities can be deliberately and systematically excluded from the assessment. This principle is important to ensure that the company does not 'cherry-pick' the areas of its activities which will show – on inspection – the most positive social and ethical performance.

Comprehensiveness in combination with the principle of inclusivity raises major practical problems, given the potential magnitude of the assessment process. A major manufacturing company may have thousands of products produced and marketed in a large number of contexts and cultures.

What this means in practice is that not everything can be covered at once, or more specifically during any one cycle. The essence of this principle is therefore that no area of the organization's activities are necessarily excluded from any particular cycle because of any unwillingness on the part of the organization – ie no 'malicious exclusion'. Over several cycles, furthermore, all of the principal stakeholder groups would be covered through an exploration of all the effects of all the organization's activities.[29]

Evolution

It is not possible, as we have here noted, to cover an entire company's 'social footprint' at one time; furthermore, it is likely that this footprint will vary over time. Furthermore, the impact and meaning given to its footprint will also vary, as the composition and expectations of key stakeholder groups change over time. The implication of this is that one-off accounting exercises are not sufficient for the needs of management – in seeking to understand what is happening – or in terms of the company's accountability to the wider public. A key principle against which the practice of SEAAR needs to be judged is therefore whether the exercise is repeated in a manner that demonstrates learning and continual challenge. That is, the process must follow an *evolutionary* path over time.

Management policies and systems

As with both financial and environmental auditing, it is not enough for an organization to get a snapshot of its performance in order to secure its learning processes. It is essential for any systematic process that the organization develops clear policies covering each accounting area, and systems and procedures that allow the accounting process itself to be controlled and evaluated and the organization's awareness and operation of policies and commitments to be assessed through an audit process.

Disclosure

The question of whether the social and ethical accounting and auditing processes are intended primarily for an internal audience, ie as a management tool, or whether they are a means of contributing to organizational learning or to strengthening public accountability, is a conflict that has figured in both the reasons *why* companies engage in the process and the *means by which* the accounting is undertaken. Clearly the focus on an internal audience obviates any need to disclose the results to the public, or even perhaps within the organization beyond the management and board. At the same time, an interest in establishing and maintaining organizational learning and a dialogue culture as well as in strengthening the company's legitimacy in the public domain would require some sort of disclosure. Where a disclosure route is chosen, the matter of quality concerns the extent to which disclosure is a formality or an active means of communication with key stakeholders and the wider public. Merely publishing a document – however comprehensive – does not constitute good practice if the document is difficult to obtain, costly, misleading, or unintelligible to key stakeholders.

Externally verified

The need for external verification concerns, again, the relative emphasis between SEAAR as a management tool and as a means of organizational learning; or as a means of strengthening accountability and legitimacy. Clearly, an emphasis towards the latter implies the need for external veri-fication of some kind. The challenge is, of course, what kind of external verification process will be of a sufficiently high professional quality and independence for it to validate the published material.

Continuous improvement

The aim of any SEAAR system must be to assess progress rather than merely retrospective performance. That is, any relevant system must be able to identify whether the organization's performance has improved over time in relation to the values, missions and objectives set by the organization and its stakeholders, as well as by those established through broader social norms. Moreover, beyond the measurement of progress is the need for a method that actively encourages 'raising the floor' of social and ethical performance.

These eight principles seem to represent the most basic dimensions of quality against which any social and ethical accounting, auditing and reporting process can and should be judged. That does not mean to say that a case where several principles are not being adhered to is necessarily 'poor' in quality. For example, the Scandinavian applications of Ethical Accounting do not include external verification (principle seven), yet this may well be because it is not required given the societal context or the particular applications. So the principles cannot, in isolation, be a basis for intercase judgement, although they can provide a checklist of things to look for in any assessment or selection process.

Scoring Quality

The eight principles are relevant in offering an initial basis for assessing the quality of any exercise in SEAAR. They are, however, too general to be of use in anything but the most basic assessment process. For example, how can one distinguish between stakeholder consultation (essentially limited and one way) and an approach to stakeholder dialogue that is intended to be more deeply participative? Similarly, there are clearly many different ways in which external verification, comprehensiveness, and disclosure can be interpreted in practice.

The approach taken here has been to consider in more depth the possible elements that define the quality of each principle set out above. Specifically, the principles have been broken down into 45 elements against which any particular social and ethical accounting and auditing process can be judged. These elements have been derived from the experience of the case studies, the broader experience of the editors and an analysis of the literature.[30]

The cases in the next section have been 'approximately rated' by these elements. The rating is approximate in that there has been no attempt to construct a numerical scoring system. To do so would imply, amongst other things, that there was some *a priori* basis on which these principles and elements can be seen to be more or less important. For example, it would be problematic to add up the smiling or gloomy faces in the table to determine which organization or method had proved more successful. This stage would require comparisons between organizations with similar aims and comparable contexts.

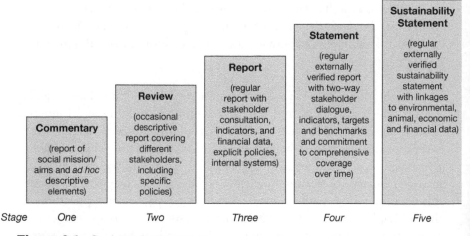

Figure 9.1: Social and ethical disclosure: assessing progress

Table 9.2: Quality rating against basic principles and elements

Case	Inclusivity	Comparability	Completeness	Evolution	Policies/ Systems	External Verification	Disclosure	Continuous Improvement
Aarhus	●	○	●	●	●	□	●	●
Ben & Jerry's Homemade, Inc.	●	○	●	●	□	●	●	○
The Body Shop International	●	○	●	●	●	●	●	●
Coop Italia	□	●	□	□	□	□	●	□
Glaxo Holdings plc	□	○	□	□	○	□	○	○
Sbn Bank	●	○	●	●	●	□	●	●
Traidcraft plc	●	●	●	●	●	●	●	●
VanCity	○	●	○	○	○	○	●	○
Wøyen Mølle	●	○	●	●	●	□	●	●

● = method seeks to address principle

○ = method partially seeks to address principle

□ = method does not adequately seek to address principle

Assessing the Quality of Disclosure

The problems of *ranking* through such scoring and weighting have already been highlighted and concern, in particular, the need to recognize legitimate differences in SEAAR processes. At the same time, there is a demand by all stakeholders to be able to assess the quality of any *disclosure* of social performance, and therefore by implication of the accounting and auditing underlying the 'discovery process'. Drawing inspiration and method from work undertaken by the United Nations Environment Programme (UNEP) and the environmental consultancy SustainAbility Ltd, we have constructed a five-stage developmental model for social and ethical reporting.

The basis of scoring an organization against the five developmental stages of social and ethical reporting is, in the main, drawn from the principles set out above and the elements in the annex to this chapter. An analysis of Glaxo's experience, for example, would place it in stage one, although the availability of some financial data would give it elements of stage three characteristics. Similarly, a major difference between Sbn Bank and Traidcraft's experience, that of external verification, would separate them into stages three and four respectively.

This five-stage model clearly does take the step of defining, to a large degree, what principles and elements are more important than others. While this is a step cautioned against by the editors themselves in earlier sections, the model does illustrate where the whole assessment of the quality of SEAAR should go in the future. Specifically, *if* there is a need to be able to judge accounting, auditing and reporting against each other, some form of developmental model will almost inevitably be used, whether formally or implicitly.

Of course, the 'inevitability' of the need for some developmental model depends, in large part, whether or not some form of certification of quality is necessary, either now or in the future.

Notes

1 Published information on corporate social and ethical accounting and auditing almost exclusively covers Western Europe and the US. Research has revealed, however, that other experiences exist. One of the most important of these is probably the ground-breaking work of the Indian industrial conglomerate Tata Industries, which is covered in Institute of Social and Ethical Accountability (1997) *Sixth Environment Foundation Windsor Castle Roundtable on Social and Ethical Accounting* Auditing and Reporting Accountability Works 1, Institute of Social and Ethical Accountability, London.

2 Nijenrode University, The Netherlands Business School/European Institute for Business Ethics (1995) *The Technology of Ethical Auditing: An Outline* Nijenrode University, Breukelen.

3 S. Zadek and R. Evans (1993) *Auditing the Market: the Practice of Social Auditing* Traidcraft/New Economics Foundation, Gateshead.

4 *The Body Shop Approach to Ethical Auditing* The Body Shop International, Littlehampton, 1996. See also the entire *Values Report* (1996) which contains all three audits.

5   P. Pruzan (1995) 'The Ethical Accounting Statement', *World Business Academy Perspectives* Vol. 9, No. 2, 1995: pp. 35–46.

6   See, for example, the paper prepared on this subject by a group of Northern non-governmental organizations, Corporate Monitoring Working Group (1996) *Monitoring Codes of Conduct*, prepared by the New Economics Foundation and the Catholic Institute for International Relations, London.

7   See, for some discussion of this, S. Zadek and P. Tiffen (1996), 'Fair Trade: Business or Campaign' *Development* Autumn 1996: 3: pp. 48–53.

8   For those interested in some of the historical background that is at best only alluded to in this section, we would suggest R. Estes (1992) 'Social Accounting Past and Future: Should the Profession Lead, Follow – or Just Get Out of the Way?' *Advances in Management Accounting*, 1: pp. 97–108; R. Estes (1995) *Tyranny of the Bottom Line: Why Corporations Make Good People Do Bad Things* Berrett-Koehler, San Francisco; R. Gray, D. Owen & K. Maunders (1996) *Accounting and Accountability: Social and Environmental Accounting in a Changing World* Prentice Hall International, Hemel Hempstead; C. Medawar (1976) 'The Social Audit: A Political View', *Accounting, Organizations, and Society*, 1(4) pp. 389–394; and S. Zadek and P. Raynard (1995) 'Accounting Works: A Comparative Review of Contemporary Approaches to Social and Ethical Accounting' *Accounting Forum* 19 (2/3) Sept/Dec.

9   D. Blake, W. Frederick and M. Myers (1976) *Social Auditing: Evaluating the Impact of Corporate Programs* Praeger, New York.

10   US Department of Commerce (1979) *Corporate Social Reporting in the United States and Western Europe: Report of the Task Force on Corporate Social Performance* US Department of Commerce, Washington, DC: p. 6.

11   See, for example, D. Logan (1993) *Transnational Giving: An Introduction to the Corporate Citizenship Activity of International Companies Operating in Europe* The Directory of Social Change, London.

12   Discussed in M. Dierkes and R. Bauer (eds) (1973) *Corporate Social Accounting* Praeger, New York.

13   A related method, known as *human asset evaluation*, sought to measure the value of productive capability of the firm's human organisation, and simultaneously the loyalty of the firm's employees and other constituencies affected by the organisation. There is a very interesting development in this approach being trialed by the Swedish insurance company, Skandia, under the title intellectual capital valuation. See Skandia (1994) *Visualising Intellectual Capital in Skandia: Supplement to Skandia's 1994 Annual Report* Skandia, Sweden.

14   US Department of Commerce (1979), op cit: p. 6.

15   John Filer, CEO of Aetna Life and Casualty, quoted in US Department of Commerce (1979), *op cit*: p. vi.

16   Allied Dunbar (1996) *The Big Picture: A Summary of the Allied Dunbar Staff Charity Fund Stakeholder Accountability Report for 1996* Allied Dunbar, Swindon: p. 2. Based on the full report, *Staff Charity Fund Review & Stakeholder Accountability Report* Allied Dunbar, Swindon.

17   See also the British equivalent of this, A. Adams, J. Carruthers, and S. Hamil (1991) *Changing Corporate Culture: a Guide to Social and Environmental Policy and Practice in Britain's Top Companies* Kogan Page, London.

18   For example, Ethibel in Belgium, and EthicScan in Canada.

19   For a brief description of this movement and related references, see A. MacGillivray and S. Zadek (1995) *Accounting for Change: Indicators for Sustainable Development* New Economics Foundation, London.

20   US Department of Commerce (1979) *op cit*: p. 8.

21   See, for example, P. Walker (1995) 'Turning Dreams into Concrete Reality', *New Economics* Winter 1995: pp. 5–9; and J. Morris (1995) 'Indicators of Local Sustainability' *Town and Country Planning*, April 1995, Vol. 64 No. 4: pp. 113–119. For a review of some of the historical and contemporary strands of work in this area, see A. MacGillivray and S. Zadek (1995) 'Accounting for Change: Indicators for Sustainable Development' WEF, London.

22   K. Davenport (1996) *Corporate Social Auditing* draft of unpublished thesis, Chapter two, p. 26.

23   P. Pruzan and O. Thyssen (1990), 'Conflict and Consensus: Ethics as a Shared Value Horizon for Strategic Planning', *Human Systems Development* 9 1990: pp. 134–152.

24   S. Zadek and P. Raynard (1995), 'Accounting Works: A Comparative Review of Contemporary Approaches to Social and Ethical Accounting', *Accounting Forum*, 19 (2/3) Sept/Dec.

25   For a more extensive description of some of the historical patterns that have been briefly alluded to in this section, see, for example, R. Gray, D. Owen, & K. Maunders (1996) *Accounting and Accountability: Social and Environmental Accounting in a Changing World* Prentice Hall International, Hemel Hempstead.

26   The principle of inclusivity can also be understood as the equivalent of the standard accounting principle of *materiality*. That is, the rights of stakeholders to choose performance indicators associated with their interests – in conjunction with the right of the organization to measure its performance against its own mission statement – is part of what secures information that is not only accurate but relevant or material.

      There is an interesting connection with Fourth Generation Evaluation here, which suffers from the methodological defect of requiring balanced power conditions from the outset of the evaluation process. See S. Zadek (1995) *Beyond Fourth Generation Evaluation* unpublished paper, New Economics Foundation, London.

27   There have been enormous strides forward in the last decade in developing more participative approaches to dialogue between institutions and their stakeholders. Some of the most interesting work has been in the development field, where participative learning methods have been developed to cope with gross imbalances of power between the dialoguing partners, for example, those that exist between development agencies and village communities in the South. See, for example, J. Pretty, I. Guijt, J. Thompson and I. Scoones (1995) *Participatory Learning and Action: A Trainer's Guide* International Institute for Environment and Development, London.

28   There has been intense activity in the area of social indicator development over the last decade, particularly since the Rio Summit under *Local Agenda 21*. A good review of some of this material is provided by A. MacGillivray and S. Zadek (1995) *Accounting for Change: Indicators for Sustainable Development* New Economics Foundation, London.

29   Note, too, that this may mean it is more realistic and relevant for a large, diversified company to develop different social and ethical accounts for different subunits instead of trying to develop one single accounting, auditing and reporting system for the whole organization.

30   A considerable debt is due to John Elkington and Andrea Spencer-Cooke for their work in benchmarking environmental reports. See in particular United Nations Environmental Programme (1994) *Company Environmental Reporting: A Measure of the Progress of Business & Industry Towards Sustainable Development* Technical Report 24, UNEP, Paris, and UNEP/SustainAbility (1996) *The Benchmark Survey: The Second International Progress Report on Company Environmental Reporting* UNEP, Paris.

STAKEHOLDER ENGAGEMENT AND DIALOGUE

Jeffrey Unerman

A key point identified by the judges for the 2003 *ACCA UK* [Sustainability Reporting] Awards was the poor quality of stakeholder identification and involvement in the submitted reports. Beyond this, stakeholder engagement as an overall activity and more specifically as part of the reporting process is becoming increasingly high on the agenda in both the public and private sectors. It is therefore more important than ever before for such processes to demonstrate a clear rationale, transparency, and impact.

(ACCA, 2005)

The above quotation encapsulates the key issues which are addressed in this chapter. It indicates that engagement and dialogue with stakeholders are increasingly recognized as crucial elements of sustainability reporting, while conceding that there is a shortage of evidence within social and environmental reports that such engagement and dialogue is actually taking place. In addressing these important issues, the aims of this chapter are to:

● explain why engagement and dialogue with a range of stakeholders are crucial elements of sustainability reporting;
● examine various theoretical perspectives regarding the prioritization of different stakeholders' needs and expectations, as identified through stakeholder dialogue, in the social and environmental reporting process;
● evaluate some of the key difficulties faced when an organization seeks to engage a broad range of stakeholders in the determination and discharge of the organization's social and environmental responsibilities, and the duties of accountability allied to these responsibilities;
● identify some of the stakeholder engagement and dialogue processes employed in practice by organizations.

But before addressing these issues, it will be helpful to define what is meant by the terms *stakeholder engagement and dialogue*. Thomson and Bebbington (2005, p. 517) provide a useful definition when they state that:

[s]takeholders are involved [in the social and environmental reporting process] in a number of different ways including, identifying what issues are important to report on, how well the company has performed on specific issues and how to communicate this performance . . . Stakeholder engagement describes a range of practices where organizations take a structured approach to consulting with potential stakeholders. There are a number of possible practices which achieve this aim including: internet bulletin boards, questionnaire surveys mailed to stakeholders, phone surveys, and community based and/or open meetings designed to bring stakeholders and organisational representatives together.

A further perspective on the role of stakeholder engagement and dialogue is provided through the Institute of Social and Ethical AccountAbility's framework, AA1000. Within this framework, dialogue between a company and its stakeholders is one of the central principles of 'good' accountability practices:

> [l]aunched in 1999, the AA1000 framework is designed to improve accountability and performance by **learning through stakeholder engagement**.
>
> It was developed to address the need for organizations to integrate their stakeholder engagement processes into daily activities. It has been used worldwide by leading businesses, non-profit organizations and public bodies.
>
> The Framework helps users to establish a systematic stakeholder engagement process that generates the **indicators, targets, and reporting systems** needed to ensure its effectiveness in overall organisational performance.
>
> (ISEA, 2005, emphasis in original)

This importance of stakeholder engagement was further emphasized by the Institute of Social and Ethical Accountability when it published a draft standard on stakeholder engagement in September 2005 (Account Ability, 2005). This draft (p. 9) states that:

> [T]he overall purpose of stakeholder engagement is to drive strategic direction and operational excellence for organizations, and to contribute to the kind of sustainable development from which organizations, their stakeholders and wider society can benefit by:

Learning:

- Identifying and understanding
    - the needs, expectations and perceptions of internal and external stakeholders;
    - the challenges and opportunities identified by those stakeholders; and,
    - the material issues of internal and external stakeholders.

Innovating:

- Drawing on stakeholder knowledge and insights to inform strategic direction and drive operational excellence.
- Aligning operations with the needs of sustainable development and with societal expectations.

Performing:

- Enhancing performance.
- Developing and implementing performance indicators that enable internal and external stakeholders to assess the organization's performance.

Having provided a broad overview of the meaning and importance of stakeholder engagement and dialogue, this chapter will now proceed to examine why these processes are central to social and environmental reporting.

THE CORE ROLE OF STAKEHOLDER ENGAGEMENT AND DIALOGUE

To understand why stakeholder engagement and dialogue are crucial elements of social and environmental reporting, it is necessary to place these elements within the context of the overall social and environmental reporting process. Several commentators have characterized social and environmental reporting as a hierarchical staged process, whereby the decisions taken at each stage in the hierarchy determine the issues to be considered and decided in the subsequent stages.

For example, Deegan and Unerman (2006) and O'Dwyer *et al.* (2005b) argue that there are four broad hierarchical stages involved in the social and environmental reporting process. Deegan and Unerman (2006, pp. 311–13) label these as the '*why – who – for what – how*' stages, which are shown in Figure 9.2. The *why* stage involves determining an organization's philosophical motivations, or objectives, for engaging in social and environmental reporting – which are likely to be closely aligned to that organization's motives for adopting (or refusing to adopt) corporate social responsibility (CSR) policies and practices. The *who* stage identifies the stakeholders to whom an organization considers itself responsible and accountable if it is to achieve its philosophical objectives for engaging in social and environmental reporting. The *for what* stage is the stakeholder engagement and dialogue stage (and the main focus of this chapter), where the social, environmental, ethical and economic expectations of these stakeholders are identified and prioritized. The *how* stage comprises the mechanisms and reports which the organization employs to address these stakeholder expectations.

Although the focus of this chapter is stage 3 from this model, decisions taken at stages 1 and 2 will clearly shape the stakeholder dialogue and engagement processes employed by any organization. The relevant aspects of these stages are explored in a little more depth below, before focusing on stage 3.

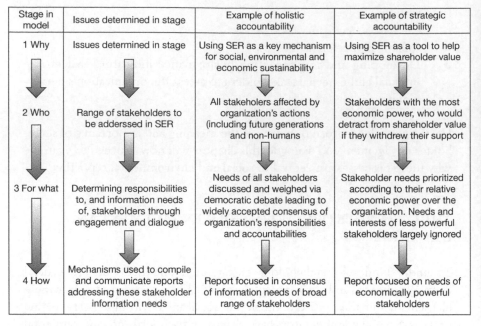

Stage in model	Issues determined in stage	Example of holistic accountability	Example of strategic accountability
1 Why	Issues determined in stage	Using SER as a key mechanism for social, environmental and economic sustainability	Using SER as a tool to help maximize shareholder value
2 Who	Range of stakeholders to be adderssed in SER	All stakeholers affected by organization's actions (including future generations and non-humans	Stakeholders with the most economic power, who would detract from shareholder value if they withdrew their support
3 For what	Determining responsibilities to, and information needs of, stakeholders through engagement and dialogue	Needs of all stakeholders discussed and weighed via democratic debate leading to widely accepted consensus of organization's responsibilities and accountabilities	Stakeholder needs prioritized according to their relative economic power over the organization. Needs and interests of less powerful stakeholders largely ignored
4 How	Mechanisms used to compile and communicate reports addressing these stakeholder information needs	Report focused in consensus of information needs of broad range of stakeholders	Report focused on needs of economically powerful stakeholders

Figure 9.2: A staged hierarchical model of the Social and Environmental Reporting (SER) process.

Stage 1: understanding organizational motives for stakeholder engagement and dialogue

While there may be a combination of different motives driving any organization's social and environmental reporting and CSR in practice, the academic literature examining these motives can be very broadly divided into two perspectives (which may be viewed as two opposite ends of a continuum). One of these perspectives regards social and environmental reporting and CSR as processes which should be aimed at transforming business practices so they become socially and environmentally sustainable. Proponents of this holistic perspective often argue that a continual drive for short-term economic sustainability (in the form of maintenance or growth in financial profits) is incompatible in practice with social and environmental sustainability, as the generation of financial profits is almost always accompanied by direct and/or indirect negative social and environmental impacts (Bebbington, 2001; Gray, 2006; Gray and Bebbington, 2000; Meadows *et al.*, 2004). From this perspective, therefore, *social and environmental reporting* can only be regarded as *sustainability reporting* if it is structured in such a manner as to help in holding the organization (or its managers) truly responsible and accountable for all of their social and environmental impacts on all stakeholders – not just for those impacts or activities prioritized by the organization's managers (Bebbington, 2001; Bebbington and Gray, 2001).

The other broad perspective regards social and environmental reporting as a tool used by managers to win or retain the support of those stakeholders who have power to influence the achievement of an organization's goals (usually maximization of profit). Various theoretical perspectives highlight how social and environmental reports can be used strategically almost as a marketing tool, aimed at aligning perceptions of an organization's social and environmental policies and practices with the ethical values of its economically powerful stakeholders (see, for example, Bailey *et al.*, 2000; Deegan, 2002; Neu *et al.*, 1998; O'Dwyer, 2002, 2003). In this context CSR is often portrayed in terms of a 'win–win' practice, whereby organizational actions which apparently reduce the negative (or increase the positive) impacts of an organization's activities on society and/or the environment also help to increase that organization's profits (Norris and O'Dwyer, 2004; O'Dwyer, 2002, 2003; Thomson and Bebbington, 2005). However, the rarely declared corollary to this argument is that any reductions in negative social and/or environmental impacts on some stakeholders which would also result in a negative economic impact (for example reduced overall short- or medium-term profits) will not be undertaken. Thus, increased profit may be regarded as the prime motive underlying CSR and social and environmental reporting within this 'win–win' perspective, which has little to do with moving the organization towards a position where it is socially, environmentally and economically sustainable (if such a position could ever exist in practice) and accountable to a broad range of stakeholders. Spence (2005) argues that the 'win–win' business case has achieved such a dominant position in business thinking and in discourse about CSR, that it effectively suppresses many arguments which may highlight the social and environmental damage caused by many business activities, thus facilitating the continued unsustainability of business. For these reasons, social and environmental reporting strategically driven by a profit-oriented, economic, motive will not be referred to as *sustainability reporting* in this chapter, but will be simply referred to as *social and environmental reporting*.

Stage 2: linking stakeholder identification to motives for reporting

Having determined the broad philosophical motives or objectives under-pinning why an organization wishes to produce a sustainability report, the next stage in the social and environmental reporting process involves identifying *to whom* the organization needs to report if it is to achieve these philosophical objectives. This identification of stakeholders has to take place after the philosophical motives for engaging in CSR and social and environmental reporting have been determined, because the range of stakeholders to be taken into consideration by any organization will be directly dependent upon its motives for engaging in CSR and social and environmental reporting. For example, an organization whose managers undertake CSR and social and environmental reporting because they believe it will maximize shareholder value will tend to focus only on those stakeholders who are able to exert the greatest economic influence on the organization's operations (Bailey *et al.*, 2000; Freeman, 1984; Freidman and Miles, 2002; Neu *et al.*, 1998; O'Dwyer, 2005b; Unerman and Bennett, 2004). Conversely, managers whose motives for engaging in CSR and sustainability reporting are grounded in a broader moral philosophy, of being responsible, responsive and account-able to all those upon whom their organization's activities might impact, are likely to be concerned with the whole of this broader range of stakeholders – rather than a narrower group of stakeholders whose needs are prioritized simply because the stakeholders' actions can impact upon the organization (Deegan and Unerman, 2006; Gray *et al.*, 1997; O'Dwyer, 2005b; Unerman and O'Dwyer, 2006).

Moving from stakeholder identification to stakeholder engagement and dialogue

Once the stakeholders who are the audience for an organization's social and environmental reporting have been identified, the third broad stage in the social and environmental reporting process is, according to Deegan and Unerman (2006), to identify the social, environmental and economic expec-tations of these stakeholders. This stage is crucial because these expectations will indicate both what behaviour these stakeholders require and consider acceptable from the organization, and the information needed by these stakeholders to enable them to judge the organization's performance in relation to these expectations.

Only once an organization knows *for what* issues its identified stake-holders regard it as being responsible and accountable can it then begin to produce a social and environmental report which addresses these specific issues. In other words, an organization cannot determine *how* to compile an effective social and environmental report – for example, to decide upon which issues to address in the report – until it has identified its stakeholders' information needs and expectations, because without this identification of stakeholders' information needs and expectations any resultant social and environmental report will be providing information which is not targeted at any particular purpose. Without appropriate targeting of the information, its purpose and impact is questionable (AccountAbility, 2005).

In such circumstances, only by luck will a social and environmental report be effective in addressing the information needs of, or discharging any duties of accountability which the organization has to, its identified stakeholders. Consequently it will be an ineffective mechanism for systematically holding the organization, and its managers, accountable for the social, environmental and economic impacts which the organization's actions may have upon its identified stakeholders. This is why stakeholder engagement and dialogue is a crucial element of social and environmental reporting (O'Dwyer, 2005b; Owen *et al.*, 2001; Owen *et al.*, 2000; Thomson and Bebbington, 2005).

Having established the importance of stakeholder engagement and dialogue to social and environmental reporting, we can now address some of the key issues and difficulties involved in the implementation of stakeholder engagement and dialogue processes.

Key issues and difficulties in stakeholder engagement and dialogue

Identifying the range of stakeholders to be considered

The first key issue which needs to be addressed in the implementation of any stakeholder engagement and dialogue process is the identification of stakeholders with whom the organization seeks to communicate. As indicated in the previous section, the range of stakeholders whose views are considered in any organization's stakeholder engagement and dialogue processes will be dependent upon the organization's (or its managers') motives for engaging in CSR and social and environmental reporting.

For an organization using social and environmental reporting strategically to help maximize shareholder value, those stakeholders with the most economic power will usually be significant in the organization's day-to-day operations. They will consequently be readily identifiable by the organization and may also be readily accessible through communication media prevalent in the areas where the organization operates. For example, a multinational corporation with a head office in a Western nation and whose products are sold primarily in Western nations may find that most of its economically powerful stakeholders are also based in Western nations. A multinational such as this can use a range of interactive communication media prevalent in Western nations (such as the internet, focus groups, opinion research) to engage in dialogue with, and to help identify, its economically powerful Western stakeholders' social, environmental and economic expectations (Swift *et al.*, 2001).

Conversely, where the motives of an organization's managers for engaging in CSR and sustainability reporting are based on a more holistic concern to be responsible and accountable for their impact on all those upon whom they have an impact, the process of identifying and engaging in dialogue with this broad range of stakeholders is likely to be much more problematic for several reasons.

Impossibility of direct dialogue and engagement with some stakeholders

Firstly, as organizational actions which take place today can, in many instances, have long-term impacts on nature and society, stakeholders affected by an organization's operations are likely to include future generations (World Commission on Environment and Development, 1987). It is difficult to conceive how an organization can engage stakeholders from future generations in dialogue today regarding current organizational responsibilities and accountabilities. Certain groups of contemporary stakeholders (such as some non-governmental organizations) might position themselves as guardians of specific interests of future generations, but engaging in dialogue with such 'proxy' stakeholder groups involves a vicarious representation of the interests of future generations which may be different from the actual interests yet to be judged by the future generations themselves (Unerman and O'Dwyer, 2006).[1]

Similar issues arise when recognizing that an organization's actions might impact on a range of non-human stakeholders today such as fauna other than humans (Singer, 1993) or, more broadly, the ecosystem (Gray, 2006; Meadows et al., 2004), and/or on some human stakeholders who are less able to articulate their own concerns and interests (for example, infants or the mentally impaired).

Addressing heterogeneous stakeholder views and expectations

Secondly, even if all stakeholders who are affected (or likely to be affected) by an organization's actions were in a position to articulate their own interests, the needs and expectations of different stakeholders are often likely to be mutually exclusive (Lehman, 1995; Neu et al., 1998; Unerman and Bennett, 2004). Faced with a range of mutually exclusive demands from different stakeholders, managers need a mechanism to determine which social, environmental and economic needs and expectations they will seek to address in their CSR and social and environmental reporting.

For managers of organizations strategically motivated to engage in CSR and social and environmental reporting by a belief that these processes will enhance shareholder value, choosing between mutually exclusive stakeholder demands is likely to be fairly straightforward – as they will simply prioritize the demands of those stakeholders with the most economic power over the organization (Adams, 2002; Bailey et al., 2000; Boyce, 2000; Buhr, 2002; Mouck, 1995; O'Dwyer, 2003). Furthermore, in situations where many of the economically powerful stakeholders of a multinational corporation are likely to share a broadly similar cultural background (because for example they are mostly from the more wealthy sections of Western nations), it may be expected that these stakeholders' broad social, environmental and economic expectations will often be similar if, as argued by some, these expectations are largely dependent upon shared cultural and social backgrounds (Lewis and Unerman, 1999). In such situations, it may be expected that multinationals whose managers regard themselves as responsible and accountable solely to those stakeholders with the most economic power over their organization will face a largely homogenous set of broad social, environmental and economic expectations and demands from their selected (often relatively wealthy, predominantly Western) stakeholders.

However, managers who are motivated to engage in CSR and sustainability reporting by a desire to minimize the negative social, environmental and economic impacts of their organization's operations on all those stakeholders who are affected by these operations will face greater problems in identifying a single set of stakeholder expectations from a wide range of often mutually exclusive expectations (Thomson and Bebbington, 2005; Unerman and Bennett, 2004).

Prioritizing stakeholder needs on the basis of maximum negative consequences

One way to identify a single set of expectations would be to prioritize the needs and expectations of those stakeholders upon whose lives the organization's operations have (or are likely to have) the greatest negative impact. But there are several problems with this method of prioritizing stakeholder needs. Firstly, it risks ignoring the views of some stakeholders upon whose lives the organization's operations cause a substantial negative impact in situations where there are other stakeholders whose lives are impacted to a much greater negative extent by the organization's operations. Secondly, it assumes that the negative impacts caused by an organization's operations on each stakeholder can be assessed with a reasonable degree of certainty. And thirdly, it presupposes that it is possible to objectively rank the negative impacts suffered by different stakeholders in order to determine which stakeholder suffers the most from the organization's operations. In practice, any ranking of this nature is likely to be based (at least in part) on the subjective perceptions of the person observing the outcome of the organization's actions, and two observers with slight differences between their respective value systems may place different weightings on different outcomes, thereby resulting in different rankings of the significance of perceived negative outcomes suffered by different stakeholders.[2]

Negotiating a consensus among mutually exclusive stakeholder views through discourse ethics

An alternative method of seeking to arrive at a single set of stakeholder expectations from among mutually exclusive competing stakeholder claims

and expectations, while still prioritizing the needs of those who are the most
negatively affected by an organization's operations, has been advocated by
Unerman and Bennett (2004). This method is based on the discourse ethics
of Jürgen Habermas (1992), which provide a theoretical model for arriving
at a consensus view of moral standards and values within a society through
the use of discourse mechanisms (see, also, Alexy, 1978).

In summary, these discourse ethics mechanisms rely upon two key
philosophical propositions. The first of these is derived from Immanuel Kant's
(1949) eighteenth-century philosophical proposition of the Categorical
Imperative (which has influenced numerous philosophers since Kant), and
judges the validity of any moral proposition by the willingness of the person
proposing this moral value to accept its validity in all possible situations. In
other words, a judgement on the morality of a particular act can only be
considered to have force if the person proposing this moral value would make
the same moral judgement no matter in what position they found themselves
in relation to the act whose morality was being evaluated. Thus, for example,
if a wealthy member of a society who owned shares in many companies but
was not reliant on paid work maintained that voluntary corporate initiatives
to protect the health and safety of employees were immoral, this moral
position would only be considered valid if this person would hold the same
view if they found themselves stripped of their wealth (and investment
income) and were then in the position of an impoverished worker who relied
upon income from employment – and had no choice regarding whether to
accept unsafe working conditions. Put another way, actions which are
considered acceptable to someone with power, wealth and privilege would
only be considered morally acceptable if that person would consider these
actions to be equally morally acceptable if they lost their power and wealth,
and were looking at (and experiencing) the outcomes of these actions from
the position of the least privileged members of society (Lehman, 1995;
Rawls, 1971).

The second key mechanism within Habermas' framework required to
arrive at a universally acceptable and accepted consensus regarding the
morality of behaviour is that each person's moral values and arguments
should be tested and evaluated through debate with others who may hold
alternative views. Habermas argues that the process in the first key stage (of
judging the moral acceptability of actions by putting oneself in the position
of others affected by the actions) is insufficient alone to arrive at a universally
accepted consensus, because each person is likely to have a different conception of the possible outcomes of particular actions on a range of different
stakeholders, and is likely to weight the significance of these outcomes
differently. Only through the process of a democratic debate, where each
person is free to articulate their own views regarding how particular acts are
likely to impact upon them, and are free to challenge the views and
arguments proposed by others, does Habermas believe that a universally
(intersubjectively) accepted and acceptable moral consensus will be arrived

at. But for this process to work, it is important that specific protocols of debate are observed so that the force of the better argument is recognized and accepted by all. The rules of debate proposed by Habermas to ensure that the debate produces and recognizes the 'best' arguments are termed an *ideal speech situation* and, in addition to requiring each participant to engage in the debate openly, honestly, and with willingness to recognize and accept the force of the better argument, they require that:

1   Every subject with the competence to speak and act is allowed to take part in a discourse.
2   a) Everyone is allowed to question any assertion whatever.
    b) Everyone is allowed to introduce any assertion whatever into the discourse.
    c) Everyone is allowed to express [their own] attitudes, desires and needs.
3   No speaker may be prevented, by internal or external coercion, from exercising [their own] rights as laid down in (1) and (2).
                    (Alexy, 1978, p. 40, as quoted in Habermas, 1992, p. 89)

However, Unerman and Bennett (2004) and Lewis and Unerman (1999) argue that, in practice, the theoretical ideal of an *ideal speech situation* is unlikely to ever be (or have been) realized in practice in the determination of organizational social, environmental and economic responsibilities and accountabilities. Among the reasons for this are that:

*   many stakeholders who are potentially affected positively or negatively by an organization's actions are not able to participate in the debate and represent their own interests because, as indicated earlier in this chapter, they may not yet have been born (future generations), may be non-human species of fauna or flora, or may not have the mental ability to articulate their own interests;
*   among those who are able to articulate their own interests, some may be better at articulating their interests than others, thus giving the more articulate a debating advantage over the less articulate in the process of discursively testing the arguments aired in the debate;
*   in practice, many people may participate in the debate strategically, aiming to further their own interests irrespective of the impacts these may have on others – rather than being open and honest regarding these impacts and rather than being willing to recognize the strength of the more compelling moral arguments.

Nevertheless, Unerman and Bennett (2004) argue that although the requirements of an *ideal speech situation* debate are unlikely to ever be realized in practice, they have the potential to inform stakeholder dialogue processes. In other words, these ideal speech procedures should not be regarded as an 'all-or-nothing', but should be regarded as one end of a continuum ranging from no democratically informed procedures to a full ideal speech situation debate (see, also, Power and Laughlin, 1996). Unerman and Bennett argue that any movement along this continuum away from managers simply taking into account the information needs of only those stakeholders with the greatest economic power over achievement of the organization's objectives, and towards a democratic debate among all stakeholders who are affected by the organization's actions, is desirable and should not be sacrificed simply because the full 'ideal speech situation' is unachievable in practice. In the context of the distinction made at the beginning of this chapter between sustainability reporting (aimed at helping realize social, environmental *and* economic sustainability) and social and environmental reporting (motivated by an imperative to increase profits irrespective of negative social and environmental impacts which may arise), any movement towards a democratic consensus in the determination of organizational social, environmental and economic responsibilities and accountability should help move us away from profit-oriented strategic social and environmental reporting and towards more holistic sustainability reporting.

An important aspect of such an 'emancipatory' debate among stakeholders regarding the social, environmental and economic responsibilities of a business is that the debate should not be controlled by the business itself (Thomson and Bebbington, 2005). Such control limits the scope of the debate, and may result in important stakeholder concerns being marginalized (Gray *et al.*, 1997). Thomson and Bebbington (2005) indicate that one possible outcome of a process of stakeholder engagement where the organization itself invites selected stakeholders to participate and determines both the agenda and the channels of communication to be used (ensuring 'difficult' issues are not adequately aired), can be the production of accounts which support and reinforce a falsely objectified 'win–win' image of organizational social and environmental impacts, whose role is 'to tell a more or less passive audience that "everything" is fine and to discourage further questioning of the organizations' (p. 521). Thomson and Bebbington (2005, p. 520) further argue that stakeholder engagement and dialogue mechanisms which would support sustainability accounting and accountability would require that:

- measures be taken to equalize power between the organization and its stakeholders (and, presumably, between different stakeholders);
- the difficulties (or impossibility) of achieving business social and environmental sustainability are explicitly recognized in the stakeholder dialogue; and
- the views of stakeholders regarding all of the impacts which the organization has on them and on the environment are accorded a central place in any social and environmental report resulting from the dialogue process.

The next section of this chapter examines evidence of stakeholder engagement and dialogue practices to see how well they measure up to the principles discussed above.

Evidence of stakeholder engagement in practice

So far this chapter has explored a variety of issues related to stakeholder engagement and dialogue from a largely theoretical perspective, explaining: why stakeholder engagement is a crucial element of the sustainability reporting or social and environmental reporting process; how the range of stakeholders that any organization's managers will seek to engage is related to their philosophical objectives for engaging in CSR; and some of the difficulties involved in seeking to identify, from amongst mutually exclusive competing stakeholder social, environmental and economic expectations, a consensus set of expectations which the organization can then address in its sustainability reporting. This section moves away from these rather abstract (but nevertheless important) theoretical considerations to examine evidence of stakeholder engagement and dialogue practices.

A broad view on the general attitude in practice among large UK corporations towards stakeholder definition and prioritization is offered by Owen et al. (2005). In a survey of managerial attitudes, they found that managers considered shareholders to be the most important group of stakeholders in social and environmental reporting. After shareholders, the ranking among managers for the importance of different stakeholder groups in sustainability reporting was: employees, environmental pressure groups, government/regulators, local communities, customers, long-term lenders and suppliers. However, this ranking cannot be regarded as applicable universally as, for example, Adams (2002) found differences between the stakeholders who were considered the most important by a sample of German managers and those considered the most important by managers in the UK.

Among the academic studies which have commented upon aspects of stakeholder dialogue mechanisms in practice are Thomson and Bebbington (2005), Swift et al. (2001), Unerman and Bennett (2004), Owen et al. (2001), O'Dwyer (2005a) and O'Dwyer et al. (2005a, 2005c).

The dialogue mechanisms mentioned by Thomson and Bebbington (2005) covered: 'internet bulletin boards, questionnaire surveys mailed to stakeholders, phone surveys, and community based and/or open meetings designed to bring stakeholders and organisational representatives together' (p. 517) in addition to focus groups and tear-off comment cards included in social and environmental reports. In commenting on the (lack of) use of the latter, Thomson and Bebbington (2005, p. 523) state:

> [t]hese forms are usually fairly small, they cover a very small set
> of questions or solicit feedback of a very general nature. All the

> evidence which exists . . . suggests that very few individuals provide
> feedback on these preprinted, enclosed feedback forms.

In addition to the dialogue mechanisms outlined by Thomson and Bebbington (2005), Swift *et al.* (2001) found evidence for the use of interviews and company newsletters.

Unerman and Bennett (2004) conducted an in-depth analysis of the use of one stakeholder dialogue mechanism employed by Shell – an internet web-forum in the form of a bulletin board of social and environmental issues hosted on Shell's website. This web-forum, which is a mechanism also used by other companies, allowed anyone with internet access and an email address to post comments on any of the topics covered by the web-forum (which included a catch-all 'other' category). Shell officials replied to many, but not all, of the comments posted by external stakeholders, but Unerman and Bennett found little evidence of external stakeholders commenting on each others' comments. They therefore concluded that the web-forum was not being used by external stakeholders as a mechanism to debate their views, but rather appeared to be used to state views with little evidence of a willingness to engage in debate which might challenge (and possibly lead to a change in) these views. Furthermore, Unerman and Bennett commented that as many stakeholders potentially affected by Shell's operations may not have access to the internet (for example those in less developed nations), and as there were no translation facilities provided for non-English language users, the web-forum could not be used in practice to engage in dialogue with all possible stakeholders. Thus, while the facilities of this web-forum had the potential to move a little way towards the realization of an 'ideal speech situation' democratic debate among stakeholders with divergent views on the social and environmental responsibilities and accountabilities of Shell, in practice it was not used by either Shell or many of its external stakeholders to conduct such a debate.

Rather than commenting upon specific stakeholder dialogue mechanisms, Owen *et al.* (2001) examined managerial attitudes towards the overall process of stakeholder dialogue and engagement. They found that while there was recognition of the importance of stakeholder dialogue and engagement in social and environmental reporting:

> [t]he views of many of the corporate respondents . . . give rise to some suspicion that their commitment to stakeholder engagement is largely confined to a desire to manage expectations and balance competing interests, whilst leaving much scope for the exercise of managerial discretion.
>
> (Owen *et al.*, 2001, p. 270)

Broadly similar insights are provided by some of the findings of O'Dwyer (2005a). Furthermore, in an interview-based study examining the perceptions of one form of stakeholder (non-government organizations) in Ireland towards corporate stakeholder engagement, O'Dwyer *et al.* (2005a) found that these stakeholders believed there was active resistance by many corporations to meaningful engagement and dialogue with some stakeholders (to the extent that some viewed the relationship between corporations and stakeholders as antagonistic).

The above attitudes by corporations towards stakeholder engagement and dialogue in practice would indicate that these measures are used strategically as part of a business case, 'win–win' oriented social and environmental reporting process which has more to do with improving economic performance than it has to do with moving us towards sustainability. However, in a further study, O'Dwyer *et al.* (2005c) found that most of the Irish NGOs who responded to a questionnaire survey considered their relationships with corporations to be amicable, indicating that antagonism between corporations and stakeholders might not be a significant impediment to meaningful stakeholder engagement and dialogue – although a majority of the respondents did not actually take the opportunities which they perceived as being available for engagement and dialogue in helping to determine corporate social and environmental responsibilities and duties of accountability.

Summary and conclusions

This chapter has explored a variety of issues related to the role of stakeholder engagement and dialogue in the process of social and environmental reporting. It located these practices in the context of the motives for organizations engaging in social and environmental reporting, with these motives only being regarded as leading to sustainability accounting if they aimed at making the organization responsible, responsive and accountable to all those stakeholders upon whom their operations may have an impact. It further discussed the problems in operationalizing stakeholder dialogue and engagement mechanisms where these are motivated by concerns to address the expectations of this very broad range of stakeholders. It outlined theoretical procedures for arriving at a consensus among competing, mutually exclusive stakeholder needs and expectations, but indicated that in practice such procedures were not evident. If we are to achieve an improvement in the sustainability of business, then stakeholder dialogue mechanisms which give greater empowerment to a broad range of stakeholders will need to be developed and employed. Otherwise, stakeholder dialogue may continue to be used to provide a fig-leaf for strategically motivated social and environmental reporting which has little to do with making business more holistically sustainable in practice.

Notes

1   It may also be considered problematic for an individual to identify today their own interests in any more than a few years into the future.
2   Nevertheless, there have been some attempts in the academic literature to rank the significance of perceived negative social and environmental consequences of organizational activities – for example in developing full cost accounting models designed to account for externalities (see, for example, Bebbington et al., 2001).

References

ACCA (2005) Improving stakeholder engagement reporting: An ACCA and the Environment Council workshop – March 2005, London: Certified Accountants Educational Trust.

AccountAbility (2005) Stakeholder engagement standard: Exposure draft. London: AccountAbility.

Adams, C. A. (2002) Internal organizational factors influencing corporate social and ethical reporting. Accounting, Auditing and Accountability Journal, 15(2): 223–50.

Alexy, R. (1978) Eine theorie des praktischen diskurses. In W. Oelmüller (ed.) Normenbegründung, Normendurchsetzung. As cited in J. Habermas (1992), Moral consciousness and communicative action. Trans. C. Lenhardt and S. W. Nicholsen. Cambridge: Polity Press.

Bailey, D., Harte, G. and Sugden, R. (2000) Corporate disclosure and the deregulation of international investment. Accounting, Auditing and Accountability Journal, 13(2): 197–218.

Bebbington, J. (2001) Sustainable development: A review of the international development, business and accounting literature. Accounting Forum, 25(2): 128–57.

Bebbington, J. and Gray, R. (2001) An account of sustainability: Failure, success and a reconceptualization. Critical Perspectives on Accounting, 12(5): 557–88.

Bebbington, J., Gray, R., Hibbitt, C. and Kirk, E. (2001) Full cost accounting: An agenda for action. London: Association of Chartered Certified Accountants.

Boyce, G. (2000) Public discourse and decision-making: Exploring possibilities for financial, social and environmental accounting. Accounting, Auditing and Accountability Journal, 13(1): 27–64.

Buhr, N. (2002) A structuration view on the initiation of environmental reports. Critical Perspectives on Accounting, 13(1): 17–38.

Deegan, C. (2002) Introduction: The legitimising effect of social and environmental disclosures – a theoretical foundation. Accounting, Auditing and Accountability Journal, 15(3): 282–311.

Deegan, C. and Unerman, J. (2006) Financial accounting theory: European edition. Maidenhead: McGraw-Hill.

Freeman, R. E. (1984) Strategic management: A stakeholder approach. Boston: Pitman.

Freidman, A. L. and Miles, S. (2002) Developing stakeholder theory. Journal of Management Studies, 31(1): 1–21.

Gray, R. (2006) Social, environmental and sustainability reporting and organisational value creation? Whose value? Whose creation? Accounting, Auditing and Accountability Journal, 19: 793.

Gray, R. H. and Bebbington, J. (2000) Environmental accounting, managerialism and sustainability. Advances in Environmental Accounting and Management, 1(1–44).

Gray, R., Dey, C., Owen, D., Evans, R. and Zadek, S. (1997) Struggling with the praxis of social accounting: Stakeholders, accountability, audits and procedures. Accounting, Auditing and Accountability Journal, 10(3): 325–64.

Habermas, J. (1992) Moral consciousness and communicative action. Trans. C. Lenhardt and S. W. Nicholsen. Cambridge: Polity Press.

ISEA (2005) 'Accountability: AA1000 Series', http://www.accountability.org.uk/aa1000/default.asp, accessed 8 June 2005.

Kant, I. (1949) The foundation of the metaphysics of morals in the philosophy of Immanuel Kant. Trans. L. W. Beck (first published in 1785 edn). Chicago: University of Chicago Press.

Lehman, G. (1995) A legitimate concern for environmental accounting. Critical Perspectives on Accounting, 6(5): 393–412.

Lewis, L. and Unerman, J. (1999) Ethical relativism: A reason for differences in corporate social reporting? Critical Perspectives on Accounting, 10(4): 521–47.

Meadows, D. H., Randers, J. and Meadows, D. L. (2004) Limits to growth: The 30 year update. London: Earthscan Publications.

Mouck, T. (1995) Financial reporting, democracy and environmentalism: A critique of the commodification of information. Critical Perspectives on Accounting, 6: 535–53.

Neu, D., Warsame, H. and Pedwell, K. (1998) Managing public impressions: Environmental disclosures in annual reports. Accounting, Organizations and Society, 23(3): 265–82.

Norris, G. and O'Dwyer, B. (2004) Motivating socially responsive decision-making: The operation of management controls in a socially responsive organisation. British Accounting Review, 36(2): 173–96.

O'Dwyer, B. (2002) Managerial perceptions of corporate social disclosure: An Irish story. Accounting, Auditing and Accountability Journal, 15(3): 406–36.

O'Dwyer, B. (2003) Conceptions of corporate social responsibility: The nature of managerial capture. Accounting, Auditing and Accountability Journal, 16(4): 523–57.

O'Dwyer, B. (2005a) The construction of a social account: A case study in an overseas aid agency. Accounting, Organizations and Society, 30(3): 279–96.

O'Dwyer, B. (2005b) Stakeholder democracy: Challenges and contributions from social accounting. Business Ethics: A European Review, 14(1): 24–41.

O'Dwyer, B., Unerman, J. and Bradley, J. (2005a) Perceptions on the emergence and future development of corporate social disclosure in Ireland: Engaging the voices of non-governmental organisations. Accounting, Auditing and Accountability Journal, 18(1): 14–43.

O'Dwyer, B., Unerman, J. and Brocklebank, C. (2005b) Non-government organisational accountability: The case of Amnesty Ireland. Paper presented at the 17th International Congress on Social and Environmental Accounting Research, University of St Andrews, St Andrews.

O'Dwyer, B., Unerman, J. and Hession, E. (2005c) User needs in sustainability reporting: Perspectives of stakeholders in Ireland. European Accounting Review, 14(4): 759–87.

Owen, D. L., Swift, T. and Hunt, K. (2001) Questioning the role of stakeholder engagement in social and ethical accounting, auditing and reporting. Accounting Forum, 25(3): 264–82.

Owen, D., Shaw, K. and Cooper, S. (2005) The operating and financial review: A catalyst for improved corporate social and environmental disclosure? London: ACCA.

Owen, D. L., Swift, T. A., Humphrey, C. and Bowerman, M. (2000) The new social audits: accountability, managerial capture or the agenda of social champions? European Accounting Review, 9(1): 81–98.

Power, M. and Laughlin, R. (1996) Habermas, law and accounting. Accounting, Organizations and Society, 21(5): 441–65.

Rawls, J. (1971) A theory of justice. Oxford: Oxford University Press.

Singer, P. (1993) Practical ethics, 2nd edn. Cambridge: Cambridge University Press.

Spence, C. (2005) Social and environmental reporting in the UK: A neo-Gramscian perspective, unpublished doctoral thesis, University of St Andrews, St Andrews.

Swift, T., Owen, D. L. and Humphrey, C. (2001) The management information systems dimensions of social accounting and accountability, CIMA Research Report. London: Chartered Institute of Management Accountants.

Thomson, I. and Bebbington, J. (2005) Social and environmental reporting in the UK: A pedagogic evaluation. Critical Perspectives on Accounting, 16: 507–33.

Unerman, J. and Bennett, M. (2004) Increased stakeholder dialogue and the internet: Towards greater corporate accountability or reinforcing capitalist hegemony? Accounting, Organizations and Society, 29(7): 685–707.

Unerman, J. and O'Dwyer, B. (2006) Theorising accountability for NGO advocacy. Accounting, Auditing and Accountability Journal, 19(3): 349–76.

World Commission on Environment and Development (1987) Our common future, the Brundtland Report. Oxford: Oxford University Press.

Chapter 10

Developing CSR strategy

IN THIS CHAPTER WE WILL:

- Explain what a strategic approach to CSR is, and why it is necessary
- Outline two main ways of thinking about CSR and strategy
- Set out the key components of a CSR strategy
- Outline a seven-step process for developing CSR strategy
- Develop an understanding of the factors that need to be taken into account when developing CSR strategy in a global context

Introduction

For many organizations, CSR has been seen as little more than an add-on to the 'real' business of making products, providing services, and generating a profit. In such companies, CSR may be regarded as simply a public relations exercise, where glossy reports or impressive sounding speeches from the chief executive are used to present a responsible image with little attention to how CSR might be integrated throughout the company. In others, CSR may be purely operational, with CSR initiatives such as a supplier code of conduct being used to prevent child labour in the supply chain, or support a recycling initiative being implemented at head office, but without an overarching direction or set of goals being established to guide managers on which CSR issues and tools to focus.

Increasingly, however, many CSR experts have called for organizations to develop a more strategic approach to CSR. After all, companies are spending large amounts of time and money on producing reports, supporting charities, or auditing their supply chains, yet often without a clear sense of exactly how this is benefiting the organization or society at large. As the strategy guru Michael Porter has written with his co-author Mark Kramer (in a follow-up to the reading featured in Chapter 7):

> [T]he fact is, the prevailing approaches to CSR are so fragmented and so disconnected from business and strategy as to obscure many of the greatest opportunities for companies to benefit society. If, instead, corporations were to analyze their prospects for social responsibility using the same frameworks that guide their core business choices, they would discover that CSR can be much more than a cost, a constraint, or a charitable deed – it can be a source of opportunity, innovation, and competitive advantage.
>
> (Porter & Kramer, 2006)

Developing CSR strategy has therefore become a major area of interest both for practitioners and researchers. Two main elements need to be considered here: developing a distinct CSR strategy and integrating CSR into business strategy.

Developing a distinct CSR strategy

One way to think about the intersection of CSR and strategy is to focus on the formulation and implementation of a distinct CSR strategy. In the same way that firms may have a marketing strategy or a human resource strategy, so too might they develop a CSR strategy. As CSR is a broad, and in many instances, relatively new activity for many companies, it is no surprise that CSR strategy and implementation are mostly talked about in terms of a project management structure (Castka et al, 2004; Industry Canada, 2005; Sachs et al, 2006). Typical steps would be a planning phase, an implementation phase, and an evaluation phase, with the last phase potentially initiating a feedback loop to build on successes and learn from mistakes:

Setting goals for CSR strategy

The first step in developing a CSR strategy is to identify the key areas where the organization wants to achieve progress. Furthermore, the organization needs to set specific targets of what to achieve in these areas and how progress towards these targets is going to be measured. For instance, Unilever's ten-year 'Sustainable Living Plan' launched in 2010 committed the company to a range of broad goals such as 'improving health and well-being', 'reducing environmental impact' and 'enhancing livelihoods'. Underpinning these goals though are around 60 concrete targets such as bringing safe drinking water to 500 million people by 2020, and doubling the proportion of the firm's product portfolio that meet the highest global health and nutrition standards by 2020.[1]

Designing CSR strategy

Knowing what you want to achieve is one thing, but knowing *how* to achieve it is another. Designing CSR strategies is a matter of working out how the firm can get from its current position to a desired future state. While many strategies may be more emergent than planned, firms implementing CSR need to consider how to set the direction of the firm to achieve their CSR goals.

Implementing CSR strategy

Sometimes implementing CSR strategy is about doing the same or similar things as usual but with CSR added on – for instance, adding social criteria to supplier evaluation tools – and sometimes it involves doing things completely differently from the start – such as practising stakeholder engagement. There are various CSR tools and techniques that can aid in the implementation process, some of which are specific to a particular CSR area (e.g. audits in the workplace or cause-related marketing in the marketplace) while some cut across areas, such as stakeholder management tools, codes of conduct, and risk management tools.

Assessing the outcomes of CSR strategy

Finally, the results of the CSR strategy need to be assessed, and much of what we discussed in the previous chapter constitutes the core elements of this stage. CSR auditing and reporting are the key tools that help companies to assess their social performance and communicate it to audiences inside and outside the company.

Numerous companies have developed distinct CSR strategies over the years. For example, the global chemicals company BASF says that in relation to its CSR strategy:

> [W]e identify the areas of activity of CSR relevant for us as a responsible company management. We set ourselves targets and consistently drive forward their implementation. The continuous change in the corporate environment makes it important to identify new challenges in good time and broaden the range of issues accordingly. We therefore constantly monitor CSR topics as part of our sustainability issue management. In this way we minimize risks for BASF at an early stage and utilize the opportunities presented by CSR to promote business.[2]

As we saw in Chapter 1, CSR is also a consideration for non-business organizations, such as NGOs and public entities, which means that they might also develop a distinct CSR strategy. For example, the Canadian government has developed a CSR strategy for the Canadian international extractive industry, which aims to enhance

CWS 10.1

Visit the companion website for more examples of CSR strategies

the ability of Canadian mining, oil and gas companies operating abroad to manage their social and environmental risks. The strategy emerged from stakeholder consultations and includes among other things commitments by the government to: promote CSR performance guidelines; disseminate information, tools and training; provide support for capacity building in developing countries; and set up a dispute resolution office.[3]

Integrating CSR into business strategy

Another way to make CSR more strategic is to consider how CSR fits into existing firm strategies – or what new firm strategies would need to be devised to take into account CSR issues and principles. That is, rather than consider just what 'CSR strategy' to develop, the idea here is to look at how CSR affects the firm's regular strategy-making. There are a range of considerations that need to be taken into account here, not least because, as anyone who has ever taken a course in strategic management will know, the question of 'what is strategy?' is not as simple as it first seems! But broadly speaking, according to Galbreath (2009) what we are basically concerned with here is how CSR fits into:

● The organization's overall *goals and mission.*
● The internal and external *strategic issues* that affect the organization's ability to achieve its mission.
● The decision about which *markets* an organization should operate in.
● The choice of *goods and services* that will be offered to customers in those markets.
● The development of the *internal resources* necessary to compete in those markets.
● The development of a distinctive and enduring *competitive advantage* that enables the organization to outperform its rivals.

CWS 10.2

Visit the companion website for more on Danone's approach to integrating CSR into its strategy

For example, if we consider the French food multinational Danone (Dannon in the US), its corporate strategy has been to re-focus on health and nutrition products, with a mission to 'bring health through food to as many people as possible'.[4] This has involved the divestment of non-core businesses such as the Kronenburg and 1664 beer brands, its Amoy cooking sauce business, and its huge biscuit division (which was sold to Kraft for 5.3 million in 2007), and expansion into baby and medical nutrition, including for vulnerable and low income populations. The company's decisions about which markets to operate in have thus been driven by its knowledge of changing societal expectations about food and nutrition, and considerations of how social responsibility can be integrated into its core strategy. This has also fed into investments into new capabilities in nutrition research and food science. In such a context, CSR is more a new imperative, a new set of goals which need to be implemented across the board in all areas of the company, rather than in a special CSR department, similar to a marketing or finance department.

Of course, these two different ways of thinking about CSR and strategy are not always so distinct. A well-designed CSR strategy should also integrate well with broader firm strategy – and integrating CSR into firm strategy will also sometimes necessitate the development of a specific CSR strategy. The point is that in navigating through readings, cases, and commentary on CSR and strategy it is important to recognize just what exactly is meant by the various authors.

Introducing the readings

Both readings in this chapter focus primarily on the first approach – developing a distinct CSR strategy – but also to varying degrees seek to integrate with core business strategy.

How do you develop a CSR strategy?

The reading by Husted and Allen looks at the process of setting up a CSR strategy – or what they call a 'corporate social strategy'. Their approach brings in a lot of relevant strategy theory, including competitive advantage, resource dependency, the resource-based view, and stakeholder management. This makes it relatively easy to see how CSR can be integrated into mainstream ideas about strategic management.

Husted and Allen set out the process of building CSR strategy in terms of seven steps (see Figure 10.1), which they contend, will enable firms to simultaneously create social and economic value. As we argued in Chapter 1, this alignment of social and economic responsibilities is a common approach in contemporary CSR theory and is explicit in the business case for CSR. What makes the reading particularly valuable is that although the authors draw on a lot of theory in developing their model, they also illustrate it with a variety of real-life examples that feature a range of different countries (including the UK, US, Spain, Mexico, Brazil, and Argentina), as well as a number of different areas of CSR engagement, including all of those featured in Section B of this book – the marketplace, workplace, community, and environment.

Globalizing CSR strategy

The second reading also focuses on the development of CSR strategy, and like Husted and Allen, the author Jeremy Galbreath also contends that 'CSR is ultimately a strategic issue, one that cannot be separated from a firm's overall strategy'. Galbreath explores CSR strategy first at the corporate level in a firm's domestic operations, and then goes on to examine the factors that need to be taken into consideration if the firm extends its CSR strategy to its overseas business units. As such, it offers a relatively rare account of global CSR strategy-making.

Figure 10.1: Husted and Allen's seven-step model of CSR strategy development

At the corporate level, Galbreath makes it clear that some of the different perspectives on CSR that were introduced in Section A also have implications for CSR strategy. That is, questions about whether CSR should only focus on shareholder returns, whether multiple stakeholder considerations should be included, or whether firms should altruistically seek to do good are not just normative questions, but they are also crucial strategic decisions to be made by the firm's leaders. As such, there is no one-size-fits-all model of CSR – different organizations will have different goals and different means to achieve them.

In terms of global considerations, the question of domestic vs. international CSR strategies has received relatively little attention in the literature (Peng & Pleggenkuhle-Miles, 2009). An important consideration here is that context will influence the type of CSR that is expected or valued in a particular community (Campbell, 2007). For example, while corporations in some countries are faced with an environment that provides incentives to strategically develop CSR programmes and explicitly articulate their CSR practices, in other countries the same activities are mandated by legislation and so provide little incentive for strategic engagement (Matten & Moon, 2008). Similarly, firms must decide whether to prioritize their attention to CSR in domestic or overseas markets (Peng & Pleggenkuhle-Miles, 2009).

Galbreath's contribution is in clearly articulating the critical factors that should influence a firm's CSR strategy when venturing overseas. Culture, regulatory environment, NGOs, and global standards, he argues, will all have an effect on the likelihood of success of a particular strategy and so therefore should be considered as part of the development of global CSR strategy.

Challenges for practice

Here are some of the key challenges of developing CSR strategy for managers. Think about how you might go about dealing with them if you were faced with the task of developing a strategic approach to CSR in your organization.

1. How do you convince the CEO and other senior managers to consider CSR as a strategic priority?
2. Is CSR strategy best developed and implemented in a CSR department or elsewhere in the organization – and if so, where?
3. How do you go about measuring the success or failure of a CSR strategy? What metrics should you use?
4. What is the best way to get resources allocated to developing and implementing a strategic approach to CSR?
5. What are the risks of getting the CSR strategy wrong?

Study questions

1. Why should organizations develop a strategic approach to CSR? What differences are there likely to be for CSR strategies in large vs. small firms, and in business vs. government organizations?
2. Discuss the specific challenges of developing strategy in relation to CSR. Is CSR any different from other management areas such as human resources, marketing or finance?
3. 'Firms don't need a CSR strategy, they need a competitive strategy that takes into account CSR.' Critically evaluate this statement using examples from practice.
4. What are the key elements of a successful CSR strategy?
5. Imagine a large multinational corporation with subsidiaries in all five continents seeking to design and implement a CSR strategy. What key problems will the company encounter if implementing a single global strategy? What solutions to these problems would you suggest?

Further reading

Burke, L. & Logsdon, J. M. (1996) 'How corporate social responsibility pays off', *Long Range Planning*, 29(4): 495–502.
This is a classic reading that provides a useful understanding of just how CSR programmes can create strategic benefits for firms. It identifies five factors – centrality, specificity, proactivity, voluntarism, and visibility – that help to assess how value is created by CSR initiatives from a strategy point of view.

Porter, M. E. & Kramer, M. R. (2006) 'Strategy and society: the link between competitive advantage and corporate social responsibility', *Harvard Business Review*, December: 78–92.
This is a follow-up piece to the reading by the same authors in Chapter 7, but rather than just focusing on philanthropy, here they also consider competitive strategy more broadly.

Endnotes

1   www.unilever.com/sustainable-living/uslp/ (Accessed 30 August, 2012).
2   www.basf.com/group/corporate/en/function/conversions:/publish/content/sustainability/dialogue/in-dialogue-with-politics/images/CSR_at_BASF.pdf (Accessed 30 August, 2012).
3   www.international.gc.ca/trade-agreements-accords-commerciaux/ds/csr-strategy-rse-stategie.aspx?view=d (Accessed 30 August, 2012).
4   www.danone.com (Accessed 30 August, 2012).

References

Campbell, J. L. (2007) 'Why would corporations behave in socially responsible ways? An institutional theory of corporate social responsibility', *Academy of Management Review*, 32(3): 946–967.

Castka, P., Balzarova, M. A., Bamber, C. J., & Sharp, J. M. (2004) 'How can SMEs effectively implement the CSR agenda? A UK case study perspective', *Corporate Social Responsibility and Environmental Management*, 11: 140–149.

Galbreath, J. (2009) 'Building corporate social responsibility into strategy', *European Business Review*, 21(2): 109–127.

Industry Canada (2005) *Corporate social responsibility: an implementation guide for Canadian business*, Ottawa: Industry Canada, http://strategis.ic.gc.ca.

Matten, D. & Moon, J. (2008) '"Implicit" and "explicit" CSR: a conceptual framework for a comparative understanding of corporate social responsibility', *Academy of Management Review*, 33(2): 404–424.

Peng, M. W. & Pleggenkuhle-Miles, E. G. (2009) 'Current debates in global strategy', *International Journal of Management Reviews*, 11(1): 51–68.

Porter, M. E. & Kramer, M. R. (2006) 'Strategy and society: the link between competitive advantage and corporate social responsibility', *Harvard Business Review*, December: 78–92.

Sachs, S., Maurer, M., Rühli, E., & Hoffmann, R. (2006) 'Corporate social responsibility from a "stakeholder view" perspective: CSR implementation by a Swiss mobile telecommunication provider', *Corporate Governance*, 6(4): 506–515.

HOW DO WE BUILD CORPORATE SOCIAL STRATEGY?

Bryan Husted and David Bruce Allen

Introduction

The sagacious management of firm resources has been at the core of strategic management theory for half a century (Penrose, 1959). In fact, if strategic management scholars agree on anything, it is that firm success rests on how firms develop and acquire, organize and deploy resources in competitive market environments.

Accordingly, strategy rarely focuses directly on wealth creation or profit, but rather on the intermediate or proximate goal of competitive advantage. Profit, in this scheme, is the end result of having a competitive advantage and leveraging it (Porter, 1980, 1985). Create competitive advantage, get your products and services to the market, and the profits should come.

In our work on social strategy, our approach to creating competitive advantage focuses on resources as well. However, unlike many in strategy, we treat external and internal resources as equally vital to firm success. In the model developed in this chapter, we consider the external environment in terms of resource dependence (Pfeffer and Salancik, 1978), and the internal firm environment from the perspective of the resource-based view of the firm (Barney, 1991).

Though intuitively resource dependence and the resource-based view RBV would seem to be an obvious pairing – external and internal resource matching – in management research this is rarely the case. The reason is a recurring theme in academics; the theories come from separate disciplines. Resource dependence comes from a sociology tradition, whereas RBV was developed by strategic management microeconomists (Popp *et al.*, 2006). Furthermore, resource dependence is a macro-level concept initially designed to describe how populations of firms deal with the external resource environment, whereas RBV focuses on the unique internal resources of individual firms that give rise to competitive advantage.

Disputing academic camps are not particular to strategy management. However, the conflict in the 1980s and 1990s between Michael Porter's industrial organization approach to strategy based on choosing the right markets, and RBV's emphasis on unique firm resources, ripped apart an integrated and more accurate concept of strategy that the field is still struggling to restore. In developing social strategy, we have chosen what we believe is a more open, inclusive, and balanced approach to strategy in which it is possible to explain why RBV is compatible both with resource dependence and industrial organization economics. Social strategy is, in this respect, a throwback to earlier strategy models that take into account the firm's internal environment (resources and values) and the organization's reliance upon and interaction with an external environment composed of both market and nonmarket factors.

This integrated approach to strategy, market or social, is also much more in line with how managers work. To begin with, no self-respecting CEO can afford to think of her or his firm either as just an actor in a competitive environment or as the owner of unique resources swimming in vast blue oceans. Rather, effective management treats with equal weight what the world is like out there (less or more stable, dynamic, munificent, etc.) and the firm's resources (better or worse or unique talent, products, finances, social capital, etc.). We should not forget, nonetheless, that the resources required by social strategy are broader than those needed for traditional market strategy. Whether acquired from the external environment or developed internally is circumstantial, though the addition of social strategy-based resources and capabilities often requires investing in relationships with nonmarket stakeholders absent in traditional market strategy formulation. As we have argued earlier, social strategy extends competitive strategy to include a broader range of inputs and, in turn, expands the possibilities of achieving new and unique strategic positions.

This, we trust, provides a fair explanation of our understanding of the raw materials of social strategy. With this in hand, we now turn to a more practice-oriented discussion of how firms may choose to develop and implement a social strategy.

Social strategy as business development

This chapter discusses the design of corporate social strategy via the logic of a business development plan for a new product or service. The raw materials of corporate social strategy are social issues and stakeholder positions on those issues. From here, firms develop social action projects that acquire key resources from the environment and build on critical firm resources which, in combination, are difficult to imitate and lead to the creation of new products and services that provide additional value for current or new customers.

The following seven-step model of corporate social strategy provides a more structured explanation of the story we have just told.

Step 1: Analyze social issue opportunities, competitive environment, and nonmarket stakeholders (environmental analysis) including potential creation of competitive advantage.

Step 2: Analyze firm resources and capabilities to see whether the firm can take advantage of those opportunities.

Step 3: Evaluate firm identity (corporate culture, values, etc.) in terms of social needs and opportunities. Most firms initiate values projects first; we suggest that they first consider the social context.

Step 4: If the firm does not have the requisite resources and capabilities, determine the means and cost of acquiring them. Frequently, alliances and other forms of collaboration are necessary.

Step 5: Create a plan integrating issues, stakeholders, identity, resources, competitive environment and expected outcomes.

Step 6: Implement the plan.

Step 7: Measure and evaluate performance.

The rest of the chapter will be devoted to reviewing the seven steps. Most of our effort will be spent on Step 1. The issues central to Steps 2, 3, 4, and 7 each have a chapter devoted to them. In our discussion of Steps 5 and 6, we will limit ourselves to discussing only those aspects particular to social strategy.

Step 1

Step 1: Analyze social issue opportunities, competitive environment, and nonmarket stakeholders (environmental analysis) including potential creation of competitive advantage.

Identify social opportunities

Too often firms engage in social issues that are tangential to the firm's business. It is no wonder that corporate initiatives based on these issues do not create value for the firm. Michael Porter and Mark Kramer (2006) have developed an approach for how firms can identify relevant issues central to the firm's business. The firm should first look "inside-out" by examining its own value chain (Porter, 1985). Each element of the value chain has significant social and environmental impacts. The primary activities of inbound logistics, operations, outbound logistics, marketing and sales, and after-sales service all provide clues as to the potential impacts of the firm on society. In addition, support activities of firm infrastructure, human resources, technology development, and procurement provide additional opportunities to affect the surround-ing social and natural environment. Thus, Porter and Kramer (2006) recommend that within the universe of all possible social causes a firm might take up, the obvious candidates are those causes that relate to impacts of the firm's value chain.[1]

Firms should then examine those aspects of the firm's environment that impact the firm's activities. This is the so-called activity of "looking outside-in." Porter's (1990) diamond model provides one way of identifying these social impacts. The diamond model examines the context for firm strategy in terms of competitive rivalry, factor (input) conditions, local demand, and the strength of related and supporting industries. The diamond represents a subset of the firm's stakeholder map, but focuses on those elements of the stakeholder map that affect a firm's competitiveness (Hillman and Keim, 2001). Thus, as we will explain in greater detail in Chapter 5, social strategy acquires high levels of centrality when firms focus on those issues that either affect its value chain or are affected by some element of the firm's value chain. It is this subset of social issues that presents strategic opportunities for the firm.

Market Environment

The market environment has been conceptualized in two very different ways. On the one hand, strategy has examined the impact of managerial perception on decision-making; given bounded rationality, it is inevitable that managers across firms have varying understandings of the market environment. Drawing from industrial economics, strategy scholars have also examined markets in terms of industry structure, often using game-theoretic techniques. In this chapter, we focus on perceptual analysis and its importance to social strategy. In Chapter 6, we will also take up game-theoretic models of industry structure.

The market environment affects the success of firm strategies (Dess and Beard, 1984; Sutcliffe and Huber, 1998) as well as the development of capabilities that permit successful implementation of those strategies. The market environment can be grouped around three fundamental constructs: dynamism, munificence, complexity (Dess and Beard, 1984; Keats and Hitt, 1988; Amit and Schoemaker, 1993; Sutcliffe and Huber, 1998). These three dimensions, derived from the environmental analysis literature, are indicators of the relationship and dependence that competitors in an industry have upon suppliers and customers, and other primary stakeholders, and are key to managerial *perception* of opportunities for engaging in social strategy.

Why the emphasis on perception rather than factual data? There are two main reasons. One, the three constructs describe features of the environment that the firm does not control and for which timely data collection can be difficult – a textbook case of bounded rationality. Second, and perhaps more importantly, different managers will interpret the same data as more or less dynamic and so on. Managerial perceptions of the environment are similar to perceptions of risk; much depends on how individuals and collectives selectively respond to and, in effect, enact their environments (Weick, 1995).[2]

With this in mind, we describe the three constructs.

Dynamism. Dynamism measures the difficulty in forecasting external events that may affect the competitive environment (Aldrich, 1979). In dynamic market environments, the availability of resources upon which the firm depends is unpredictable. Complexity indicates the number and variety of environmental influences and their impact on the competitive environment (Duncan, 1972; Dess and Beard, 1984). Complex market environments are characterized by heterogeneous resources. Munificence refers to the relative abundance or scarcity of resources to support sustained growth in a given competitive environment (Staw and Szwajkowski, 1975; Dess and Beard, 1984).[3]

Increased dynamism in an industry leads managers to take more risks and implement innovation strategies in an attempt to overcome uncertainty and minimize the effects of environments they find hard to understand (Miller, 1987; Buchko, 1994). In this context, the incorporation of social change activities into the firm's business strategy enables the firm to break away from established industry practices and organizational routines. For example, social strategy may be a viable alternative where there are abundant nonmarket resources and the availability of market resources is unpredictable. In this way, such firms avoid the pitfall identified long ago by the American jurist, Oliver Wendall Holmes, with respect to the law when he wrote, "To rest on a formula is a slumber, which prolonged means death." In dynamic environments, firms that have not yet explored the possibilities of social strategies may find them to be a singularly adaptive mechanism when faced with unforeseen market changes.

The Body Shop is a classic example of the firm that took advantage of market dynamism. As a new market entrant, The Body Shop understood that a significant customer segment had rejected traditional beauty products. In an environment of new social trends and emerging lifestyles, The Body Shop pursued innovation through social strategy. Integrating social change initiatives of women's liberation, fair trade, and animal rights, Anita Roddick's firm configured a social strategy embracing market and nonmarket activities in the pursuit of inter-related, competitive advantages in stakeholder integration, perceived product safety, closeness to women customers, etc. Anita Roddick was nearly alone in perceiving dynamism in this way in the sector and understanding how social strategy might be used to build competitive advantage.

The Body Shop extended the concept of "natural" to encompass all firm activities within the value chain, including raw materials procurement via fair trade and eliminating animal testing of cosmetics. Within the dynamic environment in which increased opportunities for innovation occurred, secondary stakeholders were able to benefit, among them indigenous peoples' rights groups, animal rights activists and environmentalists. Thus, environmental dynamism, through the innovation that it fosters, increases the likelihood that social change activities will actually satisfy stakeholders and improve their perceptions of corporate social performance, while inducing customers to pay a price premium for social value-added.

During the period of its success in the 1980s and early 1990s, The Body Shop sought to eliminate the difference between its business strategy and its social strategy. As The Body Shop has since learned, the two strategies are not identical, however great the degree of integration. When competitors responded to The Body Shop's natural product line, the firm found both its social strategy advantage undermined and its cost structure untenable. The double shock led to Ms. Roddick's dismissal as CEO and the firm's sale to L'Oreal, an organization better prepared to manage, and integrate, a reformulated business strategy with The Body Shop's trademark social strategy. As The Body Shop case poignantly pointed out, even the most successful social strategy must be properly integrated with business strategy.

Complexity. Complexity impels managers to take into account a wider range of environmental factors and resources and therefore to pursue more complex strategies (Hart and Sharma, 2004). Among the factors are new competitors, new market segments, changing government regulations, eroding margins, globalization, and new technologies. Environmental complexity provides opportunities for firms to respond with social strategies that reconfigure relationships with stakeholders, converting nonmarket needs into new market-based products and services. One unexpected place where social strategies may be especially useful is following success in complex environments, when it is normal for rigidities to set in and restrict innovation

(Howell and Avolio, 1992; Miller, 1993); social strategies can motivate management to incorporate within the planning processes the requisite variety needed to understand and respond more effectively to such environments.

For example, Leche Ram in Spain was faced with a fragmenting dairy market in which store brands, a powerful market leader, and strong regional players had boxed it into a shrinking, unprofitable segment. Through a joint project with UNICEF, "Ni un niño sin leche" ("No child without milk"), the firm relaunched the brand, returned to profitability, and became known as a CSR-focused firm. Soon it became a favorite of NGOs and embarked on a number of other social projects with the support of its employees (Martínez and Allen, 2000). In a complex environment, Leche Ram was able to forge a competitive advantage and create economic and social value.

Munificence. Perceived munificence has been related to the ability of a firm to diversify into new markets (Keats and Hitt, 1988). In industries where there is high munificence, there are general patterns of diversification and innovation (Miles and Snow, 1978). Ordinarily, we would expect that innovative social strategies would more likely be found in high munificence environments. Given a munificent environment, we would expect many firms in the industry to grow successfully.

However, there is a counter-situation, *hostility* (Miller and Friesen, 1983), in which aggressive competition and severe demand fluctuations provide an opportunity for firms that seek to differentiate themselves from their competitors in low munificence environments. It is here, we believe, that social strategy offers greater opportunities to create competitive advantage through the innovative conversion of nonmarket environmental factors into firm resources. For example, the Spanish package transportation company, MRW, was faced with a hostile environment in which UPS, Federal Express, and powerful local competitors were cutting prices as they offered increased services. Undersized and underfunded, MRW's founder and CEO, Francisco Martín Frías, decided on a social strategy that consisted of hiring handicapped workers to do routine tasks, for which MRW received government subsidies and earned plaudits for its social programs. MRW was able to convert an undervalued resource – handicapped citizens – into a firm resource, creating a competitive advantage in cost and reputation, in addition to achieving strong employee loyalty in an industry plagued with high turnover. Though the same aid is available to all firms that hire handicapped employees, MRW is the only firm in its industry that has hired significant numbers of the handicapped, invested in training, and adapted their installations and work schedules to turn what most believe is CSR into a competitive advantage.

MRW did not stop there. In the last ten years it has engaged in eighty-five social action projects, and maintains thirteen aid programs for soldiers, students, families, and other groups to send packages at a discount. Yearly since 1993, MRW has given 1 percent of gross sales to social action. MRW's marketing program consists almost exclusively of its social action programs for which it wins numerous awards and nearly constant press coverage.

For MRW, low munificence or resource scarcity created an opportunity for social strategy to create a competitive advantage. Through consistent innovation, it has nurtured this advantage and has come about as close as possible to creating a sustainable competitive advantage. In an industry driven by costs and price competition, MRW has achieved remarkable customer loyalty.

It is possible that in the future we will see more of this type of social strategy. Wayne Visser (2008) has argued that while philanthropic CSR will be hurt as a result of the Great Recession, an environment of low munificence, strategic CSR will expand.

With regard to social performance, i.e., the amount of social action engaged in by firms, the relationship to munificence is difficult to determine *a priori*. In the case of high munificence, we would expect firms to have additional resources to devote to social programs; however, we would not expect them to feel the necessity to innovate through social strategy. In the case of low munificence, only those firms that perceive that there is an opportunity to create competitive advantage through new and innovative social programs are likely to increase their social performance. In low munificence environments, firms frequently cut back on social programs. On balance, it is difficult to predict the impact of munificence on social performance.

Nonmarket environment

We conceive of the nonmarket environment as consisting of all those relationships between the firm and its stakeholders, that are not mediated by prices. Freeman's (1984: 46) now classic definition of the stakeholder broadly includes all persons or groups that "can affect or [are] affected by the achievement of an organization's objectives." Although his definition is widely debated and numerous other definitions have been offered (Mitchell, et al., 1997), it is generally agreed that stakeholders, many of whom are nonmarket stakeholders, form the fabric of the social structure in which firms operate and determine to whom the firm must respond.

At the core of stakeholder theory is the need to manage "potential conflict stemming from divergent interests" (Frooman, 1999: 193). The interaction of stakeholders with divergent interests creates the issues, which provide the opportunities and threats with respect to which firms may then position themselves through their social change activities. Strategic choices must be made; not all stakeholders can receive the same attention from firms because attention is a limited resource that must be allocated efficiently (Simon, 1947). A firm's attention and response to a stakeholder will depend largely on that stakeholder's salience (Henriques and Sadorsky, 1999).

Salience, or the "degree to which managers give priority to competing stakeholder claims" (Mitchell *et al.*, 1997), is a function of the power and legitimacy of the stakeholders as well as of the urgency of the claims made by stakeholders upon the firm (Mitchell, et al., 1997). As is the case with suppliers and customers, the power of stakeholders is directly related to the firm's dependence on the stakeholder for valuable resources (Pfeffer and Salancik, 1978; Frooman, 1999), but with the additional factor of the structure of stakeholder networks that give stakeholders their legitimacy (Rowley, 1997). Empirical research has confirmed that a high correlation exists between power, legitimacy, and urgency on the one hand and stake-holder salience on the other (Agle *et al.*, 1999). Highly salient, "mixed-motive" stakeholders represent both a potential opportunity for cooperation and a potential threat to the firm (Savage *et al.*, 1991; Frooman, 1999).

By definition, the firm depends upon mixed-motive stakeholders for specific resources. Given their capacity and disposition to cooperate as well as to threaten the firm, these stakeholders play a fundamental role for social strategy. Scholars have observed that in the presence of mixed-motive stakeholders, firms tend to develop a collaborative strategy in which they work jointly with the stakeholder to develop integrative, mutually beneficial solutions (Freeman, 1984; Savage, *et al.*, 1991; Frooman, 1999). A social strategy provides a mechanism to enable cooperation in ways that contribute to competitive advantage. Because of the complex and path-dependent nature of relationships with mixed-motive stakeholders, competitors will find it difficult to imitate this kind of relationship.

For example, Autopistas del Sol (AUSOL), an Argentine highway construction company, faced considerable opposition to a project for a northern access road to Buenos Aires, which would run through both wealthy and poverty-stricken neighborhoods (Austin *et al.*, 2004). As opposition gathered, AUSOL quickly launched a strategy to meet the concerns of these groups, transplanting trees in the wealthier neighborhoods and relocating a school and providing assistance to help legalize property claims in poorer neighborhoods – both actions taken despite contract provisions that made the government responsible to resolve these issues. The effectiveness of this strategy depended upon the close relationships developed with local activists and community leaders. By acting swiftly and fairly, AUSOL was able to turn the presence of mixed-motive, nonmarket stakeholders into a catalyst for the social strategy, enabling the firm to achieve its social and business objectives. Additionally, as in the MRW case, social approval increased employee commitment to the firm's mission and helped boost productivity. Social strategy is especially likely to create competitive advantage precisely when firms are able to help highly salient stakeholders with mixed motives meet their objectives.

Mixed-motive stakeholders represent a special and complex element of social strategy. Dependence on highly salient mixed-motive stakeholders is a powerful motivation for firms to respond to their needs and demands (Mitchell *et al.*, 1997). At the same time, mixed-motive stakeholders often have resources that can be used in collaboration with the firm to carry out social action programs (Husted, 2003). Thus, the likelihood that social strategy will achieve stakeholder satisfaction is greater when salient mixed-motive stakeholders are involved. Returning to the AUSOL example, its social strategy fulfilled the demands of local organizations and thus created high levels of satisfaction in the community, which provided it with the ability to continue with the construction project.

Step 2

Step 2: analyze firm resources and capabilities to see whether the firm can take advantage of those opportunities.

Once again, we turn to consider firm resources and capabilities. The RBV of the firm asserts that competitive advantage depends on firm resources, which, according to Barney include "all assets, capabilities, organization processes, firm attributes, information, knowledge, etc. controlled by a firm that enable the firm to conceive of and implement strategies that improve its efficiency and effectiveness," (Barney, 1991: 101). Resources encompass physical, human, and social capital. Social capital is of special interest. First, social strategy, as it often rests on relationships with mixed-motive stakeholders, frequently depends on building strong social networks. Second, when social capital can be converted into a competitive advantage it is likely to be enduring, due to its causally ambiguous nature, which makes it difficult to imitate (Dierckx and Cool, 1989). Third, social capital is also an integral component of knowledge management (Nahapiet and Ghoshal, 1998).

Clearly, there are many resources and capabilities that may have a positive impact (Russo and Fouts, 1997), but here we discuss only continuous innovation and stakeholder integration (Hart, 1995; Sharma and Vredenburg, 1998; Klassen and Whyback, 1999), both of which we believe have a significant relationship to social capital.

Continuous innovation. Social strategy often involves the introduction of needed products and services to underserved and poorly understood markets (Prahalad and Hammond, 2002) as well as the development of new products and services with social attributes (Kanter, 1999; McWilliams and Siegel, 2001). The ability to generate solutions for such underserved markets or the development of social products and services depends largely on the firm's capability for continuous innovation (Hart, 1995; Sharma and Vredenburg, 1998). Such a capability may already exist on the business side of a firm, but must be redeployed in order to facilitate the development of social strategies that create appropriable benefits for the firm as well as benefits for the community. Such innovation can be incremental or even disruptive to the extent that it breaks with current development trajectories and ways of thinking about social problems (Christensen *et al.*, 2006).

For example, Cemex, the largest cement manufacturer in Mexico, decided to target the problem of housing among low-income Mexican families where the quality of construction tends to be substandard. The *Patrimonio Hoy* project involved helping low-income families save in order to take a more rational approach to self-construction projects as well as provide access to specialized technical assistance. The only way in which the project would be successful from both a business and social point of view was the development of culturally appropriate mechanisms to motivate reliable participation. In order to develop those mechanisms, Cemex sent two anthropologists to study self-construction practices among the poor. They identified the *tanda* – a type of savings program used among neighbors in Mexico – as a culturally consonant way to develop self-enforcing agreements to foster savings. The successful use of the *tanda* mechanism permitted Cemex to provide construction materials and technical assistance in a way that benefited both the company and its communities. The firm benefited from sales in an underserved market and the community benefited from better quality housing. Without Cemex's capability for continuous innovation, *Patrimonio Hoy* would probably have remained another well-intentioned project to help the poor. Instead, Cemex was able to extract economic value and achieve its social objectives at the same time.

Stakeholder integration. We have discussed already the vital role of mixed-motive stakeholders. Recognition of their importance must, of course, be accompanied by gaining their participation through stakeholder integration. Sharma and Vredenburg (1998: 735) define stakeholder integration as "the ability to establish trust-based collaborative relationships with a wide variety of stakeholders – especially those with non-economic goals." Jones (1995) recognized that firm-stakeholder relationships based on mutual trust enable the firm to create a competitive advantage.

In addition to high-level relationship, social-capital advantage, there are also practical advantages to working closely with stakeholders. For example, incorporating stakeholders into product-design teams drives innovation (Harrison and St. John, 1996) and collective learning, which benefits both the firm and its stakeholders (Heugens *et al.*, 2002).

In classic RBV terms, stakeholder integration contributes to competitive advantage because the required skills are valuable, non-substitutable, and rare (Barney, 1991). Moreover, they are complex, causally ambiguous and therefore difficult to imitate (Teece, 1987). Finally, stakeholder integration is a dynamic capability, which can be redeployed to solve other social problems as well as business challenges (Grant, 1996; Teece *et al.*, 1997; Eisenhardt and Martin, 2000).

Dynamic capabilities are particularly valuable, increasing the likelihood that social strategy will generate new resources that, in turn, lead to competitive advantage. Dynamic capabilities can arise from apparently quite simple social action programs, provided that they integrate nonmarket stakeholders into firm activities. For example, the Chilean drugstore chain, Farmacias Ahumada, SA (FASA) engaged in a program of strategic philanthropy with an NGO dedicated to caring for impoverished senior citizens.

FASA cashiers were trained to ask for a small donation to the NGO at the checkout counter. This practice strengthened the firm's business because they found that their employees became better sales people as they developed their fund-raising skills (Austin *et al.*, 2004).

Often, the social capital and social networks of the firm (or members of the firm) are vital to forging alliances and with nonmarket stakeholders with specialized skills and social networks. Such stakeholder integration also permits collective learning and dialogue that can improve the ability of social projects to achieve their objectives and thus improve stakeholder satisfaction. For example, the Brazilian healthcare and cosmetic products company, Natura, had a longstanding collaboration with the Matilde Maria Cremm School, located in a marginalized neighborhood on the outskirts of Sao Paulo. The school was concerned about the low quality of education it provided. Natura's management believed that its relationship with the school was paternalistic and decided to reshape the relation by entering into an iterative cycle of dialogue with the school's leadership and other community groups. Eventually, Natura and the school transformed their relationship into a more balanced and productive collaboration that helped Matilde María Cremm become one of the top five in the state (Austin *et al.*, 2004). Stakeholder integration made this success possible. Natura expects to benefit from its developing capability for stakeholder integration in future business and social action programs.

Step 3

Step 3: evaluate firm culture, corporate values, identity, and ideology, etc. in terms of social needs and opportunities. Most firms initiate values projects first; we suggest that they first consider the social context.

Corporate culture is a complex subject that has proven difficult for management researchers to get a handle on. No one doubts its importance, but it's hard to know where to start. Do values drive behavior, or is it ideology? Do firms have an identity, or are there multiple identities? How do corporate identities take shape, change? To what extent can a specific type of corporate culture be a competitive advantage or handicap?

Many of us would, if we could, avoid the complex and troubling issues of corporate culture. However, when a firm decides to engage in social strategy its success or failure inevitably depends on firm characteristics and behavior that we recognize as corporate culture.

Elsewhere, we will deal with a broad range of corporate culture variables. In this section, we focus on one key firm resource – corporate values – which has been on the agendas of large firms around the world.

Interest in corporate values is not new. Andrews (1971) originally included corporate values as one of the fundamental pillars of corporate strategy, alongside the market environment and firm strengths and weaknesses. This focus on values was then lost in Porter's (1980, 1985) work with its emphasis on industry structure, which came to dominate the field of strategic management in the 1980s. However, Barney (1986) argued that corporate culture is a firm resource and can be a source of competitive advantage. As components of firm culture, values and business philosophy are potential resources of the firm and are essential to its identity (Albert and Whetten, 1985) and in the decision of the firm to include non-economic objectives within its mission and purpose.

All managerial decisions include a values component (Simon, 1947). According to Kluckhohn *et al.* (1952: 395): "A value is a conception, explicit or implicit, distinctive of an individual or characteristic of a group, of the desirable which influences the selection from available modes, means, and ends of action." The shared values, both explicit and implicit, of a socio-cultural system constitute an important part of its culture. Explicit values are captured, in large part, by the concept of ideology, which is a key element in all sociocultural systems (Geertz, 1973; Pettigrew, 1979). Implicit values are associated with universal beliefs that are customarily expressed through more explicit values. Together, these beliefs and values, explicit and implicit, form the bedrock of a company's identity – how the members of the company see the organization.

Corporate identity affects strategy by helping to channel available firm responses to opportunities and threats. This identity affects managerial decisions based on their understanding of the firm's goals and objectives, and beliefs and values about how the world works (Prahalad and Bettis, 1986; Simons and Ingram, 1997) and thus, properly understood and managed, identity, too, can be a source of competitive advantage for the firm.

Similarly, corporate values may coalesce into a strong ideological support for or rejection of social action. Undoubtedly some value systems and ideologies are more likely to produce a commitment to social action than others. Research into corporate ideology systems has provided evidence that there are at least three relevant dimensions: progressive or participative decision-making, social responsibility, and organicity (Goll and Zeitz, 1991; Goll and Sambharya, 1995). Participative decision-making emphasizes a proactive search for opportunities, based on the use of analytic decision tools, open communication channels, and participative consensus-based decision-making. Social responsibility refers to a company's commitment to participating in the solution of social problems. Finally, organicity deals with the firm's ability to adjust to new circumstances (Goll and Sambharya, 1995). This framework is certainly not exhaustive, but provides a useful place to begin to examine the relationship between specific values and their impact on social strategy and corporate social performance. Given the conceptual similarity between the resource for continuous innovation and the organicity dimension of ideology, we will forgo a discussion of the organicity dimension and focus on the other two dimensions.

Social responsibility orientation. Social responsibility orientation (SRO) clearly channels the kinds of responses that managers make to social threats and opportunities. Research indicates that managerial values act as a frame for recognizing and evaluating the importance of social issues (Kahneman and Tversky, 1984; Sharfman *et al.*, 2000) and the salience of stakeholders (Agle *et al.*, 1999). These managerial interpretations of social and environmental issues directly affect the selection of social strategies (Sharma *et al.*, 1999; Bansal and Roth, 2000; Sharma, 2000). The ability of a social strategy to create these benefits depends, in part, upon the genuine commitment of top managers to social responsibility. Jones (1995) argues that firms must demonstrate a sincere concern for ethics and socially responsible behavior in order to obtain competitive benefits from its stakeholder strategies. Socially minded consumers, for example, are unlikely to pay a price premium for social products unless they believe the firm has a sincere commitment to its social responsibilities (Menon and Menon, 1997; Maignan *et al.*, 1999). A strong commitment to social responsibility is evidenced in the firm's application of significant resources to innovative, new social change activities. It is to be expected that this innovation will lead to the development of new resources that are valuable, rare, and non-substitutable (Barney, 1986; Barney, 1991; O'Reilly and Pfeffer, 2000). However, given the explicit nature of an SRO, it is a resource that is imitable and therefore may only provide a competitive advantage in the short run. Nonetheless, firms such as MRW, which combine SRO with continuous innovation, can develop such a strong program and reputation that its competitors will believe the strategic position is unassailable.

Perhaps the greatest risk of social strategy is that it is seen as insincere. Mixed-motive stakeholders may be quite vocal when the firm's social strategy appears to be characterized by pure self-interest, rather than a social responsibility orientation. For example, after Nike was criticized for the labor practices of its overseas suppliers, the company hired Andrew Young to monitor and report on its CSR activities. Nevertheless, the firm's past history and the perceived lack of conviction by its CEO harmed its attempts to improve its social performance and led to consistent distrust and disapproval (McCawley, 2000; Dunne and Dolan, 2004). Long after Nike had resolved the sweatshop labor issues, activists and other stakeholders continued to point to Nike as the classic example of social irresponsibility. Only after almost ten years did Nike's the reputation return to levels it enjoyed prior to the crisis.

Participative decision-making. A participative decision-making (PDM) orientation is especially relevant to social strategy because this orientation includes a commitment to employees in decision-making. It shares many of the characteristics of what Miles and Creed (1995: 361) call a "human investment philosophy," because of its focus on the development of the self-governance capability by employees in order to create a learning organization. PDM appears to be positively correlated with financial performance

(Goll and Sambharya, 1995). This orientation increases the likelihood that managers will select decision-making processes and practices that foster employee participation.

Theorists argue that the involvement of employees is the key to effective environmental strategy because it fosters process innovation (Sharma and Vredenburg, 1998). Similar to the SRO, participative decision-making is related to competitive advantage because it is valuable, rare, and non-substitutable. For example, from its inception in 1850, the Levi-Strauss family promoted social values associated with caring for employees. Without progressive human resource practices, such as employee participation in decision-making, these values would rightfully be considered paternalistic. Moreover, maintaining employee benefits when a firm is growing and creating wealth is relatively easy. As we have once again been reminded during the severe recession, the first people to be hurt by declining profits are employees. Levi-Strauss faced its first serious economic difficulties in more than half a century in the 1980s when foreign imports and changing fashions resulted in severely reduced revenues and losses. They had to cut one-third of the workforce. Robert Haas, CEO, insisted that the firm ground the process in the company's core values; employees steered the process themselves, deciding on the criteria for who would be let go; outplacement and support programs were set up to aid those who lost their jobs (Howard, 1990). While many other clothing manufacturers failed in this period, Levi-Strauss managed to survive and later prosper once again (Mares-Dixon *et al.*, 1999). Employee participation provided the company with the ability to make difficult decisions that were vital for the company's economic wellbeing and to ameliorate the negative impact on employees.

Admittedly, Levi-Strauss is an unusual case; in most cases, corporate values are off-the-shelf products that those at the top have convinced themselves the rest of the firm believes in. Of course, this is precisely why a firm's values and human resource practices consistent with those values can be a firm resource and a competitive advantage.

Step 4

Step 4: if the firm does not have the requisite resources and capabilities, determine the means and cost of acquiring them. Frequently, alliances and other forms of collaboration are necessary.

One of the main arguments of this book is that social activities can be managed for competitive advantage and value creation just as we customarily do with value chain activities. Accordingly, the acquisition of needed resources and capabilities for social action programs can and should be managed within the framework of the traditional make-or-buy decision. This decision, to incorporate activities within the firm's value chain or buy from a supplier, is at the heart of corporate strategy. Recently, a third alternative, alliances, has become an increasingly important option. Within social strategy, firms then have the option either to outsource social action through charitable contributions, to internalize social projects by undertaking them in-house, or to collaborate with NGOs and other allies. In Chapter 10, we discuss the conditions under which these options are likely to occur so as to produce the greatest benefit and we offer examples of how firms have taken these decisions as well our survey research on how firms make these decisions.

By way of introduction, a brief look at two firms that we have already discussed. In deciding to go ahead with an alliance rather than develop a social action program on its own, Leche Ram accurately assessed the necessity of having a partner, like UNICEF, which could establish who should receive milk and provide the legitimization for such a program. In the 1980s, Anita Roddick at The Body Shop established alliances first with Greenpeace and then with Friends of the Earth that failed. Roddick had a clear idea of how she wanted to integrate environmental issues into the firm's activities and found neither partner willing to accede to her approach. The Body Shop set up and staffed it own environmental affairs department, took stands on issues, and designed and implemented a strategy on its own. We should add, here, that most large firms engage in traditional philanthropy, in effect outsourcing their social action programs.

Steps 5 and 6

Step 5: create a plan integrating issues, stakeholders, identity, resources, competitive environment and expected outcomes; and Step 6: implement the plan.

We will be brief. We have combined steps 5 and 6 because the strategic planning process, formulation, and implementation for social strategy is largely identical to strategic planning for any other type of strategy, though the content may be different. We have introduced the key elements of social strategy in the previous sections, nearly all of which we return to in a later chapter. The only item pending for this section is a brief discussion of the one key difference that separates social strategy planning from traditional market strategic planning.

As the objectives include both business and social value creation, top management will need to have a good understanding of both. This involves knowledge, values orientation, and experience with social strategy. In relating the story of The Body Shop, we saw a CEO who had sufficient knowledge of environmental issues and experience in managing alliances with NGOs to chart out the firm's environmental action program and its implementation. Levi-Strauss's Robert Haas did much more than lead the downsizing of the firm in a manner consistent with the firm's traditional values. Working with company employees, most of them from underprivileged backgrounds with limited education, he developed the "Aspirations Statement." Unlike most corporate values statements that merely set out general principles, Levi-Strauss's "Aspirations Statement" was applied in defining occupational roles and responsibilities, performance evaluations, employee training, and in deciding key business decisions with employee participation. Haas' knowledge of the impact of corporate values on Levi-Strauss required years of experience as he learned about the industry, the firm, and the people in it.

The social capital required to talk convincingly about values does not come easily. This we have seen at firms like Enron that prattled on about their outstanding values and people, but in practice fomented unethical and illegal practices from the top down (Gladwell, 2002). The recent severe recession is, in large part, a consequence of the failure of firms that had "committed" CEOs, but no real commitment to anything other than growing revenues, profit, and compensation.

Social strategy, we believe, requires a much more solid, long-term investment in values, including participative management practices. A strategic plan for social strategy is not for a year or even two, but must be undertaken with the idea in mind that values that drive the strategy are enduring, though the specific social action programs may change. As we have insisted from the outset, one of the distinguishing characteristics of social strategy is that once a *commitment is made, the firm will be expected by stakeholders to honor it.*

Step 7

Step 7: measure and evaluate performance.

One key difference between business strategy and social strategy is the differing ways in which they measure performance and order activities. Business strategists first look at measures of financial performance (ROI and ROE) before considering secondary benefits of activities (trust, reputation, commitment, values, identity). Proponents of social action often cite as the key benefits what business strategists may consider secondary (trust, reputation, commitment, values, identity), while arguing that these lead to improved financial and social performance. In effect, social strategy interposes intangible performance measures between strategic behavior and financial performance and social performance.

We argue that neither approach fully captures how social strategies ought to measure and evaluate performance. Direct measures of both business performance and social performance (or impact) are required. One is not of a higher order than the other. Measures of intangible benefits for the firm are important, but this is entirely different from monitoring the economic effectiveness of social action projects where the beneficiaries are external stakeholders. Measurement of social action is relatively new and not widely extended. There are, nonetheless, a number of methods for measuring the economic value of social action, such as conjoint analysis and hedonic pricing techniques. In addition, real option methods of evaluation are especially relevant to the valuation of social projects. Yet, the evaluation of social impacts is often neglected. Firms without a strategic focus have generally been uninterested in the actual effectiveness of their efforts, being content to be engaged in good social causes. A strategic focus requires the careful evaluation of the costs and effectiveness of social projects. Cost-benefit analysis can be applied to the small-scale social projects of the firm. Firms can apply and adapt techniques used in risk management, project management, and marketing analysis.

While it may be argued that as long as economic performance is satisfactory there is no need to measure social performance, we would insist that over time, if social action projects do not provide significant social benefits this will become clear to stakeholders and the firm will lose their support, damaging the social strategy and the firm's reputation and profitability.

Conclusion

Our purpose has been to provide an overview of the seven-step model to help companies build social strategies that will have a positive impact upon both financial and social performance. We have drawn upon the literatures of strategic management, stakeholder management, corporate social responsibility, and environmental management to create a model of social strategy formulation. Certainly it is not the only approach, but it represents one avenue that social strategy research ought to explore if it is to make a greater contribution to the theory of the firm and the practice of management. Nor is the model exhaustive. It can be extended by incorporating additional aspects of industry structure, stakeholder relationships, firm resources, and corporate identity.

Notes

1   Porter's value chain is not the only model available. Grant's (2009) *Contemporary Strategy Analysis* provides an excellent up-to-date review of the value chain with detailed segments on both cost analysis and differentiation.

2   Weick's landmark readings, "Toward a model of organizations as interpretation systems"(1984) and "Collective mind in organizations: Heedful interrelating on flight decks" (1993), provided theoretical and empirical support for studying collective decision-making with the same rigor and interest as individual decision-making. Like John Searle, Weick explained how action flowing from perceptual acts can be examined as part of objective reality. Allow us to recommend Weick's "The collapse of sensemaking in organizations: The Mann Gulch disaster" (1993); the reading is a beautifully told and moving story that explicates his key theoretical concepts.

3   Elsewhere we will add hostility and controllability to the mix of variables. Together the constructs provide us with a basis for analyzing market opportunities for social strategies.

References

Agle, B.R., Mitchell, R.K., and Sonnenfeld, J.A. 1999. Who matters to CEOs: An investigation of stakeholder attributes and salience, corporate performance, and CEO values. *Academy of Management Journal*, 42(5): 507–525.

Albert, S. and Whetten, D.A. 1985. Organizational identity. In L.L. Cummings and B.M. Staw (eds.), *Research in organizational behavior*, 7: 263–295. Greenwich, CT: JAI Press.

Aldrich, H.E. 1979. *Organizations and environments*. Englewood Cliffs, NJ: Prentice-Hall.

Amit, R. and Schoemaker, P.J.H. 1993. Strategic assets and organizational rent. *Strategic Management Journal*, 14(1): 33–46.

Austin, J.E., Reficco, E., Berger, *et al.* 2004. *Social partnering in Latin America: Lessons drawn from collaborations of businesses and civil society organizations*. Cambridge, MA: Harvard University Press.

Bansal, P. and Roth, K. 2000. Why companies go green: A model of ecological responsiveness. *Academy of Management Journal*, 43(4): 717–736.

Barney, J.B. 1986. Organizational culture: Can it be a source of sustained competitive advantage? *Academy of Management Review*, 11(3): 656–665.

— 1991. Firm resources and sustained competitive advantage. *Journal of Management*, 17(1): 99–120.

Buchko, A. 1994. Conceptualization and measurement of environmental uncertainty: An assessment of the Miles and Snow perceived environmental uncertainty scale. *Academy of Management Journal*, 37(2): 410–425.

Christensen, C.M., Baumann, H., Ruggles, R., and Sadtler, T.M. 2006. Disruptive innovation for social change. *Harvard Business Review*, 84(12): 94–101.

Dess, G.G. and Beard, D.W. 1984. Dimensions of organizational task environments. *Administrative Science Quarterly*, 29: 52–73.

Dierckx, L. and Cool, K. 1989. Asset stock accumulation and sustainability of competitive advantage. *Management Science*, 35(12): 1504–1511.

Duncan, R.B. 1972. Characteristics of organizational environments and perceived environmental uncertainties. *Administrative Science Quarterly*, 17(3): 313–327.

Dunne, S. and Dolan, P. 2004. The anti-corporate movement: A discourse analytic perspective. Unpublished paper presented at the 20th Colloquium of the European Group for Organizational Studies, Lyublyana, Slovenia.

Eisenhardt, K.M. and Mattin, J.A. 2000. Dynamic capabilities: What are they? *Strategic Management Review*, 21(10/11): 1105–1721.

Freeman, R.E. 1984. *Strategic management: A stakeholder approach*. Boston, MA: Pitman.

Frooman, J. 1999. Stakeholder influence strategies. *Academy of Management Review*, 24(2): 191–205.

Geertz, C. 1973. *The interpretation of cultures: Selected essays*. New York: Basic Books.

Gladwell, M. 2002. The talent myth. *The New York*, July 22, 28–33.

Goll, I. and Sambharya, R.B. 1995. Corporate ideology, diversification and firm performance. *Organization Studies*, 16(5): 823–846.

Goll, I. and Zeitz, G. 1991. Conceptualizing and measuring corporate ideology. *Organization Studies*, 12(2): 191–207.

Grant, 1996. Prospering in dynamically-competitive environments: Organizational capability as knowledge integration. *Organization Science*, 7(4): 375–387.

Grant, R.M. 2009. *Contemporary strategy analysis*, 7th edn. Malden, MA: Blackwell Publishers.

Harrison, J.S. and St. John, C.H. 1996. Managing and partnering with external stakeholders. *Academy of Management Executive*, 10(2): 46–60.

Hart, S.L. 1995. A natural-resource based view of the firm. *Academy of Management Review*, 20(4): 986–1014.

Hart, S.L. and Sharma, S. 2004. Engaging fringe stakeholders for competitive imagination. *Academy of Management Executive*, 18(1): 7–18.

Henriques, I. and Sadorsky, P. 1999. The relationship between environmental commitment and managerial perceptions of stakeholder importance. *Academy of Management Journal*, 42(7): 87–99.

Heugens, P.P.M.A.R., van den Bosch, F.A.J., and van Riel, C.B.M. 2002. Stakeholder integration: Building mutually enforcing relationships. *Business and Society*, 41(1): 36–60.

Hillman, A.J. and Keim, G.D. 2001. Shareholder value, stakeholder management, and social issues: What's the bottom line? *Strategic Management Journal*, 22(2): 125–139.

Howard, R. 1990. Values make the company: An interview with Robert Haas. *Harvard Business Review*, 68(5): 132–144.

Howell, J.M. and Avolio, B.J. 1992. The ethics of charismatic leadership: Submission or liberation? *Academy of Management Executive*, 6(2): 43–51.

Husted, B.W. 2003. Governance choices for corporate social responsibility: To contribue, collaborate or internalize? *Long Range Planning*, 36: 481–498.

Jones, T.M. 1995. Instrumental stakeholder theory: A synthesis of ethics and economics. *Academy of Management Review*, 20: 404–437.

Kahneman, D. and Tvesrky, A. 1984. Choices, values, and frames. *American Psychologist*, 39(4): 341–350.

Kanter, R.M. 1999. From spare change to real change. *Harvard Business Review*, 77(3): 122–132.

Keats, B.W. and Hitt, M.A. 1988. A casual model of linkages among environmental dimensions. *Academy of Management Journal*, 31(3): 570–598. p.68.

Klassen, R.D. and Whyback, D.C. 1999. The impact of environmental technologies on manufacturing performance. *Academy of Management Journal*, 42(6): 599–615.

Kluckhohn, C. *et al.* 1952. Values and value-orientations in the theory of action. In T. Parsons and E.A. Shils (eds.), *Toward a general theory of action*: 388–433. Cambridge, MA: Harvard University Press.

Maignan, I., Ferrell, O.C., Hult, G.T.M., and Tomas, M. 1999. Corporate citizenship: Cultural antecedents and business benefits. *Journal of the Academy of Marketing Science*, 27(4): 455–469.

Mares-Dixon, J., McKay, J.A., and Peppet, S.R. 1999. Building consensus for change within a major corporation: The case of Levi Strauss and Co. Accessed at www.mediate.org/Levi%20Strauss.pdf on May 24, 2004. Published in L.E. Susskind, S. McKearnen, and J. Thomas-Larmer (eds.), *The consensus building handbook: A comprehensive guide to reaching agreement*. Newbury Park, CA: Sage.

Martínez, J.L. and Allen, D.B. 2000, D.B. 2000. El marketing social: de la táctica a la estrategia (Social marketing: From tactics to strategy). *Harvard Deusto Business Review*, September-October: 66–74.

McCawley, T. 2000. Racing to improve its reputation: Nike has fought to shed its image as an exploiter of third-world labour. Yet it is still a target of activists. *Financial Times*, December 21, p. 14.

McWilliams, A. and Siegel, 2001. Corporate social responsibility: A theory of the firm perspective. *Academy of Management Review*, 26(1): 117–127.

Menon, A. and Menon, A. 1997. Enviropreneurial marketing strategy: The emergence of corporate environmentalism as market strategy. *Journal of Marketing*, 61: 51–67.

Miles, R.E. and Creed, W.E.D. 1995. Organizational forms and managerial philosophies: A descriptive and analytical review. In B.M. Staw.

Miles, R.E. and Snow, C.C. 1978. *Organizational strategy, structure, and process*. New York: McGraw-Hill.

Miller, D. 1987. The structural and environmental correlates of business strategy. *Strategic Management Journal*, 8: 55 76.

— 1993. The architecture of simplicity. *Academy of Management Review*, 18(1): 116–138.

Miller, D. and Friesen, P.H. 1983. Strategy-making and environment: The third link. *Strategic Management Journal*, 4(3): 221–325.

Mitchell, R.K., Agle, B.R., and Wood, D.J. 1997. Toward a theory of stakeholder identification and salience: Defining the principle of who and what really counts. *Academy of Management Review*, 22(4): 853–886.

Nahapiet, J. and Ghoshal, S. 1998. Social capital, intellectual capital, and the organizational advantage. *Academy of Management Review*, 23: 242–266.

O'Reilly III, C. and Pfeffer, J. 2000. *Hidden value: How great companies achieve extraordinary results with ordinary people.* Boston, MA: Harvard Business School Press.

Penrose, E.T. 1959. *The theory of the growth of the firm.* New York: Wiley.

Pettigrew, A.M. 1979. On studying organizational cultures. *Administrative Science Quarterly*, 24: 570–581.

Pfeffer, J. and Salancik, G.R. 1978. *The external control of organizations: A resource dependence perspective.* New York: Harper and Row.

Popp, A., Toms, S., and Wilson, J. 2006. Industrial districts as organizational environments: Resources, networks, and structures. *Management and Organizational History*, 1(4): 349–370.

Porter, M.E. 1980. *Competitive strategy*, New York: The Free Press.

— 1985. *Competitive advantage.* New York: The Free Press.

— 1990. *Competitive advantage of nations.* New York: The Free Press.

— 2006. Strategy and society: The link between competitive advantage and corporate social responsibility. *Harvard Business Review*, 84(12): 78–92.

Prahalad, C.K. and Bettis, R.A. 1986. The dominant logic: A new linkage between diversity and performance. *Strategic Management Journal*, 7: 485–501.

Prahalad, C.K. and Hammond, A. 2002. Serving the world's poor profitably. *Harvard Business Review*, 80(9): 48–57.

Rowley, T. 1997. Moving beyond dyadic ties: A network theory of stakeholder influences. *Academy of Management Review*, 22(4): 887–910.

Russo, M.V. and Fouts, P.A. 1997. A resource-based perspective on corporate environmental performance and profitability. *Academy of Management Journal*, 40: 534–559.

Savage, G.T., Nix, T.W., Whitehead, C.J., and Blair, J.D. 1991. Strategies for assessing and managing organizational stakeholders. *Academy of Management Executive*, 5(2): 61–75.

Sharfman, M.P., Pinkston, T.S., and Sigerstad, T.D. 2000. The effects of managerial values on social issues evaluation: An empirical examination. *Business and Society*, 39(2): 144–182.

Sharma, S. 2000. Managerial interpretations and organizational context as predictors of corporate choice of environmental strategy. *Academy of Management Journal* 43(4): 681–697.

Sharma, S. and Vredenburg, H. 1998. Proactive corporate environmental strategy and the development of competitively valuable environmental capabilities. *Strategic Management Journal*, 19: 729–753.

Sharma, S., Pablo, A.L., and Vredenburg, H. 1999. Corporate environmental responsiveness strategies: The importance of issue interpretation and organizational context. *Journal of Applied Behavioral Science*, 35(1): 87–108.

Simon, H.A. 1947. *Administrative behavior: A study of decision-making processes in administrative organizations.* New York: Macmillan.

Simons, T. and Ingram, P. 1997. Organization and ideology: Kibbutzim and hired labor, 1951–1965. *Administrative Science Quarterly*, 42: 784–813.

Staw, B.W. and Szwajkowski, E. 1975. The scarcity-munificence component of organization environments and the commission of illegal acts. *Administrative Science Quarterly*, 20: 345–354.

Sutchliffe, K. and Huber, G. 1998. Firm and industry determinants of executive perceptions of the environment. *Strategic Management Journal*, 19: 793–809.

Teece, D.J. 1987. Profiting from technological innovation: Implications for integration, collaboration, licensing, and public policy. In D.J. Teece (ed.), *The competitive challenge*: 185–220. Cambridge, MA: Ballinger.

Teece, D.J., Pisano, G., and Shuen, A. 1997. Dynamic capabilities and strategic management. *Strategic Management Journal*, 18: 509–533.

Visser, W. 2008. CSR and the financial crisis: Taking stock. November 4. Accessed by internet at http://csrinternational.blogspot.com/2008/11/csr-and-financial-crisis-taking-stock.html on October 23, 2009.

Weick, K.E. and Daft, R. 1984. Toward a model of organizations as interpretation systems. *Academy of Management Review*, 9(2): 284–295.

Weick, K. E. 1993. The collapse of sensemaking in organizations: The Mann Gulch disaster. *Administrative Science Quarterly*, 38(4): 628–652.

Weick, K. E. and Roberts, K. 1993. Collective mind in organizations. Heedful interrelating on flight decks. *Administrative Science Quarterly*, 38(3): 357–381.

Weick, K.E. 1995. *Sensemaking in organizations*. Thousand Oaks, CA: Sage.

CORPORATE SOCIAL RESPONSIBILITY STRATEGY: STRATEGIC OPTIONS, GLOBAL CONSIDERATIONS

Jeremy Galbreath

In 2003, *Corporate Governance* (Vol. 3 No. 3) published a series of readings on global responsibilities. Topics in this edition covered the global responsibilities of management (Pérez, 2003), the role of business schools in educating on a global perspective (Lorange, 2003) and the contradictions and consequences of global strategies (O'Higgins, 2003), among others. While we believe special issues on global responsibilities in journals such as Corporate Governance certainly add insight into an important topic, what we believe is missing are more substantive discussions of a firm's social responsibilities (hereafter referred to as corporate social responsibilities (CSR)) in the context of corporate strategy in a global context. More specifically, in his ground-breaking book on corporate strategy, Kenneth Andrews of the Harvard Business School argues that with respect to corporate strategy, strategists address what the firm might and can do as well as what the firm wants to do (Andrews, 1971). However, he also argues that strategists must address what the firm ought to do. The "ought to do", in Andrews' parlay, refers to CSR.

Unfortunately, according to Miles (1993), since the publication of Andrews' book on corporate strategy, CSR has had very limited impact on the field that has now become known as strategic management. This is unfortunate as CSR is ultimately a strategic issue, one that can not be separated from a firm's overall strategy (Andrews, 1971; Carroll and Hoy, 1984). Indeed, ignoring CSR can have dire consequences. For example, the total social costs that must be borne by US businesses due to socially irresponsible behavior (e.g. pollution, faulty/dangerous products resulting in consumer injuries, worker accidents due to poor safety conditions) is estimated at two and half trillion dollars per year (Estes, 1996).

If CSR and corporate strategy are integral, and if ignoring one's social responsibilities can render deep financial consequences (Estes, 1996; Frooman, 1997), then firms have important decisions to make. That is, firms need to decide on the type of CSR strategy they will pursue. Thus, first, as with any good decision-making exercise, a firm needs to understand what its options are with respect to CSR strategies. However, making a choice with respect to a CSR strategy in one's home base does not necessarily translate into a "global" CSR platform. Therefore, secondly, firms need to consider the nation/state of operation in relation to the home country as differences might drive different approaches to host country CSR strategies.

Given the significance of CSR as described in journals such as *Corporate Governance*, our discussion in this paper is important for four reasons: first, it conceptually develops the types of CSR strategies which firms might pursue, which is largely underdeveloped in the literature; second, it serves as a benchmark to evaluate CSR strategies across firms which in turn could serve as the basis to empirically investigate the relative value of each strategy; third, it offers practical guidance to managers, particularly managers of SMEs (small and medium enterprises), who are looking to broaden their CSR strategies globally; and fourth, it offers a point of reference for firms in emerging and transitioning economies who may be new to the CSR debate, especially as it applies to global environments.

CSR strategy: what are the options?

Although there are no precise definitions, Carroll (1979) conceptualizes CSR in the context of economic, legal, ethical and discretionary (or philanthropic) responsibilities. Enderle (2004) suggests firms have three responsibilities to society: economic; social; and environmental. The work of Carroll (1979) and Enderle (2004) are important in that they offer insight into what constitutes a firm's responsibilities. However, their work offers little guidance as to what types of strategies a firm might choose to pursue with respect to CSR. To fill this gap, we rely on standard strategic management concepts to develop our ideas.

Most conceptualizations of strategic management suggest that there are two levels of strategy making: corporate strategy; and business unit strategy. Corporate strategy is concerned with the scope of the firm in terms of the industries and markets in which it competes while business unit strategy is concerned with how the firm competes within a particular industry or market. For purposes of this paper, the perspective of "corporate" strategy is equated to the home country while "business unit" strategy is equated to the host country. This metaphor is adopted so that the discussion can be steered toward strategy decision making in the core base of operation while considering factors that might affect the "movement" of the base CSR strategy to existing or planned operations around the word. Thus, turning our attention to "corporate" strategy, four strategic options are described, including: the shareholder strategy; the altruistic strategy; the reciprocal strategy; and the citizenship strategy.

CSR strategic option 1: the shareholder strategy

The shareholder strategy represents an approach to CSR as a component of an overall profit motive, one that is focused exclusively on maximizing shareholder returns. This strategic option is best aligned with the economist Milton Friedman. Although the rise of investor capitalism and the responsibility to shareholders as the focal concern of managers gained strong momentum in the 1980s, Friedman (1962, 1970), concerned with the growth of unchecked and unquestioned demands of CSR, argued decades ago that the only responsibility of business is to provide jobs, make goods and services that are demanded by consumers, pay taxes, make a profit by obeying minimum legal requirements for operation and by engaging in open and free competition without deception or fraud. According to Friedman (1962, 1970), by pursuing maximum profit and strict accountability to the owners of capital, the wealth created is sufficient to meet any social responsibilities. Thus, a business firm that fulfils its profit maximizing obligations not only secures its own survival, but also contributes to the overall wealth and prosperity of society. Friedman's argument represents the neoclassical economic concept of self-interest, via the "invisible hand, at work in society. However, regulations (e.g. environmental, labor) or legal actions (e.g. shareholder lawsuits) may force firms with a pure profit motive into reactive strategies for CSR (Walton, 1982; Kok et al., 2001; Waddock et al., 2002). Lastly, given its pure economic focus, the shareholder strategy to CSR is predominately based on a short-term vision in that it is primarily concerned with producing better financial results over any given previous period.

Is the shareholder strategy a legitimate strategic option with respect to CSR? Certainly, as individuals who place their capital at risk, shareholders have a right to expect a return on their investment. However, Friedman (1970) argues that any use of shareholder funds beyond the means of making a profit is a misuse of those funds. Indeed, if we view a business from a property-rights perspective, a human rights case may be made against CSR in that any use of shareholder funds for non-commercial goals means "robbing" shareholders of the full value of their property rights. Friedman (1970) himself offers a caveat in that initiatives focused on social responsibility (beyond that of profit maximization) may be possible, but only if they improve the profits of the firm.

Echoing Friedman's position, some executives plainly see their responsibility to society as nothing more than maximizing shareholder value (Centre for Corporate Public Affairs, 2000). Furthermore, if a company is small or just starting out, any activity that diverts attention away from making a profit may not be beneficial to the survival of such companies (Spence *et al.*, 2003). Evidence does suggest that smaller firms are not as engaged in socially responsible behaviours (beyond profit maximization) as larger firms (Waddock and Graves, 1997). Although perhaps seen as short-sighted in today's business climate, a shareholder strategy, one based on the classic "Friedmanite" argument, is nonetheless a strategic option with respect to CSR.

CSR strategic option 2: the altruistic strategy

It has been suggested that business firms are not responsible to society, but rather that the obligation of social responsibility falls upon the managers of business firms (Andrews, 1971; Murray and Vogel, 1997). That is, although the firm can be viewed as an artificial person (Wokutch, 1990), and thus has the ability to do harm or good, it is ultimately managers that guide the firm's social responsiveness. In this sense, the personal values of managers and even their religious convictions say much about how a firm is predisposed toward social responsibility beyond profit maximization (Joyner and Payne, 2002; Angelidis and Ibrahim, 2004; Hemingway and Maclagan, 2004).

In this CSR strategic option, the interwoven relationship between the firm and its community is acknowledged and understood. Furthermore, as a member of the community, the firm recognizes that it must "give something back, in the form of philanthropy, in order to make a positive contribution to that community. Typically, philanthropic giving comes from a firm's surplus profits and is distributed according to social value and social and moral precepts; surpluses may be channelled to various kinds of social, educational, recreational, or cultural enterprises (Carroll, 1979). Although hard to identify the real underlying motives (Hemingway and Maclagan, 2004), this strategy encompasses "doing the right thing" by giving back to the community without expecting anything in return. Largely, the altruistic strategy might best be represented as an act of goodwill on the part of the firm and direct benefits may not be measured. Lastly, firms adopting this CSR strategy might contribute to social causes on an *ad hoc* or intermittent basis (e.g. after a natural disaster in the community) or they might make recurring contributions (e.g. giving to annual charity events).

CSR strategic option 3: the reciprocal strategy

Perhaps best viewed as "enlightened self-interest", this CSR strategic option is pragmatic in that it seeks to resolve the conflicts between economic objectives and intense social, moral and environmental expectations of society. Indeed, based on the public's recent view of business (Environics International, 1999), a firm's survival in modern society seems to require an awareness of social responsibility as an indispensable part of strategy. Thus, the reciprocal strategy has an interconnected, two-fold purpose: to benefit society, while providing an economic benefit to the firm.

In this strategy, firms are more proactive with respect to social responsibility. For example, an industrial firm that implements environmentally sound manufacturing that goes beyond minimum legal requirements may not only offer improved benefits to society, but may also lead to reduced regulatory intervention, which can result in positive economic benefits (Murray and Vogel, 1997; Hemingway and Maclagan, 2004). Similarly, a pharmaceuticals firm may give to a specific health-related cause (e.g. AIDS) not only to make a positive contribution to society, but to signal that they are a caring employer, thus benefiting their employee recruiting efforts, for example (Turban and Greening, 1997; Waddock *et al.*, 2002; Rosen *et al.*, 2003).

CSR strategy in this option may also be tied to partnerships, such as between the firm and a specific community group or a non-government organization (NGO) for the purpose of benefiting societal welfare while at the same time for the purpose of benefiting the firm's sales and/or reputation (Logan *et al.*, 1997). Cause-related marketing is also a technique in this strategy and is helpful in that it not only benefits community-based nonprofit organization and social causes, but it is designed to increase the firm's product sales or corporate identity (DiNitto, 1989; File and Prince, 1998).

Recognized as an investment that requires a medium to long-term horizon to accrue benefits, be they financial or other benefits such as improved employee recruitment and retention, CSR in this strategic option has a clear rationale, is generally tied to core business activities and is managed for both firm benefit as well as for positive societal returns. To measure the results, activity-based reporting (e.g. Demmy and Talbott, 1998) is a requirement in this CSR strategy because firms are more interested in specific bottom line benefits than in the altruistic strategy. Although not necessarily used for disclosure to the public, activity-based reporting is beneficial in that it allows a firm to track a given CSR investment to an actual return.

CSR strategic option 4: the citizenship strategy

The citizenship strategy takes on a broader scope than the previous strategic options for CSR. Here, a business firm recognizes that various stakeholders have different interests and expectations, including customers, employees, suppliers, specific communities, shareholders, the environment and so on. Indeed, this strategy perhaps is best described from a stakeholder perspective (Freeman, 1984; Clarkson, 1995; Donaldson and Preston, 1995). Interestingly, as far back as the 1940s, some scholars suggested that a business firm should be viewed "as a citizen in society" (Drucker, 1946, p. 137) which has responsibilities to other citizens. Thus, the citizenship strategy not only recognizes its responsibilities to potential external constituents beyond its shareholders, but to its internal constituents as well (Dawkins and Lewis, 2003).

To be sure, balancing the competing demands of the various groups that are affected by or have an interest in a firm is a feature of this strategy. However, the reality is stakeholder demands are often mutually exclusive and a firm cannot necessarily treat all stakeholders as equals (Sethi, 2003); thus, firms may categorize their stakeholders as primary and secondary (Clarkson, 1995). To address this tension while at the same time trying to be a good corporate citizen, sorting out how to reconcile the various economic and social objectives of stakeholders, although fraught with difficulty, seems to move the firm in the right direction.

By way of example, if a chemical manufacturer implements environmental production standards beyond those that are required by law but, in the process, has to lower wages to its employees to cover the costs, is this good citizenship? In another example, if a financial services firm lays off IT employees in its home base of operation in order to move jobs overseas where IT labor is cheaper, but in the process improves the socio-economic conditions of an emerging foreign economy, is this good citizenship? These examples are meant to illustrate the tensions involved in trying to meet the demands of all the firm's stakeholders, particularly in a global context.

To be sure, a key feature of the citizenship strategy is that firms proactively dialogue with their stakeholders – and integrate their findings into decision making. Indeed, in this strategy, stakeholder needs are integral to corporate strategy (as both an input and output) and social objectives are integrated with economic goals. However, given the complexity of managing multiple stakeholder needs, it is recognized that the potential benefits of the citizenship may not materialize in a short time frame; thus, the citizenship strategy is long-term focused even if at the expense of weaker short-term results. Furthermore, citizenship strategies develop means of managing and measuring their accountability (e.g. triple bottom line) to those stakeholders. In other words, be it through annual reports, corporate web site disclosure, or separate triple bottom line reports, firms adopting a citizenship approach are transparent with respect to CSR. Evidence does suggest that a citizenship-type strategy of CSR can offer tangible rewards such as improved financial results as well as intangible rewards, such as outstanding reputations (Margolis and Walsh, 2003).

Although there may be various permutations to these strategies, we believe that the four CSR strategic options presented serve as a good guide (Figure 10.2). Certainly, however, not every firm will develop CSR strategies that perfectly match these options nor will they necessarily maintain the same CSR strategy over time. Furthermore, choosing a strategic option with respect to CSR in one's base of operation doesn't necessarily translate to equivalent CSR strategies for operating in a global environment.

From home country to host country: global considerations for CSR strategy

Choosing an option with respect to setting the policy for CSR in the home country is one thing. However, while in many cases the drivers (e.g. regulatory, ethical, economic) that serve as the impetus for the development of CSR strategies are the same worldwide, the context of CSR can vary considerably between countries, reflecting the distinctive traits of countries themselves (Waddock and Smith, 2000; Rochlin and Boguslaw, 2001). Furthermore, regional – if not local community – differences all bear down on what constitutes socially responsible behaviour of a business firm (Post, 2000; Warhurst, 2001). Meeting the challenges of CSR in a global context is much more difficult than it appears. Without careful consideration of host country differences, firms might make poor decisions regarding what constitutes appropriate CSR strategies in foreign lands and cultures (Küskü and Zarkada-Fraser, 2004). This can ultimately undermine both financial results and the firm's reputation (Petrick et al., 1999).

Within a global context, business firms around the world share common language with respect to products, production, marketing, finance, profits and so on. However, they are inevitably embedded in a specific city, city-state, city-providence, city-nation, etc. For example, firms such as Coca-Cola, Sony and Shell are all based in a particular city-state – but they have

	Goal	Vehicles	Measurement	Benefactors	Benefits	Time Frame
Shareholder Strategy	Profit	Rationalization; Self-interest	Financial results	Shareholders; Others indirect	Financial	Short-term vision
Altruistic Strategy	Give back	"Check-book" Philanthropy	Donations	Community Groups and Causes	Benefits may not be measured	Intermittent; Possibly timed (e.g. annually)
Reciprocal Strategy	Mutual benefits	Public Relations; Sponsorship; Partnerships; Community activity; Volunteering; Cause Related Marketing	Activity-based reporting	The Firm and the Community	Performance; Market Goals; Human Resources	Medium-to long-term planning
Citizenship Strategy	Responsibility; Transparency; Sustainability; Accountability	Governance; Applied Ethics; Stakeholder dialogue; Input to/outflow of Corporate Strategy	Triple Bottom Line; Holistic	To firm: Survival, position, role; To partners of all sectors; To wider society	Tangible plus potentially Intangible	Long-term horizon

Figure 10.2: CSR strategic options

production facilities, suppliers, and sub-contractors operating in quite different city-states around the world. Here, aspects of the location of various stakeholders may vary widely which consequently affects CSR differently (Burton *et al.*, 2000).Thus, given the locale of where a business firm operates (or plans to operate) in the world, they are embedded within the various traditions of that particular setting. To address CSR strategy in a broader, global context, four key aspects are discussed: culture; regulatory environment; NGOs; and global standards.

Culture

Just as business firms development their own unique cultures – and strategies – in a home country, if they plan global expansion, they must operate within the context of national and even regional cultures of another country (Hofstede, 1980, 1983). According to Burton *et al.* (2000, p. 153), "Different cultures will emphasize different values; what is important to one culture at one time may not be important to another culture or even to he first culture at some time in the future. These values may affect both the role institutions assume within society and what society expects of those institutions."

Based on Burton *et al.* (2000) assessment, understanding the cultures of the countries and regions a firm is seeking to operate in is very important (cf. Schwartz, 1992; Maignan and Ferrell, 2003). By way of example, in India, ten-year olds working 12-hour days weaving rugs occurs. In Honduras, 15-year old girls working 80 hours per week producing sweaters occurs. In Bangladesh, incidents of nine-year olds working in shoe factories with imposed production quotas occurs (Quindlen, 1994). In many countries, such labor-related activities would not only be seen as appalling and quite contrary to culturally accepted norms of socially responsible behavior, but would also be in criminal violation of labor laws. However, the reality is in some countries the use of very young workers is a necessity as this keeps them off the street begging for survival or from committing criminal acts to obtain money (Greenfield, 2004). Research (e.g. Orpen, 1987; Burton *et al.*, 2000) does show that individuals view CSR differently from country to country.

The above examples do raise a fundamental issue: should the culture of a particular region or nation or should the firm's own standards (in the home country) form the basis of CSR strategy in international locations? For example, if a firm adopts a shareholder strategy with respect to CSR in the home country, will the same approach translate into an acceptable strategy in a different country of operation? Thus, firms must address the issue of whether to adapt to the socially responsible norms of a national or regional culture (a "relativism" approach) or to impose an international standard of CSR (a "universalism" approach) regardless of the cultural norms of a specific country or region of operation (Smeltzer and Jennings, 1998; Carroll, 2004).

The reality is firms must apply ethical and moral standards to address cultural differences with respect to CSR (Robertson and Fadil, 1999). In some cases, firms might choose not to do business in a given country or region due to suspect norms of socially responsible behavior. In other cases, they might compromise and conduct CSR in a manner that it opposed to the policy set in the home base of operation. Even in other cases, firms might act to offer their CSR leadership in the home base to the foreign base of operation, setting the standard for domestic businesses operating in that community. By way of example, Sony recently announced that its environmental targets and policies will be standardized, implemented and enforced in all of its global locations. In another example, in 1997, Mattel announced the creation of its Global Manufacturing Principles (GMP), a set of standards applied to all of the company-owned and contract manufacturing facilities around the world.

Lastly, understanding culture is important with respect to CSR as societal – if not stakeholder – concerns vary from country to country. For example, in Australia, Canada and China, environmental concerns take center-stage within society. In Indonesia, Turkey and the USA, improving education ranks highest among social concerns. Finally, in Brazil, Chile and South Africa, reducing poverty and homelessness are the most important social concerns (Environics International, 2002). Based on this information, while having a "universal" policy with respect to CSR globally may be an ideal in some areas (e.g. workers' rights, the environment), firms who understand the intricacies of a national or regional culture are better equipped to address local concerns of social responsibility when and where necessary (e.g. through philanthropic giving or strategic partnerships).

Regulatory environment

According to Carroll (1979, 2004), the regulatory environment, in the form of an enforceable legal framework, is a key component of CSR. In general, laws and regulations have been theorized as necessary in an economy as a response to inefficient or inequitable behavior (Posner, 1974). Indeed, a widely held view is that federal and state bodies impose laws where the marketplace has failed to ensure fair competition, safe products, fair and equitable working conditions and a clean and healthy environment.

Although firms are expected to operate within the overall regulatory framework of the land, since the 1970s the development of laws with respect to specific facets of social responsibility have been growing. For example, in the USA, laws have been implemented with respect to the environment (under the auspices of the Environmental Protection Agency, or EPA) and workplace safety standards (under the auspices of the Occupational Safety and Health Administration, or OSHA). Other laws are more global in nature.

In November, 1997, for example, 34 nations signed the OECD Convention on Combating Bribery of Foreign Public Officials in International

Business Transactions. The convention now makes bribery of foreign public officials a criminal act on an extraterritorial basis. Although in many ways seen as something unnecessarily imposed on business by the government (Harrington, 1996), the regulatory environment under which a firm must operate in a given country is yet another area of consideration with respect to global CSR strategy. Here, firms are again faced with ethic decisions regarding home versus host country considerations. For example, if a firm adopts a reciprocal strategy with respect to CSR in the home country and implements environmental production standards that go beyond those required by law as part of that strategy, should the same policy be adopted in a host country of operation where environmental laws don't even exist?

Non-government organizations (NGOs)

Historically, associations of private individuals (e.g. churches) have come together for public purposes, typically to provide services (e.g. education, health, welfare) in the community not available from the state, long before the establishment of democratic government and the concept of the welfare state (Novak, 1996). In more recent times, particularly since the 1950s, a new class of private "association" has been established which generally focuses directly on changing public policy. These local, regional and international non-governmental organizations, or NGOs, have grown to over 50,000 in number, almost double the number just 25 years ago, up from just over 1,000 in 1956 (Gordenker and Weiss, 1996; Smith, 1997).

A general definition of NGOs is "non-profit groups that combine resource mobilization, information provision and activism to advocate for changes in certain areas" (Spar and La Mure, 2003, p. 79). NGOs are generally either ideas-based – human rights, education, equality, environmental sustainability, etc. – or identity-based – indigenous, female, homosexual and the like. However, these lines may be blurring with many NGOs integrating ideas – and identity-based causes (van Tuijl, 1999).

With respect to what NGOs actually do, there are three approaches to classification: operational; advisory; and advocacy. Operational NGOs act to provide social services such as education, health and disaster relief. Advisory NGOs are involved in providing information and consulting services, for example, to mutual funds focused on socially responsible investing (SRI). Advocacy NGOs are directly involved in lobbying governments and local, national and international organizations for changes and/or adoption of socially responsible policies for businesses. They may also file resolutions on behalf of shareholders to pressure businesses into acting more socially responsibly. Although sometimes seen as questionable and unaccountable (Johns, 2001), NGOs are causing substantial changes in corporate management, strategy and governance (Doh and Teegen, 2003). Of particular interest is discerning the role and impact of NGOs in the host country to ascertain whether CSR policy set in the home country needs to be customized to the local environment.

Global standards

Lastly, just as NGOs can add pressure to businesses to act on behalf of society in many different ways, global standards, many coming from NGOs themselves, are another source of institutional pressure. The majority of CSR-related global standards are voluntary in nature, asking firms to develop and implement policies and practices on various CSR issues (Neergaard and Pedersen, 2003). The standards help users to establish a systematic process that generates indicators, targets and reporting systems necessary for effective implementation and monitoring of various CSR programs and activities. In essence, global standards are instruments designed for corporate self-regulation (Waddock et al., 2002).

A variety of global standards have emerged over the years and the Business and Social Initiatives (BSI) database, established by the International Labour Office, now lists over 400 different standards, principles and codes of conduct (Waddock et al., 2002). Some of the more recognized standards, however, include the ISO (International Standards Organization) 14000 and 14031 for the environment; Social Accountability (SA) 8000 for labor-related issues; the United Nations (UN) Declaration on Human Rights and the Environment; the Caux and Sullivan Principles for economic, social and political justice and general CSR; and the OECD (Organization for Economic Cooperation and Development) Guidelines for Multinational Enterprises for voluntary principles and standards with respect to CSR. With these and a host of other global standards covering every conceivable aspect of social responsibility, firms are faced with increasing pressure to strategically evaluate a cadre of external benchmarks as they establish CSR policy. Of course, strategic decisions here can become complicated when firms operate, or plan to operate, in multiple locations. Operating in multiple locations raises the issue of the choice of implementing a single, uniform policy worldwide with respect to CSR or whether to allow flexibility based on, for example, culture or the regulatory environment of a given country or region (Smeltzer and Jennings, 1998).

Conclusion

Although some strongly oppose any responsibility of the firm beyond the economic (Friedman, 1970), research does suggest that CSR beyond just the economic "pays" (Griffin and Mahon, 1997; Margolis and Walsh, 2001; Orlitzky et al., 2003). That is, CSR does have a positive financial benefit to firms. Conversely, the total social costs that must be born by US businesses due to socially irresponsible behavior is well over two trillion dollars per year (Estes, 1996). Such findings suggest that CSR is an area of corporate concern that can not be overlooked. In fact, CSR is argued to be essential to a firm's overall strategy (Andrews, 1971; Carroll and Hoy, 1984). Furthermore, as globalization continues to broaden its reach, firms must increasingly acknowledge and assess their responsibilities on a global scale (Pérez, 2003; Carroll, 2004). Thus, managers should pay keen attention to the matters of CSR and this paper offers some guidance as to how they might strategically approach the subject.

Specifically, from a strategic perspective, we have suggested that businesses have four CSR strategic options to consider: first, the shareholder strategy; second, the altruistic strategy; third, the reciprocal strategy; and fourth, the citizenship strategy. The shareholder strategy is based on Friedman (1970) and holds that its only responsibility to society is an economic one. The altruistic strategy, on the other hand, is one based on "giving back" to the community in the form of monetary donations to various groups and causes. The reciprocal strategy takes a more strategic approach to CSR in that it views social responsibility as good business. That is, by taking on broader social responsibilities, the firm not only offers improved benefits to society, but it also benefits in the form of financial and other tangible rewards. Lastly, the citizenship strategy is the most strategic. In the citizenship strategy, a firm identifies and dialogues with its stakeholders as part of input to corporate strategy formulation. By doing so, CSR strategy is specifically directed at individual stakeholder needs, be they employees, customers or even the environment. By offering full and open disclosure through mediums such as triple bottom line reports, firms leveraging a citizenship strategy aim for public transparency and accountability. In the end, by targeting social responsibilities towards specific stakeholders, the goal is to increase long-term value creation for those stakeholders as well as for the firm's financial and reputational position in the market. Although there certainly might be variations, these four options offer a baseline view of specific CSR strategies. However, as discussed in this paper, choosing a CSR strategy in the home base does not necessarily translate into a "global" program.

When extending a CSR strategy from home to host countries, various aspects, such as local cultures, regulatory environments, NGOs and global standards, must all be taken into consideration (Figure 10.3). Given that local cultures tend to view CSR differently (Orpen, 1987; Burton et al., 2000), firms must carefully examine the location of operation before transposing home to host CSR strategies. As with culture, regulatory environments also differ from country to country. However, some emerging regulations, such as the OECD convention on bribery of foreign officials, are universal in nature. Thus, as with culture, a thorough examination of the regulatory environment is an important consideration with respect to global CSR strategies. As for NGOs, their influence continues to increase around the world and many countries have powerful NGOs that are specifically focused

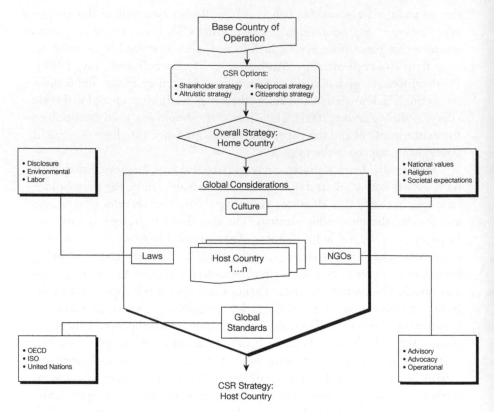

Figure 10.3: Considerations for CSR strategy in a global context

on issues of importance in the focal country. Thus, understanding the "who's who" of NGOs in any given country lends itself to informed decisions with respect to CSR strategies in that country. With respect to standards, global CSR standards such as the ISO 14000 and 14031 for the environment and the Social Accountability (SA) 8000 for labor-related issues are becoming important benchmarks for which to compare who is practicing CSR and who is not in the world. Thus, by adopting appropriate global CSR standards, firms are signalling their adherence to socially responsible practices in business, which is becoming an increasingly important means of competitive differentiation in a global economy (Waddock *et al.*, 2002).

Lastly, for scholarly consideration, we suggest researchers develop means of testing the various CSR strategies outlined in this paper. For example, case studies or survey instruments could be used to collect data on each CSR strategy. By including different industries and countries, analysis could reveal the types of CSR strategies most followed. This would be important for benchmarking similarities/differences across both industries and countries. Where financial results are collected, the results would also be important to compare and contrast the relative value of each CSR strategy. Here, the research findings would add to the growing body of evidence examining the

CSR-firm performance association, which is an important area of research content according to scholars (e.g. Margolis and Walsh, 2003).

References

Andrews, K.R. (1971), *The Concept of Corporate Strategy*, Dow-Jones Irwin, Homewood, IL.

Angelidis, J. and Ibrahim, N. (2004), "An exploratory study of the impact of degree of religiousness upon an individual's corporate social responsiveness orientation", *Journal of Business Ethics*, Vol. 51 No. 2, pp. 119–28.

Burton, B.K., Farh, J.-L. and Hegarty, W.H. (2000), "A cross-cultural comparison of corporate social responsibility orientation: Hong Kong vs United States students", *Teaching Business Ethics*, Vol. 4 No. 2, pp. 151–67.

Carroll, A.B. (1979), "A three-dimensional conceptual model of corporate performance", *Academy of Management Review*, Vol. 4 No. 4, pp. 497–505.

Carroll, A.B. (2004), "Managing ethically with global stakeholders: a present and future challenge", *Academy of Management Executive*, Vol. 18 No. 2, pp. 114–20.

Carroll, A.B. and Hoy, F. (1984), "Integrating corporate social policy into strategic management", *Journal of Business Strategy*, Vol. 4 No. 3, pp. 48–57.

Centre for Corporate Public Affairs (2000), *Corporate Community Involvement: Establishing a Business Case*, Centre for Corporate Public Affairs in Association with the Business Council of Australia, Melbourne.

Clarkson, M.B.E. (1995), "A stakeholder framework for analyzing and evaluating corporate social performance", *Academy of Management Review*, Vol. 20 No. 1, pp. 92–117.

Dawkins, J. and Lewis, S. (2003), "CSR in stakeholder expectations: and their implication for company strategy", *Journal of Business Ethics*, Vol. 44 Nos 2/3, pp. 185–93.

Demmy, S. and Talbott, J. (1998), "Improve internal reporting with ABC and TOC", *Management Accounting*, Vol. 80 No. 5, pp. 18–24.

DiNitto, E. (1989), "Marketing with a conscience", *Marketing Communication*, Vol. 14 No. 5, pp. 42–6.

Doh, J.P. and Teegen, H. (2003), *Globalization and NGOs: Transforming Business, Governments, and Society*, Praeger, Westport, CT.

Donaldson, T. and Preston, L.E. (1995), "The stakeholder theory of the corporation: concepts, evidence and implications", *Academy of Management Review*, Vol. 20 No. 1, pp. 65–91.

Drucker, P. (1946), *The Concept of the Corporation*, The John Day Co., New York, NY.

Enderle, G. (2004), "Global competition and corporate responsibilities of small and medium-sized enterprises", *Business Ethics: A European Review*, Vol. 13 No. 1, pp. 51–63.

Environics International (1999), *The Millennium Poll on Corporate Social Responsibility: Executive Brief*, Environics International, Toronto.

Environics International (2002), *Corporate Social Responsibility Monitor 2002: Executive Brief*, Environics International, Toronto.

Estes, R. (1996), *Tyranny of the Bottom Line*, Berrett-Koehler Publishers, San Francisco, CA.

File, K.M. and Prince, R.A. (1998), "Cause-related marketing and corporate philanthropy in the privately held enterprise", *Journal of Business Ethics*, Vol. 17 No. 14, pp. 1529–39.

Freeman, R.E. (1984), *Strategic Management: A Stakeholder Approach*, Pitman Publishers, Marshfield, MA.

Friedman, M. (1962), *Capitalism and Freedom*, University of Chicago Press, Chicago, IL.

Friedman, M. (1970), "The social responsibility of business is to increase its profits", *New York Times Magazine*, September 13, pp. 32–33, 122, 124, 126.

Frooman, J. (1997), "Socially irresponsible and illegal behavior and shareholder wealth", *Business and Society*, Vol. 36 No. 3, pp. 221–49.

Gordenker, L. and Weiss, T.G. (1996), "Pluralizing global governance: analytical approaches and dimensions", in Weiss, T.G. and Gordenker, L. (Eds), *NGOs, the UN & Global Governance*, Rienner Publishers, London.

Greenfield, W.M. (2004), "In the name of corporate social responsibility", *Business Horizons*, Vol. 47 No. 1, pp. 19–28.

Griffin, J.J. and Mahon, J.F. (1997), "The corporate social performance and corporate financial performance debate: twenty-five years of incomparable research", *Business and Society*, Vol. 36 No. 1, pp. 5–31.

Harrington, L.K. (1996), "Ethics and public policy analysis: stakeholders' interests and regulatory policy", *Journal of Business Ethics*, Vol. 15 No. 4, pp. 373–82.

Hemingway, C.A. and Maclagan, P.W. (2004), "Managers' personal values as drivers of corporate social responsibility", *Journal of Business Ethics*, Vol. 50 No. 1, pp. 33–44.

Hofstede, G. (1980), *Culture's Consequences: International Differences in Work-related Values*, Sage, Beverly Hills, CA.

Hofstede, G. (1983), "Dimensions of national culture in fifty countries and three regions", in Deregowski, J.D., Dziurawiec, S. and Annios, R.C. (Eds), *Expiscations in Cross-cultural Psychology*, Swets and Zeitlinger, Lisse.

Johns, G. (2001), "Protocols with NGOs: the need to know", *IPA Backgrounder*, Vol. 13 No. 1, pp. 1–16.

Joyner, B.E. and Payne, D. (2002), "Evolution and implementation: a study of values, business ethics and corporate social responsibility", *Journal of Business Ethics*, Vol. 41 No. 4, pp. 297–311.

Kok, P., Van der Wiele, T., McKenna, R. and Brown, A. (2001), "A corporate social responsibility audit within a quality management framework", *Journal of Business Ethics*, Vol. 31 No. 4, pp. 285–97.

Küskü, F. and Zarkada-Fraser, A.(2004), "An empirical investigation of corporate citizenship in Australia and Turkey", *British Journal of Management*, Vol. 15, pp. 57–72.

Logan, D., Regelbrugge, L. and Roy, D. (1997), *Global Corporate Citizenship: Rationale and Strategies*, Hitachi Foundation, Washington, DC.

Lorange, P. (2003), "Global responsibility – business education and business schools – roles in promoting a global perspective", *Corporate Governance*, Vol. 3 No. 3, pp. 126–35.

Maignan, I. and Ferrell, O.C. (2003), "Nature of corporate responsibilities: perspectives from American, French, and German consumers", *Journal of Business Research*, Vol. 56 No. 1, pp. 55–67.

Margolis, J.D. and Walsh, J.P. (2003), "Misery loves companies: rethinking social initiatives by business", *Administrative Science Quarterly*, Vol. 48 No. 2, pp. 265–305.

Miles, G. (1993), "In search of ethical profits: insights from strategic management", *Journal of Business Ethics*, Vol. 12 No. 3, pp. 219–25.

Murray, K.B. and Vogel, C.M. (1997), "Using a hierarchy-of-effects approach to gauge the effectiveness of corporate social responsibility to generate goodwill toward the firm: financial versus nonfinancial impact", *Journal of Business Research*, Vol. 38 No. 2, pp. 141–59.

Neergaard, P. and Pedersen, E.R. (2003), "Corporate social behavior: between the rules of the game and the law of the jungle", *Journal of Corporate Citizenship*, Vol. 12, Winter, pp. 43–57.

Novak, M. (1996), *The Future of the Corporation*, The AEI Press, Washington, DC.

O'Higgins, E.R.E. (2003), "Global strategies – contradictions and consequences", *Corporate Governance*, Vol. 3 No. 3, pp. 52–66.

Orlitzky, M., Schmidt, F.L. and Rynes, S.L. (2003), "Corporate social and financial performance: a meta-analysis", *Organization Studies*, Vol. 24 No. 3, pp. 403–41.

Orpen, C. (1987), "The attitudes of United States and South African managers to corporate social responsibility", *Journal Business Ethics*, Vol. 6 No. 2, pp. 89–96.

Pérez, R. (2003), "About 'global responsibilities' in management", *Corporate Governance*, Vol. 3 No. 3, pp. 78–89.

Petrick, J.A., Scherer, R.F., Brodzinski, J.D., Quinn, J.F. and Ainina, M.F. (1999), "Global leadership skills and reputational capital: intangible resources for sustainable competitive advantage", *Academy of Management Executive*, Vol. 13 No. 1, pp. 58–69.

Posner, R.A. (1974), "Theories of economic regulation", *The Bell Journal of Economic and Management Science*, Vol. 5 No. 2, pp. 335–58.

Post, J.E. (2000), *Meeting the Challenge of Global Corporate Citizenship*, Center for Corporate Community Relations, Boston College, Boston, MA.

Quindlen, A. (1994), "Out of the hands of babes", *New York Times*, November 23, p. A15.

Robertson, C. and Fadil, P.A. (1999), "Ethical decision making in multinational organizations: a culture-based model", *Journal of Business Ethics*, Vol. 19 No. 4, pp. 385–92.

Rochlin, S. and Boguslaw, J. (2001), *Business and Community Development*, The Center for Corporate Citizenship at Boston College Ford Foundation Project, Chestnut Hill, MA.

Rosen, S., Simon, J., Vincent, J.R., MacLeod, W., Fox, M. and Thea, D.M. (2003), "AIDS is your business", *Harvard Business Review*, Vol. 81 No. 2, pp. 80–7.

Schwartz, S.H. (1992), "Universals in the content and structure of values: theoretical advances and empirical tests in 20 countries", in Zanna, M.P. (Ed.), *Advances in Experimental Social Psychology*, Academic Press, San Diego, CA.

Sethi, S.P. (2003), "Globalization and the good corporation: a need for proactive co-existence", *Journal of Business Ethics*, Vol. 43 Nos 1/2, pp. 21–31.

Smeltzer, L.R. and Jennings, M.M. (1998), "Why an international code of business ethics would be good for business", *Journal of Business Ethics*, Vol. 17 No. 1, pp. 57–66.

Smith, J. (1997), "Characteristics of the modern transnational social movement sector", in Smith, J., Chatfield, C. and Pagnucco, P. (Eds), *Transnational Social Movements and Global Politics: Solidarity Beyond the State*, Syracuse University Press, Syracuse, NY.

Spar, D.L. and La Mure, L.T. (2003), "The power of activism: assessing the impact of NGOs on global business", *California Management Review*, Vol. 45 No. 3, pp. 78–101.

Spence, L.J., Schmidpeter, R. and Habisch, A. (2003), "Assessing social capital: small and medium sized enterprises in Germany and the UK", *Journal of Business Ethics*, Vol. 47 No. 1, pp. 17–29.

Turban, D. and Greening, D.W. (1997), "Corporate social performance and organizational attractiveness to prospective employees", *Academy of Management Journal*, Vol. 40 No. 3, pp. 658–72.

van Tuijl, P. (1999), "NGOs and human rights: sources of justices and democracy", *Journal of International Affairs*, Vol. 52 No. 2, pp. 493–512.

Waddock, S.A. and Graves, S.B. (1997), "The corporate social performance-financial performance link", *Strategic Management Journal*, Vol. 18 No. 4, pp. 303–19.

Waddock, S.A. and Smith, N. (2000), "Relationships: the real challenge of corporate global citizenship", *Business and Society Review*, Vol. 105 No. 1, pp. 47–62.

Waddock, S.A., Bodwell, C. and Graves, S.B. (2002), "Responsibility: the new business imperative", *Academy of Management Executive*, Vol. 16 No. 2, pp. 132–48.

Walton, C.C. (1982), "Corporate social responsibility: the debate revisited", *Journal of Economics and Business*, Vol. 34 No. 2, pp. 173–87.

Warhurst, A. (2001), "Corporate citizenship and corporate social investment: drivers of tri-sector partnerships", *Journal of Corporate Citizenship*, Vol. 1, Spring, pp. 57–72.

Wokutch, R.E. (1990), "Corporate social responsibility Japanese style", *Academy of Management Executive*, Vol. 4 No. 2, pp. 56–74..

Chapter 11

CSR, partnerships, and self-regulation

IN THIS CHAPTER WE WILL:

- Identify the role of NGOs and governments in CSR
- Examine the changing roles and divisions between companies, NGOs and governments
- Explain how CSR management can be implemented through partnerships with other businesses and NGOs
- Explain what it means to consider CSR as self-regulation
- Identify the different relationships between corporations and governments
- Explore some of the national and regional variations in these relationships

Introduction

Corporations do not have a monopoly on the 'S' in CSR. Social issues and impacts are of course much more commonly associated with the responsibilities of governments and non-governmental organizations (NGOs) than they are with business. Governments are responsible for ensuring that their citizens are protected, educated, housed, mobile, and in good health. NGOs will often focus on acute areas of need or issues needing specialized attention. So by its nature, CSR does not happen in a vacuum. Companies need always to be mindful of these other actors in the social domain – as well as the other companies that might be taking steps towards managing their social responsibilities.

The role of governments in CSR is quite a complex one. On the one hand, as we saw earlier in the book, CSR is sometimes presented as a replacement or alternative for government action. As governments have stepped back from taking on the provision of social goods, so corporations have stepped in. On the other hand, CSR is also sometimes presented as a different, or softer, form of government regulation. That is, rather than impose command and control regulation, governments have shared some of their power and encouraged firms to adopt self-regulation to ensure that societal goals are met. As we saw in Chapter 2, this is not always met approvingly by those such as Aneel Karnani, who believe only governments should be responsible for these tasks.

NGOs also play a number of roles in relation to CSR. They can be important watchdogs ensuring that irresponsible behaviour is identified and more socially responsible alternatives promoted. For example, Greenpeace waged a two-year campaign against Facebook to encourage it to 'unfriend coal' as a source of power and move to green energy. During the course of the campaign, Greenpeace supporters set a world record of 80,000 comments in one day on a single post on the campaign's Facebook page.[1] NGOs can also identify and promote best practice in CSR. For instance UNICEF, Save the Children, and the UN Global Compact worked together to produce a CSR standard for business responsibilities to children (the Child Rights and Business Principles), which was launched in 2012 along with a CSR workbook and other tools for businesses.[2]

NGOs, however, can also go further and play the role of active partner with business, working together to tackle social problems that neither alone can solve on their own. Businesses have increasingly turned to NGOs to address CSR problems because of their higher levels of trust among consumers and their enhanced credibility with local communities and other stakeholders. Increasingly, firms have found that they cannot always solve social problems alone. Consider the case of Rainforest Alliance, an environmental NGO that certifies farms, forestry operations, and tourism initiatives according to sustainability standards. Rainforest Alliance has provided its technical expertise to develop appropriate standards of sustainable management for a number of business partners as well as helping create and enforce an internationally recognized third-party certification that companies can use to demonstrate their CSR credentials to their stakeholders. Companies such as Chiquita have worked with the Rainforest Alliance to certify all of their banana plantations, while Unilever is planning to certify all of its Lipton tea plantations by 2015.[3]

The idea that business, NGOs and governments now intersect in many and diverse ways has become a critical feature of the theory and practice of CSR. There is the danger of course in advocating that CSR will solve any type of regulatory problem or governmental deficit, or that company's social programmes are best implemented through partnerships. Sometimes this may be true but also sometimes it will not. CSR doesn't always work as a form of self-regulation, and partnerships do not always achieve their desired goals. For example, the certification of sustainable forest management practices has had a limited uptake in some wood export countries such as Indonesia despite a good degree of success elsewhere (Bartley, 2010). Businesses need to be mindful of the different contexts in which these relationships play out and the different goals that the different actors are seeking to achieve.

CWS 11.1

Visit the companion website for links to these and more examples of NGO-business relationships in the area of CSR

Blurring boundaries

An important upshot of these developments is that it is becoming increasingly difficult to draw with any certainty the boundaries of the traditional sectors (Crane, 2011). The 'economic', the 'political', and the 'civil' sector (or private, public, and non-profit organizations) as labels of distinctive sets of values, ownership arrangements, purposes, and activities do still make a certain sense. Yet at the same time, there is a clear trend towards overlap and some degree of convergence. Or to put it in stronger terms, towards *category crisis* – i.e. the collapsing of binary divisions (Crane & Matten, 2008).

Just think: when businesses partner with NGOs to tackle social and political issues, or when charities develop profit-making social enterprises, or when governments delegate regulation to private actors, aren't the dividing lines between the sectors losing their sharp focus? What does it mean to refer to a private company, if in the words of Valente and Crane from Chapter 7 it has 'public responsibilities'?

These shifts have led to some fertile debates about the potential impacts of category crisis. For example, some are concerned about the degree of commercialization and marketization in the non-profit sector (Dart, 2004), while others have explored the ramifications of corporations taking on a more political role (Matten & Crane, 2005; Scherer & Palazzo, 2011)

For companies, these new intersections can place senior executives in uncomfortable positions. They may be required to navigate a landscape of overlapping interests and responsibilities and may need to think and act with a combination of business and public policy skills. Richard Haass, the US Council on Foreign Relations' President, has suggested we need to increasingly think of the 'CEO as a diplomat' (McKinsey & Company, 2009), while McKinsey managing partner Dominic Barton prefers to see managers becoming tri-sector athletes, 'able and experienced in business, government, and the social sector' (Barton, 2011: 89).

CWS 11.2

Visit the companion website for more on Haass and Barton's proposals

Introducing the readings

The two readings collected in this chapter come at the issue of business relations with other actors in two quite different ways. The first paper deals with the very practical problem of how managers might determine the options open to them with respect to their relationships with NGOs, and how these different options might support their CSR goals. The second reading takes a more theoretical perspective and examines the different relationships between government and CSR.

CSR through collaboration with NGOs

The reading by Peloza and Falkenberg addresses the question of how firms should collaborate with NGOs to achieve their CSR objectives. This is a subject that has been an important theme in the CSR literature for some time, and indeed has spawned a whole sub-field in cross-sector partnerships (see Seitanidi & Crane, 2013). The key distinguishing feature of this paper is that it makes a distinction between collaborating with one or several NGOs, and collaborating as a single firm alone, or with other firms. Each of these combinations will be better suited for particular purposes than others. There is no single solution that will work for any type of context in which business-NGO partnerships might be deployed.

The Peloza and Falkenberg reading is also interesting in that it discusses not only relationships between business and NGOs, but also between businesses. This is because companies are increasingly recognizing that, contrary to what some of the strategy specialists have argued in the previous chapter, CSR is only sometimes about gaining a competitive advantage over one's rivals. Sometimes CSR initiatives may be more about rebuilding the legitimacy of an entire industry, or ensuring that there are sufficient natural resources or productive suppliers for the industry as a whole to prosper, not just the individual firm. For example, apparel producers have collaborated on developing systems for ensuring better working conditions in supplier factories just as detergent companies have collaborated on reducing package sizes and moving to concentrated formulations. In this sense, CSR can sometimes be a *pre-competitive* practice – namely something that is in the collective interest of a wider group of ostensible rivals rather than the narrow self-interest of one (Clay, 2011).

CSR-government relations in different national contexts

The second reading focuses on the different ways that CSR is related to the practices of government. In many models of CSR, government is presented as a stakeholder of business, but few studies have explored the role of government in CSR in much detail beyond this. But governments will clearly be interested in CSR, for which there are a number of explanations (Steurer, 2010):

- CSR can help to meet government's policy objectives;
- CSR can be a complement for hard law where new regulation is undesirable or infeasible;
- CSR represents an opportunity to interact proactively and positively with business as opposed to simply through coercion;
- CSR fits with a broader trend towards soft regulation and more partnership modes of governing.

As a result, governments across the world have taken an increasing interest in CSR. As we saw in Chapter 1 (see Figure 1.1, page 9), this includes the Chinese Ministry of Commerce, the Canadian Department of Foreign Affairs and International Trade, the UK Department for Business, Innovation and Skills, and the European Commission. Each of these has a different understanding of CSR, which in turn leads to some different approaches to promoting and encouraging responsible corporate behaviour.

Gond, Kang, and Moon's reading takes inspiration from these different national approaches to CSR to provide a conceptual understanding of the range of relationships (or 'configurations' as they put it) between CSR and government. The reading provides an unusually rich and detailed account of these relationships, specifying five distinct arrangements:

1. CSR as self-government
2. CSR as facilitated by government
3. CSR as a partnership with government
4. CSR as mandated by government
5. CSR as a form of government

What this makes abundantly clear is that in both theory and practice, the relationships between CSR and government are quite heterogeneous. This is particularly the case at an international level, where, as Gond et al then go on to discuss, distinct patterns may arise due to prevailing (and at times changing) systems of governance in particular regions.

Much of the writing and research on CSR has come from the United States, but the liberal free-market economy of the US is not perfectly replicated elsewhere and so different CSR-government configurations have emerged in other parts of the world. Gond et al discuss Western Europe and East Asia, but similarly Africa, Latin America, Central Europe, and the Middle East, to name a few, would also be expected to exhibit substantial variation. Indeed, there is probably just as much, if not more heterogeneity in governments than there is in corporations across the globe, so it would be of little surprise if the approach to CSR by the governments of, say, China and Canada, or India and Italy were more distinct than the approach of Baidu and Research in Motion, or Tata Global Beverages and Illy Caffé.

Challenges for practice

Practitioners in all three sectors face challenges in managing CSR with respect to the relationships between business, government, and NGOs:

1. For corporate managers, some of the key questions are:
    a) Which issues could be 'pre-competitive' and which need to be dealt with on a strictly competitive basis?
    b) Which NGOs or other businesses are most likely to be open to collaboration and which are more likely to be in direct conflict?
    c) What are the best ways of being proactive in developing knowledge about how the other sectors work, and what their future priorities might be?

2. For NGO managers, some of the key questions are:
   a) What is the right mixture of 'carrots and sticks' (or incentives and punishments) to encourage firms to act more responsibly?
   b) What are the risks and opportunities involved in actively collaborating with business – and how can we prepare effectively for these?
   c) How much orientation to the market is enough to achieve our goals and how much could be too much for our stakeholders to accept?
3. For government managers, some of the key questions are:
   a) What CSR goals do we have and what mix of policy instruments will most effectively achieve them?
   b) How can we best work with business to solve social problems whilst still being a legitimate regulator and enforcer?
   c) What new tools and measures might we need to effectively manage our CSR relationship with business?
4. For all three sectors, the challenge will be to effectively prepare managers to be 'tri-sector athletes'. What new skill sets are required and how will managers acquire them?

Study questions

1. What role do NGOs play in the practice of CSR? How does this differ from the role of governments?
2. According to the Corporate Responsibility Coalition (CORE), many NGOs and trade unions regard CSR as a way for corporations 'to avoid the creation of regulatory and legal mechanisms as a means of ensuring that they adhere to acceptable standards of conduct'. Using examples from practice, explain whether you agree or disagree with the suggestion that CSR is about this kind of regulatory avoidance.
3. Define the concept of 'category crisis' in the context of CSR, using relevant examples to illustrate your points. How should managers prepare for category crisis?
4. Under what circumstances would a company consider partnering with multiple businesses and multiple NGOs in seeking to achieve its CSR goals? What are the main risks of doing so?
5. Investigate the approach to CSR of the government in the country in which you are from or are studying in. What specific policies and programmes are used and which of Gond et al's five configurations does it most equate to?

Further reading

Seitanidi, M. M. & Crane, A. (2009) 'Implementing CSR through partnerships: understanding the selection, design and institutionalization of nonprofit-business partnerships', *Journal of Business Ethics*, 85: 413–429.

This reading starts from where the reading by Peloza and Falkenberg ends – you've decided you want to partner with an NGO to address your CSR goals, but now you need to decide how exactly to go about it. This reading uses case study research to develop a three-stage model of selection, design and institutionalization of partnerships to explain how partnerships are actually implemented in practice.

Albareda, L., Lozano, J., & Ysa, T. (2007) 'Public policies on corporate social responsibility: the role of governments in Europe', *Journal of Business Ethics*, 74(4): 391–407.

This reading is a good companion piece to the reading by Gond and colleagues in this chapter since it provides a more in-depth look at the role of government in CSR in one of the contexts, Europe, that was briefly explored by Gond et al. The big difference is that in this paper, the different parts of Western Europe are broken down still further to show four distinct approaches across the continent. A handy list of specific CSR policies and programmes is also provided.

Endnotes

1   www.greenpeace.org/international/en/campaigns/climate-change/cool-it/ITs-carbon-footprint/Facebook/ (Accessed 30 August, 2012)
2   www.unicef.org/csr/12.htm (Accessed 30 August, 2012).
3   www.unilever.com/mediacentre/pressreleases/2007/sustainable-tea-sourcing.aspx; www.chiquita.se/eu/en/our-commitment/rainforest-alliance.html# (Accessed August 30, 2012).

References

Bartley, T. (2010) 'Transnational private regulation in practice: the limits of forest and labor standards certification in Indonesia', *Business and Politics*, 12(3).
Barton, D. (2011) 'Capitalism for the long term', *Harvard Business Review*, 89(3): 84–91.
Clay, J. (2011) 'Precompetitive behaviour – defining the boundaries', www.guardian.co.uk/sustainable-business/precompetitive-behaviour-defining-boundaries (Accessed 30 August, 2012).

Crane, A. (2011) 'From governance to Governance: on blurring boundaries', *Journal of Business Ethics*, 94(supp 1): 17–19.

Crane, A. & Matten, D. (2008) 'Fear and loathing in the JCC: unleashing the monster of "New Corporate Citizenship Theory" to confront category crisis', *Journal of Corporate Citizenship*, 29: 21–24.

Dart, R. (2004) 'The legitimacy of social enterprise', *Nonprofit Management and Leadership*, 14(4): 411–424.

Matten, D. & Crane, A. (2005) 'Corporate citizenship: towards an extended theoretical conceptualization', *Academy of Management Review*, 30(1): 166–179.

McKinsey & Company (2009) 'The CEO as diplomat: an interview with Richard Haass', www.mckinseyquarterly.com/The_CEO_as_diplomat_An_interview_with_Richard_Haass_2451 (Accessed 30 August, 2012).

Scherer, A. G. & Palazzo, G. (2011) 'The new political role of business in a globalized world – a review of a new perspective on CSR and its implications for the firm, governance, and democracy', *Journal of Management Studies*, 48(4): 899–931.

Seitanidi, M. M. & Crane, A. (eds) (2013) *Responsible business and social partnerships: a research handbook*, London: Routledge.

Steurer, R. (2010) 'The role of governments in corporate social responsibility: characterising public policies on CSR in Europe', *Policy Sciences*, 43(1): 49–72.

THE ROLE OF COLLABORATION IN ACHIEVING CORPORATE SOCIAL RESPONSIBILITY OBJECTIVES

John Peloza and Loren Falkenberg

The lack of a conclusive business case for corporate social responsibility is at the heart of the ongoing debate over the role of business in solving social and environmental problems. Although the link between CSR activities and firm financial performance is still debated, research suggests that the relationship depends, at least in part, on how the CSR initiative is executed.[1] Given that CSR initiatives are often in collaboration with NGOs, we focus on factors that influence the effectiveness of these collaborations.

Research suggests that firms are more likely to enjoy business benefits from these relationships when they go beyond simple cash donations and include expertise, access to strategic knowledge, and in-kind resources.[2] Austin positions corporate involvement along a continuum.[3] At the one end, relationships where firms make traditional donations are labeled *philanthropic*. He argues that in the *transactional* stage, greater business benefits can accrue when the firm focuses donations around specific activities (e.g., a percentage of every sale). At the other end of the spectrum are *integrative* relationships that are characterized by shared employees and activities, a relationship that approximates a joint venture.

Our framework expands previous categorization by including the potential for collaboration with other firms, or multiple NGOs. A basic form of integrative collaboration is between a single firm and a single NGO, such as the long-standing relationship between Timberland and City Year where Timberland donates financial support, products, employee volunteers, and management expertise. Another structure includes multiple firms and one NGO, such as the Responsible Care program of the chemical industry. A third structure occurs when one firm works with multiple NGOs, such as Starbucks working on a range of social and environmental issues with Oxfam, Global Exchange, and the Ford Foundation. Finally the most complex structure includes group of firms working with a group of NGOs to address broad complex social or environmental issues, such as Initiative for Responsible Mining Assurance that includes producers and retailers of precious metals working with a host of NGOs spanning both social and environmental issues.

Each collaboration structure has its own unique strengths and weaknesses, and each will allow the firm to reach its CSR objectives with varying degrees of effectiveness. It is important for managers to choose (or develop) the collaboration structure that aligns with the company's CSR objectives and operating context. For example, many of the issues at the heart of CSR objectives are part of "meta-problems"[4] such as community poverty, human rights violations, or dangers to human health. Resolution of these broad issues requires an expanded framework of collaboration; a move from a dyadic collaboration between a single firm and a single NGO, to network collaborations involving a range of firms and NGOs, each with a specific focus and expertise. However, there are operating contexts where a local CSR issue can be effectively addressed through a single company/NGO collaboration.

Although excellent progress has been made in providing guidance to managers on building deeper relationships between their firm and NGOs,[5] relatively little attention has been paid to the relationships that include multiple firms and/or multiple NGOs and the full spectrum of collaboration opportunities. Specifically, what options are available to managers in their relationships with NGOs, and how do they differ in their abilities to support the objectives of the firm? Our framework expands the traditional one firm/one NGO model of collaboration to include simultaneous multi-firm and multi-NGO collaborations. Our extension of the prevailing view of collaboration for social performance also integrates recent research on the benefits of collective action in addressing social issues.[6]

Objectives Behind CSR Programs

To order to account for both social and environmental initiatives, we adopt the definition of CSR provided by Barnett: "a discretionary allocation of corporate resources toward improving social welfare that serves as a means of enhancing relationships with key stakeholders."[7] Under this definition, the discretionary allocation of resources can be directed to internal activities that improve social welfare, or towards non-governmental organizations (NGOs) that address the specific social and environmental issues the firm has targeted. This reading focuses on CSR activities that involve relationships with NGOs. Further, we limit our consideration of collaborations to those interactions between firms and NGOs that involve corporate support beyond money (Austin's integrative stage), and those characterized by a two-way exchange of resources and expertise between the firm and NGO.

Although some stakeholders contend that corporations must assume responsibility for improving communities, pure altruistic criteria are rarely sufficient justification for the allocation of firm resources. Normative arguments for CSR are typically accompanied by an argument for the business case.[8] In linking social and financial objectives, Porter and Kramer argue that a firm can gain economic returns by tackling social and environmental issues that in turn provide advantages for the firm, such as a better educated workforce or a healthier community economy.[9] In each case, the objective of the manager is to secure the mediating process between CSR investment and economic return. For example, CSR can lead to an enhanced reputation that makes the firm more attractive to customers and is helpful in attracting and maintaining a more productive, high-quality workforce.[10] In some cases, the mediation may require the effective treatment of a social or environmental issue, and collaboration with NGOs can lead to the development of new competencies.[11] NGOs can be an external source of specialized skills and knowledge, particularly when internal development of such expertise is costly, inefficient, and time-consuming. For example, Rondinelli and London describe relationships where data and business practices are shared (e.g., between firms such as DuPont and United Parcel Service and NGOs) leading to important product redesign, manufacturing changes, and materials substation.[12] In other cases, engagement with NGOs on social and environmental issues has led to a change in the culture of the firm toward increased innovation.[13]

For each CSR initiative, successful mediation from investment to economic return will be dependent on the context of the CSR activities. The objectives of the firm within a given CSR initiative and its operating environment influence the types of collaborative relationships that should be developed. Managers should identify the economic objectives desired from the CSR activity and structure collaborative relationships that align with these objectives. For example if specific environmental expertise is required, and only accessible through a network of NGOs, it would be most appropriate for the firm to coordinate its activities within a collaboration with the NGOs. In contrast, when enhanced reputation is the goal it may be better achieved through a relationship with a single NGO.

How Should Firms Collaborate for CSR?

The framework outlined in Figure 11.1 describes four types of relationships where a firm can partner with either a single or multiple NGOs and enter into the relationship on its own or through collaboration with other firms. Although we use a broad distinction of single versus multiple actors, we recognize that the number of partners can vary widely from smaller groups of two or three partners to organizations like the World Conservation Union, which includes over 700 NGOs. Further, our framework defines collaboration for a broad range of CSR activities, incorporating efforts beyond monetary donations to include the development of social or environmental standards, exchange of expertise or technology for environmental initiatives, or service delivery for social initiatives.

Quadrant One: Focused Contribution

Collaborations involving a single firm and NGO are in quadrant one. This relationship is simple in that it involves coordinating the activities of two entities, but it can range from simple philanthropic donations to a complex and deep collaboration involving a range of resources. Although these relationships are often rooted in philanthropic donations and improve the firm's reputation, they can still lead to improved communities through significant interactions between the two organizations. An example of a high-profile collaboration, leading to a reduced environmental footprint, is the partnership between McDonald's and the Environmental Defense Fund. This enduring partnership began in the late 1980s and has resulted in the company reducing its waste through redesign or reduction of packaging by hundreds of thousands of tons. Environmental Defense provided expertise that guided McDonald's purchasing practices to significantly increase the use of recyclable materials. Initially based on a reduction in packaging, the partnership has since expanded to a reduction of energy use and an introduction of state-of-the-art technology designed to reduce the production of greenhouse gases.

A more recent example involves Unilever, the world's largest tea company, and its commitment to purchase tea from sustainable sources. As part of its commitment the company has entered into a partnership with the international environmental NGO, Rainforest Alliance, which certifies tea farms in Africa. According to both partners, the initiative improves the sustainability of farming, incomes, and livelihoods of millions. Demonstrating the competitive mindset that often accompanies such single-firm/NGO collaborations, CEO Patrick Cescau acknowledged the marketing opportunity associated with ethical responsibilities, stating that the program "provides us a means by which we can differentiate our brands from those of our competitors."

These one-on-one partnerships can create a number of benefits for firms. First, because this is a common structure there are existing "templates" upon which to build, and many managers in both firms and NGOs are experienced in managing this type of relationship.

As seen in the Unilever example, they can provide an opportunity for the firm to "own" an issue that leads to an improved reputation. This can provide the firm a means of meaningful differentiation from competitors since social factors can be a significant decision criteria for many consumers.[14] Managers are routinely advised to find a single cause or focus that is aligned with the competencies and core business of the firm because stakeholders will be less likely to question the firm's motives as self-serving.[15] Further, if managers seek a deep collaboration with an NGO, it can lead to a significant social impact on a highly focused issue. This impact can be highly focused to provide firms the opportunity to positively affect the local economic conditions, education system, or any other issue of particular relevance to the firm.

Focused contributions are particularly appropriate when a stable government is in place, there is sufficient public infrastructure to meet the basic needs of the community, and adequate environmental and employment regulations are developed. In these contexts, focused contributions can build on existing programs or solve a problem that has occurred because of cracks in the social and regulatory infrastructure. For example, focused contributions may support recreational opportunities in the community by working with a community "Boys and Girls Club" or an environmental NGO such as "Ducks Unlimited" to improve wetland habitats for waterfowl.

The limited nature of the partnership also limits the potential for leakage of intellectual property that the firm shares with the NGO. For example, King argues that because environmental groups have an incentive to disperse cleaner technology, working with more than one environmental NGO increases the chance that control over relevant intellectual property will be lost.[16]

Researchers have referred to a progression of stages in corporate citizenship and argue that firms should take on more complex CSR issues as they gain experience with CSR.[17] Mirvis and Googins outline five stages of corporate citizenship: *elementary* (marginal structure; staff driven), *engaged* (ownership of CSR with functional areas), *innovative* (coordination across functional areas), *integrated* (organizational alignment toward a single focus), and *transforming* (mainstream; part of business activities).[18] Firms in the *elementary* and *engaged* stages may be limited to collaborations with a single NGO (i.e., quadrant one) simply because they lack the management resources and expertise to manage broad CSR collaborations. In quadrant one, the

	Single NGO	Multi-NGO
Single Firm	**1-Focused Contribution Collaboration Examples:** • McDonalds/Environmental Defense Fund • Unilever/Rainforest Alliance **Examples of Objectives Achieved:** • Differentiate brand from competitors • Focused, local social impacts • Respond to NGO activism specific to firm **Key Contextual Considerations:** • Ease of management/limited resource requirements • Protects intellectual property of the firm • Susceptible to personal influence/ diversion away from core business of the firm • Firm is susceptible to charges of "buying" reputation • Temptation to focus only on PR aspects • Criticisms of undue influence over NGO	**3-Diffused Contribution Collaboration Examples:** • Starbucks/Global Exchange/ Oxfam/Oaxacan State Coffee Producers Network/Ford Foundation • BP//IDPMS/Covenant Center of Development/Swayan Shikshan Prayog **Examples of Objectives Achieved:** • Address threats to firm legitimacy from multiple sources/contexts • Differentiate brand from competitors • Access new markets **Key Contextual Considerations:** • Broader/complex social and environmental goals met simultaneously • Encourage NGO investment in firm innovation • Increased management resources to coordinate disparate NGOs • Slippery slope of involvement and responsibility
Multi-Firm	**2-Shared Contribution Collaboration Examples:** • Chemical firms/Fundación Natura • Caterpillarlar/General Motors/ White Martins/Piracicaba 2010 **Examples of Objectives Achieved:** • Protection/promotion of industry legitimacy • Address infrastructure voids **Key Contextual Considerations:** • Promotes innovative culture of the firm • Potential for broader social impact on a focused issue • Reputational benefits accrue to competitors equally • Requires trusted competitors • Potential for loss of intellectual property of he firm	**4-Communal Contribution Collaboration Examples:** • Nike/Eddie Bauer/Nordstrom/ Fair Labour Association/Human Rights First/Federation of Workers in Philippines/Cambodian Labour Association • BHP-Billiton/Rio Tinto/Newmont/ DeBeers/Tiffany/Sam's Club/ Initiative for Responsible Mining Association/International Council of Mining and Metals/Jewelers of American **Examples of Objectives Achieved:** • Address complex threat to industries • Consensus of priorities among numerous powerful social actors • Geographically dispersed social impacts

	Single NGO	Multi-NGO
Multi-- Firm	• Increased management resources and attention required • Potential for loss of NGO objectivity	**Key Contextual Considerations:** • Integrate perspectives from multiple powerful stakeholders • Significant management resources and expertise required • Requires the ability to negotiate priorities • Potential for free-riding

Figure 11.1: Strategic factors for CSR collaboration strategies

relationship is straightforward, and outcomes are relatively easy to monitor. Managers in firms in later stages of CSR development still may elect to undertake a focused collaboration because it can represent the most efficient means of reaching objectives of the CSR initiative. For example, an employee volunteer program can provide leadership training and skill development and can improve employee satisfaction through collaboration with a single NGO.

However, managers who consider this type of collaboration should be aware of its limitations. First, these relationships are susceptible to influence by senior management or other powerful decision makers who place personal relevance over the ethical responsibilities of the firm when selecting an NGO for collaboration. Decisions to work with a specific NGO can be influenced by local business networks, social contacts of managers, or even their spouses.[19] Choosing to collaborate with NGOs on the basis of personal biases can channel precious firm resources into nonproductive initiatives or initiatives that lead to reduced benefits when compared to more strategically based relationships.

The single-firm/single-NGO relationship also leaves the firm susceptible to charges of trying to "buy" reputation, as is evidenced by the case of McDonald's and recent accusations that it has focused on the relatively minor issue of packaging while ignoring its culpability in both childhood and adult obesity. Further, focus on a specific relationship may lead the firm to become more concerned with the public relations aspects of the relationship, which can restrict the development of meaningful social or environmental initiatives and the long-term potential economic benefit to the firm.[20] Finally, when there is a large discrepancy between the size of the firm and the NGO, these partnerships are open to criticisms of the firm exerting undue influence over the NGO.[21] A large firm that collaborates with a small NGO runs the risk, perhaps unintentionally, of the NGO becoming reliant on the support of the firm leading to a lack of credibility and objectivity in the relationship.

Quadrant Two: Shared Contribution

Relationships between a single NGO and multiple firms fall into quadrant two. An often-cited example of collaboration among competitors is in the chemical industry, where the Responsible Care initiative is considered a model of self-regulation. In Ecuador, the industry has developed a relationship with a single NGO, Fundación Natura, as part of its self-regulation. A benefit of the Ecuadorian model is that it helps ensure a common platform for all firms signed on to Responsible Care, leading to the establishment of best practices across the industry. The formal collaboration with Fundación Natura came after years of individual projects between the NGO and individual firms, giving both sides the opportunity to establish trust and firms the opportunity to recognize the value in an NGO partner highly focused in their industry. The collaboration has yielded several codes covering many operational aspects of member companies, including work in the areas of process safety, environmental protection, community awareness and emergency response, and occupational health management.

A second type of collaboration in this quadrant is among firms from different industries operating in the same community. An example of this type of collaboration is found in Piracicaba, Brazil, where Caterpillar has its manufacturing operations. The decision of Caterpillar to locate in the city exacerbated the shift from an agricultural to a more urban society, and the firm recognized the need to help alleviate some of the social issues arising from this footprint. The increased migration to the city led to increased unemployment, higher levels of poverty and crime, and a lack of appropriate infrastructure for the bulging population.

Caterpillar initially worked through philanthropic initiatives, exemplified by donations to NGOs focused on halting unsustainable forestry practices in local rainforests. However, a transformation occurred when the firm, partially driven by a change in perspective at company headquarters, began to consider its ethical responsibilities and seek a closer relationship with community organizations.[22] Managers sought the support of other local firms such as General Motors and White Martins (Brazil's leading supplier of industrial and medical gases) eventually leading to multiparty support for a new NGO, Piracicaba 2010. The organization has an ambitious mandate to transform the city through diversification of agricultural activities, the provision of low-income housing, and assistance with infrastructure including water and roads. In fact, the organization has moved so far beyond the initial work of Caterpillar that residents and community leaders no longer consider it a Caterpillar initiative, but rather a community-wide initiative.

Initiatives found in quadrant two illustrate the potential for co-opetition among firms. Co-opetition in these initiatives is based on recognizing that a coordinated effort is useful for solving more complex social or environmental problems, and alleviation of these social problems can benefit all firms involved. These collaborations provide a number of benefits for member firms. First, for firms facing a common threat due to the risk profile of their industry (e.g., energy exploration, mining, and chemicals), collective action can be effective at improving the conditions for the entire industry. Barnett argues that as firms evaluate industry trends, such as the threat of regulation leading to reduced profitability, investments in communal initiatives with competitors are appropriate.[23] Collaborations of this type can be found in the self-regulatory frameworks developed by industries like Responsible Care. This self-regulation serves as a means of legitimization of the entire industry and can help maintain the license to operate within firms' local communities.

Barnett also examined the life cycle of industries to argue that younger industries in need of legitimization benefit from increased collaboration among firms, as opposed to firms in declining industries where the benefits of retaining legitimacy are reduced.[24] The potential for success with multi-firm collaboration increases in industries with strong associations because of the existing infrastructure and connectivity. However, reports of industry association activity in areas beyond government lobbying efforts are limited. Although Bansal and Roth find some evidence of industry association activities beyond government lobbying,[25] Bertels and Peloza do not find industry associations active in projects related to ethical or philanthropic responsibilities of the member firms.[26] However, even when existing associations do not themselves participate in CSR (either through a form of industry self-governing body or through direct involvement) their existence can help support shared contributions. Members share existing social networks, both formal and informal, which can facilitate cooperation among member firms. Further, these can span industries to include geographically focused networks such as Chambers of Commerce. These industry-spanning networks can be particularly useful at supporting collaborations developed to tackle broad, community-wide issues such as the Brazil example mentioned earlier.

A second benefit of multi-firm collaborations is the potential for increased innovation within a firm, as demonstrated by Ahuja when he showed that network participation in the chemical industry network was related to the number of patents secured by the firm.[27] The knowledge that is shared among network members can lead to innovative ideas or practices, particularly if the organizations are not direct competitors. Thus, networks that encompass a broad base of firms and NGOs are more likely to share knowledge and benefit from the resulting innovation. Even when a practice is widely known, networks speed diffusion by providing specific information on costs and benefits of a practice in more detail and in a more persuasive manner than other forms of diffusion.

A shared contribution collaborative structure is particularly appropriate when firms are operating in communities with institutional voids. For example, the collaboration started by Caterpillar with a local NGO resulted in the development of basic infrastructure needs, which the government was either unwilling or unable to provide. Developing public infrastructure can be expensive and require integration of expertise and assets. Firms co-operating through an NGO can share the expense and resources, and long-term maintenance can be ensured because the NGO stays in place while members of the collaboration may shift. Governments monitoring firms engaged in shared contribution strategies, especially those developed under industry self-regulation structures as presented here, have the responsibility to ensure that self-regulation does indeed provide meaningful impacts for stakeholders to whom the firm is responsible. Should self-regulation become a means for shirking firm responsibility, governments can encourage action through either consultation with collaboration members, or through direct legislation.[28]

As noted, this type of collaboration can play a critical role in self-regulation. An NGO can facilitate agreement on acceptable operating standards and play the third-party role in terms of visibly controlling and monitoring standards agreed upon by the member companies.[29] Key outcomes for this type of self-regulation are a "level playing field" for member companies, a shift from reactive to proactive standards (that is, problems will be prevented rather than solved), and a reduction in negative advocacy.

Finally, the relationships found in quadrant two highlight the potential for solving social issues beyond the scope of single firms. Companies that operate within an industry or within a limited geographic area can collectively make a larger social impact than one company alone. Whether the partner companies are from the same industry or the same community, they will share common social issues that require attention and can more effectively deal with the issue, which in turn creates a more economically sustainable enterprise for all firms.

Notwithstanding the benefits provided by the collaborations found in quadrant two, this strategy is not appropriate for all firms. Several limitations restrict their potential value for some firms. First, because the relationships involve multiple firms, the benefits gained through differentiation from industry competitors are diminished. For example, when multiple firms from the chemical industry claim participation in the Responsible Care initiative, they lose the ability to distinguish their firm from others (although they can differentiate themselves from firms in other industries, which can provide value in a tight labor market, for example). Involvement in such collaborations limits the ability of consumers to make purchases on social as well as economic criteria. As such, this type of collaboration is better suited to firms with similar reputations for CSR or that engage in other distinguishing CSR activities. This strategy is also suitable for firms with weak CSR reputations, as participation is the rising tide that lifts all boats, or association with other firms with strong reputations for CSR will improve the reputation of the firm.[30]

A second restriction on the value of collaborations in quadrant two is that participation requires a high degree of trust and ability to work together on the part of member firms. This problem is alleviated when all firms face a similar threat, but it is less clear in situations where participating firms come from a range of industries and have different cultures and CSR goals.

Firms participating in this type of collaboration need to contribute more resources and expertise than those in quadrant one. These collaborations are characterized by increased consultation with stakeholders, increased involvement and contact with other innovative companies through forums and professional meetings, and dedication of resources and performance measurement from the Board to the plant level. Because of these requirements, firms should ideally be in the innovative or integrative categories of the stages outlined by Mirvis and Googins before undertaking this type of collaboration.[31]

Next, the converse of a benefit of only working with a single NGO— limited opportunity for loss of intellectual capital—is true for quadrant two. The potential for leakage in intellectual capital is increased when firms work together through CSR. Therefore, this type of relationship is more suited to initiatives that do not involve direct application of expertise or technology from firms, as is the case with many environmental initiatives and relevant technologies. Social initiatives are more appropriate, as are environmental initiatives that involve standards or level playing fields as in the case of Responsible Care.

Finally, when multiple firms collaborate through a single NGO the relationship is open to charges of conflicts of interest or undue pressure since the NGO is highly dependent on the goodwill of member firms. The relationship has the potential to evolve into complicity if the NGO ceases to bring external objectivity and credibility to the initiative, and the NGO itself becomes a target of criticism from concerned stakeholders. Therefore, collaborations found in quadrant two are most suited to either firms that have a high degree of existing credibility with respect to CSR, or when firms have the ability to partner with an existing NGO that also has a high degree of credibility within the NGO community.

Quadrant Three: Diffused Contribution

Quadrant three contains relationships where a company works simultaneously with multiple NGOs in CSR initiatives. A high-profile example is Shell's Camisea project in the Amazon region of Peru. After painful lessons with the Brent Spar in the North Sea and the Ogoni in Nigeria, Shell worked to limit its "footprint" in Peru. Staff identified over 350 relevant stakeholders including indigenous populations, environmental NGOs, and local governments, which resulted in formal collaborations with over 40 organizations. This collaboration led to significant modifications to the firm's original plans, such as a redesign of the power source for the project.[32]

A diffused contribution approach is appropriate when firms have signifi-cant, focused operations in a local area with voids in the business infra-structure. In such instances, basic infrastructure can be improved through partnerships with a range of NGOs with local knowledge. When BP wanted to offer fuel-efficient stoves to people living in rural India, for example, it lacked the retail and distribution infrastructure needed to make the project work and it lacked the local knowledge to tap into the network of small shops and informal traders. Through collaboration with three NGOs—IDPMS, Covenant Centre of Development, and Swayam Shikshan Prayog—the collaboration succeeded in building a viable distribution strategy for the region. The partnership also worked to refine the design and safety features of the stove, with the NGOs providing training and support for retailers and users.[33]

Another example of a firm increasing the social impact of their actions through a coalition of NGOs is the work between Starbucks and a range of NGOs working in the coffee-growing regions of Mexico. The firm has a good relationship with Global Exchange on the issue of fair trade coffee, ensuring that local farmers are paid a fair price for their products. However, in 2002 Starbucks began a pilot project to work with Oxfam (which is dedicated to fighting hunger and poverty), the Oaxacan State Coffee Producers Network (which represents the thousands of local Mexican farmers and cooperatives), and the Ford Foundation (which supports the promotion of democratic values and international cooperation and fights poverty and social injustice). Through this broader network of NGOs, the firm is able to make a broader impact on the local community. The goals of this collaboration are to create a sustainable community across a range of issues, each intertwined within the community, reduce their negative social footprint, and to improve the sustainability of Starbucks and the coffee-growing regions in Mexico. Argenti reports that both sides of the collaboration developed a mutual respect and an understanding of the issues faced by other partners, demonstrating the effectiveness of combining expertise through collaboration.[34]

Because collaborations of this type are effective at addressing complex, broad social and environmental issues faced by the firm, they are appropriate for firms with a broad base of international operations, a firm that is domi-nant within a local community, or firms with dominant market shares within their industries.[35] In the first instance, when a firm has highly dispersed operations geographically, it is less likely to possess local knowledge or even be able to identify key ethical responsibilities in areas further from the home country. Important knowledge is obtained from building coalitions with local NGOs possessing expertise (i.e., quadrant two). In the second instance, when a firm dominates a local community, it can effectively tackle complex issues through a coalition of community groups.[36] Given that NGOs have a singular focus, and a firm must manage multiple issues that span across multiple constituencies, managers can obtain expertise and skill needed to manage specific issues from the more-focused NGO. The corporate manager becomes the coordinator of resources and consultations across NGOs and stakeholders.

In the third case, a dominant firm within an industry can become a target for a multitude of issues and be affected by negative activism.[37] For example, when H.B. Fuller was blamed for children sniffing glue in Latin America, the problem was not the glue but rather a series of problems within the community. In these situations, corporations need to be visibly working with NGOs to diffuse the negative activism and develop appropriate philanthropic programs.

Two benefits of this type of collaboration stem from greater access to information. First, collaborating with a single NGO can lead to information asymmetry about community needs, while an expanded network of NGOs leads to enhanced knowledge on both emerging community issues and potential solutions. Second is increased access to specialized technology and training. King points out numerous examples where nonprofits have invested in technology that is then used by firms, such as the work of the Alliance for Environmental Innovation's development of a more efficient delivery box for UPS or the training provided by Conservation International to farmers that strengthened the supply of shade-grown coffee offered by Starbucks.[38] However, King argues an inherent problem for NGOs that develop special-ized technologies or expertise is that the company loses any incentive to support the NGO once they have accessed the needed resource. In a collab-orative network with multiple NGOs, investment costs and risks are diffused across organizations and thus investment is more likely to occur.

Firms in the *innovative* and *integrated* stages of the Mirvis and Googins model are most likely to maximize the value from this form of collaboration because they have the appropriate organizational infrastructure to manage more sophisticated CSR strategies. For example, Argenti outlined how Starbucks' multi-NGO collaborations developed after Starbucks worked with and became aware of the myriad of issues associated with production of coffee.[39]

This collaborative structure is effective in communities where govern-ments are not building public infrastructure or where local leaders have minimal resources to support community projects. When there is limited public infrastructure, multiple groups are needed to build the missing components; and coordination through a focal point is required to limit duplication. In situations where the local leadership is stable and community-oriented, NGOs can develop effective programs for solving a variety of complex problems beyond the resources of the leaders. In this situation, a business can leave the coordinating role to local leaders, but still needs to support a group of NGOs to address the problems identified by the community.

The benefits provided by these collaborations are not without challenges, the most pressing of which is the need for dedicated expertise to managing the NGO partners. Managing these collaborations requires considerable skill and experience, since NGOs have unique cultures from firms and often have competing priorities from stakeholders limiting their flexibility to cooperate.[40]

A focused administrative structure is critical for a strategy of diffused contributions to ensure managers are not inadvertently dragged into initiatives unrelated to the firm's strategy. Collaborations with NGOs can lead to increased expectations for support, because cooperation is seen as an invitation to bring a concern forward and the company's willingness to add social and environmental issues to its agenda. Indeed, Argenti reports that managers worry that by entering into joint agreements with NGOs, they are potentially opening a floodgate.[41]

Quadrant Four: Communal Contribution

Quadrant four contains multi-party collaborations that include NGOs and corporations, with multiple representatives from each group. These collaborations are appropriate for what Selsky and Parker refer to as "meta-problems," issues exceeding the scope of a single organization.[42] They require multi-institutional collaborative efforts across stakeholders, such as forums, partnerships, negotiations and planning to have social impact.[43] Managers that collaborate with multiple NGOs can tap into existing networks of communication among NGOs that is already taking place on an informal basis. Indeed, Hendry finds a large number of informal relationships among environmental NGOs around data sharing, collective planning of activities, and lawsuits.[44] However, these collaborations can be highly complex, and require a long-term focus for both the firm and NGO.

Communal contribution is particularly appropriate when the issue occurs in dispersed geographic locations, environmentally sensitive areas, or in developing countries where local regulatory institutions are not yet mature. Although communal contributions can be effective at addressing institutional voids where governments are not able to fully provide public resources, governments in these situations can take a leadership role is defining priority issues and connecting firms with appropriate NGOs. They can also use public policy (e.g., tax policy and deductibility of firm resources dedicated to CSR initiatives) to encourage collaboration between firms and NGOs.

A high-profile example of multi-firm, multi-NGO collaboration is the Fair Labor Association (www.fairlabor.org). The association is composed of over 20 apparel manufacturers (such as Nike, Eddie Bauer, and Nordstrom) and dozens of NGOs. Each member plays a vital role in areas such as consultation, monitoring, and verification. The advisory board of the FLA is composed of an international roster of NGOs from various perspectives including Human Rights First and the National Council of Churches based in New York, the Federation of Free Workers in the Philippines, and the

Cambodian Labour Association among others. The Workplace Code of Conduct of the FLA addresses a broad range of issues including exploitation (forced and child labor), work environment (harassment and abuse, discrimination, health and safety), and employment criteria (collective bargaining, wages and compensation). The result is comprehensive oversight of a myriad of issues across dozens of nations. In short, involvement for member companies provides methods for managing different ethical responsibilities and increases the social impact of their activities.[45]

Another example is the Initiative for Responsible Mining Assurance (IRMA; www.responsiblemining.net) developed to respond to the ethical responsibilities of firms working in the mining of precious metals. The operations of these firms have been linked to severe human rights and environmental abuses in some of the world's most vulnerable countries and regions. Members of IRMA include gold and diamond mining companies such as BHP-Billiton, Rio Tinto, Newmont, and DeBeers, jewelry retailers such as Tiffany's and Wal-Mart/Sam's Club, and associations such as the International Council of Mining and Metals and the Jewelers of America. These firms and associations collectively collaborate with NGOs that provide expertise on a range of environmental (e.g., Canadian Boreal Initiative, Conservation International and World Wildlife Fund) and social (e.g., Oxfam America, Pembina Institute) issues arising from mining operations. The mandate of the organization is to tackle a broad range of ethical responsibilities of member firms, including independently verifying compliance with environmental, human rights, and social standards for mining operations.

Given the scale of these issues, one of the primary benefits of the collaborations in quadrant four is that they allow for remediation of complex issues that can detract from firm or industry performance. In particular, the collaboration between firms and NGOs provides significant support to the nonprofit sector thereby ensuring resources for the NGO to tackle social and environmental issues. Connectivity for young NGOs leads to legitimacy, resource sharing and a more efficient use of donor support.[46] Further, Brass and colleagues[47] note relationships with established actors are particularly valuable in situations where output is difficult to directly evaluate, as it is within the NGO sector.

By broadening both firm and NGO partners, managers balance critical social and environmental issues generally involving competing stakeholder expectations as to a "right" approach. Inclusive approaches such as this are most critical when firms are operating in conditions with visible ethical dilemmas (e.g., animal rights, military contracting). In these situations, there are competing stakeholder values and a lack of agreement on the "right" choice. For example, companies such as Shell have environmentalists attempting to limit Shell's operations while many local community governments want to expand it. Companies can never resolve competing demands so they must visibly identify priorities and develop policies and programs to ensure that the priorities are met.[48] Coordinated strategic planning between

NGOs and corporations is also needed because community problems are like peeling an onion; the most visible issue is composed of a number of underlying problems. Complex problems are best addressed through multiple approaches, where both firms and NGOs cooperate and combine resources (i.e., expertise, supplies, and funds) of different organizations. Indeed, although measurement on the social and environmental aspects of CSR is often lacking,[49] effectiveness of CSR is best considered at a collective rather than organizational level (e.g., AIDS in Africa).[50]

The largest limitation to pursuing the strategy outlined in quadrant four is the significant expertise and resources necessary to manage the initiative. Firms in the fifth stage of the Mirvis and Googins framework—*transforming*—are best suited to engage in this type of collaboration. These firms are characterized by an interest in leadership on issues related to CSR, and firms in this stage are able, both structurally and culturally, to maintain relationships with multiple organizations.

Another limitation to quadrant four is that it is limited to initiatives where a collaborative mindset is present rather than a goal of developing a distinct reputation or niche, since both firms often seek to create legitimacy and differentiation within their industry, and NGOs seek to gain credibility and sustainable funding.[51] Both sides of this equation face pressures to differentiate and compete for resources, and many are unwilling to collaborate on such a broad scale due to a fundamental difference in values, organizational structure, and common experience. Paul Gilding, a former executive - director of Greenpeace International stated: "When it comes to market transformation, the problem is that NGOs are almost completely ignorant of how markets and business work, while business is largely ignorant of how to work with NGOs."[52] In this context, managers in both firms and NGOs fear a loss of control in the relationship. Thus collaborative projects between firms and NGOs are more stressed (i.e., lower trust, higher misunderstandings) than those in the traditional alliances between firms.[53]

A competitive mindset among firms can also deter this type of collaboration. In their study of CSR within a local community, Bertels and Peloza found that competitive forces among firms, both within and across industries, lead to a steady stream of "one-upmanship."[54] This ratcheting effect begins when firms in higher-profile industries feel pressure to engage in CSR at a higher level than firms from other industries. When this level is matched by larger firms in other industries, it becomes a new standard among community firms. To move to a collective focus, a more collaborative mindset is needed. Further restriction on this type of collaboration is evident in a study by Bansal and Roth who found that firms that exceeded industry standards for CSR were persecuted by their peers for raising the informal standard (i.e., cost base) for all firms within the industry.[55]

One of the most significant risks with multi-party collaborations— especially for companies that compete within the same industry—is that one or more of the participants will free ride by not fairly contributing to a project. Because free riding is less likely by NGOs that require visibility to receive future funding, the potential for free riding among firms occurs in quadrants two to four.

Even in situations where free riding is recognized, there can be powerful incentives for leading members of the collaborations to sustain the institutions created. Studies of the chemical industry's Responsible Care Initiative, for example, demonstrate that despite the presence of free riders, the program still provides active members with benefits that sustain the program. Such programs can act as powerful deterrents to government-imposed legislation or action by activist groups. Lenox analyzes data from chemical companies over a ten-year period, including firms that were both active in the initiative and firms that were not (i.e., free riders).[56] Firms could free ride because of the lack of explicit monitoring and sanctioning mechanisms. He found that active self-regulators had improved financial performance, while the free riders received reputation benefits by merely joining the Responsible Care Initiative. However, leading firms are still motivated to maintain the institution of Responsible Care for the legitimacy it offers and the potential to address ethical responsibilities.

Conclusion

Our framework for the collaboration among firms and NGOs adds a new dimension to the existing view of collaboration in the social responsibilities of firms. It provides criteria for managers to apply when seeking to optimize both the social/environmental and economic impacts from joint initiatives between their firms and NGOs. It also shifts the underlying logic from one of pure competition to recognizing the potential for co-opetition. Although the benefits of communal strategies across firms are well documented,[57] the prevailing view among both managers and researchers appears to be that competitive CSR strategies are best suited to deliver economic benefits to the firm. For example, reputational benefits that are secured by one firm are often assumed to be at the expense of other firms, either competitors within the same industry or firms within the same community.[58] Managers should undertake efforts to connect with existing networks to support opportunities for collaborative involvement with other firms, NGOs, or both. Doing so will provide skills and preparation that will allow them to consider a broader range of collaboration options in their CSR initiatives.

Our framework provides a menu of options for managers looking to match the goals and contextual factors associated with their CSR activities and to ensure that the value of their CSR investment is maximized. Faced with multiple choices to implement an initiative, managers can prioritize among objectives that deliver differentiation from industry competitors versus social impacts that benefit the entire industry. Although such prioritization will depend on the specific situation of the firm, careful consideration of our framework helps facilitate the process.

Further, the framework assists firms that wish to pursue more than one priority with different structures and initiatives in the most effective manner. For example, firms with overseas operations that face allegations of sweatshops may prioritize the objective of legitimacy with governments and activists. Working collaboratively with other firms that are facing a similar issue and with NGOs that have expertise can help protect legitimacy of the entire industry. At the same time, a firm can undertake a CSR initiative to conserve energy at HQ with the objectives of cost savings and employee empowerment to promote efficiency. With this initiative, a focused collaboration with a single NGO with expertise in energy conservation would be an efficient structure to pursue. In each initiative, measurement of performance against targets is critical. In the first example, measures such as media coverage may be appropriate, while in the second case employee satisfaction and expenses are appropriate.

Thus, although at a corporate level CSR initiatives are often centered around a small number of focused priorities for the firm (e.g., fit with the business strategy or core competencies of the firm), collaboration strategies can vary across a range of initiatives. Further, the availability of suitable NGOs or firms with which to collaborate may also present a limitation to full consideration of each strategy.

Our examination of the benefits of various forms of collaboration also makes progress toward uncovering the mechanisms by which CSR can impact the financial performance of the firm. Smith highlighted that the implementation of CSR holds many challenges, and given the reliance of firms on NGOs to execute CSR initiatives, the choice of collaboration structure is at the heart of the implementation challenge.[59] In a recent meta-analysis of the relationship between CSR and financial performance, Margolis and colleagues call for a movement away from the broad question to an increased examination of the mechanics of how firms successfully engage in CSR.[60] We respond to their call for increased attention to the structures pursued by managers that enable them to reach CSR objectives. By examining the moderating factors between CSR collaboration strategy and benefits for the firm, we link the relationship between firm motives and performance outcomes.

As seen here, both firms and NGOs can benefit from extending their view of collaboration in CSR. For company managers, collaboration with either multiple firms and/or multiple NGOs can often deliver performance against key corporate motives to a greater extent than collaboration between a single firm and NGO. Managers must explicitly examine their objectives and initiate the proper collaboration structure accordingly.

Notes

1. See, for example: Marc Orlitzky, Frank Schmidt, and Sara Rynes, "Corporate Social and Financial Performance: A Meta-Analysis," *Organization Studies*, 24/3 (2003): 403–441; Joshua Margolis and James P. Walsh, "Misery Loves Companies: Rethinking Social Initiatives by Business," *Administrative Science Quarterly*, 48/2 (June 2003): 268–305; N. Craig Smith, "Corporate Social Responsibility: Whether or How?" *California Management Review*, 45/4 (Summer 2003): 52–76; David J. Vogel, "Is There a Market for Virtue? The Business Case for Corporate Social Responsibility," *California Management Review*, 47/4 (Summer 2005): 19–45.

2. David Hess, Nicolai Rogovsky, and Thomas W. Dunfee, "The Next Wave of Corporate Community Involvement: Corporate Social Initiatives," *California Management Review*, 44/2 (Winter 2002): 110–125.

3. James E. Austin, "Strategic Collaboration Between Nonprofits and Businesses," *Nonprofit & Voluntary Sector Quarterly*, 29/1 (March 2000): 69–97.

4. John W. Selsky and Barbara Parker, "Cross-Sector Partnerships to Address Social Issues: Challenges to Theory and Practice," *Journal of Management*, 31/6 (December 2005): 849–873.

5. See, for example, Austin, op. cit.; Ida E. Berger, Peggy Cunningham, and Minette E. Drumwright, "Mainstreaming Corporate Social Responsibility: Developing Markets for Virtue," *California Management Review*, 49/4 (Summer 2007): 132–157; Michael Yaziji, "Turning Gadflies into Allies," *Harvard Business Review*, 82/2 (February 2004): 110–115.

6. For recent work on the benefits of communal strategies for firms, see Michael L. Barnett, "Finding A Working Balance Between Competitive and Communal Strategies," *Journal of Management Studies*, 43/8 (December 2006): 1753–1773; Michael L. Barnett, "Waves of Collectivizing: A Dynamic Model of Competition and Cooperation Over the Life of an Industry," *Corporate Reputation Review*, 8/4 (Winter 2006): 272–292.

7. Michael L. Barnett, "Stakeholder Influence Capacity and the Variability of Financial Returns to Corporate Social Responsibility," *Academy of Management Review*, 32/3 (July 2007): 794–816.

8. Smith, op. cit.

9. Michael Porter and Michael Kramer, "The Competitive Advantage of Corporate Philanthropy," *Harvard Business Review*, 80/12 (December 2002): 57–68.

10. For research on the consumer audience, see, for example, Donald R. Lichtenstein, Minette E. Drumwright, and Bridgette M. Braig, "The Effect of Corporate Social Responsibility on Customer Donations to Corporate-Supported Nonprofits," *Journal of Marketing*, 68/4 (October 2004): 16–32. For research on the employee stakeholder, see Daniel Turban and Daniel Greening, "Corporate Social Performance and Organizational Attractiveness to Prospective Employees," *Academy of Management Journal*, 40/3 (June 1997): 658–672.

11. See, for example, Petra Christmann, "Effects of 'Best Practices' of Environmental Management on Cost Advantage: The Role of Complementary Assets," *Academy of Management Journal*, 43/4 (August 2000): 663–680; Stuart Hart, "A Natural-Resource-Based View of the Firm," *Academy of Management Review*, 20/4 (October 1995): 986–1014; Michael Porter and Claas van der Linde, "Green and Competitive: Ending the Stalemate," *Harvard Business Review*, 73/5 (September/October 1995): 120–134.

12. Dennis A. Rondinelli and Ted London, "How Corporations and Environmental Groups Cooperate: Assessing Cross-Sector Alliances and Collaborations," *Academy of Management Executive*, 17/1 (February 2003): 61–76.

13. Rosabeth Moss Kanter, "Spare Change to Real Change," *Harvard Business Review*, 77/3 (May/June1999): 122–132.

14. Minette E. Drumwright, "Company Advertising With a Social Dimension: The Role of Noneconomic Criteria," *Journal of Marketing*, 60/4 (October 1996): 71–87.

15. Carolyn J. Simmons and Karen L. Becker-Olsen, "Achieving Marketing Objectives Through Social Sponsorships," *Journal of Marketing*, 70/4 (October 2006): 154–169.

16. Andrew King, "Cooperation Between Corporations and Environmental Groups: A Transaction Cost Perspective," *Academy of Management Review*, 32/3 (July 2007): 889–900.

17. Zadek provides a case study of Nike's development from an ignorance of social issues to leading advocate. Simon Zadek, "The Path to Corporate Social Responsibility," *Harvard Business Review*, 82/12 (December 2004): 125–133.

18. Philip Mirvis and Bradley Googins, "Stages of Corporate Citizenship," *California Management Review*, 48/2 (Winter 2006): 104–123.

19. Joseph Galaskiewicz, "An Urban Grants Economy Revisited: Corporate Charitable Contributions in the Twin Cities, 1971–81, 1987–89," *Administrative Science Quarterly*, 42/3 (September 1997): 445–471.

20. Porter and Kramer, op. cit.

21. Donald H. Schepers, "The Impact of NGO Network Conflict on the Corporate Social Responsibility Strategies of Multinational Corporations," *Business & Society*, 45/3 (September 2006): 282–299.

22. A case study of the Caterpillar experience in Brazil is available: Margaret Griesse, "Caterpillar's Interactions with Piracicaba, Brazil: A Community-based Analysis of CSR," *Journal of Business Ethics*, 73/1 (June 2007): 39–51.

23. Barnett (December 2006), op. cit.; Barnett (Winter 2006), op. cit.

24. Barnett (Winter 2006), op. cit.

25. Pratima Bansal and Kendall Roth, "Why Companies Go Green: A Model of Ecological Responsiveness," *Academy of Management Journal*, 43/4 (August 2000): 717–736.

26. Stephanie Bertels and John Peloza, "Running to Stand Still: Managing CSR in an Era of Ratcheting Expectations," *Corporate Reputation Review*, 11/1 (2009): 56–72. A collection of papers in a forthcoming issue of *Corporate Reputation Review* ("Beyond Corporate Reputation: Managing Reputational Interdependence") is dedicated to the study the relationships between firm and industry reputations.

27. Gautam Ahuja, "Collaboration Networks, Structural Holes and Innovation: A Longitudinal Study," *Administrative Science Quarterly*, 45/3 (September 2000): 425–455.

28. For a review of firms' efforts to self-regulate and influence public policy on issues related to the environment, see Ans Kolk and Jonatan Pinkse, "Multinationals' Political Activities on Climate Change," *Business & Society*, 46/2 (June 2007): 201–228.

29. Ian Maitland, "The Limits of Business Self-Regulation," *California Management Review*, 27/3 (Spring 1985): 132–148.

30. Barnett argues that similarities among firms will lead to increased investment in collaborative initiatives. Barnett (December 2006), op. cit.

31. Mirvis and Googins, op. cit.

32. More information on this case study is available from James E. Post, Lee E. Preston, and Sybille Sachs, *Redefining the Corporation: Stakeholder Management and Organizational Wealth* (Stanford, CA: Stanford Business Books, 2002).

33. Brugmann and Prahalad provide additional detail of IBM's experience in India. Jeb Brugmann and C.K. Prahalad, "Cocreating Business's New Social Impact," *Harvard Business Review*, 85/2 (February 2007): 80–90.

34. A comprehensive review of the relationships between Starbucks and NGOs can be found in Paul A. Argenti, "Collaborating with Activists: How Starbucks Works with NGOs," 47/1 (Fall 2004): 91–116.

35. Barnett provides an excellent review of the incremental benefits that accrue to leading firms when they invest in initiatives that benefit not only the institutional entrepreneur but other firms as well. Barnett (December 2006), op. cit.

36. Keith G. Proven, Mark A. Veazie, Lisa K. Staten, and Nicolette I. Teufel-Shone, "The Use of Network Analysis to Strengthen Community Partnerships," *Public Administration Review*, 65/5 (September/October 2005): 603 613.

37. Kathleen Rehbein, Sandra Waddock, and Samuel B. Graves, "Understanding Shareholder Activism: Which Corporations Are Targeted?" *Business & Society*, 43/3 (September 2004): 239–267.

38. King, op. cit.

39. Argenti, op. cit.

40. Proven et al., op. cit.

41. Argenti, op. cit.

42. Selsky and Parker, op. cit.

43. Turcotte and Pasquero review some of the challenges unique to multiparty collaboration. Marie-France Turcotte and Jean Pasquero, "The Paradox of Multistakeholder Collaborative Roundtables," *The Journal of Applied Behavioral Science*, 37/4 (December 2001): 447–464.

44. Jamie R. Hendry, "Taking Aim at Business: What Factors Lead Environmental Non-Governmental Organizations to Target Particular Firms?" *Business & Society*, 45/1 (March 2006): 47–86.

45. Aaron Chatterji and David Levine, "Breaking Down the Wall of Codes: Evaluating Non-Financial Performance Measurement," *California Management Review*, 48/2 (Winter 2006): 29–51.

46. Eugene Bardach, *Getting Agencies to Work Together: The Practice and Theory of Managerial Craftsmanship* (Washington, D.C.: The Brookings Institute, 1999); Mark A. Hager, Joseph Galaskiewicz, and Jeff A. Larson, "Structural Embeddedness and the Liability of Newness Among Nonprofit Organizations," *Public Management Review*, 6/2 (June 2004): 159–188.

47. Daniel J. Brass, Joseph Galaskiewicz, Henrich R. Greve, and Wenpin Tsai, "Taking Stock of Networks and Organizations: A Multilevel Perspective," *Academy of Management Journal*, 47/6 (December 2004): 795–817.

48. Schepers, op. cit.

49. Margolis and Walsh, op. cit.

50. Keith G. Provan and H.B. Milward, "A Preliminary Theory of Interorganizational Network Effectiveness: A Comparative Study of Four Community Mental Health Systems," *Administrative Science Quarterly*, 40/1 (March 1995): 1–33.

51. Simon Zadek, *The Civil Corporation: The New Economy of Corporate Citizenship* (London: Earthscan, 2001); Hildy Teegan, Jonathan P. Doh, and Sushil Vachani, "The Importance of Nongovernmental Organizations (NGOs) in Global Governance and Value Creation: An International Business Research Agenda," *Journal of International Business Studies*, 35/6 (November 2004): 463–483.

52. Quoted in Argenti, op. cit., p. 108.

53. Barbara Parker and John W. Selsky, "Interface Dynamics in Cause-Based Partnerships: An Exploration of Emergent Culture," *Nonprofit and Voluntary Sector Quarterly*, 33/3 (September 2004): 458–488; Rondinelli and London, op. cit.

54. Bertels and Peloza, op. cit.

55. Bansal and Roth, op. cit.

56. Michael J. Lenox, "The Role of Private Decentralized Institutions in Sustaining Industry Self-Regulation," *Organization Science*, 17/6 (November/December 2006): 677–690.

57. Barnett provides an extensive review of the benefits of communal investments beyond those explored here. Barnett (December 2006), op. cit.

58. Bertels and Peloza, op. cit.

59. Smith, op. cit.

60. Joshua Margolis, Hillary Anger Elfenbein, and James P. Walsh, "Does it Pay to be Good? A Meta-Analysis and Redirection of Research on the Relationship Between Corporate Social and Financial Performance," working paper, Harvard Business School.

THE GOVERNMENT OF SELF-REGULATION: ON THE COMPARATIVE DYNAMICS OF CORPORATE SOCIAL RESPONSIBILITY

Jean-Pascal Gond, Nahee Kang and Jeremy Moon

Introduction

This paper explores the relationship between government and corporate social responsibility (CSR). CSR, as a field of corporate discourse and practice, has recently been described as a new form of self-regulation (Vogel, 2010) which enhances the 'economization of the political' (Shamir, 2008, pp. 1–4), and as that which could free corporations from governmental pressures under a *façade* of morality (Banerjee, 2008; Shamir, 2004a). Yet, the CSR movement raises broader governance issues with globalization (Gibbon & Ponte, 2008; Scherer & Palazzo, 2011; Thompson, 2008), and it is associated with new forms of both business involvement in new governance (Moon, 2002) and market politicization (Micheletti, 2003; Michelleti, Føllesdal & Stolle, 2004). These latter trends create new opportunities for governments to regulate corporate behaviours through CSR as well as to deploy CSR for governance purposes. Hence, governments' interest in CSR grows, shaped by a range of motivations and contexts, including the welfare state crisis (Midttun, 2005), the relational state and new governance (Moon, 2002), new social demands (Kjaergaard & Westphalen, 2001), national competitiveness (Hodge, 2006) and sustainable development (European Commission, 2002). Despite the growing evidence of government agency in relation to CSR, both historically and comparatively, the government-CSR relationship is counter-intuitive to many, and therefore remains largely overlooked, particularly in theoretical and conceptual terms.

In exploring CSR-government relationships we refute two common assumptions about CSR. The first is that CSR is exclusively about what government policy or regulation does not require of business or that which occurs beyond the requirements of government and the law (McGuire, 1963; McWilliams & Siegel, 2001, 2011). The second assumption we address is that CSR is simply a smokescreen for deregulation (Shamir, 2004a, 2004b, 2005, 2008) and thus, to mix our metaphors, window-dressing for irresponsible behaviour (Jones, 1996; Shamir, 2004a, 2004b, 2008; Banerjee, 2008). In demonstrating that both of these assumptions misrepresent the empirical reality of CSR with serious consequences for policy (e.g. undermining of the ability of governments to engage in CSR or denying the governments' deliberate use of CSR to enhance regulation through market pressures), we offer a typology of the relationship between CSR and government that accounts for their multiple configurations of interaction.

Building on insights from political science, economic sociology, legal studies and organization theory, we propose a typology that maps a wide range of CSR-government configurations and that recognizes the central role of government agency in this relationship. Thus we explore CSR not only as self-government (voluntary and non-enforceable) or as an alternative form of government (substitute for government), but also as self-regulation which is facilitated by government, coordinated in partnerships with government, and mandated – either directly or indirectly – by government.

We then use this framework as a conceptual tool with which to explore empirically the variety of ways in which governments engage with CSR in a comparative historical perspective. Here, we focus on Western Europe and East Asia. The choice of the two regions is based on the fact that their national governance systems, often described as either 'organized' or 'coordinated', differ from the more 'liberal' system of governance associated with the US (Dore, 2000; Hall & Soskice, 2001), and therefore can shed light on CSR-government relationships not limited to the conventional notion of 'CSR as self-government', which originates from the US. Moreover, the two regions allow a valid comparison with the US as they have relatively well-developed and stable systems of governance (albeit to varying degrees). The choice of national case studies within the two regions is not meant to be representative but indicative of the common and varying CSR-government relationships.

We attribute the neglected variety of CSR-government configurations to two main factors that have been downplayed in the extant studies on CSR. First, inadequate attention has been paid to the important differences in the way in which CSR has 'travelled' (or diffused) and has been mediated by the national governance systems, and, second, there has been insufficient emphasis placed on the role of the government (or government agency) in the CSR domain. Our empirical analysis suggests that in the CSR domain, as in other areas, 'market-building is state-building' (Fligstein, 1996). Governments can and do mobilize corporations purposively and strategically through CSR, either for liberalizing specific areas of social and political life (Shamir, 2004a, 2008) or for enhancing indirectly market and civil society pressures on corporations to behave in a socially responsible manner (McBarnet, 2007; Vogel, 2010; Zerk, 2006). Finally, we discuss how the typology of CSR-government relationships we propose can help further our understanding of socio-economic hybridization at the intersection of the business, political and society spheres, and in uncovering processes that govern the so-called 'self-regulation' that have been overlooked in prior debates.

Our paper takes the following path. We begin by discussing the concept of CSR as conventionally understood, pointing to the fact that much of the extant CSR literature does not allow sufficient room for government and, as consequence, for regulation and public policy in relation to CSR. We go on to explain our conceptual framework for CSR-government configurations. We then apply this framework to selected countries in Western Europe and East Asia in a comparative historical perspective. In so doing we compare and contrast the national directions of change in CSR-government relationships as well as the key drivers and issues of CSR in the respective countries. Hence, we are able to specify a set of possible shifts from one CSR-government configuration to another. We proceed to explain these findings with respect to the way CSR has travelled to the different national governance systems, the path-dependent change from one configuration to another, as well as the strategies of government policies therein. Finally, we conclude with a discussion on the findings, presenting CSR as neither a matter of self-regulation nor an acceptable face of deregulation. Instead, we present it as a more nuanced regulatory phenomenon which is reflective of a multi-national or even global (as opposed to US specific) concept, enacted in national settings of governance and as a feature of wider regulatory strategies. We finally discuss how our conceptualization of the CSR-government relationships can inform future research on the government of self-regulation.

Conventional views of CSR

CSR refers to corporate actions that focus on enhancing stakeholder relations while aiming at enhancing social welfare (McBarnet, 2007). Crouch recently proposed to define CSR more specifically as 'corporate externality recognition', that is, 'behaviour by firms that voluntarily takes account of the externalities produced by their market behaviour, externalities being defined as results of market transactions that are not themselves embodied in such transactions' (2006, p. 1534). Such an approach overlaps the widely diffused definition by the European Commission of CSR as 'a concept whereby companies integrate social and environmental concerns in their business operations and in their interaction with their stakeholders on a voluntary basis' (European Commission, 2001, p. 6).

At an empirical and descriptive level, CSR has been approached as a set of corporate practices and discourses shaped by a range of actors in the organizational field (Shamir, 2005, 2008). At a theoretical and analytical level, CSR is a more controversial concept (Crane, Matten, McWilliams, Moon & Siegel, 2008; Gond & Moon, 2011a) that has been subject to scrutiny and debates since the term emerged in the early 1950s (Bowen, 1953; Heald, 1970).

The conventional views of CSR are dominated by two key assumptions perpetuated by both CSR advocates and their critics. The first common assumption, associated with the critics of CSR and more broadly of neo-liberalism, is that CSR is a smokescreen for deregulation (Hanlon, 2008; Shamir, 2005) and, possibly, a window-dressing for irresponsible behaviour (Banerjee, 2008; Gond, Palazzo & Basu, 2009; Jones, 1996). According to this view, corporations actively shape the CSR organizational field in order to 'de-radicalize' CSR and ultimately to undermine its potential for social reform (Banerjee, 2008; Shamir, 2004a). Corporations do so by co-opting, supporting or creating 'market-friendly' NGOs that frame the notion of CSR in ways that are amenable to business interests (Shamir, 2004a, 2005). Such corporate reframing of CSR also involves a 'commodification' process whereby social responsibilities are addressed only to the extent to which they support the development of new market opportunities (Shamir, 2008). Hence, it would be wrong to consider CSR as an 'emancipatory social project' or a 'counter hegemonic force' to the dominant neo-liberalism (Santos, 2002, p. 146). Rather, social responsibility is a subtle and yet an effective response from the capitalist system to the threat of further governmental regulations. As noted by Shamir, corporate CSR discourse and practice fit neatly with an approach to neo-liberalism that focuses on 'responsibilization' and stresses new modes of governance through 'market-embedded morality' (2008, p. 1). CSR can thus be regarded as an illustration of the capitalist system's capacity to 'recycle' its own critique and to find new moral justifications of its perpetuation (Boltanski & Chiapello, 2005 [1999], pp. 7–12). It represents one of the last 'complex effects of domination' created by management to hide its increasing control over social life (Boltanski, 2009, pp. 190–3), and some would go even further to suggest that CSR could be the 'brand new spirit of capitalism' (Kazmi, Leca & Naccache, 2008). By this reasoning, the current development and diffusion of CSR would achieve a 'silent takeover' by corporations of political and social spheres (Hertz, 2002), which was a concern shared by the earlier CSR thinkers (Bowen, 1953; Chamberlain, 1973; Levitt, 1958).[1]

The second assumption, firmly underpinned by neo-liberalism and central to many definitions of CSR influenced by the US experience, is that CSR is what government policy or regulation does not require of business or that which occurs beyond the requirements of government and the law (McGuire, 1963; McWilliams & Siegel, 2001, 2011). This view has been termed the 'dichotomous view of CSR and government', in which corporations undertake social responsibilities entirely on a voluntary basis and governments administer public policy (Moon & Vogel, 2008, pp. 304–7). This notion of the separation between markets and politics echoes Milton Friedman's (1970) dictum that hired professional managers are responsible for running businesses (on behalf of their owners) and that elected politicians and public officials are accountable for, experienced in and trained for government. Friedman's view of business is that it lacks both accountability and capacity to address matters beyond economic interests. This perspective, endorsed by the mainstream economics and management studies literatures, considers CSR to be either a form of philanthropy that has ethical and normative dimensions or business strategy that has an instrumental dimension (Porter & Kramer, 2006). In both cases, CSR is conceptualized as a form of self-government which exists alongside government and the public system of governance (Margolis & Walsh, 2003; McBarnet, 2007, pp. 13–27). Thus, government and CSR coexist, but have no obvious relationship. This view leaves no room for the role of government in CSR.

Missing in discussions on CSR is the fact that, both historically and comparatively, national governments have always had a relationship with CSR and continue to have influence on CSR. This is because markets and politics cannot be neatly separated in reality (Chang, 2002; Dahl & Lindblom, 1992 [1953]; Fligstein, 1996), and as such government agency becomes important as it allows room to contemplate strategic engagement with neo-liberalism through CSR. The reliance on market mechanisms for governing corporate behavior – for instance through the diffusion of the 'shareholder model' of corporate governance in the US since the 1980s (Fligstein & Markowitz, 1993) – does not equate to a retreat by the state but rather an active engagement by government to define the rules and mechanisms shaping the new mode of governance (Fligstein, 1996, 2001). In the case of CSR, scholars of legal studies have noted that the reliance on market mechanisms through CSR is a way to enhance market pressures on corporations, and thus to complement rather than supplant the legal framework by moving beyond the 'command and control' approach to legislation (McBarnet, 2007; Zerk, 2006).

By and large, works on CSR that build on the two aforementioned assumptions have failed to acknowledge the institutional embeddedness of market mechanisms within broader systems of governance that reflect social relations as well as the national legal and political governance systems (Chang, 2002; Granovetter, 1985; Polanyi, 1957, 2001 [1944]). In so doing, they share a common blind spot: both miss the underlying yet crucial role of the government in CSR, exercised both indirectly through the mobilization of market mechanisms and directly through the legal and regulatory shaping of private CSR initiatives.

We, therefore, propose a different and competing view of CSR by challenging the strict boundaries between market (private business) and state (public) responsibilities prevalent in extant CSR literature, and in turn open a realm in which the relationship between CSR and government can be explored (Kallio, 2007, pp. 170–1). We draw on the national governance systems literature (Boyer, 2005; Hollingsworth & Boyer, 1997) – under whose rubric we include the 'national business systems' (Whitley, 1992, 1999) and the 'varieties of capitalism' approach (Amable, 2003; Hall & Soskice, 2001; Streeck & Yamamura, 2001; Yamamura & Streeck, 2003) – to give attention to the national institutional frameworks within which corporations operate (Crouch, 2006; Kang & Moon, 2010; Matten & Moon, 2008; Moon & Vogel, 2008; Vogel, 2010). Without going into the debate on 'agency versus structure', these works are useful in that they view corporations as actors, but ones which are constrained (and enabled) by the broader institutional settings in which they operate (Crouch, 2006; Deeg & Jackson, 2007), and therefore, embedded in their respective national governance systems. CSR is seen as reflecting (and serving) the broader patterns of social responsibility of businesses within these systems (Jackson & Apostolakou, 2009; Kang & Moon, 2010; Matten & Moon, 2008). Such a perspective allows more room to investigate CSR in relation to the varied modes of governance and the roles of government.

Configuring CSR-government relations

We propose a repertoire of configurations of the CSR-government relationships to investigate the various ways in which government can influence and strategically promote CSR. Theoretically, our repertoire is informed by prior works on the relationships between law and CSR (McBarnet, 2007; Zerk, 2006), those on the private regulation of corporate conduct (Vogel, 2005, 2010), and on the studies that explore the role of government in CSR (Albareda, Lozano, & Ysa, 2007; Fox, Ward & Howard, 2002; Moon, 2002; Moon & Vogel, 2008; Steurer, 2010). Empirically, our analysis relies on comparative case studies of national CSR. We build on these conceptual resources and empirical evidences to theorize CSR-government relationships as reflecting different balances of governmental and business responsibilities embedded in divergent national governance systems.

Table 11.1 presents the outcome of our analysis and distinguishes five distinct modes of coordination between corporations and government over the content and process of CSR initiatives: (1) CSR as self-government, (2) CSR as facilitated by government, (3) CSR as partnership with government, (4) CSR as mandated by government and, finally, (5) CSR as a form of government. In what follows, we specify each configuration by describing the coordination mode underpinning the relationship as well as the locus of power over the content and process of CSR within each configuration, which is related to the degree to which the CSR initiatives are legally binding and enforceable.

In reality, some government policies and some CSR initiatives will often reflect several of these relationships as do national stages of CSR-government development. Moreover, the relationships that we posit often underpin or overlie one another. Most obviously, CSR as self-government (or self-regulation) is fundamental and is the base to all the relationships. This holds even, paradoxically, where CSR is mandated directly or indirectly by government, as corporations can always elect to disregard government incentives and partnership obligations and even regulations.

CSR as self-government

CSR as a form of self-government operates alongside government, and conforms to a traditional, philanthropic view of CSR in which business makes discretionary contributions to society quite independently of government (Heald, 1970). These contributions often reflect more societal business than governmental business relationships, and thus the contributions of business are akin to those of citizens providing mutual support (Carroll, 2008; Moon *et al.*, 2005). Within this configuration, CSR initiatives are defined and designed at the discretion of corporations. These initiatives are by nature 'extra legal' (McGuire, 1963; McWilliams & Siegel, 2001, 2011) and correspond to what McBarnet has described as 'CSR beyond the law' (2007, pp. 13–31). Yet, they may complement governmental actions by filling institutional and legal voids in an 'implicit' understanding of what is required for business social legitimacy (Matten & Moon, 2008), but not as a result of coordination of the two actors (Vogel, 2010, pp. 81–3).

CSR as facilitated by government

Governments can go further and facilitate CSR through endorsement in the forms of speeches and other means of giving their imprimatur to business contributions to society (e.g. awards, kitemarks). The Australian and Danish governments introduced peak business leaders' forums to enable government to engage business concerning topics of their responsibility (Fox *et al.*, 2002). Such modes of facilitation do not necessarily rely on any form of legal development.

However, facilitation can also refer partially to what has been described as 'CSR through law' (McBarnet, 2007) as found in public procurement policies (McCrudden, 2007a, 2007b; Zerk, 2006, pp. 38–9), which encourage business responsibility through rules about access to public-sector markets (e.g. through product requirements, ethnic/gender make-up of the workforce and sourcing of materials). In so doing, government shapes CSR initiatives indirectly by selecting *ex post* specific CSR initiatives regarded as valuable. *Ex ante*, governments can also facilitate CSR through subsidies to businesses (e.g. for voluntary participation in public employment or training policies) or to business associations which advocate, advance and implement CSR (Moon & Richardson, 1985). Government can even play a role in encouraging the formation of business associations for CSR (e.g. Business in the Community [BITC] UK: Moore, Richardson & Moon, 1989, p. 50).

The support of BITC in the UK is a case of such indirect stimulation of CSR through the creation of an intermediary organization that would subsequently support CSR initiatives. Another common form of endorsement is through tax incentives for corporate charitable giving. In these cases, the government exercises an *ex ante* control over corporate resource allocations in CSR initiatives.

Table 11.1: Five CSR-government configurations

Relationship type	Description	Mechanism of coordination	Influence of corporations	Influence of the legal framework	Illustrations
1. CSR as self-government	Corporate discretion independent of but alongside government	Absence of coordination, disconnection or coincidence of private and public initiatives	*Strong* Little state interference in CSR initiatives	*Weak* Typical case of 'CSR beyond law' to society, strategic CSR	Philanthropic contributions
2. CSR as facilitated by government	Governments provide incentives for CSR or encourage CSR through rhetoric	*Ex ante* governmental influence through the design of incentive systems and *ex post* encouragement through rhetoric	*Strong – medium* Governments contribute to CSR but it is mainly driven by corporations	*Medium* CSR indirectly shaped by legal intervention Indirect form of 'CSR through law'	Governmental subsidies, tax expenditures, imprimatur; socially responsible public procurement
3. CSR as a partnership with government	Governments and business organizations (and often civil society) combine their resources and objectives	Various modes of coordination and interaction of government and business resources and strategies	*Strong – medium* State likely to influence weakly the content and strongly the process of CSR initiatives	*Medium* Indirect mobilization of the legal framework for shaping CSR	Multi-actor institutions to deliver social goods or norms/codes using some governmental resources (as above)
4. CSR as mandated by government	Governments regulate for CSR	*Ex ante* governmental framing of CSR initiatives through the control of outcomes or disclosure	*Medium – weak* State likely to influence strongly the content of corporate CSR initiatives	*Strong* CSR shaped by the legal framework; direct form of 'CSR through law'	French law on social reporting (NRE); UK Companies Act amendment
5. CSR as a form of government	Firms act as if they were governments where there are government deficits	Firm level or through stakeholder processes/institutions	*Strong* State power vacuum, delegation or substitution by CSR	*Weak* Corporations act as government 'CSR for law'	CSR in pre-welfare state; post-privatization; global governance; new/'wicked' issues

Source: Adapted from Fox *et al.* (2002) and McBarnet (2007) with authors' additions.

CSR as partnership with government

Governments can also shape CSR further through partnerships (Moon and Willoughby, 1990; Moore et al., 1985, 1989). Fox et al. (2002) and Ward (2004) report several illustrations of such partnerships, especially in developing countries and often in the extractive sectors, such as the Philippines' mining industry or the oil industry in Angola. Partnerships between government and CSR can occur with individual companies or with business associations. There is often a mix of complementary resources that the two bring into the partnership; for instance, governments often bring fiscal and regulatory capacity whereas companies bring their networks, employees and knowledge to bear in addressing problems (Fox et al., 2002). The partnership often also involves civil society organizations representing communities, religious or labour organizations or the environment. Civil society organizations bring their close understanding of social expectations and of social problems as well as legitimatization to the partnerships. Partnerships can be developed to address local issues (e.g. local economic partnerships), national issues (e.g. the UK's CSR Academy to improve SMEs' understanding of CSR) and even global issues (e.g. the US Apparel Industry Partnership, the UK Ethical Trade Initiative). Through their various modes of coordination, partnerships reflect a range of possible power balances between government and corporations. Partnerships provide governments with more opportunity to frame CSR policy and its deployment than simple facilitation.

CSR as mandated by government

Although the idea of governmental mandate of CSR is counter-intuitive as it appears to obviate corporate discretion, there are a number of reasons to include this relationship that overlaps with 'CSR through law' (McBarnet, 2007, pp. 31–45). First, governments have used 'soft law' to encourage CSR, often as a means of experimenting with new approaches to business responsibility. As noted by Ayres and Braithwaite (1992), regulation can be used in a variety of ways which fall short of coercion and punishment. For example, a number of governments have required companies to report their social, environmental and ethical impacts without specifying the particular behaviour they deem responsible (Berthoin-Antal & Sobzack, 2007). Specifically, the UK government has used disclosure as a tool in enacting legislation 'which not only encouraged, but in practical terms necessitates, the adoption of CSR policies by major companies' (McBarnet, 2007, p. 32).[2]

Second, a number of governments have underpinned various regulations with the rhetoric of CSR in order to legitimatize these regulations. The French government's introduction of an obligation on companies to make a 'bilan social' or social statement in 1977 was a means of providing information about employment conditions and industrial relations broadly defined

(Igalens & Nioche, 1977). In 2006, the Chinese Communist Party at its sixth plenum of the Sixteenth Party Central Committee set the definitive requirements for companies to implement CSR as part of a general reinforcement to its Building Harmonious Society policy of 2004.

Third, legal frameworks have been mobilized proactively by NGOs in ways that turn initially 'voluntary' CSR initiatives or code of conducts into legally binding obligations. As a result, 'CSR as self-government' has sometimes ultimately been turned into 'CSR as mandated by government'. For instance, private litigation has transformed what was initially seen as CSR as a public relations stunt into a legally binding commitment in the case of *Kasky vs. Nike*. Nike's initial claim in its CSR report that its suppliers adhered to its code of conduct which did not permit sweated labour was judged false and misleading and thus in violation of California's legislation on unfair competition and false advertising (see Parker, 2007 for an in-depth discussion). Also, a 2005 European Directive included, under restrictive circumstances, non-compliance by a company with its code of conduct as an instance of misleading commercial practice (McBarnet, 2007, p. 41). Legal interventions in other CSR-related domains such as contractual law (McBarnet & Kurkchiyan, 2007), international law (Zerk, 2006) and criminal law (Voiculescu, 2007) have the potential to reinforce such a consolidation of CSR as 'soft law', as the voices of suppliers, intergovernmental and international organizations or domestic governmental bodies are brought into the legal process.

Within such a configuration the locus of control over CSR initiatives lies principally with government although corporate cooperation with the law and NGOs can also be a factor.

CSR as a form of government

CSR as an (alternative) form of government reflects a dichotomous relationship between business and government. Within this configuration, business initiatives do not necessarily complement government's action but are a functional substitute for this action. Corporations, through CSR, can substitute for government in terms both of social roles and over the definition and control of their own activities (Crane, Matten & Moon, 2008, ch. 3). From a legal perspective, this corresponds to what has been described as 'CSR for law' (McBarnet, 2007, pp. 44–54), although it can also be regarded as 'CSR instead of law'. This substitution may refer to inherent limits of the 'command and control' approach in the law. Yet, this is often negatively regarded by those both on the right (Friedman, 1970; Levitt, 1958) and on the left (Hertz, 2002; Monbiot, 2001), as a usurpation of the proper responsibilities of government and as undermining democratic accountability.

However, companies can act in government-like ways which are not necessarily malign (Melé, 2008). Corporations can provide social benefits (e.g. recreation opportunities, library and education facilities for workers, their families and communities), as was the case in the UK prior to the emergence of the welfare state in the nineteenth century (Moon, 2005). In modern times, and less developed parts of the world, corporations provide such social benefits where there are serious governance deficits (e.g. withdrawal of government services in Kenya [Muthuri, Moon & Chapple, 2009], as well as in the transitional economies of Eastern Europe [Strange, 1996]). The international arena is another sphere in which companies have taken to self-regulation to cover environmental and social conditions in their supply chain (Scherer and Palazzo, 2008, 2011) where governments, national or international, have proved unwilling or unable to regulate cross-border activities. The most obvious example of a joint initiative by international corporations is the UN Global Compact which is 'principle-led' but other initiatives involve closer forms of self and social regulation of supply chains (e.g. Ethical Trade Initiative, Marine Stewardship Council). Businesses can also act like governments in the way they address a host of new issues for which regulation may be premature or too blunt an instrument.

Each configuration reflects a specific mode of coordination between corporations and government over the content and process of CSR, related to the degree of legal binding and of the enforceability of CSR initiatives. Taken as a whole they represent a continuum ranging from situations within which government dominates CSR (CSR as mandated by government), through situations of mixed powers (CSR as facilitated and partnered by government), to situations where corporations are more likely directly or indirectly to shape CSR (either CSR as self-government or CSR as a form of government).

These five configurations can be regarded as 'ideal-types' of CSR-government relationships in the Weberian sense, as they are based on 'the one-sided accentuation of one or more points of view and by the synthesis of a great many diverse, more or less present and occasionally absent concrete individual phenomena' (Weber, 1949, p. 90). According to Weber, an ideal type is not a 'hypothesis' but one that 'offers guidance to the construction of hypotheses' (Weber, 1949, p. 90). Typologies such as the above have been proved useful to theory-building in organization studies (Doty & Glick, 1994; Fiss, 2007, Fiss, 2011; Mintzberg, 1983), and so in what follows we rely on them to illuminate empirically the variety of possible CSR-government relationships across space and time in order to theorize the dynamic processes whereby these relationships are formed in national contexts. In particular, we explore empirically how CSR-government relations differ within and across Western Europe and East Asian countries, how these countries have seen shifts from one configuration to another in recent years. The purpose here is to highlight these configurations and their dynamics rather than to derive new findings on CSR in the countries of the two regions.

Exploring CSR-government configurations in Western Europe and East Asia

Western Europe

There were some nineteenth-century patterns of industrial paternalism and philanthropy (CSR as self-government) shared by the US and Western European countries, particularly where industrialization preceded the welfare state, as in the cases of the UK (Marinetto, 1999; Moon, 2005), the Netherlands (Cramer, 2005) and France (Beaujolin & Capron, 2005). They were often associated with the religious convictions of business leaders (Acquier, Gond & Igalens, 2011), and reflected some of the imperatives of industrialization, such as maintaining a loyal and well-functioning workforce (Rowlinson & Hassard, 1993). The divergence between Western Europe and the US occurred with the advent of the European welfare state from the late nineteenth to mid-twentieth century, but particularly after the Second World War, as the European welfare state replaced philanthropic provision, shifting the configuration from 'CSR as self-government' to 'CSR as mandated by the government'. Interestingly, where industrialization tended to parallel or follow the growth of the welfare state (e.g. Germany, Scandinavia), there was little evidence of corporate philanthropy; rather, the responsibilities of business were driven or framed by governments in a style more reminiscent of the New Deal period in the US.

The divergent trajectories of twentieth-century business responsibility can be understood with reference to the respective national governance systems. The Western European governance systems, which are embedded in the organized (or coordinated) model of capitalism, have tended to be characterized by more concentrated financial systems, more regulated education and labour systems, and cultural systems more sceptical about business and confident about government than in the liberal market model of capitalism (Hall & Soskice, 2001; Amable, 2003; Boyer, 2005). As such, their governance systems reflect varying balances of neo-corporatist and state forces. This has informed the nature of businesses and their responsibilities have been implied, supported and reinforced by the negotiated outcomes of neo-corporatist processes and state engagement. These have covered many of the areas which in the US have been subject to corporate discretion such as health insurance, training, higher education, arts or community services (Matten & Moon, 2008).

Since the last quarter of the last century, 'CSR as self-government' has gradually been supplemented by 'CSR as mandated by government', albeit at different rates and from different starting points. As Table 11.2 shows, these differences reflect distinctive European features and motivations (Habisch *et al.*, 2005; Maignan & Ralston, 2002; Matten & Moon, 2008). As argued by Matten and Moon (2008), this change can be attributed partly to the organizational challenges (or isomorphic pressures) associated with the imperatives of managing businesses in a highly globalized environment (DiMaggio & Powell, 1983; Meyer, 2000; Meyer, Boli, Thomas & Tamirez, 1999). European businesses have become subject to numerous 'coercive isomorphisms' in the form of soft-, social- and self-regulation, including various inter-governmental initiatives (e.g. the OECD Guidelines for Multi-National Companies, the UN Global Compact), collective business initiatives (e.g. the Global Reporting Initiative) and new socially responsible investment criteria (e.g. Dow Jones Sustainability Index, Domini Social Index, FTSE4 Good). They are also the subject of 'mimetic processes' whereby European businesses join business associations for CSR, sign up to new principles, codes and standards (e.g. Business in the Community, UK or CSR Europe). Finally, new 'normative pressures' have emerged with such issues as sustainable development and labour standards in supply chains, which are not in the remit of traditional welfare states. These new normative expectations are not only highlighted by sometimes critical media which have enhanced consumer awareness, but are also addressed by business and professional associations, business schools, business media and non-government and government organizations with whom companies interact (Vogel, 2010). In fact, iso-morphic pressures have been exerted and the changes carried out by so-called 'CSR entrepreneurs' aiming either at reforming local institutions (Boxenbaum, 2006; Boxenbaum & Battilana, 2005) or at building new CSR products and markets (Boxenbaum & Gond, 2006) based on the notion of CSR as self-government.

The pressures for change in CSR at an organizational level have been further complemented by the structural and institutional shifts in the broad national governance systems from an organized to a liberal market model of capitalism (Kang & Moon, 2010; Moon, 2002). With the advent of neoliberalism, neo-corporatist institutions and state power have come under pressure. Labour unions are less able to secure nation-wide employee protec-tion and remuneration, and neo-corporatist policy-making systems have become less hierarchical and consensual, affording more business discretion and self-regulation (Molina & Rhodes, 2002). At the same time, over the last quarter century the roles of governments have tended not only to decline in terms of the share of the economy accounted for by public sectors, but also to change in terms of mode where the prevailing trend towards deregulation has encouraged governments to rely less on their authority and more on markets and networks (McBarnet, 2007; Moon, 2002).

Notwithstanding pressures for change at various levels of the economy and society and, as a consequence, elements of convergence between CSR in Western Europe and the US, some differences persist, as change is often an incremental and path-dependent process (Streeck & Thelen, 2005). Despite the shift in the national governance system as noted above, remnants of neocorporatist and state traditions prevail (Matten & Moon, 2008). CSR in Europe is more closely organized with and through business associations, be they national or even European (e.g. CSR Europe). European CSR is also

Table 11.2: The changing social responsibility doctrine in Western Europe

Period	Stage of development	Key concept	Corporate legitimacy	Main motivations
1880–1900	Spread of industrialization; philanthropy	Self-government: philanthropy/ paternalism alongside regulatory state	Context of labour movements, industrial regulation	Mixed: religious, legitimacy, productivity
1900–1945	Growth of welfare state; narrowing of business SR	Self-government: philanthropy/ paternalism alongside various state forms	Contested by labour/socialist movements/ governments; incorporated in fascist systems	Legitimacy (often linked with nationalism)
1945–1980	Consolidation of welfare state; expansion of industrial state; growth of neo-corporatism; narrowing of business SR	Implicit role in enabling and mandating government/ modest self-government in philanthropy	Incorporation in mixed economy/ welfarism	Legitimized in Social Democracy/ Christian Democracy/ Liberalism/ Conservatism. Marginal values-led motivation
1980–present	Liberalization/ privatization/new governance; globalization yields wider corporate discretion	Explicit CSR: community, market, workplace, environment	Global citizenship; focus on individual firm (as opposed to business in general or collectively)	Legitimacy, stakeholder approval, business strategy

Source: Compiled by authors.

much more closely aligned with government policies, both as facilitated by various forms of endorsement and as in partnership with government (Habisch *et al.*, 2005). For instance, Albareda *et al.* (2007, pp. 395–6) conclude that fifteen of the European governments' policies for CSR are 'relational' in that they were designed to improve collaboration between governments and business and civil society stakeholders.

This reference to the EU reminds us that engagement with CSR is not simply the purview of national government. Indeed there is some interaction between these different levels, as illustrated by the impact of the EU Commission's directive on sustainable public procurement which appears to have been adopted by most member states (Steurer, 2010, p. 64). As Grodzins (1966) observed, federal systems are less about strict differentiation of levels of government, more about mutual contagion, much as in a marble (as opposed to a layer) cake. This is clearly also true of the EU which balances elements of supra-national with inter-governmental power. Thus, while a characterization of the EU CSR system is beyond the reach of this paper, we assume that it is infused by multiple national CSR systems. In addition, sub-national governments have also been able to employ the range of instruments we have noted above for national governments. For example, as McCrudden (2007a) has noted, the Northern Ireland government has encouraged a specific form of responsible business behaviour particularly by using their considerable powers of public procurement.

Naturally, there are also variations in the way national governments engage with CSR within Europe. The UK is regarded as leading in European (and global) CSR (Vogel, 2005), and also as having the most advanced public policies for CSR (Aaronson, 2003; Stiftung-GTZ, 2007). The UK combines 'CSR as self-government' with a wide range of government policies designed to facilitate CSR in the combined forms of endorsement, partnerships and mandate (Moon, 2004), emphasizing the CSR contribution not only to international responsibilities and reputations of UK companies (e.g. by the Ethical Trade Initiative), but also, and increasingly, to national competitiveness (Hodge, 2006). Reflecting their state traditions and industrial relations, the Scandinavian countries generally place greater emphasis on co-responsibility for an inclusive society and dynamic labour market, and as such CSR reflects partnership relations with government. For instance, in Denmark, a major CSR threshold was the government-business partnership to address labour market problems in the 1990s, which remains a key focus of CSR (Morsing, 2005). Meanwhile, Germany, like France (Berthoin-Antal & Sobzack, 2007), is a relatively late enthusiast for CSR as self-government and remains a relatively statist one, preferring CSR as mandate and introducing numerous labour, social affairs and governance laws.

While differences within Europe persist, this is expected to narrow with time, certainly for the EU member states, given the prevalence of the EU as the supra-national regulatory body and its interest in CSR. Since the Lisbon Summit in 2000, the EU has looked to business, and specifically CSR, to fill the gap between the objective of economic competitiveness and the goal of increased social and economic standards. This broad goal has informed various uses of CSR including the global positioning of the EU as an 'ethical power'. Perhaps reflecting the changes undergone by the member states due both to the organizational and structural-institutional pressures discussed earlier, there has been a shift since the initial EU emphasis on 'CSR as mandate' to a greater emphasis on less restrictive and binding CSR-government configurations. For instance, the EU Commission (2006) has sought to facilitate CSR through the publication of Green Papers and supporting discussions (e.g. the Multi-Stakeholder Forum on CSR in 2004).

East Asia

The kind of industrial paternalism and philanthropy shared by Western Europe and the US in the nineteenth century can also be found in East Asian businesses (in Japan, South Korea and, more recently, China) in the twentieth century as industrialization preceded the welfare state. After all, the East Asian governance systems share some similarities with those of Western Europe, conforming more closely to organized rather than liberal market models of capitalism (Dore, 2000; Streeck & Yamamura, 2001). For instance, as in Western Europe, East Asian governance systems can be characterized by more concentrated financial systems, more regulated education and labour systems, and cultural systems more sceptical about business and confident about government (Whitley, 1992, 1997).

Despite sharing similar features, there is a subtle but critical difference between the two governance systems: there is an absence of strong neo-corporatist institutions, or a tradition of voluntary association between organized interests, in East Asian governance systems. This makes their governance systems more statist than those of Western Europe (Kang, 2010; Orrù, Biggart & Hamilton, 1997), whether this be through strong 'administrative guidance' (Japan and South Korea) (Amsden, 1989; Evans, 1995; Johnson, 1982) or through state ownership and control (China). This feature has informed the nature of East Asian corporations and the state-oriented nature of their responsibilities. Large flagship businesses were either public entities (SOEs) or perceived to be pseudo-public entities even when private property rights were respected (e.g. the *chaebol* in South Korea) (Kang and Moon, 2010; Kim, 1997; Mafune, 1988) and as such it has long been a common practice for business leaders to proclaim their responsibility for national growth (You & Chang, 1993).

There was a strong sense of industrial paternalism, reflecting the imperatives of the importance of workers being regarded as human capital and of maintaining industrial peace in 'catch-up' development. CSR consisted of the provision of social and economic infrastructure for workers and their families, such as housing, education and medical facilities, not dissimilar to those found in the nineteenth-century US and Western Europe. However, what differed is that philanthropy was not driven by the religious convictions of the business leaders (CSR as self-government), but rather by government initiatives (CSR as mandate), as CSR became a way of substituting for the absence and late emergence of the welfare state. Therefore, CSR in Japan and South Korea went further to include social protection measures for the core workforce, ranging from long-term employment to legal sanctioning of the priority of wage claims over creditors in case of bankruptcy (You & Chang, 1993). CSR in the form of corporate welfare schemes tied workers' interests to those of businesses. Notwithstanding certain 'pathologies' associated with the quality of employment and work-life balance (e.g. long working hours) (Fukukawa & Moon, 2004; Welford, 2004), and weak representation rights within the firm, large businesses in Japan and South Korea shared welfare responsibilities that in other national governance systems would be seen as belonging to government.

East Asian businesses have not been immune to the organizational and institutional challenges described above in relation to Western Europe. In fact, these pressures have been magnified in the cases of South Korea and China due to further democratization and transition to a more market-based economy, respectively. Where organizational pressures are concerned, as corporations grow and go global, they have become subject to similar isomorphic pressures. However, the kind of 'CSR entrepreneurialism' aiming at either reforming local institutions or building new CSR products and markets based on the notion of CSR as self-government is at a very early stage, although this is expected to grow with rising consumer awareness (on China, see Garner & Chan, 2005; Gerth, 2010).

Again, similarly to in Western Europe, there have been structural and institutional pressures for change in CSR, as policies of liberalization, deregulation and privatization challenge the traditional interventionist role of the state. What differs from Western Europe is that the absence of strong neocorporatist institutions amid the shrinking realm of the state has generally meant a more fundamental shift towards more 'liberal' governance systems; for example, South Korea in the post-1997 period (Kang, 2010; Pirie, 2005), but also to a smaller degree China where there has been a rise of a new generation of private entrepreneurs (Tsai, 2005, 2006).

However, as discussed above, change is a path-dependent process, and, while governments in East Asia are becoming less interventionist in their approach to the market, the remnants of strong state exist (Kang, 2010; Tiberghien, 2007; Woo-Cumings, 1999). As a consequence, the notion of CSR as mandate still prevails but there is also evidence of other configurations emerging in order to tackle new CSR-related problems. For example, in response to the growing concerns regarding Chinese business activity in Africa, China has embarked on a partnership with a more 'experienced' partner, Britain's Department for International Development (DFID), with the intent of monitoring and controlling the social and environmental impact of Chinese investments in the region.

While CSR continues to be largely mandated, what has changed is that the key CSR issues of interest to the government have diversified to go beyond human capital and employment relations to encompass a broader set of issues reflecting the times. These include 'good' corporate governance, especially after the Asian and global financial crises (Gourevitch & Shinn, 2005; Walter, 2008), sustainable development, in response to the growing international and regional concerns for climate change, and the status of East Asia as a large carbon emitter. For a diverse mix of CSR-government configurations to emerge, the role of civil society is likely to be vital (Vogel, 2010). As it stands, civil society remains relatively weak in South Korea and Japan in comparison to their Western European counterparts, and closely bound to the state, and has been conspicuously absent as a driver of CSR in China.

Explaining the varying trajectories: national governance systems, path-dependency and government agency

National framing of CSR-government configurations

Western Europe and East Asia demonstrate important differences in the way in which CSR has 'travelled' (or been diffused), mediated by the national governance systems of the two regions. While CSR has become a global management concept, CSR at the national level is in fact implemented differently to reflect variations in national governance systems. The CSR development trajectories of the two regions suggest that national governance systems are likely to have influenced the CSR-government configuration when CSR emerges within, or is imported to, a given country. For instance, contrary to the US where CSR as self-government has been the dominant form of CSR-government configuration, reflecting its 'liberal' governance system, that in Western European countries reflects governance systems underpinned by traditions of neo-corporatism and state engagement. In East Asian countries, the CSR-government configuration has been mandated, reflecting their statist governance systems. Future empirical research can generalize these findings and evaluate systematically the likelihood of specific configurations' emergence within a variety of national governance systems.

> *Proposition 1:* National governance systems shape the emergence of specific CSR-government configurations during the process of CSR diffusion.

Path dependence in CSR-government configuration shifts

Once a given configuration of CSR-government has emerged in a country, the shift to another configuration seems to be path dependent. Our empirical analysis of successive configuration shifts in Western Europe and East Asia highlights these trends. For instance, the UK – a country which, by European standards, had relatively strong CSR as a form of self-government – has evolved indirectly but progressively towards more government-led forms of CSR. In the late 1990s and the 2000s, these relationships were further complemented by CSR as mandated by government (e.g. pension fund and company reporting) (Moon, 2004). In contrast, numerous continental European countries adopted a reverse move, from more to less government-controlled approaches to CSR. Hence, several countries with *a priori* divergent national governance systems (e.g. UK vs. Germany or France) converged progressively on specific configurations that represent a more balanced equilibrium between government and corporation (e.g. CSR as a partnership or CSR as facilitated by government). This move holds true increasingly for the relatively more democratic and liberal countries of East Asia (e.g. Japan and South Korea vs. China) as the government becomes less interventionist and civil society becomes more empowered.

> *Proposition 2:* Once a CSR-government configuration has been adopted to reflect the national governance system, the shifts to other configurations are likely to be path dependent.

Government agency in CSR-government configuration shifts

One factor explaining the neglected variety of CSR-government relationships is the inadequate attention paid to the role of the government in prior CSR research. Although governments themselves figure in accounts of national governance systems, their role is mostly passive. This is because governments are not considered as key actors in the CSR organizational field, but rather as arenas where different interests are played out.

However, in the context of government policies for CSR (rather than CSR *per se*), we find that state tradition and government agency play a critical role. In particular this is reflected in choices about the nature of the CSR-government relationships, but also, and more fundamentally, about the uses of CSR. Thus specific government strategies inform the extent to which CSR is used either as a means of supplementing and complementing governance of social and environmental issues or as a means of regulating business itself. In line with prior works highlighting the role of government bodies in the import of managerial practices (Djelic & Quack, 2003; Djelic & Sahlin-Anderson, 2006; Frenkel, 2005), our analysis suggests that governments play an active and crucial role in shaping the adoption of a specific CSR-government configuration as well as in governing the shift from one configuration to another. Hence, governments can strategically mobilize CSR either to enhance or to retract their support from private initiatives aimed at managing social and environmental issues. This is most clearly observable in China where government agency is noticeably strong, and where, as discussed earlier, the government has mandated CSR policies to control the private sector.

> *Proposition 3:* Governments themselves play a crucial role in shaping the shifts of CSR-government configurations during the process of CSR diffusion by using CSR strategically either to enhance or to weaken their involvement in social and environmental issues.

Implications and discussion

Variety of CSR across governance systems

The three propositions generalize the CSR development trajectories of the two regions. These propositions are intended to lend support to future investigations on complexities of government-CSR configurations across diverse contexts. They can be tested at different levels, from the local, through national and regional, to global levels. They can also be used to uncover the path dependency of CSR development and its relationship to broader shifts in national or regional governance systems. The European context presents an especially attractive case for studying these propositions, as CSR practices are advanced and have been shaped through a variety of initiatives at the national as well as regional (EU) levels through government agency.

Although we have broadly defined CSR and thus treat this concept as an homogeneous entity, arguably CSR is a complex organizational and institutional phenomenon that encompasses several dimensions (Crouch, 2006; Gond & Crane, 2010) that are not all susceptible to being shaped in the same manner by the government or the national governance systems (Campbell, 2007). Some authors have proposed approaching CSR as 'corporate stakeholder responsibility' and suggest studying how corporations address the needs and claims of their various stakeholders (Barnett, 2007; Freeman, Harrison & Wicks, 2007; Jamali, 2008). This perspective could be used in future research to refine our propositions; for instance, in considering how national governance systems and governments shape CSR investments toward specific stakeholders. In addition, Basu and Palazzo (2008) have distinguished discursive, cognitive and behavioural components to CSR. The repertoire of CSR-government relationships we have proposed can be instrumental in identifying which relationships are likely to influence CSR in its discursive, cognitive or behavioural facets.

The government of CSR

Our study demonstrates that CSR is emerging not only as a global management concept, but also as systems of government and governance, emphasizing that the association of CSR with government should no longer be counter-intuitive. We have highlighted the extensive range of CSR-government relationships (Table 11.1). CSR as self-government conventionally sits alongside a functioning system of liberal market governance, although it also underpins other CSR-government relationships. Beyond that there are more interventionist government policies, from encouraging (through facilitation and partnering) to mandating in the forms of 'soft' and 'hard' regulations. There is also the manifestation of CSR as government, where corporations act as if they were governments. This is mainly associated with underdeveloped governance systems and issues 'between' the developed and the developing worlds in MNC supply chains. Future research could investigate whether developing countries are more likely to see this specific configuration emerge as a primary form of CSR. It could also explore evolutions from this configuration to other possible configurations and contrast these paths with what has been observed in East Asia and Western Europe.

Notwithstanding the common themes, there are considerable national differences. Although the US could have been considered the cradle of explicit CSR, in Western Europe there has been the clearest development from CSR as implicit to CSR as self-government which is strongly encouraged, facilitated and partnered by government. In East Asia, there has been a relatively recent growth of CSR as self-government, and where governments have encouraged CSR there has been a strong emphasis on mandate-type policies.

CSR has emerged as a feature of the variety of 'new governances', confirming Moon's conclusion (with reference to the UK) that CSR had 'moved from the margins of governance to occupy a more mainstream position, entailing partnerships with government and non-profit organisations' (2002, p. 406). But national configurations of CSR and their differing relationships to national governments are increasingly connected to the emerging global systems of governance. Thus, national companies, business associations, NGOs and governments are connected through international institutions, commitments to global standards, the adoption of global practices and participation in these new governance entities (Moon & Vogel, 2008; Scherer & Palazzo, 2008, 2011).

There is a paradox here. On the one hand, CSR is part and parcel of a more liberalized environment emphasizing autonomy and 'bottom-up' and problem-oriented, multi-sector governance instruments. On the other hand, in contrast to the US model of CSR as self-regulation, other governments are more conspicuous in exploiting CSR for their own purposes. We characterize these developments as a maturation of CSR in which, from the perspective of business, there is a shift from the relative isolation of CSR as self-government to a contribution to governance which is more engaged and socially regulated and, albeit to varying extents, governmentally regulated.

Looking briefly to future research agendas, first, there is a clear need for greater evaluation of contribution of CSR to governance and of the role of government policies therein (Gendron, Lapointe & Turcotte, 2004). How does CSR improve society? Do government policies stimulate improvements in business social performance or do they simply mimic that which business is already adopting? Second, there is also a clear need for comparative research into the compatibility, convergence, difference or divergence of government policies for CSR. This is important for businesses whose activities straddle national boundaries as well as for policy-makers to better understand the effectiveness of their policies. This is especially important at the international level in which global, regional, national and sectoral policies coexist.

Reconsidering socio-economic hybridization through CSR

In considering government as central to the analysis of CSR, our study introduces a crucial yet missing component in the contemporary discussions of the socio-economic hybridization process that seems to characterize contemporary institutionalization of CSR. Prior accounts of this process have given focus to the 'corporatization of civil society' (Shamir, 2004a, pp. 681–5) or the 'economization of the political' (Shamir, 2008, pp. 1–4), but have failed to identify the 'visible hand' of government in the CSR markets that grow at the intersections of the market and civil society. Hence, they miss the process of 'politicization of the economic' (or 'market politi-cization') that are also constitutive of socio-economic hybridization through CSR, thereby overlooking the fact that 'socially responsible' market-building also involves governmental and legal intervention (Fligstein, 1990). Yet, for CSR markets, as in the case of other markets, 'an increase in economic exchange causes actors to push for more rule making and more state capacity to govern' (Fligstein & Sweet, 2002, p. 1208). This paper has proposed tools to investigate government agency in socio-economic hybridization through CSR and calls for uncovering the processes whereby governments shape this hybridization. Recognizing the presence and influence of government in CSR opens new avenues for research. For instance, this invites future studies to examine the politics of market-building through CSR, evaluating how governments influence the construction of CSR initiatives (e.g. fair trade), and how non-corporate actors might engage with governments to create platforms that support their CSR agendas.

Conclusion

In this paper, our goal was to revisit the relationship between CSR and government which has been sidelined in prior economic sociology discussions of social responsibility. We critically reviewed prior assumptions on the CSR-government relation and contributed to the emerging literature on political CSR in four ways. First, we reintegrated government as a distinctive actor in institutional dynamics surrounding CSR. Second, we proposed the variety of capitalism perspective to conceptualize the role of government in CSR. Third, we developed a theoretically grounded typology of CSR-government relations and showed how it can be used empirically as an analytical tool to investigate the role of government across time and space. Fourth and finally, we explained how the reintegration of government in CSR analysis calls for a reconsideration of the idea that CSR refers unilaterally to a process of society's commodification, corporatization or de-politicization. In contrast to this view, we offer an approach to CSR as an opportunity for market repoliticization and the development of new modes of governance.

Acknowledgements

The authors would like to thank the participants in the European Academy of Management (EURAM) Annual Conference, Liverpool, UK, 11–14 May, 2009, for their constructive comments, also the participants in the CRISES seminar held at HEC Montréal, CA, 26 January 2011. Nahee Kang would also like to thank the Economic and Social Research Council in the UK for the postdoctoral fellowship that enabled her to co-write this paper while based at the International Centre for Corporate Social Responsibility, Nottingham University Business School, UK.

Notes

1   Several of these early testimonies on CSR can be found in the first volume of Gond and Moon (2011b).
2   The UK government did so in adopting legislation according to which UK pension funds had to disclose whether or not they were taking into account social, environmental and ethical decisions. Although UK pension funds had no obligation to report on the CSR policies of the companies they invested in, they all decided to do so for reputational reasons. This in return produced a cascading effect on corporations that were pushed to report on extra-financial information in order to satisfy institutional investors' requests for CSR information (McBarnet, 2007).

References

Aaronson, S. (2003). CSR in the global village: The British role model and the American laggard. *Business and Society Review*, *108*, 309–38.

Acquier, A., Gond, J.-P. & Igalens, J. (2011). La religion dans les affaires: La responsabilité sociale de l'entreprise: Les sources religieuses de la responsabilité sociale de l'entreprise. Note Fondapol. Paris: Fondapol. Available at: http://www.fondapol.org.

Albareda, L. J., Lozano, M. & Ysa, T. (2007). Public policies on corporate social responsibility: The role of governments in Europe. *Journal of Business Ethics*, *74*, 391–407.

Amable, B. (2003). *The diversity of modern capitalism*. Oxford: Oxford University Press.

Amsden, A. H. (1989). *Asia's next giant: South Korea and late industrialization*. New York and Oxford: Oxford University Press.

Ayres, I. & Braithwaite, J. (1992). *Transcending the deregulation debate*. New York: Oxford University Press.

Banerjee, S. B. (2008). Corporate social responsibility: The good, the bad and the ugly. *Critical Sociology*, *34*, 51–79.

Barnett, M. L. (2007). Stakeholder influence capacity and the variability of financial returns to corporate social responsibility. *Academy of Management Review*, *32*(3), 794–816.

Basu, K. & Palazzo, G. (2008). Corporate social responsibility: A process model of sensemaking. *Academy of Management Review*, *33*(1), 122–36.

Beaujolin, F. & Capron, M. (2005). France: Balancing between constructive harassment and virtuous intentions. In A. Habisch, J. Jonker, M. Wegner & R. Schmidpeter (Eds.), *Corporate social responsibility across Europe*. New York: Springer.

Berthoin-Antal, A. & Sobzack, A. (2007). Corporate social responsibility in France: A mix of national traditions and international influences. *Business and Society*, *46*, 9–32.

Boltanski, L. (2009). *De la critique: Précis de sociologie de l'émancipation*. Paris: Gallimard.

Boltanski, L. & Chiappello, E. (2005 [1999]). *The new spirit of capitalism*. London: Verso.

Bowen, H. R. (1953). *The social responsibilities of the businessman*. New York: Harper & Row.

Boxenbaum, E. (2006). Corporate social responsibility as institutional hybrids. *Journal of Business Strategies*, *23*, 45–64.

Boxenbaum, E. & Battilana, J. (2005). Importation as innovation: Transposing managerial practices across fields. *Strategic Organization*, *3*, 355–83.

Boxenbaum, E. & Gond, J.-P. (2006). *Importing socially responsible investment in France and Quebec*. DRUID working paper.

Boyer, R. (2005). How and why capitalisms differ. *Economy and Society*, *34*(4), 509–57.

Campbell, J. (2007). Why would corporations behave in socially responsible ways? An institutional theory of corporate social responsibility. *Academy of Management Review*, *32*(3), 946–67.

Carroll, A. B. (2008). A history of corporate social responsibility: Concepts and practices. In A. Crane, A. McWilliams, D. Matten, J. Moon & D. Siegel (Eds.), *The Oxford handbook of corporate social responsibility* (pp. 19–46). Oxford: Oxford University Press.

Chamberlain, N. W. (1973). *The limits of corporate responsibility*. New York: Basic Books.

Chang, H.-J. (2002). Breaking the mould: An institutionalist political economy alternative to the neo-liberal theory of the market and the state. *Cambridge Journal of Economics*, *26*(5), 539–59.

Cramer, J. (2005). Redefining positions in society. In A. Habisch, J. Jonker, M. Wegner & R. Schmidpeter (Eds.), *Corporate social responsibility across Europe* (pp. 87–96). Berlin and Heidelberg: Springer.

Crane, A., Matten, D. & Moon, J. (2008). *Corporations and citizenship*. Cambridge: Cambridge University Press.

Crane, A., Matten, D., McWilliams, A., Moon, J. & Siegel, D. (Eds.) (2008). *The Oxford handbook of corporate social responsibility*. Oxford: Oxford University Press.

Crouch, C. (2006). Modelling the firm in its market and organizational environment: Methodologies for studying corporate social responsibility. *Organization Studies*, *27*, 1533–51.

Dahl, R. H. & Lindblom, C. E. (1992 [1953]). *Politics, economics and welfare*. Chicago, IL: University of Chicago Press/New Brunswick, NJ: Transaction Publishers.

Deeg, R. & Jackson, G. (2007). Towards a more dynamic theory of capitalist diversity. *Socio-Economic Review*, *5*, 149–79.

DiMaggio, P. & Powell, W. (1983). The iron cage revisited: Institutional isomorphism and collective rationality in organizational fields. *American Sociological Review*, *48*, 147–60.

Djelic, M.-L. & Quack, S. (2003). *Globalization and institutions: Redefining the rules of the economic game*. Cheltenham: Edward Elgar.

Djelic, M.-L. & Sahlin-Anderson, K. (2006). *Transnational governance: Institutional dynamics of regulation*. Cambridge: Cambridge University Press.

Dore, R. (2000). *Stock market capitalism: Welfare capitalism*. New York: Oxford University Press.

Doty, D. H. & Glick, W. H. (1994). Typologies as a unique form of theory building: Toward improved understanding and modelling. *Academy of Management Review*, *19*, 230–51.

The European Union Commission (2001). *Promoting a European framework for corporate social responsibility*. Green Paper of the European Commission. COM(2001) 366, July. Brussels: The EU Commission.

The European Union Commission (2002). *Corporate social responsibility: A business contribution to sustainable development*. Brussels: The EU Commission.

The European Union Commission (2006). *Implementing the partnership for growth and jobs: Making Europe a pole of excellence on corporate social responsibility*. Brussels: The EU Commission.

Evans, P. (1995). *Embedded autonomy: States and industrial transformation*. Princeton, NJ: Princeton University Press.

Fiss, P. C. (2007). A set-theoretic approach to organizational configurations. *Academy of Management Review*, *32*(4), 1180–98.

Fiss, P. C. (2011). Building better causal theories: A fuzzy set approach to typologies in organization research. *Academy of Management Journal*, *54*(2), 394–420.

Fligstein, N. (1990). *The transformation of corporate control*. Cambridge, MA: Harvard University Press.

Fligstein, N. (1996). Markets as politics: A political-cultural approach to market institutions. *American Sociological Review*, *61*, 656–73.

Fligstein, N. (2001). *The architecture of markets: An economic sociology of capitalist societies*. Princeton, NJ: Princeton University Press.

Fligstein, N. & Markowitz, L. (1993). Financial reorganization of American corporations in the 1980s. In W. J. Wilson (Ed.), *Sociology and the public agenda* (pp. 185–206). Beverly Hills, CA: Sage.

Fligstein, N. & Sweet, A. (2002). Constructing markets and politics: An institutionalist account of European integration. *American Journal of Sociology*, *107*, 1206–43.

Fox, T., Ward, H. & Howard, B. (2002). *Public sector roles in strengthening corporate social responsibility*. Washington, DC: The World Bank Group.

Freeman, R. E., Harrison, J. S. & Wicks, A. C. (2007). *Managing for stakeholders: Survival, reputation, and success*. New Haven, CT: Yale University Press.

Frenkel, M. (2005). The politics of translation: How state-level political relations affect the cross-national travel of management ideas. *Organization*, *12*, 275–301.

Friedman, M. (1970). The social responsibility of business is to increase its profits. *New York Times Magazine*, September 13, 122–6.

Fukukawa, K. & Moon, J. (2004). A Japanese model of corporate social responsibility? *Journal of Corporate Citizenship*, *16*, 45–59.

Garner, J. & Chan, V. (2005). *The rise of the Chinese consumer: Theory and evidence*. Chichester: John Wiley and Sons.

Gendron, C., Lapointe, A. & Turcotte, M.-F. (2004). Social responsibility and the regulation of the global firm. *Industrial Relations / Relations Industrielles*, *59*(1), 73–100.

Gerth, K. (2010). *As China goes, so goes the world: How Chinese consumers are transforming everything*. New York, NY: Hill and Wang.

Gibbon, P. & Ponte, S. (2008). Global value chains: From governance to governmentality? *Economy and Society*, *37*(3), 365–92.

Gond, J.-P. & Crane, A. (2010). Corporate social performance disoriented: Saving the lost paradigm? *Business and Society*, *49*(4), 677–703.

Gond, J.-P. & Moon, J. (2011a). Introduction: Corporate social responsibility in retrospect and prospect. In J.-P. Gond & J. Moon (Eds.), *Corporate social responsibility: Critical perspectives on business and management*. Oxford: Routledge, in press.

Gond, J.-P. & Moon, J. (Eds.) (2011b). *Corporate social responsibility: Critical perspectives on business and management*. Oxford: Routledge, in press.

Gond, J.-P., Palazzo, G. & Basu, K. (2009). Reconsidering instrumental corporate social responsibility through the Mafia metaphor. *Business Ethics Quarterly*, *19*, 55–8.

Gourevitch, P. A. & Shinn, J. (2005). *Political power and corporate control: The new global politics of corporate governance*. Princeton, NJ: Princeton University Press.

Granovetter, M. (1985). Economic action and social structure: The problem of embeddedness. *American Journal of Sociology*, *91*, 481–93.

Grodzins, M. (1966). *The American system: A new view of the government of the United States*. New York: Rand McNally.

Habisch, A., Jonker, J., Wegner, M. & Schmidpeter, R. (2005). *Corporate social responsibility across Europe*. Berlin: Springer.

Hall, P. & Soskice, D. (2001). *Varieties of capitalism: The institutional foundations of comparative advantage*. Oxford: Oxford University Press.

Hanlon, G. (2008). Re-thinking corporate social responsibility and the role of the firm: On the denial of politics. In A. Crane, D. Matten, A. McWilliams, J. Moon & D. Siegel (Eds.), *The Oxford handbook of corporate social responsibility* (pp. 156–72). Oxford: Oxford University Press.

Heald, M. (1970). *The social responsibility of business: Company and community, 1900–1970*. Cleveland, OH: Case Western Reserve University Press.

Hertz, N. (2002). *The silent takeover*. London: Arrow.

Hodge, M. (2006). The British CSR strategy: How a government supports the good work. In J. Hennigfeld, M. Pohl & N. Tolhurst (Eds.), *The ICCA handbook on corporate social responsibility*. London: Wiley.

Hollingsworth, R. & Boyer, R. (1997). *Contemporary capitalism: Institutional embeddedness*. Cambridge: Cambridge University Press.

Igalens, J. & Nioche, J.-P. (1977). A propos du bilan social, trois voies de l'innovation sociale. *Revue Française de Gestion, 12–13*, 193–9.

Jackson, G. & Apostolakou, A. (2009). Corporate social responsibility in Western Europe: An institutional mirror or substitute? *Journal of Business Ethics, 94*(3), 371–94.

Jamali, D. (2008). A stakeholder approach to corporate social responsibility. *Journal of Business Ethics, 82,* 213–31.

Johnson, C. (1982). *MITI and the Japanese miracle: The growth of industrial policy*. Stanford, CA: Stanford University Press.

Jones, M. T. (1996). Missing the forest for the trees: A critique of the social responsibility concept and discourse. *Business and Society, 35*, 7–41.

Kallio, T. J. (2007). Taboos in corporate social responsibility. *Journal of Business Ethics, 74*, 165–75.

Kang, N. (2010). Globalisation and institutional change in the state-led model: The case of corporate governance in South Korea. *New Political Economy, 15*(4), 519–42.

Kang, N. & Moon, J. (2010). *Institutional complementarity between corporate governance and CSR: A comparative institutional analysis of three capitalisms*. Centre for Organisations in Development Working Paper Series 3. University of Manchester.

Kazmi, B.-A., Leca, B. & Naccache, P. (2008). *Corporate social responsibility: The brand new spirit of capitalism*. Paper presented at the Critical Management Studies Research Workshop, Los Angeles.

Kim, E. M. (1997). *Big business, strong state: Collusion and conflict in South Korean development, 1960–1980*. Albany, NY: SUNY Press.

Kjaergaard, C. & Westphalen, S.-Å. (2001). *From collective bargaining to social partnerships: New roles of social partners in Europe*. Copenhagen: The Copenhagen Centre.

Levitt, T. (1958). The dangers of social responsibility. *Harvard Business Review, 36*, 41–50.

Mafune, Y. (1988). Corporate social performance and policy in Japan. In L. E. Preston (Ed.), *Research in corporate social performance and policy*. Greenwich, CT: Jai Press.

Maignan, I. & Ralston, D. A. (2002). Corporate social responsibility in Europe and the US: Insights from businesses' self-presentations. *Journal of International Business Studies, 33*, 497–515.

Margolis, J. D. & Walsh, J. P. (2003). Misery loves companies: Whither social initiatives by business? *Administrative Science Quarterly, 48*, 268–305.

Markowitz, L. (2008). Can strategic investing transform the corporation? *Critical Sociology, 34*(5), 681–707.

Marinetto, M. (1999). The historical development of business philanthropy: Social responsibility in the new corporate economy. *Business History, 41*, 1–20.

Matten, D. & Moon, J. (2008). 'Implicit' and 'explicit' CSR: A conceptual framework for a comparative understanding of corporate social responsibility. *Academy of Management Review, 33*, 404–24.

McBarnet, D. (2007). Corporate social responsibility beyond law, through law, for law: The new corporate accountability. In D. McBarnet, A. Voiculescu & T. Campbell (Eds.), *The new accountability: Corporate social responsibility and the law* (pp. 9–56). Cambridge: Cambridge University Press.

McBarnet, D. & Kurkchiyan, M. (2007). Corporate social responsibility through contractual control? Global supply chains and 'other-regulation'. In D. McBarnet, A. Voiculescu & T. Campbell (Eds.), *The new accountability: Corporate social responsibility and the law* (pp. 59–92). Cambridge: Cambridge University Press.

McCrudden, C. (2007a). *Buying social justice: Equality, government procurement and legal change.* Oxford: Oxford University Press.

McCrudden, C. (2007b). Corporate social responsibility and public procurement. In D. McBarnet, A. Voiculescu & T. Campbell (Eds.), *The new accountability: Corporate social responsibility and the law* (pp. 93–118). Cambridge: Cambridge University Press.

McGuire, J. (1963). *Business and society.* New York: McGraw-Hill.

McWilliams, A. & Siegel, D. (2001). Corporate social responsibility: A theory of the firm perspective. *Academy of Management Review, 26,* 117–27.

McWilliams, A. & Siegel, D. (2011). Creating and capturing value: Strategic corporate social responsibility. *Journal of Management.* Retrieved from http://jom. sagepub.com/ content/early/2010/10/ 12/0149206310385696.short? rss = 1&ssource = mfr.

Melé, D. (2008). Corporate social responsibility theories. In A. Crane, A. McWilliams, D. Matten, J. Moon & D. Siegel (Eds.), *The Oxford handbook of corporate social responsibility* (pp. 47–82). Oxford: Oxford University Press.

Meyer, J. W. (2000). Globalization: Sources and effects on national states and societies. *International Sociology, 15,* 233–48.

Meyer, J. W., Boli, J., Thomas, G. & Ramirez, F. O. (1999). The changing cultural content of the nation-state: A world society perspective. In G. Steinmetz (Ed.), *State and culture: New approaches to the state after the cultural turn* (pp. 123–43). Ithaca, NY: Cornell University Press.

Micheletti, M. (2003). *Political virtue and shopping: Individuals, consumerism, and collective action.* New York: Palgrave Macmillan.

Micheletti, M., Føllesdal, A. & Stolle, D. (2004). *Politics, products, and markets: Exploring political consumerism past and present.* New Brunswick, NJ: Transaction Publishers.

Midttun, A. (2005). Realigning business, government and civil society: Emerging embedded relational governance beyond the (neo) liberal and welfare state models. *Corporate Governance: The International Journal of Business in Society, 5,* 159–74.

Mintzberg, H. T. (1983). *Structure in lives: Designing effective organizations.* Englewood Cliffs, NJ: Prentice Hall.

Molina, O. & Rhodes, M. (2002). Corporatism: The past, present and future of a concept. *Annual Review of Political Science, 5,* 305–31.

Monbiot, G. (2001). *Captive state: The corporate takeover of Britain.* London: Pan.

Moon, J. (2002). The social responsibility of business and new governance. *Government and Opposition, 37,* 385–408.

Moon, J. (2004). *Government as a driver of corporate social responsibility.* International Centre for Corporate Social Responsibility Research Paper Series, 20. Nottingham University Business School.

Moon, J. (2005). CSR in the UK: An explicit model of business-society relations. In A. Habisch, J. Jonker, M. Wegner & R. Schmidpeter (Eds.), *Corporate social responsibility across Europe* (pp. 23–36). New York: Springer.

Moon, J. & Richardson, J. J. (1985). *Unemployment in the UK: Politics and policies.* Aldershot: Gower.

Moon, J. & Vogel, D. (2008). Corporate social responsibility, government, and civil society. In A. Crane, A. McWilliams, D. Matten, J. Moon & D. Siegel (Eds.), *The Oxford handbook of corporate social responsibility* (pp. 303–23). Oxford: Oxford University Press.

Moon, J. & Willoughby, K. (1990). Between state and market in Australia: The case of Local Enterprise Initiatives. *Australian Journal of Public Administration, 49,* 23–37.

Moon, J., Crane, A. & Matten, D. (2005). Can corporations be citizens? Corporate citizenship as a metaphor for business participation in society. *Business Ethics Quarterly*, *15*, 427–51.

Moore, C., Richardson, J. J. & Moon, J. (1985). New partnerships in local economic development. *Local Government Studies*, *11*, 19–33.

Moore, C., Richardson, J. J. & Moon, J. (1989). *Local partnership and the unemployment crisis in Britain*. London: Allen & Unwin.

Morsing, M. (2005). Denmark: Inclusive labour market strategies. In A. Habisch, J. Jonker, M. Wegner & R. Schmidpeter (Eds.), *Corporate social responsibility across Europe* (pp. 23–36). New York: Stringer.

Muthuri, J., Moon, J. & Chapple, W. (2009). Implementing 'community participation' in corporate community involvement: Lessons from Magadi Soda Company in Kenya. *Journal of Business Ethics*, *85*, 431–44.

Orrù, M., Biggart, N. & Hamilton, G. (1997). *The economic organization of East Asian capitalism*. Thousand Oaks, CA: Sage.

Parker, C. (2007). Meta-regulation: Legal accountability for corporate social responsibility. In D. McBarnet, A. Voiculescu & T. Campbell (Eds.), *The new accountability: Corporate social responsibility and the law* (pp. 207–39). Cambridge: Cambridge University Press.

Pirie, I. (2005). The new Korean state. *New Political Economy*, *10*(1), 27–44.

Polanyi, K. (1957). Economy as instituted process. In K. Polanyi, C. M. Arenseberg & H. Pearson (Eds.), *Trade and market in the early empires: Economies in history and theory*. Glencoe, IL: The Free Press.

Polanyi, K. (2001 [1944]). *The great transformation: The political and economic origins of our times*. Boston, MA: Beacon Press.

Porter, M. E. & Kramer, M. R. (2006). Strategy and society: The link between competitive advantage and corporate social responsibility. *Harvard Business Review*, *84*, 78–92.

Rowlinson, M. & Hassard, J. (1993). The invention of corporate culture: A history of histories of Cadbury. *Human Relations*, *6*, 299–326.

Santos, B. D. S. (2002). *Toward a new legal common sense: Law, globalization and emancipation*. London: Butterworths.

Scherer, A. & Palazzo, G. (2008). Globalization and corporate social responsibility. In A. Crane, D. Matten, A. McWilliams, J. Moon & D. Siegel (Eds.), *The Oxford handbook of corporate social responsibility* (pp. 413–31). Oxford: Oxford University Press.

Scherer, A. & Palazzo, G. (2011). The new political role of business in a globalized world: A review of a new perspective on CSR and its implications for the firm, governance, and democracy. *Journal of Management Studies*, *48*(4), 899–931.

Shamir, R. (2004a). The de-radicalization of corporate social responsibility. *Critical Sociology*, *30*(3), 669–89.

Shamir, R. (2004b). Between self-regulation and the Alien Tort Claims Act: On the contested concept of corporate social responsibility. *Law and Society Review*, *38*(4), 635–64.

Shamir, R. (2005). Mind the gap: Commodifying corporate social responsibility. *Symbolic Interaction*, *28*, 229–53.

Shamir, R. (2008). The age of responsibilization: On market-embedded morality. *Economy and Society*, *37*, 1–19.

Steurer, R. (2010). The role of government in corporate social responsibility: Characterising public policies on CSR in Europe. *Policy Sciences*, *43*, 49–72.

Stiftung-GTZ (2007). *The CSR navigator: Public policies in Africa, the Americas, Asia, and Europe*. The Bertelsmann Stiftung and The Deutsche Gesellschaft für Technische Zusammenarbeit.

Strange, S. (1996). *The retreat of the state: The diffusion of power in the world economy*. Cambridge: Cambridge University Press.

Streeck, W. & Thelen, K. (2005). *Beyond continuity: Institutional change in advanced political economies*. Oxford: Oxford University Press.

Streeck, W. & Yamamura, K. (2001). *The origins of non-liberal capitalism: Germany and Japan in comparison*. Ithaca, NY: Cornell University Press.

Thompson, G. F. (2008). The interrelationship between global and corporate governance: Towards a democratization of the business firm? In A. Scherer & G. Palazzo (Eds.), *Handbook of research on global corporate citizenship* (pp. 476–98). Cheltenham: Edward Elgar.

Tiberghien, Y. (2007). *Entrepreneurial states: Reforming corporate governance in France, Japan, and Korea*. Ithaca, NY: Cornell University Press.

Tsai, K. (2005). Capitalist without class: Political diversity of private entrepreneurs in China. *Comparative Political Studies*, *38*(9), 1130–58.

Tsai, K. (2006). Adaptive information institutions and endogenous institutional change in China. *World Politics*, *59*(1), 116–41.

Vogel, D. (2005). *The market for virtue: The potential and limits of corporate social responsibility*. Washington, DC: Brookings Institute.

Vogel, D. (2010). The private regulation of global corporate conduct: Achievements and limitations. *Business and Society*, *49*(1), 68–87.

Voiculescu, A. (2007). Changing paradigms for corporate criminal responsibility: Lessons from corporate social responsibility. In D. McBarnet, A. Voiculescu & T. Campbell (Eds.), *The new accountability: Corporate social responsibility and the law* (pp. 399–429). Cambridge: Cambridge University Press.

Walter, A. (2008). *Governing finance: East Asia's adoption of international standards*. Ithaca, NY: Cornell University Press.

Ward, H. (2004). *Public sector roles in strengthening corporate social responsibility: Taking stock*. The World Bank.

Weber, M. (1949). *The methodology of the social science*. Glencoe, IL: The Free Press.

Welford, R. (2004). Corporate social responsibility in Europe, North America, and Asia. *Journal of Corporate Citizenship*, *17*, 33–52.

Whitley, R. (1992). *Business systems in East Asia: Firm, markets and societies*. London: Sage.

Whitley, R. (1999). *Divergent capitalisms: The social structuring and change of business systems*. Oxford: Oxford University Press.

Woo-Cumings, M. (1999). *The developmental state*. Ithaca, NY: Cornell University Press.

Yamamura, K. & Streeck, W. (2003). *The end of diversity? Prospects for German and Japanese capitalism*. Ithaca, NY: Cornell University Press.

You, J.-I. & Chang, H. J. (1993). The myth of free labour market in Korea. *Contributions to Political Economy*, *12*, 29–46.

Zerk, J. A. (2006). Multinationals and corporate social responsibility: a new regulatory agenda. In J. A. Zerk (Ed.), *Multinationals and corporate social responsibility: Limitations and opportunities in international law* (pp. 7–59). Cambridge: Cambridge University Press.

CSR masala at the Tata Group

The India-based Tata Group is one of the world's largest conglomerates. With more than 100 companies across 80 countries, the group operates in seven business sectors – communication and information technology, engineering, materials, services, energy, consumer products, and chemicals. This includes global brand names such as Tetley Tea, Taj Hotels, and Jaguar and Land Rover cars, as well as national Indian icons such as Tata trucks, Titan watches, Tata tea, Tata salt, and the Tata Nano car. The Tata Group companies employ some 425,000 people and generates revenues of more than $80 billion annually.[1] In the 2010s Tata regularly ranked as one of the top 50 most valuable brands in the world.[2]

History and relevance of CSR at Tata

The origins of the Tata Group can be traced to 1868 when Jamsetji N. Tata started a small trading company with $400. Nearly 150 years later the group is still associated with the Tata family and remains well-known for its founder's vision of a business based on strong values and a sense of community responsibility. 'In a free enterprise,' Jamsetji N. Tata is quoted as saying, 'the community is not just another stakeholder in business, but is in fact the very purpose of its existence.'[3] The slogan of the company is 'Leadership with trust'. As the company website puts it: 'Our practice of returning to society what we earn evokes trust among consumers, employees, shareholders and the community. We are committed to protecting this heritage of leadership with trust through the manner in which we conduct our business.'[4]

The group is well-known in India for its commitment to social responsibility. The company has pioneered numerous social initiatives in the country. For example, in 1912, 36 years before it became law in India, Tata instituted a mandatory eight-hour work day. From 1917, it offered schooling to its employees' children. Its policies on provident funds, paid leaves, maternity benefits, grievance redress, and profit sharing were far ahead of the times and exemplified beyond-compliance leadership.

Today, the group remains a CSR leader in India and is building a unique global reputation for social responsibility. By 2012, no less than 42 Tata companies had signed up to the UN Global Compact, the highest number of any business group globally.[5] Moreover, a recent report assessing the CSR initiatives of the top 500 firms in India, gave only 12 businesses its highest ranking, three of which were Tata companies (Tata Consultancy Services, Titan, and Tata Steel).[6] According to the same report, more than one fifth of the top 100 had no CSR initiatives in place at all. Less than a third of India's largest companies report on CSR issues, and 'many Indian companies lack the systematized corporate responsibility policies and practices of their foreign peers' (Balch, 2012). Indeed, in the early 2010s, when the Indian government proposed that companies should spend 2 per cent of their profits on CSR, the Tata Group as a whole was already spending an impressive 3 per cent of its net profits on development-related programmes – with some Tata companies having reached 20 per cent during the previous decade.[7] That said, the company has not been without its critics. For instance, the launch by Tata Motors of the Tata Nano in 2009 was greeted with dismay by many environmentalists who saw the introduction of such an affordable car in India as a precursor to huge environmental and traffic congestion problems given India's already overstretched infrastructure. The company was also forced to pull out of the factory proposed to build the Nanos in Singur, West Bengal, after a major controversy over the land acquisition process in the lead-up to the factory's construction. Clearly managing CSR in a huge global company such as Tata poses a number of significant challenges.

Organizational structure

Looking at the sheer size of a multinational conglomerate like the Tata Group, the problems faced in implementing a company-wide CSR policy are clearly evident. With such organizations working in a globalized economy and having business operations across multiple sectors, to have a unified CSR vision and a code of conduct cutting across geographies and industries is a hugely complex undertaking.

The Tata group is not immune to this challenge of joining up all the parts of its CSR management – or as an Indian cook might put it, of combining the individual CSR spices to create a perfect CSR masala (mixture). Having business operations in 80 countries and with 67 mergers and acquisitions in the past decade alone,[8] the group faces multiple hurdles in formulating and implementing a cohesive CSR strategy. This is due to different legal jurisdictions, varied auditing methodologies, adaptability issues of local cultures and huge resource requirements.

The group itself is a complex structure, with ownership resting in several philanthropic family foundations, and operating through two principal holding companies, Tata Sons and Tata Industries (see Figure 1). Of these, Tata Sons holds the bulk of the shares in all key Tata companies and owns the Tata name and trademark. Tata Industries is responsible for promoting Tata's entry into new and high tech businesses.

At a group level, there are two main entities that offer support and direction to the individual Tata companies in their CSR endeavours. These entities – Tata Council for Community Initiatives (TCCI) and Tata Quality Management Services (TQMS) – report to the Group Corporate Centre (GCC), which is the apex decision-making body that defines and directs the business endeavours of the Tata Group.[9] With top management being part of the GCC, the organizational support for the two group-level CSR management functions is fairly well-assured.

Tata Council for Community Initiatives

The group's first steps towards formalizing its CSR strategy across its multiple businesses came in 1994 in the form of TCCI. The council was formed to bring

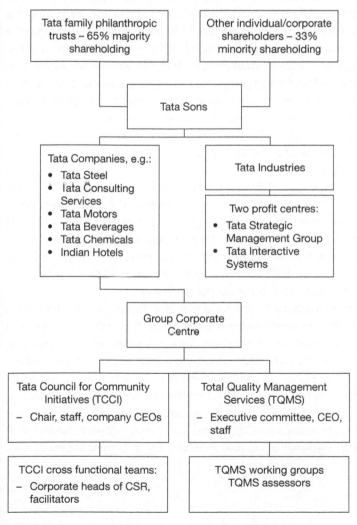

Figure 1: CSR management structure at the Tata Group

together the best practices within the Tata Group in the sphere of CSR. It comprises CEOs from more than 50 Tata Companies – the CEO of every company that signs the brand agreement with the Tata Sons holding company is required to join the TCCI. 'Within each firm, a Corporate Head Social Responsibility (always a senior executive) manages a cross-functional CSR team of facilitators with specific responsibilities for community development, environmental management and volunteering . . . TCCI operates across Tata companies as a network of more than 200 trained facilitations and over 28, 000 volunteers' (Nadkarni & Branzei, 2008). The TCCI is the focal point for Tata companies signed up to the UN Global Compact, and assists Tata companies in CSR reporting according to the Global Reporting Initiative.[10]

The council has published frameworks such as the Corporate Sustainability Protocol and the Tata Index for Sustainable Human Development (TISHD), which are intended to serve as guides for Tata companies. For example, the TISHD 'provides guidelines for Tata companies looking to fulfil their social responsibilities' through the establishment of a common framework for directing and measuring the community work that Tata companies undertake.[11] At the end of an assessment a score card is generated out of 1000 points, which highlights the achievement of the company on the parameter of human excellence.[12] Recently, when a scorecard was generated for a number of Tata Group companies, the group average came to 454 points, reflecting that on average, the group assessed that its companies were building capacities for human achievement. Variance across the group, however, was substantial. While companies like Tata Steel excelled on the index with 712 points, Tata's hotel business, the Taj Group, scored a much lower 255 points (Nadkarni & Branzei, 2008).

More recently, TCCI formulated the Corporate Sustainability Protocol, which is an extension to the TISHD. The protocol is aimed at helping the group companies put together their CSR reports. It measures an organization's performance on several levels, such as its strategy and commitment towards sustainability; levels of community engagement; and risk management and mitigation policies with respect to social and environmental issues. For each level, points are allocated on the processes in place to meet these objectives and the output generated.

While these frameworks have been made available to the group companies, TCCI's directives cannot be mandated across them. According to the vice-president responsible for group corporate sustainability at Tata, 'no group level resource can ever mandate anything to companies. Companies have independent boards and are fiercely autonomous.'[13] The onus of becoming more sustainable hence lies at an individual company level, with the role of TCCI limited to offering advice, tools, and shared learning on a range of CSR issues. For instance, at the annual conference organized by TCCI, Tata company CEOs and facilitators meet to share their experiences and group leaders help evolve meaning and a common direction for best practice.

Tata Quality Management Services

TQMS is a division of the Tata Sons holding company and has broad responsibility for providing value to Tata companies around performance enhancement and competitiveness.[14] One area of CSR activity TQMS is involved with is facilitating understanding and implementation of the Tata Code of Conduct, which serves as a guide to Tata employees on core business ethics practices and principles. This it tackles through training, interventions, and development of reference materials. As part of its mandate, TQMS has also been entrusted with facilitating climate change initiatives in all group companies. Its role is to build awareness on climate change, establish current carbon footprints of the Tata companies, and help them in identifying and acting on mitigation measures.[15] Part of its vision is that by 2013, 'all group companies [will] have the lowest carbon footprint in their relevant business segments'.[16]

Similar to TCCI, TQMS's governance structure comprises a working group that has members from the senior leadership teams of several group companies. To accelerate the process of developing a low carbon strategy, TQMS has partnered with external consultants such as Ernst & Young and McKinsey & Co for expertise. By 2009, TQMS had helped map the carbon footprint of 12 Tata companies including the 'five jewels' (Tata Steel, Tata Chemicals, Tata Power, Tata Motors, and Tata Consultancy Services). TQMS then helped develop abatement strategies both for the long and short term for the 12 companies. In the next phase of implementation, TQMS will help map the carbon footprint of a further 11 Tata companies. In this way, TQMS seeks to set examples that will translate into capability building and creation of change agents to replicate such initiatives across all companies.[17]

Beyond these group level initiatives around CSR management, there are also numerous activities developed by the individual Tata companies, of which Tata Steel and Tata Consulting Services provide some interesting comparisons.

CSR at Tata Steel

Tata Steel, part of Tata Sons, is a $20 billion company and the seventh largest steel manufacturer in the world. With more than 30,000 employees worldwide, it has operations in more than 20 countries and a presence in over 50.[18]

Being a natural resources intensive business, Tata Steel faces a challenging CSR environment, yet has a long history of CSR engagement and is frequently cited as one of the leading Indian exponents of responsible business.[19] It is one of the few companies from the subcontinent listed in the Dow Jones Sustainability Index.

The 100-year-old flagship plant of Tata Steel is located in the city of Jamshedpur (named after the Tata Group Founder). The plant covers around a fourth of the land area of the city, leading to Jamshedpur popularly being referred to 'steel city'. Sharing such ties and dependency, a Tata enterprise – Jamshedpur Utilities & Services Company (JUSCO) – was created with the specific purpose of improving the quality of life for the communities where Tata Steel manufactures. Spending about

$22 million each year, JUSCO provides services in the area of water, power, infrastructure, public health, and horticulture, while its education department manages 25 of the 183 schools in the city.[20] The company also created its corporate NGO – Tata Steel Rural Development Society (TSRDS) – to develop and lead its community programmes. TSRDS is responsible for planning and implementing initiatives with partnering institutions in the field of health, education, infrastructure, land and water management, sports, livelihood, and empowerment.

With Tata Steel being itself a pioneer in CSR in India (for example it was an early adopter of the Global Reporting Initiative in 2002), the frameworks provided by TCCI might be expected to have only fairly minimal impact on the organization's efforts. But TCCI's directives have certainly shaped the company's framework for understanding CSR. According to one senior manager in the Tata Steel Corporate Sustainability Office, the TCCI provides the 'big picture' framework for 'wealth creation and distribution in multiple forms' (Tata Services Limited, 2010: 92) Also, TQMS helped Tata Steel map and develop abatement strategies for their environmental footprint.

CSR at Tata Consultancy Services

Tata Consultancy Services (TCS) is another Tata Sons subsidiary, but one in a very different business to Tata Steel. TCS is an IT services and business solutions provider. As such, being a service provider, TCS's CSR initiatives vary significantly from those at Tata Steel. In the area of environmental responsibility TCS focuses on reducing its energy needs, instituting green IT, building green offices, and promoting resource efficiency. In the community, the firm's main emphasis is on education, especially IT education. It seeks to make a positive social impact by promoting IT literacy amongst the underprivileged, creating IT capability in times of natural disasters, and running curriculum development partnerships and employee volunteer programs with engineering schools. Moreover, with two thirds of Tata Sons being owned by various philanthropic trusts and Tata Sons, in turn, owning 75 per cent of TCS, nearly 49 per cent of the dividend paid out by TCS every year goes towards funding philanthropic work (Tata Services Limited, 2010: 92).

Compared with Tata Steel, TCS is a relative newcomer to CSR, and its immediate social impacts are nowhere near as evident as for its 'smokestack' sister company. But as a Tata company it has a significant CSR legacy to live up to, and with group CSR management capabilities in place such as TCCI and TQMS, there is no shortage of encouragement and tools to support it in its endeavours. By the 2010s, TCS was ranking as one of India's top companies in terms of its CSR performance.

Study questions

1.   What are the main opportunities and challenges in developing and implementing CSR strategy for a global conglomerate such as Tata? To what extent
do you think that the company has effectively met these challenges and
capitalized on these opportunities?
2.   What is the corporate social strategy of the Tata Group? Analyze the group's
approach to CSR in terms of Husted and Allen's seven-step corporate social
strategy framework presented in Chapter 10.
3.   What is the relationship of individual Tata company CSR strategies and
practices to those of the Tata Group as a whole? What degree of variation or
integration is preferable?
4.   Download the most recent CSR or sustainability report of either Tata Steel or
TCS. Evaluate the company's approach to social reporting according to the
eight quality principles set out by Zadek and colleagues in Chapter 9 – inclusivity, comparability, completeness, evolution, management policies, disclosure,
externally verified, continuous improvement.
5.   To what extent can the Tata approach to CSR management be explained by the
company's Indian roots? Explain with reference to Gond and colleagues' analysis
of international variations in 'CSR-government configurations' from Chapter 11.

Endnotes

1   www.tata.com/aboutus/sub_index.aspx?sectid=8hOk5Qq3EfQ=
2   www.business-standard.com/india/news/tata-movesin-apple-led-global-brand-
pecking-order/468370/
3   www.tatapower.com/sustainability/policies.aspx
4   www.tata.com/aboutus/readings/inside.aspx?artid=CKdRrD5ZDV4=
5   www.tata.com/reading.aspx?artid=IV/tF5W9eeQ=
6   www.telegraphindia.com/external/display.jsp?mode=details&id=27752
7   www.tata.com/ourcommitment/readings/inside.aspx?artid=wE7I6Bvf3LQ=
8   www.tata.com/htm/Group_MnA_YearWise.htm
9   www.tata.com/aboutus/readings/inside.aspx?artid=HRrcG3jvdLA=&sectid=
sqvi8BnCJpo=
10   www.tata.com/reading.aspx?artid=IV/tF5W9eeQ=
11   Ibid.
12   www.csridentity.com/tata/Sustainability%20Reporting.pdf (Page 23)
13   Personal correspondence with Anant Nadkarni.
14   www.tataquality.com/UI/APage.aspx?SectionId=030509112833197201
15   www.tataquality.com/UI/APage.aspx?SectionId=030509112915897872
16   www.tataquality.com/UI/APage.aspx?SectionId=030509112833197201
17   www.tataquality.com/UI/APage.aspx?SectionId=011209173342823173
18   www.tatasteelindia.com/corporate-citizen/social/building-community-network.
asp; www.tata.com/company/profile.aspx?sectid=jsA69xFbDUA=

19   Elankumaran et al, 2005.
20   http://readings.economictimes.indiatimes.com/2010-09-30/news/27588839_
     1_samriddhi-tractor-forbes-marshall; www.juscoltd.com/; www.tatagrowthshop.
     com/sustainability/jamshedpur-glance.htm

References

Balch, O. (2012) 'Country briefing: India', *Ethical Corporation*, April: 11–19.
Elankumaran, S., Seal, R., & Hashmi, A. (2005) 'Transcending transformation:
     enlightening endeavours at Tata Steel', *Journal of Business Ethics*, 59(1/2):
     109–119.
Nadkarni, A. G. & Branzei, O. (2008) 'The Tata way: evolving and executing
     sustainable business strategies', *Ivey Business Journal*, (March/April): www.ivey
     businessjournal.com/topics/strategy/the-tata-way-evolving-and-executing-
     sustainable-business-strategies.
Tata Services Limited (2010) 'A journey towards an ideal', www.csridentity.com/tata/
     A%20Journey%20Towards%20an%20Ideal.pdf.

Chapter 12

The future of CSR in a global context

IN THIS CHAPTER WE WILL:

- Revisit the case for and against CSR
- Understand the current state of CSR
- Introduce social entrepreneurship and social innovation as future areas of CSR
- Assess new social movements as drivers of CSR
- Understand how new trends in regulation will shape CSR
- Discuss CSR as an emerging profession in management
- Reflect on the future of CSR as an academic subject

CSR – is it a good idea then?

Coming toward the end of our journey through the world of CSR, it is time to revisit some of our starting points. Let's begin with one of the more delicate issues we highlighted back in Chapter 2, namely the contested status of the field in the wider context of business practice, research, and teaching. Remember, there are a number of prominent voices out there, both in the literature as well as in practice, who still think that CSR should not exist and is just a lot of 'hot air' (Stern, 2009).

In Section B we studied the key *practical* responses to this contention in four distinct fields of corporate activity – marketplace, workplace, community, and the ecological environment. Here, we discovered that CSR has indeed enjoyed a rather broad uptake and application by companies. Taking a closer look at why companies do these things we have learned that companies can operate more successfully if they cater to new expectations from customers, employees, local communities, and wider public concerns about the natural environment. Most of what we discussed, however, would not necessarily pacify the critics. CSR sceptics, such as Milton Friedman (1970), would in fact be quite happy with most of what companies do today under the name of CSR – after all, the rationale is that it contributes to the bottom line by lowering costs, providing new market opportunities, enhancing employee efficiency, etc. Aneel Karnani (see Chapter 2) would perhaps hasten to add that CSR is therefore a misnomer for such activities and that corporations, by pretending to be 'socially responsible', are just fooling us into believing they are interested in the public good – while in reality they are doing these things simply to make yet more money.

Be that as it may, it is in Section C – where we talked about the management of CSR – that it became clear that we can make a reasonably solid case for arguing that CSR deserves its own place in the management curriculum. After all, for whatever reasons companies engage in CSR, we are definitely able to circumscribe a fairly distinct set of instruments, tools and practices that companies apply when they 'do CSR'. We have studied, among others, new forms of reporting, new approaches to strategy and new ways of interacting with other societal actors – all of which warrant the differentiation of CSR as a new field of business practice.

So, our preliminary conclusion is that even if companies are not turning into 'do gooders' (Portney, 2008: 267) when they practise CSR, they definitely engage with societal demands using a distinct and evolving subset of management practice. Therefore, at the end of this book, there can be little doubt that CSR is indeed a legitimate new member in the sub-disciplines of management, alongside the usual suspects such as marketing, finance, human resource management, or strategy.

This is, however, not the whole story. Some of the themes we discussed in the course of this book suggest that CSR is maybe a little more than just another field of management with the same purpose as the business management of old, namely to make a profit. Take, for instance, the reading by Valente and Crane (Chapter 7): a good deal of what corporations are doing in developing countries or other places with poor public governance clearly transcends a narrow business case rationale. Or think of Utting's discussion of equality in the workplace (Chapter 6): companies have to address discrimination and, more generally, respect basic human rights not just because of any associated promise of profit. In the short term, such measures invariably cost valuable resources to implement and there is hardly any direct revenue or other gain to offset these costs. In fact, a growing number of CSR issues are just fuelled by a general rise in the breadth and depth of public expectations towards business. It appears that CSR faces a number of challenges that are more related to what we discussed in Chapter 2 under the label of a 'social licence to operate'.

It is in this growing set of social expectations that CSR can be seen as a basic condition to operate. This indeed gives critics of CSR a real headache. They would probably shout for the government to 'rescue' corporations from these undue demands on their licence to operate. We have seen in particular in the three integrative case studies that in many instances governments just are not up to their textbook role anymore. This book has showcased that companies become involved in furthering the public good without an immediate and quantifiable contribution to the bottom line. CSR, in those instances, is more than pure and simple profit maximization. Rather, it is often the overarching enabling condition of business success to begin with. Throughout the book we have time and again come across the reasons why these activities are pursued by private companies: the role of business in contemporary society has changed and the social expectations of what companies should provide to society have significantly broadened. This is only further highlighted by the media storm and public outrage that ensues when business scandals are exposed.

The future of CSR – some trends and perspectives

In this final concluding chapter we will sketch out some of the implications of our discussions about CSR over the last 11 chapters. We will see that these evolve around the two key themes just mentioned: what is the relationship between the business value and the social value that a business creates? And what does it say about the changing role of business in society when we see a number of management activities that obviously are not immediately linked to plain old profits? The latter aspect has surfaced every now and then throughout our discussions in this book; at the end of our journey though it is worth fleshing it out a little more by looking at the dynamics and future developments in CSR.

New business models: social entrepreneurship and social innovation

Figure 12.1 provides an overview of future developments in CSR in the context of new models for business. As discussed throughout the book the question of creating social value is at the core of the CSR project. But social value may be a means to an end, or an end itself, just as economic value (or profits) can be a means or a goal. Different combinations of these two goals give rise to different forms of CSR.

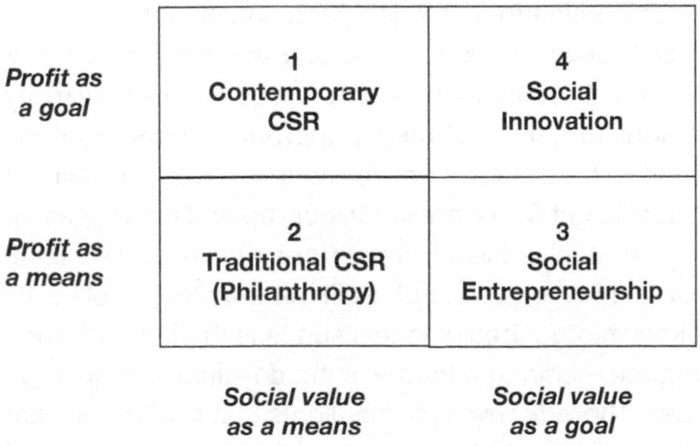

Profit as a goal	**1** Contemporary CSR	**4** Social Innovation
Profit as a means	**2** Traditional CSR (Philanthropy)	**3** Social Entrepreneurship
	Social value as a means	*Social value as a goal*

Figure 12.1: Future developments in CSR

Contemporary CSR

In a standard business – regardless of whether it is a family-owned SME or a multibillion dollar publicly listed corporation – social value creation however has to be aligned with the core purpose of the business, which in most cases consist of profit generation, in many cases even profit maximization. Most of the book has in fact focused on segment 1 of Figure 12.1: firms address consumer demand for fair trade, implement diversity policies for their employees or set up recycling programmes because the social value of those measures serves as a means to generate profits. All along the value chain, throughout all the functional operations of the business, well-run companies are aware that successful integration of societal expectations will ultimately contribute to the bottom line. Sometimes this contribution is short-term and quantifiable in a simple business case analysis; in other situations the contribution of CSR to the bottom line is more long-term and indirect and is a fundamental basic condition of the 'licence to operate' for the business.

Traditional CSR

We have also discussed the approach of traditional CSR represented in segment 2. For these companies CSR is an activity that is mostly driven by the desire to share some of their business success with their wider societal environment. Sponsorship of sports teams, funding of arts and music, employee volunteering to help the homeless, or endowments given to universities – all these are seen as something a 'good corporate citizen' should do in 'giving back' to society, in order to be a responsible member of society. This is the top level of Carroll's 'pyramid of CSR', which we discussed in Chapter 3. These activities generally do not pursue a direct profit goal as they are not linked to the core business – other than creating some general good will or positive brand recognition. In most cases companies also do not have a strategic intent with these activities. The choice of project or stakeholder group may depend on the owner, the CEO or the employees' personal preferences, or some commitment to local communities (e.g. the local soccer or hockey team) or wider societal concerns (e.g. contribution to earthquake or tsunami relief).

Sometimes, however, philanthropists have gone beyond this approach. Frank (2007), in his entertaining portrait of the 'superrich' in America describes how many of those philanthropists have applied a more strategic approach to philanthropy. Rather than just giving away money, for example, one former investment banker set up a company with the explicit goal to get 500 wells in Ethiopia up and running within a year. The companies set up by such philanthropists are run as professional businesses – the only difference is that the goal is not profit but the creation of social value. Probably the most well-known organization in this space is the Bill & Melinda Gates Foundation,[1] whose purpose – among others – is the development of drugs for currently untreatable diseases. The latter example highlights that businesses that are set up just to reach a certain social goal often venture into highly uncertain and risky endeavours. Similar to 'venture capital' they are often referred to as 'venture philanthropy' (Van Slyke & Newman, 2006) as both are similar in approach and execution – with the only difference being that the latter approach is primarily interested in social outcomes as a goal of the organization.

This area is, however, not just the domain of rich people and philanthropists. In many countries globally we have seen the rise of businesses whose goal is not profit but to create social value. This leads us to segment 3, namely social entrepreneurship

Social entrepreneurship

Social entrepreneurship can be described as 'a process involving the innovative use and combination of resources to pursue opportunities to catalyze social change and/or address social needs' (Mair & Marti, 2006: 37). That is, the primary goal of social entrepreneurship is social value creation, yet it typically leverages the power of markets, and the profit motive to achieve those goals.

Social enterprises have grown considerably over the last two decades and are now a phenomenon in both developing and developed countries. The most prominent example for this type of business from the developing context is probably the Grameen Bank in Bangladesh, a microfinance institution with the social purpose to enable poor rural families to set up small businesses.[2] Founded in 1976 by Nobel Prize winner Muhammad Yunus, Grameen Bank also illustrates why the terminology of 'entrepreneurship' has become popular for this type of business: they are often initiated and run by charismatic entrepreneurs who – similar to 'for-profit' entrepreneurs – have a vision for their business, run it professionally and successfully, albeit for a different purpose than traditional businesses.

While Grameen Bank and Yunus get a great deal of recognition for their microcredit business, the types and purposes of social enterprises are very many and varied. Another example of such a social entrepreneur is British celebrity chef Jamie Oliver who with his Fifteen restaurant in London set up a social enterprise whose purpose is to provide under-privileged young people with training and jobs in the catering industry.[3] The UK in some ways can be seen as a leader in this space, with the 'Community Interest Company', introduced in 2005 as a legal charter for social enterprises.[4]

CWS 12.1

Visit the companion website for more international examples in the field of social entrepreneurship

Social innovation

The latest trend in CSR, however, is businesses which attempt both profit and social value as part of their business goals. This area of 'social innovation' (segment 4, Figure 12.1) describes businesses (or projects within larger companies) that take a specific social need as a business opportunity. One of the long-standing definitions views social innovation as a situation where companies take 'community needs as opportunities to develop ideas and demonstrate business technologies, to find and serve new markets, and to solve long-standing business problems' (Moss Kanter, 1999: 124).

We have discussed some examples of these approaches in Chapter 5 in the reading by Prahalad and Hammond, who introduced the BOP approach as one emerging area of social innovation. As discussed in Integrative case 3, the new Tata Nano car is also a good example here: while addressing a social need (safe transportation), Tata provides a solution that at the same times contributes to its bottom line. Companies in this space, rather than talking about CSR tend to prefer the language of 'CSO', corporate social opportunity (Grayson & Hodges, 2004).

Beyond the developing world, social innovation and the idea of running a company with dual, or even multiple purposes has gained significant traction in the US, where the model of the 'Benefit Corporation' as a new legal form of company has emerged.[5] Those companies, commonly referred to as 'B-Corps' are set up with the deliberate 'corporate purpose to create a material positive impact on society and the environment' and the fiduciary duties of the management include the successful attainment of those goals. The B-Corp was first implemented as a new legal charter of corporations in Delaware and by 2012 had been adopted in seven other states, and the designation of certified B-Corporation had been given to more than 500 companies.

Social entrepreneurship and social innovation clearly are among the most vibrant new business models and contemporary areas of development in CSR. They have been popularized in many ways – through government initiatives, business associations, and in the popular business press. The most widely received example of the latter is Michael Porter's concept of 'shared value' (Porter & Kramer, 2011) as an approach to social innovation, where businesses pursue simultaneously economic and social value.

New social movements

Social movements are collective efforts to change society, comprising people united by a common set of beliefs about a preferred state of the world (Den Hond & De Bakker, 2007). Social movements, represented by NGO groups, activists, and others looking to change corporate behaviour have long played a role in shaping the context in which CSR has emerged and become institutionalized. Earlier in this book we came across the definition of CSR as 'the economic, legal, ethical, and discretionary *expectations* that society has of organizations at a given point in time'.[6] Expectations by society therefore are one of the key starting points for CSR and it follows that as those expectations change with the development of new social movements, so does the nature of what CSR is intended to achieve (Den Hond & De Bakker, 2007; Vogel, 2000). Arguably, the development of CSR has been very much influenced by the rise of the environmental movement in the 1970s and 1980s (Hoffman, 2001) and by the anti-globalization movement in the early 2000s (Eschle & Maiguashca, 2005).

Among the latest wave of such movements we have seen the rise of the so-called 'Occupy Wall Street' movement.[7] After gaining global attention with a symbolic 'occupation' of Wall Street (or more precisely, Zuccotti Park, a little square close to

Wall Street in downtown Manhattan) the movement spread in less than a month during the autumn of 2011 to more than 900 cities globally. In the 'Declaration of the Occupation of New York City', the campaign Occupy Wall Street articulates a long list of concerns about irresponsible corporate behaviour with the following preface: 'We come to you at a time when corporations, which place profit over people, self-interest over justice, and oppression over equality, run our governments'.[8]

Regardless of whether we agree with this assessment or not, there is little doubt that from a CSR perspective this new social movement has raised issues that are likely to stay on society's agenda for some time to come (Trudell, 2012). Among the many issues the movement claims to focus on, the aftermath of the financial crisis has been prominent. In the context of large amounts of public funds committed to 'save' financial institutions and large corporations (often leaving public finances in many countries in a state that has initiated more or less severe austerity measures), the Occupy movement has chiefly focused on corporations and highlighted some of their detrimental effects on society. One of the movement's signature slogans was to be 'the ninety-nine percent', while large companies, and their wealthy investors and leaders were deemed to be representative of the 'one percent'. In this way, business has been portrayed as a force for growing income and wealth gaps in many countries. The Occupy movement thus represents concerns that many people across the world share: that business chiefly serves the interests of shareholders and senior management, while infringing the interests of workers, customers and the wider public.

Again, as we said above, studying social movements from a business perspective is not so much concerned with the question whether the Occupy movement was right and had an accurate grasp of what they proclaimed to be concerned about. The central question from a CSR perspective is whether the movement is strong enough, and represents societal unrest deeply enough rooted in wider society, so that it might shape the 'expectations' on business and thus enter the CSR agenda. Dominic Barton, global managing director of McKinsey, put this in fairly unequivocal terms in a *Harvard Business Review* reading in 2011:

> Business leaders face a choice: They can reform the system, or watch as the government exerts control . . . there is growing concern that if the fundamental issues revealed in the crisis remain unaddressed and the system fails again, the social contract between the capitalist system and the citizenry may truly rupture, with unpredictable but severely damaging results.
>
> (Barton, 2011)

One of the reasons the environmental movement became so crucial for business over the last four decades lies in the fact that it changed the legal framework of business in the long term. With politicians representing (or 'pandering to' as some would put it) popular demands, the concerns of the Occupy movement might eventually inform the legislative agenda, and thus have direct consequences on how business is run. An example of this can be seen in the discussion of the 'Buffet rule'

CWS 12.2

Visit the companion website for more material on the Occupy movement and the business response to it in the US.[9] In 2011, the billionaire investor Warren Buffet publicly declared that he thought it was unfair that his secretary was paying a higher percentage of tax on her salary than Buffet himself did. He argued that there is little justification for people with middle-class incomes to pay a higher percentage of taxes than millionaires. The Buffet rule, supported by the Obama administration, suggests that people with more than $1 million income should be taxed at 30 per cent minimum. This led to a virulent debate on how to reform the tax system in the US – with potentially significant implications for companies and their shareholders. This turns our attention to another significant area of future development in CSR, namely regulation.

CSR between private and public regulation

In Chapter 1 we identified one of the core characteristics of CSR to be that it is 'voluntary'. This somehow suggests that CSR and regulation appear to be mutually exclusive terrains – certainly if it means mandatory governmental regulation. On a second look though, as we have seen in the previous chapter, the relation between CSR and regulation is not that simple. This is largely due to the fact that the contemporary landscape of business regulation only rather loosely resembles what has been our traditional understanding of hard, command-and-control, regulation. This is due to the rise of two phenomena for business: i) the advent of globalization has created regulatory spaces beyond the traditional nation state level; and ii) regulation today is often issued, monitored, enforced, and sanctioned by private, rather than just public or governmental actors. The new landscape of regulation therefore evolves along two core dimensions, 'national-transnational' and 'private-public', as Figure 12.2 illustrates. All four types of regulation have experienced significant innovation in institutionalizing more responsible business practices.

National public regulation

Let us first have a look at the regulatory efforts of national state governments as the traditional source of business regulation. This type of regulation is continuing to shape the CSR agenda of business. Over the last two decades, various national governments have initiated reforms and created an infrastructure for CSR. Perhaps the most pronounced efforts were made by the Blair administration in the UK in the late 1990s, by creating a cabinet-level position on CSR, a CSR academy, and a fairly wide-ranging framework for CSR (Kinderman, 2012). Similar efforts have recently taken place in Canada, most notably the Office of the Extractive Sector CSR Counsellor in the Ministry of Foreign Affairs and International Trade.[10] While CSR is, in principle, by its very nature voluntary, the role of regulation here is different from classic imperative governmental regulation and has best been described as an 'orchestrating' or coordinating role of governments. Similar efforts can be reported from most Western democracies, with a growing momentum in emerging economies. Most pronounced are recent efforts in China and India, with the latter, for example, launching a set of national voluntary CSR guidelines in 2011.

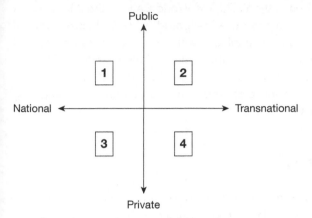

Figure 12.2: Basic dimensions of CSR-related regulation

Next to these fairly soft forms of regulation we have also seen in recent years a rising appetite among governments to change many of the frameworks that govern business practices in a more substantial way. In the US, the 2010 Dodd-Frank Act aimed at reforming Wall Street[11] and the subsequent instituting of a Bureau of Consumer Protection[12] are just some examples of this trend. In a similar vein, France introduced mandatory reporting on CSR in 2003 (Ioannou & Serafeim, 2012). India, too, has looked to complement its voluntary guidelines with some hard regulation in the form of the 2011 Companies Bill, which mandates companies above a certain size to institute a CSR committee, develop a CSR policy, and, most controversially of all, set aside a minimum 2 per cent of net profits to achieve the goals of the CSR policy.[13]

This ongoing appetite of nation-states to regulate responsible business behaviour – alongside the direct impact – will certainly fuel much of future voluntary CSR initiatives as one of the reasons companies adopt CSR has always included to forestall and thus avoid more regulation.

CWS 12.3

Visit the companion website for details of these and other CSR initiatives by governments in different countries

Transnational public regulation

Following the trend of globalization of business, we have also seen significant inter-governmental regulation at the transnational level (segment 2) in the last two decades. Many of the regional trading agreements and economic treaty systems, most notably in the EU, have created frameworks and regulation for responsible business practices. Addressing climate change, for instance, is a fairly well established issue on the CSR agenda of many North American companies (Hoffman, 2005; Kolk & Pinkse, 2005); in Europe it is by now part of the regulatory framework due to the European Emission Trading System established in 2005 (Eberlein & Matten, 2009).

Beyond these CSR-related initiatives, the EU Commissions on Trade, Competition, and Labour have also taken rather incisive measures to protect the interests of wider stakeholders. In a similar vein, recent debates on regulating 'tax-havens' at the G20 meetings have fuelled a renewed interest in transnational regulation. A number of initiatives at the WTO, the World Bank or the IMF have led to rules and procedures that at times have instigated more inclusive forms of corporate stakeholder engagements, in particular with regard to environmental and human rights issues. Last but not least, the United Nations with its 'Global Compact'[14] has for well over a decade now been playing a key role in providing a set of norms and interactive learning platforms with the objective of instigating responsible business practices.

National private regulation

Arguably the main growth in CSR related regulation we have seen and continue to observe is in the area of private regulation (self-regulation). This means regulation which is authored by companies, industry associations or other transnational bodies, sometimes with inclusion of NGOs, and very rarely with inclusion of governments (Bernstein & Cashore, 2007). Among the main drivers for private regulation by business are the avoidance of first-mover disadvantages and the reduction of uncertainty. When, for example, the mining multinational DeBeers attempted to deal in a responsible way with the problem of diamonds mined from conflict zones ('blood diamonds'), it faced potential competitive disadvantage if their global competitors were to continue the practice and avoid the costs or lost revenues related to a responsible approach. A collectively accepted, industry-wide, set of rules, such as the 'Kimberley Process'[15] not only potentially created a 'level playing field' in the industry, but also created a common reference point in terms of industry best practice. Furthermore, industry agreements also counter the problem that the behaviour of one company can potentially taint the reputation of all players in an industry, regardless of their individual behaviour.

Relatively rare, however are strict examples of *national private regulation* (segment 3) since most CSR issues today transcend national borders and most industries are increasingly global in reach. We witness national collective self-regulation particularly in instances where businesses in a country want to avoid regulation by their government. A good example is the 'Towards Sustainable Mining' principles develop by the Mining Association of Canada,[16] which could be interpreted as a straightforward attempt at avoiding governmental regulation. Unsurprisingly, an attempt by parliament to make responsible practices in the Canadian mining industry mandatory was finally voted down in 2010.[17]

Transnational private regulation

Most instances of self-regulation are coming in the form of transnational private regulation (segment 4). Examples of transnational private regulation are abundant. One longstanding example here is the Marine Stewardship Council,[18] an effort initially led by Unilever and the WWF to create an industry framework for sustainable management of fisheries in the North Atlantic; the most recent – and potentially a game changer in CSR – is the new ISO 26000 norm issued by the International Standards Organization.[19] Similar to its sisters ISO 9000 or ISO 14000 on quality and the environment respectively, ISO 26000 was released in 2010 as a new global standard for CSR. Unlike its predecessors, however, it is not a standard whose adoption by companies will be certified. Rather, it is meant as a standard that provides a 'process guideline' for companies on how to implement CSR. This hints at a trend in transnational regulation of CSR: companies see the desire to institution-alize CSR in their industries by standardizing it and creating a common understanding of what this new management practice is really about – but not to be held formally accountable for their behaviours or impacts. Thus, the expectation for the future is towards a more structured, universally shared and widely accepted understanding of CSR, but not necessarily a more tightly regulated one (Schwartz & Tilling, 2009).

> **CWS 12.4**
>
> Visit the companion website for more examples of CSR-related self-regulation by industry

Assessing the outcomes of CSR

The critical reader of this book, in particular readers with some management experi-ence, might by now lean back and wonder about one particular bias of our account of CSR. Clearly, most of our discussions have focused on management concepts, practices, areas of application, and tools and strategies of implementation of CSR. One area that so far has received rather scant attention is the question of how exactly we can measure, assess, and evaluate the concrete effects and outcomes of CSR 'out there' in society. Admittedly, we have covered the subject to some extent in Chapter 9 where we discussed reporting and auditing questions of CSR. In general, however, the discussion on corporate social performance (CSP) is rather different from, say standard financial performance in business. CSP, in theory and practice, for the most part has focused on the resources companies put *into* CSR: how much money has been invested, what policies have been put in place, what programmes have been implemented, or more generally – what the company has 'done' in the area of CSR (Wood, 1991). Most of the non-financial reports of companies today would still mostly concentrate on these aspects.

There is, however, growing demand for a change of perspective in this area. After all, what would we think of a company who could tell us in detail about all the resources they invested in developing and manufacturing their products – but had no clear indication of what the financial impact of all those measures were? Clearly, the measurement of financial outcomes in terms of revenues and profits is a core element of managing and assessing firm performance. It is no little surprise, then, that currently one of the hottest areas of development in CSR – both in theory and practice – is the question of how better to assess the impacts of CSR in terms of CSP. This effort, however, proves to be considerably more complex than measuring financial perfor-mance, which at least can be assessed in dollars and cents. The concrete impact of an education or healthcare project by a company is more difficult to ascertain. And even when results are quantifiable, such as in some areas of environmental performance, different CSR outcomes are often not comparable and require different types of metrics.

The area of CSP therefore is one of the most dynamic fields of future development in CSR. This becomes even more of a demand for businesses that – as discussed earlier in this chapter – are set up with the specific goal of creating some form of social outcome, value, and change, such as social enterprises or social innovation businesses. The more businesses are focusing on such social goals – and the more resources are dedicated even to traditional CSR – the more companies want to know what exactly the social impact of their CSR expenditures actually is. This certainly is a challenge for academic research in CSR and – fuelled by the rise of social enterprises and social innovation – there seems to be a reinvigoration of research into the question of how to generate a better understanding and management of the outcomes of CSR (Gond & Crane, 2010; Salazar et al, 2012).

Careers in CSR

At the end of a book that may be used as part of a professional education programme, many readers might ask themselves how CSR might concretely relate to their professional lives. In other words, are there careers to be made in CSR?

The generic answer to this question is an emphatic 'yes' – CSR has certainly emerged as a specific job profile and recruitment specification since the early 2000s (Cartland, 2010). It might be more of a challenge, however, to characterize what exactly the typical career might look like. Looking at the careers of many of our students as well as at some of the career guides out there it appears that we can identify three main trajectories (Grant, 2009; Mohin, 2012).

- *Dedicated CSR professionals.* Over the past two decades, CSR has given rise to not only a plethora of consultancies, think tanks, and specialized advisory firms, but also a rise in the number of CSR-related professionals in 'traditional' professional service and law firms. They include the big consulting and auditing firms, such as McKinsey or Accenture, which have seen growing markets in advizing business in CSR reporting, auditing, and general CSR-related strategy consulting (Fernandez Young et al, 2003).
- *Managers working in CSR roles/departments within companies.* According to some surveys, more than 90 per cent of CSR jobs are in companies and more than two thirds work in teams of five employees or less. For two thirds of these CSR managers, it is their first job in CSR and more than half are internally recruited (ACCSR, 2007). These numbers seem to point to a commonly encountered experience of CSR professionals, which is that sound knowledge of, and experience in, the core business of an organization is often a vital stepping stone into a more specialized CSR role.
- *Line managers with some CSR responsibility as part of their brief.* Next to those two categories of specialized CSR manager there is also a growing demand from recruiters for literacy in CSR as part of a regular line manager role in companies. As such the main brief may be in accounting, marketing,

HR, or operations, but some knowledge of CSR is increasingly desired in many of these jobs, in particular in leading-edge industries and companies.

Table 12.1. provides an overview of the actual activities of CSR professionals. This suggests that the major skills necessary for CSR professionals tend to be in the reporting and communications realm with expertise in environmental issues also important. We might also add to the list those social innovators and entrepreneurs starting their own organizations with social objectives, or indeed to work for and lead NGOs.

It is more of an open question regarding the extent to which CSR is yet a far-reaching career trajectory in an organization. Certainly in the professional services sector, CSR has largely been a field of growth for these firms, providing some CSR professionals with an exciting growth-driven working environment. With demand in CSR consulting and services still growing this realm of CSR work can indeed be considered a promising career path, although there is also clearly some variation according to the ups and downs of economic cycles.

The picture is a little more muddled when we look to CSR managers within larger organizations. The surveys and guides cited earlier tend to suggest that most jobs are not actual line management functions but rather small teams reporting to the communication/PR/public affairs function, or sometimes to the board directly. As the jobs in most cases do not contribute directly to the bottom line – in fact mostly are a cost for the organization – it might be rather hard to build up credentials to move up in the corporate hierarchy. This is somewhat echoed by the salaries for CSR managers, which seem to be slightly below average compared to other management positions at the same level. Whether the fact that the CSR industry is dominated by women – where there tends to be a gender pay gap anyway – is relevant here is an open question (around two thirds of CSR managers are female according to ACCSR, 2007, and Cartland, 2010).

The real motivator, however, of moving into a CSR job for many professionals is the intrinsic value of the day to day work. According to one survey, CSR managers cite as the top three benefits of their work (ACCSR, 2007: 15):

- To work in an area that is aligned with my personal values
- To deal with important issues
- To promote positive change between my organization and society

CWS 12.5

Visit the companion website for links to various platforms where CSR-related jobs are advertised

Table 12.1: Top five activities of CSR professionals in the UK

Mainstream corporations	Professional Service Firms
1. **Community involvement**	1. Reporting
2. **Reporting**	2. External marketing
3. **Environment**	3. Environment
4. **Internal marketing**	4. Climate change
5. **Climate change**	5. Community involvement

Based on data reported by Cartland (2010)

Among the bottom two benefits the respondents listed:

- Pay and reward increases
- Promotion within my organization

These findings are reflected in a study of CSR/sustainability professionals, which found that for such people the key attraction to their work lies in a pivotal role of values, inspiration, expertise, empowerment, strategic thinking, and social contribution as sources of meaning (Visser & Crane, 2010). What is more, when it comes to CSR we have discovered some fascinating blurring of boundaries between the NGO and activist camp and the corporate sphere. Examples are the Greenpeace board member and youngest ever president of the Sierra Club Adam Werbach[20] or the founder of the Canadian Green Party Jim Harris.[21] Werbach began his corporate career consulting for Walmart and now works in a senior sustainability role for the advertising multinational Saatchi & Saatchi while Harris runs his own consultancy advizing Fortune500 companies on how to become more sustainable. The main motivation for these individuals to move into business is the hope that companies with their financial resources and economic power can affect positive social and environmental change rather quicker than NGO campaigns or political processes. This is a rather recent phenomenon and CSR-related roles in some way are the natural corporate setting for such intentions; it remains an open question, however, how far activism can succeed within the bureaucratic confines of the corporate world.

Finally in terms of CSR careers we might reflect on the formal qualifications needed to progress in the industry. These are largely provided by training courses and the study of CSR as an academic subject.

Future perspectives on CSR as an academic subject

At the end of our journey through the world of CSR it might indeed be worth spending a moment to reflect on the status of this topic within the wider teaching curriculum in business education. Given the contested nature of the topic, it is no surprise that business schools have struggled and in most cases have only reluctantly opened up to the CSR[22] agenda. It is just a little more than a decade ago that one of our colleagues noted that there is an 'intellectual bias against business ethics' in business schools and that teaching and research in CSR is seen as a 'field of study [. . .] falling somewhere on the vector between ambivalence and disdain' (Hosmer, 1999: 91, 102).

Luckily, there is good news. Recent surveys all paint a picture which identifies CSR as a solid part of the curriculum. Two thirds of business schools in Europe and North America now have a compulsory CSR course in most of their programmes and, for instance, 90 per cent of North American schools offer at least an optional course to their full time MBAs (Moon & Orlitzky, 2011). In addition, the number of postgraduate and even undergraduate specialist programmes is also growing, not to mention PhD programmes in CSR and related subjects. This advance does not only apply to the teaching curriculum, but also academic research has begun to take the subject seriously: a study of the top 50 business schools in the *Financial Times* MBA rankings found that two thirds of these top schools have a dedicated research centre or institute in CSR (Jones Christensen et al, 2007). It should be added that most of these surveys were just concentrating on the business school as the most obvious place of business education, although CSR has also entered the teaching and research agenda in a number of other academic departments, including law, politics, sociology, and international development.

CWS 12.6

Visit the companion website for links to numerous academic courses, research centres and institutes in CSR

It might be worth asking though if this is just an ephemeral trend soon to be overtaken by other management fashions. To answer this question we can look to the drivers of the rise in CSR. One of the key findings of the surveys so far is the importance of student interest in fuelling schools' attention to CSR – in other words, business schools may just be following the demand of their customers to integrate CSR offerings into their curriculum (Matten & Moon, 2004; Moon & Orlitzky, 2011). This is also reflected in a rapid growth in student organizations around the topic. At the international level the most well-known player is Net Impact, which has more than 30,000 members organized in local 'chapters' in more than 300 universities globally.[23] We see a growing trend among students to use their business education and skills to impact social change – along the lines of the emerging trends of social entrepreneurship and innovation discussed earlier. Or, as the Net Impact mission states, many CSR students aspire to be 'change-makers who are using our jobs to tackle the world's toughest problems'.

Next to students, interest from the business community also plays a part in driving CSR education. Indeed, the first page of a Google search on 'CSR education' will list not some programme of a leading university but CSR training offered by companies such as Accenture, Intel, SAP, or the Indian Jindal Steel&Power.[24] In part this interest is, again, fuelled by current and future employees of business. A 2008 survey by PriceWaterhouseCoopers among 'millennials' (people who entered the workforce after January 2000) came to this conclusion:

> Corporate responsibility is critical – 88% of millennials said they will choose employers who have corporate social responsibility (CSR) values that reflect their own and 86% could consider leaving an employer if CSR values no longer matched their expectations.
>
> (PriceWaterhouseCoopers, 2008: 5)

These are, of course, the espoused preferences of just one stakeholder group. Next to the general trend – specifically discussed in Section B of this book – of growing and changing stakeholder demand, the changing conditions in the wider economic setup of many countries and indeed the global economy have put business not only more on the spot but also in a more pivotal position with regard to expectations towards wider positive social change.

The first aspect here – a rise of critical scrutiny – has certainly been a response to corporate scandals and the financial crisis. Next to these movements critical of business we see, second, a growing trend in the public to accept business influence and power in society as it is, while at the same time attempting to 'use' business to address the most pressing contemporary social issues. The rise of social entrepreneurship and innovation is just one indicator of this trend. One might not necessarily go as far as some scholars who see CSR as one of the fundamental conditions for the survival of Western democracy – through supplementing and, by default, substituting the modern welfare state (Crouch, 2011). It is fairly clear though that many of the most pressing contemporary social and environmental challenges – be it cutbacks of the welfare state, unemployment, extreme weather events, or resource shortages – can only be tackled by an increasing involvement of the private sector. As we learned throughout this book, this involvement can be 'forced' by national laws; more often than not though, companies' engagement in these arenas has been voluntary. As such, these developments provide a solid basis for the expectation that we have just seen the beginnings of CSR as a core element of successful management of businesses.

Challenges for practice

Secure an interview with a CSR professional or practitioner. Seek to understand:

1. What path has their career taken?
2. Do they have a CSR or other relevant qualification? Have they found it helpful in their work?
3. What professional groups or associations does the interviewee belong to? Are they of value?
4. What do they see as key capabilities for their role?
5. How do they see their future career developing?

Study questions

1. Locate the case studies in this book and any other CSR examples you are familiar with on Figure 12.1. Try to find examples for each quadrant.
2. CSR has come a long way in the last 50 years:
    a) What do you anticipate CSR will look like in another 50 years' time?
    b) What role do you think regulation will play?
    c) To what extent would you expect this to vary in different national contexts?
3. Find a biography of someone you consider to be a CSR leader, either in a film, book or magazine.
    a) Try to identify what you consider to be their key qualities and capabilities.
    b) Do the same exercise for a social entrepreneur. Reflect on any similarities or differences in the capabilities identified.
4. Reflect again on the question we raised earlier in this book (Chapters 1 and 2) about whether CSR is a new phenomenon. What elements of CSR have a

long standing tradition from the very beginning of the industrial revolution? What elements of CSR are specific to the late twentieth and early twenty-first century? In which direction do you expect the CSR agenda to evolve?

Further reading

Barton, D. (2011) 'Capitalism for the long term', *Harvard Business Review*, 89(3): 84–91.
The financial crisis that began in the late 2000s has led to pressing questions about the societal value of our current capitalist system. As key protagonists of capitalism, corporate leaders have begun to take up these questions and Dominic Barton's reading is one such example. Writing as the Global Managing Director of the consulting giant McKinsey & Co., he suggests that overcoming short-termism, shareholder dominance, and lack of commitment to a firm through dispersed ownership are key steps towards a capitalist system that allows companies to live up to their responsibilities beyond short-term profit maximization.

Mair, J. & Marti, I. (2006) 'Social entrepreneurship research: a source of explanation, prediction, and delight', *Journal of World Business*, 41(1): 36–44.
Johanna Mair and Ignasi Marti provide an overview of the burgeoning field of both emerging business practice and research in social entrepreneurship. The area is of interest as CSR-related concerns – in this book often discussed as an add-on to 'normal' business operations – in social enterprises are at the core of the purpose of these businesses. The discussion around this new form of firm is interesting not only as a new future area of business practice and research but also provides a backdrop for discussions about the general social purpose of private business enterprise in the first place.

Endnotes

1   www.gatesfoundation.org (Accessed 29 June, 2012).
2   www.grameen-info.org (Accessed 29 June, 2012).
3   www.fifteen.net (Accessed 29 June, 2012).
4   www.cicregulator.gov.uk (Accessed 29 June, 2012).
5   www.bcorporation.net (Accessed 29 June, 2012).
6   Chapter 3, reading by Schwartz & Carroll, emphasis added.
7   http://occupywallst.org (Accessed 29 June, 2012).
8   www.nycga.net/resources/declaration (Accessed 29 June, 2012).
9   www.whitehouse.gov/economy/buffett-rule (Accessed 29 June, 2012).
10   www.international.gc.ca/csr_counsellor-conseiller_rse (Accessed 29 June, 2012).

11 www.sec.gov/about/laws/wallstreetreform-cpa.pdf (Accessed 29 June, 2012).
12 www.ftc.gov/bcp/index.shtml (Accessed 29 June, 2012).
13 http://readings.economictimes.indiatimes.com/2012-07-22/news/32777534_
1_csr-activities-new-companies-bill-corporate-social-responsibility (Accessed
29 June, 2012).
14 http://unglobalcompact.org (Accessed 29 June, 2012).
15 www.kimberleyprocess.com (Accessed 29 June, 2012).
16 www.mining.ca/site/index.php/en/towards-sustainable-mining.html (Accessed
22 June, 2012).
17 http://openparliament.ca/bills/40-3/C-300 (Accessed 22 June, 2012).
18 www.msc.org (Accessed 22 June, 2012).
19 www.iso.org/iso/home/standards/management-standards/iso26000.htm
(Accessed 22 June, 2012).
20 www.fastcompany.com/magazine/118/working-with-the-enemy.html
(Accessed 22 June, 2012).
21 www.jimharris.com (Accessed 22 June, 2012).
22 As discussed earlier in this book, CSR is often taught under different labels,
which most commonly include business ethics, sustainability, corporate
citizenship, and business and society.
23 www.netimpact.org (Accessed 22 June, 2012).
24 This refers to a search conducted 27 June, 2012.

References

ACCSR (2007) *The CSR manager in Australia: research report on working in corporate social responsibility*, Melbourne: Australian Centre for CSR.
Barton, D. (2011) 'Capitalism for the long term', *Harvard Business Review*, 89(3): 84–91.
Bernstein, S. & Cashore, B. (2007) Can non-state global governance be legitimate? An analytical framework', *Regulation & Governance*, 1(4): 347–371.
Cartland, A. (2010) 'Who works in CSR? Staffing and recruitment in CSR', in M. Pohl & N. Tolhurst (eds) *Responsible business: how to manage a CSR strategy successfully*, Chichester: John Wiley, 43–63.
Crouch, C. (2011) *The strange non-death of neo-liberalism*, Cambridge: Polity.
Den Hond, F. & De Bakker, F. G. A. (2007) 'Ideologically motivated activism: how activist groups influence corporate social change activities', *Academy of Management Review*, 32: 901–924.
Eberlein, B. & Matten, D. (2009) 'Business responses to climate change regulation in Canada and Germany – lessons for MNCs from emerging economies', *Journal of Business Ethics*, 86(2): 241–255.
Eschle, C. & Maiguashca, B. (eds) (2005) *Critical theories, international relations and 'the anti-globalization movement'*, London: Routledge.
Fernandez Young, A., Moon, J., & Young, R. (2003) *The UK corporate social responsibility consultancy industry: a phenomenological approach.* Nottingham: No. 14-2003 ICCSR Research Paper Series, ISSN 1479-5124.

Frank, R. (2007) *Richistan: a journey through the American wealth boom and the lives of the new rich*, New York: Crown Publishers.

Friedman, M. (1970) 'The social responsibility of business is to increase its profits', *The New York Times Magazine*, 13 September: 13, 32–33, 122–126.

Gond, J. P. & Crane, A. (2010) 'Corporate social performance disoriented: saving the lost paradigm?' *Business & Society*, 49(4): 677–703.

Grant, E. A. (2009) *Careers with a conscience*, Philadelphia: Wetfeet, Inc.

Grayson, D. & Hodges, A. (2004) *Corporate social opportunity: seven steps to make corporate social responsibility work for your business*, Sheffield: Greenleaf.

Hoffman, A. J. (2001) *From heresy to dogma: an institutional history of corporate environmentalism* (expanded edn), Palo Alto, CA: Stanford University Press.

Hoffman, A. J. (2005) 'Climate change strategy: the business logic behind voluntary greenhouse gas reductions', *California Management Review*, 47(3): 21–46.

Hosmer, L. T. (1999) 'Somebody out there doesn't like us: a study of the position and respect of business ethics at schools of business administration', *Journal of Business Ethics*, 22: 91–106.

Ioannou, I. & Serafeim, G. (2012) 'The consequences of mandatory corporate sustainability reporting', Harvard Business School Research Working Paper No. 11-100.

Jones Christensen, L., Peirce, E., Hartman, L. P., Hoffman, W. M., & Carrier, J. (2007) 'Ethics, CSR, and sustainability education in the *Financial Times* top 50 global business schools: baseline data and future research directions', *Journal of Business Ethics*, 73: 347–368.

Kinderman, D. (2012) '"Free us up so we can be responsible!" The co-evolution of corporate social responsibility and neo-liberalism in the UK, 1977–2010', *Socio-Economic Review*, 10(1): 29–57.

Kolk, A. & Pinkse, J. (2005) 'Business responses to climate change: identifying emergent strategies', *California Management Review*, 47(3): 6–20.

Mair, J. & Marti, I. (2006) 'Social entrepreneurship research: a source of explanation, prediction, and delight', *Journal of World Business*, 41(1): 36–44.

Matten, D. & Moon, J. (2004) 'Corporate social responsibility education in Europe', *Journal of Business Ethics*, 54(4): 323–337.

Mohin, T. (2012) *Changing business from the inside out: a tree-hugger's guide to working in corporations*, San Francisco, CA: Berrett-Koehler.

Moon, J. & Orlitzky, M. (2011) 'Corporate social responsibility and sustainability education: a trans-Atlantic comparison', *Journal of Management & Organization*, 17(5): 583–603.

Moss Kanter, R. (1999) 'From spare change to real change: the social sector as beta site for business innovation', *Harvard Business Review*, 77(3): 122–128.

Porter, M. E. & Kramer, M. R. (2011) 'Creating shared value', *Harvard Business Review*, 89(2): 62–77.

Portney, P. R. (2008) 'The (not so) new corporate social responsibility: an empirical perspective', *Review of Environmental Economics and Policy*, 2(2): 261–275.

Prahalad, C. K. & Hammond, A. (2002) 'Serving the world's poor, profitably', *Harvard Business Review*, 80(9): 48–57.

PriceWaterhouseCoopers (2008) *Managing tomorrow's people. Millennials at work: perspectives from a new generation*, www.pwc.com/managingpeople2020.

Salazar, J., Husted, B., & Biehl, M. (2012) 'Thoughts on the evaluation of corporate social performance through projects', *Journal of Business Ethics*, 105(2): 175–186.

Schwartz, B. & Tilling, K. (2009) '"ISO-lating" corporate social responsibility in the organizational context: a dissenting interpretation of ISO 26000', *Corporate Social Responsibility and Environmental Management*, 16(5): 289–299.

Schwartz, M. S. & Carroll, A. B. (2003) 'Corporate social responsibility: a three domain approach', *Business Ethics Quarterly*, 13(4): 503–530.

Stern, S. (2009) 'The hot air of CSR', *Financial Times*, 2 February.

Trudell, M. (2012) 'The Occupy movement and class politics in the US', *International Socialism Journal*, 12(133), www.isj.org.uk (online journal).

Van Slyke, D. M. & Newman, H. K. (2006) 'Venture philanthropy and social entrepreneurship in community redevelopment', *Nonprofit Management and Leadership*, 16(3): 345–368.

Visser, W. & Crane, A. (2010) 'Corporate sustainability and the individual: understanding what drives sustainability professionals as change agents', http://ssrn.com/abstract=1559087.

Vogel, D. (2000) 'Ideas, ideologies, and social movements: the United States experience since 1800', *Business History Review*, 74(3): 550–552.

Wood, D. J. (1991) 'Corporate social performance revisited', *Academy of Management Review*, 16: 691–718.

Subjects Index

Absenteeism 283, 284, 287

Accountability 10, 13, 14, 16, 18, 65, 74, 115, 234, 257, 261, 268, 270, 301, 306–308, 310, 311, 313, 400, 402, 404, 406, 410, 412, 418, 419, 425, 426, 428, 430, 436, 439, 477, 478, 482–484, 519, 525

Accounting (social accounting) 4, 38, 46, 47, 91, 148, 226, 336, 401, 403, 405, 406, 409–413, 415–420, 422, 436, 439, 564

Activists 5, 45, 53, 62, 87, 216, 264, 266, 306, 310, 373, 375, 456, 459, 464, 512, 558

Adam Smith 49

Affirmative action 122

Africa 1, 2, 54, 203–208, 224, 254, 255, 293, 303, 311, 318, 402, 492, 498, 510, 532

Agency theory 78, 178, 179, 186

Agriculture 204, 226, 227, 231, 255, 269, 301, 302, 303, 309, 317, 318, 319, 324, 362, 366, 367, 373, 382, 394, 502,

Altruistic strategy 483

America, 17, 44, 65, 68, 136, 193, 214, 241, 278, 293, 336, 340, 362, 396, 455, 500, 561, 566

Angola 524

Animal rights activists 53, 456

Animal testing 409, 456

Apartheid 206

Apparel industry 45, 524

Arab Spring 20, 207

Argentina 447

Arts and culture 206

Asia 8, 11, 136, 203, 211, 224, 293, 303, 349, 360, 367, 371, 402, 492, 517, 518, 527, 531–534, 536

Auditing (social auditing) 14, 124, 242, 257, 263, 269, 272, 314, 354, 399, 401 406, 409 411, 413, 415–420, 422, 425, 427, 429, 431, 433, 435, 437, 439, 443, 445, 546, 563, 564.

Australasia 17

Australia 10, 18, 227, 386, 480

Automobile Industry 46, 352, 368, 369, 377, 383, 384,

Autonomy 13, 263, 536

Bangladesh 6, 16, 223, 224, 479, 557

Ban-Ki Moon 69

Belgium 240

Big society 18

Board of directors 125, 285, 312

BOP Market 226, 228–231, 232, 234, 217, 224, 225,

Bottom of the Pyramid (BOP) 32, 213, 217, 222–226, 233, 234, 262, 301

Boycott 44, 45, 119, 214

Branding 13, 14, 54, 213, 218, 245–248, 250

Brazil 17, 211, 221, 264, 316, 352, 447, 480, 502, 503
Brent Spar 45, 505
Bribery, 480, 481, 483
Britain/British 17, 35, 38, 52, 134, 214, 344, 385, 413, 557
Business case for CSR 11, 21, 39, 44, 49, 215, 261, 269, 283, 447
Business ethics 68, 89, 91, 105, 115, 122–124, 126, 127, 409, 549, 566
Business responsibility 5, 71, 80, 83, 84, 522, 524, 527

Calorie labelling 10
Canada 7, 46, 240, 253, 255, 375, 444, 480, 492, 560, 562
Carbon emissions 10, 204, 384
Carbon footprint 10, 352, 386, 549
Carbon market 387
Cause-related marketing 77, 80, 94, 124, 213, 218, 238, 247, 248, 250, 294, 328, 329, 330, 346, 445, 476, 478
Charitable giving 285, 293, 294, 334, 522
Charities 12, 15, 39, 64, 240, 247, 289, 294, 329, 347, 443, 490
Chemical industry, 255, 367, 496, 502–504
Child labour 216, 253, 264, 443
Chile 480
China 7, 15, 19, 20, 118, 119, 211, 216, 221, 227, 231, 255, 265, 352, 361, 362, 365, 369, 384, 480, 492, 532, 560
Chinese Ministry of Commerce 7, 491
Chinese Government 11
Citizenship strategy 483
Civil society 12, 15, 16, 32, 64, 65, 237, 238, 260, 265, 268, 269, 273, 295, 310, 517, 523, 524, 529, 532, 534, 537
Civil society organisation (CSO) 15, 16, 558
Climate change, 17, 69, 349, 350, 352, 355, 362, 371, 372, 373, 374, 375, 376, 377, 378, 379, 380, 381, 382, 384, 387, 388, 394, 395, 532, 549, 561
Code of ethics 116
Collective bargaining 265, 509
Common good 63, 89, 91, 95, 403
Community organisations, 15, 16, 502
Community relations, 261, 294, 312
Competitive advantage, 46, 78–80, 315, 333, 338, 345, 444, 446, 447, 451–454, 456–465, 491

Competitors, 51, 79, 80, 113, 142–144, 148, 151, 157, 231, 237, 241, 242, 250, 277, 318, 336–338, 342, 345, 346, 376, 377, 380, 392, 393, 403, 455, 456. 457, 459, 464, 499, 500, 502, 503, 504, 511, 562
Compliance, 7, 8, 10, 54, 65, 92, 109, 111–113, 118–120, 123, 126, 263, 265, 266, 267, 271, 292, 293, 393, 405, 509, 546
Consequentialist 113, 114, 118, 122
Consumer (s) 11, 32, 44–47, 50–52, 62, 65, 67, 79 80, 109, 112, 113, 120, 141, 143–146, 148–150, 156, 159, 162, 163, 216, 218, 233, 237, 239, 240, 243, 245–247, 249, 266, 269, 271, 278, 280, 282, 284, 285, 312–314, 316, 360, 378, 382, 383, 404, 410, 413, 464, 472, 474, 489, 499, 504, 545, 528, 532, 545, 556, 561
Consumer protection 112
Consumer sovereignty 237
Continental European 17, 533
Corporate governance, 18, 37, 63, 134, 135, 218, 336, 472, 473, 520, 532
Corporate citizenship, 37, 69, 70, 74, 75, 81–84, 124, 277, 285, 292, 302, 305, 403, 499
Corporate community involvement/ investment, 108, 291, 293
Corporate constitutionalism, 81, 94
Corporate image 245
Corporate marketing 246
Corporate misbehaviour 3, 15
Corporate social performance (CSP) 47, 49, 50, 56, 87, 88, 93, 95, 126, 456, 463, 563, 564
Corruption 19, 20, 64, 222, 268, 272, 300, 302, 335, 336
Cross-sector partnerships 294, 491
CSR brand 216, 247
CSR industry 247, 565
CSR initiative 10, 56, 495, 497, 501, 512
CSR institutions 266
CSR instruments 14, 268, 269
CSR market 241, 246, 238, 537
CSR movement 20, 263, 270, 516
CSR practitioners 5, 400
CSR programmes 54, 56, 279–280, 281, 286–289, 300,
CSR standards 4, 484
CSR strategy 15, 28, 39, 50–56, 212, 399, 400, 443, 444, 445, 446, 447,

448, 449, 473, 475, 476, 477, 478,
479, 481, 483, 484, 546, 547, 551,
Customers 3, 6, 13, 46, 49, 51, 52, 56, 67,
79, 80, 88, 118, 135–137, 141, 143,
144, 147–149, 155, 156, 162, 163, 195,
203, 205, 206, 212, 213, 215, 216, 218,
223, 224, 226, 227, 230–235, 240–244,
246, 247, 249, 256, 258, 277, 278, 288,
292, 312, 314, 317, 329, 332, 333, 335,
338, 339, 341, 342, 346, 359, 365, 370,
375, 376– 378, 382, 383, 386, 391,
392, 394, 396, 397, 403, 437, 446, 453,
455, 456, 459, 476, 483, 497, 553, 559,
567

Deforestation 264, 361, 362
Democracy 44, 48, 136, 301, 306, 308,
529, 568
Democratic 30, 204, 238, 306, 316, 428,
434, 436, 438, 481, 506, 525, 534
Democratic Republic of Congo 204
Denmark 242, 405, 406, 410, 415, 530
Developed countries 16–18, 41, 54, 223,
228, 255, 292, 349, 359, 363, 557
Developed economies 18, 360– 362, 365,
370
Developing countries, 18–20, 31, 41, 55,
64, 64, 80, 204, 211, 216, 217, 222,
230, 231, 233, 253, 255, 262, 264,
267, 269, 292, 295, 299, 300, 301,
302, 305, 313, 322, 325, 331, 333,
335, 336, 341, 352, 362, 363, 371,
385, 466, 508, 524, 536, 554
Developing world 15, 17, 19, 40, 41, 212,
222, 223, 227, 300, 367, 371, 402, 558
Digital divide 52, 55, 56, 234
Disclosure 116, 148, 336, 375, 387, 406,
415, 416, 418, 419–422, 476, 477,
483, 484, 523, 524
Discrimination 68, 265, 509, 554
Distributive justice 89
Diversity 5, 21, 66, 255, 325, 379, 394,
410, 415, 417, 556
Domini Social Index 528
Dow Jones Sustainability Index 47, 528,
549

East Asia 136, 492, 517, 518, 527, 531
Eastern Europe 68, 360, 526
Ecological environment, 2, 212, 349, 351,
353, 355, 359, 361, 363, 365, 367,
369, 371, 373, 375, 377, 379, 381,
383, 385, 387, 553.

Ecological footprint 360
Economic development 8, 203, 207, 225,
232, 299, 339, 359
Economics 70, 76, 82, 104, 121, 124,
127, 152, 230, 409, 415, 452, 454, 519
Ecuador 502
Education 17–20, 28–30, 55, 67, 226,
227, 231, 294, 299, 300, 304, 310,
313, 314, 316, 321, 322, 331, 334,
341, 343, 344, 346, 363, 396, 413,
414, 462, 467, 480, 481, 499, 525,
527, 531, 550, 563, 564, 566, 567
Emerging/transitional economies 20, 362
Employee 43, 67, 108, 110, 112, 116,
125, 143–145, 157, 193, 238, 242,
254, 255, 258, 264, 277–281,
283–289, 293, 294, 328–330, 372,
394, 395, 457, 459, 465, 467, 476,
496, 501, 512, 528, 550, 554, 556
Employee volunteering 67, 294, 556
Employers 254, 255, 263, 271, 280, 281,
284, 294, 342, 567
Energy industry 350
England 28, 36
Enlightened self-interest 8, 11, 36, 37, 43,
50, 77, 80, 215, 254, 475
Entrepreneurship 553, 555, 557, 558,
567, 568
Environment, 3, 7, 8, 10, 15, 18, 20, 29,
36, 46, 52, 55, 56, 62, 68, 69, 76, 79,
83, 84, 86, 87, 89, 90, 95, 115, 140,
142, 150, 153–156, 159, 163, 164,
169–171, 174, 179, 185, 186, 192,
194–197, 206, 212, 237, 245, 246,
248, 253, 255, 284, 295, 305, 308,
329, 331, 333, 335, 336, 349–353,
355, 358, 359, 361, 363, 365–367,
369, 371, 373, 375, 377, 379, 380,
381, 383, 385, 387, 396, 404, 422,
429, 432
Environmental challenges 360, 362, 568
Environmental performance 47, 51, 53,
263, 267, 369, 563
Environmental pollution 268
Environmental protection 18, 19, 64, 90,
257, 394, 480, 502
Environmental responsibility 425, 438,
439, 550
Environmental scanning 150, 153, 154,
186
Equality of opportunity 254, 268
Equator Principles 263, 393
Ethical branding 213, 218, 248, 250

Ethical consumers 46, 218, 235, 237, 239, 247, 249, 250
Ethical differentiation 244
Ethical market(s) 238
Ethical marketing 68, 243
Ethical principles 89, 109, 114, 120, 122, 123
Ethical trade 236, 524, 526, 530
Ethics 47, 68, 69, 75, 76, 89, 91, 93, 105, 109, 113–116, 118, 119, 121–124, 126, 127
Ethiopia 556
Europe 4, 15, 18, 28, 29, 38, 68, 69, 158, 203, 211, 254, 293, 317, 358, 402, 405, 409, 413, 527, 528, 530, 536, 561, 566
European Commission 15, 38, 491, 516, 518
European Companies 17, 18
European CSR 17, 528
European Union (EU) 8, 10, 38, 255, 352, 374, 375, 377, 384, 529, 530, 535, 561
Exploitation 43, 55, 217, 225, 363, 509
External verification 406, 410, 416, 419, 420, 422
Externalities 9, 10, 30, 92, 152, 354, 518
Extractive industries 266, 272, 361, 524, 562
Exxon Valdez 192

Fair Trade 46, 51, 52, 236, 238, 240, 243, 247, 248, 268, 271, 272, 301, 411, 456, 506, 537, 556
Fairness 89, 109, 225, 257, 261, 355
Family 14, 33, 183, 207, 281, 361, 396, 402, 465, 545, 546, 547, 556
Far East, 17, 18
Feminist ethics 89
Feminist 47, 89
Finance 4, 12, 249, 266, 324, 376, 383, 387, 391–394, 446, 478, 554
Financial crisis 27–31, 391, 392, 559, 567
Financial performance 49, 63, 77, 87, 126, 152, 215, 401, 402, 464, 467, 495, 511, 512, 563
Financial services industry 391
Food Industry 4, 10, 17, 43, 46, 62, 214, 216, 217, 242, 296, 353, 373, 446
Foreign direct investment (FDI) 19, 207, 262, 322, 371
France 47, 242, 379, 405, 527, 530, 533, 561
Free rider 89, 337, 340, 346

Freedom 17, 48, 89, 164, 182, 265, 329
Freedom of association 265
Full disclosure 116

Genetically modified organisms 17
Germany 28, 54, 324, 333, 368, 527, 530, 533
Global Manufacturing Principles (GMP) 480
Global Reporting Initiative (GRI) 263, 266, 404, 408, 528, 548, 550
Global Sullivan Principle 89, 95
Global warming 17
Globalization 18, 30, 37, 38, 43, 48, 82, 83, 261, 268, 269, 300, 333, 456, 483, 516, 529, 558, 560, 561
Goodwill 49, 329, 330, 341, 342, 344–346, 475, 505
Governance 18, 19, 31, 37, 38, 63, 70, 134, 135, 179, 206, 218, 222, 302, 309, 310, 311, 312, 316, 336, 400, 492, 516, 517, 549, 554
Government 5, 10, 11, 15, 20, 28, 30, 32, 37, 38, 40, 43, 48, 49, 55, 64, 65, 70, 78, 83, 86, 116, 120, 134, 142–149, 151, 156, 157, 159–161, 163, 192, 194, 195, 207, 229, 237, 238, 273, 295, 299–306, 308, 309, 316, 321– 323, 325, 339, 341, 343, 344, 358, 367, 368, 373, 374, 377, 380, 384, 388, 394, 402, 417, 437, 446, 456, 457, 459, 488–492, 499, 503, 516–527, 529–537, 546, 554, 558, 559, 562
Great East Japan earthquake 294, 350, 353
Greenhouse gas emissions 54, 352, 368, 374
Greening of industry 360
Greenwash 246, 369, 375
Gross Domestic Product (GDP) 14, 206, 224, 270

Health and safety 32, 111, 116, 118, 143, 144, 219, 254, 255, 263, 264, 314, 434, 502, 506, 509
Healthcare 4, 17–20, 28, 41, 54, 55, 57, 204–206, 230, 271, 294, 462, 563
Housing 4, 20, 28, 35, 254, 304, 321, 322, 335, 366, 392, 460, 461, 502, 531
Human capital 307, 318, 531, 532
Human resource management 12, 192, 212, 254, 294, 333, 444, 450, 454, 465, 478, 554, 565

Human rights 3, 10, 15, 18, 19, 20, 44, 45, 52, 54, 89, 90, 95, 118, 137, 212, 253, 256, 257, 261, 265, 266, 267, 273, 275, 299, 304, 305, 310, 314, 316, 318, 404, 474, 481, 482, 496, 508, 509, 554, 562

India 4, 79, 119, 205, 226, 227, 228, 229, 230, 231, 232, 264, 291, 293, 333, 353, 362, 353, 362 365, 384, 396, 479, 506, 545
Indigenous peoples 264, 266, 456, 481, 505
Indonesia 264, 365, 480, 489
Industrial revolution 4, 35
Integrative social contract theory 82, 89, 94
Internal marketing 258, 278, 279, 281, 287, 565
Investors 6, 18, 41, 47, 50, 51, 56, 192, 195, 216, 218, 245, 328, 336, 374, 376, 377, 403, 559
ISO 14000/1 364, 385, 482, 484
ISO 26000 256, 404, 563
ISO standards 350

Japan 17, 157, 158, 294, 350, 358, 375, 400, 405, 501, 502, 504
Job security 144, 273
Justice 30, 89, 90, 95, 109, 113, 114, 257, 261, 305, 353, 396, 400, 482, 559

Key Performance Indicators (KPIs) 53, 54
Kyosei, 91

Labour standards 30, 253, 256, 257, 264, 266, 276, 528
Latin America 224, 227, 230, 255, 349, 360, 369, 371, 492, 507
Learning 55, 227, 233, 242, 264, 311, 324, 331, 341, 342, 418, 419, 426, 461, 462, 464, 548, 562
Legal/law 5–8, 10, 20, 30, 43, 71, 75, 77, 86, 87, 104–106, 108–113, 115–127, 148, 168, 172–178, 197, 198, 211, 254, 261, 266, 267, 270, 292, 320, 335, 473, 474, 476, 480, 484, 491, 516, 517, 519, 520, 521, 522, 523, 524, 525, 526, 530, 531, 537, 545, 546, 557–559, 564, 567, 568
Lesotho 204
Licence to operate 32, 554, 556
Life-cycle analysis 382

Lobbying 86, 148, 264, 270, 481, 503
Local Agenda 21 414
Local communities 10, 11, 3, 18, 293, 312, 344, 373, 397, 437, 489, 503, 553, 556
Logistics 12, 353, 385, 454

Malaysia 292, 365, 405
Marketing 11, 12, 77, 80, 86, 116, 118, 163, 214–217, 224, 227, 229, 235, 236, 237, 238, 240, 242, 243, 245, 247, 249, 250, 278, 281, 329, 333, 346, 375, 387, 429, 444, 446, 454, 458, 468, 478, 499, 554, 564
Mexico 134, 224, 321, 394, 397, 447, 460, 461, 506
Microcredit/microfinance 16, 19, 217, 223, 225, 227, 230, 302, 309, 317, 318, 321, 394, 557
Middle East 20, 203, 207, 394, 402, 492
Military 44, 207, 309, 313, 509
Mobile telecommunication 1, 20, 203–209, 227
Morality/moral 32, 36, 42, 56, 68, 79, 85, 90, 95, 106, 109, 113, 114, 115, 116, 117, 120, 122, 123, 134, 138, 168, 172–178, 181, 182, 196, 197, 198, 210, 267, 268, 270, 292, 301, 370, 413, 430, 434, 435, 475, 480, 516, 519
Morocco 344
Mozambique 204
Multinational Corporation (MNCs) 17, 18, 19, 122, 222, 225, 228, 231, 232, 234, 257, 304, 322, 431, 432, 536

Natural resources 331, 333–335, 351, 353, 361, 491, 549
Netherlands 7, 10, 45, 240, 360, 375, 527
New social movement 559
Nigeria 18, 44, 45, 304, 505
Nobel Peace Prize 16
Non-governmental organization (NGO) 5– 7, 10, 12, 15, 16, 18, 41, 44, 53, 267, 316–319, 376, 387, 461, 462, 476
North America 29, 203, 395, 409, 413, 566
North Africa 20, 207
Northern Europe 136
Norway 410
Nuclear power 185, 379

OECD Guidelines for Multinationals 256
Ogoni people 310, 505

Oil industry 3, 44, 45, 134, 146, 163, 192, 267, 301, 303, 353, 356, 361, 373, 377, 374, 376, 377, 378, 381, 382, 383, 386, 446, 524
Olympics, 330
Organizational learning 418, 419
Organizational structure 378, 510, 546
Outsourcing 227–229, 254, 309, 332, 336, 385, 466
Owners13, 29, 134, 135, 141–144, 146, 147, 168, 183, 192, 195, 282, 474, 519

Participation 70, 173, 234, 261, 269, 280, 286, 301, 304, 353, 383, 395, 461, 465, 467, 503, 504, 522, 536
Paternalism 36, 527, 529, 531
Paternalistic capitalism 36, 37, 42, 43, 55
Peru 230, 505
Pharmaceutical industry 31, 39, 40, 41, 42, 43, 48, 54, 56, 57, 120, 230, 301, 324, 344, 347, 476,
Philanthropy/philanthropic 4, 6, 9, 11, 17, 36, 39, 41, 64, 67, 71, 77, 78, 83, 105–108, 110, 115, 117, 122, 124, 127, 190, 218, 247, 262, 278, 291–295, 300, 302, 306, 312, 314, 321, 328–348, 396, 412, 461, 458, 466, 473, 475, 478, 480, 495, 498, 502, 503, 507, 519, 521, 523, 527, 529, 531, 546, 547, 550, 555–557
Philippines 227, 292, 500, 508, 524
Philosophy/philosophical 11, 42, 68, 70, 75, 77, 82, 87, 90, 91, 113, 136, 140, 156, 159, 160, 162, 164, 212, 294, 352, 354, 410, 427, 429, 430, 434, 437, 463, 464
Politics/political 4, 7, 8, 18, 19, 20, 21, 28, 30, 36, 42, 44, 45, 64, 68–70, 76, 80, 81, 82, 83, 85, 90, 92, 93, 94, 95, 96, 142, 143, 144, 145, 147, 148, 149, 150, 152, 193, 194, 195, 207, 222, 267, 268, 269, 270, 302, 304, 305, 306, 309, 310, 311, 313, 317, 318, 320, 321, 322, 325, 352, 354, 359, 363, 374, 376, 399, 400, 402, 482, 490, 516, 517, 519, 520, 537, 566, 567
Pollutants/pollute/polluting/pollution 3, 10, 36, 38, 45, 63, 79, 111, 117, 120, 235, 237, 268, 292, 331, 335, 349, 350, 351, 352–353, 358, 359–370, 394, 403, 472,
Population growth 349, 359, 361–363
Portfolio analysis 150–152, 154

Poverty 1, 37, 63, 206, 221, 227, 228, 234, 243, 261, 262, 302, 306, 317, 319, 320, 353, 359, 361–363, 366, 370, 371, 400, 459, 480, 496, 502, 506
Power 17, 32, 44, 48, 49, 64, 76, 80–82, 93, 94, 96, 134, 137, 146–150, 169, 171, 174–198, 207, 208, 216, 223, 224, 226, 228, 230, 232, 233, 237, 249, 268–282, 292, 300, 301, 305, 306, 310, 316, 320, 349, 363, 368, 371, 375, 376, 379, 385, 566–568
Pressure groups 44, 245, 437
Pricing 41, 54, 203, 215, 272, 468
Principles 81, 85, 86, 89, 91, 93, 107, 114, 117, 168. 169, 180, 181, 187, 196, 272, 294, 417–421, 526, 560
Prisoners' dilemma 161
Privacy 52, 164, 204
Private sector 12, 14, 16, 32, 38, 261, 301, 302, 303, 306, 311, 313, 314, 320, 325, 534, 568
Procurement 12, 47, 206, 229, 385, 454, 456, 522, 523, 529, 530
Product quality 46, 243
Product safety 20, 32, 38, 119, 456
Production 12, 17, 80, 86, 163, 212, 214, 237, 249, 33, 334, 340, 352, 353, 358, 362, 365, 369, 372, 374, 376, 381, 382, 383, 385, 394, 410, 436, 477, 478, 479, 481, 498, 507
Profit 6–8, 13, 14, 32, 41–43, 49, 53, 61, 63–65, 67, 93, 111, 170, 203, 223, 229, 314, 324, 330, 347, 379, 380, 396, 414, 426, 429, 436, 443, 451, 467, 474, 475, 478, 481, 490, 536, 546, 547, 554–557, 559
Profitability 11, 32, 36, 63, 91, 120, 320, 457, 468, 503
Property rights 40, 135, 181, 387, 474, 531
Public relations 6, 120, 148, 153, 163, 233, 293, 306, 308, 312, 316, 328, 345, 346, 404, 443, 478, 501, 525
Public affairs 39, 86, 148, 153, 163, 174, 192, 474, 565
Public interest 4, 16, 30, 31, 61, 62, 65, 86, 314, 412–414
Public opinion 65, 350, 375
Public legitimacy 12, 15
Public policy 74, 85, 86, 93, 95, 149, 174, 302, 304, 305, 308, 322, 371, 481, 490, 508, 517, 519

Public sector 1, 12, 14, 37, 47, 299, 305, 313, 314, 409, 522
Public service 14, 301, 302, 305–310, 314, 320,-323, 325.
Purchasing 45–47, 224, 226, 228, 245, 256, 363, 376, 413, 498

Race to the bottom 30, 31
Ralph Nader 151
Rawlsian principles 89
Recession 4, 29, 31, 48, 458, 465, 467
Recycled products 238
Regulation 3, 10, 15, 17, 19, 30–32, 43, 64, 65, 85, 92, 152, 153, 157, 186, 255, 273, 301, 302, 309, 318, 352, 354, 358, 368, 372, 374, 375–377, 384, 399, 405, 561–563
Religion/ religious 75, 82, 114, 117, 193, 316, 475, 484, 524, 527, 529, 531
Reporting (Environmental, Ethical, CSR, Social, Sustainability Reports and Reporting) 4, 13, 14, 20, 22, 47, 51, 52, 192, 242, 247, 257, 263, 267, 312, 354, 371, 399, 400, 401–442, 443, 445, 464, 476, 477, 478, 482, 483, 523, 524, 525, 546, 548, 551, 554, 561, 563, 564, 565
Reputation 44–47, 50, 80, 135, 152, 236, 243–245, 253, 258, 282, 283, 294, 330, 338, 342, 348, 375, 387, 546, 562
Reputational risk management 213, 218, 246, 247, 250
Respect 5, 8, 10, 19, 42, 49, 54, 78, 81, 86, 91, 95, 106, 107, 109, 114, 480–484, 490, 505, 506, 518, 548, 554
Retail 43, 46, 152, 224, 242, 263, 271, 279, 280, 402, 412, 413, 506
Rights 3, 10, 15, 18–20, 40, 44, 45, 52, 53–55, 90–93, 95, 109, 113, 114, 117, 118, 123, 481, 482, 489, 500, 508, 509, 531, 554, 562
Russia 17, 20, 310, 352, 394

SA8000, 90, 265, 268, 269
Scandinavia 136, 175, 409, 527
Second World War 29, 527
Security 44, 69, 144, 221, 266, 273, 299, 300, 304, 313, 315, 349, 353
Self-regulation 15, 32, 65, 273, 354, 399, 482, 488, 489, 491, 493, 495, 497, 499, 501, 503–505, 507, 509, 511, 517, 519, 521, 525, 527, 537, 562

Selling 32, 116, 120, 149, 155, 215, 222, 236, 240, 359, 396
Shareholder 1, 6, 11, 12, 13, 20, 28, 29, 30, 42, 43, 44, 48, 49–51, 55, 56, 57, 62, 63, 64, 65, 67, 77, 78, 94, 109, 113, 134, 135, 156, 236, 301, 306, 312, 314, 315, 332, 336, 376, 388, 392, 401, 403, 437, 475, 476, 477, 478, 479, 484, 485, 520
Shareholder value 42, 43, 49, 77, 78, 94, 135, 236, 301, 314, 428, 430–432, 474
Singapore 291
Small and medium-sized enterprise (SMEs)/small business, 12, 13, 14, 22, 72, 207, 224, 226, 297, 310, 321, 343, 356, 404, 473, 524, 556, 557
Social enterprise/entrepreneur 6, 8, 12, 15, 16, 39, 490, 557
Social auditing 14, 124, 263, 269, 411
Social capital 232, 319, 452, 460–462, 467
Social contract theory 42, 82, 83, 89, 94
Social marketing 118, 278
Socially responsible investing (SRI) 47, 481
Solidarity 243
Sourcing 14, 52, 215, 216, 243, 247, 265, 281, 322, 522
South Africa 18, 40, 55, 149, 194, 195, 204–206, 221, 230, 264, 293, 301, 312, 413, 480
South Korea 17, 531, 532, 534
Soviet Union (Former) 360
Stakeholder analysis 142, 153, 196
Stakeholder democracy 136
Stakeholder engagement 37, 38, 52, 53, 404, 406, 424–428, 430, 431, 436–439, 445, 562
Stakeholder management 11, 74, 86–89, 95, 124, 140–167, 173–175, 445, 447, 468
Stakeholder map 141–143, 153, 155, 158, 159, 454
Stakeholder model 134, 135
Stakeholder theory 88, 89, 133–202 197, 458
Stakeholders 11, 52, 54, 113, 125, 133–202, 266, 270, 403, 417, 419, 420, 425, 432, 434, 437, 438, 448, 453, 455, 456, 458–460, 466, 477, 483, 505, 508
Standard of living 225, 239, 266, 363, 366, 371

Stewardship 15, 79, 241, 268, 351–353, 365–369, 405, 526, 562
Strategic CSR 247, 278, 458
Strategic management 88, 134, 136, 140, 141, 150, 152–155, 405, 446, 447, 451, 452, 463, 468, 472, 473
Strategic philanthropy 108, 124, 291, 293, 294, 328–330, 461
Strategic planning 140, 149, 152, 154, 163, 378, 466, 509
Strategic review 150, 152–154
Suppliers 6, 11, 13, 19, 45, 47, 52, 54–56, 67, 79, 86, 88, 134, 147, 155, 216, 245, 256, 263, 333, 336, 339, 353, 384, 385, 455, 459, 464, 476, 479, 491, 525
Supply Chain 8, 20, 47, 206, 216, 228, 237, 256, 261, 265, 301, 314, 315, 317–319, 353, 373, 374, 377, 378, 380– 387, 443, 526
Survival economies 361, 362
Sustainability 8, 14, 47, 64, 69, 74, 90, 91, 124, 203, 206, 241, 242, 247, 349, 351–354, 358, 359, 362–365, 367–371, 373, 378, 392, 403, 404, 420, 424, 425, 428–431, 433, 436, 437, 439, 445, 478, 481, 489, 498, 506, 566
Sustainable development 7, 16, 19, 37, 69, 79, 90, 91, 95, 261, 268, 335, 353, 361, 363, 364, 366, 368, 426, 516, 528, 532

Taiwan 17
Tanzania 204, 205, 311, 344
Tax 30, 63, 204, 271, 272, 293, 329, 333, 366, 396, 397, 401, 508, 522, 523, 560
Terrorist 38, 39, 140
Thailand 291
Third Sector 12, 15
Tobacco industry, 3, 47, 50, 116, 117, 126, 214, 328,
Total quality management 364, 547
Traditional CSR 66, 67, 292, 555, 556, 564
Trust 12, 13, 32, 146, 161, 244, 294, 311, 312, 386, 453, 461, 467, 489, 502, 504, 510, 545
Turkey 338, 480

UN Conference on Trade and Development (UNCTAD) 270

UN norms 266, 267
Unions 6, 142, 143, 144, 146, 148, 149, 150, 155, 156, 170, 195, 254, 255, 256, 259, 265, 266, 268, 269, 273, 395, 493, 528
United Kingdom (UK) 6, 10, 18, 243, 254, 395
United Nations (UN) 1, 19, 42, 62, 69, 89, 90, 218, 224, 233, 256, 266, 267, 268, 299, 312, 324, 341, 352, 387, 422, 482, 484, 562
United Nations Declaration on Human Rights and the Environment 482,
United Nations Environment Program (UNEP) 422
United Nations Framework Convention on Climate Change (UNFCCC) 352, 368,
United Nations Global Compact 69, 89, 95, 256, 257, 263, 265, 266, 267, 272, 285, 299, 304, 489, 526, 528, 546, 548
United Nations' Millennium Developments' Goals 19
United States of America (USA) 4, 6, 8, 14, 17, 28–30, 71, 134, 204, 205, 211, 271, 227–231, 236, 336, 342, 358, 360, 362, 480. 492
Universal Declaration of Human Rights 90, 259, 266
Utilitarianism 95, 107, 109, 114, 123

Values 4–9, 11, 44, 49, 51–53, 55, 75, 76, 84, 90, 92, 93, 115, 140, 181, 184, 186, 192, 194, 217, 240, 243, 244, 245, 248, 250, 258, 277, 281, 282, 288, 320, 329, 403, 410, 413, 417, 419, 429, 434, 452, 453, 462–467, 475, 479, 484, 490, 506, 509, 510, 529, 545, 565–567
Venture capital 343, 556
Vietnam 255, 294
Virtue 36, 185, 193, 215
Voluntarism 10, 136, 159, 160, 162, 192

Western Europe, 17, 492, 517, 518, 526–529, 531–533, 536
Working conditions 4, 15, 19, 28, 253–256, 261, 262, 264, 265, 322, 434, 480, 491

Author Index

Aaronson, S. A. 19, 530
Abell, D. 166
Abrahamson, E. 377
ACCA. 425
AccountAbility. 426, 430
ACCSR. 564, 565
Ackerman, R. 84
Acquier, A. 527
Adams, C. A. 432, 437
Agle, B. R 14, 77, 87, 95, 134, 137, 292,
    458, 459, 461; also co-author of
    section168–202,
Ahlstedt, L. 172, 177
Ainina, M. F. 478
Albareda, L. J. 521–529
Albert, S. 463
Aldrich, H. E. 455
Alexy, R. 434, 435
Alford, H. 91, 95
Alkhafaji, A. F. 170, 172, 177
Allen, D. B. 10, 78, 239, 457; also co-
    author of section 451–472
Allianz/WWF. 383
Allison, G. 165
Alsop, R. 49
Altman, B, 75, 83
Amable, B. 520, 527
Amit, R. 455
Amsden, A. H. 531
Andrew, L. 234
Andrews, K. R. 104, 472, 475, 483

Andriof, J, 83, 97
Angelidis, J. A. 105, 475
Apostolakou, A. 521
Aragon-Correa, J. A. 373
Araki, T. 136
Argandoña, A. 89, 91
Argenti, P. A. 506
Athos, A. 152
Auger, P. 218
Aupperle, K. E. 104, 105, 108, 125
Austin, J. E. 459, 462, 495
Avolio, B. J. 457
Ayres, I. 524

Babbie, Earl. R. 125
Bailey, D. 429, 430, 432
Balch, O. 546
Ball, A. 14
Balzarova, M.A. 444
Bamber, C. J. 444
Banerjee, S. B. 516, 518, 519
Bansal, P. 373, 464, 510
Barnett, M. L. 497, 503, 535
Barney, J. B. 79, 452, 460, 461, 463, 464
Bartley, T. 489
Barton, D. 490, 559
Basu, K. 518, 535
Battilana, J. 528
Bauer, R. 84
Baumann, H. 460
Bayon, R. 386

Beard, D. W. 455
Beaujolin, F. 527
Bebbington, J. 16, 425, 428, 429, 431, 433, 436–438, 440
Bendell, J. 353
Bendheim, C. 87
Bennett, M. 432–436
Berger, I. E. 379
Berkhout, F. 376
Berle, A. A. 13
Berman, S. 77, 87
Bernstein, S. 562
BERR. 7
Bertels, S. 503, 510
Berthoin-Antal, A. 524, 530
Best, M. 234
Bettis, R. A. 463
Bhambri, A. 184
Bhattacharya, C. B. 45, 218. 246, 257; also co-author of section 277– 290
Biehl, M. 564
Biggart, N. 530
Birchall, J. 376
Blair, J. D. 172, 174, 176, 178, 459
Blomstrom, R, L. 104
Boatright, J. R. 105
Bodwell, C. 474, 476, 482, 484
Boguslaw, J. 478
Boiral, O. 375
Boli, J. 528
Bollier, D. 118
Boltanski, L. 519
Bonini, S. M. J. 376
Bourlakis, M. 256
Bowen, H. R. 74, 518, 519
Bowerman, M. 431
Bowie, N. 88, 89, 172, 173, 176
Boxenbaum, E. 528
Boyce, G. 432
Boyer, R. 520, 527
Bradbury, H. 351
Bradley, J. 437, 438
Braithwaite, J. 524
Brammer, S. 17, 293
Brams, S. 166
Brandy, F. 94–96
Branzei, O. 548
Brass, D. J. 509
Brenner, S. N. 171, 172, 173, 174, 176, 187
Brewer, T. 85
Brocklebank, C. 431
Brodzinski, J. D. 478

Broekhoff, D. 385, 387
Brooke, J. 119
Brooks, L. 119
Brown, A. 474
Brown, D. 402
Brown, T. J. 5, 45
Browning, L. 396
Brummer, J . 75
Bryne, J. A. 116
Buchholz, R. A. 105, 121
Buchko, A. 455
Buhr, N. 432
Burke, B. 78
Burton, B. K. 89, 105, 479, 483
Butler, Jr. J. K. 105
Buysse, K. 373

Cadbury, A. 117
Campbell, J. L. 449, 535
Cannon, T. 68
Capron, M. 527
Carbon Trust. 386
Carey, J. 91
Carrier, J. 567
Carroll, A. B. 5, 23, 60, 70, 73, 75, 83, 87, 89, 95, 104–109, 110–114, 116–119, 121, 108, 172, 173, 176–179, 190, 195, 291, 292, 472, 475, 480, 483, 521, 569; also co-author of section 104–132
Cartland, A. 564, 565
Cashore, B. 562
Cassel, D. 89
Castka, P. 444
CDP. 375
Centre for Corporate Public Affairs. 474
Chakravarthy. R. 165
Chamberlain, N. W. 519
Chan, V. 532
Chang, H. J. 520, 531
Chappell, T. 238
Chapple, W. 291, 292, 526
Charan, R. 152
Cheney, G. 245
Chiappello, E. 519
Child, J. 29
Chrisman, J. 14
Christensen, C. 79, 80, 94, 460
Christensen, J. 567
Christensen, L. T. 245
Clair, J. A. 351
Clark, A. 396

Clarkson, M. 127, 171, 173, 175, 177, 178, 183, 476, 477
Clay, J. 491
CNN. 120
Cobb, R. 182, 238, 246
Cochran, P. 87, 95
Cochran, P. L. 105
Colbert, B. 90
Collinson, D. 16
Commission of the European Communities. 6, 10, 15, 69
Context. 404
Cook, J. 376
Cool, K. 460
CORE. 6
Cornell, B. 172, 173, 177
Cowton, C. J. 218
Craig, T. 79
Cramer, J. 527
Crane A. 68, 69 70, 136, 237, 238, 243, 244, 245, 247, 249, 293, 490, 491, 518, 522, 525, 535, 564, 566; also author of section 235–252 and co-author of section 299–328
Creed, W. E. D. 464
Crook, C. 30
Crouch, C. 518, 520, 535, 568
Cunningham, P. H. 379
CWS. 248
Cyert, R. M. 179

Dacin, P. A. 5, 45
Daft, R. 186, 468
Dahl, R. L, 180, 184
Dahl, R.H. 520
Danish Commerce and Companies Agency. 405
Dart, R. 490
Davenport, K. 414
Davies, I. A. 243
Davis, J. J. 246
Davis, K. 5, 81–82, 93, 94, 104, 114, 118, 181
Dawkins, J. 477
Dawkins, R. 187
De Bakker, F. G. A. 558
De Colle, S. 135
De George, R. 114, 115, 123
de Graaf, G. 14
Deeg, R. 520
Deegan, C. 427, 429, 430
Deephouse, D. L. 137
Delmas, M.A. 373

Demmy, S. 476
Den Hond, F. 558
Dennis, B. S. 105
Derry, R. 122
Desmond, J. 237, 249
Dess, G. G. 239, 455
Devinney, T. M. 218
Dey, C. 243, 430, 436
DeYoung, K. 120
Dierckx, L. 460
Dill, W. 147
Dillard, J. 402
DiMaggio, P. 179, 181, 528
DiNitto, E. 476
Dion, M. 83
Djelic, M. L. 534
Dlugolecki, A. 374
Doh, J. P. 15, 17, 481
Dolan, P. 464
Donaldson, T. 42, 82, 83, 88, 89, 94, 95, 114, 116, 123, 134, 138, 173, 178, 179, 476
Donati, P. 92
Donnelly, J. 90
Dore, R. 517, 531
Doty, D. H. 526
Downey, H. K. 186
Drucker, P. 476
Drumwright, M. E. 379
Duncan, R. B. 455
Dunfee, T. 82, 83, 89, 94, 123
Dunn, C. 89
Dunne, S. 464

Eberlein, B. 561
Eckhardt, G. M. 218
Eesley, C. 373
Egg Corporation of Australia. 10
Eisenhardt, K. M. 461
Elankumaran, S. 4, 552
Elder, C. D. 182
Elfenbein, H. A. 512
Elkington, J. 15,
Ellmen, E. 118
Emery, F. 166
Emmett, D. 166
Emshoff, J. 86, 164, 165
Enderle, G. 473
Environics International. 475, 480
Epstein, E, M. 104
Ernst & Young. 373
Eschle, C. 558
Estes, R. 472, 473, 483

Ethical Performance. 5
Etzioni, A. 96, 180, 184, 187, 198
Evan, W, 88, 89, 95, 143, 165, 172, 173, 177, 198
Evans, P. 531
Evans, R. 430, 436; also co-author of section 409–424
Eyestone, R. 182, 184

Fadil, P. A. 480
Falkenberg, L, 490, 491; also co-author of section 495–515
Farh, J. L. 479, 483
Feinberg, J. 114
Fennel, S. 15
Fernandez Young, A. 564
Ferrell, O. C. 479
File, K. M. 476
Financial Times. 116
Fiss, P. C. 526
Fitzpatrick, D. 396
Fligstein, N. 517, 520, 537
Follesdal, A. 516
Fort, T. 91
Fouts, P. A. 377, 460
Fowler, R. 385, 387
Fox, M, 476
Fox, T. 521, 523
Francken, M. 375
Frank, R. 556
Frederick, R. E. 114; also author of
Frederick, W. C.75, 93, 186, 195, 197
Frederick, W. E. 118
Freeman, I. 16
Freeman, R. E. 86, 88, 89, 90, 95, 114, 115, 119, 133–134, 135, 136, 165, 166, 172, 173, 175, 176, 184, 198, 430, 458, 459, 476, 535; also author of section 140–168
French, J. R. P. 180
Frenkel, M. 534
Friedman, A. L. 218, 430
Friedman, M, 27, 30, 92, 94, 104, 292, 474, 482, 519, 525, 554
Friedman, R, 92
Fries, J. 405
Friesen, P. H. 458
Frooman, J. 77, 458, 459, 473
Frynas, J. G. 19
Fukukawa, K. 531

Galaskiewicz, J. 509
Galbraith, J. K. 237

Galbreath, J. 446, 447, 449; also author of 472–487
Gamble, A. 135
Ganesan, S. 216
Gann, D. M. 376
Garner, J. 532
Garriga, E. 69, 214, 402; also co-author of section 74–104
Gedajlovic, E. 16
Geertz, C. 463
Gendron, C. 536
George, M. 216
Gerth, K. 532
Ghoshal, S. 460
Gibbon, P. 516
Gilbert, D. R. 173, 89, 114, 115, 119, 176
Gillenwater, M. 385, 387
Gioia, D. A. 29
Gladwell, M. 467
Gladwin, T. 90, 97
GlaxoSmithKline. 41
Glick, W. H. 526
Global Sullivan Principles, 89, 95
Goll, I. 463, 465
Gond, J. P 518, 527, 528, 535, 538, 564; also co-author of section 516–544
Goodman, N. 165
Goodpaster, K. 91
Googins, B. 499, 505, 507, 510
Gordenker, L. 481
Goshal, S. 29
Gourevitch, P.A. 532
Graafland, J.J. 254
Granovetter, M. 187, 520
Grant, E. A. 564
Grant. R. M. 461, 468, 564
Graves, S. 77, 87, 474–476, 482, 484
Gray, B. 85
Gray, R. 16, 428, 430, 432, 436
Grayson, D. 12, 293, 558
Green, R. 122
Greenfield, W.M. 479
Greening, D. 85, 476
Greer, C. R. 186
Greve, H. R. 509
Grey, R. 16
Griffin, J. J. 77, 482
Grodzins, M. 530
Grubb, M. 379
Gruber, V. 218
Guah, T. R. 17
Guerrera, F. 135

Habermas, J. 406, 434, 435
Habisch, A. 475, 527, 529
Hall, P. 517, 520, 527
Hambrick, D. C. 186
Hamel, G. 243
Hamilton, G. 531
Hamilton, K. 386
Hammond, A. 80, 94, 217, 460, 558; also
    co-author of section 221–235
Handy, C. 29
Hanlon, G. 518
Hannan, M. T. 179
Harrington, K. V. 105
Harrington, L. K. 481
Harrison, J. 79, 135, 461, 535
Hart, S. 79, 80, 94, 351, 354, 373, 456,
    460; also author of 358–371
Harte, G. 429, 430, 432
Hartman, L. P. 567
Harvey, F. 387
Hashmi, A. 4, 552
Hasnaoui, A. 16
Hatfield, J. D. 108
Hayibor, S. 77
Heald, M. 75, 518, 522
Hegarty, W. H. 105, 479, 483
Heinzl, J. 120
Hemingway, C. A. 475, 476
Henderson, D. 29,
Henriques, A. 404
Henriques, I. 458
Herman, S. W. 114
Hertin, J. 376
Hertz, N. 519, 525
Hess. D. 293
Hession, E. 437, 438
Heugens, P. P. M. A. R. 461
Higgins, D. 386
Higgins, M. 80
Hildebrand, D. 246
Hill, C. W. L. 172, 173, 177, 186
Hillman, A. 79, 454
Hintz, G. 376
Hirschman, A. 166
Hockerts, K. 242, 243
Hodge, M. 516, 530
Hodges, A. 12, 293, 558
Hofer, C. 166
Hoffman, A. J. 349, 372, 376, 379, 558,
    561
Hoffman, R. 444
Hoffman, W. M. 114
Hofstede, G. 479

Hollingsworth, R. 520
Hopwood, A. 405
Hosenball, M. 116
Hosmer, L. T. 566
Houlder, V. 396
House, J. C. 384
Howard, B. 521
Howard, J. 235
Howard, R. 465
Howell, J. M. 453
Hoy, F. 472, 483
HSBC. 392
Huber, G. 455
Hudsonvoice. 120
Hult, G. T. M. 464
Humphrey, C. 431, 437, 438
Hunt, K. 431, 437, 438
Husted, B. W. 10, 78, 239, 459;
    also co-author of section
    451–472
Hyman, J. 385, 387

Ibrahim, N. 105, 475
Igalens, J. 525, 527
IIRC. 405
Industry Canada. 444
Ingram, P. 463
Ioannou, I. 561
ISEA. 426

Jackson, G. 520, 521
Jackson, J. 105, 237
Jaffe, A.B. 384
Jahnukainen, I. 172, 177
Jamali, D. 15, 353, 535
Jennings, M. M. 479, 482
Jensen, M. 78, 92, 94, 139, 179
Johns, G. 481
Johnson, C. 531
Jones Christensen, L. 567
Jones, R. E. 105
Jones, T. 75, 84–85, 87, 95, 96, 170, 172,
    173, 177, 179, 182, 184, 186, 292,
    461, 464, 516, 518
Jonker, J. 527, 529
Josephson, M. 115
Joyner, B. E. 475

Kahneman, D. 464
Kaku, R. 91, 95
Kallio, T. J. 520
Kaltenheuser, S. 118
Kanari, N. 352

Kang, N. 520, 521, 528, 532; also co-author of section 516–544
Kant, I. 88, 89, 95, 96, 107, 114, 434
Kanter, R. M. 460
Kapstein, E. B. 48
Kaptein, M. 87
Karnani, A. 29, 32, 215, 217, 489; also author of section 61–65
Kay, S. 77
Kazmi, B. A. 519
Keats, B. W. 455, 457
Keim, G. 77, 79, 454
Kelly, G. 135
Kempshall, M. 91
Kennelly, J. 90, 97
Keshishian, T. 15, 353
Keykhah, M. 374
Kim, E. M. 531
Kinderman, D. 560
King, A. 499, 375, 507
Kitson, A. 248
Kjaergaard, C. 516
Klassen, R. D. 460
Klein, N. 39
Klonoski, R. 104
Kluckhohn, C. 463
Knickerbocker, F. T. 377
Koenig, R. 166
Kok, P. 474
Kolk, A. 372, 373, 374, 376, 377, 379, 561; also co-author of section 371–390
Korschun, D. 257, 258; also co-author of section 277– 290
Kotha, S. 87
KPMG. 402
Kramer, M. 23, 73, 78, 94, 97, 244, 295, 372, 379, 444, 497, 519, 558; also co-author of section 328–348
Kreiner, P. 184
Kurkchiyan, M. 522, 538
Kusku, F. 478
Kuznetsov, A. 20
Kuznetsova, O. 20

La Mure, L. T. 481
Lager, F. 118, 238
Lane Keller, K. 244
Langtry, B. 173, 174, 176, 177
Lansing, P. 119
Lapointe, A. 536
Lash, J. 373, 375, 376
Lasthuizen, K. 14
Laufer, W. S. 404

Laughlin, R. 436
Leca, B. 519
Lehman, G. 432, 434
Lenox, M.J. 373
Leroy, P. 375
L'Etang, J. 104
Levitt, T, 97, 104, 519, 525
Levy, D. 372, 373, 375, 376, 377, 379
Lewis, E. 247
Lewis, L. 433, 435
Lewis, S. 477
Lindblom, C. E. 519
Lindgreen, A. 5
Litz, R. 79.
Livesey, S. 245, 247
Logan, D. 476
Logsdon, J. 75, 78, 83, 84, 93, 94
London, T. 497
Lorange, P. 154, 155, 472
Lowry, R. P. 118
Lozano, M. 521–529
Luce, D. 166

Macalister, T. 396
Maclagan, P. W. 475, 476
Maclay, C. M. 234
MacLeod, W. 476
MacMillan, J. 149
Mafune, Y. 531
Mahon, J. 77, 91, 182, 482
Maignan, I. 71, 464, 479, 527
Maiguashca, B. 558
Mair, J. 557
Mak, H. 250
Makower, J, 104
Mallot, M. J. 104
March, J. G. 179
Mares-Dixon, J. 465
Margolis, J. D. 49, 477, 482, 485, 512, 520
Marinetto, M. 527
Maritain, J. 90, 91
Markowitz, L. 520
Marshall, S. 402
Marti, I. 557
Martin, R. L. 49, 57
Martinez, J. L. 457
Mason, P. A. 186
Matten, D. 5, 17, 18, 28, 68–70, 72, 136, 254, 293, 449, 490, 518, 520–522, 525, 527, 561, 567; also co-author of 391–398
Mattin, J. A. 461
Maurer, M. 444

McBarnet, D. 518, 520–525, 528, 538
McCarthy, A. D. 105
McCawley, T. 464
McCrudden, C. 522, 530
McDonald, J. 166
McGill, A. 84
McGowan, R. 91
McGuire, J. 104, 516, 519, 522
McIntosh, M. 83
McKay, J. A. 465
McKenna, R. 474
McMahon, T. 75
McWilliams, A. 77, 214, 460, 516, 518,
    519, 522
Meadows, D. H. 428, 432
Meadows, D. L. 428, 432
Means, G. C. 13
Meckling, W. 78, 179
Mele, D. 91, 525; also co-author of
    section 74–104
Mendonca, L.T. 376
Menon, A, 80, 94, 247, 351, 464
Menon, J. 392
Merton, R. 143
Meyer, A. 243
Meyer, G. D. 105
Meyer, J. W. 179, 375, 528
Micheletti, M. 518
Middlemiss, N. 244, 246
Midttun, M. 516
Miles, G. 472
Miles, R. 165, 464, 457
Miles, S. 218, 430
Miller, A. 239
Miller, D. 455, 457
Miller, R. L. 105
Miller, S. G. 105
Mintzberg, H. T. 526
Mirvis, P. 499, 505, 507, 510
Mitchell, A. 238, 244
Mitchell, R. K. 14, 77, 87, 458, 459, 464;
    also co-author of section 168–202
Mohin, T. 564
Molina, O. 528
Monbiot, G. 525
Monks, R. 376
Montanari, J. 80, 94
Montiel, I. 375
Moon, J. 5, 17, 18, 28, 70, 72, 254, 291,
    292, 297, 449, 492, 516, 518–522,
    524–528, 530, 531, 532, 533, 536,
    538, 564, 566, 567; also co-author of
    section 516–544

Moore, C. 522, 524
MORI. 45
Morsing, M. 14, 530
Moss Kanter, R. 557
Mouck, T. 432
Murray, K. 80, 94, 475, 476
Muthuri, J. 292, 526
Muzzio, D. 166

Naccache, P. 519
Nadkami, A. G. 548
Nahapiet, J. 460
Nasi, J. 136, 172, 173, 175, 176, 177, 195
Nasi, S.195
National Consumer Council. 246
Naughton, K. 116
Naughton, M, 91, 95
Neergaard, P. 482
Negandhi, A. 165
Nelson, K. A. 119
Neron, P. Y. 70, 66
Neu, D. 429, 430, 432
Neubaum, D. 16
Newell, P. 292
Newman, H. K. 557
Nicholls, A. 16, 243
Nicholson, M. J. 119
Nielson, A. 10
Nioche, J. P. 525
Nix, T. H. 174
Nix, T. W. 459
Norris, G. 429
Novak, M. 481
Nystrom, P. 165

O'Dwyer, B. 16, 403, 429, 430, 431, 432,
    437, 427, 430, 438
O'Neil, H. M. 105
O'Higgins, E. R. E. 472
O'Reilly III, C. 464
Öberseder, M. 218
Ogden, S. 77, 87
Okereke, C. 372, 376
Orlitzky, M. 215, 482, 566, 567
Orpen, C. 479, 483
Orru, M. 530
Orts, E. 122
Ouchi, W. 158
Overdorf, M. 79
Owen, D. L. 403, 431, 437, 438

Pablo, A. L. 464
Paine, L. S. 121

Palazzo, G, 70, 490, 516, 518, 526, 535, 536
Palmatier, R. W. 216
Paolella, M. S. 376
Parent, M. M. 137
Parker, B. 508
Parker, C. 525
Parks, D. 186
Parma, B. L. 135
Parsons, T. 76, 92, 181
Pascale, R. 152
Paul, K. 195
Paulson, A. 120
Pavelin, S. 17, 293
Payne, D. 475
Pedersen, E. R. 482
Pedwell, K. 429, 430, 432
Peirce, E. 567
Peloza, J. 503, 510; also co-author of section 495–515
Peng, M. W. 449
Penrose, E. T. 451
Peppet, S. R. 465
Perez, E. 396
Perez, R. 472, 483
Perrini, F. 14
Perrow, C. 187
Peters, T. 162
Peterson, S.R. 384
Petrick, J. A. 478
Pettigrew, A. M. 463
Pfeffer, J. 166, 179, 180, 186, 422, 459, 464
Phillips, R. 89, 95, 134
Pineau, J. L. 352
Pinkse, J. 372, 374, 376, 379, 561; also co-author of section 371–390
Pinkston, T. S. 105, 464
Pirie, I. 532
Pisano, G. 79, 461
Pleggenkuhle-Miles, E. G. 449
Po, Ip. 20
Poitras, G. 110
Pojman, L. P. 114
Polanyi, K. 520
Ponte, S. 516
Pope John Paul II, 91
Popkin, S. 77
Popp, A. 452
Porter, M. E. 23, 73, 78, 94, 97, 238–239, 241, 242, 244, 295, 372, 373, 379, 444, 451, 454, 463, 479, 519, 558; also co-author of section 328–348

Portney, P. R. 554
Portnoy, P. R. 384
Posner, L. P. 117
Posner, R.A. 480
Post, F. R. 107, 108
Post, J. 84, 85, 86, 89, 93, 95, 478
Powell, W. 179, 181, 528
Power, M. 436
Prahalad, C. K. 79, 80, 243, 460, 463, 558; also co-author of section 221–235
Preston, L. 75, 84, 85, 86, 88, 89, 93, 95, 134, 138, 173, 178, 179, 476
PriceWaterhouseCoopers. 567
Prince, R. A. 476
Pruzan, P. 415; also co-author of section 409–424

Quack, S. 534
Quindlen, A. 479
Quinn, D. 96
Quinn, J. 79, 478

Raiffa, H. 166
Ralston, D. A. 527
Ramirez, F.O. 528
Ramus, C. A. 375
Randers, J. 428, 432
Rappeport, A. 353
Raven, B. 180
Rawls, J. 432
Reed, D. 166, 173, 176
Reficco, E. 459, 462
Regelbrugge, L. 476
Reidenbach, R. E. 117
Reingold, R. N. 119
Reinhardt, F. L. 372, 373, 378
Reisch, M. 119
Revkin, A. C. 387
Rhodes, M. 528
Rice, F. 118
Richardson, J.J. 522, 524
Rinaldi, L. 353
Roberts, K. 468
Robertson, C. 480
Robin, D. P. 117
Rochlin, S. 478
Roddick, A. 238
Rogovsky, N. 293
Roman, R. 77
Rondinelli, D. A. 497
Rosen, S. 476
Rosenkopf, L. 377
Ross, S. 78

Ross, W. D. 115
Roth, K. 464, 510
Rothschild, W. 166
Rowan, B. 179, 375
Rowley, T. 87, 77, 459
Rowlinson, M. 527
Roy, D. 476
Rude, R. 75, 85
Ruggie, J.G. 273, 273
Ruggles, R. 460
Rugman, A. M. 373
Ruhli, E. 444
Russo, M. V. 377, 460
Rutherford, R. 13
Rynes, S. L. 215, 482

Sachs, S. 89, 444
Sadorsky, P. 458
Sadtler, T. M. 460
Sæverud, I. A. 377
Sahlin-Anderson, K. 534
Salancik, G. 166, 180, 186, 422, 459
Salazar, J. 564
Sambharya, R. B. 463, 465
Santos, B. D. S. 519
Saunders, C. B. 105
Saunders, L. 396
Sauters-Sachs, S. 89
Savage, G. T. 172, 174, 176, 178, 195, 459
Schendel, D. 166
Scherer, A. G. 70, 490, 516, 526, 536,
Schlegelmilch, B. B. 218
Schmidpeter, R. 13, 475, 527, 529
Schmidt, F. L. 215, 482
Schneeweis, T. 104
Schoemaker, P. J. H. 455
Schwartz, B. 563
Schwartz, M. S. 73, 87, 569; also co-author of section 104–132
Schwartz, S. H. 479
Scott, W. R. 179, 181
Seal, R. 4, 552
Seitanidi, M. M. 491
Selsky, J. W. 508
Sen, S. 45, 218, 246, 257; also co-author of section 277– 290
Serafeim, G. 561
Sethi, S. P. 37, 84, 95, 119, 477
Sexty, R. W. 105
Shallari, S. 352
Shamir, R. 516, 517, 518, 519, 537
Shapiro, A. C. 172, 173, 177

Sharfman, M. P. 464
Sharma, S. 373, 456, 460, 461, 464, 465
Sharp, J. M. 444
Shaw, B. 107, 108
Shearer, J. W. 118
Shinn, J. 532
Shrivastava, P. 90
Shuen, A. 79, 461
Shulman, J. 16
Siegel, D. 77, 214, 460, 518
Sigerstad, T. D. 464
Silverstein, D. 116
Simanis, E. 235
Simms, C. 235
Simon, H. A. 458, 463
Simon, J. 476
Simon, Y. 90
Simons, T. 463
Singer, P. 432
Skapinker, M. 32,
Skjærseth, J.B. 377
Smeltzer, L. R. 479, 482
Smith, A. 49
Smith, E. T. 91, 118
Smith, J. 481
Smith, N. C. 20, 28, 40, 42; 45, 48, 208, 214, 215, 478; also author of section 35–61
Smith, T. 91
Smith, W. J. 80, 105
Snow, C. C. 457
Sobzack, A. 524, 530
Social Investment Forum, 47
Solomon, R. 96, 122
Sonnenfeld, J. A. 459, 464
Sorkin, A. R. 28
Sormunem, J. 186
Soskice, D. 517, 520, 527
Spar, D. L. 481
Sparkes, R. 218
Spence, C. 429
Spence, L. J. 13, 14, 29, 72, 256, 292, 297, 353, 475
Spencer, B. A. 105
St. Clair, L. 84
St. John. C. 79, 461
Starbuck, W. 165
Starik, M. 173–176, 192
Stavins, R. N. 384
Staw, B. W. 455
Stead, E. 90
Stead, J. 90
Stead, W. E. 351

Stern, N. 350
Stern, S. 553
Sternberg, E. 29
Steurer, R. 521, 530, 491
Stiftung-GTZ. 530
Stolle, D. 516
Stone, C. D. 105
Strange, S. 526
Streeck, W. 520, 531, 528
Strong, K. C. 105
Strudler, A. 122
Sturdivant, F. 86
Suchman, M. C. 181, 184, 375
Sugden, R. 429, 430, 432
Sulmasy, D. 91
Sundgren, A. 104
SustainAbility. 49, 51
Sutchliffe, K. 455
Swaen, V. 5
Swanson, D. 93, 95, 96, 105
Sweet, A. 537
Swift, T. 431, 437, 438
Szwajkowski, E. 455

Talbot, J. 476
Tam, P. 44
Taschini, L. 376
Tata Services Limited. 550
Teal, T. 118
Teece, D. 79, 461
Teegen, H. 15, 481
Terrachoice. 246
The Clarkson Centre for Business Ethics. 89
The Economist. 30, 44
The European Union Commission, 516, 518, 530
The Netherlands Business School/European Institute for Business Ethics. 409
Thea, D. M. 476
Thelen, K. 528
Thomas, G. 528
Thompson, G. F. 516
Thompson, J. K, 171, 172, 176
Thomsen, C. 13
Thomson, I. 425, 429, 431, 433, 436–438
Thyssen, O. 415
Tiberghien, Y. 532
Tichy, N. 84
Tickell, S. 41
Tilling, K. 563
Toffel, M.W. 373

Tolhurst, N. 68
Tomas, M. 464
Toms, S. 452
Treanor, J. 392, 395, 396, 397
Trevino, L. 96, 119
Trexler, M. 385, 387
Triggle, N. 10
Trist, E. 166
Trudell, M. 559
Tsai, K. 532
Tully, S. 68
Turban, D. 476
Turcotte, M. F. 536
Turner, G. 386
Tvesrky, A. 464

UK Department of Trade and Industry (DTI). 37
Unerman, J. 16, 405, 427, 430, 431, 432–436, 437, 438; also author of section 424–442
United Nations Global Compact, 69
United Nations. 90
US Department of Commerce. 412, 414
Utting, P, 25, 258, 554; also author of 260–277

Valente, M, 295, 490; also co-author of section 299–328
Van de Ven, A. 166
Van de Ven, B. 254
Van den Bosch, F. A. J. 461
van der Linde, C. 242
van der Linde, G. 379
Van der Wal, Z. 14
Van der Wiele, T. 474
Van Huijstee, M. M. 375
van Luijk, H. J. L. 71
Van Marrewijk, M. 75, 91
Van Riel, C. B. M. 461
Van Slyke, D. M. 557
Van Tuijl, P. 481
Van Tulder, R. 87
Varadarajan, P. 80, 94, 247
Velasquez, M. 91, 114
Verbeke, A. 373
Victor, D. G. 384
Vidaver-Cohen, D. 83
Vincent, J. R. 476
Visser, W. 12, 68, 71, 293, 458, 566
Vogel, C. M. 475, 476
Vogel, D. 38, 86, 95, 215, 516, 517, 520, 521, 522, 528, 530, 532, 536, 558

Voiculescu, A. 525
Votaw, D. 75
Vredenburg, H. 460, 461, 464, 465, 375

Waddock, S. 77, 87, 474–478, 482, 484
Walley, N. 379
Walsh, J. P. 49, 477, 482, 485, 512, 520
Walter, A. 532
Walton, C. C. 474
Ward, H. 521, 523
Warhurst, A. 478
Warren, R. 20
Warsame, H. 429, 430, 432
Wartick, S. 75, 87, 95, 105, 182
Watantada, P. 250
Waterman, R. 162
Watson, R. 77, 87
Weaver, G. 96
Webb, T. 18
Weber, K. 6, 16
Weber, M. 180, 181, 526
Wegner, M. 527, 529
Weick, K. E. 455, 468
Weiss, J. 89, 105
Weiss, S. 118
Weiss, T. G. 481
Weitz, B. 216
Welford, R. 531
Wellington, F. 373, 375, 376
Wernerfelt, B. 79
Werre, M. 93
Westpac. 52
Westphalen, S. A. 516
Wheeler, D. 90
Whetten, D. A. 463
Whitehead, B. 379
Whitehead, C. J. 172, 174, 176, 178, 459
Whitley, R. 520, 531
Whyback, D. C. 460
Wicks, A. C. 87, 89, 95, 134, 135, 173, 176, 535

Wijnberg, N. 89
Williamson, O. 179, 183
Willoughby, K. 524
Wilson, E. O. 187
Wilson, G. 165
Wilson, H. 395
Wilson, J. 452
Windsor, D. 77, 171
Wokutch, R. E. 105
Woo-Cumings, M. 532
Wood, B. J; co-author of 168– 202
Wood, D. J. 75, 77, 78, 83, 84, 87, 88, 93, 94, 95, 105, 182, 184, 190, 195, 458, 459, 563; also co-author of section 168–202
World Business Council for Sustainable Development (WBCSD). 19, 37, 90
World Commission on Environment and Development (WCED). 90, 432
World Economic Forum (WEF). 37, 262
World Health Organization. 40,
Wright, C. 243, 386, 387
Wüstenhagen, R. 242, 243

Yager, J. 31
Yamaji, K. 91
Yamamura, K. 520, 531
Yankee, J. A. 108
You, J. I. 531
Young, R. 564
Ysa, T. 521–529
Yunus, M. 6, 16, 319, 320, 557

Zadek, S. 16, 97, 216, 430, 436; also co-author of section 409–424
Zahra, S. 16
Zarkada-Fraser, A. 478
Zeitz, G. 463
Zerk, J. A. 517, 520–522, 525
Zigarelli, M. 117

Companies and Organisations

&Beyond 313–315
3M 117, 118
ABB 367
Accenture 564, 567
AccountAbility (Formerly known as institute of Social and Ethical Accountability, ISEA) 404
Adobe Systems 342
Aeroquip Corporation 364
Africa Now 318
Air Canada 253
Akzo Nobel 365
Allied Dunbar 412
America Online 343
American Apparel 241
American Express 193, 336, 340
Amnesty International, 15, 16
Anglo-American 68, 293
Apple 19, 216, 335
Aptech 227
Aracruz Celulose 366
Arthur Andersen 116
AT&T 146, 163
Autopistas del sol(AUSOL) 459, 460
AVIVA 403
Avon 345

B&Q 47, 241
Baidu 492
Bamburi Cement 308, 309

Banco Real 321
Bank of America (BOA) 28
Barclays 383, 386, 392, 403
BASF 365, 445
Bechtel Corporation 316
Ben and Jerry's 39, 46, 118, 124, 237, 243
Bertelsmann 293
BHP Billinton 509
Black water worldwide 299
BMW 69, 368, 382, 385
Body Shop 39, 46, 118, 121, 124, 237, 243, 409, 416, 421, 456, 466
Bourneville 35
British American Tobacco 214
British Petroleum (BP) 52, 134, 135, 137, 211, 236, 267, 280, 378, 383, 384, 500, 506
British Telecom 52, 385
BSkyB 386
Burroughs Wellcome 40
Burt's Bees 243
Business for Social Responsibility 8, 11, 37
Business in the Community (BiTC) 37, 212, 292, 522, 528

Cadbury 28, 35, 36, 117, 236, 254
Cafedirect 46, 243
Carlsberg 214

Carnegie 28
Carrefour 211
Caterpillar 502
Caux Roundtable Principles for Business 91
CEMEX, 321, 460, 461
Centrica, 385
Chevron, 267, 383
Chick-fil-A 117
Chiquita 489
Chisso 116
Chrysler Corporation 119
Cisco 278, 330, 331, 335, 337, 340, 341, 342, 345, 346
Cisco Networking Academy 331, 335, 340, 341
Cisco systems 278, 330, 331, 335, 337
Citibank 226
Citigroup 225, 376, 403
Clorox 243
Coca-Cola 55, 56, 353, 373, 478
College Retirement Equities Fund 336
Community Development Bank 16
Conservation Corporation Africa 313
Coop Italia 412, 416, 421
Cooperative Group 248
Co-operative Bank 218, 248
Corporate Responsibility Coalition 6, 10
Credit Suisse 386
Credit Union 416
CSR Academy 524, 560

Daimler/Mercedes 69
Dandin Group 230
Daniel Salt and Sons 36
Danone, 217 446
Day Chocolate 243
DeBeers 509, 562
Dell 383
Deloitte Touche Tohmatsu 277
Delta Airlines 277
Deutsche Bank 67, 392
Deutsche Post DHL 353
Dow Chemical 365, 367
Dow Corning 116, 119
Dream works SKG 334, 340
Ducks Unlimited 499
Duke 28
Dunlop Tire Corporation 365
DuPont 227, 367, 497

Eaton 119
Ecotricity 242

Ecover 218, 240
Eddie Baker 508
Edward Jones 47
Electricite de France 379
Electricity 242
Endangered Species Chocolate 236
Enron 29, 38, 116, 121, 467
Enron Worldcom 29, 38
Ericssomn 229
Ernst & Youn, 549
Essent 376
Exxon Mobil, 69, 335, 338, 378
Exxon, 245

Fabio Rosa 316
Facebook 489
Fair Labour Association (FLA) 500, 315, 316, 508, 509
Farmacias Ahumada, SA (FASA) 461, 462
FC Barcelona Foundation 293
Federal Express 457
Fifteen 557
Film Recovery Systems 115, 121
Financial Times 266
Financial Times/London Stock Exchange (FTSE) 47, 266, 528
Firestone 116, 121
FleetBoston Financial 339, 343
Ford 116, 124, 254, 383, 403, 496, 500, 506
Ford Foundation 506
Forest Stewardship Council 241, 268, 351
Foxconn 19, 216
Friends of the Earth 466

Gap 14, 84, 104, 221, 245, 263, 267, 272, 295, 343, 354, 402, 404, 473, 530, 565
Gates Foundation 344, 556
General Electric (GE) 11, 116, 120, 121, 135, 278, 382
General Motors (GM) 29, 42, 193, 500, 502
GlaxoSmithKline 40, 42, 272
Global Exchange 496
Goldman Sachs 386
Google 20, 382, 385, 386, 567
Global Business Coalition (GBC) on HIV 16
Global Climate Coalition (GCC) 16
Grameen Bank 6, 16, 319, 320, 339, 340, 557,

Grameen Telecom 223
Grand Circle Travel 338, 339
Green Mountain coffee Roasters, 281
GreenPeace 15, 16, 45, 466, 489, 510, 566
GS, 272
Gyandoot 227

H.B Fuller 507
H.J Heinz 118
Heinekan 301
Hewlett-Packard 231, 232, 342
Hindustan Lever 225, 229, 231
Home Depot 47, 277
Honey Care Africa 318, 319
Honeywell 190
HSBC 19, 212, 386, 387, 391–397

IBM 156, 193, 278, 343, 346, 382
Illy Caffe 492
Intel 567
Interface Carpets 249, 325, 352
International Corporate Governance Network 336
International Labour Organization (ILO) 1, 6, 256, 257
International Standards Organization (ISO) 482
ITC 229
ITT 152

Jindal Steel & Power 567
John Manville corporation 116, 124
Johnson & Johnson 117, 121, 124, 152
Just Desserts 190
JWT 207

KFC 10, 214
Kodak 193
KPMG 272, 402
Kraft 236
Kroger, 293
Krupp 28

Lafarge 308
Leche Ram 457, 466
Levi Strauss 118, 190, 465–467
Lockheed Aircraft 116
London Stock Exchange 266
L'Oreal 243, 456

Mabati Rolling Mills 306
Macy's 293

Magadi Soda Ash 305, 307, 315, 320, 321, 323
Malden Mills 118, 121
Marathon Oil 146
Marine Stewardship Council 15, 526, 562
Markle Foundation 233
Marks and Spencer 247, 386
Mattel 480
Max Havelaar 240,
McDonalds 10, 211, 243, 245, 253, 378, 498, 501
McKinsey and Company 232, 549, 559, 564
Me to We Style 240
Mercedes 69, 254, 384
Merck 40, 118, 121
Microsoft 55, 69, 211
MIT Media Lab 229
Mobil 146, 335, 338
Monsanto 236, 367
MRW 457–459, 464
Munich Re 374

Napster 117, 121
National Australia Bank 386
Natura 462
Neste Oil 383
Nestle 116, 211
Net Impact 567
New Economics Foundation 409, 415
New England Telephone 155, 156
Newmont 509
News Corp 386
Nike 8, 44, 45, 54, 216, 245, 314, 402, 464, 500, 508, 525
n-Logue 230
Nordstrom 500, 508
Novartis 40

Oxfam 16, 41, 42, 264, 269, 496, 500, 506, 509
OECD (Organization for Economic Cooperation and Development) 256, 263, 268, 272, 480, 482, 483, 484, 528

Panduit 342
Parmalat 29
Pepsi 55, 119, 121
Pfizer 40, 294, 344, 346
Philip Morris 89, 328, 367
Pioneer Hibred 227
Pizza Hut 10
Port Sunlight 35, 254

Pret a Manger 10
PricewaterhouseCoopers (PwC) 283,
    567, 386
Proctor and Gamble 151, 124, 156, 163,
    351
PRODEM 227
Puma 314

Rainforest Alliance 489
Reckitt Benckiser 386
Research in Motion 492
Rhino Records190
Rio Tinto 52, 246, 500, 509
Royal Bank of Scotland (RBS) 28
Royal Dutch/ Shell 45, 51, 310, 381

Saatchi & Saatchi 566
Safaricom 204
Safeco 335
Safeway 293
Sainsbury's 243, 353
Saltaire 36
SAP 277, 567
Save the Children 15, 489
SbN Bank, 409, 410, 416, 421, 422
SC Johnson 335
Sears 156
SEKEM 317–319, 324
Seventh Generation 366
Shell 44, 45, 51–54, 69, 211, 243, 267,
    304, 310, 381, 383, 384, 402, 438,
    478, 505, 509
Siberian Urals Aluminum company
    (SUAL) 310
Smith & Wesson 120, 121
Sony 367, 478, 480
Southwest Airlines 376
Starbucks 37, 43, 44, 52, 55, 271, 496,
    500, 506, 507
StarKist 118
Stonyfield Farms 46
Stora Enso 383
Sun Microsystems 342
SustainAbility Ltd 422
Swiss Re 374, 386

TARAhaat 226
Target 40, 65, 204, 226, 236, 241, 244,
    288, 341, 344, 345, 371, 376, 386,
    460, 505, 507
Tata 4, 7, 217, 293, 305, 323, 399, 400,
    492, 545–550, 552, 558
TATA Global Beverage 492

TATA Group 305, 545–552
Telefonia 230
Tesco 247
Tiffany's 509
Timberland 118, 190, 283, 496
TNT 386
Tom's of Maine 237, 240
Toronto-Dominion Bank 386
Total 81, 206, 224, 229, 262, 267, 272,
    303, 340, 342, 343, 363, 364, 393,
    472, 482, 547
Toyot 211, 293, 353, 377, 383
Traidcraft 243, 409, 415, 416, 421
TransFair 240
Triodos 240
Turiya Group 301

U.S. Steel 146
Unilever 15, 67, 69, 211, 225, 243, 247,
    264, 269, 294, 373, 382, 444, 489,
    498, 499, 500, 562
Unilever- Indonesia 264
Union Carbide 119, 121, 124
United Parcel Service (UPS) 457, 497,
    507
United State Postal Service 14
Unocal 44, 267
US Airways 376

Vodacom 204–206
Vodafone 1, 2, 20, 203–207, 254
Voxiva 230

Walker Information 46
Walmart 120, 121, 211, 216, 242, 253,
    262, 271, 282, 378, 566, 509, 566
Westinghouse 193
Westpac 52
White Martin 502
Woolworth 293
Worldcom 29, 38
World Business Council for Sustainable
    Development (WBCSD) 16, 19, 37, 38,
    50, 53, 90
World Economic Forum 8, 37, 84, 89,
    262, 300
World Bank 1, 8, 40, 266, 300, 311, 316,
    325, 360, 393, 562
World Commission on Environment and
    Development (Brundtland Report) 90,
    95
World Health Organization (WHO) 40, 361

World Trade Organization (WTO) 40,
    361
Worldwide Fund For Nature (WWF) 15,
    376, 383, 387, 395, 562

Xe, 299
Xerox Corporation 365, 367

Yahoo 386